THOMAS CARLYLE BY WHISTLER

ENJOYMENT OF LITERATURE

by

RALPH P. BOAS

PROFESSOR OF ENGLISH
WHEATON COLLEGE, NORTON, MASS.

and

EDWIN SMITH

CLASSICAL HIGH SCHOOL, SPRINGFIELD, MASS.

HARCOURT, BRACE AND COMPANY

NEW YORK CHICAGO

[n · 5 · 53]

PRINTED IN THE U. S. A.

TO

WILLIAM C. HILL

PRINCIPAL OF THE CENTRAL HIGH SCHOOL
SPRINGFIELD, MASSACHUSETTS

A WORD TO THE TEACHER

Teachers who have used the authors' *An Introduction to the Study of Literature* will recognize in *Enjoyment of Literature* a rewritten and expanded version of the older book. Its aim is, as before, to provide teachers with material which will enable high-school students to read literature with zest, appreciation, enjoyment, and understanding.

Every effort has been made to provide a thorough, comprehensive, humanized companion to the student's reading. This book may well be available merely for consultation by sophomores and juniors, but it should be the constant companion for the senior. For example, when he studies *Macbeth* or *Hamlet* he should also study—and master—Part Three, Drama; when he studies Milton's *Minor Poems* or a collection of modern poets he should also study—and master—Part One, Poetry. For this reason the book should be in the hands of the students themselves. This fact explains why so much of the illustrative material is taken from books read in the average secondary school course.

This book is, furthermore, designed as a flexible, helpful assistant to the teacher. It does not impose a method on the teacher; it will fit any method which the individual teacher sees fit to use. All progressive teachers have come to believe that literature ought to be taught as *literature*, the revelation in artistic form of an author's vision of life, be that vision expressed in prose or poetry, lyric or epic, drama or essay. When students leave school they do not read "classics" with notes and introductions. They read literature as they find it and where they find it. What they need for an understanding of literature, an appreciation of literature, an impulse toward good literature, is a knowledge of literary forms as they will meet them outside the classroom. Some help toward making reading really enjoyable has to be given the student; this book aims to give that help in such a way as to appeal to high-school boys and girls and conserve the teacher's time and energy.

We have made considerable reference to great works of literature which the student ought to come to know but which at the moment may be wholly new to him. Every effort has been made to increase the literary background of the student. It is not necessary to use the whole book during one year, nor is it necessary to assign any part of it for a continuous series of lessons. It ought to be constantly available for the many problems of appreciation and understanding which constantly arise as the class studies fiction, poetry, drama, and essay.

Primarily the book is for twelfth-year students, but portions of it may be used for those in their tenth or eleventh year of school. Younger students can easily grasp the technical part of literary study; for instance, methods of telling a story, methods of revealing character, romance and realism, figures of speech, use of word music, meter in poetry, the construction of the drama, and so on. Such sections can be taken up separately, in short assignments, as occasion arises. For older students are designed the pages dealing directly with literary appreciation and interpretation—for instance, style, truth and artistic beauty, the nature of poetry, the difficulties facing the dramatist, the manner and method of the essayist. Whole chapters will also be useful for review in preparation for College Board Examinations or in a survey of the forms of literature. The exercises are accordingly varied in difficulty, the more definite ones being for younger students, the more comprehensive ones for those who have begun to read and think for themselves.

Many sections are planned especially to aid in the appreciation of classics studied in school. Pages on such books as *Ivanhoe*, *Silas Marner*, *Kidnapped*, *The House of the Seven Gables*, *The Merchant of Venice*, *As You Like It*, *A Midsummer Night's Dream*, *Twelfth Night*, *Julius Caesar*, *Hamlet*, *Macbeth*, *Idylls of the King*, *The Vision of Sir Launfal*, and *The Ancient Mariner* may be easily found by consulting the index and occasionally assigned in connection with the reading of these books.

We have tried to maintain old time-tested ideals of literary worth, but we recognize that the advancing years have opened new horizons. The study of literature is now regarded as a joyous adventure rather than as an intellectual discipline. The great increase in leisure nowadays makes guidance in reading more important than ever before. Progressive teachers now recognize that many students read detective stories and light romances and that such reading has its value as recreation. The teacher's task now is not to frown upon such reading, but to show its relation to more lasting literature which, in time, students may feel to be more permanently rewarding. This book recognizes varying needs and various levels of enjoyment and aims at adaptability to actual taste and daily literary and dramatic experience.

The many changes in this new book will, we hope, make it more useful in the newer methods of teaching. Especially we have aimed at stimulating that most valuable of all educational experience, self-directed activity by the student. Some of the changes are as follows:

1. Chapters have been shortened and centralized about a single theme. Hence the book should be more valuable since it is more easily adapted to assignments of reasonable length and to self-directed use by students.

2. Exercises are divided into three groups: Comprehension Questions, which will enable the student to test himself; Problems in Appreciation, which will enable the student to make new ideas concrete; and Questions on Books Studied, which will train the student to apply new ideas to material already studied.

3. General critical material has been consolidated with the study of specific forms, thus stimulating thought and removing the difficulty of critical vagueness.

4. Summaries have been consistently used to clarify and consolidate the various chapters.

5. The historical chapters have been completely rewritten and there is now available a group of extended discussions of the great writers of English Literature. These discussions provide much fuller material in a more comprehensive and concentrated manner. Hence the student is provided with an introduction to the main stream of English Literature in a form which will stimulate him to exploration in an interesting field.

6. Number one of the Comprehension Questions at the end of each chapter lists the new words and important concepts of the chapter.

Thus is provision made for supplying the student with the vocabulary for handling, discussing, criticising, and thinking about the various types of literature.

7. Many new illustrations have been provided which emphasize the main theme of the book, Literature for Enjoyment.

All these changes aim at making the book a usable and teachable classroom textbook.

The general plan of the book and Parts IV and V are by Mr. Boas; Parts I, II, III, and all the exercises and suggestions for study are by Mr. Smith.

R. P. B.
E. S.

A WORD TO THE STUDENT

This book has been placed in your hands because your teacher wishes you to learn the enjoyment which comes from reading good books with intelligent appreciation. With your teacher as a guide, you are engaged upon an intellectual adventure, the search for a knowledge of the great minds of the past and for the beauty and wisdom which their imaginations have woven into great poems, stories, plays, and essays.

Here you will find information about books and writers which should be a part of every educated person's background. Here, too, you will find material which you can use in connection with class assignments in literature, "book reports," and preparation for examinations. Above all, you will be helped to read and study literature so that books will become for you the open door to an enjoyable and profitable mental life.

These are some of the specific ways in which this book will be of use to you.

1. *This book may be used as a source of information.*

There are certain elementary facts about literature which all students need to know. This book explains these facts clearly to you with many examples. It also contains exercises which will drive home these facts so that they will stick in your mind. For example, one has to know about figures of speech and about meter and pattern in poetry. Here you will find these facts and hundreds of others simply presented. Moreover an attempt is made to do more than present them; their value and significance are pointed out so that you may have at least the beginnings of critical discrimination.

2. *This book is planned as a direct stimulus to literary appreciation.*

Such a discussion as Chapter III, "Sharing the Poet's World," should help any student to respond to the emotional appeal of poetry. Chapter VIII, "Sensing the Music of Poetry," will quicken your ear for both the music and the meaning of any poem. Chapter XVII, "Testing the Truth of a Story," ought to help you to be a bit more specific about such a phrase as "true to life." Chapter XXIV, "How to Study Plot Construction," will throw new light upon the next play or motion picture which you see. In all the chapters there are comments on the value of specific types of literature. These comments will help you to know a good book when you see one, to distinguish between the temporary and the permanent, the artificial and the true, the flashy and the genuine.

3. *This book is planned to help you in independent study.*

One of the greatest joys in life is the joy of discovery. There is nothing which gives so much pleasure and profit as finding out things by ourselves. Throughout the chapters you will find exercises and references specially designed to help you in independent study. Varied and extensive as are the references, however, they touch only a small portion of the great treasure house of English literature. With the scores of suggestions given here as a guide, you can find a source of endless pleasure and profit on the shelves of your school or public library.

4. *This book will be valuable for review in the senior year after the regular reading list has been completed. Such review will be found useful for coördinating and reëstablishing what otherwise might be random impressions or half-shaped memories.*

Naturally your memories of the various books read in your years at school are bound to become somewhat vague by the time you have reached the senior year. A study of the chapters on poetry, prose fiction, drama, and essay will make these vague memories definite, and will enable you, moreover, to see the books in a new light—as examples of the art of literature.

5. *This book is designed to be a constant companion in all your study of literature.*

Matters that need to be "looked up" in connection with books which you study in school, matters like figures of speech, meters in poetry, the technique of story telling, the Elizabethan theater and playwrights, the lives and works of great writers—all these and many more are explained and illustrated here. Here are subjects for compositions and reports which cover a wide range of material, tastes, and abilities. For instance, you will find exercises on different plays, novels, poems, and authors which can be adapted to many kinds of assignments, from writing a triolet to reviewing a novel by Conrad. Here are sketches and studies of authors, explanations of literary technique, studies and appreciations of types of literature, and exercises of many kinds in the understanding and enjoyment of books. All these are for your use as you need them.

6. *This book may be used in preparation for examinations.*

The use of this book ought to help you to generalize upon your reading and to compare and classify books. Nine-tenths of the books and authors discussed in this book appear in the reading lists of the College Entrance Examination Board and other examining bodies. Many of the exercises are modeled directly upon the usual type of questions asked on examination papers.

7. *The main object of the book.*

Our main object is to help you to appreciate and enjoy good books. If you can learn to understand and enjoy the best that poetry, fiction, drama, biography, and essays have to offer, you will never find life dull or time slow. But of course you must bring something to a book if you expect to get something out of it. You must be ready to yield your understanding and imagination to an author if he is to give you in turn the full richness of his experience with life. And you can do that more easily if you understand something of him, his times, and his purposes; of the nature of the difficult art which he practices; of the strange force of genius which impels him to re-create for you out of his reactions to life a meaning, a pattern, a mood that wake a response in you. . . . Some of these things this book attempts to make clear. Some can only be felt through imaginative sympathy, and this sympathy is what we should like to arouse and cultivate in you in such chapters as "Enjoying Poetry," "Sharing the Poet's World," "How the Poet Uses Word Pictures and Sounds," "Understanding the Thought in Poetry," "Sensing the Music of Poetry," "Testing the Truth of a Story," "Why Books Live," "Characterization in Drama." Chapters like these are designed to be read in your senior year as you are coming to evaluate books with some critical and imaginative judgment; the chapters dealing with facts and definitions can easily be mastered and used earlier in your course, while you are reading books which require this sort of explanation.

This book, then, should be useful to you in many ways; but we hope it will be of service in the one way that really matters: We hope it will help you to know and love good books.

THE AUTHORS

CONTENTS

PART ONE: POETRY

PART TWO: PROSE FICTION

PART THREE: DRAMA

PART FOUR: THE ESSAY AND OTHER PROSE NON-FICTION

PART FIVE: THE GREAT WRITERS

LIST OF ILLUSTRATIONS

Part One

POETRY

WHY do people read poetry? That is what many students would like to know. It seems incredible to them, so they tell us, that people really can enjoy it. Yet even these very objectors usually get involuntary pleasure from the tale of "our good old grinnin', gruntin' Gunga Din" or of the Highwayman and Bess, the landlord's black-eyed daughter. Nor can they be heard strenuously objecting to the reading of a ballad by Robert W. Service or "The Wreck of the Julie Plante" or "Johnnie's First Moose" from William Henry Drummond's *Habitant* poems. And once they can be persuaded to try Masefield's *Right Royal, Enslaved,* and *Reynard the Fox,* or perhaps Benét's *John Brown's Body* or MacLeish's *Conquistador,* they are usually willing to admit that poetry does give pleasure after all. From then on, they too are ready to enjoy poetry that does more than merely tell a story—first, lyrics of simple understandable emotions like "Trees" and "Sea-Fever"; then poems that plumb more deeply into the human spirit, that say more and say it more subtly and truly. Of course there are many intermediate stages between enjoyment of Robert W. Service and Browning, between Kipling and Walter De la Mare, but the imaginative journey is a fascinating one that will repay the traveler many times over.

Poetry must be felt through the imagination. Can one analyze the sources of pleasure to be found in poetry? That is what Part I attempts to do, but it can do that, of course, only in a very meager and limited way. Much of that pleasure depends on the reader's imagination and sensitiveness. Like the lonely traveler in De la Mare's "The Listeners" (page 88), he must be sensitive to the overtones of spirit, hearkening in an air stirred and shaken by the poet's words till he feels in his heart their strangeness, till he, too, feels the silence surge softly backwards as he lays down his book and leaves the moonlit world of the spirit to rejoin the world of men. Such pleasure, of course, cannot be learned or taught, really. All that we can do here is talk about it a little in the hope that another, too, may feel himself

> Lord of the fruits of Tartary,
>   Her rivers silver-pale!
> Lord of the hills of Tartary,
>   Glen, thicket, wood, and dale!
> Her flashing stars, her scented breeze,
> Her trembling lakes, like foamless seas,
> Her bird-delighting citron-trees
>   In every purple vale! [1]

[1] Quoted from Walter De la Mare's *Songs of Childhood* by permission of Henry Holt and Company.

CHAPTER 1

ENJOYING POETRY

Poetry affords opportunity for pleasurable recognition. In the first place, poetry gives us the pleasure of recognition. That is, in a way, a proof that it is widely read. We all flush with involuntary pleasure when we hear an allusion to Joyce Kilmer's "Trees" or to Alan Seeger's "I Have a Rendezvous with Death," because we know about them.

Poetry appeals to the imagination. But the feeling of pleasurable recognition is only a minor reason for our enjoyment of poetry. When we read in a novel [1] that the heroine, as she looked out into the moonlit winter night, quoted softly to herself:

> Deep on the convent-roof the snows
> Are sparkling to the moon,

it does give us pleasure if we recognize the poem; but it gives us pleasure even if we do not. The reason is not far to seek. Poetry stimulates the imagination. It enables us to see in our imagination the beauty of the snow "sparkling to the moon" and to feel the cold stillness of the winter night. It recreates for us the beauty of "October's Bright Blue Weather"

> When on the ground red apples lie
> In piles like jewels shining,
> And redder still on old stone walls
> Are leaves of woodbine twining.

In the dead of winter "The Vision of Sir Launfal" carries us back to June when

[1] *Main Street.*

The cowslip startles in meadows green,

and

The buttercup catches the sun in its chalice.

There is no wonderland to which poetry cannot take us through the imagination, whether it be deep under the sea in

Sand-strewn caverns, cool and deep,
Where the winds are all asleep;
Where the spent lights quiver and gleam;
Where the salt weed sways in the stream

or in that ideal land of

magic casements, opening on the foam
Of perilous seas, in faery lands forlorn.

Poetry takes us back into the Middle Ages with Keats in "The Eve of St. Agnes" or leaves us

Alone, alone, all, all alone,
Alone on a wide, wide sea

with the Ancient Mariner. It transports us to a snowbound New England homestead,

Content to let the north-wind roar
In baffled rage at pane and door,

with Whittier, or brings us once more to the time when

A boy's will is the wind's will,
And the thoughts of youth are long, long thoughts.

Small wonder, then, that poetry is universally read. Through its appeal to the imagination it offers us the surest escape from the stern reality of facts.

Appreciation of great poetry comes gradually. Of course the inexperienced reader need not expect to get an emotional reaction from all great poetry as soon as he reads it. There are certain stages along this journey toward appreciation of imaginative beauty, and it is far better to begin with spontaneous enjoyment of Longfellow, Lowell, and Whittier than to give up poetry in disgust just because one can see nothing to "Lycidas," "Comus," "Prometheus Unbound," or "Saul." If you have never cared much for poetry, why not begin with some popular story poem? Almost every boy likes Kipling, and who is to blame a boy if he gets a thrill out of "Gunga Din"? On the other hand, who is to blame you if, having been dragged to the Pierian spring of Milton, you refuse to drink thereof? It is not without preparation that one comes to enjoy:

Hence, vain deluding Joys,
   The brood of Folly without father bred!
How little you bested,
   Or fill the fixèd mind with all your toys!
Dwell in some idle brain,
   And fancies fond with gaudy shapes possess,
As thick and numberless
   As the gay notes that people the sun-beams,
Or likest hovering dreams,
   The fickle pensioners of Morpheus' train.
But, hail! thou Goddess, sage and holy!
Hail, divinest Melancholy!

It is useless to tell you to hail "divinest Melancholy" if you cannot, from your perspective, see that "Il Penseroso" is a better poem than "Gunga Din." But there are fine poems that everyone can enjoy: "Fuzzy-Wuzzy," the "big black boundin' beggar" who broke a British square; "Danny Deever," whom "they're hangin' in the mornin' "; "The Highwayman," who "rode with a jewelled twinkle . . . under the jewelled sky"—to say nothing of *Dauber*, *Right Royal*, *The Everlasting Mercy*, and *Enslaved*, or Mr. Chesterton's superb "Lepanto" with its:

Dim drums throbbing, in the hills half heard,

Stiff flags straining in the night-blasts cold
In the gloom black-purple, in the glint old-gold,
Torchlight crimson on the copper kettle-drums,
Then the tuckets, then the trumpets, then the cannon, and he comes.
Don John laughing in the brave beard curled,
Spurning of his stirrups like the thrones of all the world,

Holding his head up for a flag of all the free.
Love-light of Spain—hurrah!
Death-light of Africa!
Don John of Austria
Is riding to the sea.[1]

Poetry sharpens appreciation of Nature. Once you have acquired a taste for poetry, however, you should not miss the pleasure that comes from reading poems that have nothing to do with stories at all, poems that picture in words the world about you. Perhaps it is "Sea-Fever" with:

a gray mist on the sea's face and a gray dawn breaking,

and

a windy day with the white clouds flying,
And the flung spray and the blown spume, and the sea-gulls crying,

or the woods of Robert Frost, so "lovely, dark and deep," or Kew in lilac time where

The cherry-trees are seas of bloom and soft perfume and sweet perfume,

Perhaps it is Rupert Brooke's "Grantchester":

Ah God! to see the branches stir
Across the moon in Grantchester!
To smell the thrilling-sweet and rotten
Unforgettable, unforgotten
River-smell, and hear the breeze
Sobbing in the little trees,[2]

or Amy Lowell's "The Garden by Moonlight" with

A black cat among roses,
Phlox, lilac-misted under a first-quarter moon,
The sweet smells of heliotrope and night-scented stock,

or Walter De la Mare's "April Moon," that brings

[1] Used by permission of Dodd, Mead and Company, Inc.
[2] Copyright, 1915, by Dodd, Mead and Company, Inc.

More lovely shade than light,
That, setting, silvers lonely hills
Upon the verge of night.[1]

Poetry intensifies enjoyment of common experiences. At other times, human sympathy is so direct and artless that it meets with immediate and universal human response. That is why most of us understand at once the feeling of Rupert Brooke's "The Great Lover":

These I have loved:
White plates and cups, clean-gleaming,
Ringed with blue lines; and feathery, faëry dust;
Wet roofs, beneath the lamp-light; the strong crust
Of friendly bread; and many-tasting food;
Rainbows; and the blue bitter smoke of wood;
And radiant raindrops couching in cool flowers;
And flowers themselves, that sway through sunny hours,
Dreaming of moths that drink them under the moon;
Then, the cool kindliness of sheets, that soon
Smooth away trouble; and the rough male kiss
Of blankets; grainy wood; live hair that is
Shining and free; blue-massing clouds; the keen
Unpassioned beauty of a great machine;
The benison of hot water; furs to touch;

Voices in laughter, too; and body's pain,
Soon turned to peace; and the deep-panting train;
Firm sands; the little dulling edge of foam
That browns and dwindles as the wave goes home;
And washen stones, gay for an hour; the cold
Graveness of iron; moist black earthen mold;
Sleep; and high places; footprints in the dew;
And oaks; and brown horse-chestnuts, glossy-new;
And new-peeled sticks; and shining pools on grass;—
All these have been my loves.[2]

All these are very simple poems about simple experiences, and yet they have given a great deal of pleasure to many people, a pleasure which you, too, can easily share.

Poetry stirs the imagination. But when the poet's imagination leaves this earth and goes soaring with Shelley among skylarks and

[1] Reprinted by special permission of and arrangement with Henry Holt and Company.
[2] Copyright, 1915, by Dodd, Mead and Company.

clouds and west winds, or drifting with Keats far back into the past when a Grecian urn was new, the inexperienced reader is apt to become uneasy. In reading Keats, he wants to know exactly who this "Belle Dame sans Merci" is, and why Keats should yearn to "fade far away, dissolve, and quite forget," or be "half in love with easeful Death" just because he has heard a nightingale that

> In some melodious plot
> Of beechen green, and shadows numberless,
> Singest of summer in full-throated ease.

Walter De la Mare, also, piques such a reader. He cannot help being interested, perhaps exasperated, by "The Listeners"; but he wants to know who this traveler is who is knocking on the moonlit door as his horse champs the grasses of the forest. And who are these listeners who stand

> . . . listening in the quiet of the moonlight

> . . . thronging the faint moonbeams on the dark stair

> Hearkening in an air stirred and shaken
> By the lonely Traveller's call?

And why, if

> . . . they heard his foot on the stirrup,
> And the sound of iron on stone,
> And how the silence surged softly backward,
> When the plunging hoofs were gone [1]

—why didn't they reply? In short, what does the poem mean?

Poetry should not be taken too literally. Now it is really too bad that all people cannot enjoy poetry once it gets beyond the range of one's intimate experience with "familiar matter of today that has been and may be again." But one must be something of a poet himself to enjoy the very best in poetry. One must develop within himself something of the poet's sensitiveness to men and Nature and to the unseen, but not unreal, world of spirit. One's imagination must be able to soar away from the literal if one is to enjoy Spenser, Milton,

[1] Reprinted by special permission of Henry Holt and Company.

Blake, Shelley, Keats, Francis Thompson, De la Mare. If one has or cultivates that type of imagination, one's joy in reading poetry is as satisfying and as incommunicable as religious ecstasy. For the sensitive reader there is a deep and mournful pathos in lines like the following four excerpts from Shakespeare, which probably would leave unmoved thousands of devotees of Edgar Guest. But such lines are touchstones. Try them and see if you, too, feel their poetry:

> When to the sessions of sweet silent thought
> I summon up remembrance of things past.

or

> Not poppy, nor mandragora,
> Nor all the drowsy syrups of the world
> Shall ever medicine thee to that sweet sleep
> Which thou ow'dst yesterday.

or

> I'll bury thee in a triumphant grave.
> A grave? O, no! a lantern, slaughter'd youth,
> For here lies Juliet, and her beauty makes
> This vault a feasting presence full of light.

or

> Fear no more the heat o' the sun,
> Nor the furious winter's rages;
> Thou thy worldly task hast done,
> Home art gone, and ta'en thy wages:
> Golden lads and girls all must,
> As chimney-sweepers, come to dust.

Poetry goes deep into human experience. Naturally, the more deeply the poet's thought and feeling penetrate into life, the more deeply will the reader have to think and feel if he is to understand and sympathize. Shakespeare has passages in his sonnets and in his greatest plays that can be appreciated only after some experience with life.

The four preceding passages from Shakespeare all require thought to be understood, experience to be felt. They illustrate perfectly that it is perhaps through poetry that we gain our profoundest appreciation of life. There is scarcely a feeling of which man is capable that does not find expression in some great poem, for the poet recreates for us, not only a picture or a sensation, but also the feeling that goes with it. His expression of these things in words gives us keen pleasure. Thus it is that poetry helps us to understand and sympathize. The poet is keenly sensitive, not only to the claims of beauty, but also to the claims of human sympathy. Through sympathy, he has gained understanding. Broad human sympathy is best exemplified in the works of the greatest poets like Chaucer, Shakespeare, and Browning, who deal primarily with human beings, but it is not confined to those three.

It sometimes is hard for us to understand quite all that a poet wants us to see and feel, but a genuine feeling for poetry, once aroused, grows with the growth of the reader's mind and spirit. Because poetry appeals to our sense of beauty, because it expresses what we feel and cannot ourselves express, and because it helps us to understand and sympathize with life, it makes our lives richer. If you wish to test this statement, read again any great poem with which you have been familiar since childhood, and notice how much unconscious pleasure, appreciation, and understanding have been added to your life because of it. Any simple lyric like "Sweet and Low" or "Crossing the Bar" or even something from *A Child's Garden of Verses* will afford you convenient proof. Such poems are in themselves answers to the question, "Why read poetry?" Poetry offers pleasure to all, but of course, like all other arts, it offers the most to those who have the most imagination, sympathy, and sensitiveness to give to its appreciation.

Summary. One enjoys poetry because it stimulates the imagination, increases appreciation of nature and human experiences, arouses a feeling for beauty, and quickens the sense of kinship with our fellow men. But appreciation of the best poetry comes gradually and grows with the growth of capacity to see and feel and understand.

Note. All the poems listed in the exercises for these chapters can be found in one or another of the following anthologies:

Twentieth Century Poetry, Drinkwater, Canby, and Benét
Modern Verse, Anita Forbes
Golden Numbers, Wiggin and Smith
English Poetry, Its Principles and Progress, Gayley, Young, and Kurtz
The New Poetry, Monroe and Henderson
British Poets of the Nineteenth Century, Page
The Golden Treasury, Palgrave
The Oxford Book of English Verse, Quiller-Couch

The Little Book of Modern Verse, Rittenhouse
Adventures in English Literature, Schweikert, Inglis, and others
Open Gates, Spaulding
Modern American and British Poetry. Untermeyer
Yesterday and Today, Untermeyer
Contemporary Poetry, Wilkinson
New Voices, Wilkinson

COMPREHENSION QUESTIONS

1. Why is it easier to enjoy Kipling and Masefield than Milton?
2. Why do beginners in poetry often fail to understand or enjoy Keats and Shelley?
3. What qualities of mind and temperament must a reader have if he is to enjoy the highest type of poetry?
4. What passages in the following poems can anyone enjoy regardless of his knowledge of poetry?

Chesterton	"Lepanto"
Coleridge	"The Ancient Mariner"
Kipling	"Gunga Din," "Danny Deever," "Fuzzy-Wuzzy"
Lowell	"The Vision of Sir Launfal"
Milton	"L'Allegro"
Noyes	"The Highwayman"
Tennyson	"The Brook"
Whittier	"Snowbound"

5. State in your own words the three most important reasons why people enjoy poetry. Can you cite a poem to illustrate each of your reasons?
6. What do we mean by saying that poetry appeals to the imagination? Find and bring to class a poem which has this appeal.
7. Name some common human feelings or experiences about which poems have been written.
8. What are the human experiences that form the basis of each of the poems quoted in this chapter? Which are the easiest and which are the most difficult to understand?
9. Find and bring to class three poems that you think show sympathetic understanding of three different human emotions.
10. Find and bring to class:
    (*a*) a poem you have always enjoyed, (*b*) a poem you have outgrown, (*c*) a poem you have learned to enjoy, (*d*) a poem you have never enjoyed. Try to analyze your reactions to these poems finding out what reasons underlie them.

PROBLEMS IN APPRECIATION

1. Select a half-dozen or more poems that really are the result of something deeply felt and sincerely thought—all the better if they represent conflicting points of view. For example take:

Arnold	"Dover Beach"
Browning	"Rabbi Ben Ezra"
T. S. Eliot	"Ash Wednesday"
Hardy	"In a Wood"
Ralph Hodgson	"The Song of Honour"
Keats	"Ode on a Grecian Urn"
Millay	"Renascence"
Shakespeare	146th Sonnet
Tennyson	"Ulysses"
Thompson	"The Hound of Heaven"
Wordsworth	"Ode on Intimations of Immortality"

In each poem what has been felt and what ideas have these feelings stirred in the poet? Then, what ideas and feelings have been communicated to you? Are you the richer for any of them?

2. Memorize the following poem. How can it add to your appreciation of life? What common human experience does it suggest with: (*a*) Time, (*b*) Beauty? How can you state its philosophy in everyday language?

LOVELIEST OF TREES

Loveliest of trees, the cherry now
Is hung with bloom along the bough,
And stands about the woodland ride,
Wearing white for Eastertide.

Now, of my threescore years and ten,
Twenty will not come again,
And take from seventy springs a score,
It only leaves me fifty more.

And since to look at things in bloom
Fifty springs are little room,
About the woodlands I will go
To see the cherry hung with snow.

A. E. HOUSMAN

3. Memorize the following selection from Milton's "L'Allegro." Try to write a description or a poem of your own expressing the same morning-

mood of gladness. Bring to class a photograph or drawing that this mood suggests. How can this poem add to your enjoyment of life?

While the plowman, near at hand,
Whistles o'er the furrowed land,
And the milkmaid singeth blithe,
And the mower whets his scythe,
And every shepherd tells his tale
Under the hawthorn in the dale.

❦

Russet lawns, and fallows gray,
Where the nibbling flocks do stray;
Mountains on whose barren breast
The laboring clouds do often rest;
Meadows trim with daisies pied;
Shallow brooks, and rivers wide.
Towers and battlements it sees
Bosomed high in tufted trees,
Where perhaps some Beauty lies,
The Cynosure of neighboring eyes.

❦

When the merry bells ring round,
And the jocund rebecks sound
To many a youth and many a maid
Dancing in the checkered shade;
And young and old come forth to play
On a sunshine holiday.

4. Here is a poem that has given lasting pleasure to many. The novelist Virginia Woolf feels that this may last long after our age and its problems have been forgotten. How do you feel about it? Try to point out its haunting word music. What does it *say?* What *feelings* does it wake in you? What common experiences lie behind it?

When I am dead, my dearest,
Sing no sad songs for me;
Plant thou no roses at my head,
Nor shady cypress tree;
Be the green grass above me
With showers and dewdrops wet;
And if thou wilt, remember,
And if thou wilt, forget.

I shall not see the shadows,
I shall not feel the rain;
I shall not hear the nightingale
Sing on, as if in pain:
And dreaming through the twilight
That doth not rise nor set
Haply I may remember,
And haply may forget.

CHRISTINA ROSSETTI

CHAPTER 2

DISTINGUISHING BETWEEN POETRY AND PROSE

Difficulties of distinguishing between poetry and prose. It is difficult to put into exact words the difference between poetry and prose. The dividing line is often shadowy because much so-called prose has poetic qualities and much so-called poetry, prosaic qualities. A good deal of what we commonly regard as prose is, in essence, poetry, and a good deal more of what we commonly regard as poetry is, in essence, prose.

We are likely to classify any writing that has rhyme and rhythm as poetry, and any other writing as prose. The two examples given below seem to refute this theory. The one in rhyme and meter has not a spark of poetic fire; in the one without rhyme and meter the poetic fire is unquenchable. A recent critic [1] has pointed out that David's lament over Jonathan:

> Thy love to me was wonderful, passing the love of women,

is instinct with the breath of poetry, whereas Pope's metrical paraphrase of it,

> Thy love was wondrous, soothing all my care,
> Passing the fond affection of the fair,

is not much more than artificial affectation. The same critic suggests that the hopeless pathos of Isaiah's

> The sun shall be no more thy light by day; neither
> for brightness shall the moon give light unto thee,

[1] J. L. Lowes, *Convention and Revolt in Poetry.*

is shattered forever in Pope's rhymed version,

> No more the rising Sun shall gild the morn
> Nor ev'ning Cynthia fill her silver horn.

The same observation must strike you at once when you compare Addison's hymn,

> The spacious firmament on high,
> With all the blue ethereal sky,
> And spangled heavens, a shining frame,
> Their great Original proclaim

with its Biblical equivalent,

> The heavens declare the glory of God; and the firmament sheweth His handywork.

It is clearly evident that many of the beautiful passages in the King James version of the Bible, though they are not in metrical form, are more eloquently poetical than all the rhymed couplets in existence. These verses from the twelfth chapter of Ecclesiastes you have only to read aloud to feel the power of their rhythm:

> Remember now thy Creator in the days of thy Youth, while the evil days come not, nor the years draw nigh, when thou shalt say, I have no pleasure in them;
>
> While the sun, or the light, or the moon, or the stars, be not darkened, nor the clouds return after the rain:
>
> In the day when the keepers of the house shall tremble, and the strong men shall bow themselves . . . and those that look out of the windows be darkened,
>
> And the doors shall be shut in the streets . . . and he shall rise up at the voice of the bird, and all the daughters of music shall be brought low;
>
> Also when they shall be afraid of that which is high, and fears shall be in the way, and the almond tree shall flourish, and the grasshopper shall be a burden, and desire shall fail: because man goeth to his long home, and the mourners go about the streets:
>
> Or ever the silver cord be loosed, or the golden bowl be broken . . . or the wheel broken at the cistern
>
> Then shall the dust return to the earth as it was: and the spirit shall return unto God who gave it.

There is hardly an element of all that we usually regard as poetry which is not found in this passage. Here are pictures, symbols, images, phrases haunted with the accumulated connotations of man's centuries of experience with life and death. Nor is the Bible alone in possessing this poetic quality. It is found in a good deal of the best English prose, from the glowing pulsations of the finest paragraphs of Ruskin and Carlyle to the elusive lilt in the dialogue of the Irish plays of Yeats and Synge. Such passages illustrate the difficulty of distinguishing between poetry and prose. There are, however, three general characteristics of poetry, one specific, the others necessarily vague.

Regularity of metrical pattern. The most tangible characteristic of poetry is rhythm secured by regularity of metrical pattern. Much prose has every element of poetry except this of metrical pattern. But all poetry, even free verse, has some pattern of recurrent rhythm or rhyme, or both.

The poet's use of words. The second characteristic of poetry is that the poet uses words with imaginative insight to suggest more than they may be defined to mean. In general, the main function of words in prose is to make statements, to convey ideas and facts clearly; in poetry the main function of words is to arouse moving suggestions. This use of suggestive words stirs our feelings and imaginations. We have all experienced the baffled sensation of lacking appropriate words with which to express our feelings or thoughts; and most of us have found these feelings and thoughts expressed definitively in a passage from one of the great poets. The essence of a thousand love stories, for instance, is suggested—not stated—in a single stanza by Robert Burns:

> Had we never loved sae kindly,
> Had we never loved sae blindly,
> Never met—or never parted,
> We had ne'er been broken-hearted.

The staggering conception of eternal damnation has been summed up in a few words in Dante's *Inferno*. Over the gates of Hell, Dante says, are these words:

> All hope abandon, ye who enter here.

The thundering significance of these few words has caught and held the imagination of generations. Such passages as these are remarkable for what they suggest rather than for what they directly state.

Feeling created through poetic suggestion. The poet creates feeling through the suggestive power of words. It is the power of words in themselves to arouse our imaginations and to create feeling that the poet uses with greatest effect. This is the power of poetic suggestion.

A majority of the words which we use have a double significance—that is, they have a *denotation*, or a dictionary meaning, and a *connotation*, or a wealth of suggested meanings. The word *home* is an obvious example. The dictionary definition of home is "a dwelling place" or "the abode of one's family." But how much more than that does it mean to each of us! To some it means father and mother. To some it means good things to eat and cosy attics on rainy days, or the smell of burning leaves, or

> the velvet, imperial crowd—
> The dahlias that reign by the gardenside,

or the swish of

> ladies' skirts across the grass,

or

> the unmeaning beat
> Of ghostly finger-tips of sleet

on the windowpane. All these memories are flashed to the mind in images of forgotten sights, sounds, and smells by that one word *home*. As we have already seen, it is the poet's power of using words so that their connotative meaning arouses our imaginations and our feelings that is his chief gift. Single vivid phrases presenting images tinged with feeling are characteristic of poetry.

Suggestive restraint. The poet may, by restraint, suggest other things than sensations and pictures. Often a single phrase will reveal the depth of a human heart. How much is suggested in a few words by Ophelia's simple response to Hamlet's brutal

> I did love you once!

The only words her heart can utter are,

> I was the more deceiv'd,

and there are no more pathetic lines in all Shakespeare. How much pathos is condensed into one line in Wordsworth's "Michael" when the poet says that the old father, heartbroken over his son's selfishness and weakness, went forth many a day to work at clearing the land

> And never lifted up a single stone.

Denotation and connotation. The denotation of words in poetry is, of course, important, even though connotation is of more value than exact definition. One has to know that "charlock" is wild mustard in order to get the picture in

> and shone far-off as shines
> A field of charlock in the sudden sun
> Between two showers,

and that a "shallop" is a light, swift boat in order to appreciate the adaptation of sound to sense in

> The shallop flitteth silken-sail'd.

It is also well to know that "mews" and "peewits" are shore birds like our gulls in order to visualize

> The flights of mew and peewits pied
> By millions crouched on the old sea wall,

and one must look up "eygre" to learn that it means a tidal wave in order to feel the force of

> So farre, so fast the eygre drave,
> The heart had hardly time to beat,
> Before a shallow seething wave
> Sobbed in the grasses at oure feet:
> The feet had hardly time to flee
> Before it brake against the knee,
> And all the world was in the sea.

It is necessary to understand the denotation of words before we can fully appreciate their connotative value.

Sometimes, however, we lay too much stress upon the denotation of proper names which at times have a connotative value quite disproportionate to their importance as allusions to history. For instance, we frequently spoil the finest figure in Keats' sonnet "On First Looking into Chapman's Homer" by stressing the error of making Cortez and not Balboa the discoverer of the Pacific. To Keats the name Cortez stood just as effectively as that of Balboa for all the breathless, crowded suggestions of romance and discovery that he felt when he first read Chapman's "Homer":

> like stout Cortez, when with eagle eyes
> He star'd at the Pacific—and all his men
> Look'd at each other with a wild surmise—
> Silent, upon a peak in Darien.

What if historically it was Balboa? Is not Cortez just as valuable for purposes of suggestion? Why ruin that breathless picture by reminding ourselves of the facts of history? We do not need a geography in hand to enjoy the richness of these lines from Keats:

> Manna and dates, in argosy transferr'd
> From Fez; and spiced dainties, every one,
> From silken Samarcand to cedar'd Lebanon.

As far as poetic suggestion is concerned, the chief value of proper names is their connotative value. Therefore besides knowing their literal meaning, we ought to be sure that words convey to us the suggestion which the poet wishes them to convey.

Poetic language in prose. Many prose writers also use words which arouse our feelings and our imagination by the power of suggestion. For instance, Hawthorne's choice of figurative language to suggest his meaning is often instinctively poetic. When he says that Phoebe was as "pleasant about the house as a gleam of sunshine falling on the floor through a shadow of twinkling leaves"; when he describes the garden as a "green-play-place of flickering light and shade," and the humming bird as "a thumb's bigness of burnished plumage," he is using words much as a poet does, to suggest moods and pictures. But as his words have no metrical pattern, they are not poetry. Moreover, poetical prose, however beautiful, does not usually linger in the memory as does poetry. It is the poet rather than the prose writer who uses words primarily for purposes of suggestion instead of primarily for purposes of direct statement. To the poet, words in themselves are beautiful. A poet's statement of this feeling for words may be found in Anna Hempstead Branch's "Her Words" from *Songs for My Mother:*

My mother has the prettiest tricks
  Of words and words and words.
Her talk comes out as smooth and sleek
  As breasts of singing birds.

She shapes her speech all silver fine
  Because she loves it so.
And her own eyes begin to shine
  To hear her stories grow.

And if she goes to make a call
  Or out to take a walk
We leave our work when she returns
  And run to hear her talk.

We had not dreamed these things were so
  Of sorrow and of mirth.
Her speech is as a thousand eyes
  Through which we see the earth.

God wove a web of loveliness,
  Of clouds and stars and birds,
But made not anything at all
  So beautiful as words.

They shine around our simple earth
  With golden shadowings,
And every common thing they touch
  Is exquisite with wings.

There's nothing poor and nothing small
  But is made fair with them.
They are the hands of living faith
  That touch the garment's hem.

They are as fair as bloom or air,
  They shine like any star,
And I am rich who learned from her
  How beautiful they are.[1]

[1] Reprinted by permission of and arrangement with Houghton Mifflin Company.

The poet's attitude toward the world about him. The third and most fundamental characteristic of poetry lies in the poet's way of looking at things. His sensibilities are keener than those of other men. His imagination is more quickly aroused. Others, looking out of their windows, feel vaguely the beauty of spring; the poet translates that feeling into an imaginative picture of

> . . . daffodils,
> That come before the swallow dares, and take
> The winds of March with beauty.

The poet's senses are keener: odor, sound, touch, and taste make an immediate appeal to him. He sees and hears with finer sensibilities than other men, and writes of

> The coming musk-rose, full of dewy wine,
> The murmurous haunt of flies on summer eves.

Then, too, his emotions are more deeply stirred. Most of his writing is done under stimulus of the strong feelings created in him by his imagination. Life to him is, first of all, an imaginative experience. To him

> the meanest flower that blows can give
> Thoughts that do often lie too deep for tears.

The poet and Nature. For the poet Nature is rarely disassociated from feeling. He observes that

> The rainbow comes and goes,
> And lovely is the rose;
> The moon doth with delight
> Look round her when the heavens are bare;
> Waters on a starry night
> Are beautiful and fair;

and this beautiful picture creates in him a feeling which causes him to add,

> But yet I know, where'er I go,
> That there hath passed away a glory from the earth.

Sometimes his imagination carries him further than this, and he associates himself with Nature till he becomes one with her, as Shelley does in his invocation to the West Wind:

Make me thy lyre, even as the forest is:
What if my leaves are falling like its own?
The tumult of thy mighty harmonies
Will take from both a deep autumnal tone,
Sweet though in sadness. Be thou, Spirit fierce,
My spirit! Be thou me, impetuous one!

The poet's attitude toward man. In his attitude toward man, also, the poet is moved primarily by his imagination. Perhaps because of this, he sees into the heart of man and interprets truly what he sees there. Tennyson, for instance, in his shorter lyrics of purely personal emotion has given almost perfect expression to the feeling of grief for

what has been
And never more will be

which is common to us all. In this ability to speak for all mankind the poet is the representative of the race. He feels for all the world when he cries:

Rough wind, that moanest loud
Grief, too sad for song;
Wild wind, when sullen cloud
Knells all night long;
Sad storm, whose tears are vain,
Bare woods, whose branches strain,
Deep caves and dreary main,—
Wail, for the world's wrong!

The poet's yearning for ideal beauty. Perhaps it is the very keenness of the poet's sensibilities which sometimes makes the beauty of the world almost an intolerable pain to him, inspiring him with a restless dissatisfaction with things as they are. All of us, no doubt, feel a vague discontent, a

desire of the moth for the star,
Of the day for the morrow,
The devotion to something afar
From the sphere of our sorrow.

Like Keats, when we hear the nightingale, we, too, are filled with a sort of divine discontent even while we are under the hushed spell of moonlight and leaves, through which the song of the bird is fading,

Past the near meadows, over the still stream,
Up the hill-side . . . buried deep
In the next valley-glades.

We, too, should like to escape where we can quite forget what he among the leaves has never known:

The weariness, the fever, and the fret,

the solitude and fear and pain and grief and all

The dreary intercourse of daily life.

Like Matthew Arnold, we have seen the moonlight on the ocean and,

the long line of spray
Where the sea meets the moon-blanch'd land.

But in us as in him, this beauty has touched a chord of melancholy, a sad reflection that,

the world, which seems
To lie before us like a land of dreams,
So various, so beautiful, so new,
Hath really neither joy, nor love, nor light,
Nor certitude, nor peace, nor help for pain;

Men and women, it is true, feel vaguely these deep-hidden emotions. They know the sad sense of exile, the inarticulate nostalgia of the soul,

Strange, piteous, futile thing,

seeking release

From dusty bondage into luminous air.

But the poet feels these things more keenly, and expresses them more beautifully and insistently. He cannot "cry, 'Content' to that which grieves his heart," though he knows with Meredith

Ah, what a dusty answer gets the soul
When hot for certainties in this our life!

For all poets, as for Keats, all too often, Melancholy

> dwells with Beauty—Beauty that must die;
> And Joy, whose hand is ever at his lips
> Bidding adieu.

The poet seeks an answer to life's riddle. But as the poet feels the incompleteness and dissatisfactions of life more keenly than ordinary people, he often has, too, a mystical, intuitive vision of its meaning. Francis Thompson can say, in spite of all,

> Such is; what is to be?
> The pulp so bitter, how shall taste the rind?
> I dimly guess what Time in mists confounds;
> Yet ever and anon a trumpet sounds
> From the hid battlements of Eternity;
> Those shaken mists a space unsettle, then
> Round the half-glimpsed turrets slowly wash again.[1]

Tennyson can continue blindly steadfast in his faith in an ultimate meaning to life:

> O, yet we trust that somehow good
> Will be the final goal of ill,
>
> That not a worm is cloven in vain;
> That not a moth with vain desire
> Is shrivell'd in a fruitless fire,
> Or but subserves another's gain.
>
> Behold, we know not anything;
> I can but trust that good shall fall
> At last—far off—at last, to all,
> And every winter change to spring.[2]

Even in the midst of the "still sad music of humanity," Wordsworth can feel:

> . . . a sense sublime
> Of something far more deeply interfused,
> Whose dwelling is the light of setting suns,
> And the round ocean and the living air,
> And the blue sky, and in the mind of man;
> A motion and a spirit, that impels
> All thinking things, all objects of all thought,
> And rolls through all things.[3] . . .

[1] "The Hound of Heaven."
[2] "In Memoriam."
[3] "Lines Composed a Few Miles above Tintern Abbey."

And Browning can afford to be defiant to life's incompleteness

All we have willed or hoped or dreamed of good shall exist;
  Not its semblance, but itself; no beauty, nor good, nor power
Whose voice has gone forth, but each survives for the melodist
  When eternity affirms the conception of an hour.
The high that proved too high, the heroic for earth too hard,
  The passion that left the ground to lose itself in the sky,
Are music sent up to God by the lover and the bard;
  Enough that he heard it once: we shall hear it by and by.[1]

This sympathy and this ability to express what we all feel but cannot all say are the supreme gifts of the poet to us—consolation in hours of despair, loneliness and pain; sympathy and understanding in moments of joy. It is from him, too, that we get our truest sympathy for those about us, through him that we hear

The still, sad music of humanity,
Nor harsh nor grating, though of ample power
To chasten and subdue.

All this is only another way of saying that the poet's imagination is more sensitive to all that touches it than other men's. Through it, his very senses are made more keen; he sees and hears and feels in the world about him subtle beauty or ugliness which quite escape us. Through it, also, he is able to interpret what he feels so that there is nothing that his imagination touches

But doth suffer a sea-change
Into something rich and strange.

Here, then, are ample reasons why an appreciation of poetry makes one's knowledge of life more keen and his understanding of it more sympathetic. The language of poetry is the truest language of the human heart.

Summary. Although the dividing line between prose and poetry is difficult to draw, poetry generally has a metrical pattern (where prose has not); the poet stresses the suggestive power of words (where the prose writer stresses exact meanings); and, most important of all, the poet looks on the life and the world about him as an emotional, imaginative experience (where the prose writer is more likely to stress the intellectual side of experience).

[1] "Abt Vogler."

COMPREHENSION QUESTIONS

1. *Vocabulary:* rhyme, rhythm, meter, connotation, denotation, poetic suggestion, nostalgia, intuition, vision, mystical, mysterious, illogical, frustration.
2. Name and explain in your own words the three chief qualities which distinguish poetry from prose.
3. Find and bring to class some verses which seem to you to have none of the qualities of poetry except rhyme and meter.
4. Find and bring to class one passage of prose which seems to you to be poetical in feeling and imagination.
5. Explain and illustrate the difference between the connotation and the denotation of words.
6. Why does the poem "Her Words" from *Songs for My Mother*, quoted in this chapter, help to illustrate the poet's feeling for words?
7. Name a common experience that would not stir the feelings of the ordinary practical man but that would arouse deep feeling in a poet.
8. Why does the poet so often associate sadness with beauty?
9. What are some of the evidences of the incompleteness and disillusionments of life which particularly stir the poet?
10. Find a poem in which the poet expresses his sadness about some common human trouble.
11. Why do so many poets write about the passing of time and the fading of beauty?
12. Find a poem in which the poet expresses confident faith which he feels but cannot explain.

PROBLEMS IN APPRECIATION

1. The foregoing pages on the poet's attitude toward man and Nature and the riddle of human destiny will perhaps help you to understand some of the most beautiful and noble poems ever written. Here are a few which express the poet's feeling for beauty, his sensitiveness, his divine discontent, his faith and courage and intuitive vision. See how these poems illustrate the poet's attitude toward life. But first, of course, you must read and study them for themselves; then you can see their relationship to the larger field of all poetic instinct and aspiration:

Arnold	"Dover Beach"
Browning	"Rabbi Ben Ezra," "Abt Vogler"
Ralph Hodgson	"The Song of Honour"
Keats	"Ode on a Grecian Urn," "Ode on Melancholy," "Ode to a Nightingale"

Thompson	"The Hound of Heaven"
Wordsworth	"Lines Composed a Few Miles above Tintern Abbey"

2. The following poems are particularly good illustrations of the fact that poets see and feel more intensely than ordinary people, that experiences which do not seem matters of intense feeling to unimaginative, practical men and women of common sense are often of great emotional significance to poets. Point out in at least three of these poems the lines that would seem exaggerated to a man with no imagination. Is the poet's sensitiveness too great, or has his feeling a real significance that has escaped the ordinary man?

Byron	"To the Ocean"
William H. Davies	"Leisure"
De la Mare	"The Mother Bird"
Hardy	"The Darkling Thrush"
Ralph Hodgson	"The Bull," "Eve," "The Song of Honour"
A. E. Housman	"Loveliest of Trees"
Keats	"Ode to a Nightingale," "Ode on Melancholy"
Shelley	"To a Skylark," "The Cloud," "Ode to the West Wind"
Wordsworth	"I Wandered Lonely as a Cloud," "The Solitary Reaper"

3. In these poems compare and contrast the varying attitudes toward the one universal human experience, death:

Rupert Brooke	"The Dead"
Browning	"Prospice"
Bryant	"Thanatopsis"
Robert Frost	"Out, Out—," "The Death of the Hired Man"
Gray	"Elegy Written in a Country Churchyard"
Christina Rossetti	"Song" (see p. 13)
Alan Seeger	"I Have a Rendezvous with Death"
Shakespeare	Hamlet's Soliloquy, Claudio's Soliloquy in *Measure for Measure*
Tennyson	"Break, Break, Break" (see p. 43)
Katharine Tynan	"Easter"
Louis Untermeyer	"Matter"

Henry Vaughan	"Beyond the Veil"
Whitman	"When Lilacs Last in the Dooryard Bloomed"
Wordsworth	"She Dwelt among the Untrodden Ways" (see p. 42)
Elinor Wylie	"Hymn to Earth," "Bells in the Rain"

4. Another subject that particularly occupies the thoughts and feelings of poets is the passing of time and the toll it takes. Show how this idea enters into the following poems. Quote the most eloquent lines. Compare and contrast the different attitudes:

Arnold	"Rugby Chapel"
Browning	"Earth's Immortalities," "Time's Revenges," "Love among the Ruins"
Herrick	"Counsel to Girls"
Hodgson	"Time, You Old Gypsy Man"
A. E. Housman	"With Rue My Heart Is Laden," "When First My Way"
Keats	"Ode on a Grecian Urn" (see p. 100), "When I Have Fears"
Masefield	"On Malvern Hill," *Sonnets*
Lizette Woodworth Reese	"Tears"
Edwin Arlington Robinson	"Monadnock through the Trees"
Carl Sandburg	"Cool Tombs," "Grass"
Stevenson	"A Lad That Is Gone," "We Uncommiserate Pass into the Night"
Tennyson	"Tears, Idle Tears"

5. Practically all poets are concerned deeply with beauty. They are touched at once by it, and, more than this, it awakens in them an unfulfilled desire for beauty beyond that this earth can offer. Try to trace both these characteristics in the following poems:

Rupert Brooke	"Blue Evening," "Grantchester"
Grace Hazard Conkling	"After Sunset"
William H. Davies	"The Kingfisher," "The Moon"
De la Mare	"The Listeners" (p. 88), "Silver," "Tartary" (p. 2), "Arabia"
Camilla Doyle	"The Prettiest Things"
Keats	"Ode to a Nightingale" (p. 40), "Ode on a Grecian Urn" (p. 100)
Vachel Lindsay	"The Chinese Nightingale"

Masefield	"On Growing Old"
Noyes	"The Barrel-Organ," "The Flower of Old Japan"
Shelley	"To a Skylark," "The Cloud," "The Question"
Sara Teasdale	"Spring Night," "Barter," "Stars"

6. Find in any contemporary anthology evidence that poetry can be found in the most commonplace subjects:

locomotives	windmills	steel mills	brickyards
subways	birds	boats in a fog	water
stone walls	fishes	ships	
swimming	automobile riding	donkeys	

Compile your own list for a short essay on the poetry of the commonplace.

7. In June, 1932, the College Entrance Examination Board quoted this passage from Hazlitt's essay "On Poetry in General" to see whether the students taking the examination really did see a relationship between poetry and life. Read it carefully several times *after you have familiarized yourself with some of the poetry listed below.* Can you quote passages from these poems which seem to you to illustrate either favorably or unfavorably what Hazlitt says?

> Poetry is the language of the imagination and the passions. It relates to whatever gives immediate pleasure or pain to the human mind. It comes home to the bosoms and businesses of men; for nothing but what so comes home to them in the most general and intelligible shape can be a subject for poetry. Poetry is the universal language which the heart holds with Nature and itself. . . . It is not a mere frivolous accomplishment . . . the trifling amusement of a few idle readers or leisure hours—it has been the study and delight of mankind in all ages. Many people suppose that poetry is something to be found only in books, contained in lines of ten syllables, with like endings: but wherever there is a sense of beauty, or power, or harmony, as in the motion of a wave of the sea, in the growth of a flower that "spreads its sweet leaves to the air, and dedicates its beauty to the sun,"—*there* is poetry, in its birth. . . . There is no thought or feeling that can have entered into the mind of man, which he would be eager to communicate to others, or which they would listen to with delight, that is not a fit subject for poetry.

A study of the following poems should supply you with material illustrative of Hazlitt's remarks:

Arnold	"Dover Beach" (page 85), "The Buried Life"
Rupert Brooke	"The Soldier," "The Great Lover" (page 7), "Grantchester"
Browning	"Rabbi Ben Ezra," "Saul"
Coleridge	"The Ancient Mariner"
De la Mare	"The Listeners" (page 88), "Old Susan," "All but Blind" (page 93)
Wilfred W. Gibson	"The Ice-Cart," "Geraniums," "Solway Ford"
Gray	"Elegy Written in a Country Churchyard"
Ralph Hodgson	"The Song of Honour," "Eve" (page 90), "The Bull"
A. E. Housman	*A Shropshire Lad, Last Poems*
Keats	"Ode to a Nightingale" (pages 40-41), "Ode on a Grecian Urn" (page 100)
Masefield	*Dauber, The Everlasting Mercy, King Cole, Sonnets*
Millay	"Renascence"
Noyes	"The Forest of Wild Thyme"
Carl Sandburg	*Chicago Poems*
Shelley	"To a Skylark"
Tennyson	"Break, Break, Break" (page 43), "Tears, Idle Tears" (page 170), "Morte d'Arthur," "Ulysses"

8. Some of the following words and phrases have connotative power; others have not. Some are suggestive but not necessarily poetic. Make a list of the ones that to you are poetic (suggestive) or prosaic (literal) and those that are doubtful. Explain your reasons for each choice. What do the connotative words suggest to you personally?

stout Cortez	deep	summer	copper
eternity	Golgotha	cousins	ink
multitudinous seas	stars	margin	arbitration
silken Samarkand	democracy	Spain	collection
cedar'd Lebanon	1914	Penelope	example
affections	palms	Priscilla	fugue
development	sticks	Mary	shortstop
alone	Mandalay	Alexander	Orpheus
Happy Warrior	Hoboken	Robert E. Lee	prairies
Gorgeous East	Cathay	tiger	Tartary

barbaric pearl	Virginia	ant	Norse
light	Judas	angles	blotting paper
machine	octogenarian	perpendicular	fire box
carburetor	violets	Sphinx	subject
still	cabbages	electricity	Mr. Wilkinson, a clergyman
dark	sea	Snowbound	

9. Here is a poem which is a very good example of the way poets look at life. The scientific, practical, and prosaic point of view about the stars does not satisfy Walt Whitman. To him, the contemplation of Nature is an emotional experience; he is impatient of mere facts. Show how this poem illustrates a difference between poetry and prose. Can you think of other experiences to which a poet might react as he did to the learned astronomer? Is his mood wholly confined to poets, or do ordinary people also feel it?

When I heard the learn'd astronomer,
When the proofs, the figures, were ranged in columns before me,
When I was shown the charts and diagrams, to add, divide, and measure them,
When I sitting heard the astronomer where he lectured with much applause in the lecture-room,
How soon unaccountable I became tired and sick,
Till rising and gliding out I wander'd off by myself,
In the mystical moist night-air, and from time to time,
Look'd up in perfect silence at the stars.

10. In each of the following passages pick out the words and phrases which have the *power of suggestion.* What do they suggest: color? sound? mood? odor? touch? taste? feeling? heat? cold? fear? softness? hardness? Have any of the proper names connotative value? Be specific in your discussion.

(*a*) While he from forth the closet brought a heap
Of candied apple, quince, and plum, and gourd;
With jellies soother than the creamy curd,
And lucent syrops, tinct with cinnamon;
Manna and dates, in argosy transferr'd
From Fez; and spiced dainties, every one,
From silken Samarcand to cedar'd Lebanon.

KEATS

(*b*) These delicates he heap'd with glowing hand
On golden dishes and in baskets bright
Of wreathed silver: sumptuous they stand
In the retired quiet of the night,
Filling the chilly room with perfume light.

KEATS

(c) The lustrous salvers in the moonlight gleam.

KEATS

(d) Noiseless as fear in a wide wilderness.

KEATS

(e) The silver, snarling trumpets 'gan to chide.

KEATS

(f) Death, like a friend's voice from a distant field
Approaching thro' the darkness, call'd; the owls
Wailing had power upon her, and she mixt
Her fancies with the sallow-rifted glooms
Of evening and the moanings of the wind.

TENNYSON

(g) the wan day
Went glooming down in wet and weariness.

TENNYSON

(h) Silver sails all out of the west.

TENNYSON

(i) Disdain and scorn ride sparkling in her eyes.

SHAKESPEARE

(j) How sweet the moonlight sleeps upon this bank.

SHAKESPEARE

(k) Alone, alone, all, all alone,
Alone on a wide, wide sea!

COLERIDGE

(l) The fair breeze blew, the white foam flew,
The furrow follow'd free;
We were the first that ever burst
Into that silent sea.

COLERIDGE

(m) There is not wind enough to twirl
The one red leaf, the last of its clan,
That dances as often as dance it can,
Hanging so light, and hanging so high,
On the topmost twig that looks up at the sky.

COLERIDGE

(n) Deep in the shady sadness of a vale
Far sunken from the healthy breath of morn,
Far from the fiery noon, and eve's one star,
Sat gray-hair'd Saturn, quiet as a stone,
Still as the silence round about his lair;
Forest on forest hung about his head

Like cloud on cloud. No stir of air was there,
Not so much life as on a summer's day
Robs not one light seed from the feather'd grass,
But where the dead leaf fell, there did it rest.

KEATS

(*o*) Coldly, sadly descends
The autumn-evening. The field
Strewn with its dank yellow drifts
Of wither'd leaves, and the elms,
Fade into dimness apace,
Silent;—hardly a shout
From a few boys late at their play!
The lights come out in the street,
In the school-room windows;—but cold,
Solemn, unlighted, austere,
Through the gathering darkness, arise
The chapel-walls.

ARNOLD

(*p*) at midnight,
When soft the winds blow,
When clear falls the moonlight,
When spring tides are low;
When sweet airs come seaward
From heaths starr'd with broom,
And the high rocks throw mildly
On the blanch'd sands a gloom;
Up the still, glistening beaches,
Up the creeks we will hie,
Over banks of bright seaweed
The ebb-tide leaves dry.
We will gaze, from the sand-hills,
At the white, sleeping town;
At the church on the hillside—
And then come back down.
Singing: "There dwells a loved one,
But cruel is she!
She left lonely for ever
The kings of the sea!"

ARNOLD

(*q*) The lights begin to twinkle from the rocks;
The long day wanes: the slow moon climbs: the deep
Moans round with many voices.

TENNYSON

(*r*)

O mother Ida, many fountain'd Ida
Dear mother Ida, harken ere I die.
For now the noonday quiet holds the hill;
The grasshopper is silent in the grass:
The lizard, with his shadow on the stone,
Rests like a shadow, and the winds are dead.
The purple flower droops: the golden bee
Is lily-cradled.

TENNYSON

(*s*)

One seem'd all dark and red—a tract of sand,
  And some one pacing there alone,
Who paced forever in a glimmering land,
  Lit with a low large moon.

One show'd an iron coast and angry waves.
  You seem'd to hear them climb and fall
And roar rock-thwarted under bellowing caves,
  Beneath the windy wall.

TENNYSON

(*t*)

The gray sea and the long black land;
And the yellow half-moon large and low;
And the startled little waves that leap
In fiery ringlets from their sleep,
As I gain the cove with pushing prow,
And quench its speed i' the slushy sand.

Then a mile of warm sea-scented beach;
Three fields to cross till a farm appears;
A tap at the pane, the quick sharp scratch
And blue spurt of a lighted match,
And a voice less loud, thro' its joys and fears,
Than the two hearts beating each to each!

BROWNING

CHAPTER 3

SHARING THE POET'S WORLD

There are three elements to be found in any poem. These are:

(1) *The imagination.* As we have seen, one of the chief differences between prose and poetry lies in the greater sensitiveness of the poet's imagination. It is chiefly through his imagination that the poet makes his appeal to our senses, our feelings, and even our intellects.

(2) *The thought of the poem.* Many poems present through the medium of the imagination ideas which are well worth the reader's serious study, though these ideas are more often suggested than directly stated, because the poet finds it more natural and more effective to express himself through suggestion than through direct statement. Some of the deepest and most enduring thoughts that have come to man have been expressed through the medium of poetry.

(3) *The form.* Form is the technical means by which the poet expresses his feelings or his ideas, through sound, images, pattern, and other devices. This is the most tangible, as well as the most technical, part of the study of poetry.

One of the chief functions of the imagination in poetry lies in its power to create feeling. One may read prose in the pursuit of information or ideas or just to get a good story, but if a man likes poetry at all, he likes it because it appeals to some sort of emotion that he has himself felt or can understand.

Universality of appeal. The chief standard by which we judge the emotional appeal of a poem is its universality. Almost without exception all great works of art have dealt with the eternal passions, aspirations, and regrets that fall to the lot of every human being, whether they flow from

old, unhappy, far-off things,
And battles long ago;

or from

Some natural sorrow, loss, or pain
That has been, and may be again.

Indeed no matter how trite the subject matter of a poem or how slipshod and sentimental its language, it is sure of an appreciative audience if it touches a familiar chord.

What most of us need to learn, however, is how to distinguish between the trite, sentimental, or cheap expression of a universal theme, which we find in songs like "The Vacant Chair," and the artistically perfect expression of the same theme in a poem like Tennyson's "Break, Break, Break." It is true that the surest touchstone of enduring quality in a work of art is the universality of its appeal; but this alone is not enough to stamp a work of art as great or even to make it a work of art at all. Whittier's "Barefoot Boy," for instance, is not a great poem, but it appeals to a reminiscent, somewhat sentimental feeling that we all have toward boyhood. That much loved Hoosier poet, James Whitcomb Riley, certainly did not write a great poem in "A Life Lesson," but he did make an instant appeal to all of us who have suffered from broken dollies and broken teasets and broken hearts and who are wistfully aware that

the rainbow gleams
Of . . . youthful dreams
Are things of the long ago.

Assuredly, a universal emotional appeal will make a poem popular, bringing pleasure and comfort to many, but it cannot be taken as a guarantee of greatness. There must be other tests of greatness, of which universality of appeal is only one element.

Sentimentality and self-consciousness. Besides being universal, the emotion inspired by a poem must be genuine, not affected, and it must be justified, not sentimental. *By sentimentality we mean reveling in emotion for its own sake. It is feeling that is not justified by the circumstances, or language that exaggerates the emotion the poet seeks to arouse.* But how can the inexperienced, impressionable reader know what is sentimental and what is justifiable? This question is not always easy to answer. There are, however, a few common symptoms of the more obvious kinds of sentimentality. One is self-consciousness. *The sentimental person is always thinking first of himself. He luxuriates in his own feelings, calling on others to witness them.* For example, there is Orlando's speech to the Duke and his followers in *As You Like It:*

> But whate'er you are
> That in this desert inaccessible,
> Under the shade of melancholy boughs,
> Lose and neglect the creeping hours of time;
> If ever you have look'd on better days,
> If ever been where bells have knoll'd to church,
> If ever sat at any good man's feast,
> If ever from your eyelids wip'd a tear
> And know what 'tis to pity and be pitied,
> Let gentleness my strong enforcement be:
> In the which hope I blush, and hide my sword.

And in the same play we find Silvius explaining to all and sundry "what 'tis to love":

> It is to be all made of sighs and tears;
>
> It is to be all made of faith and service;
>
> It is to be all made of fantasy,
> All made of passion and all made of wishes,
> All adoration, duty, and observance,
> All humbleness, all patience, and impatience,
> All purity, all trial, all observance.

It is no wonder that Rosalind cries out upon this extravagant sentimentality, calling it

> the howling of Irish wolves against the moon

for she, many fathoms deep in love though she is, is not a sentimentalist. She knows that "Men have died from time to time and worms have eaten them, but not for love."

Sentimentality and self-pity. Self-pity is particularly unpleasant and discreditable. When Tennyson makes Elaine talk in the unnatural style she affects on her deathbed, singing her little song of love and death, making fine epigrams about Lancelot, and giving such elaborate directions for her funeral, the reader feels slightly sticky with sentiment. It is all too self-conscious, too artificial, too much assumed for effect. It falsifies Elaine's character, and almost nullifies the effect of the genuinely touching and restrained scene with Lancelot in the garden that precedes it. The trouble is not with the situation; innocent idealism and hero worship are not, if properly presented, sentimental motives at all. The trouble is that both Tennyson and Elaine are more concerned with the effect they are making than with realities. Tennyson made the same mistake with the Queen's final repentance in "Guinevere"; but in "Geraint and Enid," he handled Enid's meek joy at her deliverance much better. Here, because he did not say too much, Tennyson escaped the pitfall of sentimentality. The greatest writers learn to avoid this pitfall. With all the dangers confronting him in his delineation of Viola, Ophelia, Desdemona, Cordelia, Perdita, and Miranda, Shakespeare never once struck a false note. We, too, must learn to distinguish between true and false feeling. We should beware of that song in which,

> The hours I spent with thee, dear heart,
> Are as a string of pearls to me.
>
> Each hour a pearl, each pearl a prayer
> To still a heart in absence wrung,
>
> O memories that bless and burn,
> O barren gain, and bitter loss.
>
> My rosary! my rosary!

However justified the feeling may be, the language exaggerates it beyond all proportion, for the whole poem revels in self-conscious self-pity. Back in the early days of this century, people used to sing a somewhat limp song:

> Sing me to sleep, thy hand in mine,
> Our fingers as in prayer entwine

without realizing that they should not want to feel quite that way on so slight a provocation even if they could. A little later their children would quaver out falsetto notes bewailing the fact (?) that

It seems like a year since I've seen you, dear,
Yet I know it's been only a day,

without realizing that, after all, they could not feel quite so grieved as that about it. The feeling in such verse is not justified. And for the present generation, let radio crooners and torch singers supply the horrible examples.

Poetic sensibility that is not sentimentality. Sometimes, however, it is difficult to decide whether the emotional appeal of a poem is real and justified. This is because great poets often write poems expressing great emotion on subjects which seem to us not to warrant so much feeling. Keats is often misjudged in this respect. One of his most beautiful poems, the "Ode to a Nightingale," is a case in point. It begins,

My heart aches, and a drowsy numbness pains
  My sense, as though of hemlock I had drunk,
Or emptied some dull opiate to the drains
  One minute past, and Lethe-wards had sunk:

O, for a draught of vintage! that hath been
  Cool'd a long age in the deep-delved earth,

  That I might drink, and leave the world unseen,
And with thee fade away into the forest dim:

Fade far away, dissolve, and quite forget
  What thou among the leaves hast never known,
The weariness, the fever, and the fret

And leaden-eyed despairs.

Now this doubtless seems like strong language to many people who may never have heard a nightingale, or who, even if they have, have never felt quite that way about it. Certainly it offers a problem as to the justice of the emotional appeal of the poem, although the power of the language leaves no question of its sincerity. What we must do here is to yield ourselves to the spell of the imaginative picture that Keats has created. That is real, based on a genuine experience beautifully recreated in phrase after phrase laden with poetic suggestion of gardens and dim trees drenched with moonlight and dew, and flooding it all, the song of the bird,

Perhaps the self-same song that found a path
  Through the sad heart of Ruth, when, sick for home,
  She stood in tears amid the alien corn;
    The same that oft-times hath
Charm'd magic casements, opening on the foam
Of perilous seas, in faery lands forlorn.

No one who has had the emotional experience of yielding to the imaginative appeal of this poem will stop to question further; he can only be grateful that the song of the nightingale so long ago should have created such a lasting heritage of beauty for us. There is no better way of judging the sincerity and enduring justice of a poem than by studying the power and beauty of its language. Words that evoke passion and beauty by their sheer connotative power can hardly be called sentimental.

Restraint the opposite of sentimentality. In general, however, the poet establishes his sincerity by what he does not say rather than by what he does, that is by *suggestive restraint.*

The lady doth protest too much, methinks,

says Queen Gertrude of the Player Queen in *Hamlet.* And, indeed, to protest too much is one of the surest ways of creating an impression of insincerity and thus of losing the reader's sympathy. In *Twelfth Night,* for instance, there is a significant difference between the extravagant, though beautiful, sentimentality of Orsino's.

That strain again! it had a dying fall:
O, it came o'er my ear like the sweet sound,
That breathes upon a bank of violets,
Stealing and giving odor!

Away before me to sweet beds of flowers:
Love-thoughts lie rich when canopied with bowers,

and the simple pathos of Viola's,

She never told her love,
But let concealment, like a worm i' the bud,
Feed on her damask cheek.

Of course, the failure to repress one's feelings does not necessarily mean that the feeling is insincere. There are times when the strength of the poet's feelings reaches an ecstasy of love, despair, or hate that makes restraint impossible. In general, however, the poet gains far greater effect by suggesting all that he feels in a few simple words than by attempting to tear a passion to tatters.

Instances of an intense emotional effect secured through restraint may be found in most of the really great poets. Shelley's "Ozymandias," Wordsworth's "Lucy" poems, Tennyson's "Break, Break, Break," and Matthew Arnold's "Requiescat" suggest themselves at once. Indeed, it is significant that four of the supreme lyrics of grief in our language are expressed in the simplest of words. The hours of aching loneliness that one feels for those he has loved and lost are here concentrated into a few quiet stanzas. Two of these lyrics may be quoted to show the power of restraint.

She dwelt among the untrodden ways
   Beside the springs of Dove,
A Maid whom there were none to praise
   And very few to love:

A violet by a mossy stone
   Half hidden from the eye!
Fair as a star, when only one
   Is shining in the sky.

She lived unknown, and few could know
   When Lucy ceased to be;
But she is in her grave, and oh,
   The difference to me!

WORDSWORTH

Here is the deepest personal feeling suggested in the most direct and simple terms. The two simple figures in the second stanza create a complete picture in themselves and perfectly suggest all that must have existed for Wordsworth in that friendship. The last two lines

But she is in her grave, and oh,
   The difference to me!

are so poignant in their connotation of heartbroken grief that they have become well-nigh proverbial.

The second illustration is Tennyson's "Break, Break, Break":

Break, break, break,
  On thy cold gray stones, O Sea!
And I would that my tongue could utter
  The thoughts that arise in me.

O, well for the fisherman's boy,
  That he shouts with his sister at play!
O, well for the sailor lad,
  That he sings in his boat on the bay!

And the stately ships go on
  To their haven under the hill;
But O for the touch of a vanish'd hand,
  And the sound of a voice that is still!

Break, break, break,
  At the foot of thy crags, O Sea!
But the tender grace of a day that is dead
  Will never come back to me.

This poem, written at "five o'clock in the morning between blossoming hedges" far inland, has become, in its perfect blending of imagery, tone color, and restraint, part of our common language of grief. Surely it is a convincing proof that a few words are often more significant than a great many.

Continuity of appeal. We must also be sure that there is no break in the feeling of a poem from beginning to end. You have doubtless noticed in a theater that the actor whose big scene is once spoiled by careless laughter cannot usually get back his grip on the feelings of the audience. This principle is doubly true in lyric poetry where the emotional spell is necessarily a brief one. A single prosaic line in the most impassioned lyric in the world is almost sure to ruin the whole poem. Tennyson's "Maud," for instance, contains some love poetry of a very high order, but the genuine ecstasy of one section is broken by this stanza,

I kiss'd her slender hand,
She took the kiss sedately;
Maud is not seventeen,
But she is tall and stately.

A few stanzas so tempting to one's sense of the ridiculous as this would ruin any poem.

Range of emotional power. There are two other standards by which we may judge the appeal of a poem to our feelings, though they are considerations which need not necessarily have any bearing upon its greatness. The first of these is the range of emotional power displayed in a poem. This does not concern the lyric, since most lyric poetry is the expression of a single mood. Judged by this standard some of our greatest poets take a comparatively low place. Keats' range is practically limited to the marvelous portrayal of beauty in its appeal to the senses. Wordsworth's greatness lies in his power of infusing the simplest of themes with tragic, sometimes almost exalted, intensity and beauty. Coleridge lives for a few passages of simple descriptive power, and for two or three single poems like "Christabel" and "The Ancient Mariner," that reach imaginative heights of a strange, unearthly kind which no other poet has attained.

Poe's poetry has little claim to immortality except its sheer music unencumbered by ideas. Burns is the great song writer. Some poets live for a single lyric. But we place Shakespeare and Milton and Browning high at the head of the list of English poets because they display a range of powers far beyond that of the others. The sensuous richness of Keats' imagery and the white radiance of Shelley's imagination, "pinnacled dim in the intense inane," are beyond the reach of any other single poet. But Shakespeare is beyond Keats and Shelley and all others, not in the one particular in which they surpass him, but in the stupendous length and breadth and depth of his power to understand and to express almost the whole range of human feeling. Therefore, although range of imagination does not enter into our estimate of lyrical poetry, it is a most important consideration as far as the relative greatness of individual poets is concerned.

Depth of emotional appeal. The other standard by which we measure the relative emotional value of a poem is the comparative depth of feeling it expresses. Obviously a gay little lyric like Constable's

> Diaphenia like the daffadowndilly,
> White as the sun, fair as the lily,

or a sweetly insincere one like Carew's

> Ask me no more where Jove bestows,
> When June is past, the fading rose;
> For in your beauty's orient deep
> These flowers, as in their causes, sleep,

cannot be ranked as great poetry, though they are charming of their kind. This difference in depth, however, should not lead us to lay too great stress upon comparative rank of feeling. A poem is meant to be a joy for what it is, not criticized for not being what it was never intended to be.

An excellent opportunity for studying relative depth of the emotional appeal in poetry is to be found in two poems dealing with the love of home, one by Longfellow and one by William Ernest Henley. Longfellow's is a quiet, pleasant little lyric with a gentle fluttering of dovelike feeling.

> Stay, stay at home, my heart, and rest;
> Home-keeping hearts are happiest,
> For those that wander they know not where
> Are full of trouble and full of care;
>   To stay at home is best.
>
> Weary and homesick and distressed,
> They wander east, they wander west,
> And are baffled and beaten and blown about
> By the winds of the wilderness of doubt;
>   To stay at home is best.
>
> Then stay at home, my heart, and rest;
> The bird is safest in its nest;
> O'er all that flutter their wings and fly
> A hawk is hovering in the sky;
>   To stay at home is best.

As you see, this is not a very profound feeling nor is it intended to be. The meter and the rhymes are suggestive of no deeper agitation than a quiet rustling of wings to rest. But the other poem, a more passionate variation of the same general theme, has all the throbbing eagerness of the homesick heart.

It runs, in part, as follows:

> O, Falmouth is a fine town with ships in the bay,
> And I wish from my heart it's there I was today;
> I wish from my heart I was far away from here,
> Sitting in my parlor and talking to my dear.
>   For it's home, dearie, home—it's home I want to be.
>   Our topsails are hoisted, and we'll away to sea.
>   O, the oak and the ash and the bonnie birken tree
>   They're all growing green in the old countrie.

O, there's a wind a-blowing, a-blowing from the west,
And that of all the winds is the one I like the best,
For it blows at our backs, and it shakes our pennon free,
And it soon will blow us home to the old countrie.
  For it's home, dearie, home—it's home I want to be.
  Our topsails are hoisted, and we'll away to sea.
  O, the oak and the ash and the bonnie birken tree
  They're all growing green in the old countrie.

When you have studied a bit more the details of poetic technique, you will be able to pick more than one flaw in this little poem, but you will never be able to challenge the conviction of the homesick pound of its rhythm and its yearning refrain. If you would carry the comparison further, there are many other poems which afford excellent opportunity for studying the depth of emotional appeal and the power with which it is expressed in poetry. Among these are Burns'

My heart's in the Highlands, my heart is not here;
My heart's in the Highlands, a-chasing the deer,

and Allan Cunningham's

Hame, hame, hame, hame, fain I wad be
O hame, hame, hame, to my ain countrie!

and that famous section from Scott's "Lay of the Last Minstrel" beginning

Breathes there the man with soul so dead,
Who never to himself hath said,
This is my own, my native land!

and, perhaps best of all, Browning's "Home Thoughts from Abroad"

Oh, to be in England,
Now that April's there,
And whoever wakes in England
Sees, some morning, unaware,
That the lowest boughs and the brushwood sheaf
Round the elm-tree bole are in tiny leaf,
While the chaffinch sings on the orchard bough
In England—now!

Summary. The emotional appeal of a poem may be judged by its *universality*, *justice*, *restraint*, *continuity*, *range*, and *depth*. If it expresses a feeling common to all human beings it is *universal;* if it is not marred by sentimentality, it is *justified;* if it suggests more than it says, it is *restrained;* if it is unbroken throughout the poem, it has *continuity.* Some poets express a *wider range* and *greater depth* of feeling than others. The greatest poetry can meet all these tests.

COMPREHENSION QUESTIONS

1. *Vocabulary:* universality, sentimentality, continuity, restraint, range, depth.
2. What do we mean by "universality of appeal"? Find a poem which expresses a universal feeling. Why is universality of feeling not a guarantee of poetic greatness?
3. What do we mean when we say that the feeling of a poem is not justified?
4. Explain in your own words the meaning of sentimentality. Why are self-pity and self-consciousness almost always indications of sentimentality? Find a poem or a song that you think is sentimental.
5. Why is Keats' "Ode to a Nightingale" not considered a sentimental poem?
6. What do we mean by *suggestive restraint* in poetry? Why is restraint an indication that a poem is not sentimental? Use poems by Wordsworth and Tennyson quoted in this chapter as examples of restraint.
7. Explain and illustrate why a break in the continuity of a poem is likely to ruin it.
8. What do we mean by a poet's range of emotional power? Why do we call Shakespeare the greatest of English poets?
9. Find and bring to class three poems dealing with the same emotion with three different degrees of depth.

PROBLEMS IN APPRECIATION

1. Discuss the similarities and the differences of the emotional appeal in the following poems. Relative depth? Various means of creating feeling? Which appeals most to the feelings you yourself have felt?

Rupert Brooke	"Grantchester"
Browning	"Home Thoughts from Abroad"
Burns	"My Heart's in the Highlands"
Allan Cunningham	"Loyalty"
Longfellow	"My Lost Youth"
Moore	"The Harp That Once through Tara's Hall"

Riley	"The Old Swimmin' Hole"
Scott	"My Native Land"
Stevenson	"Blows the Wind Today"
Whittier	"Snowbound"

2. What is the mood of each of the following poems? Is it a mood common to most people or only to a few? Is it a deep mood? Does it seem to you justified? sincere? Is it kept up throughout the poem? Have you felt it yourself? Is it unknown to you? Have you read poems which express the same mood? Do they express it better? not so well? Explain.

Rupert Brooke	"Grantchester," "Blue Evening"
Chesterton	"Lepanto," "The Donkey"
De la Mare	"The Sunken Garden," "Tartary," "Old Susan"
Robert Frost	"Birches," "The Road Not Taken"
Ralph Hodgson	"The Song of Honour," "The Bull," "Eve"
Kipling	"Recessional"
Amy Lowell	"The Garden by Moonlight," "Lilacs," "Patterns"
Edgar Lee Masters	"Lucinda Matlock," "Father Malloy"
Carl Sandburg	"Cool Tombs," "Lost," "A Fence," "At a Window"
Sara Teasdale	"Water Lilies," "Barter," "Stars"

3. Here are ten moods with ten poems to match them. On a separate sheet of paper list the poems and opposite each write the mood:

love	homesickness	love of Nature	courage
friendship	religious faith	pity	
grief	patriotism	despair	

Arnold	"Dover Beach"
Browning	"Home Thoughts from Abroad" "Rabbi Ben Ezra"
Henley	"England, My England"
Hodgson	"The Bull"
Christina Rossetti	"A Birthday"
Shakespeare	29th Sonnet
Tennyson	"Break, Break, Break" "Crossing the Bar"
Wordsworth	"Lines Composed a Few Miles above Tintern Abbey"

REQUIESCAT

Strew on her roses, roses,
  And never a spray of yew!
In quiet she reposes:
  Ah, would that I did too!

Her mirth the world required;
  She bathed it in smiles of glee.
But her heart was tired, tired,
  And now they let her be.

Her life was turning, turning,
  In mazes of heat and sound.
But for peace her soul was yearning,
  And now peace laps her round.

Her cabin'd, ample spirit,
  It flutter'd and fail'd for breath.
To-night it doth inherit
  The vasty hall of death.

MATTHEW ARNOLD

(*a*) Consider carefully the emotional element in this poem. (*b*) To what feelings does it appeal? (*c*) Does it appeal to more than one emotion? (*d*) Is that emotion universal? sincere? justified? (*e*) How can you tell whether or not it is sincere and justified? (*f*) Is it sustained throughout? (*g*) Is the poem effective because of unrestrained vehemence of expression? (*h*) How is its mood created? (*i*) What instances are there of feeling secured through sound? (*j*) Are there any phrases remarkable for poetic suggestion? (*k*) What figures of speech do you find? (*l*) Are there any that appeal to you? (*m*) Are there expressions that you do not understand? (*n*) Is there any line which seems to you truly great for its power of suggestion? (*o*) Bring to class a poem which you yourself have found and answer these questions about it.

5. In any anthology:
(*a*) Find poems that express well feelings you yourself have felt. (*b*) Find poems that could appeal only to a certain class of readers. (*c*) Find poems that would appeal to anyone. (*d*) How great a range of feeling is there in the book? (*e*) How many means of creating feeling? (*f*) Find a mood created through pictures and sound. (*g*) Find several poems which show relative depth and power to express love, grief, patriotism, love of home, gayety, humor, and so on.

6. Here are moods and sensations you have doubtless felt. Select the one that comes back to you most vividly and try by means of suggestive word pictures and word rhythms to express this mood in a little poem so that your feeling will be communicated to others. Perhaps it would be better to have your word pictures based on actual experience.

homesickness	grief	Christmas joy	exhilaration
friendship	spring restlessness	weariness	
loneliness	autumn restlessness	heat	

Can you find poems by others, such as Bliss Carman's "A Vagabond Song," for "autumn restlessness," that express these moods?

CHAPTER 4

HOW THE POET USES WORD PICTURES AND WORD SOUNDS

Feeling created through word pictures. There are many ways in which emotional effects in poetry are secured, two of which deserve special consideration. The first of these is by word pictures. Read *The Idylls of the King*, noticing how faithfully the word pictures not merely reflect, but actually create the mood of the story. In "The Coming of Arthur," when all were transfigured by

> A momentary likeness of the King,

the Knights stood rejoicing:

> Far shone the fields of May thro' open door,
> The sacred altar blossom'd white with May,
> The sun of May descended on their King,
> They gazed on all earth's beauty in their Queen,
>
> Then while they paced a city all on fire
> With sun and cloth of gold, the trumpets blew,
> And Arthur's knighthood sang before the King:—
> "Blow trumpet, for the world is white with May!"

And in "Gareth and Lynette," when the kingdom is in the heyday of its glory, we find that:

> . . . The birds made
> Melody on branch, and melody in mid air.
> The damp hill-slopes were quicken'd into green,
> And the live green had kindled into flowers,
> For it was past the time of Easter-day.

In the later idylls the pictures reflect the sultry heat of summer and the electric stillness that foretells the coming storm. In "Lancelot and Elaine"

> . . . tremulous aspen-trees
> And poplars made a noise of falling showers,

the casement stood wide for heat, and the dawn

> shot red fire and shadows

flaring blood-red on Elaine's face; and

> she mixt
> Her fancies with the sallow-rifted glooms
> Of evening, and the moanings of the wind.

Later, in "The Holy Grail," the landscape takes on an unearthly gloom lighted only by the Holy Vessel:

> Fainter by day, but always in the night
> Blood-red, and sliding down the blacken'd marsh
> Blood-red, and on the naked mountain top
> Blood-red, and in the sleeping mere below
> Blood-red.

Lancelot's mad, remorseful quest takes place over waste fields and on

> the naked shore,
> Wide flats, where nothing but coarse grasses grew,

and in lonely mystic castles, where he saw

> No bench nor table, painting on the wall
> Or shield of knight, only the rounded moon
> Thro' the tall oriel on the rolling sea.

Still later, in "The Last Tournament," the morning of the tournament of Dead Innocence

> Brake with a wet wind blowing,

and

> The sudden trumpet sounded as in a dream
> To ears but half-awaked, then one low roll
> Of autumn thunder, and the jousts began;
> And ever the wind blew, and yellowing leaf,
> And gloom and gleam, and shower and shorn plume
> Went down it.
>
> Then fell thick rain, plume droopt and mantle clung,
> And pettish cries awoke, and the wan day
> Went glooming down in wet and weariness.

And when Arthur returned from his heartsick quest against the Red Knight,

> he climb'd,
> All in a death-dumb autumn-dripping gloom,
> The stairway to the hall, and look'd and saw
> The great Queen's bower was dark,—about his feet
> A voice clung sobbing till he question'd it,
> "What art thou?" and the voice about his feet
> Sent up an answer, sobbing, "I am thy fool
> And I shall never make thee smile again."

In "Guinevere,"

> One low light betwixt them burn'd
> Blurr'd by the creeping mist, for all abroad,
> Beneath a moon unseen albeit at full,
> The white mist, like a face-cloth to the face,
> Clung to the dead earth, and the land was still,

and

> she to Almesbury
> Fled all night long by glimmering waste and weald,
> And heard the spirits of the waste and weald
> Moan as she fled, or thought she heard them moan.
> And in herself she moan'd, "Too late, too late!"
> Till in the cold wind that foreruns the morn,
> A blot in heaven, the raven, flying high,
> Croak'd.

"The Passing of Arthur" culminates the series with some of the most effective mood painting in Tennyson. Every scene is saturated with gloom, with wet and cold and weariness. After the last, dim, weird battle of the west,

the pale King glanced across the field
Of battle,

and saw that

only the wan wave
Brake in among dead faces, to and fro
Swaying the helpless hands, and up and down
Tumbling the hollow helmets of the fallen,
And shiver'd brands that once had fought with Rome,
And rolling far along the gloomy shores
The voice of days of old and days to be.

No detail is omitted which might deepen the emotional tone of the poem. The

dolorous day
Grew drearier toward twilight falling,

and over the scene,

the sea-wind sang
Shrill, chill, with flakes of foam.

Sir Bedivere concealed Excalibur in

the many-knotted waterflags,
That whistled stiff and dry about the marge,

and when the three queens with crowns of gold came to take Arthur on the barge, he heard rise from them

A cry that shiver'd to the tingling stars,
And, as it were one voice, an agony
Of lamentation, like a wind that shrills
All night in a waste land, where no one comes
Or hath come, since the making of the world.

He stood long,

Revolving many memories, till the hull
Look'd one black dot against the verge of dawn,
And on the mere the wailing died away.
But when that moan had past for evermore,
The stillness of the dead world's winter dawn
Amazed him, and he groan'd, "The King is gone."

Courtesy of the Metropolitan Museum of Art

A GRECIAN URN

Fired by the perfect beauty of an antique vase such as this John Keats wrote his "Ode on a Grecian Urn."

Courtesy of *Vanity Fair*

ISADORA DUNCAN'S RUSSIAN DANCERS

The impulse to rhythmic beauty finds expression in the dance as well as in poetry.

Use of pictures to suggest mood. There is no quality more common to poetry than this constant use of picture-making words to create mood. Many times these pictures are painted in detail, but more often they are suggested in a few words. How many pictures of cold are suggested, for instance, in each line of the opening stanza of "The Eve of St. Agnes":

> St. Agnes' Eve—Ah, bitter chill it was!
> The owl, for all his feathers, was a-cold;
> The hare limp'd trembling through the frozen grass,
> And silent was the flock in woolly fold:
> Numb were the Beadsman's fingers, while he told
> His rosary, and while his frosted breath,
> Like pious incense from a censer old,
> Seem'd taking flight for heaven, without a death,
> Past the sweet Virgin's picture, while his prayer he saith.

It would be difficult to point out a better example of words to create a single vivid impression in one line. No description of cold has ever been more compelling than that one line,

> The owl, for all his feathers, was a-cold.

Another instance of feeling created by pictures is found in Shakespeare's Seventy-Third Sonnet:

> That time of year thou mayst in me behold
> When yellow leaves, or none, or few, do hang
> Upon those boughs which shake against the cold,
> Bare, ruin'd choirs, where late the sweet birds sang.
> In me thou seest the twilight of such day
> As after sunset fadeth in the west,
> Which by and by black night doth take away,
> Death's second self, that seals up all in rest.
> In me thou seest the glowing of such fire
> That on the ashes of his youth doth lie,
> As the death-bed whereon it must expire
> Consumed with that which it was nourished by.
> That thou perceivest, which makes thy love more strong,
> To love that well which thou must leave ere long.

Consider the emotional effect of cold and desolation created here by just the two lines

Upon those boughs which shake against the cold,
Bare, ruin'd choirs, where late the sweet birds sang,

and you will begin to realize the magic power that very simple words may have to suggest feeling through pictures.

The first way, then, by which a poet creates feeling is through pictures, sometimes painted in detail and sometimes suggested in just a few words.

Feeling created through sound. The second common way by which the poet may create feeling is by the use of sound. We shall discuss the importance of sound in poetry somewhat in detail later; here we merely wish to suggest a few of the ways in which it helps to arouse a mood. Probably our first pleasure from the Mother Goose lines and limericks of our childhood came purely from the effect that the mere sound of the words and the swing of the meter had upon our feelings. One does not need to know the meaning of *tintinnabulation* or *Runic rhyme* to get the mood of

How they tinkle, tinkle, tinkle,
In the icy air of night!
While the stars, that oversprinkle
All the heavens, seem to twinkle
With a crystalline delight;
Keeping time, time, time,
In a sort of Runic rhyme,
To the tintinnabulation that so musically wells
From the bells, bells, bells, bells,
Bells, bells, bells—
From the jingling and the tinkling of the bells.

Neither does one need to study the Cavalier spirit in song to catch that spirit just from the sound of Browning's

Marching along, fifty-score strong,
Great-hearted gentlemen, singing this song.

Hampden to hell, and his obsequies' knell,
Serve Hazelrig, Fiennes, and young Harry as well!
England, good cheer! Rupert is near!
Kentish and loyalists, keep we not here.

What difference does it make to us whether we know who Hazelrig, Fiennes, Rupert, or even Hampden were? The poem sweeps us along till we fall in with its rhythmic tread whether we know what it means or not.

Two other poets who take our feelings by storm by the very spirit of their rhythm are Scott and Burns. One does not have to read beyond the first stanza of

Oh, young Lochinvar is come out of the west,
Through all the wide Border his steed was the best,

Pibroch of Donuil Dhu
  Pibroch of Donuil,
Wake thy wild voice anew,
  Summon Clan Conuil.

Faster come, faster come,
  Faster and faster,
Chief, vassal, page and groom,
  Tenant and master,

or

Come fill up my cup, come fill up my can,
Come saddle your horses, and call up your men;
Come open the West Port and let me gang free,
And it's room for the bonnets of Bonny Dundee!

in order to be completely captured by the spirit of the whole poem. And of course that spirit is here created by sound alone. Even the careless rhymes of many of Scott's lyrics are happily lost in the sheer galloping beat of the meter, so absolutely does his rhythm fit his mood.

Appropriate rhythms enhance emotional effect. Robert Burns, too, is as great as the greatest in his adaptation of sound to feeling. Perhaps this is why he is our greatest song writer, for song is the most natural example of rhythmic expression of emotion, and no writer has had a gift of spontaneous song to compare with that of Burns. It is small wonder that

O, my luve is like a red, red rose,
  That's newly sprung in June.
O, my luve is like the melodie,
  That's sweetly play'd in tune!

and

Ye flowery banks o' bonie Doon,
  How can ye blume sae fair?
How can ye chant, ye little birds,
  And I sae fu' o' care?

and

Scots, wha hae wi' Wallace bled,
Scots, wham Bruce has aften led,
Welcome to your gory bed
  Or to victorie!

and

O, wert thou in the cauld blast
  On yonder lea, on yonder lea,
My plaidie to the angry airt,
  I'd shelter thee, I'd shelter thee.
Or did Misfortune's bitter storms
  Around thee blaw, around thee blaw,
Thy bield [1] should be my bosom,
  To share it a', to share it a',

have become a part of the common vocabulary of love, grief, patriotism, and tenderness.

We must not make the mistake, however, of thinking that only stirring emotions are expressed by sound. The monotony of the regularly recurring accents and the deep-toned, melancholy vowels of

Break, break, break,
On thy cold gray stones, O Sea!

are more than half the secret of the effect of the poem on our feelings. The endless, hopeless weariness of the Queen's life of penance is suggested by the dragging meter of

The days will grow to weeks, the weeks to months,
The months will add themselves and make the years

And mine will ever be a name of scorn

[1] Shelter.

in Tennyson's "Guinevere." And the effect of dreary isolation in these lines from "The Passing of Arthur" is achieved as much by the mere sound of the words as by the appropriate imagery:

> and from them rose
> A cry that shiver'd to the tingling stars,
> And, as it were one voice, an agony
> Of lamentation, like a wind that shrills
> All night in a waste land, where no one comes,
> Or hath come, since the making of the world.

Summary. Skillful word pictures in poetry not only reflect the mood of the poet but actually create the mood in the mind of the reader. The second common way by which the poet affects the reader is by the use of appropriate word sounds and rhythms.

COMPREHENSION QUESTIONS

1. Find and bring to class two poems which illustrate how pictures in poetry help to create mood.
2. Find and bring to class two poems which illustrate how the sound of the poem affects the emotion of the reader.
3. Can you cite examples outside of literature of the power of sounds to arouse feeling?
4. Find pictures which seem to you to suggest or create *moods*. Explain your choice.
5. In any collection of poems:
   (*a*) Find pictures that appeal to you either because of their familiarity or strangeness. (*b*) Find pictures that suggest a clearly defined mood, such as *peace*, *gloom*, *happiness*, or *weariness*. (*c*) Find pictures suggested in a few words and some painted in detail. (*d*) Write a description of the scene suggested to you by the pictures in some poem; be sure that your description creates a central mood. (*e*) Try to recast your description in poetic form.
6. Read each of the following aloud. What is the feeling created by each one? Explain in detail how a large part of that feeling is created by sound. Is the feeling due to some other element? Is the feeling universal or limited? Is it deep or light? Does it seem to you justified? sincere?

(*a*)
> Here, where the world is quiet,
> Here, where all trouble seems
> Dead winds' and spent waves' riot

In doubtful dreams of dreams;
I watch the green field growing
For reaping folk and sowing,
For harvest time and mowing,
A sleepy world of streams.

SWINBURNE

(*b*) In the afternoon they came unto a land
In which it seemed always afternoon.
All round the coast the languid air did swoon,
Breathing like one that hath a weary dream.
Full-faced above the valley stood the moon;
And like a downward smoke, the slender stream
Along the cliff to fall and pause and fall did seem.

TENNYSON

(*c*) Sigh no more, ladies, sigh no more,
Men were deceivers ever,
One foot in sea and one on shore;
To one thing constant never.

SHAKESPEARE

(*d*) 'Twas brillig, and the slithy toves
Did gyre and gimble in the wabe:
All mimsy were the borogoves,
And the mome raths outgrabe.

LEWIS CARROLL

(*e*) The moving Moon went up the sky,
And nowhere did abide;
Softly she was going up,
And a star or two beside.

COLERIDGE

(*f*) The waves beside them danced, but they
Outdid the sparkling waves in glee:
A poet could not but be gay,
In such a jocund company!
I gazed—and gazed—but little thought
What wealth the show to me had brought.

WORDSWORTH

(*g*) Now glory to the Lord of Hosts, from whom all glories are!
And glory to our Sovereign Liege, King Henry of Navarre!

MACAULAY

CHAPTER 5

HOW THE POET CONVEYS IDEAS BY FIGURES OF SPEECH

The imagination and figures of speech. Through his imagination the poet is often able to see resemblances and differences which escape most of us. He can use this sort of imagination to combine or associate ideas, pictures, moods, or sensations in such a way as to make his meaning doubly clear and forceful.

Figures of speech in daily conversation. Of course, to a certain extent, we all express ideas in terms of figures of speech. For instance, when we think of cold, our imagination creates for us a picture of something associated in our minds with cold—ice, or wind, or perhaps a polar bear. When we try to express the idea of dullness we instinctively think of something dull or blunt, possibly a hoe. When we wish to express forcefully the idea of thickness, we search about in our minds for something which we associate with thickness, and we say, perhaps, that the fog is so thick that we could cut it with a knife. If we wish to impress our hearers with the fact that our automobile was going very fast, we say it flew like a bird—or we leave off the direct comparison, implying it in the one word, "flew." We also express ourselves in this way through finding differences instead of similarities between things. Thus we make our idea of cold more intense by thinking of something that is hot. Our mind conjures up a picture of a day in June with its buttercups and daisies when

> . . . there's never a leaf nor a blade too mean
> To be some happy creature's palace;

and in that way make the cold outside seem more bitter. Or perhaps we try to gain an effect by exaggeration—by making mountains out of our molehills. Still again, we unconsciously substitute certain words for others closely associated with them. Thus we speak of reading Dickens instead of his books, and of watching the kettle, instead of the water in it, boil. Our imagination supplies us with many similar ways of making our meaning more effective. Most of these ways are figures of speech. A figure of speech, then, is any departure from the plain or ordinary way of expressing oneself for the purpose of making the meaning more effective.

The simile. The first and most common figure of speech is the simile; for instance:

> The bride hath paced into the hall,
> Red as a rose is she.

A simile is a directly expressed comparison. It usually contains the words "like" or "as," but we should beware of placing too much stress on this fact because not all expressions containing these words are comparisons. We use similes constantly in our daily speech, but our similes are often commonplace or exaggerated, or inappropriate. "Teeth as white as pearls," for instance, is a simile so common that it has lost its force. The poet, however, uses similes with more care and with more imagination. To him, similes always reveal a new or unexpected resemblance between objects or ideas that may at first seem dissimilar. His similes often throw an unexpected light on his meaning or bring out some hidden beauty that would escape our less appreciative glance. They are like rays of light that make dim places beautiful, or like the moonlight that casts a mysterious charm over places which seem prosaic or ugly in the common light of day.

What makes a simile effective. To be effective, a simile should not be based on too great a similarity. It should always give a little thrill of surprise and pleasure to the reader. To say that an apple is as round as an orange is not effective; the objects compared are alike in too many respects. A simile is perhaps most likely to be effective if the objects compared are alike in only one respect. On the other hand, although the objects compared in a simile must not be too much alike, they must not be too different, unless one wishes them to be so for purposes of burlesque. No one would, for instance, say that an apple is as round as a tower. A simile, however, should not be commonplace. The similes of eyes blue as violets and of hair like fine-spun gold have lost by constant repetition their original force. Similar examples, from the pine "like a lonely sentinel" to the childish rhyme,

> Sugar is sweet, and so are you,

will occur to you at once. If a figure of speech is to make the meaning more effective, it should not be "weary, stale, flat, and unprofitable."

The most important thing about a simile, however, is that it should arouse in the mind of the reader exactly the suggestion that the poet wishes to give. Here, as always in poetry, the power of poetic suggestion is most necessary. Things that do not look at all alike may possess a hidden resemblance which the poet shows to be appropriate and compelling. But unless the resemblance is appropriate, the simile falls flat or becomes ridiculous. Sometimes we fail to see things as the poet sees them.

Inappropriate similes. In Oliver Wendell Holmes' famous little burlesque, "The Ballad of the Oysterman," he says of a drowned maiden,

> Her hair drooped round her pallid cheeks,
> like seaweed on a clam.

At once you realize that there are many points of actual similarity between the things compared here, but you also feel at once that the comparison is highly inappropriate. Why? Merely because the suggestions aroused by seaweed and clams are so far removed from pathos that the comparison causes laughter rather than tears. In other words, the poetic suggestion of the figure is inappropriate. In Tennyson's *Idylls of the King* among many beautiful similes there occasionally occurs a simile almost as inappropriate as that of Holmes. In "Gareth and Lynette" Tennyson, wishing to suggest the fierce brightness of the Noonday Sun's shield, uses this comparison:

> As if the flower,
> That blows a globe of after arrowlets
> Ten thousand-fold had grown, flash'd the fierce shield,
> All sun.

In "The Last Tournament" Tennyson wishes to suggest how the drunken Red Knight, after defying King Arthur, fell from his horse. To do so, he uses this simile:

But let the drunkard, as he stretch'd from horse

Down from the causeway heavily to the swamp
Fall, as the crest of some slow-arching wave,
Heard in dead night along that table-shore,
Drops flat, and after the great waters break
Whitening for half a league, and thin themselves,
Far over sands marbled with moon and cloud,
From less and less to nothing.

No one would deny the vivid beauty of the picture here, but no one could defend, either, the use of such a picture to describe a drunken man falling off a horse. Tennyson makes a similar mistake in "The Princess" where he describes eight "daughters of the plow" working at the Princess Ida's university by saying:

Each was like a Druid rock;
Or like a spire of land that stands apart
Cleft from the main, and wail'd about with mews.

As Henry Van Dyke remarks, "the image is grand—just a little too grand for a group of female servants summoned to eject three masculine intruders from the university!" In all these examples the similes are inappropriately strained to the breaking point.

Appropriate similes. The thing to consider in studying any figure of speech, then, is the suggestion the poet wishes to convey. If it does convey that suggestion forcefully, it is a good figure; if it conveys another suggestion or a confusing mixture of suggestions it is a poor figure.

Some similes are so appropriate that they linger in the memory. Tennyson has many such successful similes. In "Geraint and Enid," wishing to suggest the beauty of the silk gown which Earl Doorm offers to Enid, he says:

one among his gentlewomen
Display'd a splendid silk of foreign loom,
Where like a shoaling sea the lovely blue
Play'd into green.

This gives the reader an exact image of the color, and a picture as well. In "Lancelot and Elaine" he wishes to suggest the concentrated fury with which Lancelot's kith and kin bore down upon him in the tournament:

> They couch'd their spears and prick'd their steeds, and thus,
> Their plumes driv'n backward by the wind they made
> In moving, all together down on him
> Bare, as a wild wave in the wide North Sea,
> Green-glimmering toward the summit, bears, with all
> Its stormy crests that smoke against the skies,
> Down on a bark, and overbears the bark
> And him that helms it; so they overbore
> Sir Lancelot and his charger.

In spite of the somewhat involved sentence structure, this simile adds beauty and vitality to the passage and, best of all, does create the impression of concentrated fury which the author wished to convey. In "Sohrab and Rustum" Matthew Arnold wishes to suggest the idle wonder with which Rustum regarded

> The unknown adventurous youth, who from afar
> Came seeking Rustum, and defying forth
> All the most valiant chiefs.

To do this he uses two similes so perfect in their suggestion and yet so unexpected that they would not have occurred to any mind except a poet's:

> And Rustum came upon the sand, and cast
> His eyes toward the Tartar tents, and saw
> Sohrab come forth, and eyed him as he came.
> As some rich woman, on a winter's morn,
> Eyes through her silken curtains the poor drudge
> Who with numb blacken'd fingers makes her fire—
> At cock-crow, on a starlit winter's morn,
> When the frost flowers the whiten'd window-panes—
> And wonders how she lives, and what the thoughts
> Of that poor drudge may be; so Rustum eyed
> The unknown adventurous youth, who from afar
> Came seeking Rustum, and defying forth
> All the most valiant chiefs; long he perused
> His spirited air, and wonder'd who he was.
> For very young he seem'd, tenderly rear'd;
> Like some young cypress, tall, and dark, and straight,
> Which in a queen's secluded garden throws

Its slight dark shadow on the moonlit turf,
By midnight, to a bubbling fountain's sound—
So slender Sohrab seem'd, so softly rear'd.

Comparisons from contemporary poets. Contemporary poetry makes a point of selecting similes and other figures of speech that are unusual and yet most startlingly appropriate. Poems by Amy Lowell, Robert Frost, Edgar Lee Masters, William Rose Benét, Edna St. Vincent Millay, and Carl Sandburg are excellent material for a study of the use of comparisons.

Here are a few comparisons from the work of modern poets. Elinor Wylie in "Sea Lullaby," thus tries to suggest the beauty and cruel treachery of the sea:

A treacherous smiler
With teeth white as milk,
A savage beguiler
In sheathings of silk,

Her bright locks were tangled,
She shouted for joy,
With one hand she strangled
A strong little boy.

Now in silence she lingers
Beside him all night
To wash her long fingers
In silvery light.[1]

Sara Teasdale finds these comparisons for a description of a spring night in a city park:

The park is filled with night and fog,
  The veils are drawn about the world,
The drowsy lights along the paths
  Are dim and pearled.

Gold and gleaming the empty streets,
  Gold and gleaming the misty lake,
The mirrored lights like sunshine swords,
  Glimmer and shake.[2]

[1] By permission of Alfred A. Knopf, Inc.
[2] From *Rivers to the Sea* by Sara Teasdale. By permission of The Macmillan Company, publishers.

Carl Sandburg makes metaphors and similes in his "Nocturne in a Deserted Brickyard":

Stuff of the moon
Runs on the lapping sand
Out to the longest shadows.
Under the curving willows,
And round the creep of the wave line,
Fluxions of yellow and dusk on the waters
Make a wide dreaming pansy of an old pond in the night.[1]

Metaphors. The second most common figure of speech is the *metaphor*. A metaphor is a comparison implied rather than stated. When Burns wrote:

O, my luve is like a red, red rose,
  That's newly sprung in June.
O, my luve is like the melodie,
  That's sweetly play'd in tune,

he used similes to express what his love meant to him. If he had not made the direct comparison but had said, "My luve is a red, red rose," and "My luve is a melodie," he would have been using metaphors. When Tennyson said of Guinevere:

Sea was her wrath, yet working after storm,

he meant that her wrath was *like the sea;* but he condensed his simile into a metaphor.

Difference between metaphor and simile. "The simile is a comparison of one thing to another, a comparison pointed out by such words as *like* or *as*. A metaphor, on the other hand, occurs when we omit the *like* or *as* and call the thing the other thing to which we would compare it if we were using a simile." [2]

Human thought often expressed in metaphors. Metaphors are extremely common both in poetry and in daily speech. Indeed, most of our slang is metaphorical. One of the greatest living poets, Robert Frost, recently expressed his conviction that metaphor, man's way of expressing himself through associated images, is at the core of all genuine poetry. He pointed out how difficult it is to express ourselves

[1] Reprinted by permission of and arrangement with Henry Holt and Company.
[2] Quoted from Luella B. Cook's *Using English*, Book Two.

at all unless we resort to metaphors. Of course, as he was careful to remark, no metaphor can completely get at the truth of things, but probably metaphorical language comes closer to it than the literal definitions of scientists. Indeed, most of our literary, scientific, political, and philosophical language sooner or later becomes metaphorical in its attempts to explain things. We constantly use metaphors like "machine age," "sales talk," "air-mindedness," "Red Russia," "clean living," "spread-eagle oratory," "princes of the church," "public servants," "bluebloods," "sea dogs," "yes-men," "the Promised Land," "commodity dollars." But we seldom realize that all these and many more are only comparatively (in other words, metaphorically) true. By means of indirect comparisons, we struggle to say what we really mean. To the poet, truth without metaphor is unthinkable. He simply cannot express himself literally, and no one can understand him who tries to read him literally. Consider, to choose obvious examples out of thousands, how impossible it would be to read "The Ancient Mariner," or *Macbeth* without a metaphorical sense to help you.

Similes and metaphors in "The Ancient Mariner." In "The Ancient Mariner" we find the mariner with his "glittering eye," to be "long, and lank and brown" as is the "ribbed sea sand." The ship is idle as "a painted ship upon a painted ocean" underneath a "hot and copper sky" and a "bloody sun." The water, "like a witch's oils, burnt green, and blue, and white." The track of the water snakes is a "flash of golden fire." The Mariner's "black lips" are "baked," and the sky and sea "lay like a load" on his weary eye. But a "spring of love gushes" from his heart and he hears a song "like all instruments, like a lonely flute, an angel's song, that makes the heavens be mute." The sails make a pleasant noise like that "of a hidden brook" in the "leafy month of June that to the sleeping woods all night singeth a quiet tune." On his return the bay is "clear as glass," and the moonlight "steep'd in silentness" the steady weathercock. But his soul has been "alone on a wide, wide sea," and he must pass from land to land telling his story to those who need it, a story which, stripped of its metaphors, would be pretty childish reading. But clothed in them it is illuminated with truth and beauty.

Similes and metaphors in *Macbeth*. In *Macbeth* we find the protagonist almost always speaking metaphorically. His "seated heart knocks at his ribs." He thinks of himself as "standing on the bank and shoal of time" as "prick'd on by vaulting ambition," as having "bought golden opinions from all sorts of people." He is like "withered murder aroused by his sentinel, the wolf, moving like Tarquin with stealthy steps towards his design." He has "murdered sleep that knits up the ravell'd sleave of care, [sleep] the balm of hurt minds." His bloody hands will "the multitudinous seas incarnadine, making the green one red." He has put "rancours in the vessel of his peace" and given his "eternal jewel" to the devil. His mind is a "rack" on which he lies in "restless ecstasy." He is "cabin'd, cribb'd, confin'd, bound in to saucy doubts and fears." Life to him is a "fitful fever," a "brief candle," "a walking shadow," a "poor player that struts and frets his hour upon the stage," "a tale told by an idiot." In his memory is a "rooted sorrow," and in his brain are "written troubles" that will not be erased. His way of life has fallen into "the sear and yellow leaf." He is in "blood stepp'd in so far that, returning were as tedious as go o'er." He yearns for a "sweet oblivious antidote" that will "cleanse the stuff'd bosom of that perilous stuff which weighs upon the heart." Strip the play of its metaphors and all of its power and most of its truth would disappear.

Allegory. A figure of speech closely allied to metaphor and simile is *allegory*. An allegory is the description of one thing under the likeness of another. It is a sort of expanded metaphor in the form of a story usually teaching some truth or belief which the reader is left to discover. For instance, if we say, "Man's progress toward salvation is like the journey of a man who abandons home, friends, and all earthly pursuits in order to seek a distant city," we are using a simile. If we say, "Man's progress toward salvation is the journey of a man who abandons home, friends, and all earthly pursuits in order to seek a distant city," we are condensing that simile into a metaphor. But if we tell the story of a man's journey toward a distant city in such a way that at every point the reader realizes that our story is really the likeness of any man's progress toward salvation in this world, we have expanded our metaphor into an allegory. This particular allegory is Bunyan's *Pilgrim's Progress*, perhaps the most perfect example of prose allegory. A simple illustration of the difference between allegory, metaphor, and simile is this:

Simile: Israel is like a vine brought out of Egypt and planted in Palestine.

Metaphor: Israel is a vine brought out of Egypt and planted in Palestine.

Allegory: God brought a vine out of Egypt and planted it in Palestine.

Allegory is a very common way of teaching a lesson. The parables in the New Testament are allegories, and so are Æsop's fables.

The *Idylls of the King* as an allegory. The most striking example of this figure which you will come across in your reading of poetry is Tennyson's *Idylls of the King.* In "Gareth and Lynette," for instance, the description of the gate is allegorical. The whole idyll of "The Holy Grail" may be interpreted allegorically. In this idyll the visions of Percivale are an allegorical way of saying that Percivale must give up sensual pleasures, domestic happiness, wealth, and fame if he intends to seek the vision of God. In fact the whole series of idylls represents the eternal war between the powers of good and evil that goes on in the heart of any man who seeks to make himself perfect. Many of the characters, such as the Lady of the Lake, the three Queens, Merlin, and even Arthur himself may be reduced to mere allegorical figures.

Difficulties of writing allegory. Allegory is a good way of teaching a lesson but it is often a confusing way of telling a story. If the allegorical meaning is kept clear throughout, the characters are likely to become mere abstractions; if, on the other hand, the characters and events become interesting in themselves, the allegorical meaning is likely to drop out of sight. The *Idylls of the King* illustrate this difficulty. The allegorical meaning appears only at intervals, and the lesson might perhaps have been as well taught by the story without the aid of allegory. Tennyson himself became somewhat irritated at being frequently asked to explain the allegorical significance of this or that passage or character. He often said that the *Idylls* could be read intelligently without regard to the allegory; but there are passages which seem to require the allegorical interpretation.

Personification. It is interesting to see how closely related to similes and metaphors most figures of speech are. Probably the majority of them are based on either similarity or contrast. There is *personification,* for instance. Personification is the figure of speech by which we speak of things that are not persons as though they were

Courtesy of the Metropolitan Museum of Art

THE PARTHENON

Even in its ruins the Parthenon shows the stately dignity and the calm power of Greek art.

© Underwood & Underwood, N.Y.

DOWNTOWN NEW YORK

Modern literature must interpret the beauty and power of modern life, which is unlike anything in the past.

LITCHFIELD CATHEDRAL, ENGLAND

The imagination which finds beautiful expression in poetry finds equally beautiful expression in architecture.

persons. This is a figure that is as natural for the child as for the poet. It is natural for a little girl to think of her doll as a person because by that simple expedient she can make it more real. It was natural for the pagans of antiquity to personify the forces of Nature as gods and goddesses because in that way they could give expression to their instinctive feeling that these forces were guided by some Intelligent Power for some purpose which they could but dimly comprehend. The poet, especially in his simpler moods, uses personification frequently. Stevenson's little poem about the wind is an almost perfect example of both the naturalness and the effectiveness of personification. It is natural for the child to say:

I saw you toss the kites on high
And blow the birds about the sky;
And all around I heard you pass,
Like ladies' skirts across the grass—
    O wind, a-blowing all day long,
    O wind, that sings so loud a song!

I saw the different things you did,
But always you yourself you hid.
I felt you push, I heard you call,
I could not see yourself at all—
    O wind, a-blowing all day long,
    O wind, that sings so loud a song!

O you that are so strong and cold,
O blower, are you young or old?
Are you a beast of field and tree,
Or just a stronger child than me?
    O wind, a-blowing all day long,
    O wind, that sings so loud a song! [1]

The use of personification alone gives vitality to the child's imaginative conception of the wind here, and it also helps us to put ourselves in the child's place and enjoy the poem more. Personification is most valuable in thus quickening the imagination. The marvelous lines in *Romeo and Juliet*,

Night's candles are burnt out, and jocund day
Stands tiptoe on the misty mountain tops,

[1] Reprinted by permission of and arrangement with Charles Scribner's Sons

are fairly alive with their suggestion of coming Dawn. This is also true of Horatio's words in *Hamlet:*

> But, look, the morn, in russet mantle clad,
> Walks o'er the dew of yon high eastern hill.

Hyperbole. The figure of speech called *hyperbole* is one that is used far too freely in everyday speech. Hyperbole is exaggeration for effect. To say that we laughed till we thought we should die, for instance, is an example of the unnecessary, pointless hyperbole frequent in daily conversation. With the poet, hyperbole is useful for the rush of powerful suggestions it carries with it, as in the following passage from Jean Ingelow's "The High Tide on the Coast of Lincolnshire":

> So farre, so fast the eygre drave,
> The heart had hardly time to beat,
> Before a shallow seething wave
> Sobbed in the grasses at oure feet:
> The feet had hardly time to flee
> Before it brake against the knee,
> And all the world was in the sea.

The Elizabethans, as you may have noticed, were very fond of hyperbole, and sometimes used it with overwhelming force as in Macbeth's:

> What hands are here? ha! they pluck out mine eyes.
> Will all great Neptune's ocean wash this blood
> Clean from my hand? No, this my hand will rather
> The multitudinous seas incarnadine,
> Making the green one red.

Hyperbole is an interesting figure to watch because it is so very powerful when effective, and, when ineffective, so very flat.

Apostrophe. *Apostrophe,* like hyperbole, may be easily abused. It is a form of address in which the absent are addressed as though present, the inanimate as though animate, the dead as though living. It occurs frequently in poetry. In the following examples the absent are addressed as though present:

> Oh Romeo, Romeo! wherefore art thou Romeo?

Come into the garden, Maud,
For the black bat, night, hath flown.

In these, inanimate objects are addressed as though animate:

Roll on, thou deep and dark blue Ocean—roll!
Ten thousand fleets sweep over thee in vain.

Blow, blow, thou winter wind,
Thou art not so unkind
As man's ingratitude.

O Rome! my country! city of the soul!

In these, the dead are addressed as though living:

Milton! thou shouldst be living at this hour:
England hath need of thee.

O my son Absalom, my son, my son, Absalom,
Would God I had died for thee!

Apostrophe usually represents an excited state of feeling. If it seems the natural overflow of powerful feelings, it is likely to arouse similar feelings in the reader; if it is used carelessly, or too frequently, it defeats its own end.

Antithesis. A figure that is the opposite of the simile is the *antithesis*. Antithesis is another word for *contrast*. We all know the effectiveness of putting black against white, the little against the great, the bright and gay against the drab and sullen. The poet uses this device often. Notice the contrast between the first two lines and the last two lines of the following stanza from Byron's "The Destruction of Sennacherib." This stanza illustrates, too, the use of simile and antithesis in a single passage:

Like the leaves of the forest when summer is green,
That host with their banners at sunset were seen:
Like the leaves of the forest when autumn hath blown,
That host on the morrow lay wither'd and strown.

This is rather an obvious use of antithesis. Sometimes the poet uses antithesis for less easy but more startling effects. In the following selection from Tennyson's "The Last Tournament" notice the remarkable contrast between the scene of barbarous massacre in the first lines and the marvelously vivid effect of lonely quiet in the final line.

Then the knights, who watch'd him, roar'd
And shouted and leapt down upon the fallen,
There trampled out his face from being known,
And sunk his head in mire, and slimed themselves;
Nor heard the King for their own cries, but sprang
Thro' open doors, and swording right and left
Men, women, on their sodden faces, hurl'd
The tables over and the wines, and slew
Till all the rafters rang with woman-yells
And all the pavement stream'd with massacre.
Then echoing yell with yell, they fired the tower,
Which half that autumn night, like the live North,

Made all above it, and a hundred meres
About it, as the water Moab saw
Come round by the east, and out beyond them flush'd
The long low dune and lazy-plunging sea.

Irony. *Irony* is a deliberate discrepancy between what one says and what one means by what one says. It is a figure by which we make our words convey the opposite meaning from what they say. It is not, however, used to deceive, but rather to make the meaning more effective. An excellent example of irony is Antony's funeral oration in *Julius Caesar;* here he refers to the conspirators as "honorable men" when he wishes the crowd to feel that they are actually traitors. In "Guinevere" Tennyson makes the little novice praise Guinevere in such a way that the irony of her words is apparent both to the queen and to the reader, although the novice herself is unaware of it. Used in everyday speech irony is sometimes called sarcasm. It is considered an ignoble but powerful weapon. In literature, it is the classic device for arousing emotions ranging from scorn to pity.

Metonymy. *Metonymy* means change of name. In this figure the name of one object is substituted for that of another closely associated with it in our minds. Metonymy is almost as common as metaphor in our daily speech. When we say that we read Shakespeare instead of his books, we are substituting the author for his works. When we say that gray hairs should be respected, we mean that old age should be respected; and we are substituting one phrase for another associated with it. When we say the kettle boiled, or his head whirled, or he writes a beautiful hand, or the pen is mightier than the sword, we are using metonymy. Metonymy combines brevity with concreteness and is therefore of great value in poetry. Usually it passes unnoticed. When Tennyson says,

> And called for flesh and wine to *feed his spears,*

> About his feet
> *A voice clung* sobbing,

he is using metonymy which adds brevity and suggestiveness to his lines.

Epigram. *Epigram* originally meant an inscription on a monument. As such inscriptions were usually short, compressing as much as possible into a few words, epigram has come to mean any saying in prose or poetry which says something true or wise in a brief pointed manner. Caesar's "Veni, vidi, vici" is a famous illustration. Most poetry is not primarily epigrammatic, but epigrams occur in poetry fairly often. You will find the most famous epigrams in English poetry in Pope and Dryden, the brilliant literary leaders of the late seventeenth and early eighteenth centuries. Here are a few famous ones from Pope:

> Hope springs eternal in the human breast;
> Man never *is*, but always *to be* blest.

> 'Tis education forms the common mind;
> Just as the twig is bent the tree's inclined.

> A little learning is a dangerous thing;
> Drink deep, or taste not the Pierian spring.

> Honor and shame from no condition rise;
> Act well your part, there all honor lies.

Summary. In summary we may define briefly the figures of speech:

Simile—a direct comparison
Metaphor—an implied or indirect comparison

Allegory—an implied comparison expanded into a story or description
Personification—speaking of something that is not a person as if it were
Antithesis—contrast for effect
Hyperbole—exaggeration for effect
Apostrophe—rhetorical address to a person or thing that is absent, or dead, or inanimate
Irony—in expression, making one's words imply the opposite of what they literally mean; in situations or events, a state of affairs that is the opposite of what it seems or of what was expected
Metonymy—substitution of one word for another closely associated with it
Epigram—a short, witty saying, usually true

Figures of speech are of small consequence in themselves. Their value in poetry cannot be learned by merely cataloguing them. It is not enough to recognize a figure of speech when you see it. Figures of speech are used for a purpose; unless they fulfill that purpose they have no value. If they do not increase the suggestive power of a passage by throwing an unexpected light on its significance, by making it more vivid, by increasing its emotional appeal, or by adding clearness, force, or beauty, the poem is better off without them.

COMPREHENSION QUESTIONS

1. *Vocabulary:* simile, metaphor, allegory, antithesis, hyperbole, apostrophe, irony, metonymy, epigram, personification.
2. Define the term *figure of speech.*
3. Define each of the figures of speech explained in this chapter.
4. What is the most essential quality that a figure of speech should have?
5. Make a list of your own of metaphors common in daily speech suggested by the list on page 68.
6. Make a summary of the metaphors in a well-known poem, for instance "Snowbound" or "The Vision of Sir Launfal," following the plan used with "The Ancient Mariner" in this chapter.
7. In what way is an allegory really a metaphor?
8. How does metonymy contribute both brevity and concreteness to our daily speech? Cite examples.
9. Bring to class examples of all the figures of speech in this chapter.

PROBLEMS IN APPRECIATION

1. Here are similes and metaphors for study. Some are better than others. See if you can discover which of them fail to suggest what the author intended them to. Do any of them convey a mixture of suggestions?

Are any of them beautiful in themselves but inappropriate as comparisons? As you study each one, ask yourself the following questions:

What are the things compared? Are they like or unlike? Are they alike in more than one respect? Are they commonplace? Are they too dissimilar? Do they seem to be straining for effect? What is the poetic suggestion of the comparison? Does the figure add clearness, force, beauty, or mood to the passage?

(*a*) To suggest bitterness in a man's heart:

But ever after, the small violence done
Rankled in him and ruffled in his heart,
As the sharp wind that ruffles all day long
A little bitter pool about a stone
On the bare coast.

TENNYSON

(*b*) To suggest beauty, dignity, and spiritual light in a man:

His hair, a sun that ray'd from off a brow
Like hill-snow high in heaven, the steel-blue eyes,
The golden beard that clothed his lips with light.

TENNYSON

(*c*) To suggest modesty in a girl:

A violet by a mossy stone
Half hidden from the eye!
Fair as a star, when only one
Is shining in the sky.

WORDSWORTH

(*d*) To suggest sudden joy:

Haply I think on thee and then my state,
Like to the lark at break of day arising
From sullen earth, sings hymns at heaven's gate.

SHAKESPEARE

(*e*) To suggest an unpleasant smile:

Thereat the Lady stretch'd a vulture throat,
And shot from crooked lips a haggard smile.

TENNYSON

(*f*) To suggest the incalculable power of an idea let loose among men:

Hark! the rushing snow!
The sun-awakened avalanche! whose mass,
Thrice sifted by the storm, had gathered there

Flake after flake, in heaven-defying minds
As thought by thought is piled, till some great truth
Is loosened, and the nations echo round,
Shaken to their roots, as do the mountains now.

SHELLEY

(*g*) To suggest the mystery, beauty, and fragility of life:

Life, like a dome of many-colored glass,
Stains the white radiance of Eternity,
Until Death tramples it to fragments.

SHELLEY

(*h*) To suggest vague longing:

The desire of the moth for the star,
Of the night for the morrow,
The devotion to something afar
From the sphere of our sorrow.

SHELLEY

(*i*) To suggest eternal separation from what one loves:

Who renders vain their deep desire?
A God, a God their severance ruled!
And bade betwixt their shores to be
The unplumb'd salt, estranging sea.

ARNOLD

(*j*) To suggest the growth of love:

So day by day it grew, as if one should

Slip slowly down some path worn smooth and even
Down to a cool sea on a summer day.

MORRIS

(*k*) To suggest dawn:

Like a lobster boiled, the morn
From black to red began to burn.

BUTLER

(*l*) To suggest a beautiful, highborn maiden:

A damsel of high lineage, and a brow
May blossom, and a cheek of apple-blossom,
Hawk-eyes; and lightly was her slender nose
Tip-tilted like the petal of a flower.

TENNYSON

(*m*) To suggest a desolate old man on a cold winter's day:

But the wind without, was eager and sharp,
Of Sir Launfal's gray hair it makes a harp,
And rattles and wrings
The icy strings,
Singing, in dreary monotone.

LOWELL

(*n*) To suggest the peace and quiet of a home at twilight:

And the night shall be filled with music,
And the cares, that infest the day,
Shall fold up their tents, like the Arabs,
And as silently steal away.

LONGFELLOW

(*o*) To describe gentle and tender melancholy:

A feeling of sadness and longing,
That is not akin to pain,
And resembles sorrow only
As the mist resembles the rain.

LONGFELLOW

(*p*) To describe a ship becalmed:

Day after day, day after day,
We stuck, nor breath nor motion;
As idle as a painted ship
Upon a painted ocean.

COLERIDGE

(*q*) To suggest the pain and bitterness of estrangements from friends:

They stood aloof, the scars remaining,
Like cliffs which had been rent asunder;
A dreary sea now flows between.
But neither heat, nor frost, nor thunder,
Shall wholly do away, I ween,
The marks of that which once hath been.

COLERIDGE

(*r*) To suggest the hot sun in a tropical sky:

All in a hot and copper sky,
The bloody Sun, at noon,
Right up above the mast did stand,
No bigger than the Moon.

COLERIDGE

(*s*) To suggest a pleasant, soft, cool sound:

A noise like a hidden brook
In the leafy month of June,
That to the sleeping woods all night
Singeth a quiet tune.

COLERIDGE

(*t*) To suggest a worn-out civilization:

A broken spring in a factory yard,
Rust that clings to the form that the strength has left
Hard and curled and ready to snap.

T. S. ELIOT

(*u*) To suggest the nature of experience:

Yet all experience is an arch wherethro'
Gleams that untravell'd world whose margin fades
Forever and forever.

TENNYSON

(*v*) To suggest human dissatisfaction and disillusionment with life:

Ah, what a dusty answer gets the soul
When hot for certainties in this our life!

MEREDITH

2. Here are various figures of speech. Identify each one and comment on its poetic value. Is it striking? beautiful? illuminating? appropriate? moving? What is its poetic suggestion?

(*a*) Then a soldier,
Full of strange oaths and bearded like the pard,
Seeking the bubble reputation
Even in the cannon's mouth.

SHAKESPEARE

(*b*) I will kill thee a hundred and fifty ways.

SHAKESPEARE

(*c*) Arthur with a hundred spears
Rode far.

TENNYSON

(*d*) Tiger, tiger, burning bright
In the forests of the night.

BLAKE

(*e*) She is coming, my own, my sweet;
Were it ever so airy a tread,
My heart would hear her and beat,

Were it earth in an earthy bed;
My dust would hear her and beat,
Had I lain for a century dead,
Would start and tremble under her feet,
And blossom in purple and red.

TENNYSON

(*f*) In various talk th' instructive hours they past,
Who gave the ball, or paid the visit last;
One speaks the glory of the British Queen,
And one describes a charming Indian screen;
A third interprets motions, looks, and eyes;
At ev'ry word a reputation dies.

POPE

(*g*) Sport that wrinkled Care derides,
And Laughter holding both his sides.

MILTON

(*h*) O Wild West Wind, thou breath of Autumn's being,
Thou, from whose unseen presence the leaves dead
Are driven like ghosts from an enchanter fleeing,

Yellow, and black, and pale, and hectic red,
Pestilence-stricken multitudes!

SHELLEY

(*i*) Down swept the chill wind from the mountain peak,
From the snow five thousand summers old.

LOWELL

(*j*) Disdain and scorn ride sparkling in her eyes.

SHAKESPEARE

(*k*) Sharp misery had worn him to the bones.

SHAKESPEARE

(*l*) O, beware, my lord, of jealousy;
It is the green-eyed monster which doth mock
The meat it feeds on.

SHAKESPEARE

(*m*) this fell sergeant, death,
Is strict in his arrest.

SHAKESPEARE

(*n*) Good name in man and woman, dear my lord,
Is the immediate jewel of their souls.
Who steals my purse steals trash; 'tis something, nothing;
'Twas mine, 'tis his, and has been slave to thousands;

But he that filches from me my good name
Robs me of that which not enriches him
And makes me poor indeed.

SHAKESPEARE

(*o*) Not poppy, nor mandragora,
Nor all the drowsy syrups of the world,
Shall ever medicine thee to that sweet sleep
Which thou ow'dst yesterday.

SHAKESPEARE

Make a similar list of figures of speech you encounter in any anthology of modern verse. For a list of good anthologies see page 10.

3. The following poem is really an allegory describing the cost to a human being when his fate chooses to make him an artist, a genius. What does it mean? In what sense is it an allegory, that is, an expanded metaphor? Express the same idea literally. Can you invent another metaphor or allegory for it?

A MUSICAL INSTRUMENT

What was he doing, the great god Pan,
  Down in the reeds by the river?
Spreading ruin and scattering ban,
Splashing and paddling with hoofs of a goat,
And breaking the golden lilies afloat
  With the dragon-fly on the river.

He tore out a reed, the great god Pan,
  From the deep cool bed of the river:
The limpid water turbidly ran,
And the broken lilies a-dying lay,
And the dragon-fly had fled away,
  Ere he brought it out of the river.

High on the shore sat the great god Pan,
  While turbidly flow'd the river;
And hack'd and hew'd as a great god can,
With his hard bleak steel at the patient reed,
Till there was not a sign of a leaf indeed
  To prove it fresh from the river.

He cut it short, did the great god Pan
  (How tall it stood in the river!),
Then drew the pith, like the heart of a man,
Steadily from the outside ring,
And notch'd the poor dry empty thing
  In holes, as he sat by the river.

"This is the way," laugh'd the great god Pan
  (Laugh'd while he sat by the river),
"The only way, since gods began
To make sweet music, they could succeed."
Then, dropping his mouth to a hole in the reed,
  He blew in power by the river.

Sweet, sweet, sweet, O Pan!
  Piercing sweet by the river!
Blinding sweet, O great god Pan!
The sun on the hill forgot to die,
And the lilies revived, and the dragon-fly
  Came back to dream on the river.

Yet half a beast is the great god Pan,
  To laugh as he sits by the river,
Making a poet out of a man:
The true gods sigh for the cost and pain,—
For the reed which grows nevermore again
  As a reed with the reeds in the river.

ELIZABETH BARRETT BROWNING

4. Can you think of metaphors or similes to suggest?

sudden surprise
dismay
the sounds of dry leaves and twigs in winter woods
white snow on black branches
sunset seen through bare boughs
lights at night
the sounds and odors of a May twilight
gleaming rails seen from a railway train
the feeling of diving into a cool wave on a hot day
a bathing beach
the power of habit to transform personality
street sounds

Can you make one or more of these the basis of a short poem or description? Can you make up a similar list for yourself?

CHAPTER 6

UNDERSTANDING THE POET'S SYMBOLS AND IMAGES

The poet's images. Closely allied to figures of speech are *symbols* and *images*. By image we mean a word picture that stands for an idea in the poet's mind. A picture may incidentally help to create a mood, but unless it stands for an idea in the poet's mind, we do not think of it as an image. In Tennyson's "Crossing the Bar" the lines:

Sunset and evening star

and

Twilight and evening bell

are pictures that stand for the idea of quiet consummation and lasting peace that death brings to us all. Instead of making a direct statement of his idea, the poet paints a word picture which suggests his idea. In Lowell's lyric:

Violet! sweet violet!
Thine eyes are full of tears;
Are they wet
Even yet
With the thought of other years?

it is difficult to attach any definite idea to the suggested picture of the violet, but in Wordsworth's:

A violet by a mossy stone
Half hidden from the eye!

the picture is felt clearly to stand for a trait of character, modesty, which is an idea. Shelley's reference to the violet,

> Odors, when sweet violets sicken,
> Live within the sense they quicken,

does more than create a mood; it also serves as an image of the idea of the imperishable quality of beauty. In Matthew Arnold's "Dover Beach" the picture of the sea creates a mood, and it also stands in Arnold's mind as the living image of an idea:

> The sea is calm to-night,
> The tide is full, the moon lies fair
> Upon the straits;—on the French coast the light
> Gleams and is gone; the cliffs of England stand,
> Glimmering and vast, out in the tranquil bay.
> Come to the window, sweet is the night-air!
> Only, from the long line of spray
> Where the sea meets the moon-blanch'd land,
> Listen! You hear the grating roar
> Of pebbles which the waves draw back, and fling,
> At their return, up the high strand,
> Begin, and cease, and then again begin,
> With tremulous cadence slow, and bring
> The eternal note of sadness in.

And, as if he feared lest we fail to perceive that this picture is but the image of an idea to him, he proceeds to explain:

> Sophocles long ago
> Heard it on the Ægean, and it brought
> Into his mind the turbid ebb and flow
> Of human misery; we
> Find also in the sound a thought,
> Hearing it by this distant northern sea.

Then he explains in even more elaborate detail just what idea this picture stands for in his mind. To him that ebbing tide with its "melancholy, long, withdrawing roar" is but the image of the ebbing tide of Faith:

> The Sea of Faith
> Was once, too, at the full, and round earth's shore
> Lay like the folds of a bright girdle furl'd.
> But now I only hear

Its melancholy, long, withdrawing roar,
Retreating, to the breath
Of the night-wind, down the vast edges drear
And naked shingles of the world.
Ah, love, let us be true
To one another! for the world, which seems
To lie before us like a land of dreams,
So various, so beautiful, so new,
Hath really neither joy, nor love, nor light,
Nor certitude, nor peace, nor help for pain;
And we are here as on a darkling plain
Swept with confused alarms of struggle and flight,
Where ignorant armies clash by night.

Contemporary poetry has laid great stress upon the use of images; indeed, certain contemporary poets have called themselves "imagists." But the more conservative modern poets have also used images freely. Edwin Markham chooses these images to describe the character of Abraham Lincoln:

The color of the ground was in him, the red earth;
The smack and tang of elemental things:
The rectitude and patience of the cliff;
The good-will of the rain that loves all leaves;
The friendly welcome of the wayside well;
The courage of the bird that dares the sea;
The gladness of the wind that shakes the corn;
The pity of the snow that hides all scars;
The secrecy of streams that make their way
Under the mountain to the rifted rock;
The tolerance and equity of light
That gives us freely to the shrinking flower
As to the great oak flaring to the wind—[1]

In "Frost Tonight" Edith M. Thomas gives us a picture that suggests both a mood and an idea:

Apple-green west and an orange bar;
And the crystal eye of a lone, one star . . .
And, "Child, take the shears and cut what you will,
Frost to-night—so clear and dead-still."

[1] Reprinted from "Lincoln, the Man of the People" with the permission of the author.

Then I sally forth, half sad, half proud,
And I come to the velvet, imperial crowd,
The wine-red, the gold, the crimson, the pied,—
The dahlias that reign by the garden side.

The dahlias I might not touch till to-night!
A gleam of shears in the fading light,
And I gathered them all,—the splendid throng,
And in one great sheaf I bore them along.

. . . .

In my garden of Life with its all late flowers
I heed a Voice in the shrinking hours:
"Frost to-night—so clear and dead-still" . . .
Half sad, half proud, my arms I fill.[1]

An image, then, is a mental picture built up by the poet's words and used, not merely to create a mood but also to stand for an idea.

The poet's symbols. *A symbol* is much like an image except that it is not necessarily a picture. It is any concrete object used to stand for an abstract idea. The cross, for instance, is a symbol for Christianity, the crescent for Mohammedanism, the stars and stripes for the United States. The use of symbols is natural. Certain objects are almost universally used to stand for certain ideas. The Rock of Gibraltar serves as a symbol for anything firm and unshakable. Mountains have always stood in men's minds for the eternal strength and patience of God.

I will lift up mine eyes unto the hills, from whence cometh my help,

cried the Psalmist. Similarly the sea has always been a symbol for the vast unknown deep whence came the soul of man and whither it will return again,

When that which drew from out the boundless deep
Turns again home.

Dangers of symbolism. Poetic suggestion, as you can readily see, is at the very core of symbolism. Nothing is more suggestive than a good symbol, but nothing is more confusing than a vague, uncertain one. If it is to have force, there must be no doubt in the mind of the reader as to what the symbol suggests. The *Idylls of the King*, being allegorical, naturally contains many symbols, some of which, like

[1] Reprinted by permission of and arrangement with Houghton Mifflin Company.

Excalibur, are clear; but others of which, like Merlin's Siege Perilous, are vexingly vague. In Tennyson's "Flower in the Crannied Wall" there is a definite, effective symbol wherein a tiny flower stands for the whole mystery of existence:

> Flower in the crannied wall,
> I pluck you out of the crannies,
> I hold you here, root and all, in my hand,
> Little flower—but *if* I could understand
> What you are, root and all, and all in all,
> I should know what God and man is.

Suggestive power of symbols. On the other hand symbolism should not be too literal. Its whole value depends on its fertile suggestiveness. Here is a modern poem in which the symbols and images are effective not so much because they are clear cut and definite as because they are subtly suggestive. Here the very elusiveness of the symbolism is part of its fascination. There are few more haunting poems in English than Walter De la Mare's "The Listeners":

> "Is there anybody there?" said the Traveller,
> Knocking on the moonlit door;
> And his horse in the silence champed the grasses
> Of the forest's ferny floor:
> And a bird flew up out of the turret,
> Above the Traveller's head:
> And he smote upon the door again, a second time;
> "Is there anybody there?" he said.
> But no one descended to the Traveller;
> No head from the leaf-fringed sill
> Leaned over and looked into his grey eyes,
> Where he stood perplexed and still.
> But only a host of phantom listeners
> That dwelt in the lone house then
> Stood listening in the quiet of the moonlight
> To that voice from the world of men:
> Stood thronging the faint moonbeams on the dark stair,
> That goes down to the empty hall,
> Hearkening in an air stirred and shaken
> By the lonely Traveller's call.
> And he felt in his heart their strangeness,
> Their stillness answering his cry,
> While his horse moved, cropping the dark turf,
> 'Neath the starred and leafy sky;
> For he suddenly smote on the door, even

Louder, and lifted his head:—
"Tell them I came, and no one answered,
That I kept my word," he said.
Never the least stir made the listeners,
Though every word he spake
Fell echoing through the shadowiness of the still house
From the one man left awake:
Ay, they heard his foot upon the stirrup,
And the sound of iron on stone,
And how the silence surged softly backward,
When the plunging hoofs were gone.[1]

There is no mistaking the magic of this poem. It casts a spell over the imagination that no reader ever quite escapes. And when the silence surges softly backward and the plunging hoofs are gone, the reader returns to reality with a start. But what does it mean? The image of a man knocking on a closed door, listening vainly for a response from irresponsive silence, feeling all the time in his heart a strangeness, a stillness answering his cry—that image calls up a host of connotations. It is drenched with significance, but to label it with one dogmatic interpretation would be impertinent folly. Perhaps with Christina Rossetti, the Listeners would say,

Aloof, aloof, we stand aloof, so stand
Thou too aloof, bound with the flawless band
Of inner solitude; we bind not thee;
But who from thy self-chain shall set thee free?

Perhaps the Traveller is like a poet knocking at the Door of the Spirit, seeking an answer to the eternal question of life itself. Perhaps Mr. De la Mare would say to us that each feels in his heart the strangeness and stillness of an Unseen Reality which he can never make articulate. The symbols and images here have value for the many fascinating possibilities they suggest; they would be spoiled by too definite an explanation. It is significant, subtle symbolism of this sort that is at the heart of all poetic meanings.

Here is another very suggestive modern poem, almost as famous as "The Listeners." It is Ralph Hodgson's "Eve." Apparently it gives us an image of Mother Eve tempted by the glittering wiles of the Serpent in the Garden of Eden:

[1] Reprinted by permission of and arrangement with Henry Holt and Company.

Eve with her basket, was
Deep in the bells and grass,
Wading in bells and grass
Up to her knees,
Picking a dish of sweet
Berries and plums to eat,
Down in the bells and grass
Under the trees.

Mute as a mouse in a
Corner the cobra lay,
Curled round a bough of the
Cinnamon tall. . . .
Now to get even and
Humble proud heaven and
Now was the moment or
Never at all.

"Eva!" Each syllable
Light as a flower fell,
"Eva!" he whispered the
Wondering maid,
Soft as a bubble sung
Out of a linnet's lung,
Soft and most silverly
"Eva!" he said.

Picture that orchard sprite,
Eve, with her body white,
Supple and smooth to her
Slim finger tips,
Wondering, listening,
Listening, wondering,
Eve with a berry
Half-way to her lips.

Oh had our simple Eve
Seen through the make-believe!
Had she but known the
Pretender he was!
Out of the boughs he came,
Whispering still her name,
Tumbling in twenty rings
Into the grass.

Here was the strangest pair
In the world anywhere,
Eve in the bells and grass

Kneeling, and he
Telling his story low. . . .
Singing birds saw them go
Down the dark path to
The Blasphemous Tree.

Oh what a chatter when
Titmouse and Jenny Wren
Saw him successful and
Taking his leave!
How the birds rated him,
How they all hated him!
How they all pitied
Poor motherless Eve!

Picture her crying
Outside in the lane,
Eve, with no dish of sweet
Berries and plums to eat,
Haunting the gate of the
Orchard in vain. . . .
Picture the lewd delight
Under the hill tonight—
"Eva!" the toast goes round,
"Eva!" again.[1]

This poem, like "The Listeners," is apparently simple in its words, pattern, pictures, and situation. But actually its effect is the result of extremely subtle rhythm and imagery. It is more real and more pitiful than either the half-mythical subject or the half-playful style would seem to warrant. And the reason for this, of course, is that, whether the reader believes in the Bible story or not, the poem forces on him a sad conviction of the tragedy of lost innocence. Anyone who has irrevocably closed the gate of happiness on himself is as desolate to contemplate as Eve in the poem

crying
Outside in the lane,
Eve, with no dish of sweet
Berries and plums to eat,
Haunting the gate of the
Orchard in vain.

[1] From *Poems* by Ralph Hodgson. By permission of The Macmillan Company, publishers.

But it is to be remembered that the pity which this poem inspires might easily have been turned into moralizing sentimentality if the author had tried to be more explicit. The symbols and images are effective here not because they teach a lesson but because they suggest with beautiful restraint the common human experience of bartering true values for false ones.

Summary. Symbols and images, then, are ways of effectively suggesting an idea. An image is a word picture that stands for an idea; a symbol is a concrete object that stands for an idea. The suggestion aroused by each must be understandable but it need not be dogmatically explicit.

COMPREHENSION QUESTIONS

1. *Vocabulary:* symbols, images, concrete, abstract, values, explicit.
2. Define symbol. Find three examples of symbols familiar to us all in our everyday life.
3. What is the difference between a symbol and an image?
4. Find a poem which uses an image to suggest a mood or an idea. Explain what the image is and whether or not you think it expresses the idea clearly and appropriately.

PROBLEMS IN APPRECIATION

1. Music, when soft voices die,
Vibrates in the memory;
Odors, when sweet violets sicken,
Live within the sense they quicken.

Rose leaves, when the rose is dead,
Are heap'd for the belovèd's bed;
And so thy thoughts, when thou art gone,
Love itself shall slumber on.

SHELLEY

By means of images this poem suggests the value of all beautiful things. Each image suggests a special kind of appeal to one's sense of the beautiful—beauty of sound, of odor, of touch, of sight, of thought. What are the images here? What truth do they suggest?

2. Over the shoulders and slopes of the dune
I saw the white daisies go down to the sea,
A host in the sunshine, an army in June,
The people God sends us to set our hearts free.

The bobolinks rallied them up from the dell,
The orioles whistled them out of the wood;
And all of their singing was, "Earth, it is well!"
And all of their dancing was, "Life, thou art good!" [1]

BLISS CARMAN

Do the pictures here suggest a mood or an idea or both? If both, are the two separate or essential each to each? Has the sound anything to do with the mood or the idea? Would it have been possible to express the same idea as well by different pictures or different moods? Is the poem, as a philosophy of life, the result of a special mood felt on a special occasion, or could it be always true? Compare and contrast it with Louis Untermeyer's poem, "Mockery."

3. Here is a little poem from Walter De la Mare's *Peacock Pie* that does more than create a mood and paint a picture. It suggests the author's philosophy of life and implies that there are reasons for intellectual humility. Can you describe:

(*a*) the mood of the poem, (*b*) its pictures, (*c*) its philosophy?

All but blind
In his chambered hole
Gropes for worms
The four-clawed Mole.

All but blind
In the evening sky,
The hooded Bat
Twirls softly by.

All but blind
In the burning day
The Barn-Owl blunders
On her way.

And blind as are
These three to me,
So, blind to Some-one
I must be.[2]

4. Find the symbols and images in the following poems. Tell what each symbol or image represents. Discuss the meaning and the effectiveness of each.

[1] "Daisies," by Bliss Carman; reprinted by permission of and by arrangement with Small, Maynard and Company.

[2] Reprinted by permission of and arrangement with Henry Holt and Company.

Rupert Brooke	"The Great Lover"
Adelaide Crapsey	"The Warning," "Triad," "November Night"
De la Mare	"All but Blind"
Emily Dickinson	"Suspense," "Indian Summer," "A Cemetery"
T. S. Eliot	"Portrait of a Lady," "Sweeney among the Nightingales"
Robert Frost	"Mending Wall," "Birches," "The Onset," "Snow Dust"
Henley	"Margaritae Sorori"
Ralph Hodgson	"The Bull," "Stupidity Street"
Longfellow	"Oft Have I Seen"
Masefield	"Cargoes"
Lizette Woodworth Reese	"Tears," "Apples"
Carl Sandburg	"Cool Tombs," "Clean Curtains," "Grass"
Humbert Wolfe	"Journey's End"

5. A poet, of course, must make abstract ideas and feelings concrete—that is, related to something we can see or feel or hear or touch—if he is to communicate an emotion to the reader. How is this done in the following poems? What is the abstract idea or feeling in each, and what is the symbol or image that gives it imaginative life?

De la Mare	"Nod"
Emily Dickinson	"Chartless"
Robert Frost	"Mending Wall," "Birches"
Ralph Hodgson	"The Bull," "Eve"
Holmes	"The Chambered Nautilus"
Vachel Lindsay	"The Congo"
Masefield	"Sea-Fever," "Cargoes"
Alice Meynell	"The Shepherdess"
J. C. Squire	"The Discovery"

6. The following poem contains many images to suggest coolness. Pick them out. Which words have the power of suggesting this sensation to you? Which should you like most to think of on a hot day?

BALLADE MADE IN THE HOT WEATHER

Fountains that frisk and sprinkle
The moss they overspill;
Pools that the breezes crinkle;
The wheel beside the mill,
With its wet, weedy frill;

Wind-shadows in the wheat;
A water-cart in the street;
The fringe of foam that girds
An islet's ferneries;
A green sky's minor thirds—
To live, I think of these!

Of ice and glass the tinkle,
Pellucid, silver-shrill;
Peaches without a wrinkle;
Cherries and snow at will,
From china bowls that fill
The senses with a sweet
Incuriousness of heat;
A melon's dripping sherds;
Cream-clotted strawberries;
Dusk dairies set with curds—
To live, I think of these!

Vale-lily and periwinkle;
Wet stone-crop on the sill;
The look of leaves a-twinkle
With windlets clear and still;
The feel of a forest rill
That wimples fresh and fleet
About one's naked feet;
The muzzles of drinking herds;
Lush flags and bulrushes;
The chirp of rain-bound birds—
To live, I think of these!

Envoy

Dark aisles, new packs of cards,
Mermaidens' tails, cool swards,
Dawn dews and starlit seas,
White marbles, whiter words—
To live, I think of these! [1]

W. E. HENLEY

7. Try to write for yourself a short poem which will make real one of the following ideas, experiences, or sensations by means of symbols or images:

drowsiness	loyalty	motherhood
coldness	religious feeling	compassion for human suffering
being left alone	joy at being home again	disillusionment
dread		

Make your own list of similar subjects.

[1] Reprinted by permission of and arrangement with Charles Scribner's Sons

CHAPTER 7

GRASPING THE THOUGHT IN POETRY

It is not growing like a tree
In bulk, doth make man better be;
Or standing long an oak, three hundred year,
To fall a log at last, dry, bald, and sere:
A lily of a day
Is fairer far in May,
Although it fall and die that night;
It was the plant and flower of light.
In small proportions we just beauties see;
And in short measures, life may perfect be.

Poetry deals with thought as well as feeling. If there were nothing more to poetry than the qualities discussed in Chapters 1–6, it would be difficult to see why this stanza from one of Ben Jonson's poems is great poetry. It has no definite mood; it makes no strong appeal to the emotions. It is not primarily the expression of feeling; it is not just a beautiful picture, or a startling figure of speech. True, there is an image, the image of the lily, "the plant and flower of light." But this image is valuable because it expresses an idea, the idea that perfection is not necessarily measured in terms of time or space or size. The lily, which blooms and dies in a single day, is said to be as perfect as anything in the world. Here we come upon a new beauty in poetry. This is the beauty of ideas. Poetry deals with thought as well as feeling.

How the poet's imagination works. Sometimes a poet is not content merely to create pictures, feelings, or sounds. He feels in the beauty which he sees a deeper significance than can be expressed in terms of mere feeling or sensation. He looks out of his window and sees a tree; his imagination is stirred by its beauty and he writes:

I think that I shall never see
A poem lovely as a tree.

Then his imagination roves and he attributes to the tree feelings such as human beings have. He writes:

A tree whose hungry mouth is prest
Against the sweet earth's flowing breast;

A tree that looks at God all day,
And lifts her leafy arms to pray;

A tree that may in summer wear
A nest of robins in her hair;

Upon whose bosom snow has lain;
Who intimately lives with rain.

With his imagination still more deeply stirred, he feels an underlying spiritual significance in his imaginative experience with the tree. He is touched with reverence at the thought that God made such beauty for him to see. He concludes his poem with a childlike simplicity that conveys a lesson in humility:

Poems are made by fools like me,
But only God can make a tree.[1]

The poet expresses his ideas imaginatively. The poet, feeling a truth, expresses it through his imaginative insight. He may have beliefs which he cannot prove to be true, but his imagination finds comparisons that help to make clear the reasons for his faith. Thus the poet says:

I never saw a moor,
I never saw the sea;
Yet know I how the heather looks,
And what a wave must be.

[1] From *Trees and Other Poems* by Joyce Kilmer; copyright, 1914, by George H Doran Company, publishers. Reprinted by permission of and arrangement with the publishers.

I never spoke with God,
Nor visited in Heaven;
Yet certain am I of the spot
As if the chart were given.[1]

EMILY DICKINSON

Difference between ideas expressed in prose and in poetry. Poetry expresses its deepest truths through the medium of the imagination, whereas prose reasons out its truths through analysis. The propositions of Euclid are intellectual and analytical; they must therefore be expressed in prose. But man's hunger and thirst after righteousness, his burning passion for truth and beauty have their deepest roots in his heart; he must therefore express them in terms of imagination and feeling, which are the language of poetry.

"Beauty is truth, truth beauty,"—that is all
Ye know on earth, and all ye need to know,

says the poet, expressing his idea as a passionate conviction. Only through imaginative sympathy with the poet can this difficult idea be grasped; it cannot be coldly reasoned out. That is why many analytical, literal-minded people cannot understand poetry. They are not in the habit of arriving at ideas through the imagination. "The heart has its reasons that reason knows not of," said a wise Frenchman who, though he was a mathematician, was thinking then like a poet.

The poet teaches truths largely through suggestion. His preference for suggestion rather than direct statement is one of his chief differences from the prose writer. For instance, suppose he wishes to teach that all things save God's greatness are transient. Instead of a detailed sermon he writes a suggestive little story containing a symbol for his idea:

A certain pasha, dead five thousand years,
Once from his harem fled in sudden tears,

And had this sentence on the city's gate
Deeply engraven, *Only God is great.*

So those four words above the city's noise
Hung like the accents of an angel's voice.

[1] Copyrighted by Little, Brown, and Company. Reprinted with the permission of Little, Brown, and Company and of Mrs. Martha Bianchi.

And evermore, from the high barbican,
Saluted each returning caravan.

Lost is that city's glory. Every gust
Lifts, with dead leaves, the unknown pasha's dust.

And all is ruin—save one wrinkled gate
Whereon is written, *Only God is great.*[1]

THOMAS BAILEY ALDRICH

Thought suggested through a picture. Suppose the poet is impressed not so much with the greatness of God as with the futility of human greed and cruelty, passion and arrogance. Instead of a sermon he gives us a picture that impresses his idea on us unforgettably. See what Shelley teaches with wonderful restraint in "Ozymandias":

I met a traveller from an antique land
Who said: "Two vast and trunkless legs of stone
Stand in the desert. Near them, on the sand,
Half sunk, a shattered visage lies, whose frown,
And wrinkled lip, and sneer of cold command,
Tell that its sculptor well those passions read
Which yet survive, stamped on these lifeless things,
The hand that mocked them and the heart that fed.
And on the pedestal these words appear—
'My name is Ozymandias, king of kings:
Look on my works, ye Mighty, and despair!'
Nothing beside remains. Round the decay
Of that colossal wreck, boundless and bare
The lone and level sands stretch far away."

As a final example, let us take one of the great poems in our literature, Keats' "Ode on a Grecian Urn." [2] In this poem it is the transience of human life in contrast to the immortality of beauty that impressed the poet. He has just seen a Grecian urn, buried for centuries in the dust of a forgotten age and now brought to life as perfect and as

[1] Reprinted by permission of and arrangement with Houghton Mifflin Company.

[2] An *ode* is a poem, varying in length and in metrical form originally designed to be sung or set to music, but now usually merely the lyric expression of some noble, exalted, dignified, or beautiful sentiment. It is often based on the figure of speech called *apostrophe*. Keats' odes are famous examples.

eloquently beautiful as when it was made. This sets him wondering. The pictured border of the urn, showing the inhabitants of a little Greek village setting out with joy and reverence to celebrate a religious holiday stirs his imagination. Where are they now? And yet this cold and beautiful urn is still untouched by time; and on it is crystallized forever the whole scene: the soft pipes; the bold lover, for whom the loved one can never fade; the happy boughs that can never shed their leaves; the happy love and joy of that spring morning, forever warm and still to be enjoyed. Surely, the poet thinks, Beauty alone endures, and shall endure long after he who saw the Grecian urn and we who read his poem are dust. And so, he argues, Beauty is Truth, for both are eternal. But his way of arriving at this conclusion is not logical at all; it is based wholly on the feelings with which his experience has fired his imagination. He shows us the picture. He feels that we shall feel, as he does, how inevitable and remorseless is the power of time to destroy all things lovely, and yet how triumphant is the power of art to preserve forever one lovely moment. Thus, he says, the idealized truth of art transcends the incomplete, unsatisfying, temporal truth of experience. But the poet does not reason all this out logically. He glimpses the truth and utters a poignant exclamation:

Thou still unravish'd bride of quietness,
  Thou foster-child of silence and slow time,
Sylvan historian, who canst thus express
  A flowery tale more sweetly than our rhyme:
What leaf-fring'd legend haunts about thy shape
  Of deities or mortals, or of both,
    In Tempe or the dales of Arcady?
  What men or gods are these? What maidens loth?
What mad pursuit? What struggle to escape?
    What pipes and timbrels? What wild ecstasy?

Heard melodies are sweet, but those unheard
  Are sweeter; therefore, ye soft pipes, play on;
Not to the sensual ear, but, more endear'd,
  Pipe to the spirit ditties of no tone:
Fair youth, beneath the trees, thou canst not leave
  Thy song, nor ever can those trees be bare;
    Bold Lover, never, never canst thou kiss,
  Though winning near the goal—yet, do not grieve;
She cannot fade, though thou hast not thy bliss,
    For ever wilt thou love, and she be fair!

Ah, happy, happy boughs! that cannot shed
  Your leaves, nor ever bid the Spring adieu;
And, happy melodist, unwearied,
  For ever piping songs for ever new;
More happy love! more happy, happy love!
  For ever warm and still to be enjoy'd,
    For ever panting, and for ever young;
All breathing human passion far above,
  That leaves a heart high-sorrowful and cloy'd,
    A burning forehead, and a parching tongue.

Who are these coming to the sacrifice?
  To what green altar, O mysterious priest,
Lead'st thou that heifer lowing at the skies,
  And all her silken flanks with garlands drest?
What little town by river or seashore,
  Or mountain-built with peaceful citadel,
    Is emptied of this folk, this pious morn?
And, little town, thy streets for evermore
  Will silent be; and not a soul to tell
    Why thou art desolate, can e'er return.

O Attic shape! Fair attitude! with brede
  Of marble men and maidens overwrought,
With forest branches and the trodden weed;
  Thou, silent form, dost tease us out of thought
As doth eternity: Cold Pastoral!
  When old age shall this generation waste,
    Thou shalt remain, in midst of other woe
  Than ours, a friend to man, to whom thou say'st,
"Beauty is truth, truth beauty,"—that is all
    Ye know on earth, and all ye need to know.

Thought in poetry not hidden. Keats' "Ode on a Grecian Urn" shows that suggestion is often more moving than direct preaching. The poet does not hide his thought. He wishes our imagination to grasp the suggestion of what he has said because to him the imagination is more luminous than reason. Keats had no desire to mystify us; he wished us to grasp the meaning he saw in that picture; and he thought we should see it in the light of the imagination more clearly than if it were given us by means of a card catalogue.

The poet may teach directly. The poet can also tell us directly what he thinks. Many a sermon lingers in our minds because it is cast in rhythmic form. This is true of Carlyle's:

So here hath been dawning
Another blue Day:
Think wilt thou let it
Slip useless away.

Out of Eternity
This new Day is born;
Into Eternity,
At night, will return.

Behold it aforetime
No eye ever did:
So soon it forever
From all eyes is hid.

Here hath been dawning
Another blue Day:
Think wilt thou let it
Slip useless away.

Carlyle's poem, of course, is really little more than a jingling moral challenge. Except for the suggestion about eternity in the second and third stanzas, it has very little poetry about it. Nevertheless, great poetry can have really intellectual content. The great poets of the seventeenth and eighteenth centuries, especially Milton, Donne, Herbert, Crashaw, and Vaughan, and many of our modern poets, especially T. S. Eliot, Conrad Aiken, Thomas Hardy, Lascelles Abercrombie, Robinson Jeffers, and Hart Crane, have sometimes fused intellect and emotion. To illustrate that poetry may deal nobly and profoundly with ideas as well as with intuitive emotional glimpses, we quote these three "thought poems." The first is Shakespeare's One Hundred and Forty-Sixth Sonnet, a thoughtful reflection on values that, if it does not make an immediate ascetic of the reader, at least impels his respectful attention:

Poor soul, the center of my sinful earth,
Foil'd by these rebel powers that thee array,
Why dost thou pine within and suffer dearth,
Painting thy outward walls so costly gay?
Why so large cost, having so short a lease,
Dost thou upon thy fading mansion spend?
Shall worms, inheritors of this excess,
Eat up thy charge? is this thy body's end?

Then, soul, live thou upon thy servant's loss,
And let that pine to aggravate thy store;
Buy terms divine in selling hours of dross;
Within be fed, without be rich no more:
  So shalt thou feed on Death, that feeds on men,
  And Death once dead, there's no more dying then.

This sonnet has both emotional and intellectual content. The reader who has not known what it is to "pine within and suffer dearth" or to "within be fed, without be rich no more" can hardly apprehend the emotion of the poem. Yet any reader can find in the sonnet a philosophy of life, asceticism as opposed to hedonism, for instance, well worth arguing about on a purely intellectual basis.

The second "thought poem" is a speech from one of the most intellectual of Shakespeare's plays, *Troilus and Cressida.* Here the theme stresses the desirability of clear-eyed cynicism and worldly wisdom. Experience does indeed teach men to be prepared for oblivion and ingratitude. The many-sided truth of this poem can be illustrated again and again, not only from history but from contemporary personalities. See if you can paraphrase and illustrate all that Shakespeare says here. Some of the phrases, as always in his poetry, are worth lingering over, so packed are they with human emotions and intellectual content:

Time hath, my lord, a wallet at his back,
Wherein he puts alms for oblivion,
A great-sized monster of ingratitudes;
Those scraps are good deeds past, which are devour'd
As fast as they are made, forgot as soon
As done. Perseverance, dear my lord,
Keeps honor bright; to have done is to hang
Quite out of fashion, like a rusty mail
In monumental mockery. Take the instant way;
For honor travels in a strait so narrow,
Where one but goes abreast . . .

For time is like a fashionable host
That slightly shakes his parting guest by the hand,
And with his arms outstretch'd, as he would fly,
Grasps in the comer: welcome ever smiles,
And farewell goes out sighing. O, let not virtue seek
Remuneration for the thing it was;
For beauty, wit,

High birth, vigor of bone, desert in service,
Love, friendship, charity, are subjects all
To envious and calumniating time.
One touch of nature makes the whole world kin,
That all with one consent praise new-born gawds,
Though they are made and molded of things past,
And give to dust, that is a little gilt
More laud than gilt o'er-dusted.
The present eye praises the present object.

The third "thought poem" is from the great eighteenth-century poet, Alexander Pope. Since the wave of romanticism that swept over all European literature in the nineteenth century, it has been fashionable to belittle the poets of the previous century, Thomson, Pope, and lesser lights. But Pope was something more than a brilliant aphorist. He had something to say, and he said it so clearly and brilliantly that we are mistakenly inclined to think of him as superficial. But these opening lines from Epistle II of his *Essay on Man* ought to dispel that illusion.

Know then thyself, presume not God to scan;
The proper study of mankind is man.
Plac'd on this isthmus of a middle state,
A being darkly wise and rudely great;
With too much knowledge for the sceptic side,
With too much weakness for the Stoic's pride,
He hangs between, in doubt to act or rest;
In doubt to deem himself a God or beast;
In doubt his mind or body to prefer;
Born but to die, and reasoning but to err;
Alike in ignorance, his reason such,
Whether he thinks too little or too much:
Chaos of thought and passion, all confus'd;
Still by himself abus'd or disabus'd;
Created half to rise and half to fall;
Great lord of all things, yet a prey to all;
Sole judge of truth, in endless error hurl'd;
The glory, jest, and riddle of the world!

It doesn't matter that these ideas were not new, even to Pope. What matters is that they are expressed not merely with brilliance but with genuine suggestive power. For all their apparent ease and finish, one can linger over them as profitably as over the two previously quoted selections from Shakespeare. There are more ideas, if less beauty, in Pope's lines than in Keats' "Ode on a Grecian Urn," and like that great poem, they suggest more than they say.

Dangers of sermonizing in poetry. Any way of presenting ideas that is imaginatively appropriate is effective in poetry, but a poem that preaches without stirring our feelings is not poetry at all; it has none of the qualities of poetry except rhyme and meter. That is why we do not call a writer like Edgar Guest a real poet. Not that there is any objection to his wholesome homilies on the home, the family cheerfulness, respect for the old, love for children, or kindness to animals. One might as reasonably object to the Boy Scout oath. Most of what Edgar Guest says is true; but nothing that he says is ever poetry, for the essence of poetry is suggestive beauty or emotion. Everyone knows Ella Wheeler Wilcox's lines:

> It is easy enough to be pleasant
> When life flows along like a song,
> But the man who's worth while is the man who can smile
> When everything goes dead wrong!

Everyone would probably concede their truth, but only the extremely naïve would fancy them to be poetry. As a matter of fact, the emphasis upon ideas is why romantically poetic people do not care for Dryden, Pope, Dr. Johnson, Addison, or even Longfellow and Lowell when they begin to moralize in verse. But one should not on that account belittle intellectual poetry. Ideas as well as emotions can be stirring.

The four essentials in understanding poetry. All that we have been saying about the intellectual element in poetry may be summarized in a few statements.

Great poetry can be fundamentally intellectual. Indeed many of our best contemporary poets, such as T. S. Eliot, Ezra Pound, Robinson Jeffers, Conrad Aiken, and Hart Crane, are difficult to read because their poetry is so packed with profound and subtle thought. It is even likely that the poetry of the immediate future will, as T. S. Eliot prophesies, be necessarily difficult. Modern man is so harried by seemingly insoluble problems that his literature must reflect these difficulties. And they are difficulties which so challenge his intellect and so engage his energies with social conflicts that purely personal emotions seem by contrast less significant than they used to be. Today a lyric poet who writes, however beautifully, of merely personal feelings, is sometimes under-estimated because his work does not attack the knotty intellectual problems of the hour. Hence such exquisite and perfect poetry as that of Walter De la Mare or Sara Teasdale attracts less attention among the discerning than these gifted authors really deserve.

But the great poems of thought express their thought by suggestion rather than by direct statement. Ideas come to us in poetry suffused with emotional connotations; it is the suggestive power of a poem that makes it great, whether it suggest personal experience or social concepts. You will note that the passages from Shakespeare quoted in this chapter are packed with figures of speech which *suggest* ideas and experiences that it would take pages to explain in detail. Even the simple poems dealing with elementary ideas like "Trees," "Ozymandias," or "A Turkish Legend" gain their effect by suggestive language. And a great and difficult modern poem like T. S. Eliot's "The Waste Land" is intelligible to the reader only in so far as he can grasp the allusions and implications packed in each stanza; if he misses these "objective correlatives," as Mr. Eliot calls them, he finds himself in a waste land indeed, but a waste land stored with plenty to which he has lost the key.

The chief means by which the poet manages to suggest his ideas to us are symbols, images, and figures of speech. Notice how in most of the poems quoted in this chapter these devices (the same sort of thing that Mr. Eliot designates as "objective correlatives") are used to wake an emotional and intellectual response in the reader. An oak, a lily, a "tree that looks at God all day," a moor, the sea, a "wrinkled gate," "two vast and trunkless legs of stone," a Grecian urn, a "fading mansion," "time with a wallet on his back," a rusty mail, a fashionable host, "a being darkly wise and rudely great," "the glory, jest and riddle of the world"—all these are the symbols, images, metaphors, personifications, allegories by which the poet tells us what he means. "Why doesn't he say it and be done with it?" you ask. Because he can better stir our imaginations and our feelings and so more effectively convince us if he is suggestive rather than explicit. The various poetic devices have the same effect upon emotions as a musical background to a play or a ceremony; they evoke the mood appropriate to the meaning.

To get the meaning out of a poem *we must first be sure that we are reading its symbols, images, or figures of speech aright.* A mere vague, sentimental reaction will not do. If the symbol, for instance, represents an idea, we shall have to use our reason as well as our emotions in discovering what that idea is. To do that we must *study the language of a poem, phrase by phrase and stanza by stanza with concentration.* We should not slide easily over things that we don't understand or jump to superficial conclusions about vague phrases. And *we must re-create for ourselves the meaning of the poem or phrase clearly and unsentimentally without trying to insert into it our own ideas or our own emotional reactions.* In conclusion, we add without explanation, a seventeenth-century poem by George Herbert (1593–1633). See what you can make of it. What is the central symbol? How does it express the central idea? Put each stanza into your own words. Trace the development of the thought from stanza to stanza.

THE PULLEY

When God at first made Man,
Having a glass of blessings standing by—
Let us (said He) pour on him all we can;
Let the world's riches, which disperséd lie,
Contract into a span.

So strength first made a way,
Then beauty flow'd, then wisdom, honor, pleasure:
When almost all was out, God made a stay,
Perceiving that, alone of all His treasure,
Rest in the bottom lay.

For if I should (said He)
Bestow this jewel also on My creature,
He would adore My gifts instead of Me,
And rest in Nature, not the God of Nature:
So both should losers be.

Yet let him keep the rest,
But keep them with repining restlessness;
Let him be rich and weary, that at least,
If goodness lead him not, yet weariness
May toss him to My breast.

Summary. Besides appealing to the imagination, poetry also appeals to the intellect. It makes its appeal through suggestion rather than through direct statement, however, and in this way often conveys profoundly true or beautiful ideas so we see them in the light of reason as well as of imagination. The poet's chief means of suggestion are symbols, images, and figures of speech. Modern poetry tends to become increasingly difficult because modern life is beset by increasingly difficult intellectual problems.

COMPREHENSION QUESTIONS

1. *Vocabulary:* thought, feeling, ideas, imagination, didacticism, ascetic, cynicism, didactic, romanticism, aphorist, hedonism.
2. What is the chief difference between the way in which ideas are expressed in poetry and the way in which they are expressed in prose?
3. Make a list of three ideas which you think are appropriate material for prose but not for poetry. Explain your choice.
4. Make a list of three ideas which you think could well be expressed in poetry. What quality have these that makes them inherently poetic instead of prosaic?
5. Why is it dangerous to attempt to preach in poetry?
6. What are the chief devices by which the poet suggests ideas?

PROBLEMS IN APPRECIATION

1. Paraphrase two of the following poems in such a way as to trace the progress of the thought from stanza to stanza or from line to line. Where do the divisions or transitions in the thought come? Are the ideas directly expressed or merely suggested? Are they brought home by images, symbols, allegory, or stories? If so, how are the divisions of the poem related to its thought?

Arnold	"Self-Dependence"
Browning	"Rabbi Ben Ezra," "A Grammarian's Funeral," "The Statue and the Bust," "Saul," "Abt Vogler"
Hardy	"In a Wood," "The Darkling Thrush," "An Ancient to Ancients"
Ralph Hodgson	"The Song of Honour"
Robinson Jeffers	"Boats in a Fog"
Kipling	"Recessional," "If"
Masefield	"The Passing Strange," "The Chief Centurions," "Be with Me, Beauty"
Lola Ridge	"Reveille"

E. A. Robinson	"The Master," "The Gift of God," "For a Dead Lady"
Tennyson	"Ulysses"
Thompson	"The Hound of Heaven"
Wordsworth	"Lines Composed a Few Miles above Tintern Abbey," "Ode on Intimations of Immortality"
Henry Wotton	"The Character of a Happy Life"

2. Summarize as briefly as possible the ideas suggested by one of the following poems. State briefly whether or not you think these ideas true. How are they suggested by the poet? Does the medium of suggestion (symbol, image, etc.) seem to you appropriate?

Arnold	"Self-Dependence," "Shakespeare"
Browning	"Prospice," "Abt Vogler," "The Patriot," "Memorabilia"
Clough	"Say Not the Struggle Naught Availeth"
Gray	"Elegy Written in a Country Churchyard"
Herbert	"Virtue"
Ralph Hodgson	"The Song of Honour"
Kipling	"Recessional"
Longfellow	"Weariness"
Lovelace	"To Althea from Prison," "To Lucasta, on Going to the Wars"
Masefield	"What Am I, Life?"
Edgar Lee Masters	"Father Malloy," "Lucinda Matlock," "Anne Rutledge," "Rutherford McDowell," "Arlo Will," "Webster Ford," "Doc Hill," "Hare Drummer"
Lizette Woodworth Reese	"Tears"
Christina Rossetti	"Uphill"
Carl Sandburg	"Chicago," "At a Window," "The Poor," "The Road and the End," "Killers," "Choose," "Joy," "The Great Hunt," "Our Prayer of Thanks," "To a Contemporary Bunk Shooter"
Edward R. Sill	"Opportunity"
Thompson	"The Hound of Heaven"

3. The following poem is a good example of a poet's teaching a lesson directly and yet not sounding too prosaic.

A TALISMAN

Take Temperance to thy breast,
While yet is the hour of choosing,
As arbitress exquisite
Of all that shall betide;
For better than fortune's best
Is mastery in the using,
And sweeter than anything sweet
The art to lay it aside.[1]

LOUISE IMOGENE GUINEY

What is the lesson here? What passages seem more poetic than prosaic? Do you think the poem has value for its truth? Has it any poetic value? What parts of it are directly stated? Is any more suggested than is literally expressed?

4. Having read the *Idylls of the King*, write an essay on the allegorical significance of the *Idylls*. In this essay you should point out the allegorical meaning of the idylls as a whole, and you should explain what scenes and characters and passages in each individual idyll can be interpreted allegorically. Then you should conclude the essay with a paragraph commenting on the truth or falsity of the teaching of the *Idylls:*
   (*a*) Which of the *Idylls of the King* have the least allegory in them? (*b*) Why is it that these idylls are more effective as stories than the ones that are more directly allegorical? (*c*) Is it possible to read the *Idylls* understandingly without reference to their allegorical significance? (*d*) In what respects is Arthur made less satisfactory as a human character by the fact that he is also an allegorical type?

5. Paraphrase these passages from the *Idylls of the King* carefully noting particularly how the thought is carried from line to line. Point out thought divisions. Is any use made of symbols, images, or figures of speech? In each case comment on the truth or falsity of the ideas, illustrating by examples from your own experience or the experience of people you know about:
   (*a*) King Arthur to Sir Bedivere, "The Passing of Arthur," lines 408–423, (*b*) King Arthur on the quest for the Grail, "The Holy Grail," lines 869–915, (*c*) Sir Tristram on the ideals of the Round Table, "The Last Tournament," lines 650–698.

[1] Reprinted by permission of and arrangement with Houghton Mifflin Company.

© Underwood & Underwood, N.Y.

CLOISTERS AT CANTERBURY CATHEDRAL, ENGLAND

About this old cathedral cluster venerated traditions in English religious life.

Courtesy of the Metropolitan Museum of Art

"I think that I shall never see
A poem lovely as a tree."

Courtesy of the Metropolitan Museum of Art

"NORTHEASTER," BY WINSLOW HOMER
"Sea was her wrath yet working after storm"

6. Here is an exercise which could easily be used as a game. The A list represents an idea expressed by some poem in the list. The B list is a symbol used in some poem in the list to suggest one of the ideas in the A column. The C list gives the poems in which these ideas and symbols appear. Read the poems first, then see which member of the class can first match correctly the proper idea, symbol, and poem.

A

(1) A poet is made only at the cost of pain and isolation from his fellows.
(2) Discovering a great book is like discovering a new world.
(3) A beautiful sight recollected in tranquillity gives us ever-renewed pleasure.
(4) How mysterious is the power of God Who has created creatures of power, beauty, and terror as well as of helpless innocence.
(5) Work is sometimes both a benediction and an escape from worldly trouble.
(6) Romance has gone out of commerce since the advent of the machine age.
(7) Life is too short for one to miss an opportunity to enjoy beauty.
(8) The idealist protests against barriers between men; the realist finds them necessary.
(9) Experience widens our horizons.
(10) Man cannot escape the relentless pursuit of God's love.
(11) One should guard one's thoughts lest they escape one's control.
(12) Personal connotations may give rich meaning to a trivial experience.

B

(1) guarded sheep
(2) a field of daffodils
(3) an arch
(4) a wall
(5) a reed
(6) an eagle's feather
(7) a laborer praying in a cathedral
(8) "stout Cortez"
(9) "quinquireme of Nineveh" and "stately Spanish galleon"
(10) a pursuing dog
(11) a cherry tree in bloom
(12) a tiger

C

(1) Blake	"The Tiger"
(2) Elizabeth Barrett Browning	"A Musical Instrument"
(3) Browning	"Memorabilia"
(4) Robert Frost	"Mending Wall"
(5) A. E. Housman	"Loveliest of Trees"

(6) Keats	"On First Looking into Chapman's Homer"
(7) Longfellow	"Oft Have I Seen"
(8) Masefield	"Cargoes"
(9) Alice Meynell	"The Shepherdess"
(10) Tennyson	"Ulysses"
(11) Thompson	"The Hound of Heaven"
(12) Wordsworth	"Daffodils"

CHAPTER 8

SENSING THE MUSIC OF POETRY

The room was so still that the tick of the clock was the only sound to be heard except the voice that was holding its hearers fascinated. The principal slipped into the back of the room unnoticed, and beheld the problem of all past English teachers leaning over his desk spellbound by a poem. Then the principal himself fell under the spell of the voice and the enchanting story. He, too, listened breathlessly, while the redcoat troops bound the landlord's black-eyed daughter up to attention. He strained his ears to hear the horse's hoofs, "*tlot-tlot, tlot-tlot*, in the distance." He waited in suspense until the musket shattered the moonlight and the life of the black-haired girl.

John caught his breath and leaned forward again. Would they get him? Yes, they did.

> they shot him down on the highway,
> Down like a dog on the highway,
> And he lay in his blood on the highway, with the bunch of lace at his throat.

And to cap the climax the ghost of the highwayman comes back, so they say.

> And still of a winter's night, they say, when the wind is in the trees,
> When the moon is a ghostly galleon tossed upon cloudy seas,
> When the road is a ribbon of moonlight over the purple moor,
> A highwayman comes riding . . .
> Up to the old inn-door.

The teacher laid down the book and there was a long sigh from the class. They came back to the schoolroom with a start, but the spell of the moonlight and the tragic story still hung over them. They dreaded to have it broken.[1]

[1] "Making Things Make Themselves" by Vera E. Fawcett: *English Journal*, June, 1924. Reprinted by permission of the author and the editor.

Here is the poem which held them spellbound:

THE HIGHWAYMAN

Part I

I

The wind was a torrent of darkness among the gusty trees,
The moon was a ghostly galleon tossed upon cloudy seas,
The road was a ribbon of moonlight over the purple moor,
And the highwayman came riding—
        Riding—riding—
The highwayman came riding, up to the old inn-door.

II

He'd a French cocked-hat on his forehead, a bunch of lace at his chin,
A coat of the claret velvet, and breeches of brown doe-skin;
They fitted with never a wrinkle: his boots were up to the thigh!
And he rode with a jeweled twinkle,
        His pistol butts a-twinkle,
His rapier hilt a-twinkle, under the jeweled sky.

III

Over the cobbles he clattered and clashed in the dark inn-yard,
And he tapped with his whip on the shutters, but all was locked and barred;
He whistled a tune to the window, and who should be waiting there
But the landlord's black-eyed daughter,
        Bess, the landlord's daughter,
Plaiting a dark red love-knot into her long black hair.

IV

And dark in the dark old inn-yard a stable-wicket creaked
Where Tim the ostler listened; his face was white and peaked;
His eyes were hollows of madness, his hair like moldy hay,
But he loved the landlord's daughter,
        The landlord's red-lipped daughter,
Dumb as a dog he listened, and he heard the robber say—

V

"One kiss, my bonny sweetheart, I'm after a prize to-night,
But I shall be back with the yellow gold before the morning light;
Yet, if they press me sharply, and harry me through the day,
Then look for me by moonlight,
        Watch for me by moonlight,
I'll come to thee by moonlight, though hell should bar the way."

VI

He rose upright in the stirrups; he scarce could reach her hand,
But she loosened her hair i' the casement! His face burnt like a brand
As the black cascade of perfume came tumbling over his breast;
And he kissed its waves in the moonlight,
(Oh, sweet black waves in the moonlight!)
Then he tugged at his rein in the moonlight, and galloped away to the West.

Part II

I

He did not come in the dawning; he did not come at noon;
And out o' the tawny sunset, before the rise o' the moon,
When the road was a gipsy's ribbon, looping the purple moor,
A red-coat troop came marching—
Marching—marching—
King George's men came marching, up to the old inn-door.

II

They said no word to the landlord, they drank his ale instead,
But they gagged his daughter and bound her to the foot of her narrow bed;
Two of them knelt at her casement, with muskets at their side!
There was death at every window;
And hell at one dark window;
For Bess could see, through her casement, the road that *he* would ride.

III

They had tied her up to attention, with many a sniggering jest;
They had bound a musket beside her, with the barrel beneath her breast!
"Now keep good watch!" and they kissed her.
She heard the dead man say—
Look for me by moonlight;
Watch for me by moonlight;
I'll come to thee by moonlight, though hell should bar the way!

IV

She twisted her hands behind her; but all the knots held good!
She writhed her hands till her fingers were wet with sweat or blood!
They stretched and strained in the darkness, and the hours crawled by like years,
Till, now, on the stroke of midnight,
Cold, on the stroke of midnight,
The tip of one finger touched it! The trigger at least was hers!

V

The tip of one finger touched it; she strove no more for the rest!
Up, she stood up to attention, with the barrel beneath her breast,
She would not risk their hearing; she would not strive again;
For the road lay bare in the moonlight;
        Blank and bare in the moonlight;
And the blood of her veins in the moonlight throbbed to her love's refrain.

VI

Tlot-tlot; tlot-tlot! Had they heard it? The horse-hoofs ringing clear;
Tlot-tlot, tlot-tlot, in the distance? Were they deaf that they did not hear?
Down the ribbon of moonlight, over the brow of the hill,
The highwayman came riding,
        Riding, riding!
The red-coats looked to their priming! She stood up, straight and still!

VII

Tlot-tlot, in the frosty silence! *Tlot-tlot,* in the echoing night!
Nearer he came and nearer! Her face was like a light!
Her eyes grew wide for a moment; she drew one last deep breath,
Then her finger moved in the moonlight,
        Her musket shattered the moonlight,
Shattered her breast in the moonlight and warned him—with her death.

VIII

He turned; he spurred to the West; he did not know who stood
Bowed, with her head o'er the musket, drenched with her own red blood!
Not till the dawn he heard it, his face grew gray to hear
How Bess, the landlord's daughter,
        The landlord's black-eyed daughter,
Had watched for her love in the moonlight, and died in the darkness there.

IX

Back, he spurred like a madman, shrieking a curse to the sky,
With the white road smoking behind him, and his rapier brandished high!
Blood-red were his spurs in the golden noon; wine-red was his velvet coat;
When they shot him down on the highway,
        Down like a dog on the highway,
And he lay in his blood on the highway, with the bunch of lace at his throat.

. . . .

X

And still of a winter's night, they say, when the wind is in the trees,
When the moon is a ghostly galleon tossed upon cloudy seas,

When the road is a ribbon of moonlight over the purple moor,
A highwayman comes riding—
Riding—riding—
A highwayman comes riding, up to the old inn-door.

XI

Over the cobbles he clatters and clangs in the dark inn-yard;
And he taps with his whip on the shutters, but all is locked and barred;
He whistles a tune to the window, and who should be waiting there
But the landlord's black-eyed daughter,
Bess, the landlord's daughter,
Plaiting a dark red love-knot into her long black hair.[1]

ALFRED NOYES

Sound one of the chief means of securing rhythm. One of the chief differences between poetry and prose is that in poetry there is a rhythm secured by some regular pattern of accent or quantity, or both, whereas in prose there is only the indefinite rhythm of speech. Through sound we get the effect of the rhythm.

Sound also creates feeling. Sound is also one of the chief ways of creating feeling in poetry; and the appeal to the emotions is one of the principal characteristics of poetry. Perhaps it has never occurred to you that the language of most emotions is naturally rhythmical. Why do crowds at a football game seek to express themselves in rhythmic cheering? Anyone who has taken part in an athletic contest knows the feeling of intense loyalty, the burning desire to fight to the finish, that is aroused in him by hearing the rhythmic chant of "Fight, Fight, Fight, Fight" from the bleachers. Why is it that the most primitive races express themselves by rhythmic yells, swaying dances, and the steady regular beat of tom-toms? The first literary utterance of any race is poetry, largely because it is man's nature to express feelings rhythmically.

What interests us is not the fact so much as the means by which the poet creates feeling by sound.

How the poet uses meter. His first means is, of course, rhythm secured by meter. Meter is the name by which we refer to the arrangement of lightly and heavily stressed syllables in lines; in other words,

[1] From *Collected Poems*, Vol. I, by Alfred Noyes; copyright, 1913, Frederick A. Stokes Company. Reprinted with the permission of the publishers.

it corresponds to the beat in music. When the beats come fast and irregularly, there is a corresponding impression of haste, excitement, and breathlessness created, thus, in "The Holy Grail":

> for every moment glanced
> His silver arms and gleamed, so quick and thick
> The lightnings here and there to left and right
> Struck, till the dry old trunks about us, dead,
> Yea, rotten with a hundred years of death,
> Sprang into fire.

and in "The Passing of Arthur"

> Dry clashed his harness in the icy caves
> And barren chasms, and all to left and right
> The bare black cliff clanged round him as he based
> His feet on juts of slippery crag that rang
> Sharp-smitten with the dint of armed heels.

Many of the passages already quoted—Scott's shorter lyrics, Burns' songs, Browning's "Home Thoughts, from Abroad," and Tennyson's "Break, Break, Break"—illustrate the effect of meter. There are many other illustrations. For purposes of comparison read aloud the following passages from "Gareth and Lynette." In the first you will notice that the meter is hurried, uneven, with accents tumbling against each other in unexpected places. It is the account of Gareth and the Morning Star, and the meter serves largely to create the feeling of breathless haste, violence, and excitement that is essential to the passage.

> all at fiery speed the two
> Shock'd on the central bridge, and either spear
> Bent but not brake, and either knight at once,
> Hurl'd as a stone from out of a catapult
> Beyond his horse's crupper and the bridge
> Fell, as if dead; but quickly rose and drew,

And Gareth lash'd so fiercely with his brand
He drave his enemy backward down the bridge,
The damsel crying, "Well-stricken, kitchen-knave!"
Till Gareth's shield was cloven; but one stroke
Laid him that clove it grovelling on the ground.

The other passage comes before Gareth's fight with the Evening Star. Notice how slowly and wearily the meter drags itself along, without spirit or interest, and what utter indifference it suggests. Tennyson creates this mood largely through the meter.

With slow steps from out
An old storm beaten, russet, many-stain'd
Pavilion, forth a grizzled damsel came,
And arm'd him in old arms, and brought a helm
With but a drying evergreen for crest,
And gave a shield whereon the star of even
Half-tarnish'd and half-bright, his emblem, shone.

In this song from Shakespeare's *Cymbeline* notice how the meter pours out exultant joy up to the climax:

Hark! Hark! the Lark at Heaven's gate sings
And Phoebus 'gins arise,
His steeds to water at those springs
On chaliced flowers that lies;
And winking Mary-buds begin
To ope their golden eyes:
With everything that pretty bin,
My Lady sweet, arise!
Arise, arise!

Now, for purposes of contrast, turn to the weary monotony of the rhythm in this passage from *Macbeth:*

Tomorrow and tomorrow and tomorrow
Creeps in this pretty pace from day to day,
To the last syllable of recorded time.
And all our yesterdays have lighted fools
The way to dusty death. Out, out brief candle!
Life's but a walking shadow, a poor player
That struts and frets his hour upon the stage
And then is heard no more. It is a tale
Told by an idiot, full of sound and fury,
Signifying nothing.

As a final example, read Kipling's poem "Boots" which so famously re-creates the rhythm of marching soldiers:

We're foot—slog—slog—slog—sloggin' over Africa!
Foot—foot—foot—foot—sloggin' over Africa—
(Boots—boots—boots—boots—movin' up an' down again!)
There's no discharge in the war!

Feeling created through the sound of words regardless of meter. In the foregoing selections, however, the very sound of the words is partially responsible for the emotional effect. The harsh consonants in the description of Gareth's fight with the Morning Star and the weary sibilants creeping through the description of the arming of the Evening Star have quite as much to do with the feeling as the meter has.

Onomatopœia. Sound is also important in poetry because it often helps to make the meaning more vivid. Frequently the poet tries to make the sound of words indicate their sense, sometimes by direct imitation, sometimes by suggestion. The fascinating device by which the poet uses words the sound of which suggests their sense, is *onomatopœia.* As far as sound is concerned, it is the most directly suggestive device that the poet can use. Furthermore, it is as common in our daily speech as it is in poetry. A good many of our words, such as *bang*, *crash*, *crack*, *roar*, *wail*, probably owe their existence to the instinctive effort of someone to make the sound of his words suggest their sense. In the field of poetry the use of onomatopœia varies from the most obvious imitation of sounds as in Poe's "The Bells" or Vachel Lindsay's "The Congo," "The Santa Fé Trail," and "General William Booth Enters into Heaven," to the most discriminating choice of words to suggest sounds as in Tennyson's:

I heard the ripple washing in the reeds,
And the wild water lapping on the crag.

There is scarcely a sound that cannot be suggested by onomatopœia. Suppose it is the galloping of horse's hoofs. There is that most famous example from Virgil:

Quadrupedante putrem sonitu quatit ungula campum.

There is the deliberate imitation in the beat of many a "horseback poem," for instance, Browning's "How They Brought the Good News from Ghent to Aix":

> Then I cast loose my buffcoat, each holster let fall,
> Shook off both my jack-boots, let go belt and all,
>
> Called my Roland his pet-name, my horse without peer;
> Clapped my hands, laughed and sang, any noise, bad or good
> Till at length into Aix Roland galloped and stood,

and there is the American's favorite, "Paul Revere's Ride." Suppose the poet wishes to suggest the sound of water. One thinks at once of Southey's "The Cataract of Lodore" and of Tennyson's "Brook" with its varied suggestions of running water from the noisy

> I chatter, chatter as I flow
>
> I babble on the pebbles,

to the drowsy

> I murmur under moon and stars.

Then there are hundreds of isolated lines filled with suggestions of the shifting music of the waters from the roll of

> The league-long roller thundering on the reef,

and the hiss of

> A shallow seething wave
> Sobbed in the grasses at our feet,

to the quiet of

> Save for some whisper of the seething seas.

All other sounds, too, find expression through this familiar device. One can hear the swish of silk in

> And the silken, sad, uncertain rustling of each purple curtain,

and the noise of battle in

Shocks, and the splintering spear, the hard mail hewn,
Shield-breakings, and the clash of brands, the crash
Of battle-axes on the shatter'd helms,

and the murmuring accents of "folk at their prayers" in the old Latin hymn

Pie Jesu, Domine,
Dona eis requiem.
Miserere, Domine,
Dona eis requiem,

and the faint answer of echoes borne "from distance beyond distance" in

O, sweet and far from cliff and scar,
The horns of Elfland faintly blowing!

Blow, bugle, blow, set the wild echoes flying
And answer, echoes, answer, dying, dying, dying.

One hears the booming, hurried beat of drums in

The double double double beat
Of the thundering drum,

and the lonely wail of the wind in

A wind that shrills
All night in a waste land where no one comes,
Or hath come since the making of the world,

and the murmur of bees in

The broad ambrosial lines of lofty lime
Made noise with bees and breeze from end to end,

and the exultant rush of a victorious army in:

Mine eyes have seen the glory of the
coming of the Lord;
He is trampling out the vintage where
the grapes of wrath are stored;
He hath loosed the fateful lightning
of His terrible swift sword;
His truth is marching on.

Word music. The final reason that sound is important in poetry is that it is often the most important source of beauty. The poet often uses words quite apart from either the meaning they suggest or the mood they create, just because he likes the sound of them. Thus beauty of sound alone is often one of the charms of poetry. Some poets, for instance Poe and Swinburne, have very little else to give us, but that is enough. This musical quality in poetry we shall call *word music.* One does not have to know anything at all about the mood or context of the following passages in order to enjoy the music of their sound:

Silver sails all out of the west,

or

The long, low dune and lazy-plunging sea,

or

Thou still unravish'd bride of quietness,
Thou foster-child of silence and slow time,

or

I wield the flail of the lasting hail,
And whiten the green plains under,
And then again I dissolve it in rain.
And laugh as I pass in thunder,

or

No growth of moor or coppice,
No heather-flower or vine,
But bloomless buds of poppies,
Green grapes of Proserpine,
Pale beds of blowing rushes
Where no leaf blooms or blushes
Save this whereout she crushes
For dead men deadly wine,

or

O world! O life! O time!
On whose last steps I climb
Trembling at that where I had stood before;
When will return the glory of your prime?
No more—Oh, never more!

Out of the day and night
A joy has taken flight;
  Fresh spring, and summer, and winter hoar,
Move my faint heart with grief, but with delight
    No more—Oh, never more!

Indeed it is a question whether the passage from Swinburne's "The Garden of Proserpine," the next to last of the preceding quotations, has much of any meaning apart from its music.

Three kinds of rhyme. The ways in which word music is secured are rather tangible and easily analyzed. These methods may seem a little mechanical when they are analyzed, but poets employ them more or less unconsciously. The most obvious device for securing musical effect is *rhyme.* Rhyme is identity or close similarity between stressed sounds in corresponding places. There are three general kinds of rhyme: middle rhyme or assonance, end rhyme, and beginning rhyme or alliteration.

Assonance is much used in French and Spanish poetry and is coming into increasing prominence among modern poets. It consists in pairing the same vowel sounds in a verse, or verses, without regard to the consonants. It is a vowel rhyme found where the consonants do not rhyme at all. Here are examples:

The laughing *leaves* of the *trees divide,*
And *screen* from *seeing* and *leave* in *sight*
The god pursuing, the maiden hid.

But when the *waves* touched the marble *base*
And steps the fish over twice a *day.*

The *weeds* that *grew green* from the graves of its roses.

Alliteration we shall treat separately.

When we say *rhyme,* then, we mean rhyme occurring at the end of lines, as in:

Sweet is true love tho' given in vain, in *vain;*
And sweet is death who puts an end to *pain,*

or rhyme occurring at the middle and end of a line as in:

I bring fresh *showers* for the thirsting *flowers*
  From the seas and the streams;
I bear light *shade* for the leaves when *laid*
  In their noonday dreams.

This latter sort of rhyme is sometimes called *internal rhyme.* In the first and third lines, the word at the end rhymes with the word in the middle of the line; but in the second and fourth lines the rhymes occur at the end only. This passage also illustrates two other differences in rhymes. The rhymes *streams* and *dreams, shade* and *laid,* are called *masculine rhymes.* A masculine rhyme is one ending with accented syllables. The rhyme *showers* and *flowers* is called *feminine rhyme.* A feminine rhyme is a rhyme in two syllables, the first of which is accented.

Rhyme scheme. The pattern of rhymes in a poem is called its *rhyme scheme.* In analyzing a rhyme scheme, one uses letters of the alphabet to indicate the various rhymes as they occur. The first rhyme is called *a;* the second rhyme is called *b,* and all the words rhyming with it *b;* the next rhyme is called *c,* and so on. Here is a very artificial rhyme scheme from Tennyson:

Her song the lintwhite swelleth, *a*
The clear-voiced mavis dwelleth, *a*
  The callow throstle lispeth, *b*
The slumbrous wave outwelleth, *a*
  The babbling runnel crispeth *b*
The hollow grot replieth *c*
  Where Claribel low-lieth. *c*

Notice that all these rhymes are feminine rhymes with the scheme *a a b a b c c*. Considered as masculine rhymes, the ends of all the lines rhyme. The resulting effect is forced and unnatural, but it is an interesting experiment. The rhyme scheme of the following passage from Tennyson is used in his "In Memoriam." This effective rhyme scheme knits the first and last lines of a four-verse stanza by rhyme.

Ring out, wild bells, to the wild sky, *a*
  The flying cloud, the frosty light: *b*
  The year is dying in the night; *b*
Ring out, wild bells, and let him die. *a*

The following stanza from Swinburne's "A Forsaken Garden" illustrates a more elaborate rhyme scheme.

In a coign of the cliff between lowland and highland, *a*
  At the sea-down's edge between windward and lee, *b*
Walled round with rocks as an inland island, *a*
  The ghost of a garden fronts the sea. *b*
A girdle of brushwood and thorn encloses *c*
  The steep square slope of the blossomless bed *d*
Where the weeds that grew green from the graves of its roses *c*
    Now lie dead. *d*

Dangers in rhyme schemes. There are a few obvious traps into which poets in their use of rhymes often fall. First of all, they sometimes wrench the accent of a word to make it rhyme; or, even worse, they use as rhymes sounds which are not closely similar. In "The Eve of St. Agnes" Keats, intentionally or unavoidably, rhymes *howl, foul,* and *soul, moon* and *crone, thing* and *evening, do* and *woe, sleet* and *violet!* Scott is often careless of rhymes, as in "Gathering Song of Donald the Black" where he rhymes *glen and* with *pennon, shelter* with *altar, come* with *groom.* Byron and Browning are also sometimes careless in this respect.

Exaggerated rhymes result in humor. Sometimes poets lay hold of words and make them rhyme, whether they will or no. Like Humpty Dumpty in *Through the Looking Glass,* these gentlemen will tolerate no nonsense from rhymes and meters, and so their blithe independence produces an irresistibly humorous effect. The best example of this imperturbable good humor you can find in the work of Ogden Nash, specifically in his cheerful volume entitled *Hard Lines.* Here you can find Mr. Nash briefly dismissing the Bronx with an unequivocal "No, thonx!" and congratulating himself:

For not having tried to impress my girl but being naturaler with her and naturaler;
So that now instead of having to marry and all that I can continue to be a careless baturaler.

In his leisure moments he reflects with fine disregard of rhyme and meter:

I would live all my life in nonchalance and insouciance
Were it not for making a living which is rather a nouciance,

and suspects that

those people are utterly unreliable
Who say they'd be happy on a desert island with a copy of the Biable
And *Hamlet* (by Shakespeare) and *Don Quixote* (by Cervantes)
And poems by Homer and Virgil and perhaps a thing or two of Dante's.[1]

But unless you can be as innocently gay with rhymes and meters as Mr. Nash and his ilk, you had better stick to the conventions of rhyming.

Danger of hackneyed rhymes. Poets sometimes make their verses monotonous by using the same rhymes over and over again. After reading a page or two of their work one feels sure that *dreams* will rhyme with *gleams*, *mist* with *amethyst*, *bright* with *light*, *flowers* with *hours*, *gold* with *old* or *cold*.

Over-complex rhyme schemes. Another danger in the use of rhymes is that of making the rhyme scheme too complex. Such a scheme, for instance, as *a a b c c b d d b e e b f f b* is too elaborate. Unless the reader follows a rhyme scheme subconsciously, expectantly waiting for the recurring sounds, there is little use in it.

Alliteration. A second common device for securing word music is *alliteration.* Alliteration is the repetition of initial consonant sounds throughout a line or lines. It is thus similar to rhyme though different in position. Sometimes, as in the following quotation from "The Scythe Song," it is highly appropriate to the sense of the poem, but often it is of value merely as beautiful sound in itself.

Hush, ah, hush, the Scythes are saying,
Hush, and heed not, and fall asleep;
Hush, they say to the grasses swaying;
Hush, they sing to the clover deep!
Hush—'tis the lullaby Time is singing—
Hush, and heed not, for all things pass;
Hush, ah, hush! and the Scythes are swinging
Over the clover, over the grass! [2]

ANDREW LANG

Of course the alliteration of the s sounds in this poem is suggestive of the swish of scythes in the grass; and the rhythmic sway of the meter

[1] Reprinted by permission of Simon and Schuster, Inc.
[2] Reprinted by permission of and arrangement with Longmans, Green and Company.

reminds us of the regular sweep of the mower's arms as they work. But even without these connotations the passage would have musical value secured by alliteration. In the lines:

> The fair breeze blew, the white foam flew,
> The furrow follow'd free,

from "The Ancient Mariner," the meter and the alliteration of f's give the impression of speed, but the alliteration is also musical in itself. More often than not, alliteration is used without any particular suggestive value merely because it is pleasing to the ear. The alliteration in:

> Elaine the fair, Elaine the lovable,
> Elaine, the lily maid of Astolat;

in

> Silver sails all out of the west;

in

> The mild-eyed melancholy Lotos-eaters came;

in

> Pale, beyond porch and portal,
> Crowned with calm leaves, she stands
> Who gathers all things mortal
> With cold immortal hands;
> Her languid lips are sweeter
> Than love's who fears to greet her
> To men that mix and meet her
> From many times and lands

is beautiful sound, indeed, with more value in its music than in any meaning it suggests. An excellent example of alliteration that contributes word music, onomatopœia, and mood, all perfectly blended, can be found in Rossetti's poem "Chimes," which suggests its idea by giving bell sounds which echo each other in haunting overtones.

Tone color through effective vowel and consonant sounds. Other devices for securing word music are to be found in the use of certain vowel and consonant sounds. The deeper toned vowels, as in:

Break, break, break,
On thy cold gray stones, O Sea,

always give a deep and melancholy music to verse, a music with "the eternal note of sadness." Other vowel sounds, such as the open ones in

O sweet and far from cliff and scar,

are invaluable in suggesting a sweeter, more distant music. The liquid consonants, l, m, n, and r, invariably soften the whole tone of a line, as in:

Lost love—labor and lullaby
And lowly let love lie.

Late love-longing and life-sorrow
And love's life lying low;

and

O Mistress mine, where are you roaming?

and

I murmur under moon and stars
In brambly wildernesses;
I linger by my shingly bars,
I loiter round my cresses.

The sibilant consonants, s and soft c, also add soft, whispering sounds to word music, and f and v sounds help to create lightness and swiftness as well as softness. Tennyson's song,

O Swallow, Swallow, flying, flying South,
Fly to her, and fall upon her gilded eaves,
And tell her, tell her, what I tell to thee,

illustrates the musical effect of liquids and sibilants as well as of f and v sounds.

Sibilants must be used sparingly, however, or they will give an unpleasant hissing sound to the verse, as in Tennyson's purposely ugly line

Then stuttering thro' the hedge of splintered teeth
Yet strangers to the tongue.

Word music in blank verse. In blank verse, which does not depend on rhyme, the word music is partly created by *end-stopped* and *run-on lines* and by *cesuras.*

An end-stopped line is a line with a pause in the sense at its end where the reading voice drops, thus:

Thou wast not born for death, immortal Bird!
No hungry generations tread thee down.

or

How sweet the moonlight sleeps upon this bank!

A run-on line is a line which has no pause at the end, in which, therefore, the sense is carried on into the next line, thus:

Perhaps the self-same song that found a path
Through the sad heart of Ruth, when, sick for home,
She stood in tears amid the alien corn,

or

And watched the curled white of the coming wave
Glass'd in the slippery sand before it breaks,

or

As on a dull day in an ocean cave
The blind wave feeling round his long sea-hall
In silence.

In the following passage the first two lines are run-on, the third is followed by a pause, and the last is end-stopped.

Till notice of a change in the dark world
Was lispt about the acacias, and a bird,
That early woke to feed her little ones,
Sent from a dewy breast, a cry for light.

A cesura is a definite pause within a line, thus:

To die, || to sleep; ||
To sleep: || perchance to dream: || ay, || there's the rub;
For in that sleep of death what dreams may come
When we have shuffled off this mortal coil,
Must give us pause: || there's the respect
That makes calamity of so long life.

In the following stanza from one of the few successful lyrics in blank verse, Tennyson's "Tears, Idle Tears," the first three lines are run-on and the last two end-stopped. There are cesuras in the third and last lines.

Ah, sad and strange as in dark summer dawns
The earliest pipe of half-awakened birds
To dying ears, || when unto dying eyes
The casement slowly grows a glimmering square;
So sad, || so strange, || the days that are no more.

There is also an effective example of these devices in Matthew Arnold's "Dover Beach":

Listen! || you hear the grating roar
Of pebbles which the waves draw back, and fling,
At their return, up the high strand,
Begin, || and cease, || and then again begin,
With tremulous cadence slow, || and bring
The eternal note of sadness in.

Hear the effect of cesuras in the line:

Begin, || and cease, || and then again begin.

The cesuras suggest the pause, the silence, and then the crash of waves again with monotonous regularity. These three devices, of course, keep blank verse, or any verse, from being monotonous, and they also give what is known as *paragraph rhythm* to the poem. Paragraph rhythm is the rhythm which flows from line to line, pausing, gathering new force, and flowing on again.

Musical effect by haunting refrain. Another common device for securing word music is the use of *refrain.* We often remember a poem because its musical and appropriate refrain lingers in our minds. All the songs in the *Idylls of the King* have refrains, from Lynette's:

Shine sweetly: twice my love hath smiled on me,

and Merlin's,

Rain, rain, and sun! a rainbow in the sky!

to the little novice's hauntingly sad and appropriate

Late, late, so late! and dark the night and chill!
Late, late, so late! but we can enter still.
Too late, too late! ye cannot enter now!

The refrains in "Tears, Idle Tears" with their subtle variations, in the "Bugle Song," and in "Sweet and Low" are other notable examples.

A great part of the effect of Rossetti's "Sister Helen" is secured by the refrain:

'Why did you melt your waxen man,
Sister Helen?
To-day is the third since you began."
"The time was long, yet the time ran,
Little brother,"
(O Mother, Mary Mother,
Three days to-day, between Hell and Heaven!)

The popular ballads of the Middle Ages made constant use of refrain, so that today their literary imitators use it often in narrative poetry. It would be interesting to collect the refrains in the ballads of poets from Scott to Alfred Noyes, Masefield, and Kipling just to see how much they really owe to medieval ballads like "Edward," "Lord Randal," and "Barbara Allen's Cruelty."

Summary. Sound is important in poetry because it is the chief source of rhythm, onomatopœia, and word music without which poetry could scarcely exist. *Rhythm* adds greatly to the emotional effect of poetry. *Onomatopœia* is imitating sounds by words, either directly or suggestively. *Word music* is secured by rhymes, alliteration, assonance, rhyme scheme, long and open vowels, liquid and sibilant consonants, cesuras, end-stopped lines, run-on lines, and musical refrains.

COMPREHENSION QUESTIONS

1. *Vocabulary:* rhythm, beats, word music, rhyme, alliteration, assonance, long vowels, sibilant consonants, liquid consonants, cesura, end-stopped lines, run-on lines, onomatopœia, open vowels.
2. State two reasons why sound is more important in poetry than in prose.
3. Find a poem in which sound helps to create mood.
4. Find a poem in which the sound is beautiful in itself, regardless of the mood or meaning of the poem.
5. Define *onomatopœia.* Cite examples from poetry or everyday speech.
6. Find examples of alliteration in poetry and in everyday speech.
7. Explain the difference between masculine and feminine rhymes; between internal and end rhymes.
8. Explain and illustrate what is meant by end-stopped lines, run-on lines, cesuras.
9. What vowel and consonant sounds are most musical? Which ones are harsh?
10. Summarize the chief means by which the poet secures word music.

PROBLEMS IN APPRECIATION

1. Analyze the word music of one of the following poems. Look especially for such devices as alliteration, deep-toned and open vowels, liquid and sibilant consonants, end-stopped and run-on lines, cesuras, effectively varied rhythms, haunting refrains, musical shifts in the meter:

Arnold	"The Forsaken Merman"
Chesterton	"Lepanto"
De la Mare	"Nod," "Arabia," "Silver," "The Listeners," "Tartary"
Keats	"La Belle Dame sans Merci," "Ode on a Grecian Urn," "Ode to Autumn"
Vachel Lindsay	"The Congo," "The Chinese Nightingale," "The Santa Fé Trail"
Masefield	*Reynard the Fox, Enslaved, Salt Water Ballads, King Cole*
Alfred Noyes	"The Flower of Old Japan"
Poe	"The Bells," "Ulalume," "The Raven"
Rossetti	"The Blessed Damozel"
Shelley	"To a Skylark," "Indian Serenade," "To Night"

Tennyson	Songs from *The Princess*, "The Passing of Arthur"
William Butler Yeats	Song from *The Land of Heart's Desire*

2. It might be interesting for you to try your own hand at manipulating words to get certain rhythmic and tonal effects. For instance, can you: (*a*) Write a little poem of two stanzas, the first in a slow rhythm, the second quick; the first using deep vowels and heavy stresses, the second using alliteration and liquid consonants? (*b*) Find imitative expressions for ten different everyday sounds? (*c*) Write a poem of ten lines of blank verse using alliteration, cesuras, end-stopped and run-on lines, and shifting pace.

3. Read the following poems aloud several times. Try to bring out the full value of musical vowel and consonant sounds, but do not overemphasize the word music so that it becomes lush. Pay special attention to variations of pace secured by variations of meter. Bring out any onomatopœia that you find so that your hearers will feel its presence, but do not bludgeon their ears with it. In short, give the sound of the poem its full emotional and tonal value.

Arnold	"The Forsaken Merman"
William Rose Benét	"The Horse Thief"
Chesterton	"Lepanto"
Coleridge	"The Ancient Mariner," "Christabel"
T. A. Daly	"Da Leetla Boy," "Mia Carlotta," "Between Two Loves"
De la Mare	"The Listeners," "Nod," "Tartary," "Silver"
William H. Drummond	"Johnnie's First Moose," "The Wreck of the Julie Plante"
Dryden	"Alexander's Feast"
Joyce Kilmer	"Rouge Bouquet"
Kipling	"Boots," "Gunga Din"
Vachel Lindsay	"The Congo," "The Santa Fé Trail," "General William Booth Enters into Heaven," "The Chinese Nightingale"
Masefield	"Tewkesbury Road," *Reynard the Fox*, "Sea-Fever," *King Cole*
Alfred Noyes	"The Highwayman," "The Barrel-Organ," "Forty Singing Seamen"

Tennyson — "The Passing of Arthur," "The Holy Grail," "The Lotus Eaters"

4. Here are examples of onomatopœia. Read each aloud to see what the poet is attempting to suggest. Is the onomatopœia in each passage imitative or merely suggestive? Is it secured by meter or by sound regardless of meter? What letters and sounds in each passage are most suggestive?

(*a*)
As I ride, as I ride,
To our Chief and his Allied,
Who dares chide my heart's pride
As I ride, as I ride?

Do I glide unespied
As I ride, as I ride?

BROWNING

(*b*) Oilily bubbled up the mere.

TENNYSON

(*c*)
By the margin, willow-veil'd,
Slide the heavy barges trail'd
By slow horses; and unhail'd
The shallop flitteth silken-sail'd
Skimming down to Camelot.

TENNYSON

(*d*)
I bubble into eddying bays,
I babble on the pebbles.

TENNYSON

(*e*)
And all around I heard you pass
Like ladies' skirts across the grass.

STEVENSON

(*f*) From the church came the murmur of folk at their prayers.

ARNOLD

(*g*)
Down, down, down;
Down to the depths of the sea!

ARNOLD

(*h*) When down swung the sound of a far-off bell.

ARNOLD

(*i*)
While I nodded, nearly napping, suddenly there came a tapping,
As of some one gently rapping, rapping at my chamber door.

POE

(*j*)
Tlot-tlot; tlot-tlot! Had they heard it? The horse-hoofs ringing clear;
Tlot-tlot, tlot-tlot, in the distance? Were they deaf that they did not hear?

Down the ribbon of moonlight, over the brow of the hill,
The highwayman came riding,
Riding, riding!
The red-coats looked to their priming! She stood up, straight and still!

NOYES

(*k*) Dim drums throbbing, in the hills half heard

Stiff flags straining in the night-blasts cold.
In the gloom black-purple, in the glint old-gold,
Torchlight crimson on the copper kettle-drums,
Then the tuckets, then the trumpets, then the cannon, and he comes,
Don John laughing in the brave beard curled,
Spurning of his stirrups like the thrones of all the world.[1]

CHESTERTON

(*l*) Dead, long dead,
Long dead!
And my heart is a handful of dust,
And the wheels go over my head,
And my bones are shaken with pain,
For into a shallow grave they are thrust,
Only a yard beneath the street,
And the hoofs of the horses beat, beat,
Beat into my scalp and my brain,
With never an end to the stream of passing feet,
Driving, hurrying, marrying, burying,
Clamor and rumble, and ringing and clatter;

TENNYSON

(*m*) Great rats, small rats, lean rats, brawny rats,
Brown rats, black rats, gray rats, tawny rats,
Grave old plodders, gay young friskers,
Fathers, mothers, uncles, cousins,
Cocking tails and pricking whiskers,
Families by tens and dozens,
Brothers, sisters, husbands, wives—
Followed the Piper for their lives.

BROWNING

(*n*) And at evening evermore,
In a Chapel on the shore,
Shall the Chaunters sad and saintly,
Yellow tapers burning faintly
Doleful Masses chaunt for thee,
Miserere, Domine!

[1] Used by permission of Dodd, Mead and Company, Inc.

Hark! the cadence dies away
On the quiet moonlight sea;
The boatmen rest their oars and say,
Miserere, Domine.

COLERIDGE

(o) Wailing, wailing, wailing, the wind over land and sea,
And Willy's voice in the wind, "Oh mother, come out to me!"

TENNYSON

(p) So we'll go no more a-roving
So late into the night,
Though the heart be still as loving
And the moon be still as bright.

BYRON

(q) Dry clashed his harness in the icy caves
And barren chasms, and all to left and right
The bare black cliff clanged round him, as he based
His feet on juts of slippery crag that rang
Sharp-smitten with the dint of armed heels—
And on a sudden, lo, the level lake
And the long glories of the winter moon.

TENNYSON

5. One could not ask for a better example of the close relationship between sound and emotion than "Nod," the little slumber poem by Walter De la Mare. Besides that, it is also an eloquent illustration of all that is said about word music on pages 123–132. The best way to enjoy it is to read it aloud, not once but repeatedly. Try it. Then you can talk or write about it in connection with the material on pages 123–132.

6. Try your hand at fitting sounds to moods in a poem of from four to eight lines which is suggested by one of the following topics:

slumber	struggle	sport
good cheer	monotony	boredom
a lament	wind and sea	
excitement	hunting	

CHAPTER 9

UNDERSTANDING THE RHYTHMS OF POETRY

Accents and time intervals. Like music, poetry is divided into certain time intervals; that is, in each are a certain number of beats or accents coming at more or less regular intervals of time. In English poetry there may be a highly irregular number of syllables coming between the heavily accented beats, but the beats themselves usually come with some regularity. The syllables in a line correspond roughly to the notes, and the beats to the time in music.

Terminology for the number of beats. The technical names for these beats and syllables are borrowed from the Greek. A line with only one accent is called *monometer;* for example,

Away!

A line with two accents is called *dimeter;* for example,

Take her up tenderly,
Lift her with care;
Fashion'd so slenderly
Young, and so fair!

A line with three heavily accented beats is called *trimeter;* for example,

Oh, to be in England
Now that April's there.

A line with four heavily accented beats is called *tetrameter;* for example,

> The stag at eve had drunk his fill,
> Where danced the moon on Monan's rill,
> And deep his midnight lair had made
> In lone Glenartney's hazel shade.

A line with five heavily accented beats is called *pentameter;* for example,

> How sweet the moonlight sleeps upon this bank.

A line with six heavily accented beats is called *hexameter;* for example,

> This is the forest primeval. The murmuring pines and the hemlocks
>
> Stand like Druids of eld, with voices sad and prophetic.

A line with seven heavily accented beats is called *heptameter;* for example:

> Oh East is East, and West is West, and never the twain shall meet.

A line with eight heavily accented beats is called *octameter;* for example:

> Once upon a midnight dreary, while I pondered, weak and weary.

Most common accent patterns in English. Trimeter, tetrameter, and pentameter are the most common beats in English verse. Monometer is found usually in single lines, not in whole stanzas. Dimeter is not usually kept throughout a poem unless the poet wishes to rain blows thick and fast to gain speed. A good example of dimeter used for this purpose is Scott's "Gathering Song of Donald the Black.'

Hexameter is occasionally found, notably in Longfellow's "Evangeline" and in some of Byron's lyrics. Byron, too, sometimes uses heptameter. Kipling has become known for his use of the heptameter. Octameter is rare. A line with seven or eight stresses almost always breaks in two and therefore is better written as two lines.

The foot in poetry. You will notice that the beats come more or less regularly but that the lightly stressed syllables between the beats vary in number. One of these time intervals measured by a heavily accented beat is called a *foot.* The line is named for the number of heavily accented beats; the foot is named for the number of syllables and the position of its accent. These names, too, are borrowed from the Greek. A foot of two syllables with the accent on the second syllable is called an *iambus;* for example,

˘ ′
defy

A foot of two syllables with the accent on the first syllable is called a *trochee;* for example,

′ ˘
happy

A foot of two syllables with the accent evenly divided between them, neither being stressed more than the other is called a *spondee;* for example,

′ ′
gray stones

A foot of three syllables with the accent on the first syllable is called a *dactyl;* for example,

′ ˘ ˘
merrily

A foot of three syllables with the accent on the third syllable is called an *anapest;* for example,

˘ ˘ ′
intercede

A foot of three syllables with the accent on the second syllable is called an *amphibrach;* for example,

◡ / ◡
Flow gently

Terminology for lines of poetry. If a line of two accents contains chiefly iambic feet, we call it *iambic dimeter.* In other words, we name the line pattern from the number of heavily accented syllables plus the prevailing foot in the line; for example,

◡ / ◡ / ◡ / ◡ / ◡ /
This ci|ty now | doth like | a gar|ment wear
◡ / ◡ / ◡ / ◡ / ◡ /
The beau|ty of | the mor|ning si|lent bare,

Here are five heavy accents to a line, and each foot is made up of a lightly stressed syllable. The whole line is therefore *iambic pentameter. Iambic pentameter, trimeter,* and *tetrameter* are the most common English meters, for the English language seems naturally to fall into iambic beats.

If a foot has three syllables, with the heavy stress on the third one, we call it *anapestic.* This, too, is a common line pattern in English, particularly for rapidly moving verse. Here, for instance, are lines in which there are four accents, or feet, and in which each foot is an anapest. The line pattern is therefore *anapestic tetrameter* (four beats, the prevailing foot having three syllables of which the last is heavily stressed):

◡ ◡ / ◡ ◡ / ◡ ◡ / ◡ ◡ /
The Assyrian came down like the wolf on the fold,
◡ ◡ / ◡ ◡ / ◡ ◡ / ◡ ◡ /
And his cohorts were gleaming in purple and gold.

This is a favorite meter with Byron and Kipling.

If a foot has three syllables with the heavy stress coming on the middle one, we call it an *amphibrach.* Hence if a line is composed mainly of amphibrachs we call it *amphibrachic.* Here is an example of *amphibrachic tetrameter:*

◡ / ◡ ◡ / ◡ ◡ / ◡ ◡ /
Flow gently, sweet Afton, among thy green braes,
◡ / ◡ ◡ / ◡ ◡ / ◡ ◡ /
Flow gently, I'll sing thee a song in thy praise.

Sometimes the accented syllable stands first in the foot. A foot of two syllables, the first of which is accented, is called a *trochee*. Hence if a line is made up of accents occurring chiefly in a succession of trochaic feet we call it *trochaic tetrameter*. Here are six such lines:

I should like to rise and go (rest)
Where the golden apples glow— (rest)
Where below another sky (rest)
Parrot islands anchored lie (rest)
And watched by cockatoos and goats, (rest)
Lonely Crusoes building boats. (rest)

If a foot has three syllables with the accent on the first one, it is called a *dactyl*. A line composed mainly of *dactyls* is called *dactylic*. Here is an example of *dactylic tetrameter:*

Warriors and chiefs should the shaft of the sword
Pierce me in leading the Host of the Lord.

There are two other kinds of feet commonly found in English poetry. One is the *spondee* which consists of two heavily stressed syllables as in "Gray stones, O sea." Another is the *amphimacer* which consists of a lightly stressed syllable coming between two heavily stressed syllables as in "first and last." The following stanza by Coleridge was designed to help beginners remember the names of meters; perhaps it will help you:

Trochee trips from long to short;
From long to long in solemn sort
Slow spondee stalks; strong foot, yet ill able
Ever to come up with dactyl trisyllable;
Iambics march from short to long;

THE TOWER OF LONDON

With this famous building is associated much of English history and legend which have found imaginative expression in historical novels.

ST. JOSEPH'S CHAPEL, GLASTONBURY ABBEY, ENGLAND

"Bare, ruin'd choirs"

With a leap and a bound the swift Anapests throng;
One syllable long with one short at each side
Amphibrachys hastes with a stately stride;
First and last being long, middle short Amphimacer
Strikes his thundering hoofs, like a proud high-bred racer.

Here, too, is a little poem by Robert Herrick, "Ode to Ben Jonson," which has lines of iambic monometer, dimeter, trimeter, tetrameter, and pentameter:

Ah Ben!	monometer
Say how or when	dimeter
Shall we, thy guests,	dimeter
Meet at those lyric feasts,	trimeter
Made at the Sun,	dimeter
The Dog, the Triple Tun;	trimeter
Where we such clusters had	trimeter
As made us nobly wild, not mad;	tetrameter
And yet each verse of thine	trimeter
Outdid the meat, outdid the frolic wine.	pentameter

You will notice in the examples above that a rest may at any time be substituted for one of the lightly stressed syllables, though never for an accented one. This chiefly occurs at the end of a line, but not always, if a pause within the line is desirable. An example is:

Break, break, break !

Lines like this are called *truncated lines.*

Sometimes, too, you will find an extra, unaccented syllable added at the end of the line. And no doubt you could find many examples of individual feet that do not conform to the patterns we have defined.

Lightly stressed syllables at the end of a line make a *feminine ending;* for example,

When the lamp is shattered. 1
The light in the dust lies dead; 2
When the cloud is scattered, 3
The rainbow's glory is shed. 4

Lines 1 and 3 have feminine endings. Lines 2 and 4, ending on an accented syllable, are masculine endings.

Scansion of poetry. Most poetry is comparatively easy to scan, but you will not go far before you discover that many lines of English verse simply will not squeeze into the Greek patterns we have enumerated above. So long as the meters are plain iambics or anapests, you will have no trouble, for the English language naturally fits these rhythms. But the minute the poet begins to shift his rhythms for effect, substituting one foot for another without warning, you will be troubled as to how to analyze this meter. For instance, omitted syllables will bother you sometimes, and at others you will find extra syllables at the beginning or end of your line. Dactylic meters, which are comparatively easy to scan in Virgil, you will find troublesome in "Evangeline." But do not let these irregularities trouble you; they do not matter so long as the poet gets the rhythmic effect he wishes at the moment. The difficulty arises from the fact that these terms were borrowed from Greek, where they suited the rhythm of the language, and superimposed upon English where they do not always fit. Classical meter was based upon regular time intervals and not upon a variety of stresses, so that accurate use of dactyls, amphibrachs, amphimacers, and spondees is almost impossible in English. The English poet will shift his heavy beats and add or subtract his light ones to suit the mood of his poetry. The recurring heavy stresses give stability to the line; but you cannot be sure at what intervals they will occur. For instance you *can* be sure that each line of blank verse will have five beats, but you cannot be at all sure as to how many lightly stressed syllables will come between these beats. To illustrate this, you have only to try to scan a few pages of the *Idylls of the King* or *Hamlet*, or some of the contemporary blank verse of Robert Frost or Edwin Arlington Robinson. Our poetic rhythms are derived from Anglo-Saxon, not Greek, sources, and we do not rigidly follow the Greek patterns. For example, our modern free verse has recurrent rhythms so far as heavy beats go, but it disregards rigid stanza forms entirely. "Dover Beach" is not bound by any definite stanzaic pattern, but its recurrent rhythm is definitely felt. One does not need to reduce

> The days will grow to weeks, the weeks to months,
> The months will add themselves and make the years

to classical terminology in order to feel the rhythmic effect. One can get the feeling of hesitation in

First as in fear, step after step, she stole
Down the long tower stairs, hesitating

without worrying about its irregular feet. And one can hear the breathless mutter in

Muttering and murmuring at his ear, "Quick, Quick!"

and the gallop of horses in

The sound of many a heavily galloping hoof

and the dignified roll of congregational music in

Singing the hundredth Psalm, that grand old Puritan anthem,

even if one does not know much about Greek meter. Nevertheless these names help to make metrical effects tangible and lead to a keener appreciation of the poet's art.

Meter fits the mood. The meter of a poem should be adapted to the mood of the subject matter. In the selections quoted, it is clear that the meter is skillfully varied in order to suggest the mood which the poet wishes to create. Often within the same poem the meter is shifted to harmonize with the changing mood. When the meter is inappropriate for the mood, the poem necessarily loses in effectiveness.

Summary. Meter is the recurring flow and rhythm of poetry. It is based on combinations of heavy and light stresses. The names of these stresses are borrowed from the Greek. Lines of poetry are divided into accent intervals called feet. Meter should be adapted to subject matter.

COMPREHENSION QUESTIONS

1. *Vocabulary:* accent, interval, monometer, dimeter, tetrameter, pentameter, hexameter, heptameter, iambus, trochee, anapest, amphibrach, dactyl, spondee, amphimacer, truncated lines, masculine and feminine endings.

2. The student should learn the terms listed above and be able to give examples of each one. Otherwise the subject of meter will always be a source of irritation to him.

PROBLEMS IN METRICS

1. Scan the following passages and give the proper metrical name to each line. Note variations and state what is gained by them.

(*a*)

Oh, talk not to me of a name great in story;
The days of our youth are the days of our glory;
And the myrtle and ivy of sweet two-and-twenty
Are worth all your laurels, though ever so plenty.

BYRON

(*b*)

Scots, wha hae wi' Wallace bled;
Scots, wham Bruce has aften led!
Welcome to your gory bed,
Or to victory!

BURNS

(*c*)

Stars of the summer night!
Far in yon azure deeps,
Hide, hide your golden light!
She sleeps!
My lady sleeps!
Sleeps!

LONGFELLOW

(*d*) And the silken, sad, uncertain rustling of each purple curtain
Thrilled me—filled me with fantastic terrors never felt before.

POE

(*e*)

Blow, blow, thou winter wind,
Thou art not so unkind
As man's ingratitude;
Thy tooth is not so keen,
Because thou art not seen,
Although thy breath be rude.

SHAKESPEARE

(*f*)

Sleep, sleep, beauty bright,
Dreaming in the joys of night;
Sleep, sleep; in thy sleep
Little sorrows sit and weep.

BLAKE

(*g*) Tears, idle tears, I know not what they mean,
Tears from the depth of some divine despair
Rise in the heart, and gather to the eyes,
In looking on the happy autumn-fields
And thinking of the days that are no more.

TENNYSON

Take her up tenderly,
  Lift her with care;
Fashion'd so slenderly
  Young, and so fair!

HOOD

(*i*) We look before and after,
  And pine for what is not:
Our sincerest laughter
  With some pain is fraught;
Our sweetest songs are those that tell of saddest thought.

SHELLEY

2. Try your own hand at writing single lines of:

   (*a*) iambic tetrameter, (*b*) iambic trimeter, (*c*) iambic pentameter, (*d*) trochaic dimeter, (*e*) dactylic trimeter, (*f*) anapestic heptameter, (*g*) spondaic tetrameter.

3. Try writing:

   (*a*) a simple stanza of four verses of simple alternating iambic tetrameter and trimeter, (*b*) two verses in iambic pentameter.

CHAPTER 10

DISTINGUISHING THE VARIOUS PATTERNS OF POETRY

As we have seen, one of the most tangible differences between poetry and prose is that the words of poetry are arranged in some definite pattern of rhythmically harmonious verses. Some poetic patterns are simple, some complex; most of them except those of free verse are more or less rigid in form.

Pattern, stanza, and verse. *Pattern* in poetry is the plan according to which a stanza is built up. A *stanza* is a definitely arranged group of rhythmically harmonious verses. The structural unit of the stanza is the *verse* which is a single line of poetry. We determine the pattern of a poem either by its stanza form or by its verse form. If a poem is not divided into stanzas, we determine its pattern by its metrical name and its rhyme scheme. If a poem is divided into stanzas, we determine its pattern by the number of verses in a stanza, by the metrical name of these verses, and by the rhyme scheme of the whole stanza.

Blank verse. Among the most common forms in English poetry is *blank verse* which is unrhymed iambic pentameter. As we have already seen, the rhythm in blank verse is saved from monotony and given what is known as paragraph structure by the skillful use of end-stopped and run-on lines and cesuras. It is the easiest kind of poetry to write poorly and the hardest to write well, for it depends on exceedingly subtle variations in the meter for perfect rhythm and tone color. The best blank verse in English is found in Shakespeare's plays, in Milton's *Paradise Lost,* in sections of Tennyson's *Idylls of the King,* in Matthew Arnold's "Sohrab and Rustum," in Keats'

"Hyperion," and in Wordsworth's "Lines Composed a Few Miles above Tintern Abbey." The *Idylls of the King* are not perfect blank verse but they offer numerous examples of the varied effects that may be secured by it. Sections of "The Passing of Arthur" are particularly worth study for the shifting accents and the surging ebb and flow of the rhythm. The *Idylls of the King* contain interesting experiments in the adaptation of sound to both sense and mood.

Rhymed couplets and heroic couplets. The *rhymed couplet* is a poem made up of iambic tetrameter lines rhyming successively *a a b b c c*, etc.

> Around their prows the ocean roars
> And chafes beneath their thousand oars.

The *heroic couplet* has the same rhyme scheme and the same iambic foot, but it is pentameter (five-stress) instead of tetrameter (four-stress).

> Fair tresses man's imperial race ensnare,
> And beauty draws us with a single hair.

Couplets are easy to write, and are effective in light, epigrammatic verse or any verse that requires speed. They are, however, difficult for slow movement as they are in constant danger of becoming monotonous and trivial. For this reason Keats refers to them scornfully as "rocking-horse" meter. Some modern poets have used couplets skillfully in long poems without making them monotonous. They achieve their effect by variation in the rhyme scheme and by the use of end-stopped and run-on lines and of cesuras. John Masefield's *Reynard the Fox* is a particularly striking example of what may be done with this pattern of the rhymed couplet. Dryden and Pope, poets of the seventeenth and eighteenth centuries, are famous for their brilliant use of the heroic couplet.

Tercet. The *tercet* pattern is a stanza form made up of three verses, usually, but not always, iambic tetrameter, rhyming variously. Sometimes stanzas in this pattern are knit together by rhyming the last line of one stanza with the first line of the next. Sometimes the three lines of a stanza rhyme; for example,

> Standing, with reluctant feet,
> Where the brook and river meet
> Womanhood and childhood fleet!

Quatrain. The *quatrain* is a four-verse stanza. The most familiar form of the quatrain is the old English ballad meter, which is a stanza made up of alternating iambic tetrameter and iambic trimeter lines rhyming *a b c b*, as in:

> The sheriff dwelled in Nottingham
> He was fain he was agone
> And Robin and his merry men
> Went to the wood anon.

This may be varied by making all the lines of equal length or by changing the rhyme scheme. A familiar variation is the "In Memoriam" stanza named from its use in Tennyson's poem. This is iambic tetrameter in all four verses rhyming *a b b a*, for example:

> He is not here; but far away
> The noise of life begins again,
> And ghastly thro' the drizzling rain
> On the bald street breaks the blank day.

The quatrain is an easy and popular pattern susceptible of many variations. In narrative verse it has been found most natural. Many of our most-loved American poems by Longfellow and Whittier are in this pattern.

Quintet. A five-line stanza is called a *quintet.* It is not very common in English, but it is the pattern of one of our most famous poems, Shelley's "To a Skylark":

> Hail to thee, blithe spirit!
> Bird thou never wert,
> That from heaven or near it
> Pourest thy full heart
> In profuse strains of unpremeditated art.

Notice in this poem the remarkable effect of soaring exaltation secured by the additional length of the last verse.

Sestet. A six-line stanza is called a *sestet*. Many poems are made up of sestet stanzas consisting of three sets of couplets. For examples, see "The Nutbrowne Maid," Collins' "How Sleep the Brave!" William Morris' "Shameful Death," Byron's "The Isles of Greece," and Rossetti's "The Blessed Damozel." We quote an illustration from Shakespeare's *Twelfth Night*.

O mistress mine, where are you roaming?
O, stay and hear; your true love's coming,
  That can sing both high and low:
Trip no further, pretty sweeting,
Journeys end in lovers meeting,
  Every wise man's son doth know.

Rime royal. The most important form of the seven-line stanza is the *rime royal* used by Chaucer, and more or less enthusiastically adopted in our day by John Masefield. This stanza consists of seven iambic pentameter verses rhyming *a b a b b c c.* The effect, you will notice, comes from repeating the last rhyming sound in the final couplet. Here is a sample from Chaucer's "The Parlement of Foules":

A garden saw I ful of blosmy bowes,
Upon a ryver in a grene mede,
There as that swetnesse everemore inow is,
With floures white, blewe, yelwe, and rede;
And colde welle stremes, nothyng dede,
That swymmen ful of smale fisches lighte,
With fynnes rede and skales sylver bryghte.

Octave. The eight-line stanza is called an octave. It is common and provides opportunity for much ingenuity in the interweaving of rhymes. We quote a familiar example from Burns:

Duncan Grey cam here to woo,
  Ha, ha, the wooing o't,
On blythe Yule night when we were fou,
  Ha, ha, the wooing o't:
Maggie coost her head fu' high,
Look'd asklent and unco skeigh,
  Gart poor Duncan stand abeigh;
Ha, ha, the wooing o't!

Ottava rima. The most famous form of the octave is the *ottava rima*, borrowed by Byron from the Italian. It is an eight-line iambic pentameter stanza rhyming *a b a b a b c c*. It is the pattern of much of Byron's "Don Juan," and of Keats' "Isabella," from which latter we quote a stanza:

> O Melancholy, linger here awhile!
>   O Music, Music, breathe despondingly!
> O Echo, Echo, from some sombre isle,
>   Unknown, Lethean, sigh to us—O sigh!
> Spirits in grief, lift up your heads, and smile;
>   Lift up your heads, sweet Spirits, heavily,
> And make a pale light in your cypress glooms,
> Tinting with silver wan your marble tombs.

The Spenserian stanza. The *Spenserian stanza* is a nine-verse stanza the first eight verses of which are iambic pentameter while the ninth verse contains an extra foot. It rhymes *a b a b b c b c c*. It derives its name from Edmund Spenser, an Elizabethan poet who used it in his greatest poem, *The Faerie Queene.* It is the meter of Shelley's "Adonais," of Byron's "Childe Harold's Pilgrimage," and of Keats' "The Eve of St. Agnes." It is well adapted to beautiful variations of word music and to elaborate imagery. Ideas can be effectively developed in this stanza where the added length of the final line gives an excellent opportunity for climax. Notice the effective climax in the last line of this Spenserian stanza from Byron's "Childe Harold's Pilgrimage":

> There was a sound of revelry by night,
> And Belgium's capital had gathered then
> Her beauty and her chivalry, and bright
> The lamps shown o'er fair women and brave men,
> A thousand hearts beat happily; and when
> Music arose with its voluptuous swell,
> Soft eyes look'd love to eyes which spake again
> And all went merry as a marriage-bell;
> But hush! hark! a deep sound strikes like a rising knell!

And notice the shifting music rising to a superb climax in the final stanza from "Adonais," one of the most beautiful uses of this pattern in our language:

The breath whose might I have invoked in song
Descends on me; my spirit's bark is driven,
Far from the shore, far from the trembling throng
Whose sails were never to the tempest given;
The massy earth and spherèd skies are riven!
I am borne darkly, fearfully, afar;
Whilst burning through the inmost veil of Heaven,
The soul of Adonais, like a star,
Beacons from the abode where the Eternal are.

Sonnet. One of the most famous stanzaic forms is the fourteen-line stanza, usually in iambic pentameter, known as the sonnet. It was introduced from Italy into England in the sixteenth century in the form commonly known as the Elizabethan sonnet. In this form it consists of three quatrains and a concluding couplet; the verse is iambic pentameter rhyming in a regular scheme; for instance, Shakespeare's famous thirtieth sonnet:

When to the sessions of sweet silent thought
I summon up remembrance of things past,
I sigh the lack of many a thing I sought,
And with old woes new wail my dear time's waste:
Then can I drown an eye, unused to flow,
For precious friends hid in death's dateless night,
And weep afresh love's long-since cancell'd woe,
And moan the expense of many a vanish'd sight:
Then can I grieve at grievances foregone,
And heavily from woe to woe tell o'er
The sad account of fore-bemoaned moan,
Which I new pay as if not paid before.
  But if the while I think on thee, dear friend,
  All losses are restor'd, and sorrows end.

In the seventeenth century, Milton adapted to English the Italian or Petrarchan form consisting of an octave, without, however, following the Italian practice of keeping the thought in the octave and sestet separate. In Milton's sonnets the thought unrolls itself throughout the entire fourteen lines, as in this one on his blindness:

When I consider how my light is spent
  Ere half my days in this dark world and wide,
  And that one talent which is death to hide
  Lodged with me useless, though my soul more bent

To serve therewith my Maker, and present
  My true account, lest he returning chide,
  "Doth God exact day-labor, light denied?"
  I fondly ask. But Patience, to prevent

That murmur, soon replies, "God doth not need
  Either man's work or his own gifts. Who best
  Bear his mild yoke, they serve him best: His state
Is kingly; thousands at his bidding speed,
  And post o'er land and ocean without rest;
  They also serve who only stand and wait."

The rhyme scheme of the Shakespearean Sonnet, as you will see, is *a b a b, c d c d, e f e f, g g,* each quatrain and the final couplet being a rhyming unit.

The rhyme scheme of the Italian Sonnet is, for the octave, *a b b a, a b b a,* and for the sestet somewhat varied, principally *c d e, c d e;* or *c c, d d, e e.*

Old French forms. There are several very interesting and intricate stanza patterns which are commonly called the Old French forms, because they are revivals of stanzas developed and perfected by the French in the fourteenth and fifteenth centuries. In the nineteenth century many English poets, notably Andrew Lang, Austin Dobson, Henley, Swinburne, and Rossetti, sought to try their skill with them. They necessitate concentration upon form, of course, but they are a challenge to any poet's skill, and very popular as media for light and graceful verse. The most common of these are the *ballade,* the *rondeau,* the *triolet,* the *villanelle,* and the *pantoum.* We are here giving examples which will perhaps enable you most profitably to figure out for yourself the requirements of these patterns. The ballade, rondeau, and triolet you will find in constant evidence in magazines like *Life, Judge, Vanity Fair,* and *The New Yorker.* The others are less common. For other examples of French forms, such as the *roundel, sestina, pantoum,* and *kyrielle,* the interested student should consult Helen Louise Cohen's *Lyric Forms from France,* Gleeson White's *Ballades and Rondeaus,* or Untermeyer and Davidson's *Poetry: Its Appreciation and Enjoyment.* We have already quoted a ballade in our chapter on symbols and images, pages 94–95, Henley's "Made in Hot Weather." If you will turn to it, you will easily see how adaptable this form is to light emotions.

Rondeau. As a sample of the rondeau, here is the familiar but now strangely ironical "In Flanders Fields":

In Flanders fields the poppies blow
Between the crosses, row on row,
  That mark our place; and in the sky
  The larks, still bravely singing, fly
Scarce heard amid the guns below.

We are the Dead. Short days ago
We lived, felt dawn, saw sunset glow,
  Loved and were loved, and now we lie
    In Flanders fields.

Take up our quarrel with the foe:
To you from failing hands we throw
  The torch; be yours to hold it high.
  If ye break faith with us who die
We shall not sleep, though poppies grow
    In Flanders fields.[1]

Villanelle. Here is a villanelle, by Cosmo Monkhouse:

Beautiful, distracting Hetty,
  This was how it came to be
As we strolled upon the jetty.

I had danced three times with Netty,
  She had flirted with Dobree,
Beautiful, distracting Hetty.

I was humming Donizetti,
  Hurt was I and angry she,
As we strolled upon the jetty.

As she leveled her Negretti,
  With provoking nicety,
Beautiful, distracting Hetty.

Suddenly she flashed a pretty,
  Half-defiant glance at me,
As we strolled upon the jetty.

And our quarrel seemed so petty
  By the grandeur of the sea!
Beautiful, distracting Hetty,
As we strolled upon the jetty.

[1] Reprinted by kind permission of Dr. Thomas McCrae.

Triolet. Here is a triolet by Arlo Bates:

Wee Rose is but three,
  Yet coquettes she already.
I can scarcely agree
Wee Rose is but three,
When her archness I see!
  Are the sex born unsteady?—
Wee Rose is but three,
  Yet coquettes she already.

Free verse. There has been a tendency on the part of modern poets to revolt from definite patterns. Strict metrical laws and definite rhyme schemes seem to them irksome. They have therefore adapted the rhythm and rhyme scheme of their verses to the feeling of their poems without regard to definite stanza forms. In their revolt from conventional forms they call their metrical effects *free verse.* Free verse has certain definite characteristics:

It is bound to no fixed rhyme scheme. It may have rhymes some of the time, or all of the time, or not at all.

It uses whatever metrical measures seem best to fit the mood or thought of the poem. Some lines are long and some are short; free verse is not bound to have any special number of accents in any given lines.

Its rhythm is *organic.* That is it varies with the emotion and ebbs and flows through the whole poem so that the result is not merely a series of chopped-up lines. To illustrate this read aloud and analyze James Stephens' "The Shell" or Carl Sandburg's "Grass," quoted below. Then try to reduce a passage of prose, such as the description of the burning ship in Conrad's *Youth* to free verse. You will see that prose has rhythms of speech and emotion in it, but that in free verse, these rhythms are more lyrical, more variously adapted to the mood.

Thus you see that the patterns of free verse, though not bound by set rules, are characterized by recurring rhythms, ebbing and flowing through the stanza, and that they are often but not invariably, *rhymed.* Free verse is not formless; it has design based on rhythm but the design is not a rigid pattern. Amy Lowell's "Patterns" is an excellent example of free verse form that is truly organic.

THE SHELL

And then I pressed the shell
Close to my ear
And listened well,
And straightway like a bell

Came low and clear
The slow, sad murmur of the distant seas,
Whipped by an icy breeze
Upon a shore
Wind-swept and desolate.
It was a sunless strand that never bore
The footprint of a man,
Nor felt the weight
Since time began
Of any human quality or stir
Save what the dreary winds and waves incur.
And in the hush of waters was the sound
Of pebbles rolling round,
For ever rolling with a hollow sound.
And bubbling sea-weeds as the waters go
Swish to and fro
Their long, cold tentacles of slimy gray.
There was no day,
Nor ever came a night
Setting the stars alight
To wonder at the moon;
Was twilight only and the frightened croon,
Smitten to whimpers, of the dreary wind
And waves that journeyed blind—
And then I loosed my ear . . . O, it was sweet
To hear a cart go jolting down the street. [1]

JAMES STEPHENS

GRASS

Pile the bodies high at Austerlitz and Waterloo.
Shovel them under and let me work—
        I am the grass; I cover all.

And pile them high at Gettysburg
And pile them high at Ypres and Verdun.
Shovel them under and let me work.
Two years, ten years, and passengers ask the conductor:
        What is this place?
        Where are we now?

        I am the grass.
        Let me work.[2]

CARL SANDBURG

[1] From *Collected Poems* by James Stephens. By permission of The Macmillan Company, publishers.
[2] Reprinted by permission of and arrangement with Henry Holt and Company.

It is a mistake however to think of free verse as the exclusive product of recent years. Poets have always broken away from conventional patterns whenever they have found a freer pattern more suited to their purposes. Matthew Arnold's "The Strayed Reveller" and "Philomela," for example, are almost as much free verse as Amy Lowell's "Patterns." And Walt Whitman and Emily Dickinson, of course, never bothered to be conventional in their patterns. Within the past five years, contemporary poets have tended more and more to return to conventional forms. At present the most generally admired of them in America—Edna St. Vincent Millay, Robert Frost, Edwin Arlington Robinson, Conrad Aiken, and Robinson Jeffers; in England, John Masefield, Alfred Noyes, Walter De la Mare, W. H. Davies, G. K. Chesterton, W. W. Gibson, and Ralph Hodgson—have written principally in the conventional metrical patterns.

The pattern and the subject matter. The poet chooses a pattern which fits his subject matter. The sonnet is excellent for the development of a single idea by first giving illustrations (in the octave) and then stating the idea directly (in the sestet). The Spenserian stanza is an excellent pattern in which to work up to a climax at the end of the stanza; it is also well adapted to elaborate ornamentation. The ottava rima has the advantage of being neither too long nor too short; it is also well adapted to musical expression. The quatrain is appropriate for any simple story or simple feeling that requires simple expression. The couplet gives an excellent opportunity for driving ideas home brilliantly so that they will linger in the mind; it also gives rapidity of movement. Blank verse is the best medium for the expression of profound or dignified feeling, or noble ideas. The pattern of a song should be spontaneously lyrical, with haunting refrains or lilting music.

Tennyson's "The Bugle Song" illustrates the blending in a perfect pattern of meter, rhymes, choice of words, and stanza form.

The splendor falls on castle walls
  And snowy summits old in story:
The long light shakes across the lakes,
  And the wild cataract leaps in glory.
Blow, bugle, blow, set the wild echoes flying,
Blow, bugle; answer, echoes, dying, dying, dying.

O hark, O hear! how thin and clear,
  And thinner, clearer, farther going!
O sweet and far from cliff and scar
  The horns of Elfland faintly blowing!
Blow, let us hear the purple glens replying:
Blow, bugle; answer, echoes, dying, dying, dying.

O love, they die in yon rich sky,
  They faint on hill or field or river;
Our echoes roll from soul to soul,
  And grow for ever and for ever.
Blow, bugle, blow, set the wild echoes flying,
And answer, echoes, answer, dying, dying, dying.

The appropriateness of every detail of the pattern is here apparent. The echoes are wonderfully suggested in the internal rhymes, in the choice of vowel sounds, and in the lingering feminine endings of the refrain. The refrain itself is perfectly suggestive of answering echoes; it has just enough variation in each stanza to carry the thought and the music on from one stanza to another. Practically every device for securing tone color is used here: beautifully varied vowel sounds, liquid and sibilant consonants, rhymes exquisitely tuned to both feeling and sense. Many of Tennyson's poems are splendid illustrations of pattern of sound and color and feeling perfectly blended. "Sweet and Low" is an obvious example. "Maud" is a poem which he loved to read aloud, because in it music and form shift instinctively with the feeling.

Ballads. There are three special types of poetry which deserve at least brief notice: ballads, light verse, and songs. Ballads, strictly speaking, are simple narrative poems, usually in quatrains, dealing with the adventures of heroes of the people, like Robin Hood, or describing simple dramatic episodes or situations. They are very old, and usually anonymous. Usually they deal with one incident—a knight poisoned, a man dying for love, a battle won, a deed of heroism or cleverness. They are almost always *objective;* that is, they tell a story without much description or attempt at characterization and without any intrusion of the author's personality, ideas, or feelings. Often, as in "Edward," which we quote, the story is told in the form of a dialogue, with questions and answers. As frequently as not, ballads make use of a refrain and other semi-literary devices such as stock epithets and repetition of words and phrases. Almost always they appealed to the common people rather than to more sophisticated audiences in court and castle. One should not, however, think of them as primitive and artless. Many of them, "Edward," "Lord Randal," "Sir Patrick Spens," "The Twa Corbies," "The Wife of Usher's Well," to mention only a few, are told with great dramatic effect and conscious artistry. Indeed most of the devices of these early ballads are to be found in modern narrative verse from "The Lady of the Lake" down to Stephen Vincent Benét's "John Brown's Body." We call modern narrative poems which imitate the form and purpose of ballads, only with more attention to pictorial background and human psychology, *literary ballads*. Scott's "Lochinvar," and "Jock of Hazeldean," Coleridge's "The Ancient Mariner," Whittier's "Skipper Ireson's Ride," Longfellow's "Paul Revere's Ride," Kipling's "Danny Deever," and Noyes' "The Highwayman" are all good examples of how the modern literary artist makes use of artistic devices of his unknown predecessors in this field. We append here a modernized version of a very old and very famous ballad, "Edward." You may have heard the dramatic musical setting of this by Loewe which Lawrence Tibbett used in making a Victor record:

EDWARD

"Why does your sword so drip with blood,
  Edward, Edward?
Why does your sword so drip with blood,
  And why so sad are ye, O?"
"O I have killed my hawk so good
  Mother, mother,
O I have killed my hawk so good
  And I had no more than he, O."

"Your hawk's blood was never so red,
  Edward, Edward,
Your hawk's blood was never so red,
  My dear son, I tell thee, O."
"O I have killed my red-roan steed,
  Mother, mother,
O I have killed my red-roan steed,
  That was so fair and free, O."

"Your steed was old and your stable's filled,
  Edward, Edward,
Your steed was old and your stable's filled,

Now say what may it be, O."
"It was my father that I killed,
Mother, mother,
It was my father that I killed,
Alas, and woe is me, O."

"What penance will ye do for that,
Edward, Edward?
What penance will ye do for that,
My dear son, now tell me, O."
"I'll set my feet in yonder boat,
Mother, mother,
I'll set my feet in yonder boat,
And I'll fare over the sea, O."

"What will ye do with your towers and hall,
Edward, Edward?
What will ye do with your towers and hall,
That are so fair to see, O?"
"I'll let them stand till down they fall,
Mother, mother,
I'll let them stand till down they fall,
For here nevermore may I be, O."

"What will ye leave to your babes and your wife,
Edward, Edward?
What will ye leave to your babes and your wife,
When ye go over the sea, O?"
"The world's room—let them beg through life,
Mother, mother,
The world's room—let them beg through life,
For them nevermore will I see, O."

"And what will ye leave to your own mother dear,
Edward, Edward?
And what will you leave to your own mother dear,
My dear son, now tell me, O?"
"The curse of Hell from me shall ye bear,
Mother, mother,
The curse of Hell from me shall ye bear:
Such counsel ye gave to me, O!"

Light verse. Light verse, sometimes called *vers de société*, is the name applied to light and graceful but sophisticated poems dealing with such subjects as love, the vanity of women, the egotism of men, conviviality, or even sheer nonsense, in a pleasantly humorous or cynical vein. Light verse is difficult to write; for even though it often verges on tenderness and sentimental compliment, as in Bret Harte's "Her Letter," and even though it is often cynically disillusioned especially about love, as in Dorothy Parker's *Enough Rope*, it should always avoid serious sentiment and it should never become bitterly satirical. It frequently brushes close to the pathos and irony of human relationships yet it must always remain smiling. If it verges on nonsense, it is in the greatest danger of all, for it takes a genius like Lewis Carroll or W. S. Gilbert to make nonsense "come right," so that it will have some point and still remain nonsense. In the writing of nonsense verse English and American poets are still peerless. In fact, the work of W. S. Gilbert, Lewis Carroll, F. Gelett Burgess, Oliver Herford, and Eugene Field, is part of a great tradition in English literature.

The greatest writers of *vers de société* were probably the Roman poets Horace and Catullus. In English literature the Cavalier poets—1590–1670—Robert Herrick, Thomas Carew, Edmund Waller, John Suckling, and Richard Lovelace are the surest and lightest in their touch. The eighteenth-century wits (except for Goldsmith and Cowper) were too ill-natured for this sort of thing, and the romanticists, Byron, Shelley, and Keats, too emotional. It was only in the late nineteenth century that some of the writers in the Old French forms whom we have mentioned succeeded in reviving light verse in just the right spirit. In our own country we may well be proud of as well as amused by T. A. Daly, Dorothy Parker, Arthur Guiterman, F. P. Adams, Samuel Hoffenstein, Newman Levy, Ogden Nash, and John V. A. Weaver. Perhaps T. A. Daly and John V. A. Weaver verge too dangerously on the sentimental, and the others on the cynical, but in general books like *Carmina*, *Enough Rope*, *Poems in American*, *Poems in Praise of Practically Nothing*, *Opera Guyed*, and *Hard Lines* are refreshing antidotes to both ill-nature and sentimentality.

Songs. Songs are, it need hardly be said, poems that are primarily intended to be sung. Such are the songs in Shakespeare's plays, many of them, such as, "Hark, hark, the lark!" "Who is Sylvia?" "Under the greenwood tree," "It was a lover and his lass," and "Blow, blow, thou Winter Wind," so spontaneously lyrical that they have been set to music many times by gifted composers. Such a song is Ben Jonson's "To Celia," known everywhere as "Drink to me only with thine eyes." Such, too, are most of Burns' great songs, which were often written to old Scotch airs, and Tom Moore's "The Last Rose of Summer," "Oft, in the stilly night," and "Believe me, if all those endearing young charms." Others, written with no particular air in mind, are so inherently singable that they have since been repeatedly set to music. Tennyson's famous songs from *The Princess*, "Sweet and Low," and "The Bugle Song," are known to everyone. Similar in effect to these are his "Crossing the Bar," Longfellow's "Stars of the summer night" from *The Spanish Student*, and Kipling's "The Gipsy Trail." There is also a sort of lyric the very words of which are so musical that they seem to sing themselves to the mere despair of any attempt at musical setting. The greatest English writer of this kind of poetry is Shelley, and probably the greatest example from all his lyrics is the famous "To Night." Of this poem John Addington Symonds says,

> I once asked an eminent musician . . . why Shelley's lyrics were ill-adapted to music. She made me read aloud to her . . . those lovely lines "To Night." Then she pointed out how the verbal melody was intended to be self-sufficing . . . how full of complicated thoughts and changeful images the verse is, how packed with consonants the words are, how the tone of emotion alters, and how no one melodic phrase could be found to fit the daedal woof of the poetic emotion.[1]

You see, words, to be set to music, must not contain too many consonants, particularly k's, w's, d's, b's, and s's (that is why Italian and Spanish are the best languages for singers) and the thought must not be filled with complicated ideas and images, or run on from one line to the next. The emotion, too, must be simple and definite. Shelley's songs are word music in themselves. Burns' and Shakespeare's are words for music. We quote below one of Burns' best-loved songs, which you probably know only as a poem, and Shelley's "To Night":

John Anderson, my jo,[2] John,
  When we were first acquent,
Your locks were like the raven,
  Your bonnie brow was brent [3]

[1] Quoted in *An Introduction to Poetry* by Hubbell and Beaty, pp. **60–61.**
[2] sweetheart
[3] smooth

But now your brow is beld,[1] John,
  Your locks are like the snaw;
But blessings on your frosty pow,[2]
  John Anderson, my jo!

John Anderson, my jo, John,
  We clamb the hill thegither;
And monie a canty [3] day, John,
  We've had wi' ane anither;
Now we maun totter down, John,
  And hand in hand we'll go,
And sleep thegither at the foot,
  John Anderson, my jo.

TO NIGHT

Swiftly walk o'er the western wave,
    Spirit of Night!
Out of thy misty eastern cave,
Where all the long and lone daylight,
Thou wovest dreams of joy and fear,
Which make thee terrible and dear,—
    Swift be thy flight!

Wrap thy form in a mantle gray,
    Star-inwrought!
Blind with thine hair the eyes of Day;
Kiss her until she be wearied out,
Then wander o'er city, and sea, and land
Touching all with thine opiate wand—
    Come, long sought!

When I arose and saw the dawn,
    I sighed for thee;
When light rode high and the dew was gone,
And noon lay heavy on flower and tree,
And the weary Day turned to his rest,
Lingering like an unloved guest,
    I sighed for thee.

Thy brother Death came, and cried,
    Wouldst thou me?
Thy sweet child Sleep, the filmy-eyed,
Murmured like a noontide bee,
Shall I nestle near thy side?
Wouldst thou me?—And I replied,
    No, not thee!

[1] bald [2] head [3] happy

Death will come soon when thou art dead
    Soon, too soon—
Sleep will come when thou art fled;
Of neither would I ask the boon
I ask of thee, belovéd Night—
Swift be thine approaching flight,
    Come soon, soon!

Summary. Pattern is the name for the stanza-structure of a poem. Pattern is determined by the number of lines in a stanza, the prevailing meter of each line, and the rhyme scheme. Some common patterns are:

Blank verse—unrhymed iambic pentameter
Couplets—lines in iambic tetrameter or pentameter rhyming consecutively
Tercet—a three-verse stanza
Quatrain—a four-verse stanza
Quintet—a five-verse stanza
Sestet—a six-verse stanza
Rime royal—a seven-verse stanza in iambic pentameter rhyming *a b a b b c c*
Ottava rima—an eight-verse stanza in iambic pentameter rhyming *a b a b a b c c*
Spenserian stanza—a nine-verse stanza with the first eight in iambic pentameter and the ninth in iambic hexameter, rhyming *a b a b b c b c c*
Sonnets—fourteen-verse iambic pentameter stanzas. The Italian sonnet has thought divisions of eight lines (*octave*) followed by six (*sestet*). The Shakespearean sonnet has three quatrains and a concluding couplet. The rhyme scheme in each is rigid
The Old French forms—rigid and artificial patterns, the most common of which are the *ballade*, *rondeau*, *triolet*, and *villanelle*
Ballads—simple narrative poems usually in quatrains
Light verse—verse of light emotional tone written with great social ease and wit
Songs—poems written for music

COMPREHENSION QUESTIONS

1. *Vocabulary:* pattern, stanza, verse, blank verse, rhymed couplet, heroic couplet, tercet, quatrain, quintet, sestet, rime royal, ottava rima, Spenserian stanza, sonnet, Old French forms, *ballade*, *rondeau*, objectivity, *triolet*, *villanelle*, free verse, ballads, light verse, songs.
2. Some of these stanza patterns a student should know thoroughly. These are: blank verse, couplet, quatrain, sonnet, free verse.

Others, he should learn to recognize by experience in reading them. The *triolet*, *rondeau*, and *villanelle* should not be memorized; they are best studied by examining the poems themselves.

3. Explain and illustrate what we mean by *paragraph rhythm in blank verse.*
4. Find three different arrangements of the quatrain pattern.
5. Explain and illustrate the difference between the Shakespearean sonnet and the Italian sonnet.
6. What are the chief characteristics of the ballad?
7. What is the chief difference between the literary ballad and the folk ballad?
8. What characteristics of the ballad do you find in the following poems?

   "The Ancient Mariner" "The Highwayman"
   "Danny Deever" "The Wreck of the Hesperus"

9. Bring to class examples of light verse by one of the following contemporary writers:

   T. A. Daly Samuel Hoffenstein
   F. P. Adams John V. A. Weaver
   Dorothy Parker Ogden Nash

10. What qualities are necessary in a poem designed to be set to music?
11. Why is Shelley's poem "To Night," quoted in this chapter, difficult to set to music or to sing?
12. Why do the songs of Burns and Shakespeare appeal to composers?
13. Find and bring to class from some contemporary magazine like *Life*, *Judge*, or *The New Yorker* examples of *ballades*, *rondeaux*, *triolets*, *villanelles*.
14. Find settings of songs by Shakespeare, Burns, Scott, and Tennyson. The Victor record catalogue will help you here.

PROBLEMS IN METRICS

1. Give the metrical name of each line in the following stanzas. Give the rhyme scheme of each stanza. Which are masculine and which feminine rhymes? Indicate end-stopped and run-on lines and cesuras. What is the name of the stanza pattern of each?

   (*a*)
   So nigh is grandeur to our dust,
   So near is God to man,
   When Duty whispers low "Thou must,"
   The Youth replies, "I can."

   EMERSON

(*b*) Shut in from all the world without,
We sat the clean-winged hearth about,
Content to let the north wind roar
In baffled rage at pane and door,
While the red logs before us beat
The frost line back with tropic heat.

WHITTIER

(*c*) I slip, I slide, I gloom, I glance,
Among my skimming swallows;
I make the netted sunbeam dance
Against my sandy shallows.

TENNYSON

(*d*) 'Tis not enough no harshness gives offence,
The sound must seem an echo to the sense:
Soft is the strain when Zephyr gently blows,
And the smooth stream in smoother numbers flows;
But when loud surges lash the sounding shore,
The hoarse, rough verse should like the torrent roar:
When Ajax strives some rock's vast weight to throw,
The line, too, labours, and the words move slow.

POPE

(*e*) Oh for boyhood's painless play,
Sleep that wakes in laughing day,
Health that mocks the doctor's rules,
Knowledge never learned of schools,
Of the wild bee's morning chase,
Of the wild-flower's time and place,
Flight of fowl and habitude
Of the tenants of the wood.

WHITTIER

(*f*) I will paint her as I see her.
Ten times have the lilies blown,
Since she looked upon the sun.

And her face is lily-clear,
Lily-shaped, and dropped in duty
To the law of its own beauty.

ELIZABETH BARRETT BROWNING

(*g*) The irresponsive silence of the land,
The irresponsive sounding of the sea,
Speak both one message of one sense to me:—
"Aloof, aloof, we stand aloof; so stand
Thou too aloof, bound with the flawless band

Of inner solitude; we bind not thee;
But who from thy self-chain shall set thee free?
What heart shall touch thy heart? What hand thy hand?"

And I am sometimes proud and sometimes meek,
And sometimes I remember days of old
When fellowship seemed not so far to seek
And all the world and I seemed much less cold,
And at the rainbow's foot lay surely gold,
And hope felt strong and life itself not weak.

CHRISTINA GEORGINA ROSSETTI

(*h*) And she forgot the stars, the moon, and sun,
  And she forgot the blue above the trees,
And she forgot the dells where waters run,
  And she forgot the chilly autumn breeze;
She had no knowledge when the day was done,
  And the new morn she saw not: but in peace
Hung over her sweet Basil evermore,
And moisten'd it with tears unto the core.

KEATS

(*i*) A casement high and triple-arch'd there was,
All garlanded with carven imag'ries
Of fruits, and flowers, and bunches of knot-grass,
And diamonded with panes of quaint device,
Innumerable of stains and splendid dyes,
As are the tiger-moth's deep-damask'd wings;
And in the midst, 'mong thousand heraldries,
And twilight saints, and dim emblazonings,
A shielded scutcheon blush'd with blood of queens and kings.

KEATS

(*j*) Ah, cool night-wind, tremulous stars!
Ah, glimmering water,
Fitful earth-murmur,
Dreaming woods!
Ah, golden-hair'd, strangely smiling Goddess,
And thou, prov'd, much enduring,
Wave-toss'd Wanderer!
Who can stand still?
Ye fade, ye swim, ye waver before me—
The cup again!

Faster, faster,
O Circe, Goddess.
Let the wild, thronging train,
The bright procession
Of eddying forms,
Sweep through my soul!

MATTHEW ARNOLD

(*k*) Let me not to the marriage of true minds
Admit impediments. Love is not love
Which alters when it alteration finds,
Or bends with the remover to remove:
O, no! it is an ever-fixed mark,
That looks on tempests and is never shaken;
It is the star to every wand'ring bark,
Whose worth's unknown, although his height be taken.
Love's not Time's fool, though rosy lips and cheeks
Within his bending sickle's compass come;
Love alters not with his brief hours and weeks,
But bears it out even to the edge of doom.
If this be error and upon me proved,
I never writ, nor no man ever loved.

SHAKESPEARE

2. What is the pattern of:

Joseph Auslander	"Remember Me, Gulls!"
Elizabeth Barrett Browning	"How Do I Love Thee"
Frances Cornford	"To a Fat Lady Seen from the Train"
T. A. Daly	"A Song to One"
Robert Frost	"Birches"
Masefield	"Dauber"
Alfred Noyes	"A Song of Sherwood"
E. A. Robinson	"The House on the Hill"
James Stephens	"The Shell"
Tennyson	"To Virgil," "Tears, Idle Tears"

3. It is rather easy, and a great deal of fun, to try one's hand at pattern-making. You surely can write quatrains and couplets and no doubt often have done so just for amusement. Why not try writing three different quatrains with three different rhyme schemes?

The *triolet* is rather easy to write, too, for once you have written the first two lines, you have only three more to do. Try your hand at one.

The *villanelle*, too, is an interesting exercise to work out, though slightly more difficult than the *triolet*. Perhaps you can write as clever a one as "When I saw you last, Rose," by Austin Dobson.

Almost anyone can write a crude ballad. Can you write one? Here is what you need to start with:

(*a*) A simple subject dealing with one dramatic incident—say the last period of a big game, or a deed of heroism such as you might find recorded in a newspaper.

(*b*) Quatrains of alternating iambic tetrameter and trimeter rhyming a b c b.

(*c*) A refrain.

Couplets are easy and amusing to write. Why not try writing a class prophecy in couplets?

Try to develop an idea in the sonnet form. First think of the idea, then of two illustrations of it. Let your octave develop the illustrations and your sestet apply them to the idea. Or let octave and sestet develop opposite ideas. For example see:

Keats	"On First Looking into Chapman's Homer"
Siegfried Sassoon	"Dreamers"
Louis Untermeyer	"Mockery"
Wordsworth	"The World Is Too Much with Us"

4. Here is a poem from *The Princess* by Tennyson which is worth studying for many reasons: its metrical pattern (it is one of the few successful blank verse lyrics in English); its expression of the poetic feeling for nature, man, time, and human destiny; its word music; its images; its universality. See if you too can find all these qualities in it:

Tears, idle tears, I know not what they mean,
Tears from the depth of some divine despair
Rise in the heart, and gather to the eyes,
In looking on the happy autumn-fields,
And thinking of the days that are no more.

Fresh as the first beam glittering on a sail,
That brings our friends up from the underworld,
Sad as the last which reddens over one
That sinks with all we love below the verge;
So sad, so fresh, the days that are no more.

Ah, sad and strange as in dark summer dawns
The earliest pipe of half-awaken'd birds
To dying ears, when unto dying eyes
The casement slowly grows a glimmering square;
So sad, so strange, the days that are no more.

Dear as remember'd kisses after death,
And sweet as those by hopeless fancy feign'd
On lips that are for others; deep as love,
Deep as first love, and wild with all regret;
O Death in Life, the days that are no more!

5. Here is a list of ten good narrative poems. Read one of them and try to discover what it gains by being told in verse.

Examine the *form:*

(*a*) What is the pattern? (*b*) How is it varied for effect? (*c*) Can you find rhythmic variations in pace that help out in the poem but that would be impossible in prose? (*d*) How does sound, especially word music and onomatopœia, help to create feeling in the poem?

Examine the *suggestive power:*

(*a*) How do pictures help out? (*b*) How are emotions made more vivid through poetic suggestion? (*c*) How do figures of speech stir the imagination?

Examine the *type:*

(*a*) What traces of the influence of old ballads, metrical romance, or epics can you find—extended similes? refrains? repetition of epithets? dialogue form? dramatic suggestiveness? (*b*) Is the story romantic, tragic, fanciful, realistic, or allegorical? (*c*) Make a list of the qualities that stamp it as poetry rather than prose. (*d*) Which seem to you most "modern" in conception and execution?

Arnold	"Sohrab and Rustum"
Stephen Vincent Benét	*John Brown's Body*
Coleridge	"The Ancient Mariner"
Keats	"The Eve of St. Agnes"
Masefield	*Reynard the Fox*, *Enslaved*
Morris	"The Haystack in the Floods"
Lola Ridge	*Firehead*
Edwin Arlington Robinson	*Lancelot*
Rossetti	"The King's Tragedy"

OUTLINE FOR STUDYING AN ANTHOLOGY

(1) Select a poem (not too long) that you like for at least two reasons; then commit it to memory. State your reasons for selecting it.

(2) Find one poem that seems to you to offer a good example of imaginative characteristics; one that illustrates the rhythmic quality of poetry; and one that illustrates the feeling for beauty.

(3) Select one poem that appeals to your imagination because of its familiarity and one that appeals to you because of its strangeness.

(4) Select a poem that secures its emotional appeal through:

(*a*) pictures, (*b*) rhythm, (*c*) the poetic connotation of its diction, (*d*) word music.

(5) Find examples of close relationship between *rhythm* or *sound* and *feeling.* Explain.
(6) Find an example of a poem that uses an *image* to express a mood or an idea.
(7) Find three Nature pictures that appeal to you. Find a detailed word painting. Find a picture created through poetic suggestion.
(8) Find a poem that secures its effect through suggestion rather than through direct statement, that is, one that suggests more than it says.
(9) Quote twelve passages illustrating the power of poetic suggestion.
(10) Find two similes that are:
(*a*) good because of the similarity of the things compared, (*b*) good because of their connotation, (*c*) too strained or too commonplace or too unlike.
(11) Find three metaphors that seem to you good. Find two examples of effective personification. Find two examples of onomatopœia. Find two examples of metonymy (define). Find two examples of symbols (explain).
(12) Find examples of word music secured by:
(*a*) alliteration, (*b*) rhyme, (*c*) use of both masculine and feminine rhymes, (*d*) end-stopped and run-on lines, (*e*) deep-toned vowels, (*f*) soft consonants, or liquid and sibilant consonants.
(13) Find a poem with a thought expressed through:
(*a*) similes or metaphors, (*b*) symbols, (*c*) images, (*d*) allegory, (*e*) the sonnet form.
(14) Find one poem the thought of which strikes you as either true or interesting, or both, and state that thought in your own words.
(15) Find a poem the inspiration of which is in:
(*a*) Nature, (*b*) personality (character), (*c*) human relationships, (*d*) universal human experience, (*e*) the commonplace in man or Nature, (*f*) literature, (*g*) music, (*h*) painting, (*i*) human history, (*j*) God or religion, (*k*) social or economic problems.
(16) Find a poem that is helped by simplicity of pattern and of language.
(17) Find a poem that uses a complicated pattern.
(18) Find a sonnet. Give its metrical name and its rhyme scheme.
(19) Find a poem in blank verse. Give its metrical name. Find an irregular verse in it. Find an end-stopped line; a run-on line.
(20) Find a poem written in quatrains. Give the metrical name of its verses and its rhyme scheme, (k) social or economic problems.
(21) Find examples of:
(*a*) couplets, (*b*) a *triolet*, (*c*) a *ballade*, (*d*) a *rondeau*, (*e*) a *villanelle*, (*f*) a Shakespearean sonnet, (*g*) an Italian sonnet, (*h*) a quintet (an-

alyze it), (*i*) a sestet (analyze it), (*j*) rime royal, (*k*) Spenserian stanza, (*l*) *ottava rima.*

(22) Find an effective use of refrain—one that has a haunting effect on the melody and on emotional appeal.

(23) Find a poem that varies its meter for a purpose and state what is gained by the variation.

(24) Find a pattern that seems to you free from any definite rhyme scheme or metrical plan.

(25) Find lines with the prevailing foot iambic; trochaic; anapestic; dactylic.

(26) Find examples of:

(*a*) spondees, (*b*) omitted syllables, (*c*) unaccented syllables added at the end of a verse.

Part Two

PROSE FICTION

THERE is probably not a high-school student in the country who has not at some time or other wondered why he is asked to read some of the novels which form part of his course in English. It might be some fun, he argues, to read *Tarzan of the Apes* or *Beau Geste*, but to him there is neither fun nor profit to be had from *The House of the Seven Gables*. Why must teachers pick out "the driest books they can find" when there are so many that are exciting and easy to read? Part Two attempts to furnish an honest answer to that question.

The writing of novels is a difficult art, and the relationship of novels to life can be felt only after one has had experience with both. But even young readers can learn why some stories are better told than others, why some characters in fiction live in the memory while others are forgotten at once, what books have to tell us about human beings and their problems. Perhaps, too, they can learn to appreciate why one author's way of expressing himself is full of life or beauty and another's merely flat and ordinary.

Before reading Part Two you will be wise to renew your acquaintance with three or four of the novels usually read in high schools, say *Silas Marner, The House of the Seven Gables, Ivanhoe, Kidnapped, A Tale of Two Cities,* and *The Rise of Silas Lapham;* otherwise you will not see the force of some of the illustrations. But do not be discouraged if you find many references to books you have not read; they are mentioned in the hope that you will become interested, and wish to know and love them. A wealth of unexplored riches in the world of fiction lies ahead of you.

CHAPTER 11

WHY READ FICTION?

What is prose fiction? Prose fiction is the name for stories in prose about imaginary happenings to imaginary people. Sometimes some of these characters and events are true to fact, but in the main a novel or romance is the creation of the imagination. Probably most of the events in *All Quiet on the Western Front* actually happened, but they have been so rearranged and recombined that they constitute fiction, not history.

Universal appeal of fiction. Almost everyone reads fiction, for almost everyone likes a good story. Very early in our lives we discover an almost limitless source of pleasure in these imaginary happenings to our imaginary friends. There are few girls who have not at some time laughed and cried with Meg, Jo, Beth, and Amy, or Heidi or Anne of Green Gables. There are few small boys who have not dashed breathlessly through the concoctions of Mr. Edgar Rice Burroughs, or crouched in terror with Tom Sawyer and Huck Finn as they listened in the upper room to the murderous plottings of Injun Joe. And there ought to be few grown-ups who do not, occasionally at least, return to listen in at the Mad Tea Party with Alice and the Hatter and the March Hare and the Dormouse.

Fiction is a source of entertainment. What are the reasons for the fascination that these imaginary people and happenings have for us? That question has more answers than you would at first suppose. Probably everybody, at any rate, reads stories sometimes just for entertainment. Men who turn out thrillers with the speed and gusto of Sax Rohmer, Edgar Wallace, J. S. Fletcher, or James Oliver Curwood hardly expect to do more than help the reader pass an exciting hour or two. A book like Tarkington's *Gentle Julia* or *Claire Ambler* or Mrs. Rinehart's pleasant *Tish* stories or Zane Grey's *Riders of the Purple Sage* lays no claim to being great literature or, indeed, literature at all; but it provides entertainment for which we are grateful.

Fiction is an escape from everyday life. Another reason is that we seek, unconsciously, to leave for a time our humdrum lives and petty troubles and identify ourselves with characters in an imaginary world—often a world which we can never hope to know in actuality. For this reason, too, we enjoy escaping from our own age of hustling and worried commercialism to "the days of old when knights were bold," and Robin Hood eluded the Sheriff of Nottingham; when Jim Hawkins, crouched in the apple barrel, listened to the sea dogs plotting against his life; when David Balfour and Alan Breck fled for their lives through the dust and heat of the Scotch heather; when Huck Finn lay under the stars and heard the night sounds and smelled the river smells on the Mississippi, years and years ago. For this reason, too, we like to read about the lives of people who live in lands and climates different from our own. The mysterious odors and sounds and sights of India, for instance, are made romantically real to us by Kipling's *Kim;* the strange fascination of the East, and the brooding languors of tropical nights and phosphorescent seas is ours for the reading of Conrad's *Lord Jim, Almayer's Folly, An Outcast of the Islands,* or "Youth"; the forests of Guiana come beautifully alive for us in W. H. Hudson's *Green Mansions;* all the healthy gusto and good cheer of an early Victorian Christmas is re-created for us when we read about that unforgettable holiday of the Pickwick Club at Dingley Dell. It would be an almost endless task to enumerate the books that can thus magically take us from our surroundings. Any high-school pupil could continue the list indefinitely himself.

In some books the story is dominant. To look more deeply into the sources of our interest in fiction, we may say that a book may hold us for any, or all, of four reasons: its story, its characters, its setting, or its theme.

In some books the story is unmistakably dominant. In this class belong the great romances of Dumas. One can scarcely believe in Dumas' characters, much less approve of them. Edward Dantés, of *The Count of Monte Cristo,* is actuated by a single motive, revenge. The long story is wholly occupied with showing how he escapes from prison and seeks his revenge. Yet it would be difficult to name a story of equal length outside of Dumas' other books in which the interest is so breathlessly sustained. Interest in incident supersedes all else, and the reader forgets the elementary characterization and the sophomoric morality of them all in the sheer rush of action.

In some books characters are dominant. Other books attract us because of their characters; it is to these, probably, that we return most often. Kipling has a short story, "The Janeites," in which he pays his tribute to a novelist who gives us practically no excitement, almost no emotion worthy of the name, no charm of setting, no descriptive power, no narrative sweep—little, in fact, but careful construction of a slight narrative and absolute fidelity to character. That novelist is, of course, Jane Austen, and the young soldier in Kipling's story could not see why his superiors were so fond of discussing her works. "Janeites," he called these enthusiasts for her whom Howells called "the divine Jane." Finally he read all six of her novels, and was exasperated to find that they were only about people, people he had always known in fact. He did not know that part of the charm of reading lies in "just people." The garrulous Miss Bates, the pompous Lady Catherine, the hypochondriac Mr. Woodhouse, the silly Mrs. Bennet, Elizabeth, and Emma are people so real that in his interest in them as fellow beings the reader forgets to wonder about what is going to happen to them. Fortunately there are many books to which we can return again and again merely because we have come to know and love their characters. More than one person has come to feel a lifelong friendship for Jane Eyre or Sam Weller or Colonel Newcome or Tom Jones or young Jolyon Forsyte. And some characters whom we do not love continue to fascinate us, none the less, so that we return to be again under the spell of the relentless Heathcliff, the half-mad Captain Ahab, the demoniac Count Dracula, or that monster created by Frankenstein. A few we have come to know with an intimacy denied us in most of our actual human contacts, so that we feel ourselves almost to have slipped into their persons; we are part and parcel of them; we have seen what they have seen, known what they have known, felt what they have felt. Such are Kristin Lavransdatter, Soames Forsyte, Isabel Archer, Jean Christophe, Lord Jim, Bazarov, the nihilist, and Raskolnikov, the murderer. One who has learned to love books for their characters need never be lonely.

In some books setting is dominant. Undoubtedly there are novels whose charm is chiefly a matter of setting. Once our imagination has been touched by a story of far away and long ago, the glamour is upon us and we want again and again to be lost in its atmosphere. One of the most beautiful of these stories is W. H. Hudson's *Green Mansions*, the romance of Abel, the fugitive, and Rima, the lovely bird girl, far away in the green forests of South America. So real does Hudson make the forest, in its mysteriously stirring life and sudden beauty and menacing gloom and ugly cruelty, and so beautiful is his conception of the lyric love of Rima and Abel that one can always return to it with fresh pleasure, fantastic though it be. This charm of setting exists for us, too, in many another tale. Once a story teller succeeds in communicating an atmosphere to the reader, he has won him.

In some books the theme is dominant. We may also read fiction because it has something to say about life and its problems; that is, it offers a commentary on life. Many writers incorporate into their books their ideas about human beings and their experiences. Practically all the important modern novelists stress theme. You cannot, for instance, have read Jack London's *The Sea Wolf* without realizing that it is something more than just the story of how Humphrey Van Weyden and Maude Brewster escaped from Wolf Larsen. If you read Wolf's talks with Humphrey and observe his actions with any attention, you see that ideas are involved here; different conceptions of the meaning of life, different standards of conduct, are in conflict. You cannot read many of Galsworthy's books without seeing that he is trying to show how human beings get mixed up in spite of themselves with the social system in which they live, how the problems of the state come, eventually, to be the problems of the individual, how the old and new are forever at war. A book like Tarkington's *Alice Adams* is not just the story of how a girl tried to bluff her way through society and failed; it shows, too, a social problem, how people who have not kept pace with the growth of their small city have to adjust themselves to new ideas, new ways of living. The problems of *Silas Marner*, of *Adam Bede*, are problems arising out of human nature; they will be of interest as long as human nature is what it is. A great many human beings are faced with the necessity of accepting the consequences of their own acts just as Godfrey Cass and Hetty Sorrel are.

A great many of us, like Silas Marner and Dolly Winthrop, are forced to grope blindly for faith in the midst of the obvious cruelties and injustices of life. Part of your appreciation of fiction depends on your ability to discover what the author has to say.

Summary. Prose fiction is the name given to any story in prose about imaginary happenings to imaginary people. It is a popular form of literature because it provides its reader with a story, acquaints him with interesting people and places, reflects life as it is lived by human beings, and presents ideas about life and its problems.

COMPREHENSION QUESTIONS

1. *Vocabulary:* the novel, plot, setting, characters, theme.
2. *Allusions:* How many of these references are familiar to you? Put in one column those that you recognize and can talk about, in another those you have read of but cannot discuss intelligently, in a third those that are wholly unfamiliar to you. Familiarize yourself with two references in your second and third columns:

Meg, Jo, Beth, and Amy	Lord Jim	Edward Dantés
Huck Finn	Raskolnikov	Emma Woodhouse
The Mad Tea Party	Isabel Archer	Elizabeth Bennet
J. S. Fletcher	The Pickwick Club at Dingley Dell	Miss Bates
Tish	Conrad	Rima, the bird girl
The Sheriff of Nottingham	Sigrid Undset	Kristin Lavransdatter
Jim Hawkins	The Sea Wolf	Soames Forsyte
David Balfour	Alice Adams	Heathcliff
		Captain Ahab

3. How would you define prose fiction in your own words?
4. What are the chief reasons for the universal popularity of fiction?
5. How does fiction enable us to live in the land of our heart's desire?
6. May books of fiction be a source of wisdom about the problems of life? Illustrate your answer from some book you have read recently.

PROBLEMS IN APPRECIATION

1. Here is a list of twenty well-known novels.

The Call of the Wild
Captains Courageous
Death Comes for the Archbishop
Emma
Ethan Frome
Henry Esmond
Ivanhoe
Jane Eyre

Kidnapped
Lord Jim
The Patrician
Pride and Prejudice
The Red Badge of Courage
The Return of the Native
The Scarlet Letter
Silas Marner
A Tale of Two Cities
Vanity Fair
The Virginian
Wuthering Heights

How many of these have you read? Classify each according to its dominant interest under four columns: plot, setting, character, and theme.

2. Add ten titles not listed here from your reading and place each in the appropriate column, according to its dominating interest.

3. Pick one book from each of your four columns and discuss orally or in a written theme such questions as:

(*a*) In which is the interest divided between plot, character, etc.? (*b*) Do any show a close relationship between character and theme or character and setting? (*c*) If there are characters who have become very real to you, name these characters and try to explain why they are so fascinating. For instance, which of these characters can you place opposite appropriate books in the list above?

Alan Breck
Miss Bates
Beatrix Esmond
Buck
Lady Catherine de Bourgh
Eustacia Vye
Godfrey Cass
Heathcliff
Sydney Carton
The Viscountess of Castlewood

(*d*) If some of these books have a theme, that is something to say about life, try to state what it is in your own words, and tell how the story and characters bring it out.

QUESTIONS ON BOOKS YOU HAVE READ

1. Choose some book you have read in which *setting* is important, for instance:

The Call of the Wild
Captains Courageous
Green Mansions
The House of the Seven Gables
Huckleberry Finn
Kim
The Shadow Line
The Scarlet Letter
Typhoon
The Virginian

(*a*) Discuss the influence of setting on plot and characters. (*b*) What scenes could not have occurred in a different setting? (*c*) What scenes take place in strikingly appropriate settings? (*d*) Which characters show especially the influence of the time and place in which they live? (*e*) Are there specific things about the setting, like the stone pits in *Silas Marner*, that are essential to the story? (*f*) Has the setting any charm of its own apart from its connection with the story and characters? (*g*) Does the setting contribute atmosphere? (*h*) Is any particular use made of the weather?

2. Choose some novel you have read in which *character* is important. (*a*) Which characters help to shape the plot? how? (*b*) What are the motives of the leading characters? (*c*) Do these motives clash at any point to keep the story moving? (*d*) Is the range of characterization wide or restricted? (*e*) Are any subordinate characters especially memorable? If so, how are they used? (*f*) What sort of people does the author portray best? (*g*) Are the characters so important that the book seems more a picture of human beings than of exciting events? Books that can be studied in this way are:

Adam Bede	*The Patrician*
The Bridge of San Luis Rey	*Pride and Prejudice*
Daisy Miller	*The Rise of Silas Lapham*
Main Street	*Silas Marner*

3. Choose some novel which you have read in which *plot* is most important. (*a*) What are the main complications of the story? (*b*) How are they combined so that different people and events are brought together? (*c*) At what point is each new complication introduced? (*d*) Do these elements ever form a chain of events that links a series of incidents into episodes, or even a series of chapters? (*e*) How is suspense maintained? (*f*) Does the movement quicken to make climaxes and then subside to rise again later, or is it a continuous flow of excitement? (*g*) Do the characters seem merely created to fit the plot, or does the plot grow naturally out of human psychology?
Suggested titles:

The Black Arrow	*Silas Marner*
Bleak House	*A Tale of Two Cities*
Guy Mannering	*The Three Musketeers*
Ivanhoe	*Treasure Island*
The Master of Ballantrae	*The Woman in White*

4. Choose some novel you have read in which *theme* is important. (*a*) State what the theme is. (*b*) Show how plot, setting, and character help to bring it out. (*c*) Does the author sacrifice any truth in his characterization in order to emphasize the theme? (*d*) Is the story in any sense propaganda? (*e*) Is the theme of importance to us, or

is it chiefly the special problem of particular individuals? (*f*) Is the theme chiefly moral, or social, or economic, or psychological? Is it a combination of some of these? (*g*) Is the action ever manipulated by the author just to bring out his point? Suggested titles:

Alice Adams	*The Red Badge of Courage*
All Quiet on the Western Front	*The Return of the Native*
The Bridge of San Luis Rey	*Romola*
Fathers and Sons	*The Shadow Line*
Moby Dick	*Silas Marner*
The Patrician	*Vanity Fair*
Pride and Prejudice	*Victory*

CHAPTER 12

DISTINGUISHING BETWEEN REALISM AND ROMANCE

What is romance? There are two kinds of fiction, realistic and romantic. Romantic fiction is primarily the kind which offers the reader an escape from reality. It often deals with distant lands and times. The things that happen in it are more exciting or mysterious or adventurous or strange than the things that happen in real life. Often it deals with such things as tournaments and besieged castles and perilous journeys through hostile country. Sometimes its characters have long journeys to go alone through forests infested with "pesky redskins," are besieged in lonely old houses, or are shut up on islands in the midst of far-away lakes, or lie in hushed hiding while a mortal foe treads close by. Sometimes romantic fiction portrays the prolonged struggle of true love against terrible and villainous odds. Sometimes there are pirates, hidden treasures, shipwrecks, thrilling flights from a close-pursuing enemy, last-minute rescues, ominous prophecies, missing heirs, disguised princes, intrigue, murder, breathless suspense. Again, romance is often pervaded by an atmosphere of strange things about to be revealed; often it deals with places and people now changed or forgotten or long since passed away. In short, romance shows life not just as it is, but as we like to imagine it to be. Perhaps no better illustration of the romantic point of view can be found than the part of *Huckleberry Finn* where Tom plans so elaborately to rescue Jim, the runaway slave. The realistic Huck is disgusted with Tom's romantic paraphernalia, but he misses half the fun.

Romantic characters are idealized. The characters of the novelist who looks at life romantically are painted in brighter colors and sketched in bolder outlines than the characters in a realistic story. They are moved by the more elemental emotions, such as love, hate, pride, loyalty, or jealousy, and they are not so subtly differentiated as the characters of a realistic novel. Edward Dantés finds one motive alone, revenge, sufficient to carry him through the pages of *The Count of Monte Cristo.* Judge Pyncheon is hardly more than a personification of greed. We don't meet people like Captain Ahab or Quasimodo, or Heathcliff, or John Silver, and so we remember them. Then, too, romantic characters are *idealized,* that is, made more good or bad or courageous or ugly or beautiful than people in real life. Romantic characters show us not so much what we are, as an enlargement of what we might be. Romantic heroes and heroines are ourselves as our dreams would have us be. You remember how Stein diagnosed Lord Jim's case for Marlowe. "He is *romantic,*" he said.

> . . . This magnificent butterfly finds a little heap of dirt and sits still on it; but man he will never on his heap of mud keep still . . . every time he shuts his eyes he sees himself as a very fine fellow—so fine as he can never be. . . . I tell you, my friend, it is not good for you to find you cannot make your dream come true, for the reason that you not strong enough are, or not clever enough. . . . Very funny this terrible thing is. A man that is born falls into a dream like a man who falls into the sea. . . . He is *romantic*—romantic. . . . And that is very bad—very bad. . . . Very good, too.

Romanticizing characters in fiction is the author's way of *making* people's dreams come true. Lord Jim kept his eyes fixed on this ideal himself, this Jim in whom he believed but whom he seemed to have betrayed so unaccountably, until he realized the ideal. We, too, get a stimulation, an exhilaration, from reading about these stirring figures of more than human size that makes us unwilling to exchange them for weaker vessels of mud and clay, like Godfrey Cass, Arthur Donnithorne, Amelia Sedley, and Tom Tulliver, human though they be.

Romantic fiction is true to life in a special way. Romantic fiction is not necessarily untrue to life. It is, indeed, often improbable. No one person's life is usually so crowded with breathless adventure as the lives of the great characters of romance are. In real life Lord Jim would probably never have had so glorious an opportunity to redeem his ideal self. In real life, Jane Eyre's honest love and courage would doubtless never have involved her in so much theatricality. Neither are people usually governed by such simple, elemental, heroic, or villainous motives as the people in romance. But in *spirit* romance is, if it be great romance, always true. It is life idealized, magnified, raised to the *n*th power. It deals with fundamentals of life—courage, devotion, love, self-sacrifice, hate, heroism—qualities that human beings *do* have. Only it takes these qualities and isolates, intensifies, or simplifies them so that we see them in a stronger light. Sydney Carton's sacrifice is a true picture of self-sacrifice—just as true as the bickerings of the Dodson sisters in *The Mill on the Floss* or the pathetic jealousies and bigotries and failures of the old men in *Vanity Fair*. Life can be heroic; only in romance it is steadily heroic.

What is realism? Realistic novelists, in contrast to romantic novelists, attempt to show life as they see it, without flinching from the facts or letting their imaginations wander into the land of the ideal. In realistic fiction the things that happen are usually things that could and do happen to a great many people in everyday life. It helps us to understand life by making it more real to us. *The Rise of Silas Lapham*, by William Dean Howells, is an excellent example of realistic fiction. Much that happens in this story is commonplace. The characters have long conversations about the sort of things that people discuss in real life; they are moved by a mixture of motives, as people are in real life; none of them is heroically good or villainously bad; at a crisis in her life the heroine behaves in a somewhat silly but unquestionably human way; throughout, things happen as they happen in real life. Such a book is not usually exciting, but it is interesting as a record of life itself, and it is significant because it deals with experiences that are common. Probably most of the greatest novels in the world are essentially realistic, some of them, it is true, equipped with a little romantic machinery to keep the plot going. Take out the plot cogs from *Silas Marner*, especially its incredible use of coincidence, and the story is almost wholly a picture of real life.

Moderate realism. Probably the first example of realistic fiction that you came across in your high-school reading was *Silas Marner*. It is evident that in this book, with the exception of the plot cogs to which we have referred, the author intended to represent life as she saw it. She wanted, on the whole, to confine herself to incidents that might have really happened. People in real life are unjustly treated, lose faith, grope for happiness, are led astray by false values, and sometimes are brought back to wholesome living by wholesome human relationships. Other people make mistakes and strive feebly to evade the consequences, sometimes realizing too late the futility of evasion. Any man, like Godfrey Cass, is likely to find that once the forces of his life are started in the wrong direction it is hard to set them aright again. Even the use of chance in the book, though a bit too conveniently arranged, has its counterpart in real life; for, as the Bible reminds us, time and chance happen to all.

George Eliot has tried to make her characters seem like real people. The motives of Godfrey, Dunstan, Silas, Eppie, and Molly Farren are all perfectly natural from a psychological point of view, as George Eliot is at frequent pains to show us. Not only do these people behave like human beings, but they talk like them. We can catch the flavor of the conversation at the Rainbow, and the tone and accent of Dolly Winthrop's voice as she talks things over with Silas. The very problems that confront the characters—the difficulties of faith, the strange intertwisting of the threads of human destiny, the seemingly inevitable operations of moral law, the mingled joys and sorrows arising from human loves and fears and hates—the whole warp and woof of the story is human. In short, *Silas Marner* is realistic.

Naturalism. Of course a modern realist of the school of Sinclair Lewis, William Faulkner, Sherwood Anderson, Theodore Dreiser, or Ernest Hemingway would hardly call *Silas Marner* realistic at all. Realism may go much further than George Eliot would have dreamed of carrying it. Realism that goes into explicit or painful or ugly physical details is usually called *naturalism.* Most such books can trace their origin to the French novelist Zola and the great Russians like Tolstoy, Dostoievsky, and Gorki. Contemporary writers of fiction are inclined to regard moderate realists like George Eliot, Thackeray, or Howells—even the incomparable Jane Austen—as a bit old-fashioned. Rather they admire the robust frankness and honest coarseness of the first of our great novelists, Fielding and Smollett. Their books usually stop at nothing painful or ugly in the attempt to show life exactly as it is. As a result they are very often more powerful and moving and sometimes more honest than George Eliot and the other Victorians, but their books are occasionally too tediously preoccupied with unpleasant details to portray life steadily and completely. Too frequently they lack a sense of proportion. Nevertheless, everyone who wants to face life courageously and honestly should, when he is ready for naturalism, read at least some books like Dreiser's *Sister Carrie* and Dostoievsky's *Crime and Punishment.*

Dangers of realism. The naturalistic school of realism does, however, suggest one word of caution to the young reader: realism does not always, in fact it does not usually, show the whole truth. Much of Sinclair Lewis' *Main Street* and *Babbitt* is true; but no one seriously considers these books the last word on American life. A book that is almost idyllic by comparison with *Main Street,* Gladys Hasty Carroll's *As the Earth Turns,* is just as true even though it is more pleasant. In fact, realism can be carried so far that it degenerates into romantic exaggeration. Thomas Hardy is a great realist, but he sometimes overworks his malicious destiny and his melodramatic crises. Edith Wharton seems deliberately to plan events in her novels so that the reader as well as the characters shall feel the force of the irony of fate. One cannot help feeling that Galsworthy too frequently underscores his characters to bring out a point, that a little humor would bring a sense of proportion to Theodore Dreiser's love for tedious and depressing details, that Ernest Hemingway's heroes ought eventually to grow up, that William Faulkner's horrors are laid on a little too thick, that James Hanley's bitter sincerity becomes hysterical and defeats its own ends. Realistic fiction, too, has its dangers.

All fiction is only imagined reality. You must be careful not to assume that realistic fiction must always be a record of things that actually can and do happen. Fiction is not just a record of things that have happened. The novelist observes life and rearranges its details to suit his purpose and he has a right to depict it as best suits that purpose. Of course Hardy has a right to end *The Return of the Native* in a welter of tragedy, or George Eliot to have Molly Farren die when and where she chooses. But both author and reader should be careful not to forget that books are, after all, imagined reality, not reality itself. And if the reader is to believe in this reality—to believe that Molly Farren *did* die as she did, that Silas *did* take the child without interference from Godfrey—the author must not distort events so that the illusion is shattered. Some books, of course, contain elements of both realism and romance. *Tom Sawyer* has scenes of perfect child psychology and scenes that read like extracts from the movies: grave robbers, a dramatic moment in a court room, a discovered treasure. *Oliver Twist,* like so many of Dickens' novels, is made up of both life and theatricality. *Green Mansions* combines fantastic romance with close and accurate observation of natural life in South America.

Summary. The two broadest classifications of prose fiction are realism and romance. Romance is fiction which enables the reader to escape from life as he sees it every day into an imaginary life that deals with events, places, or people that are out of the ordinary. Realism attempts to give an illusion of matter-of-factness, to report life as it is actually lived by most people. These two types are often combined in one novel, for all novels are imaginative rearrangements of life to suit the novelist's purpose. No novel is a literal transcript of actual experiences of actual people.

COMPREHENSION QUESTIONS

1. *Vocabulary:* realism, romance, realistic, romantic, idealism, romantic paraphernalia, coincidence, reality, imagined reality, *n*th power.
2. *Allusions:*

Captain Ahab	Molly Farren	*As the Earth Turns*
Stein	*Quo Vadis*	Zola
Quasimodo	*The Hunchback of Notre Dame*	Dostoievsky
Lord Jim		Tolstoy
Heathcliff	*Green Mansions*	Gorki
Tom Tulliver	*The Rise of Silas Lapham*	Dreiser
Amelia Sedley	*The Return of the Native*	Lewis
Arthur Donnithorne	Oliver Twist	Hemingway
Jane Eyre	Tom Sawyer	Faulkner

3. Try to explain in your own words what we mean by the terms *realistic* and *romantic* as applied to fiction.
4. Put into your own words Stein's analysis of Lord Jim on page 186. Illustrate.
5. Explain with examples, why all books, realistic or romantic, are not actually "transcripts from life," but life rearranged to make a story, or to fit the author's purposes. Show how this is done in a realistic story like *Silas Marner* and in a romantic one like *Kidnapped.*

PROBLEMS IN APPRECIATION

1. Make a list of books that you have read that are chiefly romantic, another of books that are chiefly realistic, a third of books that have both elements. In which of these lists would you place:

Alice Adams	*Oliver Twist*
As the Earth Turns	*One More Spring*
Cranford	*The Rise of Silas Lapham*
Green Mansions	*Silas Marner*
Guy Mannering	*The Three Musketeers*
The House of the Seven Gables	*Tom Sawyer*
Jane Eyre	*The Vicar of Wakefield*
Kidnapped	*Victory*
Moby Dick	*The Virginian*

2. Make a list of common subjects for realistic fiction, similar to the one on page 185 about romantic fiction. Cite examples from two books you have read.

QUESTIONS ON BOOKS YOU HAVE READ

1. Discuss *The Black Arrow* as an example of rather easily written romance. Show that Stevenson introduces a good deal of typical romantic paraphernalia without bothering to be very convincing; for instance, battles, shipwrecks, underground passages, noble outlaws, imprisoned damsels, peepholes in the tapestry, greedy barons, faithful servitors, frequent disguises, etc. If this book were written by one without Stevenson's gift for using words, would it be worth reading?

2. Point out how a realistic novelist sometimes overdoes his realism in his attempt to stress a point realistically so that his book in places becomes romantic exaggeration:
   (*a*) Sinclair Lewis in his attempt to stress drabness in *Main Street.* (*b*) Thomas Hardy in his attempt to stress unkind fate in *The Return of the Native.* (*c*) Edith Wharton in her attempt to bring out the irony of fate in *Ethan Frome* and *The House of Mirth.* (*d*) Balzac in his attempt to show filial ingratitude in *Père Goriot.* (*e*) Galsworthy in his attempt to emphasize the character of Timothy Forsyte in *The Forsyte Saga*, or class prejudices in *Fraternity*, or *The Country House.*

3. How does *The House of the Seven Gables* illustrate the theory that "Romance is not to have something happen every moment, but to make you think that something is going to happen"?

4. Compare *Guy Mannering* with *The Rise of Silas Lapham* or *Silas Marner* to illustrate the difference between the romantic and the realistic point of view.

5. Show that although *Kidnapped* is frankly a story of adventure it is a human record. Point out the large part that human nature plays in the development of the plot, and the interest that the reader feels in the human quality of David's and Alan's adventures. What little touches in the book seem especially human? (For instance, David's experiences on the island are particularly human. They have the same human quality as Robinson Crusoe's experiences in building his boat.)

6. Use Tom Sawyer's attempted rescue of Jim in *Huckleberry Finn* as an illustration of the romantic point of view, quoting freely from the book to bring out your point.

7. Use three of the following characters as examples for a paragraph on romantic figures in fiction:

Amyas Leigh	Long Tom Coffin	Dona Rita
Ben Hur	Lord Jim	Robin Hood
Brian de Bois-Guilbert	Lorna Doone	Saladin
D'Artagnan	Mary Stuart	Sydney Carton
Diana Vernon	Meg Merrilies	Uncas
Dracula	Milady de Winter	The Virginian
Hawkeye	Richard Cœur-de-Lion	
Heathcliff	Rima	

8. Make a list of your own of some books of different types of fiction you have read, for instance, realism, romance, comedy, fantasy, sea stories, stories about children, stories of the soil, detective stories, stories of adventure, ghost stories, and so on. Underline twice the books in your list which you rank as best in their class. Underline once those that you would rank as second-rate. Place a question mark after those which seem to you of debatable worth. In each case explain your choice with reference to such elements as:

   (*a*) plot interest, (*b*) characterization, (*c*) underlying idea, (*d*) use of background, (*e*) style, (*f*) truth to life, (*g*) ideas.

CHAPTER 13

HOW TO STUDY STORY BUILDING

STORY PATTERNS

A story has to have at least three elements. In the first place things must happen. The plan of these happenings is the *plot.* In the second place, what happens must happen to somebody or because of somebody. The people concerned with these happenings are the *characters* of the story. In the third place, what happens must happen somewhere at some time. The time and place supply the *setting* of the story.

Pattern, not plot, essential. Not every narrative has a plot. A disconnected record of unrelated events may be a narrative, but unless it has some sort of plan or framework to hold it together, it has no plot. A story with a plot is really a story with a plan of action. A writer, then, must have method in his narrative; he must plan what to include and what to omit, what to emphasize and what to pass over lightly. His story should progress by logical, or at least by relevant, stages to a certain definite, inevitable end. In a detective story, the reader wants to feel that each new clue helps in the solution of the mystery; in a story of adventure the reader expects each adventure to lead somewhere. Perfection in plot construction is rarely attained; and sometimes when it is attained, it is secured at the expense of other more essential qualities; but the more artistic the story, the more skillful will be the planning by which it is put together. Some few books like *Pride and Prejudice, Emma, Silas Marner, The Scarlet Letter, The Mayor of Casterbridge,* have almost perfect plot construction with no sacrifice of characterization. All of these show real insight into human nature, all present significant human situations, yet all are as carefully worked out as the most logical of detective stories. On the other hand, the structure of some books is extremely loose. Indeed some can hardly be said to have any plot at all; Willa Cather's *Death Comes for the Archbishop* and *Shadows on the Rock*, for instance, have no plot at all in the usual sense of the term; yet they have a pattern or structure.

Stories are sometimes told by diaries and letters. Early novelists followed a simple chronological plan by using diaries or letters as a device for securing clarity. What is usually called the first English novel, Richardson's *Pamela* (1740), used this method, and so did its great successor *Clarissa* and Fanny Burney's *Evelina*. It has sometimes been used, wholly or in part, ever since, from *Redgauntlet* to *Marjorie Daw*, *Dracula*, and Mary Roberts Rinehart's *The Red Lamp*. But most readers find long stories made up entirely of letters irritating to read. Notice how much more interesting *Redgauntlet* becomes once Scott drops the device. The awkward letter form even takes part of the thrill from *Dracula*.

Chronological plan is most common. In a simple story of adventure, especially adventure through a long and perilous journey, such as *Kidnapped*, *The Cloister and the Hearth*, or *Quentin Durward*, the chronological method is probably the best one possible; but even in these stories it is often necessary to go back a bit and pick up a few threads or explain what was happening meanwhile, as Stevenson does in *Treasure Island* when he interpolates the doctor's narrative. If the story is a complicated one involving many characters, the chronological method is not so easily used. In such novels, the author may have to follow Scott and carry along different sets of people in parallel order. You will remember how in *Ivanhoe*, we follow Rowena and DeBracy and Cedric up to a certain point; then we leave them and go back to the Templar and Rebecca and Isaac; leaving them, we give our attention to Locksley and the Black Knight. In this way Scott marshals his characters and events throughout the story until they are all brought together at some exciting crisis such as the siege of Torquilstone, and then separated again to be brought together once more. Such stories are really a series of more or less detached episodes which make interesting reading in themselves though they are part of the main narrative. The interest progresses from episode to episode instead of moving forward with ever-increasing power. Such *waves* *of interest* make what we call the *tempo* or *rhythm* of the story, now high and furious, now subdued. If there were no intervals between these rhythmic waves, the reader would be exhausted from lack of variety.

The anticipatory method. Of course no author is obliged to follow the chronological order in telling his story. He may anticipate the outcome, telling that first in order to emphasize what led up to it, a device familiar to movie goers. For instance, Edith Wharton's *Ethan Frome* begins by focusing the attention of a stranger in a bleak Massachusetts village on one of the natives, the crippled, prematurely old, silent, poverty-stricken, tragic Ethan Frome. The stranger sees at once that the story of Ethan's life is over, but that he has been left to linger on in some cruel trap from which there is no escape. Gradually he learns a little about the man, and once he is forced by a storm to spend the night at Ethan's farm. Then suddenly the story cuts back into the past; the stranger is forgotten; we see Ethan, a young man, waiting outside the village church to take his cousin, Mattie Silver, home from a "social." For most of the book, we follow the story of their growing love and their tragic dilemma until we see them attempting escape by suicide. Then again, with the crash of their sled into a tree, the past is shattered, and we are once more with the stranger in the Frome's kitchen. With Ethan's curt words of introduction, "and this is Miss Mattie Silver," the intolerable irony of his fate strikes the reader with more dramatic force than volumes of detail could ever have accumulated. If Mrs. Wharton had used the chronological method, her novel would have been ruined.

The retrogressive method. Another example of departure from the strict chronological method is *Lord Jim,* in which we are told at once that Jim has deserted a ship on which he was an under-officer, forgetful of all his responsibility in his cowardly fear for his own life. We see him at his own trial through the eyes of one Marlow and somehow, though he is found guilty, we agree with Marlow that he is "one of us" and not really a coward at all. Then, without warning, we are shown his boyhood, his early idealism, his job aboard the *Patna,* and in a few pages of marvelous descriptive narrative, we see the whole episode which has shattered his career. Then again we see the trial. We pause to listen to the strange effect of his case on Captain Brierly, in charge of the inquiry, a story which takes us some years ahead again. This over, we return to the trial, after which Marlow makes the acquaintance of Jim, wins his partial confidence, senses his perplexity, his pride, his inflexible, romantic idealism, and tries to help him.

Throughout the book we have glimpses of Jim, always through the experience of Marlow or some subordinate character: the wise old Stein; the elderly French lieutenant who had picked up the deserted *Patna* and its human cargo; Egstrom, the Scandinavian ship-chandler for whom Jim once worked; the contemptible agent in Patusan, Cornelius; the remarkable Malay, Doramin, and his son, Dain Waris; the girl, Jewel; the brigand, Brown. But in order really to know Jim, it is not enough for us to hear what these people say about him; we must know what they are like before we can evaluate their evidence; so we learn about them, too. And always we see Jim himself against a pictorial background we can never forget: on the bridge of the *Patna* that fatal night, in the witness box at the inquiry, on the verandah of a tropical hotel listening to Marlow, in the dugout canoe with his unloaded revolver on his lap as he proceeds up the river to Patusan, protecting Jewel and himself against the treachery in the jungle blackness, saying his last farewell to Marlow on a bit of white beach in the South Seas, keeping his final faith and meeting at last his own redemption at the hands of the natives he had meant to befriend. By this indirect, retrogressive, circling method of narration Conrad had told us what he wants us to know about Jim, and not merely what happened to him. He could have told *that* in a paragraph. The reader who will give to the book the imagination and concentration it demands will be richly repaid.

Experimental patterns. Recent novelists have experimented freely with methods of telling a story. Thornton Wilder's *The Bridge of San Luis Rey*, for instance, tells a series of episodes involving different characters relating each episode as a sort of separate "panel" in the story and unifying the whole by a common introduction and conclusion. Another form of the chronological method is what Dr. Chevalley calls the "jointed fishing rod" pattern in which the author relates what happens to a succession of generations in the same family. This is used in Butler's *The Way of All Flesh*, in Hergesheimer's *Three Black Pennys*, and in Galsworthy's *The Forsyte Saga*. A common pattern in the early twentieth-century novels is the chronological account of the development of one character, usually a young man at war with his environment. *Of Human Bondage,* by Somerset Maugham, and *Fortitude,* by Hugh Walpole, follow this scheme. Still another experiment is the "stream of consciousness" novel, in which we follow the thoughts of one character throughout a short period, often only a day, gathering our impression of his whole life from what goes on in his mind as he goes about the business of the day. Virginia Woolf's *Mrs. Dalloway* is a good example of this type, although this book does introduce a secondary theme. A difficult pattern to write and to follow is what we may call "the counterpoint" treatment, in which the lives of many seemingly unrelated characters are introduced like separate themes in a musical composition and then combined and alternated and recombined making a sort of fictional symphony. Only the sophisticated reader who is trained to understand and appreciate these "themes" or *motifs* can fully enjoy such books, however. Aldous Huxley's *Point-Counter-Point* and John Dos Passos' *Manhattan Transfer* are examples of this super-sophistication.

Sub-plots are common in the pattern. Some novels combine two or more stories in one. A minor plot carried on in connection with the main plot is called a *sub-plot.* In *Ivanhoe,* there is one story about Ivanhoe and the Lady Rowena, one about Rebecca and the Templar, and one about Prince John and King Richard. These are all carried along in such a way that one does not detract from the interest of the other but is closely connected with it. The story of Ivanhoe and Rowena is connected with that of Rebecca and Bois-Guilbert by having Rebecca, in love with Ivanhoe, nurse him back to life and by having DeBracy, a follower of the Templar, abduct Rowena so that they are all in the castle of Torquilstone at once. And as Ivanhoe's and the Templar's fortunes are inextricably bound up with those of Prince John and King Richard, all three stories are woven into one, as different colored threads are woven into one harmonious pattern. To the reader, these different plot relationships are quite clear.

Unity and clarity are necessary. To achieve mastery of construction, an author must use his material with strict artistic economy. That means that his story must be unified and it must be clear. He may weave as many stories as he chooses, but the final pattern must give the effect of being a harmonious whole. The novels already cited *do* achieve this harmony, but there are many famous novels which do not. Goldsmith thought nothing of interpolating into *The Vicar of*

Wakefield persons, scenes, even short stories and poems which had nothing to do with his main story. Thackeray inserted into *Vanity Fair* paragraphs of comment, incidents, and characters just to please himself or some reader who chanced to be following the novel in its serial form, regardless of the effect of these digressions on the structure of his novel.

Devices for securing unity. Unity can usually be gained by one of three methods: unity of related episodes happening to the same characters, as in *Pickwick Papers, The Good Companions, Huckleberry Finn;* unity of a life, in which we follow the career of some one person, seeing people and sharing in events only as they concern him, as in *David Copperfield*, and *Vanity Fair;* unity of action, in which all the episodes are combined into a harmonious whole, as in *Silas Marner*, and *Pride and Prejudice.*

Coherence is a difficult problem. Coherence in story telling demands that the ordinarily intelligent reader be able to keep things straight. Time, place, and people must not become confused in his mind. Some great novels are, in spite of their greatness, confusing. *Wuthering Heights*, for instance, suffers from having too many people telling the story, from repeated breaking-off and renewing of the thread of the narrative, from unnecessary duplication in the names of the characters. But if we once get the central motive of the story clearly in mind, namely Heathcliff's thwarted love for Catherine and his revenge, and see the other characters in relation to that motive, our difficulties vanish. Many an author uses such central motives to guide the reader. Sometimes a character helps out. For example, Pearl in *The Scarlet Letter* is the living symbol of the relationship between Hester, Chillingworth, and Dimmesdale, as well as between Hester and the community. The elaborate use of the symbolic scarlet letter, too, keeps the significance of the story clearly before us. The picture of Colonel Pyncheon in *The House of the Seven Gables* is a constant reminder of the past throughout the story. Sometimes we can follow the course of the story by concentrating chiefly in the descriptive passages. In Conrad's *Typhoon*, for instance, word pictures make the story.

GETTING THE STORY UNDER WAY

Importance of the title. From a commercial as well as from an artistic point of view the title is important, since it is the first thing a reader sees. A title should, naturally, arouse interest in the story and give some clue to its character; that is, it should be interesting and suggestive. *The Murders in the Rue Morgue, The Last Class, The Legend of Sleepy Hollow, The Man Who Would Be King, A Lost Lady, Far Away and Long Ago, Youth and the Bright Medusa*—all these are strong titles.

Brevity is a desirable quality in a title; a long title is cumbersome, a double title unnecessary. Titles like *The Shot, They, The Queen of Spades, Luck, The Black Cat, Marjorie Daw,* and *The Birthmark* are suggestive and at the same time brief. A title should also be euphonious, that is, easy to say. *The Light That Failed, A Tale of Two Cities, Wuthering Heights,* and *The Master of Ballantrae,* once pronounced, linger in the memory. Finally, a title should not be commonplace or sensational. These qualities cheapen a book in the mind of the prospective reader.

The point of view. A story may be told in the first, second, or third person. The first person often makes a story vivid and convincing, especially if it is a story of the adventures of one person or a ghost story. But "I" has limitations, as one person cannot reasonably be expected to see into the minds and motives of other characters or to be at more than one place at a time or to know all the circumstances that go to make up a story. An author sometimes tries to avoid this difficulty by making two different people, or even more, tell the story in the first person, but this device is not usually successful, as it requires the reader to shift his interest and his point of view suddenly. Some stories that are told in the first person throughout with great success are *David Copperfield, Jane Eyre, Lorna Doone, Henry Esmond, Kidnapped,* and *Huckleberry Finn. The Master of Ballantrae,* to avoid the effect of egotism, is told in the first person by a minor character.

The use of the second person in story telling is exceedingly rare. It is sometimes found in short stories, usually of child life. It produces a peculiarly vivid, intimate, reminiscent atmosphere.

On the whole the use of the third person seems most desirable for a long story. It enables the author to be omniscient, to see and to hear everything, to be sympathetic with all his characters, to portray their psychology more directly for us, and to insert his own comment if need be. Most stories are told from this point of view.

Requirements of the beginning. The beginning of a story is important because it must at once make clear the situation and the characters, explain all that the reader needs to know about what has taken place before the story opens, and arouse immediate interest. To accomplish all this is no light task.

The antecedent action. All that has happened before the story begins is called the *antecedent action.* Sometimes it is necessary to explain the antecedent action in some detail, even at the risk of detracting from the interest. Some authors reveal the antecedent action gradually; in a mystery story or a story of characters influenced by past events, this may well be done. In *The House of the Seven Gables,* Hawthorne explains the antecedent action immediately, but in so doing contrives to throw an air of mystery over the chapter that creates suspense at once and makes the reader anxious to go on. In *The Rise of Silas Lapham,* Howells makes Silas explain the antecedent action in an interview, and at the same time reveal his own character.

The first chapter. There are various ways of plunging into the first chapter. Authors of modern novels often place their characters at once in an interesting situation and begin with conversation. This is a good method if the conversation is clear and interesting and we are able to identify the speakers without difficulty. Sir Walter Scott usually chooses a romantic setting for his beginnings—the dark forest with the onrushing storm in *Ivanhoe;* the old Elizabethan inn, so full of possibilities, in *Kenilworth;* but he spends so much time in getting his narrative under way that young readers sometimes find his beginnings tiresome. Some authors begin with description, a good plan if the setting is to play an important part in the story—provided that the description is not too long. Others begin with the opening situation in good brisk narrative and lose no time in getting their story under way. Stevenson is an adept at this sort of beginning, as *Treasure Island* and *Kidnapped* demonstrate. Still others begin by focusing attention on the principal characters, which is a good method if the characters are to be few and the interest in them intense, as in *The Scarlet Letter.* One cannot lay down rules for beginning a story, but it is always interesting to see how an author uses means to an end at the very start of his story.

DEVELOPING THE ACTION

Incidents and episodes. A plot is made up of incidents and episodes. An *incident* is something that happens; an *episode* is a group of related incidents. In *Silas Marner* the staking of Wildfire is a single incident; all the incidents connected with the selling and killing of Wildfire and the consequences thereof to Silas Marner form an episode, which we might call the Wildfire episode. In *Ivanhoe* the death of the Saxon Princess, Ulrica, in the flames of Torquilstone is an incident; all the incidents connected with the events at the castle form an episode which might well be called the siege of Torquilstone.

Incidents to advance plot, to portray character, and to reveal setting. Not all incidents are necessary to the plot. Those that do advance the plot are called *plot incidents.* Those that do not directly contribute to the plot, but help to reveal character or setting are called *character incidents* or *incidents to reveal setting.* But in an artistic book all incidents contribute something toward plot, character, or setting. In *Silas Marner,* for instance, the incident about Silas and his earthenware pot has no bearing on the plot; we never hear of it again. But it does show the character of Silas. Nancy's insisting that sisters should dress alike does not help the plot, but it does reveal the character of Nancy, with her strict, unyielding, narrow ideas of right and wrong. The death of Molly in the snow, however, is essential to the plot; the whole story hinges on it. On the other hand, the scene at the Rainbow Inn does not help much either toward advancing the plot or toward throwing light on the principal characters. Its function is to reveal setting by showing us the sort of village Raveloe is; hence it has a rightful place in the story.

Symbolic incidents. Some incidents have what we may call a symbolic meaning; that is, they do more than add to plot, character, or setting; they suggest the meaning or significance of the story. Hawthorne's books are full of such incidents. Such is the midnight vigil of Hester and Dimmesdale, Pearl and Chillingworth at the scaffold in *The Scarlet Letter;* such the incidents about the soap bubbles, about the monkey, and about the dead Judge Pyncheon sitting beneath the picture of his relentless ancestor in *The House of the Seven Gables.* Nor is such symbolism found only in romantic authors like Hawthorne. In *Silas Marner* we have the symbolic breaking of the earthenware jug; in *Ethan Frome* the incidents about the pickle jar and about Zeena's rocking chair are symbolic. *The Patrician* contains much rich and poetic symbolism.

Minor crises and the climax. Besides incidents and episodes, a story usually contains a series of *minor crises,* exciting moments where the struggle of opposing forces that make up the plot is sharp and intense, to a big *climax* or turning point in the struggle. In some books there is a series of climaxes of equal importance. *Ivanhoe* is a book of this kind. In others there is but one climax, with smaller dramatic moments leading up to it. The death of the Judge is the big turning point in *The House of the Seven Gables,* but there are also exciting moments leading up to it—when he tries to force his way past Phœbe and Hepzibah to the terror-stricken Clifford, for instance, and when Phœbe departs leaving her helpless cousins alone. In *Jane Eyre* there are numerous exciting scenes leading up to the interrupted wedding and just as many points of interest thereafter. In *Kidnapped* and *Treasure Island* and *Lorna Doone* the story advances steadily from one minor crisis to another. It is these moments that add greatly to the suspense of a book and make it possible for the author to move his story onward with increasing rapidity and interest.

The obligatory scene. Another technical term used in studying fiction is the *obligatory scene.* An obligatory scene is one which the author has led us to expect and which, therefore, he is in duty bound to let us see. When in *Silas Marner,* we are told that sixteen years after Molly's death Godfrey Cass is to confess to Nancy, we feel entitled to be present at that scene; if George Eliot had not shown it to us, she would have broken faith with us. In *The House of the Seven Gables* we are made to expect that some day Judge Pyncheon will suffer the curse of the Maules, and we feel that we should be there when that dreadful event occurs. Hawthorne recognizes his obligation to the reader, giving a scene perhaps unnecessarily long. In *Jane Eyre,* we feel that we should see the solution of the mystery of the maniac imprisoned in the house; it is with an expectant thrill that we approach the outcome. In *The Master of Ballantrae* we know that the final clash between the Master and his brother is inevitable, and we should have felt cheated had it not been described for us. An author, then, should give the scenes which he has led the reader to expect.

Suspense. Of course an author must hold the interest of his readers, and to do that he must stir their emotions. A book may be great without emotional stress, as the novels of Henry James and Jane Austen demonstrate, but it cannot really sweep the reader along with it. Curiosity, sympathy, dread, anger, fear—all these the reader must feel with the characters. Suspense is a common ally of the writer of fiction.

Foreshadowing. A common way of securing suspense is *foreshadowing*—that is, by hinting as to what is to come. Stories of adventure and mystery are usually full of foreshadowing, but this device is not confined to such stories. In *The House of the Seven Gables,* Hawthorne hints that Clifford knows a secret about the house which he will ultimately reveal; that Holgrave is more intimately connected with the story of the Maules and the Pyncheons than we realize; that the Judge has done Hepzibah and Clifford a terrible wrong, that he will attempt to extort a secret from Clifford, and that he will in the end suffer the curse of the Maules. In *Silas Marner,* it is hinted that Molly may take a drop too much laudanum some day, and that Dunstan has met the fate which is afterward shown to have been his. Foreshadowing is a common and a valuable method of securing suspense, for it makes the reader anxious to see whether his suspicions will be confirmed.

Effective chapter endings. Another method is by ending a chapter effectively so that the reader will be eager to go on to the next one. When we learn that Dunstan Cass "stepped forth into the darkness" with Silas Marner's gold, we are naturally anxious to learn what became of him; and when Silas finds a human body half hidden in the snow, we are all eagerness to know what happens next. When we read in *Vanity Fair* that "Amelia was praying for George, who was lying on his face, dead, with a bullet through his heart," the dramatic close to the chapter makes it certain that we shall read on.

Withholding information. Still a third way of securing suspense is by withholding information which the reader would like to know. In *Silas Marner,* when we are not told for almost a third of the book what became of Dunstan Cass, our curiosity becomes strong indeed. In *Jane Eyre,* when we suspect that there is a mysterious person kept under lock and key in Thornfield Hall, we are naturally anxious to know more about her. In *Kidnapped,* when David and Alan become separated, we read on for several chapters to see what has become of Alan. Scott frequently leaves one group of characters in a perilous position and takes up another thread of the narrative.

Disguise. Another means of securing suspense is disguise. We like the uncertainty of not knowing whether people are what they seem or not, and if we are "in on" the disguise, the uncertainty as to whether they will be discovered. You remember how much this device adds to the excitement in *The Last of the Mohicans, The Black Arrow, The Talisman, Ivanhoe, Redgauntlet,* and many others. And where would Sherlock Holmes be without it?

Description as a means of working up suspense. One does not usually think of description as an aid to suspense, but it certainly would be impossible for the author to work up excitement without it. How could a story like *Typhoon* have been written at all without it? It gives the thrill of the fight in the Roundhouse, of the hushed and scorching hiding on the huge rock in *Kidnapped,* of the somber menace of the opening chapters of *The Return of the Native,* of the magnificent storm in *The Merry Men.* Even in quieter books a passage of description interpolated at an exciting point—for example, the passage where the Judge sends Hepzibah for Clifford in *The House of the Seven Gables*—is a valuable means of lengthening the period of uncertainty.

Surprise. A sudden shock or surprise, common to all story telling, often is effective in gripping the reader's interest. You remember the thrill in *The Lady of the Lake* when Roderick Dhu suddenly summons his hidden men and exclaims to the startled Fitz-James,

> . . . "How say'st thou now?
> These are Clan-Alpine's warriors true;
> And, Saxon,—I am Roderick Dhu!"

You remember, too, the shock of Silas Marner's sudden appearance at the Red House with Godfrey's child in his arms, of the shooting of Lorna on her wedding day in *Lorna Doone,* of the dramatic revelation of the fate of Mattie Silver in *Ethan Frome.* Sometimes the surprise is due to a deliberate "false lead" given the reader by the author, for instance, the real identity of Mr. Burchell in *The Vicar of Wakefield* and Pip's discovery that he has been wrong about Miss Havisham in *Great Expectations.* In detective stories this method is constantly used. But we ought not to feel that the surprise is a trick foisted upon us by the author; it should seem to us so logical that we should have suspected it long before.

Climax. A good climax is always effective. In all romantic fiction the "big moment" should be so genuinely stirring that we do not easily forget it. Though it is not a novel, there is no greater book for climaxes than the *Odyssey.* The Cave of Polyphemus, the Sirens, Scylla and Charybdis, Circe's witchcraft, the Land of the Dead—all these are told with a dramatic force that has made them part of the heritage of the race. "And thus he ended," says Homer when Odysseus' tale was told, and "all were hushed to silence, held by the spell throughout the dusky hall." We proceed from crisis to crisis till the coming of the final thrilling moment in which Odysseus, having proved the great bow his own, with Telemachus beside him armed with gleaming bronze, slays Antinous in the act of raising his goodly goblet. And Antinous

> sank down sidewise; from his hand the goblet fell when he was hit. . . . Roughly he pushed his table back kicking it with his foot, and scattered off the food upon the floor. The bread and roasted meat were thrown away. Into a tumult broke the suitors. They sprang from their seats and hurrying through the hall, peered at the massive walls on every side. But nowhere was there shield or ponderous spear to seize. Then they assailed Odysseus with indignation. . . . But looking sternly on them, wise Odysseus said, 'Dogs! You have been saying all the time I never should return out of the land of Troy; and therefore you destroyed my home, and, I alive, covertly wooed my wife, fearing no gods that hold the open sky, nor that the indignation of mankind would fall on you hereafter. Now for you one and all destruction's cords are knotted." As he spoke thus, pale fear took hold on all.[1]

It is a thrilling climax, one to which the story has been steadily rising, an imperishable example to writers in the grand style ever since. Nor have great writers been slow to follow it, though sometimes, as in *Jane Eyre*, and *Oliver Twist*, and *David Copperfield*, climax degenerates into mere theatricality.

Quiet climaxes. Sometimes, too, a more subtle climax is just as effective. Obvious climaxes like the discovery of Becky and Lord Steyne by Rawdon Crawley in *Vanity Fair*, or like the end of *The Scarlet Letter* and the sacrifice of Sydney Carton are moving; but more subtle ones may be just as romantic and just as thrilling. *Henry Esmond*, possibly the greatest historical romance ever written, has

[1] Translated by George Herbert Palmer. Reprinted by permission of Houghton Mifflin Company.

many. The whole scene in which Beatrix is rescued from the Pretender is a climax of shining romance, with no place for the thunders of applause that often greet the purely theatrical. As great a climax is Esmond's cry at the death of the Duke of Hamilton, the betrothed of Beatrix:

The world was going to its business again, although dukes lay dead and ladies mourned for them; and kings, very likely, lost their chances. So night and day pass away, and tomorrow comes, and our place knows us not. Esmond thought of the courier, now galloping on the north road to inform him, who was Earl of Arran yesterday, that he was Duke of Hamilton today, and of a thousand great schemes, hopes, ambitions, that were alive in the gallant heart, beating a few hours since, and now in a little dust quiescent.

Suspense not always essential. Some books are almost without the fairly obvious devices for holding the reader's interest which we have reviewed, depending instead on sheer sincerity in characterization, subtle psychological analysis, veracious reporting of daily life, beauty of style or spirit, or charm of description. There is little or no suspense in *Death Comes for the Archbishop* or *Shadows on the Rock* or *The Good Earth;* yet if sales records mean anything, these books have been laid aside with reluctance by thousands of readers, so fine is their spirit, so true and sympathetic their characterization, so beautiful their descriptive passages, so moving their simple picture of simple human beings. People do not read Henry James' *Daisy Miller* or *The American* for excitement. His study of subtle psychological relationships is enough for his admirers.

CHANCE AND HUMAN NATURE IN STORY TELLING

Mechanical devices in story telling. Authors who deliberately set out to tell a story necessarily must sometimes have to manipulate events to keep the story going. Homer had convenient gods and goddesses on whom to rely; ancient dramatists used a "god let down from a machine" (the machine being part of the furniture of the ancient Greek stage) to snatch off inconvenient characters. The novelist sometimes has to rely on letters, lost wills, missing heirs, sudden returns to life, amnesia, the United States Cavalry, people appearing out of the past, sudden deaths, and other remarkable coincidences to help them out. If these devices are made to appear reasonable and if the characters act in accordance with their own natures, the reader is willing to accept these conventions for the sake of the story. But an author should not drag in accidents to save himself from a dilemma or to prove a theory, as George Eliot drags in a flood to do away with Maggie and Tom in *The Mill on the Floss*, or as Hardy constantly uses coincidence or accident to ruin Clym Yeobright, Eustacia Vye, Tess of the D'Urbervilles, and Jude the Obscure.

Chance and human nature influence plot. In a story purporting to show life as it is, there should be no undue use of mere coincidence. Chance plays a part in our lives, it is true, and is therefore admissible as part of a story of real life, but our success or failure in life depends a good deal on ourselves, a fact which the novelist must recognize.

Silas Marner is a good case in point. Much of this story depends on the merest accident—the drawing of lots, the staking of Wildfire, the death of Molly so near to Silas' cottage. Indeed, Silas' cataleptic fits are a little too opportune to be entirely plausible. But, on the other hand, George Eliot has used human nature so skillfully that everything in the story seems to happen more because people are what they are than because of chance. The motives and reactions of Godfrey, Dunstan, Nancy, and Molly are so natural and so inevitable a part of their characters that we are inclined to discount the influence of coincidence. For if Godfrey had not been the weak, vacillating man he was, the whole story would have been different; if Dunstan had not been conceited, bullying, and deceitful, Wildfire would never have been killed; if Molly had not had a very natural desire for revenge, she would not have fallen in front of Silas' cottage, and Eppie would never have come into the story. In this work the influences of chance and character are so skillfully blended that we are forced to acquit the author of the charge of improbability. But the undue use of coincidence is a thing to watch; in a story that is supposed to represent life as it is, the important things which happen to the characters must not depend wholly on circumstances over which they have no control; human nature should play its part, too. A good deal of life is, perhaps, dependent on chance, but surely not all of it.

THE ENDING OF A STORY

The ending of a story is not so difficult as the beginning, because the story has been steadily progressing toward a preconceived end. The two dangers to be avoided in an ending are prolonging it unnecessarily after the story is over through reluctance to say farewell to the characters; and sacrificing logic and probability for the sake of making a "happy ending." It would have been a mistake for George Eliot to end *Silas Marner* by giving Godfrey Cass complete happiness after he had turned a blessing from his door for so long. A happy ending to *The Cloister and the Hearth* is impossible, and the final separation of David and Alan in *Kidnapped* is inevitable. It is an inexcusable weakness to end a story happily when its whole course has tended in the other direction. On the other hand, a story of a search for a treasure ought not to end with the treasure unattained, and a stirring bit of romantic fiction ought not to mar its ending with unnecessary gloom. We want Quentin Durward to marry Isabelle of Croye, and Sir Kenneth of *The Talisman* to be rewarded for his courage and loyalty and long-suffering. The ending of a story should, therefore, be logical and consistent, and not merely happy or unhappy to satisfy the passing mood of the reader. It should also be clear and certain; the reader does not like to be left with something unexplained.

THE DIFFICULT ART OF FICTION

All the foregoing details about the ways in which a story may be told do not, perhaps, suggest the real difficulty of the novelist's problem. It is not only that he must invent a story which will involve his characters in action and interest his reader. His work must give the effect of a designed pattern which re-creates a section of human life itself. The author must arrange his events so that they have a natural relationship to one another and yet push onward the flow of the whole narrative. His chapters must set events in motion, complicate them, flow into each other to a point which will make the reader anxious to go on. His characters must come together naturally, act and react upon each other, develop consistently, and at the same time carry on the story. His dialogue must fit the characters who use it, develop both characters and plot, and yet advance the plot. All this must be done in an appropriate framework of time and space, and perhaps serve to develop a theme as well. Consider but one good book, *Silas Marner*, in the light of these problems, one by one, and you will begin to sense the perplexing problems of the novelist and to appreciate the skill of an author who really can tell a good story well. And if you will compare this good book with a poor one, Harold Bell

Wright's *The Eyes of the World*, for instance, you will see why some books are worth reading and others are not. For such a study, see Problem 3 at the end of this chapter.

Summary

Method of narration. The author's way of telling his story varies according to his purpose. He may use letters, diaries, a straightforward chronological order of events, detached episodes, anticipations, retrogressions, or some scheme of parallel progress involving different sets of characters. He may also experiment with new patterns. If he uses sub-plots, they must be combined with the main plot. Whatever his method, his story must have unity (that is, it must be a complete whole) and coherence (that is, the reader must be able to follow it).

Getting the story under way. The *title* must be interesting, euphonious, suggestive, and not too long. The *point of view* may be from first, second, or third person, according to the author's purpose. The *beginning* must dispose of the necessary antecedent action, be clear, and arrest the attention.

Developing the action. A story involves *incidents* or happenings, and *episodes* or chains of related incidents. Incidents and episodes may advance the plot, reveal character, portray the setting, or stress the theme of the story. The story usually progresses from *minor crises* to a *climax,* or turning point. As it progresses, certain scenes become *obligatory,* that is, made necessary by what has gone before. *Suspense* may be maintained by such devices as foreshadowing, effective chapter endings, withholding information, disguise, description, surprise, or climax.

Truth to life. A story necessarily involves the element of chance or fate, but in the main it should grow out of human nature.

Ending. The ending should be reasonable and satisfactory.

Design. The whole must give the effect of a designed pattern which has re-created a section of human life.

COMPREHENSION QUESTIONS

1. *Vocabulary:* plot, logical, relevant, chronological, method of parallel progress, detached episodes, story-rhythm, sub-plots, artistic economy,

unity, coherence, focal points, incidents, episodes, symbolism, obligatory scene, suspense, foreshadowing, climax, "false leads," chance, human nature in fiction.

2. *Allusions:*

Pamela	*The Black Arrow*	*The House of the Seven Gables*
Clarissa	*Redgauntlet*	*Ethan Frome*
Evelina	*Sherlock Holmes*	*Kidnapped*
Marjorie Daw	*The Return of the Native*	*The Merry Men*
Dracula	*Emma*	*Trent's Last Case*
Quentin Durward	*The Vicar of Wakefield*	*Henry Esmond*
Ivanhoe	*Vanity Fair*	*Death Comes for the Archbishop*
Silas Marner	*Pickwick Papers*	*Shadows on the Rock*
Treasure Island	*The Good Companions*	
The Odyssey	*David Copperfield*	
Pride and Prejudice	*Wuthering Heights*	
Lord Jim	*Typhoon*	
The Last of the Mohicans	*The Scarlet Letter*	

3. Try to explain in your own words why a *plot* has to be *planned*. Show, for instance, how George Eliot probably planned in advance the plot of *Silas Marner*. What important incidents in this book were certainly in the author's mind before the story began?
4. What is meant by the chronological method? Illustrate by references to both *Kidnapped* and *Treasure Island*.
5. Explain the method of parallel progress by an analysis of the *Odyssey* and *Ivanhoe*.
6. Define and illustrate: sub-plot, obligatory scene.
7. What is meant by "artistic unity" in a story?
8. What is meant by coherence in story telling? Show how things are kept clear in the reader's mind so that he doesn't lose the thread of action in *Kidnapped, Treasure Island, Kim, Silas Marner, Ivanhoe, The Scarlet Letter*, and *Typhoon*.
9. Show the reason for the unusual method of story telling in *Ethan Frome, Lord Jim, Chance, Nostromo*, or *The Bridge of San Luis Rey*.
10. What qualities should a good title have? Give good and bad examples.
11. What qualities should a good beginning have? Illustrate. What qualities should a good ending have? Illustrate.
12. What is meant by incidents to show character, incidents to reveal setting, symbolic incidents? Illustrate each.
13. Enumerate and exemplify the chief ways of creating suspense.

THE MIDDLE TEMPLE HALL

In this magnificent Elizabethan hall, Thackeray, as a student of law, often dined. He describes the place in *Pendennis*.

Courtesy of Famous Players-Lasky Corp.

A STREET IN THRUMS

The quaint charm of life in a little Scotch village is revealed to us in Barrie's *Sentimental Tommy.*

Courtesy of Famous Players-Lasky Corp.

A SCENE FROM *HUCKLEBERRY FINN*

PROBLEMS IN APPRECIATION

1. Make a plan of the story of *Guy Mannering*, showing what outlines of the story were probably in Scott's mind before he began the story, and how he filled them in to develop it.
2. Point out and justify breaks in the chronological method in *Ivanhoe*, *Treasure Island*, *Redgauntlet*, *Silas Marner*, *Ethan Frome*, *Lord Jim*, *Victory*, *Chance*, or *Bleak House*.
3. Make an analysis of the structure of a novel, say *Silas Marner* or *The Mayor of Casterbridge* showing these things:

   (*a*) the main threads of the narrative, (*b*) the chief complications which entangle them, (*c*) the climax, or place in the story where these threads first begin to loosen, (*d*) the dénouement, or steps in the story which serve to unravel the entanglements, (*e*) the way each chapter leads to another, that is, the continuity, (*f*) the development of each chapter as a unit in itself, how it begins, what keeps it going, how it ends, what it accomplishes, (*g*) the devices for arousing and carrying over interest, (*h*) the way the characters are brought together to make a scene, the effect of their interacting on the plot, how the author gets rid of them when the scene is over, (*i*) the way the dialogue is made to seem natural and yet keep the story moving and reveal the characters, (*j*) the conclusion of the story—its logic, its satisfactoriness, (*k*) the use of description, (*l*) the relative space devoted to narration, description, exposition, and dialogue.

   You will find that an analysis of this kind will add greatly to your judgment of the art of telling a story. You have only to apply this to a good novel like *Silas Marner*, and a poor one by Harold Bell Wright or Edgar Rice Burroughs, for instance, to realize what makes one story good and another one bad.
4. In any novel point out:

   (*a*) incidents for characterization, (*b*) incidents for emphasizing setting, (*c*) plot incidents, (*d*) a chain of incidents forming an episode, (*e*) a climax, or turning point, (*f*) an obligatory scene.
5. In any story, try to find examples of suspense secured by:

   (*a*) foreshadowing, (*b*) effective chapter endings, (*c*) withholding information, (*d*) surprise, (*e*) disguise, (*f*) climax, (*g*) description, (*h*) false lead.

QUESTIONS ON BOOKS YOU HAVE READ

1. What are the chief methods of creating suspense in *The House of the Seven Gables?* Find examples of foreshadowing, of effective chapter

endings, of climax, of withheld information. Does the plot warrant the somewhat elaborate atmosphere of mystery which is thrown over it?

2. Write an essay on the influence of chance and character in *Silas Marner.* Discuss the part played by chance in stories and in real life, the reasons why the best stories grow out of character, the influence of chance and character in this particular story.

3. Discuss *Kidnapped* as a typical story of adventure through travel. What characteristics has it which are found in most stories of this type? (Fights, pursuits, disasters, disappointments, concealments, meetings with interesting characters, narrow escapes, etc., are incidents common to such stories.) Compare the story with a modern "best seller" of the same type—such as *Scaramouche, The Broad Highway,* or *Anthony Adverse.*

4. In *The Return of the Native* make a list of the episodes unfolding the plot, of the most striking scenes in the novel, of the purely preparatory or transitional scenes, and of the scenes which serve mainly to give reality to the setting. Point out some scenes which, although they add nothing to the plot, are among the best in the book.

5. Can you find and explain symbolic incidents in one of the following stories:

Dr. Jekyll and Mr. Hyde	*The Old Wives' Tale*
Ethan Frome	*The Patrician*
Fathers and Sons	*The Return*
The House of the Seven Gables	*The Scarlet Letter*
The Marble Faun	*Silas Marner*

6. Try to point out passages in which description adds greatly to atmosphere in:

Green Mansions	*The Master of Ballantrae*
The House of the Seven Gables	*The Merry Men*
Jane Eyre	*Nostromo*
Kidnapped	*The Return of the Native*
Lord Jim	"Youth"

7. In *Death Comes for the Archbishop,* Willa Cather wishes to give a picture, somewhat like a mosaic, of both legends and facts concerning a whole section of our country and its history, and of the character, struggles, and ideals of two noble human beings. All this she wished to fuse into a composite whole that should have both scope and unity, but she was not at all concerned with a plot. Can you show how she achieved this end so well that even interpolated legends fit into the picture? Show how in *Shadows on the Rock* she did the same thing with old Quebec.

8. Show how unity is given to *Vanity Fair* by means of a character, Becky Sharp; to *Pride and Prejudice*, *Emma*, and *Sense and Sensibility* by unifying the action so that it is seen from the point of view of one person; to *The Bridge of San Luis Rey* by a common theme; and to *Typhoon* or "Youth" by a common mood or setting. Useful suggestions can be found in Boas' *The Study and Appreciation of Literature*, pages 116–122.

9. Show that *Pride and Prejudice* or *Emma* fuses a number of events, many conflicting personalities and purposes into a unified story with progressive complications which rise to a climax, maintain increasing interest, and resolve themselves naturally. How are this unity and coherence secured?

10. Mr. G. K. Chesterton, poet, essayist, and himself a writer of remarkable detective stories, considers *Trent's Last Case* by Bentley perhaps the greatest detective story ever written. If this be anything like the truth, there must be some things about the book that immediately and obviously set it aside from the general rule of such books. Try to analyze it as follows:

    (*a*) In what respects does it run true to type? (For instance, in matters like the discovery of the body, clues interviewing the servants, use of newspapers, calling on Scotland Yard, appearance of an amateur detective, gradual emergence of several suspects, use of tangible objects as clues, analysis, chiefly in conversations of evidence and motives, surprise ending, subordination of love interest, clear-cut but not detailed characterization.) (*b*) In what respects is it unusual? (For instance: ingenuity of the crime, of the detective, or of the chief suspect; sudden abandonment of the case by Trent; final discovery that in spite of his cleverness he hadn't guessed right; development of the characters of Mabel, Cupples, Trent; original ideas on philosophy and psychology; clever fitting together of the pieces of the puzzle.) (*c*) What is the evidence that this book is intended not for the average reader of detective thrillers but for the man who takes an intelligent interest in ideas as well as actions? (For instance, it has little action, bloodshed, or sensationalism, but many ideas and much mental cleverness, demanding of the reader intellectual rather than emotional interest.) Has it anything to say about life apart from its interest as a detective story? (For instance, notice how the first sentence serves as a motto for the whole story.) (*d*) Try this plan of analysis on some other detective story, for instance, *The Sign of the Four* or *The Hound of the Baskervilles*. Compare the two.

CHAPTER 14

WHAT TO CONSIDER IN STUDYING THE CHARACTERS

Importance of character. The characters are usually the most interesting as well as the most profitable source of study in any story of permanent worth. In fact, as we have seen, in the most human stories the plot grows out of the characters. Many a novelist creates his characters in his imagination and then lets them work out their own story. Even in romantic fiction it is frequently the characters who are the mainsprings of the action as well as the chief source of interest. A great part of the action of *The Three Musketeers*, for instance, proceeds from the wicked machinations of Milady de Winter; *Kidnapped* is quite as much a story of character as of incident; in *The Cloister and the Hearth* one of the most charming things is the character of the hero, Gerard. In Scott's romances the subordinate characters frequently walk away with the interest at the expense of the hero and heroine. Who does not find King Louis and Duke Charles, Hayraddin and Galeotti more interesting than Quentin Durward and Isabelle of Croye? Who does not find Ivanhoe and the Lady Rowena pale before the fascinations of Rebecca and Brian de Bois-Guilbert—even before Friar Tuck, Locksley, Wamba, and Isaac?

PRINCIPAL AND SUBORDINATE CHARACTERS

This brings us to a necessary distinction between the types of characters in their relation to the plot. The *principal characters* are those with whose destinies the plot is chiefly concerned; the *subordinate characters* are those who are used to fill out the story.

Subordinate characters as instruments in the plot. The uses of subordinate characters are many. In the first place, they are often necessary instruments in carrying out the plot. If it hadn't been for the impressionable Mrs. Bardell and the unscrupulous Messrs. Dodson and Fogg, Mr. Pickwick would never have gone to jail. But for the foolish Lydia and the unprincipled Wickham, Elizabeth Bennet, in *Pride and Prejudice*, might never have come to know and love the true Darcy; and but for little Adèle, Jane Eyre would never have met Rochester at all. Sometimes, indeed, subordinate characters actually tell the story for us, as Mackellar tells of the Master of Ballantrae and his brother; as Nelly Dean and Mr. Lockwood unfold for us the tragedy of *Wuthering Heights;* and as the somewhat garrulous Marlow tells us about Lord Jim.

Subordinate characters as comic relief. Subordinate characters frequently add humor to the story. The chief source of the humor which is one of the glories of *David Copperfield*, *Oliver Twist*, *Nicholas Nickleby*, *Great Expectations*, *Bleak House*, and *Pickwick Papers* lies in characters who have no great bearing on the plot. Mrs. Gummidge,

> a lone lorn creetur, and everythink goes contrary with her;

Mrs. Micawber who, on no provocation whatever, insists upon assuring David that,

> Mr. Micawber has his faults. I do not deny that he is improvident. I do not deny that he has kept me in the dark as to his resources and liabilities both, but I never will desert Mr. Micawber;

Newman Noggs,

> a tall man, of middle age, with two goggle-eyes, a rubicund nose, a cadaverous face, and a suit of clothes—if the term be allowable when they suited him not at all—much the worse for wear, very much too small, and placed upon such a short allowance of buttons that it was quite marvelous how he contrived to keep them on;

Mrs. Wititterly,

> of a very excitable nature, very delicate, very fragile, a hot-house plant, an exotic;

Mr. Wopsle,

> united to a Roman nose and a large bald forehead;

Mrs. Pocket,

> the object of a queer sort of respectful pity because she had not married a title; while Mr. Pocket was the object of a queer sort of respectful reproach because he had never got one.

Because they are great humorous creations, the subordinate characters in Dickens often eclipse our interest in his heroes and heroines.

Subordinate characters fill in. Again minor characters help to fill in, to give life and variety when the scene requires a crowded stage. Parties, fires, shipwrecks, battles, mobs, street scenes, journeys—all these exigencies demand the introduction of minor characters. For instance, there is the party at the Red House in *Silas Marner*. We do not meet again Mrs. Crackenthorpe,

> a small blinking woman, who fidgeted incessantly with her lace, ribbons, and gold chain, turning her head about and making subdued noises, very much like a guinea pig that twitches its nose and soliloquizes in all company indiscriminately;

or Mrs. Kimble,

> the Squire's sister, as well as the doctor's wife—a double dignity, with which her diameter was in direct proportion;

or the two Miss Gunns,

> the wine merchant's daughters from Lytherly, dressed in the height of fashion, with the tightest skirts and the shortest waists, and gazed at by Miss Ladbrook (of the old Pastures) with a shyness not unsustained by inward criticism,

but we need them to give reality to the scene. There are numerous savages that are introduced in the various scenes of fighting, council, and torture in *Deerslayer* and *The Last of the Mohicans*. There are the Highlanders David meets in his journey to rejoin Alan in *Kidnapped*. There are the members of the crews in *The Nigger of the Narcissus* and *Typhoon*. There are all the crowded lively scenes of parties, and elections and stagecoaches and prisons and court rooms in *Pickwick Papers*.

Subordinate characters contribute local color. Sometimes subordinate characters help to reveal setting; that is, they contribute local color. For this purpose we are introduced to Mr. Snell and Mr. Macey and Mr. Tookey and Ben Winthrop and Jem Rodney and all the company at the Rainbow Inn in *Silas Marner*. Thus we see redskins and soldiers in *The Last of the Mohicans*, and all the members of the South American jungle village in *Green Mansions*. In any historical novel, historical characters are frequently introduced as a part of the background.

Subordinate characters as commentators. Occasionally a subordinate character will introduce comment or philosophy which the author does not care to give himself. Such a character usually makes interpretative remarks on the actions of the principal characters, thus helping to point out the significance of the story. The chief comment on the problem of faith in *Silas Marner* is given by Dolly Winthrop. In *The House of the Seven Gables*, Uncle Venner, "a miscellaneous old gentleman, partly himself but, in good measure, somebody else," who "had studied the world at street corners, and other posts equally well adapted for just observation, and was as ready to give out his wisdom as a town pump to give water" roams through the story for no other purpose than to contribute philosophy.

Subordinate characters as foils. Subordinate characters often throw light on the principal ones. Blanche Ingram in *Jane Eyre*, with her dark eyes, black ringlets, and her high features, her satirical laugh, and her "arched and haughty lip" is a mere foil to plain little Jane, who has charms denied to many a more beautiful heroine. In *Vanity Fair* many characters are brought in contact with Becky Sharp just to display her cleverness and unscrupulousness. In *Lorna Doone* minor characters sing John Ridd's praises; he cannot be expected to do it himself. As we have previously pointed out, we see Lord Jim through the eyes of many subordinate characters.

NUMBER AND RANGE OF THE CHARACTERS

Number of characters. Some great novels concern only a few people. In *The Scarlet Letter* for example, the interest centers about only four essential characters with the stern Puritan community as a background for the spiritual tragedy of their lives. In *The Marble Faun* the economy of characters is fundamentally similar though carried out less successfully. *The House of the Seven Gables* primarily concerns only five people; *Ethan Frome*, three; *Green Mansions*, two; *The Bridge of San Luis Rey*, five. Usually such novels are devoted to a profound study of a few people and their relationships with each other. On the other hand, some books have an astonishing range of characters. The people in Dickens are remarkable for both number and variety. *David Copperfield*, *Bleak House*, *Martin Chuzzlewit*, *Pickwick Papers*, *Oliver Twist*, *Nicholas Nickleby*, and the rest present a host of intensely alive, unforgettable characters, characters whose very names have become household words: Mr. Pickwick, Sam and Tony Weller, Jingle, Fagin, Bill Sikes, The Artful Dodger, Sairey Gamp, Pecksniff, Mrs. Jellyby, Dick Swiveller, and the Marchioness, Uriah Heep, the Micawbers, Barkis, the Peggottys, Traddles, Miss Mowcher, Betsy Trotwood. One could fill volumes, and volumes have been written, about the people in Dickens. Scott, too, crowds his canvas with people from all walks of life, though they are often more picturesque than profound. The great novelists, like Tolstoy, Balzac, Fielding, Turgenev, and Dostoievsky, show almost a complete picture of human society. Some contemporary authors present a wide and vivid panorama of human existence.

Authors with a limited range. Some authors are at their best with only a certain type of character. Cooper's "females" have long been ridiculed, but his romantic Hawkeye and Uncas and Chingachgook have established a tradition in pioneer and Indian fiction. In fact Cooper's Indians, Scott's knights, and Melvilles' whales have come to be more real to readers than their actual prototypes. Jane Austen, as has often been remarked, confined her characters to the upper middle-class provincial men and women of her own day; and even within this range she never attempted to show men except as a woman of her class might have had the opportunity to observe them. Kipling rarely succeeds with women characters; Charlotte Brontë had no real knowledge of men. Meredith and Henry James had no skill with simple people; Dickens is not really at home with social sophisticates. Jack London drew much of his material from rough outdoor life. Arnold Bennett portrays best humdrum provincial life in English industrial towns. And, as every reader of light fiction knows, Joseph C. Lincoln never deserts Cape Cod, Albert Payson Terhune sticks to his dogs, Zane Grey to the West, James Oliver

Curwood to the North, and P. G. Wodehouse to semi-farcical situations and characters.

The number and range of an author's characters, then, is an indication of his breadth of sympathy and of his power to fill his imaginary world with widely diverse human beings. It is always interesting to note whether a book contains few or many characters, whether they come from the same or differing walks of life, whether one type is as successfully developed as another—in short, what the range and depth of the author's power of characterization are.

STATIC AND KINETIC CHARACTERS

Characters in a story either remain fundamentally unchanged or show change and growth as the story proceeds. Those that do not change are called *static;* those that do, *kinetic.*

Kinetic characters. A novel usually takes its characters over a critical period of their lives and tries to show the effect that the circumstances of the story have upon them. In a novel, therefore, the principal characters are usually of the kinetic type, and only the subordinate ones static. A novel which delves deeply into the changes that time and circumstances bring about in a man's mind and heart is often called a *psychological* novel. George Eliot's *Romola,* for instance, is such a novel, as is also Hawthorne's *The Scarlet Letter.* The study of changing or developing character was one of the chief interests of Thackeray. We feel that Beatrix Esmond, Becky Sharp, George, Amelia, and Dobbin, in fact all the principal characters in Thackeray, develop in a certain inevitable direction, that their thoughts and habits are forming the hard mold in which their characters will ultimately be cast. Again in *The Rise of Silas Lapham* we watch the hero grow in moral strength as his fortunes decline; in *The Mill on the Floss* we watch Maggie and Tom from the time they are little children to their final tragic end, and we feel that each step in their development is the logical outcome of those that have preceded it. These characters are all kinetic; they develop, though they do not necessarily undergo violent changes.

Static characters. Romantic fiction, usually, but not always, takes a type figure and endows him with certain striking qualities without seeking to change or develop those qualities in detail as the story proceeds. In *The Three Musketeers,* D'Artagnan is perhaps a bit sadder and wiser from experience at the end, but he is in the main the same impetuous, courageous, gallant, arrogant, selfish young man that he was at the beginning. John Ridd is just as boyish and strong and wholesome, and Lorna as sweet and true at the end of *Lorna Doone* as they were in the beginning, although both have grown up in the meantime. In *The House of the Seven Gables* the Judge is the same rather heavy villain all through the book. In *The Talisman* Sir Kenneth's character undergoes no subtle change, nor does Bois-Guilbert's in *Ivanhoe*, or the Master's in *The Master of Ballantrae*. This is because a romance is interested in characters as they are rather than as they may develop. A romance is not usually psychological; its characters are thus usually static rather than kinetic.

Characters that are caricatures. Sometimes romantic characters are so exaggerated that they become caricatures, easily recognizable by a few outstanding traits or expressions, like the prominent figures in a cartoon. Dickens is a master of caricatures; almost everything said or done by his inimitable characters is exaggerated. We recognize them by their peculiar mannerisms, their startling clothes, their remarkable physiognomies, and their constantly repeated expressions. The strange creatures that live in *David Copperfield* are easily identified by their pet phrases: "I never will desert Mr. Micawber," "Janet, Donkeys!" "Barkis is willin'," "Generally speaking, I don't like boys," "Waiting for something to turn up," "lone lorn creetur." But the Micawbers, Sairey Gamps, Uriah Heeps, Bill Sikeses, and Rosa Dartles of this delightful sort of fiction, immortal though they be, must not for a moment be thought of as real people from real life. Real they are in the sense that they are astonishingly vivid, but human beings they are not. Uriah Heep is an everlasting type of false humility, Bill Sikes has come to be a synonym for brutal criminality, but in real life there are no such exaggerated types. Human nature is too complex to produce unadulterated types. Modern novelists are inclined to present human nature in all its complexity rather than with the engaging simplicity of Dickens and Scott.

WAYS OF REVEALING CHARACTER

Revealing character by description. In real life, of course, we judge a person by many things—his appearance, his actions and reactions, what he says, what others say about him, and so on. The novelist, too, uses all these ways of showing us what his people are like, and more too, for he can tell us what people are thinking about and analyze their thoughts for us.

A common method is description—a favorite with authors with a strong sense of visual impressions, like Hawthorne, Stevenson, and Conrad. It must not, however, be confused with analysis, which is concerned with the inner motives of a character. Description is a word picture of the character's appearance. To reveal character, description must do more than tell us what people look like; it must suggest the qualities which go with outward appearance. Scott, of course, goes into tedious detail in describing his people on their very first appearance; modern authors are more economical as well as more vivid. Dickens gives us pictures we always remember. Stevenson is especially adept at suggesting both appearance and personality in a few deft strokes, as in *A Lodging for the Night,* and in *The Sire de Malétroit's Door.* Any contemporary writer who knows his craft knows how to make description count toward characterization.

Revealing character by analysis. A favorite method with some authors is psychological analysis. They tell us what people are thinking and why, often in detail. Everyone who has read any book by George Eliot knows what this method is. Even in so short a book as *Silas Marner,* she explains in detail how Dunstan happened to steal the money, why Godfrey could not face consequences, why he changed, and why Nancy would not adopt the child. Part of the beginner's trouble in reading Henry James and Conrad may be traced to their fondness for analysis.

Revealing character by conversation. Conversation is a good way of showing what people are like, as any radio listener knows. What people say often shows what they are. Only to listen to the talk of Lady Catherine, Mrs. Bennett, Lydia, or Mr. Collins in *Pride and Prejudice* is to realize all you really need to know about them. In *Emma,* Miss Bates, Mr. Woodhouse, and Mrs. Elton give themselves away every time they open their mouths. In *Silas Marner* we know Dolly Winthrop by her talk. Nor is it necessary for characters to speak naturally in order to reveal themselves. Many people in Dickens, Thackeray, Fielding, or Hawthorne do not talk like real people. Yet their words tell us what they are. No one ever really talked like Mr. Jingle in *Pickwick Papers,* yet the reader can disassociate him from his stenographic style of speech. The reader who belittles the psychological truth of *The Scarlet Letter* because Hester and Pearl and Arthur Dimmesdale do not talk like real people simply betrays his own lack of imaginative appreciation; no dialogue was ever less realistic, but none was ever more self-revealing. Some contemporary novelists, most of them in fact, transcribe almost literally the commonplace language of everyday life; but a great deal of such *verbatim* reporting does not get very far with characterization, even in a book so fine in some ways as *A Farewell to Arms*.

Revealing character by incidents. Sometimes incidents, even very slight ones, will reveal character as tellingly as pages of analysis, description, or dialogue. When Silas Marner pathetically patches together the pieces of his earthenware pot even though its usefulness has gone, we are shown more vividly than in any other way that his starved soul craves something to love. Clifford's reactions toward the rose and, later, the monkey, in *The House of the Seven Gables*, are likewise revealing. So, too, is his blowing soap bubbles.

Actions of any kind may be made telling, particularly actions at a crisis in the character's life. The minister's holding his hand over his heart in *The Scarlet Letter* is significant. It makes little Pearl cry out:

> Mother, he has his hand over his heart! Is it because, when the minister wrote his name in the book, the Black Man set his mark in that place? But why does he not wear it outside his bosom, as thou dost, mother?

Significant, too, is Nancy's rigid stillness on hearing Godfrey's confession in *Silas Marner:*

> But Nancy sat quite still, only that her eyes dropped and ceased to meet his. She was pale and quiet as a meditative statue, clasping her hands on her lap. . . . He almost expected that she would presently get up and say she would go to her father's. How could she have any mercy for faults that must seem so black to her, with her simple, severe notions? But at last she lifted up her eyes to his again and spoke. There was no indignation in her voice—only deep regret.

Fiction is full of these seemingly insignificant actions which reveal character. Many are the little acts that show the shallow vanity of Hetty in *Adam Bede*, and the mixture of pride, childishness, affection, and loyalty of Alan in *Kidnapped.* In fiction, as in real life, people do significant things.

Motives and reactions. The most significant things about the characterization in a story, however, are the motives and reactions of the characters. *Motives* are the reasons which impel characters to act as they do. *Reactions* are the things they do or say because of these motives. The two greatest flaws possible in the characterization of any story are to make characters act without natural or credible motives and to make them react unnaturally to a situation just to satisfy the demands of the plot. The assigning of motives and the reactions which they cause is called *motivation.*

Motivation. Motives do not necessarily have to be reasonable—they are not always so in real life—but they must be natural and they must be consistent with what we know of the character. In *The Rise of Silas Lapham,* Penelope's motives in refusing to marry Tom because he loves her instead of her sister are not reasonable, as she herself admits, but they are entirely natural and entirely consistent with Penelope's character. One of the most human novels so far as motivation is concerned is *Bob, Son of Battle.* The motives which impel Adam M'Adam to act as he does throughout the story are conflicting and hard to unravel, but they are in accordance with his character as his past life has molded it. His reactions are often unexpected, baffling, exasperating, but no one could fail to be touched by their human quality. He baffles and irritates and touches one's heart just as many such a warped but intensely pathetic nature does in real life. Skillful examples of motivation are to be found in Barrie's *Sentimental Tommy;* in the minister's spiritual agony in Hawthorne's *The Scarlet Letter;* in the mingled, contradictory impulses of the characters in all of Thackeray's and George Eliot's novels. In romantic fiction, as we have seen, motives are much more simple and elementary than in the realistic novel; in such stories we often find characters animated by a single motive. But romantic fiction has different aims and impulses from the psychological novel; it must be judged by what it tries to do.

Reactions of characters as results of complex motives. Reactions are, of course, the tangible results of motives. In *Henry Esmond,* many motives impel Beatrix to act as she does; her heartless selfishness is the result. In *Vanity Fair* the reactions of Becky Sharp to the various situations in which she finds herself are the result of a complicated network of scheming impulses. In *Adam Bede,* the murder which Hetty Sorrel finally commits is the inevitable result of a lifetime of selfishness, vanity, and unwillingness to accept responsibility; and the reaction of Dinah to the tragedy of Hetty's life is the result of a lifetime of vastly different motives. In *Romola*, each day of Tito Melema's life is a stage in his moral degradation—an inevitable stage, the bitter lesson of which Romola tenderly points out in her talk with Lillo at the end of the book:

"It is only a poor sort of happiness that could ever come by caring very much about our own narrow pleasures. We can only have the highest happiness, . . . and this sort of happiness often brings so much pain with it, that we can only tell it from pain by its being what we would choose before everything else, because our souls see it is good. There are so many things wrong and difficult in the world, that no man can be great . . . unless he gives up thinking much about pleasure or rewards, and gets strength to endure what is hard and painful." . . .

Romola paused for a moment. She had taken Lillo's cheeks between her hands, and his young eyes were meeting hers.

"There was a man to whom I was very near, so that I could see a great deal of his life, who made almost every one fond of him, for he was young, and clever, and beautiful, and his manners to all were gentle and kind. I believe, when I first knew him, he never thought of anything cruel or base. But because he tried to slip away from everything that was unpleasant, and cared for nothing else so much as his own safety, he came at last to commit some of the basest deeds—such as make men infamous. He denied his father, and left him to misery; he betrayed every trust that was reposed in him, that he might keep himself safe and get rich and prosperous. Yet calamity overtook him."

Evaluating motives. It is the reactions of characters at a crisis in the story that best enable us to judge their motives. Many authors are true and unerring in their choice of such reactions; others falter and become inconsistent at the psychological moment. In *The Mill on the Floss*, George Eliot knew better than to make Aunt Glegg turn Maggie Tulliver off at the time of her humiliation; in *Silas Marner*, she knew well that Nancy would not leave Godfrey after sixteen years of life with him even though he confessed his past weakness. In *Jane Eyre*, we feel it natural for Jane to leave Rochester when she learns his tragic secret. In *Henry Esmond*, we expect Beatrix to react to her cousin's love as she does. And in *The Rise of Silas Lapham*, we expect the heroic refusal of Silas to stoop to dishonor even at the price of his fortune. Such reactions are illuminating; they reveal at a flash the whole worth of a character. On the other hand, some authors make their characters do and say things at a crisis merely to satisfy the exigencies of the plot. There is a good deal of unnatural hard-heartedness in Dickens that all too obviously "points a moral and adorns a tale." In some of Thomas Hardy's novels we feel that the characters occasionally act as they do in order to satisfy the author's pessimism. A study of the motives and reactions of characters in a novel is, therefore, essential for an estimate of the author's power of drawing character.

Revealing character by indirect effects. There is a sort of characterization so intangible that we cannot, as we say, "put our fingers on it" at any definite point. We can only call this indirect presentation of character. It is a process hard to define but easy to recognize, generally so subtle in its artistry that it is not often found in the ordinary competent novel. If you have read Conrad's *Victory*, you will doubtless have a fairly distinct impression of Mrs. Schomberg, the innkeeper's wife. You know that she is unhappy, haunted with sorrow and fear and brutality, patient, almost cringing, yet determined; that she is infinitely superior to her husband; that she is observant and not without courage. Yet she talks little, does little, is never analyzed, not much observed by the other characters. How does Conrad tell us so much about her? One cannot answer definitely except to say that her effect on others counts for much. Perhaps one can find better examples of this elusive, indirect, suggestive characterization in Walter De la Mare's stories than anywhere else in fiction. One is never quite sure of oneself as one reads, but one never doubts that one is under a spell.[1]

Sometimes an author reveals character by a thing so slight that it passes almost unnoticed. It is not without purpose that George Eliot makes the dog retreat under the chair as soon as Dunstan enters the room or that she tells us that even the pins in Nancy's pincushion were arranged in a systematic order from which she allowed no deviation. These little touches often reveal character as truly as long passages of direct analysis.

So much then for characterization. In conclusion, we should remember that people in a book must be *real*, either recognizable human

[1] See *The Riddle, On the Edge;* especially, "Miss Duveen," "The Almond Tree," "The Green Room," "Seaton's Aunt," "Out of the Deep."

beings or such vivid idealizations of human beings that they seem real, perhaps more real than actual persons. Whether the book be romantic or realistic, the reader must be able to identify himself with the characters. They may or may not be familiar types to him, for he likes to meet new people in fiction as well as in life, but they must be interesting and alive.

Summary. *Principal characters* are those with whom the plot is chiefly concerned. *Subordinate characters* serve as instruments in the plot, provide humor, fill in the scene, give local color, comment on the action and theme of the story, and act as foils to the main characters.

Some books and authors have a wide range of power to characterize and present many people in the course of the story. Others have a limited range and present few people.

Static characters remain unchanged throughout the story. *Kinetic* characters are developed as a result of what happens in the story.

Character may be revealed: (1) from the author's point of view by description, analysis, and conversation; (2) by actions and reactions through incidents, motives, and reactions; and (3) by indirect effects on other characters and by little touches.

COMPREHENSION QUESTIONS

1. *Vocabulary:* principal characters, subordinate characters, philosophy, range of characterization, description, analysis, indirect characterization, motives, reactions, motivation, static characters, kinetic characters.
2. *Allusions:*

Mrs. Bardell	Mr. Snell	Mr. Collins
Mr. Pickwick	Mr. Macey	Miss Bates
Wickham	Mr. Tookey	Mr. Woodhouse
Lydia	Ben Winthrop	Lady Catherine
Elizabeth Bennet	Dick Steele	Hester Prynne
Adèle	Mrs. Bracegirdle	Pearl
Jane Eyre	General Webb	Arthur Dimmesdale
Rochester	Blanche Ingram	Mrs. Schomberg
Nelly Dean	Uncle Venner	Tito Melema
Marlow	Hawkeye	Romola
Alan Breck	Uncas	Adam M'Adam

3. Explain in your own words the difference between principal and subordinate characters.

4. Make a list of the chief uses of subordinate characters. Find two examples to illustrate each item on this list, one from a book you have read in school and one from a book you have read outside of school.
5. Follow the same plan suggested in Exercise 4 above, with a list of the chief ways of revealing character.
6. What is meant by the author's range of characterization? Compare Stevenson and Dickens in this respect.
7. Illustrate from actual experience the meaning of the terms *motives*, *reactions*, and *motivation*.
8. List the chief motives of each of three characters in some book you have read recently. Check with blue pencil those that seem to you natural in the circumstances, with red those that seem to you doubtful psychology. Which of these motives affect the course of the story?
9. Follow the plan suggested in Exercise 8 with a list of the chief reactions of three characters in another book you have read recently.
10. Explain, with one example each, the difference between static and kinetic characters.
11. See Question 2 on page 183 at the end of Chapter 11 on "Why Read Fiction?" (page 177).

PROBLEMS IN APPRECIATION

1. In any novel find characterization by:
   (*a*) description, (*b*) analysis, (*c*) dialogue, (*d*) comment of others, (*e*) incidents, (*f*) little touches, (*g*) indirect method.
2. In any novel find subordinate characters used:
   (*a*) to throw light on principal characters, (*b*) to contribute humor, (*c*) to contribute philosophy, (*d*) to give an impression of numbers, (*e*) to give local color.
3. In any novel point out both static and kinetic characters.
4. In any novel point out the steps in the development of a kinetic character. Show at each point how outward events and inward motives and reactions conspired to make him act as he did. Suggestions:

Captain Ahab	in *Moby Dick* by Herman Melville
Alice Adams	in *Alice Adams* by Booth Tarkington
Axel Heyst	in *Victory* by Joseph Conrad
Fanny Bowater	in *Memoirs of a Midget* by Walter De la Mare
Godfrey Cass	in *Silas Marner* by George Eliot
Heathcliff	in *Wuthering Heights* by Emily Brontë
Henry Fleming	in *The Red Badge of Courage* by Stephen Crane
Dr. Jekyll	in *Dr. Jekyll and Mr. Hyde* by Stevenson

Lord Jim	in *Lord Jim* by Joseph Conrad
Lord Miltoun	in *The Patrician* by John Galsworthy
Molly Wood	in *The Virginian* by Owen Wister
Tito Melema	in *Romola* by George Eliot

5. Discuss the range of characterization of any novelist of whose works you have read four books.

6. In any novel point out:
   (*a*) the influence of the characters on each other, (*b*) the influence of setting on characters.

7. The following characters are good examples of indirect characterization. See if you can discover the means by which the author builds up an impression of each one that is out of all proportion to what we see and hear of him. What is the impression in each case? Refer to especially suggestive passages:
   (*a*) Annette, Soames' second wife and Fleur's mother, in Galsworthy's *The Forsyte Saga*, (*b*) Sabathier, the evil spirit who struggles for the possession of Arthur Lawford's body in Walter De la Mare's *The Return*, (*c*) Stanley, Beryl, Linda, and Kezia in Katherine Mansfield's "Prelude," (*d*) Seaton's aunt in De la Mare's "Seaton's Aunt," (*e*) Miss Duveen in De la Mare's "Miss Duveen."

QUESTIONS ON BOOKS YOU HAVE READ

1. Discuss the use of subordinate characters as shown by:

Blanche Ingram	in *Jane Eyre*
Cluny	in *Kidnapped*
Dick Steele	in *Henry Esmond*
The Dodson sisters	in *The Mill on the Floss*
The guests at the Red House	in *Silas Marner*
Gurth, Wamba, and Ulrica	in *Ivanhoe*
Hayraddin	in *Quentin Durward*
Mackellar	in *The Master of Ballantrae*
Michael Lambourne	in *Kenilworth*
Uncle Venner	in *The House of the Seven Gables*
Zerrilla	in *The Rise of Silas Lapham*

2. In *Pickwick Papers* show that the attention is not divided evenly among the groups of characters—that is, that some are more interesting than others even though their part in the story does not warrant such interest.

3. Write an essay on the element of character in *Silas Marner* discussing such details as the division between principal and subordinate characters,

the use of subordinate characters; the motives and reactions of Silas, Godfrey, and Nancy; the methods of character portrayal; examples of static and kinetic characters; the extent to which the story hinges on character.

4. In *The House of the Seven Gables* find examples of Hawthorne's fondness for making the dress of characters suggest their personality. How does this device resemble his use of other tangible means to suggest intangible ideas and feelings; for instance, Alice's posies, the well, the picture, the harpsichord, the chickens, etc.?

5. Make a list of the four main characters in *The Marble Faun* and then select from the book the phrases that best describe their outward appearance, the comments which best reveal their inward characters, and the figures of speech which present them most vividly to the reader's imagination.

6. Show how five characters in *The Bridge of San Luis Rey* are intimately connected with the theme. What part does each have in working it out?

7. What purposes are served by Uncle Venner and by the introduction of the story of Alice Pyncheon in *The House of the Seven Gables?*

8. Of the main characters in *The Return of the Native* which are the most real? why? Which, if any, seem a bit machine-made; that is, more the result of the exigencies of the plot than of the complexities of human nature? Do any seem not clearly defined?

9. In *Kidnapped* show by illustration how Stevenson takes pains to individualize interestingly even his minor characters. Give examples of people met by David in his journey who are interesting in themselves even though they have no close connection with the plot. Illustrate Stevenson's tendency to make a character stand out by emphasizing minor peculiarities of the voice, gait, appearance, etc.

10. The following are some of the most famous characters in fiction. Each name has become almost a by-word to cultivated people. How many of them do you know? Characterize those with whom you are familiar. What devices for characterization help to reveal them? What seems to you the secret of their vitality? Which of your own favorites do you miss from the list? Make out your own list of favorite characters in fiction.

Captain Ahab	Miss Bates	Betsy Trotwood
Alice	Bazarov	Bill Sikes
The Baines sisters	Becky Sharpe	Chingachgook

Christopher Vance	Isabel Archer	Nostromo
D'Artagnan	Jane Eyre	Pecksniff
Dominie Sampson	John Silver	Dr. Primrose
Elizabeth Bennet	Meg Merrilies	Mrs. Proudie
Emma Woodhouse	Mr. Micawber	Soames Forsyte
Hawkeye	Mignon	Tito Melema
Heathcliff	Colonel Newcome	

11. An outline for studying *any character in any novel:*

(*a*) Who and what is he? (*b*) Where does he live? How does his environment affect him? (*c*) What does he do in the story? (*d*) What are his chief motives? (*e*) What are his most illuminating reactions? (*f*) What are his chief traits of character and temperament? (*g*) How does he develop in the story? (*h*) What persons and events influence his development?

CHAPTER 15

SETTING AND ITS INTERACTION ON PLOT AND CHARACTER

KINDS OF SETTING

The setting of any story is its background of time and place. Setting varies in its importance.

Scenic setting. Sometimes it is merely scenic, that is, it merely helps us to visualize the scene of the action. Such a setting is usually revealed by casual description and is not of great importance in the study of the story.

Strongly localized setting. Sometimes it tries to portray the peculiarities of life in a special part of the world, such as the tropical forests of Brazil, or the fishing settlements of Brittany, or the frozen forests of Canada. Such a setting exercises a great charm over people who are interested in that scene. Numbers of people read stories just because they happen to be about Cape Cod, or the French Revolution, or the gold rush to the Yukon, even when the plot and characters are conventional and commonplace.

The essential setting. Some stories have an *essential setting*, that is, they could not be laid elsewhere because in them plot and characters depend for their very existence on the element of time and place. Poe's short story "The Fall of the House of Usher" could not well take place elsewhere. *Ivanhoe* is essentially a story of early Norman and Saxon England. The background of the ocean is necessary to *Typhoon* and the *Nigger of the Narcissus*. The house itself is an important part of *The House of the Seven Gables*, and a New England Puritan community is the best possible setting for *The Scarlet Letter*.

Setting revealed by description. It is customary for an author to describe the scene of the whole story. Sir Walter Scott seldom lets such an opportunity go by without an elaborate description. Other examples of description to reveal setting are the famous picture of the Doone valley in *Lorna Doone;* the short but adequate description of Raveloe in *Silas Marner:*

> orchards looking lazy with neglected plenty; the large church in the wide churchyard, which men gazed at lounging at their own doors in service time; the purple-faced farmers jogging along the lanes or turning in at the Rainbow; homesteads where men supped heavily and slept in the light of the evening hearth, and where women seemed to be laying up a stock of linen for the life to come;

and the charming scenes in the garden in *The House of the Seven Gables:*

> [a] green play-place of flickering light [where] the bees came and plunged into the squash blossoms [so that] Clifford heard their sunny buzzing murmur in the heart of the great yellow blossoms [and] looked about him with a joyful sense of warmth, and blue sky and green grass, and of God's free air in the whole height from earth to heaven.

Setting revealed by dialogue. Setting may also be revealed by the use of dialect in the dialogue. Thus we have Scotch dialect in *The Little Minister*, *Sentimental Tommy*, and *Bob, Son of Battle;* negro dialect in Thomas Nelson Page's stories of the South; and the New England twang in *Silas Lapham.*

Setting revealed by historical background. A common device in historical novels is to introduce historical scenes, characters, and costumes into the story. For this reason we have scenes revolving about the battle of Waterloo in *Vanity Fair;* the grand progresses of Queen Elizabeth in *Kenilworth;* the storming of the Bastille in *A Tale of Two Cities*, and the interchange of courtesies between Saladin and Richard the Lion Hearted in *The Talisman.* For this reason historical characters often appear in a novel though they have no connection with its plot. Thus we have Dick Steele in *Henry Esmond*, Spenser and Raleigh in *Westward Ho!* and a constant procession of historical figures through the pages of Scott. For this reason, too, Scott describes in detail the costumes of his characters, descriptions which he loved to write since he was an antiquarian as well as a novelist.

The symbolical setting. Occasionally an author uses symbolism in his setting in order better to bring out the significance of the story, as in *The House of the Seven Gables* in which the house, the garden, the chickens, the yellowing branch of the elm tree, Alice's posies, the harpsichord—in fact most of the elements of the setting—have a certain symbolic significance.

Symbolism in Hawthorne. No author is more fond than Hawthorne of investing scenes and objects with symbolic meaning. The supremely artistic example of this tendency in him is, of course, *The Scarlet Letter*, where the symbol, flaming on Hester's breast, hidden in the minister's heart, streaking the night sky, perpetually in the eyes and on the lips of little Pearl, is present on almost every page. Even in *The House of the Seven Gables* symbols are constantly foreshadowing the curse and the sin which is about to be expiated. Alice's posies bloom, and the elm-tree branch turns to gold in token of a moral law finally consummated. The harpsichord sounds mysteriously in warning of death. The organ grinder's monkey terrifies Clifford as a type of greed; the soap bubbles allure him as images of beauty, only to be rudely destroyed by the fleshly Judge Pyncheon. The well is bitter and brackish in memory of the wrong done to Matthew Maule, and an odd gurgle in the Judge's throat presages that he will one day have "blood to drink." Even the hens are symbolic of the decayed gentility of the Pyncheon family.

Setting and atmosphere. Most authors have a good sense of the fitness of things in choosing certain scenes for certain events. As Stevenson says in his "Gossip on Romance,"

> Some places speak distinctly. Certain dank gardens cry aloud for a murder; certain old houses demand to be haunted; certain coasts are set apart for shipwreck.

We feel that a wild night and the Devil's Bowl are the proper time and place for Adam M'Adam to discover Red Wull's guilt in *Bob, Son of Battle.* It is not only appropriate but essential that Dunstan should steal Silas Marner's money on a cold, dark, wet night. The various scenes of David's adventures in *Kidnapped* are just the places for breathless flight and hushed hiding. As we have seen, Sir Walter Scott usually chooses for beginning his stories a place that at once appeals to the imagination. Few authors fail in this choice of appropriate setting; they use time and place and weather to heighten interest.

Description reflects the mood of the story. Many story tellers use description elaborately throughout a novel. One can follow almost every passing mood in *The House of the Seven Gables* just by reading the descriptions and noting the changes in the weather as things look dark or bright for Hepzibah and Clifford. Stevenson never fails to use description effectively to create mood, and Poe's pictorial power is one of the chief sources of his morbid grip on his reader's imagination.

Over-use of description. The over-use of description to harmonize with the mood is likely to produce ludicrous results. Ruskin long ago attacked the device of making Nature sympathize too enthusiastically with the feelings of men and women. He labeled this device "the pathetic fallacy." Even Hawthorne sometimes overworked his descriptive passages. The long chapter about the dead Judge Pyncheon in *The House of the Seven Gables* is one of his worst offenses. Stories of horror, too, are prone to make altogether too conventional use of thunder and lightning and rain, just as cheap romances introduce too many twittering birds and blossoming flowers merely to make the lovers happy.

Setting and local color. Setting may often be used very elaborately for the purpose of showing how people lived at any given time and place. Most readers of Scott have suffered some annoyance at his detailed descriptions of costumes and armor and furniture and buildings which he included just to let us know how people lived and dressed in the days of Cedric the Saxon. Nevertheless, the historical novel could not well get along without such details. Thackeray, we may be sure, did not reproduce the genuine eighteenth-century atmosphere of *Henry Esmond* without patient study of the period. Even if a story has a contemporary setting, the author does not begin to write without first knowing his background. Frank Norris had to know the California wheat fields to write *The Octopus;* Ernest Poole studied life on the water fronts and among the stokers of steamers before he wrote *The Harbor*. Willa Cather spent months in the Southwest to prepare herself for *Death Comes for the Archbishop* or Tom Outland's story in *The Professor's House,* and months in Quebec for *Shadows on the Rock*. Louis Hémon lived among French peasants in Quebec before he wrote *Maria Chapdelaine*. A knowledge of setting is a prerequisite to the writing of the story.

From the Mary Harrod Northend Collection

THE HOUSE OF THE SEVEN GABLES,
SALEM, MASSACHUSETTS

Courtesy of the Metropolitan Museum of Art

"PORTIA," BY SIR JOHN MILLAIS

A famous painter expresses the graceful dignity of a charming Shakespearean heroine.

INTERACTION OF PLOT, CHARACTER, AND SETTING

Influence of the plot on the characters. Character is often influenced by plot and setting. When a character acts as he does because the plot demands it of him instead of because it is the natural course for him to take, we say that he is unduly influenced by the plot. Silas Marner's cataleptic fit and Molly Farren's overdose of laudanum are a bit too opportune to be perfectly natural; their occurrence at this particular time is demanded by the plot. If they did not act in this way at this time, the story could not go on. All that the author can do in such a case is to make the actions seem consistent with the nature of the character, as George Eliot does satisfactorily. If, however, a character is made to do violently inconsistent or unnatural things demanded of him by the exigencies of the plot, the story ceases to be a sincere and faithful picture of life. It is natural that Maisie should desert the blind artist in *The Light That Failed*, because she is a selfish, shallow girl; to have changed her nature inconsistently at the last moment to secure a happy ending would have spoiled the book. On the other hand, the conduct of some of the extremely villainous villains of Charles Reade and Dumas seems inconceivable. The jealousy of the tulip grower in *The Black Tulip* and the wickedness of Milady de Winter in *The Three Musketeers* are hard to believe; but the plot demands that these people act as they do. In judging these stories we must discount the influence of plot on character.

Influence of setting on character. The setting, or environment, of a story often exercises an interesting influence on the characters. Such an influence is apt to be true to life, for environment has its effect on all people in real life. Sometimes it is something specific about the environment that influences the characters' lives, like the stone pits in *Silas Marner*, the impregnable stronghold in *Lorna Doone*, the house in *The House of the Seven Gables*, or the huge pile of earth in *Sussex Gorse*. But more often it is the general location, the climate, the period of history, or the character of the inhabitants that is significant. Every character in *The Call of the Wild*, for instance, feels the influence of the North. In *The Last Days of Pompeii* the characters are at the mercy of the setting. The stern Puritan community in *The Scarlet Letter* leaves its lasting imprint on the minds and souls of Hester Prynne and Arthur Dimmesdale. The characters in *Westward Ho!* are animated by the enthusiasms and prejudices of the Elizabethan Age, and every individual in *The Cloister and the Hearth* is partly a product of the Middle Ages. In any novel, setting may have a decisive influence on character.

The influence of the characters on each other. The influence of one character on another is also true to life. People cannot live in communities or families without exercising an influence on each other's lives; neither can characters in a story exist independently. In *Silas Marner* the influence of character on character is clear. If Squire Cass had been a different sort of man, his sons would have turned out differently; if they had turned out differently, the whole life of Silas Marner would have been different; yet Squire Cass probably never gave Silas a thought. If Molly Farren had been different, Godfrey need never have concealed his marriage and Eppie would never have come to Silas. If Nancy had been different, Godfrey could have adopted Eppie, thereby altering the development of Silas. An example of the less tangible influences of human relationships is found in *The Rise of Silas Lapham.* Mrs. Corey cannot call on Mrs. Lapham without exercising on her a subtle influence that leads to matters of importance to both families. The unexplainable antagonism that Penelope arouses in the Corey ladies goes far toward making all their lives unpleasant and her marriage with Tom doubly difficult. This influence of character on character exists in fiction because it exists in life.

Summary. Setting is the background of the story in time and place. *Scenic setting* merely provides a pictorial background. *Local color* setting stresses the particular characteristics of special places. *Essential setting* plays an important part in the development of plot or character.

Setting may be revealed by description, dialogue, or the introduction of local characters and customs; or it may be symbolic of the meaning of the story; or it may contribute to atmosphere.

Setting, plot, and characters usually react upon one another to make the pattern of the story.

COMPREHENSION QUESTIONS

1. *Vocabulary:* setting, scenic setting, local color, essential setting, symbolic setting, atmospheric setting.

2. *Allusions:*

   Typhoon
   Lorna Doone
   The Little Minister
   Vanity Fair
   The Talisman
   Henry Esmond
   The Nigger of the Narcissus
   The House of the Seven Gables
   Sentimental Tommy
   Kenilworth
   A Tale of Two Cities
   Bob, Son of Battle
   Death Comes for the Archbishop

3. Define the term setting and illustrate it by *A Tale of Two Cities.*
4. Use a popular novel by Joseph C. Lincoln, James Oliver Curwood, or Zane Grey as an illustration of the meaning of the term *local color.*
5. How can setting help an author to create atmosphere for certain scenes in his novel? Give an example.
6. What are the chief means by which setting is emphasized?
7. Find and bring to class:
   (*a*) a good example of description to help the reader visualize the scene of the story, (*b*) a good example of description to create atmosphere, (*c*) a good example of description to give historical background, (*d*) a good example of description that is overworked.
8. Explain what is meant by symbolism in the use of setting, using *The House of the Seven Gables* as an example.

PROBLEMS IN APPRECIATION

1. In any novel look for:
   (*a*) good description for scenic background, (*b*) good description for atmosphere, (*c*) appropriate or necessary use of weather conditions.
2. What specific facts about setting are necessary to:

   Alice Adams
   The Bridge of San Luis Rey
   The Call of the Wild
   Captains Courageous
   Ethan Frome
   Green Mansions
   The House of the Seven Gables
   Kim
   The Last Days of Pompeii
   The Marble Faun
   The Mayor of Casterbridge
   Nostromo
   One More Spring
   Robinson Crusoe
   Silas Marner
   Sussex Gorse
   The Turmoil
   Typhoon
   Victory

3 In any novel in which setting affects the characters analyze as carefully as you can this effect, pointing out in detail just which of their actions and reactions are conditioned by time and place. Examples:

Almayer's Folly
The Call of the Wild
Giants in the Earth
The Good Earth
Laughing Boy
Maria Chapdelaine
The Nigger of the Narcissus
The Patrician
The Return of the Native
The Shadow Line
Shadows on the Rock
The Time of Man
Typhoon

4. In any novel in which setting is important answer these questions: (*a*) What are the chief ways by which setting is emphasized? Give examples. (*b*) Is the setting of any of the scenes especially appropriate? (*c*) Are there examples of descriptions used to create atmosphere, to increase suspense, or to reflect the mood of the story through harmony or contrast? (*d*) Has the book a distinctive atmosphere? If so, how is it secured? In which scenes is it strongest? (*e*) Is the book in any way a study of environment?

QUESTIONS ON BOOKS YOU HAVE READ

1. In one of the following novels, point out some events which take place in strikingly appropriate settings:

Guy Mannering
Jane Eyre
Kidnapped
The Last Days of Pompeii
The Return of the Native
The Scarlet Letter
Tom Sawyer
Wuthering Heights

2. Comment on the useful purpose of weather in one of the following:

Bob, Son of Battle
David Copperfield
Far from the Madding Crowd
The House of the Seven Gables
Kidnapped
The Master of Ballantrae
The Mayor of Casterbridge
The Return of the Native
The Shadow Line
Silas Marner
Typhoon
"Youth"

3. In the following pick out good description that helps the reader to visualize the scene and at the same time creates an appropriate atmosphere or mood:

Green Mansions
Indian Summer of a Forsyte
Lord Jim
Moby Dick
The Nigger of the Narcissus
The Ordeal of Richard Feverel
The Return of the Native
The Shadow Line
Shadows on the Rock
A Tale of Two Cities
The Three Mulla-Mulgars
Typhoon
"Youth"

CHAPTER 16

ANALYZING THE THEME AND STYLE OF THE STORY

THEME IN FICTION

Theme defined. Probably when you first began to read stories, you were interested chiefly in characters and what happened to them. You had never suspected that the best books are not just stories, that they have something to say, an underlying idea which we call a *theme*. Even in novels you read at school, you can see that the author is often concerned with his theme. *Silas Marner* shows that human beings need contacts with other human beings if they are not to shrivel up within themselves. It shows, too, that one's acts involve consequences and responsibilities that one cannot escape, that once a man's life takes the wrong course, it is hard to set it right again. *The House of the Seven Gables* shows the influence of the past upon the present, the slow but inevitable working out of a moral law. *Nicholas Nickleby* is a powerful attack on the brutal treatment of little children in many of the schools of Dickens' day. *Oliver Twist* reveals the sin and misery of the poor of London and the evil consequences of such sin and misery to society. *Vanity Fair* is a satire on the hypocrisy and shallowness of the fashionable society of its day.

Authors preoccupied with a theme. Some authors are so obsessed with one idea that it may be found in almost all their work. The search for spiritual peace, the constant desire to get at the meaning of life is invariably part of the novels of Tolstoy. Thomas Hardy could never escape the feeling that man is the helpless victim of forces over which he has no control. Again and again his compassion for those who are frustrated, cheated, or destroyed in the struggle for existence moves him to make such people his protagonists. In books like *Tess of the D'Urbervilles*, *The Return of the Native*, and *The Mayor of Casterbridge* hardly anybody has a chance; an unkind Fate has stacked most of the cards against human happiness. Hawthorne is preoccupied with the problem of sin and its effect on human life. Always in his books, there is a consciousness of a vague but persistently interwoven thread of evil in man's destiny.

How plot and characters illustrate theme. If a book has a theme, it is important for the reader to see how it is illustrated by plot and characters. In *The House of the Seven Gables*, the greed and unscrupulous power of Colonel Pyncheon lead him to commit a great wrong against Matthew Maule, who dies with a curse upon his lips for the whole race of Pyncheons. The story shows the working out of that curse from generation to generation until it is finally expiated by the Judge, a type figure of inherited evil stalking through the story, and by the union of the Maules and the Pyncheons through the marriage of Phœbe and Holgrave. Because of that same sin, which is really the remorseless greed of some strong man in each generation, lovely Alice Pyncheon is delivered to the hands of her tormentor; Clifford, born for a life of luxury and beauty, is confined for thirty years within gray prison walls; and gaunt old Hepzibah's life slowly decays. It is worth the student's while to study any story with an unmistakable theme to discover how plot, characters, and even setting help to illustrate the underlying idea.

Propaganda novels. Sometimes a theme is so explicit that the novel becomes outright propaganda. *Uncle Tom's Cabin*, for instance, is really a novelized tract against slavery. *Ramona* seeks to enlist sympathy for the plight of the Indians in California. Upton Sinclair's novels like *The Jungle* and *Boston* are invariably propaganda first, story afterward. H. G. Wells and Sir Philip Gibbs, English novelists, often use their craft more as a means of discussing problems than of presenting human beings. Of course a novelist may use his art to say something that he really thinks needs to be said; perhaps, indeed, he cannot help doing so. But the reader must remember that a book that is obviously propaganda, or obviously a mere means of discussing a problem, must necessarily suffer in characterization. Characters like Uncle Tom, Simon Legree, Little Eva, Ramona, and Alessandro are bound to be representative types rather than fully rounded human beings. In general a writer has to be a very great artist indeed—a Hawthorne, a Tolstoy, or a Turgenev—if he can be preoccupied with proving something and at the same time show human life justly and compassionately.

In any event, the best novels have more to tell than a story, and it is part of the reader's business to discover what it is.

STYLE IN PROSE FICTION

What style is. Style, of course, is an artist's characteristic manner of expressing himself. All artists from actresses to poets develop certain traits by which they are easily recognized. In literature we learn early that Macaulay is clear and concrete and obvious, that Ruskin is eloquent, but sometimes incoherent and scolding, that Hawthorne occasionally lets his fancy run away with him, that Dickens has a genius for caricature, that Jane Austen carefully avoids big emotions, that Chesterton is a bit too aggressively paradoxical, and Mencken a bit too savagely cynical. Part of the pleasure in reading comes from our growing power to discriminate between styles. In fact, our ability to understand books at all is partly dependent on our ability to see how style affects what the author has to say.

Three obvious facts show that style has a decisive influence on an author's subject matter: first, it is conditioned by the time and place in which the author lived; second, by his racial inheritance; third, by his individual personality and character.

Style is affected by time. Each age of literature has its own habits of thoughts and expression. The Elizabethans loved extravagant figures of speech, hyperbole, violent contrasts, intricate plays on words, good mouth-filling curses, denunciations, and other outbursts of feeling. The modern reader, on the contrary, finds it fatiguing and annoying to have to search for real meanings in a mass of rhetoric. The reader of fiction, too, soon has to face the fact that a difference in time-spirit may shut him off from the enjoyment of much that really ought to be timeless. When he reads eighteenth-century novels, for example, he adjusts himself to the eighteenth-century style. Even *The Vicar of Wakefield* demands historical perspective from the reader, lest he fail to distinguish the chaff from the wheat of that simple and charming picture of home life. So, too, a little later in the history of the novel, the reader must overlook a little priggishness and stiffness in books like *Sense and Sensibility* or *Mansfield Park* as a part of Jane Austen's upper middle-class gentility and prejudices; for if he allows himself to be irritated by these things, he will miss some of the most hard-headed, sensible, and incisively comic realism in literature. Nor should he forget that people in *Pickwick Papers* lived at a time when eating and drinking and convivial merriment took a somewhat more whole-hearted, and perhaps more wholesome, form than they do today. If he reads Hawthorne without realizing that in Hawthorne's day literary style was much more prone to fanciful language than it is today, he may miss some of the real beauty in his books.

Style is affected by race. In the second place an author's style is often inextricably bound up with his race. In Galsworthy's *The White Monkey*, Wilfrid Desert stops Michael Mont on the stairs and says with truly English bluntness, "You've got to know. I'm in love with Fleur. . . . I'm desperate, and I'll take her from you if I can," and Michael replies, "Well, as this is not a Dostoievsky novel, I suppose there's no more to be said." Thereupon Wilfrid apologizes "for being so primitive" and continues on downstairs. Here one can see at a glance the effect of nationality and of contemporary manners on the story. In a Dostoievsky novel, as Michael says, people would scarcely be so reticent. There one would expect orgies of self-analysis, self-abasement, self-expression to the *n*th degree. But our friends the Forsytes would much rather be thought unfeeling than extravagant. This same style of deprecatory sentiment and reticent idealism can be found in most English characters. Now the effect of nationality is just as apparent in American literature as in English. To realize this one has only to read Mark Twain's *A Connecticut Yankee in King Arthur's Court* or his *Innocents Abroad*. Not everything in these books is creditable to American taste (especially his treatment of the Grail legend), but one could no more mistake their American flavor than one could confuse the personalities of Maurice Chevalier and Will Rogers. For a still more striking example of racial strain in literary style, consider Joseph Conrad, the Pole who adopted English as his artistic medium. The Slavic melancholy is apparent in everything he writes, in his very choice of words such as *brooding*, *inscrutable*, *unfathomable*, *immensities*, *vastness*, *loneliness*, *mysterious*, *magnificent*, and so on. That famous description of the burning ship in "Youth" has all the melancholy mystery and magnificence and nostalgia of the Slavic temperament. Its very rhythms are un-English.

Style is affected by personality. An author's style is partly derived from his personality. Once you know an author's work well, you have really come to know the man himself; for, as has been often said, "the style is the man." If you have read a few of George Eliot's books, you know that she was profoundly interested in moral questions, that she liked to preach, that she lacked lightness and tact, that she was fond of children, that she had known religious doubt, that she understood and liked country people and country things, that she had more humor than wit, that she had studied philosophy. One reading of *Pride and Prejudice*, and you know that Jane Austen disliked sham, empty-headedness, meanness, subservience, and over-weening conceit. You know that she could see through people's social veneer, that she was not given to flattery, that she chiefly observed men as they act in the company of women, that she admired common sense and self-control, that she was conventional in her ideas, that she had both wit and humor, that she was not accustomed to giving free rein to her emotions, and that she preferred not to think of the sin and shame and misery of this world. In a similar way, the Brontë sisters emptied all the vials of their pent-up inner natures into *Jane Eyre*, *Villette*, and *Wuthering Heights*. Willa Cather's own inward poise and nobility of spirit as well as her outward experiences with men and Nature and ideas are reflected in *The Professor's House*, *Death Comes for the Archbishop*, and *Shadows on the Rock*. The complacent, disillusioned wisdom and compassionate malice of Anatole France make his books a delight or an irritation to the reader, according to his own nature. An author has to "be himself" if he is to write honestly; a reader must therefore take his view of life for what it is worth as a personal reaction.

Specific qualities to notice in style. There are, of course, specific qualities of style to be noticed in any author. Even when you began reading *Kidnapped*, *Treasure Island*, and *The Black Arrow*, you must have sensed that Stevenson was a writer who sought constantly to make his impressions sharp and vivid, that there are no vague or conventional generalities in his style. Time and again you can find him, even in *The Black Arrow* or *Prince Otto*, using just the right verb or adjective or figure of speech to make his meaning *real;* and in his best work—the storm in *The Merry Men*, the first few pages of *Markheim*, the preliminary description in *A Lodging for the Night*, the duel in *The Master of Ballantrae*, for instance—he is an artist in words with few rivals for vividness. Then as you read on, you perhaps came upon Dickens' *Pickwick Papers*, and grew to like the good fellowship of the Christmas Party at Dingley Dell, the shrewd drolleries of Sam Weller and his father, whether they discussed a "walentine" or enjoyed the discomfiture of the Reverend Mr. Stiggins at the Ebenezer Temperance Society. Like Mr. Wardle, you threw back your head and "laughed till the glasses on the sideboard rang." You had learned to relish the humor and conviviality of the man who could write, "In came Mrs. Fezziwig, one vast substantial smile." In other words, you had been captured by the Dickens' style. Later still you perhaps read *The House of the Seven Gables*, richly embroidered with poetic designs, from the fanciful hyperboles in which poor Hepzibah's gusty sighs almost blew Uncle Venner away like a dry leaf to the old-fashioned beauty of those summer afternoons in the Pyncheon garden flooded by the "yellow richness of the declining sunshine." Gradually perhaps, you came to let the charm of Hawthorne's imagery make up for some of the disappointments in his telling of the story. As you enrich your literary background, you will derive pleasure from appreciation of the qualities that distinguish one author from another. You will learn to notice how the author makes his work real by the use of sensory impressions of sound, odor, taste, touch, and color; how he gains beauty or eloquence or suggestiveness by his choice of figures of speech; how he searches for the exact word to express his meaning; how his imagination or humor or pathos or power to create atmosphere make him superior or inferior to others of his calling. The study of styles is frequently the chief means of distinguishing between the good and the mediocre in literature.

Summary. The *theme* of a story is its underlying idea. It is affected by the author's own personality and ideas. It is usually illustrated by both story and characters. Sometimes it becomes propaganda, in which case story and characters usually seem created just to make a point.

Style is the author's way of expressing himself. It is conditioned by the time in which the author lived, by his racial inheritance, and by his personality. Style shows the author's power to use language so as to make his story real to us.

COMPREHENSION QUESTIONS

1. *Vocabulary:* theme, propaganda, style, time element in style, racial element in style, sensory impressions, personal element in style.
2. *Allusions:*

Oliver Twist	*The Return of the Native*	Willa Cather
Vanity Fair	H. G. Wells	Hawthorne
Uncle Tom's Cabin	Uncle Tom	Galsworthy
Ramona	Alessandro	Mark Twain
Upton Sinclair	Elizabethans	*The Vicar of Wakefield*
Simon Legree	Dostoievsky	*Pickwick Papers*
Little Eva	Conrad	*The White Monkey*
Nicholas Nickleby	Jane Austen	Stevenson
Tess of the D'Urbervilles	George Eliot	Anatole France
The Mayor of Casterbridge		

3. Explain and illustrate what we mean by the theme of a book. You might use a short story like "The Prodigal Son" or one of Aesop's fables to illustrate your meaning.
4. Why is it that an author's interest in his theme sometimes leads him to make his characters mere mouthpieces or symbols for the expression of his ideas?
5. Why is a novel that is mainly propaganda usually not a very true picture of human life in general?
6. Define the term style.
7. Show by examples how style is characteristic of musicians, painters, actors, and athletes, just as definitely as it is of novelists.
8. What do we mean by saying that a difference in time spirit sometimes prevents us from fully enjoying books written before our own day? Can you illustrate this by showing how we sometimes fail to appreciate Elizabethan humor?
9. How does an author's nationality sometimes affect the way in which he writes? What national traits of Englishmen, Americans, Irishmen, Frenchmen, or Russians might you expect to find in their novels? Illustrate by reference to stories you have read.
10. Mention two authors you have read whose personality seems strongly impressed on their work. What passages in their books particularly illustrate this influence? Show how both author's style and the subject matter reveal the author's personality.

PROBLEMS IN APPRECIATION

1. See Exercise 4 at the end of Chapter 11 on "Why Read Fiction"? (page 183.)

2. The theme of a story may be found in:
   (*a*) social institutions or conventions, (*b*) human relationships, (*c*) character, (*d*) environment, (*e*) ethical laws, (*f*) fate, (*g*) the author's conception of the purpose and meaning of life.

   The following books illustrate one or more of these types of themes. How many can you identify with their proper type as listed above? Explain in each case how the theme of one of these novels grows out of one or more of the factors listed above.

   Alice Adams
   The American
   The Bridge of San Luis Rey
   Chance
   Dr. Jekyll and Mr. Hyde
   Ethan Frome
   The Fountain
   Fraternity
   Lord Jim
   The Patrician
   The Red Badge of Courage
   The Return of the Native
   Romola
   The Scarlet Letter
   The Shadow Line
   Silas Marner
   Victory

3. Show how the ultimate value of human love makes the theme of *The Bridge of San Luis Rey*. In what respect are the experiences of the Marquesa, Estéban, Uncle Pio, and Pepita alike? What sentences at the end of the book best point out the meaning of the story?

4. Analyze the style of any book you have recently read with special attention to the following headings:
   (*a*) proportion of narration and description, (*b*) special qualities of description, (*c*) use of sensory images, (*d*) use of figures of speech, (*e*) use of dialogue, (*f*) wit or humor, (*g*) imagination, (*h*) power to stir your feelings, (*i*) narrative sweep, (*j*) intellectual qualities, (*k*) realism, (*l*) fancy.

5. Try to form the habit of noticing how an author makes his writing *real* by the use of *definite sensory images*, that is, definite appeals to the senses—touch, taste, sight, hearing, and smell. Make collections of images of color, shape, outline, mass (sight); of sounds (hearing); of tastes, of actual impressions, of odors. You will be surprised at the number and variety of sensory nuances to be found in writing. For instance try one of the following:

Balzac	*Père Goriot*
Conrad	"Youth," *Typhoon*, *The Nigger of the Narcissus*
De la Mare	*The Return*, *Memoirs of a Midget*, *On the Edge*
Dickens	"A Christmas Carol"
Dorothy Canfield Fisher	*The Brimming Cup*
Neil M. Gunn	*Morning Tide*
Helen Keller	*Story of My Life*
Kipling	*Kim*
Katherine Mansfield	"Prelude," "At the Bay"
Masefield	*Sard Harker*, *The Bird of Dawning*
C. E. Montague	"Action"
Nordhoff and Hall	*Mutiny on the Bounty*, *Men against the Sea*
Priestley	*The Good Companions*
Elizabeth M. Roberts	*The Time of Man*
Stevenson	*Kidnapped*, "A Lodging for the Night," "The Merry Men," "The Sire de Malétroit's Door"

6. Pick out typically Elizabethan passages from *Romeo and Juliet*, *Twelfth Night*, *As You Like It*, *Henry IV*, Part I, or *Much Ado about Nothing*.

7. For a study of the effect of nationality and personality on style, consider the novels of Tolstoy, Turgenev, or Dostoievsky:
   (*a*) *Anna Karenina* or *Resurrection* as a personal revelation of Tolstoy's ideas on religion, art, politics, agriculture, the Russian peasant, morality, social and family life, labor, the purpose and meaning of life. (*b*) *Fathers and Sons*, *Smoke*, or *Virgin Soil* as examples of Turgenev's interest in the change from the old Russia to the new, as well as of his lack of complete sympathy with either. (*c*) *Crime and Punishment*, *The Idiot*, or *The Brothers Karamazov* as examples of Russian psychology in: the passion of the characters for self-abasement, their weakness of will, their capacity for suffering and self-sacrifice, their childlike simplicity, their violent passions coupled with sudden outbursts of tenderness and compassion for one another, their fondness for talk, their lack of humor in the Anglo-Saxon sense, their ability to keep faith even in the midst of moral chaos, their capacity for Christian humility and mysticism, their fatalism, their lack of self-control, their fondness for intellectual disputation, their sincerity.

QUESTIONS ON BOOKS YOU HAVE READ

1. State the theme of *The House of the Seven Gables* and show how the story illustrates it.

2. Show how *Silas Marner* emphasizes the following ideas:
   (*a*) the interrelationship in the lives of human beings, (*b*) the problem of injustice and evil in the world, (*c*) the futility of any attempt to evade moral responsibility, (*d*) the necessity of human contacts for human beings.

3. Try to find short stories with themes which come under the headings in Problem 2 above, for example:

Ambrose Bierce	"The Damned Thing"
Willa Cather	"Paul's Case"
Chekhov	"The Bet," "The Darling," "Vanka"
Kenneth Grahame	"The Roman Road,"
Hawthorne	"The Ambitious Guest," "The Birthmark," "Ethan Brand," "Dr. Heidegger's Experiment," "The Minister's Black Veil," "Rappaccini's Daughter"
Katherine Mansfield	"The Garden Party," "Bliss," "Life of Ma Parker"
Poe	"The Black Cat," "The Fall of the House of Usher," "Ligeia," "The Masque of the Red Death"
John Russell	"The Price of the Head"
Tolstoy	"The Death of Ivan Ilytch," "Master and Man"

4. Analyze Stevenson's descriptions. What is his descriptive method? For what purposes does he use description? Find examples of his fondness for specific words—to convey exactly sounds, colors, scents, facial expressions, gestures, feelings, atmosphere, touch.

5. Find examples in *Kidnapped* of Stevenson's power to portray weariness and all sorts of physical discomfort and suffering.

6. In *The Marble Faun* or *The Scarlet Letter* notice Hawthorne's fondness for repeating phrases and for piling up emphasis on certain details in order to suggest the underlying significance of what is happening. Compare his method in this with the use of "leit-motifs" in an opera. What significant details about (*a*) setting, (*b*) facial expressions, (*c*) personal peculiarities of the characters, (*d*) the symbolic use of certain tangible

objects, (*e*) the tone of voice, (*f*) gait, (*g*) gesture are given special emphasis and repeated until the reader realizes that they have an underlying significance?

7 It has been said that Hawthorne put more of himself into *The House of the Seven Gables* than into any of his other books.
(*a*) What sort of man should you imagine Hawthorne to have been? (*b*) Are there traces of Puritan ancestry, or of New England ways of thought? (*c*) How does the book indicate a preoccupation with moral questions, especially that of sin and its consequences? (*d*) What indication is there that the author was a close and loving but retiring observer of life? (*e*) What shows him to have been somewhat out of touch with the actual world of fact? (*f*) Are there indications that he was of a sensitive, imaginative nature? That he was a lover of the beautiful? (*g*) Characterize him as you think he is revealed by his work.

8. Discuss George Eliot's point of view and personality as revealed in *Adam Bede*. Find examples of:
(*a*) her sympathy with human weakness and inconsistency, combined with her stern and clear-sighted recognition of moral responsibility, (*b*) her interest in man's inward life, (*c*) her interest in people of simple birth and humble surroundings, (*d*) her fondness for children and her understanding of them, (*e*) her humor, (*f*) her interest in moral difficulties.

9. Write an essay on the style of *The House of the Seven Gables*.
(*a*) Find examples of Hawthorne's fondness for figures of speech. (*b*) Which figures predominate? (*c*) Does he use words of poetic suggestion? (*d*) Make a list of phrases or sentences which seem to you chosen with imaginative insight. (*e*) Find examples of symbolism. (*f*) Point out details in his descriptions that prove him to have been a close observer. (*g*) Find examples of his fondness for moralizing, of his ever-present sense of the moral significance of things. (*h*) Find examples of irony. (*i*) Characterize his humor. (*j*) Is his humor ever combined with pathos?

10. Write an essay on the use of the mysterious and the supernatural in Walter De la Mare.

11. It would be interesting, possibly, to try your own skill at story telling. Suppose you begin with the following steps. Write each incident suggested here as a separate composition as practice in a technical problem. Then perhaps you can write a short story that will involve all, or some, of these elements:

(*a*) *Write an incident, anything that might have happened, using sensory impressions* (touch, color, outline, taste, odor, sound); for instance, an incident in a basketball game, a swim, working in the fields, skiing, a dance. (*b*) *Write a description with a mood.* Try to use sensory impressions to create atmosphere. Include an incident if you wish, but not necessarily; for instance, a hot afternoon in a schoolroom, a girl's first ball, a funeral, in a church, a small boy sitting on the steps in the twilight, a dusty road, a theater, a subway vignette. (*c*) *Write a description of a place that will suggest the character of a person.* Accumulate details. Stress salient features. Suggest but do not mention the character of the person you are describing through his environment. Try symbolism; for instance, a boy's room, a kitchen, a hut, a living room, a farm, an apartment. (*d*) *Write an incident to show a character.* Do not use conversation but try to make the character's appearance (not forgetting details like gait, gesture, tone of voice, facial expression) and actions show what he is like. The incident may or may not be important to the character; for instance, a boy in a study room, a teacher in action, a woman in the subway or at a theater, a man in the park, anyone who has just heard something important to him, a woman on a bus. (*e*) *Write an incident to show characters, employing description and conversation.* Try to get the actual flavor of the talk; listen to people to catch the rhythm of their speech before you begin to write. Use description in brief phrases or sentences to indicate character, to fill in background, to give atmosphere; for instance, a bridge game, in a locker room, overheard on the elevator, in a hayfield, a domestic tragedy, humiliation in a schoolroom, grief, a quarrel, a high-school girl talks to a boy and to another girl, two boys discuss a personal or a practical problem, disillusionment. (*f*) *Suggest a character by showing indirectly his effect on others.* He need not even appear; for instance, a teacher, an athlete on a school team, a visiting relative, an egotist, a magnetic preacher, an actress. (*g*) *Write an incident employing all the elements* suggested in (*e*) but bring out a *theme* or underlying motif, instead of a character. Show setting, character, atmosphere if you like; but make sure that your main purpose is to bring out an idea. Be sure to suggest the idea without directly stating it. (*h*) Combining some or all of the techniques you have been practicing above, write a short narrative about some ordinary human beings who are having a common human experience, for instance, anxiety, grief, disillusionment, hope, gayety, enjoyment of outdoor life, a party, love, gratitude, surprise, pity for others, sensitiveness to beauty, music, physical action.

CHAPTER 17

TESTING THE TRUTH OF A STORY

Conflicting ideas of truth in fiction. One commonly hears people say, "I like this writer; his works are so true to life," or "I don't like this kind of book; it's too impossible," or people will exclaim over the life-likeness of some books and protest against "such nonsense" as *Green Mansions* or *The Three Mulla-Mulgars*. On the other hand, other people will object to too much realism. They do not see the use, they will say, of adding to life's miseries by depressing stories like *Ethan Frome* or *Crime and Punishment*. Give them a rousing tale of excitement or adventure like *Beau Geste* or *The Prisoner of Zenda*. What is the solution? Is all this difference of opinion just a matter of taste, or are there perhaps some criteria by which we can tell what makes a book really good, not merely popular?

Outward truth. It is well to explain at the outset that as far as "truth in life" goes there are two kinds of it in story telling. First there is fidelity to facts. A book like *Main Street* will illustrate this as well as any other. If fidelity to facts is the author's highest ideal of truth, he will strive to be an uncompromising realist. He will not introduce anything into his tale that could not have happened in real life. He will not "take sides" for or against his characters; he will try to be impartial but sympathetic. He will feel it better, however, to be cold than to be sentimental. If he cannot help feeling deeply about his subject, he will be strong and brutal and bitter rather than sweet or sentimental and poetic. You see at once that a fanciful author like Hawthorne or a sentimental one like Barrie cannot by nature be a realist of the deepest dye. If you read Arnold Bennett's *The Old Wives' Tale*, you will doubtless feel that too much tedious detail has been introduced just to build up an impression of the dullness in the routine of ordinary lives. But you will have to admit their reality. In reading *The Rise of Silas Lapham* you may have felt you could well spare some of the family conversations about Tom Corey and the Lapham girls, but you could not fairly challenge their naturalness. Of course a novelist may be a realist without going into great detail; in fact, the greatest realists have often been great artists; even more, they have often showed great restraint in choosing what to include and what to omit.

Fidelity to facts not always enough. Now of course there is no possible objection to being "true to life" in the way of great realists. But such a prosaic idea of truth sometimes cripples the imagination, and, if the author be a man of limited vision, defeats its own end, for the simple reason that mere facts are not enough. Nothing is easier to quarrel about than the facts of a given case, for the same facts seen by three different people are almost inevitably seen in three different ways. People see facts as individuals and interpret them in such different ways that one person's idea of "Mother India" or Chicago, of the Mystic Isles of the South Seas, or life in White River Junction, Vermont, for instance, is quite different from another's. Strict adherence to facts, then, is true and realistic in a somewhat narrow sense; but it does not always give us the whole truth.

Inward truth. But there is also another kind of truth to life, and that is truth of the spirit. Many a romantic, even many a frankly fantastic book, shows a truer picture of life than some merely photographic studies. If life could not be thus imaginatively envisaged with truth and sympathy, much that is greatest in literature and art would have been lost to us. Probably the painter who was the greatest artist in the actual reproduction of light and color was the Spaniard Velasquez; yet Velasquez is not necessarily on that account the greatest of artists. He reproduced physical facts, the texture of a garment, the tone of sunlight and shadow in a room with marvelous perfection; but the inward meanings of life did not interest him so much. Another Spanish artist, El Greco, hardly bothered to reproduce actual facts at all. He was not interested in giving photographic studies of Toledo, of a man, or of a saint; he sought to express the soul of these things as it appeared to him. To some observers his work is unreal, fantastic; to others, it is stripped of unessential, accidental matters of actuality till nothing remains but the inner reality itself. Such an artist, and probably a greater one, was Rembrandt. In any art there are countless illustrations of this conflict between inward and outward truth.

Impossible books that are true. Any reader of Aesop's *Fables* finds there facts that are outwardly absurd and yet inwardly true. There is an absurd common sense, a topsy-turvey logic about *Alice in Wonderland* though it is a wise child indeed who sees it. There is a bitter flavor of truth on every page of that savage work of genius, *Gulliver's Travels,* though to children it is only another fairy story. Many a schoolboy has groaned at being asked to read what he considers the "kid stuff" of the *Odyssey.* But schoolboys have not the experience or the imagination to know that the *Odyssey* is infinitely greater and truer than *Silas Marner.* From the dim pages of human legend, from the lips of an unknown poet, it brings us the authentic voice of human courage, reverence, despair, hope, loyalty, devotion. In it we see Grecian hillsides in the spring; the life and stir and daily realities of a vanished civilization; the variety and richness of human nature. And through it all we feel the strong surge of human emotion: the homesick yearning of the wandering Odysseus; the courage of men who dare the gods and the sea and the storm, even the dark land of the Dead beyond the Ocean Stream; the reverence of the human spirit for that unknown, dimly realized Spirit that shapes its destiny; the fear of men huddled in despair before the fate that bears down upon them; and the sense of honor and human dignity that makes man truly only a little less than divine. Let no cheap satire or superficial prejudice persuade you that the *Odyssey* is not true.

Final tests of truth in fiction. To judge the sum total of truth in a book, then, we should ask ourselves: first, is it true to the facts? Are the events and the dialogue a faithful representation of real life? If so, well and good; but if not, let us not condemn the book too hastily.

There are different aspects of truth. Even if a book is not true in the literal sense, is it true in spirit? That is, are the motives and reactions of the characters true? Do we feel that here is a real picture of human beings, or at least of a phase of human life? If so, we can excuse slips in dialogue and over-romantic occurrences—even the sometimes essential "long arm of coincidence."

Moral truth in the story. Then we may ask: is the moral point of view true? It is not necessary, of course, for a work of art to have a moral; but we have a right to inquire whether the author's conception of human problems, especially of right and wrong, seems to us a fair interpretation. If he is not being honest in this respect, he is giving us the most insidious kind of untruth. Even if he is being honest but seems not to see clearly because of his personal perspective, we have to accept his testimony with reservations. The reader may admire Wolf Larsen of *The Sea Wolf* in many ways, but he is not obliged to swallow his philosophy that might is right, just because of its defiant virility. And in some books, we should not only disagree but violently protest at what seems to us ethically false. We should not, for instance, care to see Hester Prynne growing weaker and Arthur Dimmesdale growing stronger, because she was courageous and he cowardly in *The Scarlet Letter*, for we know that cowardice does not breed strength. We should not feel much confidence in George Eliot's moral judgments if Godfrey Cass proved to be morally better because of his years of moral cowardice in *Silas Marner*. We may be horrified at the fate of Dr. Jekyll, but we must admit the justice of what happened to Mr. Hyde. If we read *Romola*, we feel that the moral degradation of Tito Melema was inevitable. We have a right to demand that clear moral issues be presented clearly and fairly without bias or quibbling. So much agreement between morality and art must, we suppose, be allowed.

Truth in presenting problems of human life. We should also seek to know whether the problems presented in the story are such as would occur to people in real life. Do people in real life seek to evade the consequences of their acts as Godfrey Cass did? Is it fatal to one's mental and spiritual growth to lose contact with human beings as Silas Marner did? Is it true that past generations have their influence on the present as they did in *The House of the Seven Gables?* Is it likely that men of one race could be so wholly blameless and men of another race so wholly wicked as the English and the Spanish in *Westward Ho!*? Is there justification for Tom's uncompromising fidelity to his own principles in *The Mill on the Floss?* Was Silas Lapham's financial sacrifice morally obligatory or was it a piece of quixotic idealism? Do people in real life meet problems similar to these or are they the special problems of special people? Is the solution of them in each book the right solution?

Truth in author's comment. Finally, we may ask if the ideas about life which the characters express are true, and if the author's own comment is true. Is George Eliot's comment on chance in *Silas Marner* a true observation? Do you agree with Hawthorne when he says:

> Nevertheless, if we look through all the heroic fortunes of mankind we shall find this same entanglement of something mean and trivial with whatever is noblest in joy or sorrow. Life is made up of marble and mud.

Do you agree with Holgrave's views in *The House of the Seven Gables?* What do you think of Dolly Winthrop's answer to Silas' problem of faith in *Silas Marner:*

> "Eh, there's trouble in this world, and there's things we can niver make out the rights on. And all we've got to do is to trusten, Master Marner—to do the right thing as fur as we know and to trusten. For if us as knows so little can see a bit o' good and rights, we may be sure as there's a good and a right bigger nor what we can know".

What is wrong with Adam M'Adam's philosophy of life in *Bob, Son of Battle?* What criticism can you make of the Master of Ballantrae's ethics? All these are problems and ideas that must be either truly or falsely presented. To think about them is mental stimulation. A book presents ideas as well as facts, people, and places; these, too, influence its truth.

Summary. A story may attempt to give an illusion of matter-of-factness or it may disregard the facts of everyday life in order to get at some inward truth.

The truth of a story may be tested by its presentation of everyday fact, by its moral point of view, by its presentations of problems of life, or by the ideas expressed by the author or the characters.

COMPREHENSION QUESTIONS

1. *Vocabulary:* fidelity to facts, fidelity to spirit, ethical vision, problems of life, individual, universal, artistry, reality, significance, factual.
2. *Allusions:*

The Three Mulla-Mulgars	*Gulliver's Travels*
The Old Wives' Tale	*The Odyssey*
Main Street	*The Scarlet Letter*

Ethan Frome
The Sea Wolf
Westward Ho!
Rembrandt
Bob, Son of Battle
Crime and Punishment
Alice in Wonderland
The House of the Seven Gables
Beau Geste
The Prisoner of Zenda
The Mill on the Floss
Velasquez
El Greco

3. Explain in your own words the two kinds of truth in story telling, the kind that attempts to give an illusion of matter-of-factness and the kind that disregards physical facts for the sake of inward truth.
4. Explain how Aesop's fables can be at once impossible and true.
5. Show how one of the parables in the New Testament is more concerned with inward truth than with matter-of-fact details.
6. What do we mean by saying that a novel which involves moral questions should be ethically true? Illustrate how George Eliot could have falsified the ethics of *Silas Marner*.
7. Select three novels which present problems that might naturally occur to people in real life. Are these problems naturally presented and developed?
8. What is meant by "author's comment"? Point out some examples of author's comment in George Eliot, Thackeray, Meredith, Hardy, Hawthorne, Conrad, or Thornton Wilder which seem to you true or interesting and discuss each one in the light of your own experience.
9. Read Arnold Bennett's essay "Why a Classic Is a Classic." How does it help to explain some of the books mentioned in this chapter?

PROBLEMS IN APPRECIATION

1. Point out scenes in *The Three Mulla-Mulgars* or in *Green Mansions* which are impossible yet very true to the emotional experience of human beings.
2. In any novel by a realistic author point out evidences of his careful attempt to stick closely to the facts of everyday life and to avoid the fanciful.

QUESTIONS ON BOOKS YOU HAVE READ

1. Write an essay on the problems of human life as presented in *Adam Bede* or *Silas Marner*. In it you might discuss:

   (*a*) the novelist's reasons for trying to present such problems, (*b*) the specific problems of faith, (*c*) the specific problems of attempted evasion of moral responsibility, (*d*) the specific problems of the influence of human beings on one another (all these problems are presented in these stories), (*e*) the ethical significance of the novel as a presentation of these problems.

2. Discuss, with quotations, examples, and illustrations the truth of George Eliot's comments on life.

3. What universal human problems, especially moral problems, are presented in one of the following novels:

The Brothers Karamazov	*Père Goriot*
The Fountain	*The Return of the Native*
The Good Earth	*Romola*
Kristin Lavransdatter	*The Scarlet Letter*
The Patrician	*Vanity Fair*

4. Compare and contrast the distribution of rewards and punishments in a novel by Dickens, one by George Eliot, and one by Thackeray. Which seems to you most true to life? In which is the ethical vision most clear?

5. An outline for a report of five paragraphs on any novel or play:

Paragraph one, *The story:* When and where did it happen? The effect of setting upon the plot or characters? The chief events? Are they due to human nature or to artificial manipulation? Is the method of narration coherent, unified, and interesting?

Paragraph two, *The characters:* Who and what are they? What do they do? Why? Their chief traits? How are they revealed? Their motives and reactions? Are they static or kinetic? The chief events, places, or people that influence them?

Paragraph three, *The style:* The method of narration? Influence of the author's time, race, temperament, or ideas on his presentation of the story? Prevailing mood or atmosphere? Special qualities of the style, such as eloquence, pictorial power, humor, wit, imagination, reality?

Paragraph four, *The theme:* What does the story have to say about life? How does it bring out the theme? Quote interesting ideas.

Paragraph five, *Yourself:* What were your reactions? Were they due, in any degree, to what you brought or failed to bring to the book in the way of understanding, sympathy, tastes, appreciation, etc.? What, especially, could you understand? What, if anything, puzzled, annoyed, or bored you? Do you regard your reaction to the book as a commentary on yourself, or on it, or on both? Explain.

CHAPTER 18

WHY BOOKS LIVE

Why do books endure? At last, perhaps, we are in a position to answer the questions: What makes a story a classic? Why is it that *Tom Jones*, *Pride and Prejudice*, *David Copperfield*, *Henry Esmond*, *Adam Bede*, *Wuthering Heights*, and *The Scarlet Letter* have survived and seem likely to survive for generations to come? Why have other books, perhaps far more popular in their own day, been forgotten except by students of the history of the novel? And why are some critics of contemporary novels ready to wager that *The Nigger of the Narcissus*, *Growth of the Soil*, *The Forsyte Saga*, *Kristin Lavransdatter*, *Memoirs of a Midget*, *The Three Mulla-Mulgars*, and *Death Comes for the Archbishop* will survive long after some of the best sellers like *Penrod Jashber*, *Sorrel and Son*, *The Red-Headed Woman*, *The Jade of Destiny*, *American Beauty*, and *The Magnificent Obsession* have disappeared from the library shelves.

Three standards of greatness. Of course it is difficult to predict what will survive in art and what will not. It is good for the arrogant to remember that Rembrandt was unappreciated in his day, that Beethoven, Wagner, Franck, Debussy were all regarded as destined for disgrace or oblivion, that Meredith and Conrad had to wait for recognition. But it is not likely that Kathleen Norris' *Mother*, for instance, will outlive Sigrid Undset's *The Cross*. It already seems clear that the novels of H. G. Wells will be forgotten before those of Conrad or Galsworthy. Already these favored books have gained the enthusiastic support of that devoted minority which, as Arnold Bennett pointed out in *Literary Taste: How to Form It*, keeps books alive from generation to generation. It is the infectious enthusiasm of these readers who will not willingly let a good book die that leads others to read for themselves and, eventually, to agree. But what qualities have classics which make this appreciative minority seek to keep people reading them? They have at least three.

First test: artistry. The authors of classics have usually mastered the novelist's art. Of course we do not mean that they were always perfect, but they did recognize and make use of the principles of story telling, characterization, and style, even far more than this book has attempted to suggest. Great novelists know how to tell their stories so as best to serve their purposes. They can present and develop character, make the background of time and place seem real, develop the theme so that it seems related to both characters and to real life. They have had sufficient command of language to enable them to make the whole texture of their novel alive, eloquent, true, and sometimes even beautiful. Some great novels are more artistic than others, but none has been written by an ignorant, shallow, slipshod craftsman.

Second test: vitality. Really great novels have a *vital reality.* There is no such thing as an anæmic great novel, for greatness demands vitality. It is partially this vital gusto that keeps *Pickwick Papers* and *David Copperfield* alive today. The Wellers and the Micawbers simply will not die. The same life pulsates in *Tom Jones* and *Henry Esmond.* It is less vigorous but none the less vital in *Emma,* it sweeps away the theatricality and amateurishness of *Jane Eyre* and *Wuthering Heights,* sparkles in every epigram in *The Egoist,* bursts into lyric eloquence in *The Ordeal of Richard Feverel.* It is deep, still, and solemn in *The Scarlet Letter;* it is bursting with growth in *War and Peace* and *Anna Karenina.* In this last book read only the short chapters about Levin's working in the fields with the peasants and about the death of Nikolai and you will see how literature becomes alive. This vitality may not always be pleasant, but it is always unmistakable.

Third test: significance. And last of all, a great novel must have significance; that is, it must have something to say that is worth saying. This does not mean it has to have a moral—far from it. But it must penetrate deeply enough into life so that the reader emerges with a sense of having lived and felt with human beings, and thought about them. It is in this respect that fiction is most truly a commentary on life; its intellectual power is shown not so much in arguing a point as in making us feel our kinship with our fellow men, our closeness to nature, our part in the purpose of life, whatever it may be. To do this, it must make us feel that its characters are not only particular individuals but also universal types. In a sense, their experiences must be representative; yet they must be so individual as to make each character separately alive. The literary artist, Conrad says:

speaks to our capacity for delight and wonder, to the sense of mystery surrounding our lives; to our sense of pity, and beauty, and pain; to the latent feeling of fellowship with all creation . . . which binds men to each other, which binds together all humanity—the dead to the living and the living to the unborn . . . to snatch in a moment of courage, from the remorseless rush of time, a passing phase of life . . . to arrest for the space of a breath, the hands busy about the work of the earth, and compel men entranced by the sight of distant goals to glance for a moment at the surrounding vision of form and color, of sunshine and shadows; to make them pause for a look, for a sigh, for a smile—such is the aim, difficult and evanescent, and reserved only for a very few to achieve. But sometimes, by the deserving and the fortunate, even that task is accomplished. And when it is accomplished—behold!—all the truth of life is there: a moment of vision, a sigh, a smile . . . and the return to an eternal rest.[1]

Obviously such a high artistic *credo* is for only a few. Because Homer, Chaucer, Shakespeare, Balzac, Goethe, Tolstoy, Conrad himself, have achieved this aim, their works have endured. One feels that solidarity "which binds together all humanity—the dead to the living and the living to the dead" in the *Odyssey*, in *The Canterbury Tales*, in *Hamlet* and *Faust*, in *War and Peace*, *Fathers and Sons*, *The Brothers Karamazov*, *The Scarlet Letter*, "Youth," *The Nigger of the Narcissus*, *The Three Mulla-Mulgars*. The power to suggest in an individual story the common experience of all men is the *sine qua non* of a great work of art. If you will read Tolstoy's short stories, "The Death of Ivan Ilytch" and "Master and Man," you will see that something more than a mere story is being communicated: you are sharing an universal experience. Ivan Ilytch is not merely an extremely real imaginary individual facing death; he is all men in the face of the ultimate common destiny. The simple heroism and the transfiguring sense of common brotherhood that make the theme of *Master and Man* are

[1] Quoted from the *New Review*, December, 1897. It now is the preface to *The Nigger of the Narcissus*

communicated to the reader so that he shares them. Tolstoy himself felt that this power to communicate and universalize experience is the final test of the value of art. He pointed out how characteristic it is, for instance, of the stories of the Old Testament and the parables of Christ. And undeniably, it is to be found in the greatest literature. Read for yourself a few famous short stories: the Tolstoy stories just mentioned, Chekhov's "Vanka," Katherine Mansfield's "The Garden Party," or "Prelude," Stevenson's "Markheim," Turgenev's "The District Doctor," "A Living Relic," or "A Lear of the Steppes," Kenneth Grahame's "The Roman Road," Hawthorne's "The Ambitious Guest." In every story you will find something more than a made-up yarn about imaginary people; for in each is a passing phase of life snatched and revealed in a moment of courage and vision from the remorseless rush of time. For the space of a breath, if you can sense the mystery surrounding human life, its pity and beauty and pain—if, in short, you have something in your heart and something in your head—you will pause for a look, for a sigh, for a smile. For in great books you can get your truest glimpse of the spectacle of life itself.

Summary. The enthusiasm of a few lovers of good literature keeps books alive. Such people agree that if a book is to live it should have supreme *artistry*, *vitality*, and *significance.*

COMPREHENSION QUESTIONS

1. *Allusions:*

Tom Jones	*The Three Mulla-Mulgars*
The Egoist	"Master and Man"
War and Peace	Tolstoy
Anna Karenina	Chekhov
Beethoven	Katherine Mansfield
Wagner	Kenneth Grahame
Franck	Turgenev
Debussy	Balzac
H. G. Wells	Goethe
Conrad	Sigrid Undset
Homer	*The Forsyte Saga*
Chaucer	*Memoirs of a Midget*
The Ordeal of Richard Feverel	*The Nigger of the Narcissus*
"The Death of Ivan Ilytch"	*Death Comes for the Archbishop*
The Canterbury Tales	

2. What are the three tests of enduring greatness in a novel? Apply them to one great story; for instance, "The Prodigal Son."
3. What qualities must a book have if it is to be great for its artistry? Has *The Scarlet Letter* these qualities?
4. What do we mean by *vitality* in the novel? Illustrate by citing a story which you think has vital reality and one which you think lacks this quality.
5. What do we mean by saying that a book has significance? Wherein is this different from saying that it has a moral?
6. What does Conrad mean by saying that the greatest artist "speaks to the latent feeling of fellowship which binds men together"?
7. Bring to class a poem or a short story that has an incident or situation which suggests the common experience of all men.

PROBLEMS IN APPRECIATION

1. Read two or three of the books mentioned in the sections on truth and permanent values in prose fiction and see how you would rank them as to artistry, significance, and vitality. The following short stories will afford opportunity for discussion:

Ambrose Bierce	"The Damned Thing"
Algernon Blackwood	"The Willows"
Chekhov	"Vanka"
De la Mare	"The Riddle," "Seaton's Aunt"
Gorki	"One Autumn Night"
Kenneth Grahame	"The Roman Road"
Kipling	"The Man Who Would Be King," "Muhammad Din," "Namgay Doola," "Without Benefit of Clergy"
Katherine Mansfield	"Bliss," "Miss Brill," "The Garden Party," "The Life of Ma Parker," "Prelude"
Stevenson	"Markheim"
Tolstoy	"The Death of Ivan Ilytch," "God Sees the Truth but Waits," "Master and Man"
Turgenev	"A Lear of the Steppes"

2. Put into your own words the quotation from Conrad on page 260. Try to apply it to one of the great books or stories mentioned in this chapter.

3. For any novel:
   (*a*) Does the story seem to you true to life? (*b*) If so, in what respect? (*c*) Is its truth fidelity to external facts or inward ones? (*d*) Is it true to facts as you know them? (*e*) Is everything that happens possible and probable? (*f*) Is the dialogue true to life? (*g*) Are the problems such as people in real life face? (*h*) Is the solution of the problems one that would be natural in real life? (*i*) Can you find examples of author's comment that seem to you especially true? (*j*) Do you think the author's ideas of right and wrong false, mistaken, or illogical? (*k*) Does the book present any difficult moral problem?
4. Show how *The Good Earth*, though a story of China, really is made up of the stuff of all human experience. What things in it are special and local? What things in it are common to life everywhere? Be specific.
5. Choose one of the following subjects as a topic for an essay on a novel which you have read recently:
   (*a*) the intangible charm of Walter De la Mare or Robert Nathan, (*b*) a character that stirs the imagination; for instance, D'Artagnan or Heathcliff, (*c*) life as it appears to Sinclair Lewis or Willa Cather, (*d*) a study in boys (or girls, kings, Indians, pioneers, sea-captains, soldiers, pirates, animals); for instance, Tom Sawyer, (*e*) the disadvantages of being a heroine; for instance, Jane Eyre.
6. On the jacket cover of De la Mare's *The Three Mulla-Mulgars*, Alfred A. Knopf, its publisher, asserts: "Readers of a greater age, if they can pierce through the wild adventures and the strange contrasts, catch glimpses of the mysterious and romantic pattern of life itself. *The Three Mulla-Mulgars* is not symbolism, not allegory; there is no name for its form, and there are no words for its significance. But it holds vastly more than lies on the surface and with every reading yields new emotions, profounder meanings." Of course, book jacket "blurbs" are not usually to be taken literally, but in this case the publisher is giving us the sober truth. Read the book to see if you can discover what he means by this praise. It is a good example of truth to the spirit of life rather than to its facts, as explained on pages 251–253. Underneath the fantastic details of the story, what elements that are part of "the mysterious and romantic pattern of life itself" can you find? Try this same exercise with:

James Stephens	*The Crock of Gold*
Bruce Marshall	*Father Malachy's Miracle*
W. H. Hudson	*Green Mansions*
William Beckford	*The History of the Caliph Vathek*
G. K. Chesterton	*The Man Who Was Thursday*

Robert Nathan	*One More Spring*
Elinor Wylie	*The Venetian Glass Nephew, Mr. Hodge and Mr. Hazard, Orphan Angel*
Samuel Johnson	*Rasselas*
Christopher Morley	*Thunder on the Left*

7. Sometimes it is hard to put into words our reactions to what we read. At other times, we can express those easily, but we cannot illustrate them by specific references to the book. Here is a critical comment on *Pickwick Papers*. Fill in the spaces with sentences giving definite examples from the book of the critical comment in the paragraph. Devise a similar exercise for some other book you have read, for instance *The House of the Seven Gables* or the *Odyssey*.

Pickwick Papers is far from perfect. Its story is rambling and picaresque, almost without construction . Its characters are sometimes too obvious caricatures . In its incidents it shows a tendency to make too much of too little and to repeat its effects instead of inventing new ones . Its humor isn't always so funny as it's supposed to be . Its sentimental parts seem affected and strained . And the whole book seems to us dated with a point of view unmistakably early Victorian .

Yet *Pickwick Papers* may prove to be immortal. For one thing it has several characters whom the reader can never forget. Starting out as mere caricatures, they gradually develop rich individualities that bring them to life . For another thing, the book, in spite of its exaggerations and occasional tiresomeness , has great variety. Its scenes and characters very often seem so alive that the reader lives with them . Along with this vitality goes a healthy gusto, a zest for life that one enjoys as one would a spirited holiday or a wholesome laugh . This gusto is seen not only in whole scenes, such as and in certain characters, like but in the author's choice of words and turn of phrases, as . And the whole book has a human spirit about it that is ingratiating. It makes you enjoy and appreciate more fully kindliness ; good humor ; conviviality ; generosity ; absurdity ; human eccentricities ; fun ; food ; holidays ; inns .

8. Certain phrases are likely to be misused by the beginner in criticising books. These phrases are entirely proper in the right place, but are useless if misapplied. Try to find words that express exactly what you mean; do not use these phrases unless they accurately express your meaning.

dry: This is a word best avoided in the criticism of books. A book which you do not like, which you find dull, which did not hold your attention, you should not condemn with one sweeping gesture as "dry."

very: Frequently this word is used in such a careless way that it means nothing. Do not couple it with superlative expressions, such as *fascinating, wonderful, thrilling, exciting.*

interesting: This word, proper in itself, has become hackneyed. It has thus lost its force. Find in the dictionary adjectives that express accurately different degrees of interest.

true to life: Do not overuse this phrase. Be sure, when you do use it, that you use it correctly, stating clearly in what respects the book is lifelike. The discussion in Chapter 17 will help you here.

wonderful: This is a strong word. It is best reserved for things bordering on the miraculous.

clever: Look this word up in the dictionary. It had better not be used except for extraordinary ingenuity of plot construction, successful originality of method, or brilliancy of expression. Do not refer to studies of human nature, profundity of thought, beauty of expression, or depth of feeling as "clever."

realistic: This word is best used as an antonym for *romantic.* It indicates a point of view toward life, not mere fidelity to facts. See the distinction explained in Chapter 12.

weird: This word is all right if used correctly. Look it up in the dictionary to discover its true meaning. It should not be used carelessly to indicate any vague feeling of excitement, or apprehension, or suspense.

fascinating: This, like *wonderful,* is a strong word. If you are actually held spellbound by a story or a character, you may refer to it as *fascinating.* Do not, however, use the word to indicate merely strong interest.

mysterious: This word is somewhat akin to *weird.* Do not use it to indicate mere excitement, interest, or suspense. Use it when you mean the unexplained or the unexplainable.

exciting: Use this when you really mean excitement. It is not a synonym for *interesting, mysterious,* or *unusual.*

humorous: Notice the spelling. Apply this to only those things that possess humor, not those that are merely unusual, amusing, or ironical.

typical: Beware of this word. Do not use it of characters or incidents unless they are clearly representative of their kind. Most great characters in fiction are strongly individualized, not merely typical. Becky Sharp is herself not a type of the adventuress. Jane Eyre is herself not a type of the governess. Dickens' great characters are too strongly accentuated to be "typical."

add color: Avoid this phrase unless you are sure that you use it appropriately to refer to things that give warmth, brightness, or animation to a book. Becky Sharp's schemings, subterfuges, and hypocrisies do not "add color" to *Vanity Fair.*

took the part of; portrayed: These phrases are properly applicable to actors on the stage. An actor takes the part of Hamlet, for instance. These phrases should not be applied to characters in a book.

splendid: This word applies to something of glittering brilliance or magnificence. It should not be applied to the sober things of life, however noble they may be. Dobbin in *Vanity Fair*, for instance, is not a "splendid man."

ideal: This word should be reserved for things that are perfect of their kind, things that have reached a perfection fulfilling your highest aspirations.

noble: This is another strong word, to be used carefully and sparingly. Use it only when you wish to indicate genuine nobility.

at that time; in those days; in the olden times: Never use these expressions unless you are sure that it is clear to the reader exactly what time you mean by them.

in this way; of this kind; in this manner; thus; this; these: These, too, should be definite expressions. Never use them vaguely.

description: This word should be applied only to a mental picture of how things look. Never confuse it with analysis, exposition, or narration. Not everything that is not conversation is necessarily description.

romantic: This word is the antonym of *realistic;* it does not mean sentimental or lovelorn. (See pp. 185–187.)

because: This conjunction is a causal connective. It precedes a reason given for something. Do not use it unless you are giving actual causes or reasons.

imaginary: Do not confuse this word with *imaginative.* Imaginary means created by the imagination; it does not mean having the power to imagine. An imaginary character is one that exists only in the imagination, not one that is gifted with the power of creating mental images for himself.

CHAPTER 19

HOW TO STUDY THE SHORT STORY

What the short story is. The short story is a type of prose fiction differing from the novel especially in the matter of length. It is *not* merely a story that is short. Nor are all short stories brief. For instance the books of Ruth and Esther in the Bible are no longer than Henry James' "The Turn of the Screw," and Conrad's "Youth" or "The Heart of Darkness": yet these latter are short stories, and the former are what the French call "novelettes." Irving's miniature novels *Rip Van Winkle* and *The Legend of Sleepy Hollow* are not, technically considered, short stories at all; Stevenson's "Dr. Jekyll and Mr. Hyde" is. The reason for this distinction is that the short story must be constructed according to definite artistic principles which give it a unified effect not demanded of the novel or novelette.

Poe's theory of the short story. Americans commonly assert that Edgar Allan Poe invented the form of the short story. This claim is, of course, unjustifiable. The story of the Prodigal Son in the *New Testament* is, as Clayton Hamilton triumphantly pointed out in his *A Manual of the Art of Fiction*, a practically perfect short story judged by Poe's own definitions. But Poe was the first to lay down laws for the construction of short stories, and these laws have since come to be widely accepted by both critics and short story writers. His theories, outlined in 1842 in a now famous review of Hawthorne's *Twice Told Tales*, established the following principles:

(1) A short story must create one impression.
(2) Hence it must be capable of being read at one sitting.

(3) Therefore, every word of it must contribute to the effect which the author has previously determined his story shall have.
(4) This effect must be created in the initial sentence and developed throughout the story.
(5) When it has reached its culminating point, the story must end.
(6) Only such characters as are essential to this effect should be used.

If you compare these rigid laws of artistry with Irving's ideas of a story, you will see why *Rip Van Winkle* does not come under the definition.

> For my part [said Irving] I consider a story merely as the frame on which to stretch the materials; it is the play of thought, and sentiment, and language; the weaving in of the characters, lightly yet expressively delineated; the familiar and faithful exhibitions of scenes; and the half-concealed vein of humor that is often playing through the whole—these are among what I aim at, and upon which I felicitate myself in proportion as I think I succeed.

Such a leisurely method as he describes here makes *The Legend of Sleepy Hollow* charming reading, but it will not satisfy the strict demands of Poe's art.

Brander Matthews' idea of the short story. Later critics have elaborated upon Poe's dogmas, but they have not really changed them. Thus Professor Brander Matthews remarks in an essay [1] which has since been quoted in practically all books on the short story:

> A true short story is something other and something more than a mere story which is short. A true short story differs from a novel chiefly in its essential unity of impression. In a far more exact and precise use of the word, a short story has unity as a novel cannot have it. . . . A short story deals with a single character, a single event, a single emotion, or the series of emotions called forth by a single situation. . . . The short story is the single effect, complete and self-contained, while the novel is of necessity broken into a series of episodes. Thus the short story has, what the novel cannot have, the effect of "totality" as Poe called it, the unity of impression. . . . At its best it impresses the reader that it would be spoiled if it were made larger.

Bliss Perry's comments. Seventeen years later, in 1902, Professor Bliss Perry added to Professor Matthews' comments on the restric-

[1] 1885

tions and requirements of the form. He said that if the short story deals with character, the characters must "catch the eye at once," and their development "must be hastened through striking experiences." But if it deals with action, the plot must be emphasized and the characters may be merely figures in it, as in "The Lady or the Tiger" or "The Pit and the Pendulum." If it deals with setting, "both characters and action may be almost without significance." Since it is so condensed, he concludes that it may do things a novel cannot do: pose problems without answering them, state its premises without explanation, omit details, employ symbolism. Since it deals with fragments of life, it does not demand of its author sustained power of imagination, sanity, or breadth and tolerance of view. Thus, though it is more rigidly artistic than a novel it does not demand so much depth of mind and heart. Perhaps that is why great short stories have sometimes been written by young and biased men who could not "see life steadily and see it whole," but who could fashion a tale with a keen eye for effect. Perhaps, too, that is why some of the greatest novelists who have written in both forms successfully have invariably been men who have been quite as interested in their artistic methods as in their material: Hawthorne, Hardy, De la Mare, Turgenev, Stevenson.

Clayton Hamilton's definition. Perhaps there is no better definition of the short story than Clayton Hamilton's celebrated one, first printed in *The Bookman* for February, 1904, and since repeated whenever this form has been discussed:

> The aim of the short story is to promote a single narrative effect with the greatest economy of means that is consistent with the utmost emphasis.

That means, of course, that the author must find the one method that will best achieve this "single narrative effect."

Stevenson's three ways of writing a story. The single narrative effect is what Stevenson had in mind when he said

> There are, so far as I know, three ways and three ways only of writing a story. You may take a plot and fit the characters to it, or you may take a character and choose incidents to develop it, or, lastly . . . you may take a certain atmosphere and get actions and persons to realize and express it.

Apparently he intended stories of atmosphere to include stories of setting. We should be tempted to add "theme" to his list of focal points; but he doubtless felt that theme was inherent in either a plot situation or a character, as for instance, in Hawthorne's "The Birthmark," "The Ambitious Guest," and "Ethan Brand"; or Chekhov's "The Bet," "The Darling," and "Vanka"; or Poe's "Ligeia," "The Black Cat" and "The Fall of the House of Usher."

Example of Stevenson's three methods. It is easy to see how the germ of most short stories originates in one or the other of the three elements. For instance, you can at once see that Stockton's "The Lady or the Tiger" and "The Remarkable Wreck of the *Thomas Hyke*," Stevenson's "The Sire de Malétroit's Door," and Poe's "The Pit and the Pendulum," and "The Purloined Letter" are written around plot situations. On the other hand, Stevenson's "Will o' the Mill," Kipling's "William the Conqueror," and Sinclair Lewis' "Young Man Axelbrod" begin and end with character. Poe's "Ligeia," Hawthorne's "Ethan Brand," De Maupassant's "Happiness," and Conrad's "Youth" have their inception in *theme.* As for atmosphere, read Stevenson's own words about how he came to write "The Merry Men":

> I'll give you an example—"The Merry Men." There I began with a feeling of one of those islands on the west coast of Scotland and I gradually developed the story to express the sentiment with which that coast affected me.

Later he more or less defined this feeling or "atmosphere" as:

> highland huts, and peat smoke, and the brown swirling rivers, and wet clothes, and whisky, and the romance of the past, and that indescribable bite of the whole thing at a man's heart, which is—or rather lies at the bottom of—a story.

To write that story, he chose a situation, a setting, and characters which would best express it; no other situation, setting, or characters would do.

Artistry all important in the short story. It must be clear that telling a short story is largely a matter of artistry. There is only one way to tell it with the best effect; the author must find that way. There are only a few essential characters who can enact it; the author must find them and use them, and no more. There are only a limited number of incidents by which the plot may be built up; the author must use no others. Description, narration, and dialogue cannot be used haphazardly. Every paragraph of description must be used for a purpose. Dialogue must not only be natural, it must contribute, every word of it, to plot, character, or theme; otherwise it will break the pattern of the story. The author must condense his material with unusual care; he cannot use it all. He must usually confine the action to one episode in the characters' lives—the one episode which he thinks will best serve his purpose. He cannot show life and character with the wealth of detail that the novelist uses; space does not permit it.

Necessity for condensation. Accordingly the short story writer must use the technique of story telling with more careful emphasis than the novelist. His beginnings must be briefer, with explanatory matter reduced to a minimum and devices for arousing interest sharply accentuated. Thus Poe in "The Cask of Amontillado" condenses years of antecedent action into a single sentence:

> The thousand injuries of Fortunato I had borne as I best could; but when he ventured upon insult, I vowed revenge.

In "The Masque of the Red Death" Poe begins:

> The "Red Death" had long devastated the country,

and at the end of the first three paragraphs the reader is in the very heart of the story. In "A Descent into the Maelstrom" the beginning is no less emphatic:

> We had now reached the summit of the loftiest crag. For some minutes the old man seemed too exhausted to speak.

These examples are typical of the essential condensation of the whole structure of the short story, a condensation as necessary in the middle and end as in the beginning.

Emphatic ending. The ending is, indeed, more important than the beginning. It must be dramatic, with pointed emphasis. Notice the skill with which Poe tells his stories with a gradual crescendo, up to the final climax. The victim in "The Pit and the Pendulum" is barely saved when the story ends:

> The fiery walls rushed back! An outstretched arm caught my own as I fell, fainting, into the abyss. It was that of General Lasalle. The French army had entered Toledo. The Inquisition was in the hands of its enemies.

In "The Fall of the House of Usher," the narrator has scarcely escaped when:

> There was a long, tumultuous shouting sound like the voice of a thousand waters—and the deep and dank tarn at my feet closed sullenly and silently over the fragments of the "House of Usher."

Stevenson's "Markheim" works up to a masterly close when the hero, confronting the maid upon the threshold, says with something like a smile:

> You had better go for the police. I have killed your master.

That is all. The story is over.

Artistic economy essential. Between the beginning and the ending of a short story there is also inexorable economy. Inclusion and exclusion, subordination and emphasis must be carefully planned.

Once his story is started the author must be careful to keep the emphasis wholly on the single episode he wishes to develop, rigorously excluding all irrelevant material. Whatever methods he uses to develop plot, to secure suspense, and to delineate character, he must keep an unwavering singleness of purpose. All technical details relative to the handling of plot, character, and setting have to be selected with a keen eye for the effect he wishes to produce. Only the most necessary events must be included. Only essential characters can be introduced. Setting can be emphasized only as it has bearing on plot and character. Even the methods by which these things are done must be chosen because they, of all methods, best suit the author's purpose.

The short story and the novel. One cannot wonder that so few short stories have been really great. To appreciate the careful art which goes into their construction, you could not do better than to study the analysis of Poe's "Ligeia" and "The Prodigal Son" in Clayton Hamilton's *A Manual of the Art of Fiction,* pages 195–204. But to assume that it takes greater genius to write a short story than a novel is absurd. The short story is, of course, more artistic than the novel; it demands technical craftsmanship which can be learned only after arduous practice. But the point is that *it can be learned.* What is more, it can be mastered by comparatively young people. Even writers like Hawthorne, Barrie, Stevenson, and Kipling succeeded with short stories before they attempted the novel. It takes maturity and experience with life to write a great novel: Richardson was fifty-one when he wrote *Pamela;* Fielding, forty-two when he wrote *Tom Jones;* Scott, George Eliot, William De Morgan and Conrad were all past forty before they achieved success with *Waverley*, *Adam Bede*, *Joseph Vance*, and *Nostromo*. The short story is a test of the author's craftmanship; the novel of his mind, and heart, and experience.

Great short stories come from life, not from formulas. This discussion would seem to indicate that the art of short story writing is merely a matter of finding a formula for your story and mastering the technique of developing it within the limits of that formula. As a matter of fact, whole courses in short story writing are taught on this very assumption. Plot situations and their thousands of variations are presented, catalogued, and combined in all sorts of ways for the convenience of the commercial writer. Many highly successful writers have taken Poe and his followers at their word and turned out hundreds of mechanically skillful short stories merely by mastering the technique of plot construction, character development, and so on, just as if story telling were a business completely divorced from life. O. Henry repeatedly turned the trick with great success, being sentimental, ironic, amusing, exaggerated, or surprising without giving a moment's sincere thought or feeling to what he was saying. But it simply is not true that any great story is written wholly according to a trick formula. Mature people—people who have reflected on human destiny—do not rank O. Henry with the great artists of the short story. Some even dislike the trickiness in Poe, Kipling, and Stevenson. Really great literary art comes not from mastering the tricks of a trade but from feeling and thinking about life itself and being able to express those feelings and thoughts in words. Its greatness depends partly, of course, upon the author's mastery of his artistic medium, but just as much on the sincerity and sympathy of his feeling for people and Nature and on what Henry James calls the quality of his mind. A cheap, sentimental, or shallow mind must produce cheap, sentimental, or shallow work, however cleverly it may be polished off to pass for pure gold. The stories of Katherine Mansfield, for instance, may be classified according to Stevenson's formulas, but they could never have been written just as literary exercises. Like all great art they come from the impact of life itself on a fine and sensitive spirit.

So, though stories may be, and are, written daily as mere commercial enterprises, such stories do not pretend to be, and seldom are, either art or literature.

Summary. The short story is a highly specialized type of prose fiction which must be capable of being read at a single sitting, which must deal with a single situation, create a single impression, and accomplish a single purpose. Plotting, characterization, and atmosphere must be condensed and emphasized to these ends. It therefore demands of the author more craftmanship but less range of power than the novel. But the great story, like the great novel, can never be divorced from life, or come from craftsmanship alone.

COMPREHENSION QUESTIONS

1. *Vocabulary:* short story, novel, totality, novelette, unity, atmosphere.
2. Explain in your own words why a short story is not the same thing as "any story that is short."
3. What were the chief laws that Poe laid down for the construction of the short story?
4. State Clayton Hamilton's definition of the short story. Illustrate it by reference to Poe's "Ligeia" or Hawthorne's "The White Old Maid."
5. What were the three ways in which Stevenson said one might tell a story? Do you think he should have added *theme* to his list of focal points?
6. Why is it, on the whole, easier to write a short story than a novel?
7. What are some things a novelist may include in a novel that a short story would have to omit? Illustrate by imagining what might have been added to Hawthorne's "Ethan Brand" or "The Birthmark" if they had been novels.
8. Why is a great short story always something more than a perfect working out of a literary formula?

PROBLEMS IN APPRECIATION

1. Classify the following stories under the headings of plot, character, theme, or atmosphere. Explain your classification in each case. Add two other stories to each classification:

Willa Cather	"Paul's Case"
Chekhov	"The Bet," "The Darling," "Vanka"
De Maupassant	"Happiness," "The Necklace," "A Piece of String"

De la Mare	"Miss Duveen," "An Ideal Craftsman," "The Riddle," "Seaton's Aunt"
Kenneth Grahame	"The Roman Road"
Hawthorne	"Dr. Heidegger's Experiment," "The Minister's Black Veil," "The Great Stone Face"
O. Henry	"The Gift of the Magi," "A Municipal Report," "The Third Ingredient"
W. W. Jacobs	"The Monkey's Paw"
Kipling	"The Brushwood Boy," "The Man Who Was," "The Story of Muhammad Din"
Katherine Mansfield	"The Garden Party," "The Life of Ma Parker," "Prelude"
C. E. Montague	"Action"
Poe	"The Black Cat," "Ligeia," "The Murders in the Rue Morgue"
John Russell	"The Price of the Head"
Stevenson	"The Merry Men," "The Sire de Malétroit's Door," "Thrawn Janet," "Will o' the Mill"
F. J. Stimson	"Mrs. Knollys"
Tolstoy	"The Death of Ivan Ilytch," "God Sees the Truth but Waits," "Master and Man"

2. Read Clayton Hamilton's analysis of "Ligeia" and "The Prodigal Son" in his *A Manual of the Art of Fiction*, pages 195–204. Then try the same sort of analysis with one of the following stories:

De Maupassant	"The Necklace"
Hawthorne	"Ethan Brand," "The White Old Maid"
O. Henry	"The Gift of the Magi," "The Third Ingredient"
W. W. Jacobs	"The Monkey's Paw"
Kipling	"The Man Who Was"
Poe	"The Black Cat," "The Fall of the House of Usher"
John Russell	"The Price of the Head"
Stevenson	"The Sire de Malétroit's Door"

3. How do these stories begin? Is the beginning as condensed and interesting as it should be? Does it dispose of the antecedent skillfully? On what does it focus attention at the start? Consider, for instance:

Arnold Bennett	"A Letter Home"
Conrad	"The Inn of the Two Witches"
Poe	"The Cask of Amontillado," "A Descent into the Maelstrom"
John Russell	"The Price of the Head"
F. R. Stockton	"The Remarkable Wreck of the *Thomas Hyke*"

4. Comment on the ending of the following stories. Do they stop just where they should? Explain your answer.

Hawthorne	"Ethan Brand," "The White Old Maid"
W. W. Jacobs	"The Monkey's Paw"
Poe	"The Black Cat," "The Fall of the House of Usher," "Ligeia"
John Russell	"The Price of the Head"
Stevenson	"Markheim"

5. Point out descriptive passages in these stories. Explain what each contributes to plot, setting, or atmosphere.

Poe	"The Fall of the House of Usher,"
Stevenson	"A Lodging for the Night," "Markheim," "The Merry Men," "The Sire de Malétroit's Door"

6. What are the chief events in the plot of one of the following? Is each event necessary? Explain what contributes to plot, character or atmosphere.

Arthur Conan Doyle	"The Speckled Band"
Bret Harte	"The Postmistress of Laurel Run"
O. Henry	"The Third Ingredient"
Joseph Hergesheimer	"The Token"
Fanny Hurst	"Ice Water Pl——"
W. W. Jacobs	"The Monkey's Paw"
Edison Marshall	"The Elephant Remembers"
C. E. Montague	"Action"

7. Who are the characters in one of the following? Explain why each character is necessary. Are they made interesting in themselves or are they mere figureheads for the plot?

Conrad	"Heart of Darkness," "The Inn of the Two Witches"
Kenneth Grahame	"The Roman Road"
Hawthorne	"The Birthmark," "Ethan Brand," "The Snow Image"
W. W. Jacobs	"The Monkey's Paw"
Mansfield	"Bliss," "The Garden Party," "Life of Ma Parker," "Miss Brill"
Poe	"The Fall of the House of Usher," "Ligeia," "The Tell-Tale Heart"
F. J. Stimson	"Mrs. Knollys"

8. Are any of the stories mentioned above mere exercises in developing a formula? Which of them have most and which least relation to life? Which are most and which least technically skillful?

Part Three

DRAMA

NEXT to poetry, drama is the oldest form of literature. It had its beginnings far back among the ancient Greeks, whose mighty dramatists, Aeschylus, Sophocles, and Euripides, wrote plays that have survived to our own day. Since then many of the greatest geniuses of all races have written in this form. The names of Shakespeare, Moliere, Racine, Corneille, Calderon, Goethe, Hauptmann, Tolstoy,

Chekov, Galsworthy, Shaw, Ibsen, Björnson, and O'Neill are universally familiar, for players the world over have been proud to act in their plays and audiences have been eager to see them in the theater. In Part Three we shall investigate the special nature of this literary art, its necessary connection with the business of the theater, its contribution to that accumulation of human sympathies and human ideas that makes up the imperishable literature of the world. The greatest of dramatists, fortunately for us, wrote in English, and we have used his works repeatedly as illustrations of much that we have to say. For this reason, it would be well to review some, if not all of the best-known plays of Shakespeare: *The Merchant of Venice, As You Like It, Twelfth Night, A Midsummer Night's Dream, Julius Caesar, Hamlet, Macbeth,* and *Romeo and Juliet.*

CHAPTER 20

WHAT THE DRAMA IS

Aristotle's definition. Everyone knows that a play is a situation or story designed to be acted on the stage before an audience. Yet, there has been considerable disagreement between critics as to just how to define the terms "drama" and "dramatic." The Greek philosopher Aristotle was the first to lay down definitions and rules for dramatic composition which had a determining influence on succeeding playwrights. He declared in part that "tragedy is an imitation of an action that is serious, complete, and of a certain magnitude—through pity and fear effecting the proper purgation of these emotions." According to him, tragedy must be unified in time and action and must be expressed in noble, rhythmic, and harmonious language. Later critics added the unity of place and insisted that a tragedy should develop *one* situation during *one* day in *one* place. Aristotle's theories have had an effect on dramatic composition that is still seen in some of the greatest dramas in literature. Practically all critics agree that a part of the essence of drama is *action*.

Brunetière's "struggle of wills" theory. Another man whose definition of drama has caused much discussion was the nineteenth-century French critic Brunetière. According to him, the essence of drama is *a struggle of wills*. Said he, "The theater in general is nothing but a place for the development of human will attacking obstacles opposed to it by destiny, fortune, or circumstance." At first this definition seems to fit admirably. It applies to *Macbeth* and *Julius Caesar*, and equally well to modern plays like *Magda*, *Strife*, *Candida*, *The Silver Cord*, *Anna Christie*. But there are two difficulties with that theory *as a definition*. In the first place, it applies to other forms of literature. There is a struggle of wills in *Ivanhoe,* in *Vanity Fair,* in *The Scarlet Letter,* in *The Return of the Native.* There is one also in the *Idylls of the King, Dauber, Enslaved, John Brown's Body.* And in the second place, there are some plays in which there is no struggle of wills at all; for instance in *Othello,* Othello and Desdemona do not struggle against Iago. They do not even know that he is the cause of their trouble. Again, in Barrie's *Mary Rose* there is no struggle. Mary Rose is the passive victim of her fate. In *As You Like It,* once the first act is over, there is little or no conflict; Rosalind merely amuses herself for a while. Nevertheless it is true that there are opposing forces in most plays so that the very word *dramatic* has come to imply *conflict.*

William Archer's "crisis" theory. A third theory, evolved by the famous critic William Archer, whose *Playmaking* you should certainly read if you are interested in drama, states that "the essence of drama is crisis. . . . Drama may be called the art of crisis." This too seems undeniable. Most great dramas do involve crisis, for instance, *Hamlet, Othello, Lear, Cyrano de Bergerac, Hernani.* But so do most great novels. The footprints on the sand in *Robinson Crusoe* mark a crisis. The death of Molly Farren in *Silas Marner* is a crisis. Great poems, too, contain crises; the *Iliad* and the *Odyssey* are full of them. There are crises in "Sohrab and Rustum," "Lancelot and Elaine," "Evangeline," "The Lady of the Lake." Still, a good crisis, even in fiction or poetry, has something of the theater about it; it is almost always, as we say, *dramatic.*

Maeterlinck's "situation and atmosphere" theory. The Belgian dramatist, Maurice Maeterlinck, author of *The Blue Bird, Monna Vanna,* and *Pélléas and Mélisande,* says that good drama can exist without physical action, crisis, or struggle of wills. According to him, the mere picture of an old man accepting death may be more dramatic than the conflicts and crises of all the melodramas ever written. His plays, *The Blind* and *The Intruder* illustrate this theory; they contain little or no action, no struggle—only a situation and a strong emotional atmosphere. Yet even in these plays some physical action is necessary to dramatic effectiveness, and certainly each one deals with a critical moment if not with a *struggle.*

The essence of drama. *Action,* says Aristotle, is the essence of drama; *struggle,* says Brunetière; *crisis,* says William Archer; *atmosphere,* says Maeterlinck. You see there is truth in all these theories, but all are applicable to other forms of literature as well as drama. Drama does usually involve opposing forces, a *conflict*, conscious or unconscious, of wills. It does involve *action*, it does involve *crisis*, and it does involve *atmosphere*. The mark that distinguishes it from other art forms is that it is "designed to be presented on a stage before an audience." That means, of course, that the dramatist has to rely on others to help him: his stage must be set and lighted and equipped by a producer, his words must be interpreted by men and women who may illumine or misinterpret or obscure them, and his success depends in no small degree on his ability to "get his play across" to his audience.

Summary. The drama then, is a literary composition involving *conflict*, *action*, *crisis*, and *atmosphere* designed to be acted by players on a stage before an audience. Thus it depends more than any other form on coöperation between the literary artist and those who produce, act, and witness the play.

COMPREHENSION QUESTIONS

1. *Vocabulary:* drama, dramatic, crisis, conflict, atmosphere, unity.
2. Explain in your own words what is meant by the terms *drama* and *dramatic*.
3. Why are the definitions of the drama by Brunetière, William Archer, and Maeterlinck not wholly satisfactory? To what extent is each one true?
4. Name a novel and a poem you have read that seem to you to involve *conflict*, *crisis*, and *atmosphere*. What prevents each from being drama?
5. What does the term *dramatic* mean when applied to situations outside the drama? Can you illustrate it from your reading or from life?

PROBLEMS IN APPRECIATION

1. What are the *crises* in two of these plays or stories that make them dramatic?

The Admirable Crichton
Jane Eyre
Odyssey
Oliver Twist
Pride and Prejudice
Macbeth
The Merchant of Venice
The Scarlet Letter
The School for Scandal
Silas Marner
Vanity Fair

2. What are the *opposing forces* in two of these plays? Is the struggle a conscious clash of wills? Is it inward or outward? What persons are involved in the conflict? What events come from it? Is the struggle partly influenced by character? by social conditions? by chance? Does the outcome seem natural or arbitrarily imposed by the author?

Maxwell Anderson	*Mary of Scotland*
John Lloyd Balderston	*Berkeley Square*
Barrie	*The Admirable Crichton, What Every Woman Knows*
Karel M. Capek	*R.U.R.*
Owen Davis	*Ice Bound*
Martin A. Flavin	*The Criminal Code*
Galsworthy	*The Silver Box, Strife*
Sidney Coe Howard	*The Silver Cord*
Ibsen	*A Doll's House, Rosmersholm*
Maeterlinck	*Monna Vanna, Pélléas and Mélisande*
William Vaughan Moody	*The Great Divide*
O'Neill	*The Emperor Jones, The Great God Brown, The Hairy Ape*
Rostand	*Cyrano de Bergerac*
Shakespeare	*Hamlet, Macbeth, Julius Caesar, The Merchant of Venice, A Midsummer Night's Dream, The Taming of the Shrew, Twelfth Night*
Sheridan	*The School for Scandal*
Shaw	*Candida, Caesar and Cleopatra, The Devil's Disciple*

3. Show how atmosphere makes these plays more dramatic. What is the atmosphere in each case? At what points in the play is it most apparent? How is it created?

Maxwell Anderson	*Elizabeth the Queen, Mary of Scotland*
Barrie	*Dear Brutus, Mary Rose, Quality Street*
Benavente	*La Malquerida*
Alberto Casella and Walter Ferris	*Death Takes a Holiday*
Chekov	*Uncle Vanya*
Owen Davis	*Ice Bound*
James Elroy Flecker	*Hassan*
Goethe	*Faust*
Gregorio Martinez Sierra	*Cradle Song*

Maeterlinck	*The Blind, The Intruder, Pélléas and Mélisande*
Noyes	*Sherwood*
O'Neill	*The Emperor Jones, Marco Millions*
Rostand	*Cyrano de Bergerac, Chanticleer*
Shakespeare	*King Lear, Macbeth, Romeo and Juliet, The Tempest*
Synge	*Deirdre of the Sorrows, Riders to the Sea*

CHAPTER 21

WHY THE DRAMA IS DIFFICULT TO READ

Drama is meant to be acted. The drama is difficult to read, not because it is hard to understand, but because it is meant to be not read, but acted. It has been possible to buy contemporary plays in book form, but these plays are published, usually, as a result of their successful performance on the stage. Most of the authors did not originally intend them to be read. Indeed it is doubtful that the master dramatist, Shakespeare, ever seriously considered publishing his plays; it was not until after his death that an authentic collection of his plays—the famous folio of 1623—was printed. The average dramatist writes his play in the hope that it will be publicly presented on a metropolitan stage.

A play must be visualized. Since a play is written to be seen and heard, it must be read with the imagination alert to visualize the action. Most dramatists do not put in enough stage directions to make either the actions and appearance of the characters or the stage setting of their scenes very vivid to the reader. A few, it is true, have lavished loving care and genuine literary genius upon the comment that accompanies the dialogue of their plays, but these few are conspicuous exceptions. One may read Barrie's *Quality Street*, *Peter Pan*, or *What Every Woman Knows* with as much delight as one reads his novels. For instance, he describes here Amy's room in *Alice-sit-by-the-Fire:*

The pictures on the walls are mostly studies done at school, and include the well-known windmill, and the equally popular old lady by the shore. Their frames are of fir-cones, glued together, or of straws which have gone limp and droop like streaks of macaroni. There is a cosy corner; also a milking-stool, but no cow. The lampshades have had ribbons added to them, and from a distance look like ladies of the ballet. The flower pot also is in a skirt. Near the door is a large screen, such as people hide behind in the more ordinary sort of play; it will be interesting to see whether we can resist the temptation to hide someone behind it.

The reader misses sound, movement, and background of the theater. Most dramatists have not Barrie's gift for interpretative comment. A. A. Milne imitates him, to be sure, and Shaw's plays read quite as well as they act, perhaps better. O'Neill's descriptions in *The Hairy Ape* or *The Emperor Jones* are necessary, of course, but they do not make up for the mechanical devices of the stage which enable the audience to *hear* and *see* the fear-crazed visions of Jones, the cruel contempt of the world for the outcast Yank. Thus a play that, when well acted, is most gripping, loses much of its emotional appeal in the reading. If you have seen that sincere and moving play of men in war, *Journey's End*, you will realize that neither scene nor characters can possibly be communicated to a mere reader as they are to an audience through the medium of stage or cinema. To read *Elizabeth the Queen* or *Uncle Vanya* is interesting enough. To see these plays well produced and acted by intelligent directors and players is to witness living, breathing human beings so that not only the characters but their environment for the space of two hours become alive for us. Much of this reality is lost in the reading.

The reader misses the tones of the actor's voice. Not only must we visualize the play we are reading; we must actually *hear* it. Chekhov's plotless comedies of human life, *The Cherry Orchard, Uncle Vanya, The Three Sisters,* and *The Sea Gull* are full of people as human as any to be found in drama, yet if you cannot hear the tones of their voices as well as see their somewhat stuffy provincial drawing rooms, you miss part of their humanity. Perhaps you have felt *The Rivals* or *The School for Scandal* a bit tiresome and old-fashioned; but if you could have heard Mrs. Fiske's sniffing staccato contempt as she made Mrs. Malaprop declare that "All men are Bulgarians," or have seen Ethel Barrymore's glamorous visualization of Lady Teazle, you would have realized the vitality of these old comedies. And so the little quaver in the voice of Maude Adams or Helen Hayes gave Barrie's Maggie Shand just the right tone of whimsical pathos. The wistful bewilderment of Ruth Chatterton made one pity the desolate ghost of Mary Rose, the slurred indistinctness of Pauline Lord brought to one's ears the weariness and discouragement of Anna Christie. Alice Brady and Alla Nazimova by sheer pictorial sense and insinuating vocal timbre made O'Neill's Christine and Lavinia in *Mourning Becomes Electra* more believably human than they seem to some readers of the play.

Below is the concluding scene from Martinez-Sierra's *The Kingdom of God,* which Ethel Barrymore so creditably produced a few years ago. Part of its eloquence is apparent from the printed page, but one must hear the tones of the aged Sister Gracia's voice if one is to sense fully the conviction that rings through it. The scene is in an orphan asylum in Spain, an asylum impoverished and criminally administered by the corrupt officials of the town so that the orphans have scarcely enough to eat. Led by a fine-spirited boy, Felipe, they are in open revolt when the Mother Superior, Sister Gracia, faces them with these words:

SISTER GRACIA. [*With conviction*] I am not deceiving you; I am telling you the truth: God does not will the injustice of the world. He permits it—we do not know how long—but He does not will it.

FELIPE. [*Raising his head*] Then God will be pleased if we break the heads of those who do will it.

SEVERAL CHILDREN. Yes! Yes!

SISTER GRACIA. No, no, no! The only way to remedy the evil of the world is to do good to it.

FELIPE. And who is going to do that?

SISTER GRACIA. [*Passionately*] You! You! But not by hatred, by love. You! When you are men! When you go out from here! You who have suffered injustice will know what it is and will want to make just laws. Yes, my sons, yes; the world is yours. You have overcome it with hunger, with misery, with anguish. And when you have it in your hands, make it what it ought to be. God is watching you. God has hope for you. Suffer now that you may redeem your suffering later. God sees you. God hears you. Say after me: "Lord, Lord, we give Thee thanks for this soup which is given us in Thy name. There isn't much of it; it isn't good soup, but Lord, we shall never forget the bitter taste of it. And we swear by Thy holy love that we shall be the last to eat of it." Say it with me, say it, I tell you: "We promise You that if it costs us the last drop of our blood, when we are men, there shall be no more abandoned children, no more mothers who for lack of bread and justice must carry their children in agony." [*Anxiously*] It is true, my sons, is it not, that you will make these laws when you can make them? It is true that you will create on earth the Kingdom of God?

ALL. [*Fervently*] Yes, yes, yes!

SISTER GRACIA. Thank you, my sons. And now that you have eaten, sleep. Sleep in peace. [*The children go out slowly. But Felipe does not stir; he is sitting at the table with his head on his arms, sobbing desolately. As the others leave, Sister Gracia goes over to him gently, and puts a hand on his shoulder.*] Don't cry. Men don't cry. [*Significantly*] Nor shout curses. True men suffer . . . and work . . . and hope. . . . [*The curtain falls.*][1]

Just from reading this passage you can see that *The Kingdom of God* is written in a sincere and noble spirit. But the exaltation of Sister Gracia's plea is fully communicated to the reader only if he can hear and see the whole scene.

Shakespeare must be read imaginatively. If this necessity of reading the drama imaginatively is apparent in modern plays, how much more so is it with Shakespeare where one must be constantly on the alert for stage directions implied in the text if one is to hear and see the action. Shakespeare took no pains to prepare his plays for publication; they were not published under his supervision during his lifetime, as Heywood's and Jonson's were, and many of them were not printed at all until after his death. Even then, they were filled with textual errors and inconsistencies, without clear stage directions, sometimes partly the work of collaborators, sometimes without any indication of division between scenes or acts. Yet so great is his power of suggestive language that anyone with imagination alert can hear and see and feel the whole scene. Below is the famous "Knocking at the Gate Scene" from *Macbeth.* It is one of many such in Shakespeare. The printed page contains almost no directions for players or readers, but one can catch from it the dark and cold and fear, and the awful sense of standing on the threshold of unknown and inescapable terrors; one can hear the night sounds, the heavy breathing, the tense whispers; one can almost feel the beating of the two guilty hearts as the knocking at the south entry startles them to the terrible realization of their crime. One must listen, too, for the despair and horror in Macbeth's cry:

> What hands are here? Ha! They pluck out mine eyes.
> Will all great Neptune's ocean wash this blood
> Clean from my hand? No, this my hand will rather
> The multitudinous seas incarnardine,
> Making the green one red.

[1] Translated by Edwin Smith. The whole play may be read in the Granville-Barker translation published by E. P. Dutton and Co., Inc.

One must catch the stifled anxiety of Lady Macbeth's first speech, her sudden fear and bewilderment, the gathering of courage and forced scorn in her voice as she once more takes command of the situation. Read it with these things in mind, for Shakespeare must be read this way if he is to be fully appreciated.

ACT II, SCENE II

Enter LADY MACBETH

LADY M. That which hath made them drunk hath made me bold;
What hath quench'd them hath given me fire. Hark! Peace!
It was the owl that shriek'd, the fatal bellman,
Which gives the stern'st good-night. He is about it:
The doors are open; and the surfeited grooms
Do mock their charge with snores: I have drugg'd their possets,
That death and nature do contend about them,
Whether they live or die.
MACB. [*Within*] Who's there? what, ho!
LADY M. Alack! I am afraid they have awak'd,
And 'tis not done. The attempt and not the deed
Confounds us. Hark! I laid their daggers ready;
He could not miss 'em. Had he not resembled
My father as he slept, I had done 't.

Enter MACBETH

My husband!
MACB. I have done the deed. Didst thou not hear a noise?
LADY M. I heard the owl scream, and the crickets cry.
Did not you speak?
MACB. When?
LADY M. Now.
MACB. As I descended?
LADY M. Ay.
MACB. Hark!
Who lies i' the second chamber?
LADY M. Donalbain.
MACB. This is a sorry sight. [*Looking on his hands*]
LADY M. A foolish thought to say a sorry sight.
MACB. There's one did laugh in 's sleep, and one cried "Murder!"
That they did wake each other: I stood and heard them;

But they did say their prayers, and address'd them
Again to sleep.
LADY M. There are two lodg'd together.
MACB. One cried "God bless us!" and "Amen," the other,
As they had seen me with these hangman's hands.
Listening their fear, I could not say "Amen,"
When they did say "God bless us."
LADY M. Consider it not so deeply.
MACB. But wherefore could not I pronounce "Amen"?
I had most need of blessing, and "Amen"
Stuck in my throat.
LADY M. These deeds must not be thought
After these ways: so, it will make us mad.
MACB. Methought, I heard a voice cry "Sleep no more!
Macbeth does murder sleep"—the innocent sleep;
Sleep that knits up the ravell'd sleave of care,
The death of each day's life, sore labour's bath,
Balm of hurt minds, great nature's second course,
Chief nourisher in life's feast,—
LADY M. What do you mean?
MACB. Still it cried, "Sleep no more!" to all the house:
"Glamis hath murder'd sleep, and therefore Cawdor
Shall sleep no more; Macbeth shall sleep no more!"
LADY M. Who was it that thus cried? Why, worthy thane,
You do unbend your noble strength, to think
So brainsickly of things. Go, get some water,
And wash this filthy witness from your hand.
Why did you bring these daggers from the place?
They must lie there: go carry them; and smear
The sleepy grooms with blood.
MACB. I'll go no more:
I am afraid to think what I have done;
Look on 't again, I dare not.
LADY M. Infirm of purpose!
Give me the daggers: the sleeping, and the dead
Are but as pictures: 'tis the eye of childhood
That fears a painted devil. If he do bleed,
I'll gild the faces of the grooms withal,
For it must seem their guilt. [*Exit. Knocking within*]
MACB. Whence is that knocking?—
How is 't with me, when every noise appals me?
What hands are here? Ha! they pluck out mine eyes.

Will all great Neptune's ocean wash this blood
Clean from my hand? No; this my hand will rather
The multitudinous seas incarnardine,
Making the green one red.

Re-enter Lady Macbeth

Lady M. My hands are of your colour; but I shame
To wear a heart so white. [*Knocking within*] I hear a knocking
At the south entry: retire we to our chamber.
A little water clears us of this deed:
How easy is it, then! Your constancy
Hath left you unattended. [*Knocking within*] Hark! more knocking
Get on your nightgown, lest occasion call us,
And show us to be watchers. Be not lost
So poorly in your thoughts.
Macb. To know my deed, 'twere best not know myself. [*Knocking within*]
Wake Duncan with thy knocking! I would thou couldst! [*Exeunt.*]

Reading with the imagination alert. *Julius Caesar* is full of such instances of stage directions implied in the text. "I hear a tongue," shudders Caesar, "shriller than all the music," and by that little sentence the piercing cry of the Soothsayer is described for us; but when we read the play we might not notice this. The picture of Caesar's train returning from the games is given us by the wondering comment of Brutus:

But, look you, Cassius,
The angry spot doth glow on Caesar's brow,
And all the rest look like a chidden train.
Calpurnia's cheek is pale; and Cicero
Looks with such ferret and such fiery eyes
As we have seen him in the Capitol,
Being cross'd in conference by some senators.

This is an illuminating bit of comment for a stage manager, but its pictorial value might be lost on the careless reader. Antony's dramatic gesture when he tears aside the garment covering the corpse of Caesar is not described for us; we must imagine it for ourselves from his words:

Kind souls, what, weep you when you but behold
Our Caesar's vesture wounded? *Look you here,*
Here is himself, marr'd, as you see, with traitors,

and from the words of the bystanders:

> FIRST CITIZEN: O piteous spectacle!
> SECOND CITIZEN: O noble Caesar!
> THIRD CITIZEN: O woful day!

And such a scene as the madness of the mob, which is so thrilling on the stage, cannot be realized in reading except by the deliberate effort of the imagination. Later in the play, in the tent scene, Brutus, the gentle, considerate scholar, is revealed more in the lines that suggest his actions than in any other way:

> Look Lucius, here's the book I sought for so;
> I put it in the pocket of my gown.
>
> If thou dost nod, thou break'st thy instrument;
> I'll take it from thee. . . .
> Let me see, let me see; is not the leaf turn'd down
> Where I left reading?

Reading modern plays imaginatively. Now that good plays are occasionally adapted for the talking pictures, it is easy to see the difference between merely reading a play and hearing and seeing it acted. In a sense, the dialogue, especially in a modern play where the language is not particularly distinguished, is only an outline of the action. If you have seen George Arliss in the moving picture versions of Galsworthy's *Old English*, you will realize the vital contribution of the actor to any play. *Old English* is a good character study, though an indifferent play; but as interpreted by George Arliss, it becomes a living portrait in which tone, gesture, facial expression—all these things the printed page could not indicate—speak volumes. Molnar's *The Guardsman* certainly does not seem so funny to read as it seems when acted by Alfred Lunt and Lynn Fontanne. Barrie's *The Old Lady Shows Her Medals* is rather dangerously close to sentimentality when it is read, but acted for the movies by Beryl Mercer and Gary Cooper, it takes on a good deal of poignancy and quaintness. Edward Sheldon's *Romance* seemed much less obvious and much more moving when brought to life through the personality of Greta Garbo. *The Emperor Jones*, a really fine play, loses much in the reading because the reader cannot see Jones' visions, nor can he hear the continuous, ominously beating tom-toms which so harrow the nerves in the thea ter. On the stage these things can actually be seen and heard; but if they are to be real to us as we read the play, we must constantly think of the tones and expressions and actions that go with the words. In this way the reading of a play demands constant use of the imagination.

Summary. The drama is difficult to read because it is meant to be seen and heard. Thus the reader must read it with imagination alert to conjure up the tones of the actors' voices and visualize the scenic background, costumes, action, and situation on the stage.

COMPREHENSION QUESTIONS

1. Explain with illustrations of your own three reasons why it is more difficult to read a play than a story.
2. Bring to class selections from a play by Sir James Barrie, Bernard Shaw, or Eugene O'Neill which illustrate the necessity of visualizing the scene of a play.
3. Read aloud the scenes from *The Kingdom of God* and *Macbeth* quoted in this chapter trying to indicate the tones of the speakers' voices.
4. Bring to class a good scene from Shakespeare, Sheridan, or from some modern play. Read it clearly but without expression to the class. Then read it trying to make your voice suggest the mood and meaning of each speaker. In this connection you might play to the class John Barrymore's Victor record of speeches from *King Henry VI, Part III* and *Hamlet*.
5. Bring to class pictures of some scenes from a recent Shakespearean production, for instance, the Maude Adams-Otis Skinner *The Merchant of Venice*, using them as illustrations of the necessity of visualizing the scenic background of a play.

PROBLEMS IN APPRECIATION

1. Write your own stage directions for the scene quoted from *Macbeth* in this chapter. Do not forget to indicate sounds, actors' gestures, movement, tone of voice, atmosphere as well as stage setting. Try to make your comments aids to the reader in visualizing the scene and characters, in understanding the motives, and in catching the spirit of the play.

2. Look up accounts of recent productions of Shakespearean plays, paying particular attention to new, or contrasting, or especially striking details in scenery, costuming, lighting, handling of crowds, securing of atmosphere, incidental music, etc. Productions by Sir Herbert Beerbohm-

Tree, Sir Henry Irving, Forbes-Robertson, Walter Hampden, Edward A. Sothern and Julia Marlowe, John Barrymore, Jane Cowl, Fritz Leiber, Mrs. Fiske, Eva Le Gallienne, Katharine Cornell, Otis Skinner, and others will be of interest here.

3. Study one of the following parts as if you were to be the actor or actress to play it—making notes of gestures, tone of voice, costume, make-up, stage business, effective entrances and exits, and anything else that will help to reveal your conception of the character:

Sir Andrew Aguecheek	Mercutio
Brutus	The Nurse in *Romeo and Juliet*
Cassius	Portia
Juliet	Rosalind
Mrs. Malaprop	

QUESTIONS ON PLAYS YOU HAVE READ

These exercises are on *Macbeth*, but they can easily be adapted to *Hamlet, King Lear, Othello, Julius Caesar*, and *Romeo and Juliet.*

1. Write an essay on the atmosphere of *Macbeth*, stating first what that atmosphere is, and then showing how it is created. Pay special attention to such devices as heaping-up impressions of darkness and night, of sleeplessness, of hovering evil, of blood. Underline in red the references to blood, in black those to night and darkness, in green those to sleep and sleeplessness.

2. Make a study of the lighting of the play. Make plans, directions, sketches for the arrangement of lights and shadows in the scenes listed below, for the use of colors in scenery and in costumes, for the placing of the characters in light or shadow. Try not to omit anything that would intensify the unified effect of the atmosphere and arouse the imagination of the spectator through color, light, and darkness.

(*a*) Act I, scene 1	(*g*) Act II, scene 2
(*b*) " I, " 3	(*h*) " II, " 3
(*c*) " I, " 5	(*i*) " III, " 3
(*d*) " I, " 6	(*j*) " III, " 4
(*e*) " I, " 7	(*k*) " IV, " 1
(*f*) " II, " 1	(*l*) " IV, " 2
(*m*) Act V, scene 1	

Do not forget that you can gain effects of climax, contrast, and symbolic suggestiveness by light and color as well as by other devices.

3. Make a study of the use of sound in *Macbeth.* Which scenes should you fill with clamor and excitement? When should you have quiet so deep as to give effect to slight sounds? Where should you have sudden sound crash unexpectedly to heighten dramatic effect? What sounds of Nature should you use? Where? In which passages should you rely wholly on the sound of the human voice for effect?

4. Make a study of the use of movement in *Macbeth.* Arrange the characters as you would have them on the stage in the scenes listed below. How should you arrange their crossings and recrossings, their exits and entrances, their soliloquies and asides, so far as movement alone is concerned? Upon what gestures should you lay most stress? Mark passages in the play for appropriate gestures for suiting "the action to the word," for suggested stillness or confused motion, for insane fury, for pathetic weariness, for abject terror, for rhythmic movement—all to be secured chiefly through motion.

(*a*) Act I, scene 3			(*h*) Act III, scene 4		
(*b*) " I, " 5			(*i*) " IV, " 1		
(*c*) " I, " 7			(*j*) " IV, " 2		
(*d*) " II, " 1			(*k*) " V, " 1		
(*e*) " II, " 2			(*l*) " V, " 3		
(*f*) " II, " 3			(*m*) " V, " 5		
(*g*) " III, " 2			(*n*) " V, " 8		

5. Make a study of the use of facial expression, gesture, and tone of voice in *Macbeth.* Mark certain passages for facial expressions and gestures which you think are implied in the text or which you think would be effective. Mark passages in which expression, gesture, and tone of voice are clearly indicated in the text. Investigate the history of the stage presentation of this play and see what use of these devices has been made by famous actors and actresses. Do you think that professional make-up is needed to mark the change that comes over Macbeth as the play progresses? What particular moods or traits of character should you bring out by these devices? Do you think that greater effect is made by many or few gestures? Do the parts in this play require ability to use the voice with great variety of tone and pitch? At what points do actors have to consider other parts than their own in this play in order to make contrast or similarity apparent by means of these devices?

CHAPTER 22

WHY THE DRAMA IS DIFFICULT TO WRITE

Dramatists hampered by many practical considerations. Of all the forms of literature a play is the most difficult to write well. This is not entirely because its story must be condensed into a few acts and told largely by dialogue; the difficulty is due also in no small measure to the many practical requirements which have to be satisfied before a play can be presented. A novelist or an essayist or a poet has really only himself to please; if he writes for the thrill of creating a work of art and not from commercial motives, he can write according to his conception of art; he need not bother about what other people think. But a playwright has to bother about what other people think. As we have seen, plays are written to be acted. A playwright, therefore, must convince managers of acting companies that his plays will act well. The main object of a manager is necessarily to make a play financially successful. Each manager has his own ideas of what a play should be; he may not be indifferent to the demands of art, but he may have a different artistic idea from that of the author. Accordingly, although he has accepted the play, he may ask that it be changed here and there to conform to his own standards. It is no uncommon thing for a play to be entirely rewritten after a few trial performances. A good play must satisfy the demands of the theater; and those demands usually are interpreted by a manager with experience in producing plays. Surely a play that is not suitable for theatrical performance is lacking in the first requirement of the drama. Shakespeare was himself a manager as well as a dramatist; thus he had the actual theatrical experience which made it possible for him to adapt his stories to performance on the stage.

The playwright must consider the players. The dramatist has to consider the actors and actresses who are to give life to the characters he has created. This is not a simple matter. Even after suitable players are found—sometimes a difficult task—there remains the difficulty of squaring the actor's conception of a part with the conception of the playwright. Not all playwrights are able to say of an actor what Rostand said of Coquelin, the "creator" of his Cyrano de Bergerac:

> I meant to dedicate this poem to the soul of Cyrano. But since that has slipped into you, Coquelin, it is to you that I dedicate it.

The influence of the actor. The actor, as well as the dramatist, is a creative artist and it is right that his ideas and abilities should be considered, although, of course, he should not use a part merely for the exploitation of his own personality, as movie stars too frequently do. The actor is, in the nature of things, almost as much the creator of a dramatic character as the playwright who first conceived it. A sincere and intelligent actor gives life to the dramatist's original conception, but the caprice or peculiar genius of a particular player may force him to change a part, even a whole play. Thus the famous Habañera song in *Carmen* is the result of repeated attempts by Bizet to please the prima donna who created the rôle. Shylock was played as a comic part until Charles Macklin in 1741 dared to make it tragic. People, too, used to think of Mansfield and not of Stevenson when they thought of *Dr. Jekyll and Mr. Hyde*, though now, no doubt, they think of Frederic March instead. Many parts are forever identified with great actors and actresses. The composer Debussy wondered at the marvelous way in which Mary Garden gave life to his conception of Mélisande. A whole generation of playgoers affectionately remembers Maude Adams as Peter Pan, Lady Babbie, and Maggie Shand; Ellen Terry as Portia and Imogen; Julia Marlowe as Juliet. Today we identify Anna Christie with Pauline Lord or Greta Garbo; Helena in *Uncle Vanya* with Lillian Gish; Madame Ranevsky in *The Cherry Orchard* and Christine in *Mourning Becomes Electra* with Alla Nazimova; Mrs. Malaprop with Mrs. Fiske, King Richard III with John Barrymore. And some of us get our notions of Juliet from Katharine Cornell or Eva Le Gallienne, of Portia and Shylock from Otis Skinner and Maude Adams, of Lady Teazle from Ethel Barrymore, of Mercutio from Dennis King or Fritz Leiber.

Shakespeare's plays illustrate the influence of the actor. Shakespeare probably calls Hamlet "fat and scant of breath" because the actor who first performed the part, Richard Burbage, was physically heavy. Undoubtedly some of his greatest characters were first imagined with a certain player in mind, perhaps with that player's active coöperation. It is likely that some of the scenes given to clowns and jesters and fools, especially in places where the play could very well get along without them, were written because the audience demanded a part for a popular comedian. Something of the distaste of the creative genius for this truckling to the vanity of popular favorites appears in Hamlet's famous speech to the players:

> Overstep not the modesty of nature: for anything so overdone is from the purpose of playing, whose end, both at first and now, was, and is, to hold, as 'twere, the mirror up to nature. . . . Now this overdone, or come tardy off, though it make the unskillful laugh, cannot but make the judicious grieve. . . . O, there be players that I have seen play, and heard others praise, and that highly, not to speak it profanely, that, neither having the accent of Christians nor the gait of Christian, pagan, nor man, have so strutted and bellowed that I have thought some of nature's journeymen had made men and not made them well, they imitated humanity so abominably. . . . And let those that play your clowns speak no more than is set down for them; for there be of them that will themselves laugh, to set on some quantity of barren spectators to laugh too; though in the meantime some necessary question of the play be then to be considered: that's villainous, and shows a most pitiful ambition in the fool that uses it.

This would indicate that supplying parts for a popular stock company irked Shakespeare, but the actors were there and parts had to be supplied them. And if these Launcelot Gobbos and Peters and Porters sometimes seem a bit tedious to us today, we must remember that we cannot see the droll creature who originally made them funny. Three hundred years hence Charlie Chaplin can be seen by future generations; Launcelot Gobbo we cannot see. It would be interesting to know what actor helped to suggest the creation of Falstaff, what young boy first created Portia or Viola or Rosalind, but that particular source of the greatness of Shakespeare's plays is lost to us. We can be reasonably sure, however, that these great characters owe a part of their existence to some player whose name has been long since forgotten. Since Shakespeare was himself an actor, he knew the necessity of considering the actor's as well as the dramatist's point of view.

The personality of a player as an influence on the movies. The influence of the actor may be studied with special profit in the moving pictures where the player and not the play is "the thing." It is unfortunate that an institution of such incalculable social and cultural influence as the motion picture seems to be committed to the policy of exploiting personalities instead of creating a living art. At the present writing [1] there is scarcely a popular favorite on the screen who is given an opportunity to do more than parade a much-publicized personality before the camera. Many actors and actresses of intelligence complain of this treatment, and justly so. Valentino tried in vain to escape this enslavement, but the incredible public folly at his death and funeral was eloquent testimony of the futility of his artistic ambitions. Many a popular player has objected to being rubber-stamped, stereotyped, and exhibited in stock parts. Others have held to their standards in spite of commercial allurements. True, some players have been able to use their personalities to make even the banality or silliness of their pictures seem unobjectionable, and for this the screen should thank players like Greta Garbo, Katharine Hepburn, Paul Muni, Helen Hayes, Herbert Marshall, Ramon Navarro, Lionel Barrymore, Charles Laughton, and Maurice Chevalier. But in general the screen has had a deplorable influence on public taste, and largely because it has preferred cheap and crude exhibitionism to artistic sincerity.

Literature and the screen. The lower artistic standards of the movies are especially apparent when a novel or a play is transferred to the screen. Sometimes audiences get their impressions of literature chiefly from the gross misrepresentations of the screen. Conrad's *Victory* is a case in point. Here the original elements of melodrama in the story, that is, the despicable Schomberg and the unscrupulous schemers Mr. Jones, Ricardo, and Pedro, were developed as the text suggested. But the rest of the story was mutilated without the slightest artistic scruple. Two personable but wholly inappropriate young players were engaged to play Heyst and Lena, with the result that Heyst's character, motives, and philosophy, and hence the whole meaning of the book, had to be falsified. Then a happy ending and a meretricious title were supplied, and the thing was unreeled before an unsuspecting, and probably indifferent, public as the work of that

[1] 1934.

sincere artist, Joseph Conrad. Sometimes, however, as in the case of the filming of *Little Women*, the movies do better; again, as with *Dr. Jekyll and Mr. Hyde*, they produce something which is powerful in itself but which shows little or no respect for the original text. Occasionally, as in producing plays like *Holiday*, *Street Scene*, *Berkeley Square*, *Maedchen in Uniform*, and *Cradle Song* they give a faithful representation of something worth doing. Generally, however, the exploitation of the player and the truckling to public taste have made the motion picture a doubtful blessing, to say the least. But the pity is that so much talent should go to waste, and that such a social force should be of so little benefit. With a world of great literature behind them, with a new artistic medium and a thorough knowledge of how to use it, moving pictures need only the guiding enthusiasm of a new Elizabethan age to start them on a glorious career. Doubtless there are great difficulties in the way of practical realization of an artistic ideal which depends for its success on public support, difficulties not unlike those which confronted Shakespeare and his associates three hundred years ago.

The playwright must consider the audience. No manager cares to spend time and money on a play which is not likely to meet with public favor. A play requires an audience; therefore the dramatist cannot afford to be indifferent to public opinion. This does not mean that he should consider the cheap taste of the shallow part of an audience; on the other hand, he should not ignore the legitimate arts of the theater which attract public attention. To make a play both a work of art and a theatrically effective performance requires great skill. It is not, however, an impossible task. Recent thoroughly intelligent productions of *Hamlet*, of *Romeo and Juliet*, of *The Merchant of Venice*, of *The School for Scandal*, of Drinkwater's *Abraham Lincoln*, of O'Neill's *The Emperor Jones*, *Anna Christie*, and *Ah, Wilderness!*, of Molnar's *Liliom*, of Chekhov's *Uncle Vanya*, and the prosperous existence of excellent companies in Shakespearean repertoire prove that a producer can give the best and yet be financially successful. The dramatist should be sufficiently alive to public opinion to foster the taste of that part of the public which enjoys all that is best in the theater.

Influence of the social background. Fully to understand Elizabethan plays one must understand Elizabethan social background.

In Shakespeare's day London was a small walled city of about one hundred and fifty or two hundred thousand inhabitants. It was crowded, ill-lighted, unsanitary, inadequately protected from fires, and poorly policed.[1] On the north bank of the river lived the aristocracy, but the city itself was in the hands of merchants and burghers. Outside the city at Whitehall and Westminster was the court. Inns, hotels, taverns, and theaters had to be erected outside the city walls; the theaters, on the other side of the river. But London was a hustling commercial center with traders, adventurers, soldiers, scholars, politicians, and explorers from all over the world moving through it. In its large number of transient visitors it was not unlike our New York City of today, and as in New York today its theater managers had to supply amusement for traveling visitors. There were two theatrical trusts. One was controlled by the Burbage-Shakespeare group, and one by the Henslowe-Alleyn, each owning and operating several theaters as well as going on tour in the country.

Powerful influence of the audience. Shakespeare's company played at the Globe in the summer and at the Blackfriars in the winter. The latter was suitable for indoor performances in the evening with artificial lights and catered to a less rowdy clientele than the Globe. To the Blackfriars came the aristocracy, the court, the young wits, and the university men. There, artificial lights, stage effects, and scenery could be used, and there too, this audience was brilliant, cultivated, interested in wit, ideas, poetry, and the complexities of human nature. After Queen Elizabeth died, in 1603, Shakespeare's company became the official players to the new ruler, James I; and Shakespeare had to write increasingly for this sophisticated audience. Perhaps that is why his most mature work dates from 1603 on—a period which included *Macbeth,* with its obvious flattery of the new king; *King Lear,* written deliberately beyond the limits of the conventional theater; *Othello,* an experiment in perfect plot construction; *Anthony and Cleopatra,* filled with gorgeous poetry and intellectual subtlety; and the revised and matured *Hamlet,* heavy with thought. In accounting for this flowering of genius, we must reserve some credit for one of the most brilliant audiences that has ever patronized the theater. A similar audience made possible the great Greek

[1] Dogberry and Verges in *Much Ado about Nothing* were probably justifiable satires on the stupidity of London constables.

Vandamm Studio

GEORGE ARLISS AS "SHYLOCK"

A great actor interprets with sympathy and humanity one of Shakespeare's most misunderstood characters.

Vandamm Studio

HELEN HAYES IN *MARY OF SCOTLAND*

A romantic queen lives again on the modern stage.

tragedies and the success of Molière and Racine in the France of the Grand Monarch, and of the Theater Guild and the Civic Repertory Theater in contemporary New York.

At the Globe the crowd was different. Here congregated all sorts and conditions of men: nobles and apprentices, soldiers and sailors, the burghers, visiting traders or "tourists," young blades and pick-pockets. Here the performances were in the open air, without artificial lighting, and the audience was a standing, restless, impatient mob. Here, too, action and plenty of fun and coarse melodrama were demanded, and there is evidence that Shakespeare was on the alert to give his audience what it liked.

Shakespeare and his audience. Shakespeare sometimes has whole scenes given over to processions and "dumb shows", noise and music, and exhibitions of physical skill—all things which the Elizabethans loved. *Julius Caesar* opens with a disorderly mob, probably led in the original production by a popular comedian of the Globe. In *As You Like It* there is a wrestling match at the very start, and frequent processions of foresters and rousing songs which lead Jaques to say, " 'tis no matter how it be in tune, so it make noise enough." In *Twelfth Night* there is plenty of roistering supplied by Sir Toby, who doubtless expressed the sentiments of the great majority of the audience at the Globe, and of good Queen Bess herself, when he bellowed at the puritanical Malvolio:

> Dost thou think because thou art virtuous there shall be no more cakes and ale?

Nor is Sir Toby the only source of rough and tumble amusement in the play. There is more than enough low comedy supplied by the foolish knight Sir Andrew Aguecheek, whose shallow vanity is no shallower than his own silly brain. He consoles himself for his many deficiencies with the thought that his leg

> does indifferent well in a flame color'd stock,

and remarks with some complacency,

> I knew it was I, for many do call me fool,

And for good measure are thrown in Maria, the

> most excellent devil of wit,

and the versatile Feste who turns readily from easy punning with Viola to singing wistful songs for the lovesick Orsino. In *Hamlet* and in *Macbeth* there are duels and noise, "alarums and excursions," for Shakespeare knew that his audience demanded those things; his skill lay in working them into his stories so that they helped rather than hindered. He considered his audience, giving them what they wanted without letting this consideration interfere with the development of his own ideas.

Elizabethan playwrights influenced by popular taste. Sensitiveness to public opinion is responsible for more than the casual reader realizes. Just as in the movies today, fads swept through the theatrical world and had to be capitalized. One "hit" led rival dramatists to attempt duplication. A book like Lodge's *Rosalynde* was popular; it was converted into *As You Like It.* Talk of a shipwreck swept the town; it was reflected in *The Tempest.* The success of characters like Marston's *Malcontent* led to imitation in characters like the melancholy Jaques, Don John, and Iago. There was, about 1600, a revival of interest in the tragedy of blood—alive with ghosts, revenges, stabbings in the dark, hangings, mad damsels, plots and counterplots; at once Jonson revised and revamped Kyd's *The Spanish Tragedy,* a hit eight years back, and Shakespeare took over a good bit of it for *Hamlet.* In 1598 Jonson scored a hit with his *Every Man in His Humor,* a new type of comedy in which each character had some special weakness or "humor" which made him ridiculous; Shakespeare acted in this comedy, and there is little doubt that it influenced him in his drawing of Sir Toby, Malvolio, Orsino, and Sir Andrew in *Twelfth Night.* And Jonson, earlier in his career, thought nothing of reworking for his *The Case Is Altered* a whole scene from Shakespeare's *Two Gentlemen of Verona.*

Influence of Elizabethan playwrights on each other. All dramatists borrowed or copied material from each other in their efforts to catch the public taste. The vogue of Beaumont and Fletcher's romantic plays like *Philaster* doubtless led Shakespeare to try the same type in *Cymbeline.* Earlier in his career he had imitated and outdone the leading rivals of his youth: in historical tragedy he had improved on Marlowe's *Edward II* with his own *King Richard II;* in court comedy he had bettered Lyly's earlier work with his *Love's Labour's Lost;* and in the realm of the fantastic he had quite eclipsed Peele's *Old Wives'*

Tale with *A Midsummer Night's Dream.* So close was this interrelation between playwrights and public that it is often difficult to tell who wrote what. It is possible that the Hecate scenes in *Macbeth* were by Middleton; whole sections of *The Taming of the Shrew* come from an older play; *Hamlet* is indebted to *The Spanish Tragedy* for many of its theatrical tricks; the gist of Polonius' advice in *Hamlet* and Gonzalo's ideal commonwealth in *The Tempest* may be found elsewhere; Antony's funeral speech is out of North's translation of Plutarch; the famous speech of Wolsey in *King Henry VIII* is probably by Fletcher. Certain conventions (like our stage use of the cigarette and telephone) were common property, too, so that we find the entrance reading a book, the swearing on a sword, the handling of a skull, and the use of flowers by mad persons in many plays of the time.

The playwright must consider the limitations of his theater. A dramatist is bound by the artificial limitations of his stage. On the modern stage, it is true, wonders of scenic effects can be accomplished: thunder roars and lightning flashes; cyclones sweep across the stage demolishing everything in sight, or hurling drifts of sand upon the unfortunate actors; heavy fogs cling to barges along the river making the audience shiver with fancied dampness; morning dawns mysteriously and beautifully in Canadian forests; tropical rain descends in a heavy, monotonous drizzle. Even with these possibilities there are limitations; some things cannot be attempted on the stage; then, too, there is the danger of overburdening a play with too many scenic effects, too many mechanical wonders, which distract attention from the play itself. A dramatist should confine his scenes and events to things that can be convincingly suggested on the stage unless he is to defeat his own ends. And if his stage, like Shakespeare's, is limited in scenery and in scenic possibilities, he must write his play with these limitations in mind.

Elizabethan theater influenced Shakespeare. The limitations of the Elizabethan stage were many. The stage projected a considerable distance into the amphitheater which surrounded it; there were no "wings" and no curtain; entrances had to be made from the rear of the platform, and exits were a matter of walking off without ceremony. It is interesting to see how Shakespeare adapted his plays to these difficulties. The entrance of an actor from the rear of the stage and his advance to its projecting "apron" might easily be awkward. For this reason Shakespeare often had his characters on the stage speak of those who were entering. Shakespeare took advantage of this practical difficulty using it as a means of introducing his characters to the audience. As there were no programs then, the audience had to learn from the dialogue who the characters were. Hence Shakespeare made use of lines like these as his characters approached the stage:

Yonder comes my master, your brother.

Hath not Fortune sent in this fool to cut off the argument?

Here comes Monsieur Le Beau.

Look you, who comes here: a young man and old in solemn talk.

There is, sure, another flood toward, and these couples are coming to the ark.

But soft! but soft! aside! here comes the King;
The queen, the courtiers; who is it that they follow?
And with such maim'd rites?

Sometimes these introductory comments are given with great dramatic effect as in Iago's soliloquy as Othello approaches:

> Look, where he comes! Not poppy, nor mandragora,
> Nor all the drowsy syrups of the world,
> Shall ever medicine thee to that sweet sleep
> Which thou ow'dst yesterday.

Difficulties caused by lack of a curtain. The fact that there was no curtain made it difficult to bring acts to a stirring climax. The modern dramatist rings down the curtain at the critical moment; the Elizabethan dramatist had to make his actors walk off the stage. But in his later plays Shakespeare made his scenes end effectively in spite of this difficulty. His most common methods were to leave the issue in suspense at the end of a scene, or to work up to a certain emotional pitch and end on just the right note to emphasize this pitch. Thus the first scene of Act II in *Macbeth* ends with suspense. A bell sounds softly, the signal for Macbeth to murder the sleeping king. His shuddering whisper closes the scene:

I go, and it is done; the bell invites me.
Hear it not, Duncan, for it is a knell
That summons thee to heaven or to hell.

The balcony scene in *Romeo and Juliet*, alive with the rapture and wonder of young love, sustains its mood perfectly through the last word. Had Shakespeare had all the resources of the modern stage, he could have contrived no more natural or beautiful ending:

JUL. I have forgot why I did call thee back.
ROM. Let me stand here till thou remember it.
JUL. I shall forget, to have thee still stand there,
Rememb'ring how I love thy company.
ROM. And I'll still stay, to have thee still forget,
Forgetting any other home but this.
JUL. 'Tis almost morning, I would have thee gone:
And yet no further than a wanton's bird,
Who lets it hop a little from her hand,
Like a poor prisoner in his twisted gyves,
And with a silken thread plucks it back again,
So loving-jealous of his liberty.
ROM. I would I were thy bird.
JUL. Sweet, so would I:
Yet I should kill thee with much cherishing.
Good night, good night! Parting is such sweet sorrow,
That I shall say good night till it be morrow.
[*Exit, above*]
ROM. Sleep dwell upon thine eyes, peace in thy breast!
Would I were sleep and peace, so sweet to rest!

If, however, there were dead men on the stage (as there frequently were in Elizabethan drama) the absence of a curtain made it necessary to call in someone to help remove the corpses. Thus at the end of *Hamlet*, Fortinbras and his army appear to bear off in solemn procession the somewhat numerous dead with whom the stage is strewn.

Difficulties caused by lack of much scenic equipment. But the lack of a curtain was not the only difficulty. The Elizabethan stage, though not so bare of scenery as has been generally supposed, was not equipped with the elaborate devices that we have today for the emphasis of the setting. Moreover, the performances took place in the afternoon, practically in the open air. Since the setting was not a matter of drop curtains and electrical effects, descriptive poetry had to create an imaginative picture of the needed setting. The atmosphere of the scene had to be created by the words of the author. This made it necessary for Shakespeare to develop his gift of poetic imagination.

Some of the most beautiful poetry in our language we owe to this artificial limitation of the stage. Examples are numerous: the garden scenes, the farewell scene and the tomb scene in *Romeo and Juliet*, the moonlit garden in *The Merchant of Venice*, the pictures of gloom and horror created by Macbeth's tortured imagination, the description of Cleopatra's barge in *Antony and Cleopatra*, the constantly repeated accounts of the storm in *Julius Caesar*, the description of Dover Cliffs in *King Lear*. In less detailed touches Shakespeare's practical stagecraft takes care to remind his audience of time and place. The plays are filled with such reminders:

Yon grey lines that fret the clouds are messengers of day.

The deep of night is crept upon our talk.

How ill this taper burns!

How sweet the moonlight sleeps upon this bank!

Night's candles are burnt out and jocund Day
Stands tiptoe on the misty mountain tops.

. . . 'tis bitter cold
And I am sick at heart.

But, look, the morn, in russet mantle clad,
Walks o'er the dew of yon high eastern hill.

The air bites shrewdly.

The pelting of this pitiless storm.

Blow, winds, and crack your cheeks!

Light thickens and the crow
Makes wing to the rooky wood.

Now spurs the lated traveller apace
To gain the timely inn.

. . . in the shade of these melancholy boughs.

The Elizabethan audience listened for effective language. An often-forgotten fact about Elizabethan plays is that they were written for a noisy, uncomfortable audience, standing close to the stage in a poorly lit theater. This meant, of course, that actors had to exaggerate their diction and their gestures to make an impression, so that passages like Antony's funeral oration, Mercutio's Queen Mab speech, Jaques' "Seven Ages of Man" were probably almost chanted into the upturned faces of a restless but appreciative crowd. This meant, too, that the audience was accustomed to getting impressions through the ear; the spoken word was more appreciated then than it is in our day of slovenly half-articulate enunciations. Hence the prevalence of puns, of all kinds of verbal skill, of rhythmic blank verse in plays of the period; hence the use of vivid poetry to describe and suggest the setting. The fact that these plays are longer than ours, crammed with both speech and action, indicates that actors must have spoken more rapidly and that there could have been no break in the action. Today they are given differently, so that a smart New York critic some years ago spoke of Sothern and Marlowe's revival of *Cymbeline* as "almost Episcopalian" in its lingering reverence for diction. But that is partly because our ears are not trained to take in language as Elizabethan ears were.[1]

Summary. The drama is difficult to write because the playwright must consider the interests and opinions of other people. He must coöperate with the producer, the actor, the audience and its social background, and recognize the limitations of the stage. Hence one cannot understand the Elizabethan drama without knowing something about the Elizabethan audience and the Elizabethan theater.

COMPREHENSION QUESTIONS

1. List the four principal reasons why the drama is difficult to write. Under each reason cite one example from either Shakespeare or contemporary drama.

[1] The best books on Elizabethan England are *Shakespeare's England* published by the Clarendon Press, Oxford, and *Shakespeare's Theater* by Professor Thorndike.

2. Use the moving pictures as examples of the influence of actors and actresses in changing the original conception of a story. Suggested titles:

Conrad	*Victory*
Melville	*Moby Dick*
Stevenson	*Dr. Jekyll and Mr. Hyde*
Wells	*The Island of Dr. Moreau*

3. Using a model, pictures, or diagrams, explain to the class the construction of an Elizabethan theater. Then point out how different aspects of this theater are reflected in Elizabethan plays. Use *The Merchant of Venice* or *Julius Caesar* as an example. Try the same exercise for the eighteenth-century theater with *The School for Scandal* as an example.
4. Point out how the Elizabethan audience's fondness for the following things is reflected in any Shakespearean drama:
   (*a*) full plot involving different sets of characters, (*b*) violent actions and language, (*c*) both imaginative and philosophical poetry, (*d*) puns, (*e*) plenty of low comedy, (*f*) coarse and boisterous humor, (*g*) "local" jokes.
5. Explain the different types of audiences at the Globe and the Blackfriars. How did these audiences influence Shakespeare in his writing?

PROBLEMS IN APPRECIATION

1. Investigate the history of the following actors or actresses in interpreting a rôle:
   (*a*) John Barrymore or Edwin Booth as Hamlet, (*b*) Katharine Cornell, Jane Cowl, and Eva Le Gallienne as Juliet, (*c*) Lynn Fontanne as Queen Elizabeth, (*d*) Mary Garden as Mélisande, (*e*) Helen Hayes as Cleopatra in Shaw's *Caesar and Cleopatra*, or as Mary Stuart in *Mary of Scotland*, (*f*) Charles Macklin as Shylock, (*g*) Alla Nazimova as Hedda Gabler or as Christine in *Mourning Becomes Electra*, (*h*) Mrs. Siddons as Lady Macbeth.

2. Investigate one of the following topics. They show how Elizabethan playwrights followed the taste of the day and imitated each other's work. Can you find examples from contemporary moving pictures to show how stage and screen reflect public taste?
   (*a*) the War of the Theaters, for instance, *The Poetaster;* (*b*) the Tragedy of Blood, for instance, *The Spanish Tragedy*, *Hamlet;* (*c*) the Comedy of Humors, for instance, *Every Man in His Humor*, *Twelfth Night*, and *As You Like It;* (*d*) masques, for instance, *The Tempest;* (*e*) romantic comedy, for instance, *Philaster* and *Cymbeline;* (*f*) classical tragedy based on Roman or Greek themes, for instance, *Catiline*

Vandamm Studio

HELEN HAYES AND HELEN MENKEN IN *MARY OF SCOTLAND*
Queen Mary and Queen Elizabeth confront each other in vivid drama.

AN ENGLISH MYSTERY PLAY

The play of *Noah's Ark* as given by the Shipwrights' Guild in a city square in England four centuries ago. The details are those of a performance given at the New Theater, New York, in 1911. (From a model in the Brander Matthews Dramatic Museum of Columbia University) and *Julius Caesar;* (*g*) chronicle plays, for instance, *Henry IV;* (*h*) fantastic comedies, for instance, *Old Wives' Tale, Knight of the Burning Pestle, A Midsummer Night's Dream;* (*i*) interest in ghosts, witches, revenge, etc., for instance, *Hamlet, Macbeth;* (*j*) the Malcontent, for instance, *Much Ado about Nothing, As You Like It, Timon;* (*k*) court comedies, for instance, *Love's Labour's Lost,* Lyly's plays; (*l*) comedy of the people, for instance, *The Shoemaker's Holiday.*

3. Show how the restlessness of the Elizabethan audience tended to make the action of Elizabethan plays faster at the end than at the beginning.

4. Perhaps the student would be interested to read more in detail about the nature of the drama and the Elizabethan stage. For the latter he will find *Shakespeare's England* a mine of information. Professor Thorndike's *Shakespeare's Theater* and *Tragedy,* Professors MacCracken, Pierce, and Durham's *An Introduction to Shakespeare,* Brander Mathew's *A Study of Drama* (Chapter II deals with the influence of the actor and Chapter III with the influence of the theater), and John Galsworthy's "Some Platitudes concerning the Drama"[1] are all interesting even to the beginner. Different students in the class could investigate and report on different phases of these subjects, using pictures and blackboard drawings to bring out their points.

5. It is always interesting to study the careers of actors and actresses, and sometimes such a study brings out a good deal of stimulating comment on famous characters in dramatic literature. See what you can find out about some of the following:

Sarah Bernhardt	David Garrick	Mme. Rachel
Edwin Booth	Sir Henry Irving	Ellen Terry
Kitty Clive	Richard Mansfield	
Eleonora Duse	Julia Marlowe	

Books by Edward H. Sothern, William Winter (his *Shakespeare on the Stage* is full of information), John Barrymore, Alexander Woollcott, and many others are easily available. Notebooks and collections of pictures could be made interesting for any class.

6. Make a study of the way novels and plays are transferred to the screen. First read the novel or play and then visit the movie theater trying to make a fair study of what the movies have done to it and why. What is necessarily omitted or added? What fits in with your previous conceptions? What seems to you a mistake? What is gained or lost? Have the players and director really reproduced the spirit of the book and

[1] In *The Inn of Tranquillity.*

its characters, or have they deliberately distorted or violated it for commercial reasons? Here are some plays and stories that have been filmed. You can doubtless find many others:

Alice in Wonderland	*Cradle Song*	*Moby Dick*
Anna Christie	*A Farewell to Arms*	*Night Flight*
Berkeley Square	*Frankenstein*	*Of Human Bondage*
Cimarron	*Holiday*	*The Virginian*
The Brothers Karamazov	*Little Women*	*Waterloo Bridge*

7. Investigate the practical difficulties of presenting a play in Shakespeare's day. Point out the scenes and passages which show directly the influence of the stage conditions of the time. Which of these difficulties do you think would most have affected the presentation of *Macbeth?* Contrast the presentation of this play on the Elizabethan stage and on the modern stage.

QUESTIONS ON PLAYS YOU HAVE READ

1. What practical difficulties necessarily face the producer of any of the following plays?

John Lloyd Balderston	*Berkeley Square*
Barrie	*The Admirable Crichton, Mary Rose, A Kiss for Cinderella, Peter Pan*
Drinkwater	*Abraham Lincoln*
Maeterlinck	*The Blue Bird*
O'Neill	*Dynamo, The Emperor Jones, The Hairy Ape, Marco Millions, Days Without End*
Rostand	*Chanticleer*
Shaw	*Back to Methuselah*
Shakespeare	*Macbeth, Julius Caesar, King Lear, A Midsummer Night's Dream*

2. If you were the stage manager, what practical suggestions would you make for the arrangement of the stage, for properties, for lighting, for the position of the actors, etc., in one of the following scenes from Shakespearean plays?

   (*a*) the casket scenes and the court room scenes in *The Merchant of Venice*, (*b*) the funeral scene and the tent scene in *Julius Caesar*, (*c*) the scene in the witches' cave and the banquet scene in *Macbeth*, (*d*) the heath scenes in *King Lear*, (*e*) the graveyard scene, the play scene, and the ghost scenes in *Hamlet*, (*f*) the balcony scenes, the death of Mercutio, and the tomb scene in *Romeo and Juliet*.

Try to find out how these scenes were produced on the stage in the eighteenth and nineteenth centuries. If possible, get pictures, diagrams, and newspaper clippings.

3. Explain why certain parts in plays which you have read are obviously good acting parts, for example:

Cassius	Hamlet	The Nurse in *Romeo and Juliet*
Emilia (in *Othello*)	Hedda Gabler	Rosalind
The Emperor Jones	Liliom	
Falstaff	Mrs. Malaprop	

4. Point out in one of Shakespeare's plays, parts, scenes, events, and passages which show that he had the actor's point of view.

5. Find all the things in *Macbeth* that would have pleased an Elizabethan audience. Are there any remarks put in to please any particular part of the audience? How does the study of the play from this angle help to determine the probable date of its composition?

6. Discuss the opportunities for the players in *Othello*. Was any special attention paid to the actor's point of view in the writing of this play?

CHAPTER 23

EXAMINING THE VARIOUS KINDS OF DRAMA

Tragedy. The two most fundamental divisions of the drama are *comedy* and *tragedy*. In general, *tragedy* involves the ruin of the leading characters whereas *comedy* presents temporary difficulties but ultimate success. But of course there are many variations of this general principle. To the Greeks, tragedy meant the destruction of some noble person through fate. A man like Œdipus might be morally innocent; but even though he had unknowingly violated divine law, he must suffer. To the Elizabethans, tragedy meant, in the first place, death, and in the second place, the destruction of some noble person through some flaw in his own character. His fall made the basis of the action of the play; and the unfolding of his character its human interest. Today, tragedy may not deal with noble persons or moral laws at all. It may not involve death so much as dismal life. Sometimes it shows ordinary human beings crushed by social or economic forces which they cannot control as in John Galsworthy's *Justice* and *The Silver Box*, or Hauptmann's *The Weavers*. It may show the tragedy not of the strong and noble but of the weak, foolish, mean, or deluded as in *Hedda Gabler*, *The Wild Duck*, *Rosmersholm*, or *Mourning Becomes Electra*. Occasionally tragedy has a strong moral tinge as in Tolstoy's *The Power of Darkness;* but more often its moral lies in its picture of social injustice and futility, or of human error as in Galsworthy's *Strife*, Maugham's *Our Betters*, O'Neill's *The Hairy Ape*, Elmer Rice's *Street Scene*, Gorki's *The Lower Depths*. The original purpose of tragedy was, according to Aristotle, to cleanse our hearts by filling them with pity and awe; and certainly the great tragedies of Sophocles, Shakespeare, Racine, and Goethe do have this effect. So do some modern plays like Tolstoy's *The Power of Darkness,* Hauptmann's *The Sunken Bell,* Synge's *Riders to the Sea,* Maeterlinck's *Pélléas and Mélisande;* but it is at least debatable whether plays so preoccupied with weakness, meanness, and despair as *Hedda Gabler, Desire under the Elms,* or *The Vultures,* can have just the effect Aristotle had in mind. Truly great tragedy deals with something more than physical horrors and moral decadence. But whatever its subject matter, true tragedy should develop according to laws of human nature. It should not hinge on mere caprice or irrelevant accident.

Comedy. *Comedy* is lighter drama in which the leading characters overcome the difficulties which temporarily beset them. Classical comedy from the time of Menander often involved an entertaining complication of affairs in which clever and unscrupulous but amusing fellows got the better, temporarily, of honest, well-meaning folk only to find the tables turned on them in the end. The action was tangled by complications, there were often sub-plots involving secondary characters, and the ending was usually brought about arbitrarily without regard to probability. In comedy certain type figures early made their appearance—the young lovers, one or both disguised; the miser; the scheming comic-servant; the pert maid; the confidants, male and female, of the lovers; the quick-tempered father; the harassed mother; the cowardly braggart; the parasite; the drunkard; the blundering and stupid fellow; and so on. Elizabethans took over all of these conventions bodily, but so humanized them that even absurd comedies often became quite real. An analysis of comedies like *The Alchemist, Volpone, Twelfth Night, The Taming of the Shrew,* and *A Comedy of Errors* reveals many such stock characters. Molière's *Tartuffe, The Miser, The Bourgeois Gentleman,* and others are brilliant humanizations of classic comedy patterns. And so, for that matter, are *The Rivals, The School for Scandal,* and *She Stoops to Conquer.*

Humor of situation. Humor is, of course, essential to comedy. There are three time-honored ways in which humor may be introduced into a play: through *situation,* through *character,* or through *dialogue.* Dramatic situations with humorous possibilities have been tried and tested for hundreds of years until they are now pretty well standardized. Mistaken identity, comic reversals of fortune, incongruous or absurd juxtaposition of circumstances, drinking scenes, farcical pursuits, escapes, and evasions can be found in plays from Aristophanes down through the centuries to the latest whipped-cream absurdity of Noel Coward, the insane antics of the Marx Brothers, or the hapless flounderings of Messieurs Laurel and Hardy caught once more in the web of circumstance. It is the skillful use of such sure-fire comic situations that gives certain scenes in *Twelfth Night, The Taming of the Shrew, The Rivals,* and *She Stoops to Conquer* their apparently timeless theatrical effectiveness.

Humor of characterization. A more satisfactory type of humor comes through the creation of characters who are either consciously or unconsciously funny. At the lowest end of the comic scale are frankly farcical characters, created merely to be laughed at. Such are many Elizabethan clowns, comic servants, and country bumpkins, the blundering Dogberry, the unsuspecting Mrs. Malaprop with her "nice derangement of epitaphs," and all the comic drunkards, servant girls, dialect characters, and stupid oafs of the modern theater. At the higher end are the really great comic figures of dramatic literature, ranging from the satirical portraits of Ben Jonson, Molière, Congreve, and Sheridan to the Nurse in *Romeo and Juliet* and, at the very peak, the amazing Falstaff himself. These people have rich individualities, and inexhaustible drolleries, surprises, or brilliance of their own which make them far more than mere laughingstocks going through ready-made lines in a ready-made play.

Humor of lines or manner. The third source of humor and wit may exist in a play independently, as it does in comedies of manners such as *The School for Scandal, The Way of the World,* or *Lady Windermere's Fan,* or it may derive partly from situation or character as in the case of Falstaff, who is "not only witty in himself but also the cause of wit in other men." Sometimes the wit or incongruity of certain lines in certain situations (recall plays like *Holiday, Private Lives, Paris Bound*) gives the humor; sometimes, and more often, it is the nature or manner of the person speaking. Occasionally the wit has a timeless quality that sparkles in any age quite apart from its relation to situation or character. Shakespeare, Molière, Sheridan, Congreve, Oscar Wilde, and other finished artists in high comedy have provided us with many such lines.

Farce. When comedy involves ridiculous or hilarious complications without regard for human values, it becomes *farce.* In a farce we are so busy laughing at absurdly comic happenings that we do not care whether the people are real or not. Difficulties arising from mistaken identities like those in *A Comedy of Errors* are usually farcical. When characters are animated by ridiculous motives or blocked by inconsequential trifles, the play is likely to be a farce. *The Taming of the Shrew,* with its absurd exaggeration of Katherina's bad temper and the extreme measures taken by Petruchio to overcome it, is really farce-comedy. In Oscar Wilde's *The Importance of Being Earnest* the chief obstacles in the course of true love are a young lady's unwillingness to marry anyone whose name is not Ernest and the inability of her suitor to produce any ancestors or antecedents other than the handbag in which he was found at a railway station. Many movies—from the hilariously insane concoctions of the Marx Brothers to the satirically romantic comedy of films like *Trouble in Paradise*—are farces.

Fantastic comedy. A *fantasy* is a play, sometimes, but not always, comic in spirit, in which the author gives free reign to his fancy, allowing things to happen without regard to reality. Sir James Barrie has become famous for his fondness for a whimsical dream world of this kind. His *Mary Rose, A Kiss for Cinderella, Dear Brutus,* and *Peter Pan* are notable examples of fantastic comedy. It would be a mistake, however, to think of Barrie's fancies as purely childish fairy plays. Without being bound to reality, they often convey some subtle human truth, so that underneath the apparent sentiment of *Mary Rose* and *Dear Brutus* there is really a bitter commentary on human nature and human destiny. Shakespeare tried his hand at joyous comic fantasy in *A Midsummer Night's Dream* and at poetic allegorical fantasy in *The Tempest.* Modern plays in this vein, each with its underlying allegory are Ibsen's *Peer Gynt* and *The Lady from the Sea,* Maeterlinck's *The Bluebird,* Mackaye's *The Scarecrow,* Dunsany's *If, The Gods of the Mountain,* and *King Argimenes and the Unknown Warrior,* Noyes' *Sherwood,* Josephine Preston Peabody's *The Piper,* Molnar's *Liliom,* Karel M. Capek's *The Insect World* and *R.U.R.*, and Kaufman and Connelly's *Beggar on Horseback.*

Comedy of manners. If comedy is very much concerned with exposing the artificialities and hypocrisies of polite society, filled with wit and glitter and drawing-room manners and fashionably easy morality lightly covered by airy banter, we call it the *comedy of manners.* In such plays superficial polish and style are what matters, not human nature. In the late seventeenth century under the influence of a brilliant but corrupt court this type of comedy reached its apex, though Shakespeare's successors, Beaumont and Fletcher, Massinger, and Shirley, had begun to experiment with it. Congreve's *The Way of the World* is a dazzling example of the comedy of manners, so light and brilliant and glittering in its dialogue and manner that modern actors and actresses simply cannot carry it off adequately. Farquhar's *The Beaux Stratagem* is another, but most familiar to modern audiences is Sheridan's *The School for Scandal.* Today the comedy of manners is represented by plays like Wilde's *Lady Windermere's Fan,* Maugham's *Our Betters* and *The Circle,* and in America by Philip Barry's gay comedies of wealthy American life, *Paris Bound* and *Holiday.* In Europe it is still written brilliantly, especially in France and Hungary. Depending a great deal on the audience, it always presupposes well-defined social classes with certain social conventions and values accepted by audience and actors.

Tragi-comedy. Comedy, of course, often verges on tragedy on the one hand or on bitter satire on the other. Shakespeare's *Measure for Measure* and *All's Well That Ends Well* are bitter variations of comic themes, and Jonson's *Volpone,* almost literally Roman in its framework, is one of the most bitter invectives ever penned against human greed. Molière's plays have the satire without the bitterness. Other plays, for instance *Much Ado about Nothing,* have tragic elements but are kept from being tragedies because the ending is arbitrarily made happy and because the characterization of the people in the tragic dilemma is deliberately withheld so that the audience does not take them too seriously. This is how Shakespeare skates over thin ice with the plight of the lovers in *A Midsummer Night's Dream* and the plight of Hero and Claudio in *Much Ado about Nothing.* But in *The Merchant of Venice,* Shylock is made so human that we grieve for his fate, and the play is really a tragi-comedy.

Melodrama. The opposite extreme from farce is *melodrama*—in fact so opposite are the two that they almost meet. Melodrama, too, pays almost no attention to human values; but its object is to get a thrill instead of a laugh. It is a play, usually with a happy ending, in which the interest centers in the exciting and unusual things that happen fast and mysteriously. The characters are likely to be *stock figures*—that is, types rather than strongly marked individualities—

moved by elementary motives. The good people in such a play are very good and very brave, qualities which they need if they are to survive the dangers into which they are plunged for no plausible reason except to provide another thrill for the audience. The bad people are very bad, with no redeeming feature unless tenacity of purpose may be so called. A melodrama is not to be judged too seriously. If it supplies harmless entertainment like *Broadway*, for instance, its purpose is achieved. The plot of *Hamlet*, as it originally existed, is melodramatic, but Shakespeare transformed the leading character from a figurehead of blood-and-thunder melodrama to a genuinely tragic human being.

Screen melodrama. Moving pictures have carried melodrama to absurd lengths. In the early days, screen serials used to display lovely ladies being rescued weekly from harassing perils and harrowing exploits. In *Way Down East*, a handsome young man in a fur coat, with the agility of a mountain ram, leaped across floating ice to the very edge of a roaring waterfall and snatched therefrom an unconscious damsel floating to her doom on a convenient ice floe. In the patriotic variety of early movie, infantry, cavalry, aëroplanes, and motor corps, traveling rapidly but not forgetting to bear aloft the Stars and Stripes, would rush in the nick of time to save a woman's honor or spare her feelings. Then came the period of *The Cat and the Canary* and *The Bat*, and similar thrillers, filled with sliding panels, gibbering idiots, comic servants, and shots in the dark. Of late years the movie melodrama has gone "hard" and horrible. Messieurs Dracula, Frankenstein, and Hyde have been at their blood-curdling dirty work. The Hound of the Baskervilles has been heard howling over the moors of Hollywood, and the murders in the Rue Morgue have at last been reduced to the ultimate absurdity. Sated with these horrors, the thrill-seeking public has found solace in the underworld. Here languorous ladies with expensive jewels and platinum hair look on scenes of violence and cruelty with bored indifference and vie with each other for the attentions of low-browed, sleek-haired, hard-favored rascals only to have the morning grapefruit smashed in their lovely faces to the delight of the gaping audience. Here devoted and deserted old mothers invariably wend their way over the hill to the poorhouse, having found, and with a vengeance, "how sharper than a serpent's tooth it is to have a thankless child." Here are wise-cracking reporters, never sober, always quick at repartee; steely-eyed, heavy-jowled, iron-hearted newspaper editors; incessantly jangling telephones; taxis ever ready to accommodate the fleeing criminal, machine guns a-plenty; glittering night clubs, ill-mannered detectives, innocent heroines, aristocratic grand dames, and poor but rapidly rising young heroes—all thrown together with plenty of excitement, but no regard whatever for any of the values, human, moral, or artistic, to which art is usually dedicated. Such is melodrama, but fortunately for most of us life itself is a little less nerve-wracking.

Medieval mystery plays. In the Middle Ages, the drama had its beginnings under the patronage of the church, which used dramatic representations to portray stories from the Bible and the lives of the saints to the common people. Later these plays were produced by trade guilds at different religious festivals, each guild being in charge of one play dealing with some Bible story. The plays were arranged in a series, called a cycle, designed to show, in order, the fall of man and his redemption by Christ. Some of them were written with no little dramatic skill, and many of them came directly from the people and unconsciously expressed their own ideas and lives in terms of Biblical characters. They were called *mystery plays.* The nearest modern approach to them is probably Marc Connelly's negro play, *The Green Pastures,* which in its reverence and naïve humor and pathos approximates the spirit and form of these medieval plays.

Miracle plays. As people grew tired of the constant repetition of the story of Christianity in mystery plays, they came to write little plays dealing with the lives of the saints. These, strictly speaking, were called *miracle plays.* Usually they concerned the miraculous legends about the Blessed Virgin or popular saints. Maeterlinck's *Sister Beatrice* is a modern miracle play, and Massenet's opera *Our Lady's Juggler* attempts the same sort of thing in music.

Morality plays. Mystery and miracle plays were followed by *morality plays* in which the characters were abstract virtues and vices. One of these, *Everyman,* is a solemn and moving tragedy which is still acted with great impressiveness.

The masque. The *masque* is a dramatic composition with a slight plot, usually allegorical in character and embellished with much singing and dancing. Effective costuming was important in the masque, which was usually written for performance at court or at some country house on a special occasion. In the court of James I, Ben Jonson, associated with the painter Inigo Jones, brought the masque to a high perfection. Milton's *Comus* is probably the best masque ever written. Today the form is sometimes revived by poetic dramatists for special occasions.

The chronicle play. A *chronicle play* deals directly with historical episodes and characters. Its leading figures enact the scenes of history. Such a play, however, often has a sub-plot dealing with imaginary characters, thereby adding dramatic interest to the historical narrative. Shakespeare wrote many chronicle plays. His *King Henry IV*, Part I and Part II, *King Henry V*, and *King Richard II* are the best of these. Conspicuous examples of the modern revival of interest in the chronicle play are John Drinkwater's *Abraham Lincoln* and *Oliver Cromwell*, Louis Parker's *Disraeli*, Sacha Guitry's *Pasteur*, Maxwell Anderson's *Elizabeth the Queen* and *Mary of Scotland*, and Agnes MacIntosh's *Richard of Bordeaux*.

Closet drama. Sometimes dramatic poetry is not really meant to be acted. Plays meant merely for reading are called *closet drama*. Such plays are Shelley's *Prometheus Unbound*, Byron's *Manfred*, Browning's *Pippa Passes*, Swinburne's trilogy dealing with Mary Stuart, and Hardy's *The Dynasts*.

The drama of social criticism. The *drama of social criticism*, as the early devotees of Ibsen used to love to call it, made its appearance with Ibsen's *A Doll's House* in 1879. This was our first *problem play*, that is, one written primarily to set forth some problem of human relationships as affected by social laws and customs. Of course, in a sense, problems of this kind were nothing new in the drama. But after Ibsen the drama began to be specifically concerned with the struggle of some particular individual against social conventions or injustices. In *A Doll's House*, Nora feels that she owes more to herself than to her husband and children, thus bringing herself into conflict with society's conception of marriage. In *The Wild Duck*, Gregers Werle feels called upon to force an unwelcome truth on a family that is happier in its ignorance, and the result is tragedy for the family. In *An Enemy of the People*, Dr. Stockman finds himself in conflict with the selfish interests of a whole community. After Ibsen the social drama spread over Europe and America. In England, Pinero, Galsworthy, and Shaw wrote constantly with some social problem in mind:

the fate of a "woman with a past" in *The Second Mrs. Tanqueray*, Christianity and socialism in *Androcles and the Lion* and *Major Barbara;* social injustice in *The Silver Box* and *Justice.* In France, Brieux's dramas were not so much plays as dramatic documents presenting the facts about social problems. Such plays are usually serious and absorbing and, if they do not sacrifice characterization to propaganda, may be universally significant. If, however, they distort the truth or depend for their interest on the problem they present, they lose their value the minute the problem ceases to be of interest.

Many problem plays which were considered startling in their own day, for instance *A Doll's House* itself, have already ceased to attract much interest, because people are no longer interested in the problem. It often happens, too, that the attention of the author is distracted by the problem from his story and characters. Ideas interest him more than people, and hence his people tend to become mere mouthpieces for his ideas. It is this tendency to use the drama for merely the exploiting of ideas, not for the presentation of human life, that prevents Bernard Shaw from being a really great dramatist. With the possible exception of *Candida* and *Saint Joan*, his plays are mostly filled with puppets who merely express ideas which Shaw wishes to expound or refute. In less degree this is sometimes the trouble with Galsworthy too. In *Strife* the problem of capital and labor is so absorbing that we think about it more than about the people of the play. So, too, with *The Pigeon*, we puzzle over a problem rather than watch a spectacle of life itself. Even Eugene O'Neill sometimes tends to build his dramas and characters according to formula in order better to develop a problem.

The one-act play. A form of drama which has been popular during the past two decades and which has been highly developed is the one-act play. At the time of the appearance of Maeterlinck's *L'Intruse* (*The Intruder*) in 1890, the one-act play was still an experimental form of dramatic composition. Today there are in the literature of almost every European language one-act plays which are little short of masterpieces. Merely to name the dramatists who have used this form successfully—Barrie, Pinero, Shaw, Galsworthy, Maeterlinck, Hauptmann, Chekhov, Synge, Lord Dunsany, Yeats, Lady Gregory—is to list the leading playwrights of contemporary literature. Books on one-act plays, collections by individual authors, and anthologies have sprung up in abundance; amateur and professional companies have used all the resources of modern dramatic art on their production.

The one-act play bears almost the same relation to the full-length play as the short story does to the novel.[1] It is governed by many of the same laws of structure as longer plays, but it is necessarily rigorously condensed. It must accomplish a maximum of dramatic effect with a minimum of dramatic means. Like the short story, it must deal with one dominant theme and, usually, with one dominant character. It need not necessarily take the characters at a crisis, but it must take them at a significant episode in their lives, an episode that is worthy of dramatic development. Like the short story, too, the one-act play must strive to produce a single effect; it cannot go from comedy to tragedy so readily as a full-length play. It must, also like the short story, get under way immediately, develop its complications rapidly, and end emphatically. Its methods of characterization need not differ from those in the longer play, but they must be used with concentration, economy, swiftness, and directness. The emphasis must everywhere be sure and unmistakable. The general tone of the one-act play is, however, exceedingly varied. It may be tragedy or romance, poetic fancy or brutal realism, light comedy or farce.

Summary. *Tragedy* is drama which involves the ruin of the leading characters.

Comedy is drama which involves real but temporary difficulties of the leading characters. Special types of comedy:

Farce is comedy which depends wholly upon laughable situations without regard for human values.

Fantastic comedy is comedy which deals with impossible situations in terms of ordinary human nature.

The *comedy of manners* deals satirically and superficially with polite society.

Tragi-comedy is drama which does not involve death or disaster but which verges on tragedy or bitter satire.

Melodrama—a play which depends for its interest wholly on exciting scenes and exaggerated characters.

Types of drama of historical interest:

Medieval mystery plays dealt with Bible stories and characters.

[1] See Clayton Hamilton's *Studies in Stagecraft* and Helen Louise Cohen's *One-Act Plays by Modern Authors.*

Medieval miracle plays dealt with the lives of the saints.

Chronicle plays dealt directly with historical scenes and characters.

Masques were slight plays involving much singing and dancing and costuming. They were usually allegorical.

Closet drama is meant to be read, not acted.

The *drama of social criticism* discusses social, economic, or political problems by means of a play.

The *one-act play* is a complete drama in one act.

COMPREHENSION QUESTIONS

1. *Vocabulary:* The student should learn all the terms listed above and be able to give at least one example for each.
2. Explain by reference to *As You Like It* and *Julius Caesar* the difference between comedy and tragedy.
3. Wherein does our modern conception of tragedy differ from that of the Elizabethans? Use three of the following plays to illustrate your point:

George Abbot and Ann Preston Bridgers	*Coquette*
Benavente	*La Malquerida*
Gordon Bottomley	*King Lear's Wife*
D'Annunzio	*The Daughter of Jorio, Francesca da Rimini*
James Elroy Flecker	*Hassan*
Galsworthy	*Justice, The Silver Box*
Giuseppe Giacosa	*Like Falling Leaves*
Gorki	*The Lower Depths*
Hauptmann	*Drayman Henschel, The Rats, The Weavers*
Maeterlinck	*Pélléas and Mélisande*
Masefield	*The Tragedy of Nan*
O'Neill	*The Emperor Jones, The Hairy Ape, Mourning Becomes Electra*
Pinero	*The Second Mrs. Tanqueray*
Elmer Rice	*Street Scene*
Robert Cedric Sherriff	*Journey's End*
Synge	*Deirdre of the Sorrows, Riders to the Sea*
Tolstoy	*The Power of Darkness*
Eugene Walter	*The Easiest Way*

4. Which of the common elements listed on page 315 can you find in *A Midsummer Night's Dream, Twelfth Night,* or *The Rivals?*
5. Why is *The Merchant of Venice* really a tragi-comedy?
6. Use *The School for Scandal* as an example for a definition of the comedy of manners. Do *Pygmalion, Lady Windermere's Fan,* and *The Importance of Being Earnest* fit this definition?
7. Read Stephen Phillips' *Paolo and Francesca,* or Synge's *Deirdre of the Sorrows,* or Flecker's *Hassan.* What passages in it are especially poetic? Compare them with similar passages in *Romeo and Juliet* and *Macbeth.* Which type of poetic tragedy seems to you greater? why? What qualities had Elizabethan poetic drama that are not so marked in our own?
8. Describe to the class a recent moving picture you have seen that is a good example of melodrama. What scenes and episodes mark it as such?
9. What is the chief distinction between *farce* and *comedy?* Illustrate by referring to a farcical moving picture.
10. If you have seen or read *The Green Pastures,* use it as an example of a modern mystery play. Try to get hold of a medieval mystery play and see what points both have in common.
11. Read Maeterlinck's *Sister Beatrice* as an example of a modern miracle play.
12. Find and read *Everyman* as an example of a medieval morality play. Compare it with Yeats' *The Hour Glass.*
13. Is *King Lear* really a closet drama, as Charles Lamb once asserted? Defend your answer.
14. What unpalatable human truth can you find underneath the fantasy of Barrie's *Dear Brutus, Mary Rose, The Admirable Crichton,* or *Peter Pan?*
15. Define fantastic comedy using *A Midsummer Night's Dream* or *The Tempest* as an example.
16. Explain in your own words what is meant by the drama of social criticism. Illustrate your remarks by references to one or more of the following:

Maxwell Anderson	*Both Your Houses*
Martin A. Flavin	*The Criminal Code*
Galsworthy	*The Eldest Son, Justice, Loyalties, The Mob, The Pigeon, The Silver Box, Strife*
Gorki	*The Lower Depths*
Hauptmann	*The Weavers*
Ibsen	*A Doll's House, An Enemy of the People*
George S. Kaufman and Marc Connelly	*Beggar on Horseback*

Channing Pollock	*The Enemy, The Fool*
Elmer Rice	*We the People*
Shaw	*Major Barbara, Pygmalion, The Apple Cart*
Ernst Toller	*Masse Mensch*

PROBLEMS IN APPRECIATION

1. In any Elizabethan comedy try to find examples of:
   (*a*) disguise, (*b*) mistaken identity, (*c*) comic servants, (*d*) scheming but likable rogues, (*e*) practical jokes or horseplay, (*f*) two or more pairs of lovers, (*g*) an arbitrarily happy ending, (*h*) spirited, beautiful, and loyal ladies, (*i*) confidants, (*j*) tangled cross motives, (*k*) hot-headed old men, (*l*) quarrels, (*m*) eavesdropping, (*n*) misunderstanding.

2. In any Elizabethan tragedy find examples of:
   (*a*) a potentially noble soul ruined by fate, by some weakness, by a wicked person, (*b*) moral issues in conflict, (*c*) passages of eloquence, passion, or poetry, (*d*) strong human passions aroused, (*e*) comic relief, (*f*) ideas expressed in eloquent poetry, (*g*) villains, (*h*) many characters.

3. In any Elizabethan chronicle play find:
   (*a*) famous historical scenes and characters, (*b*) under-plots dealing with common people, (*c*) comic minor characters, (*d*) patriotic motives and speeches, (*e*) political scheming, (*f*) battles, (*g*) speeches of defiance, (*h*) political argument.

4. In any farce or melodrama find evidences of sacrificing human values for amusing or exciting action.

5. In any good comedy, try to find examples of:
   (*a*) humor derived from a comic situation (classify it), (*b*) humor derived from a comic character (analyze it), (*c*) wit due to situation, (*d*) wit due to character, (*e*) wit independent of situation or character.

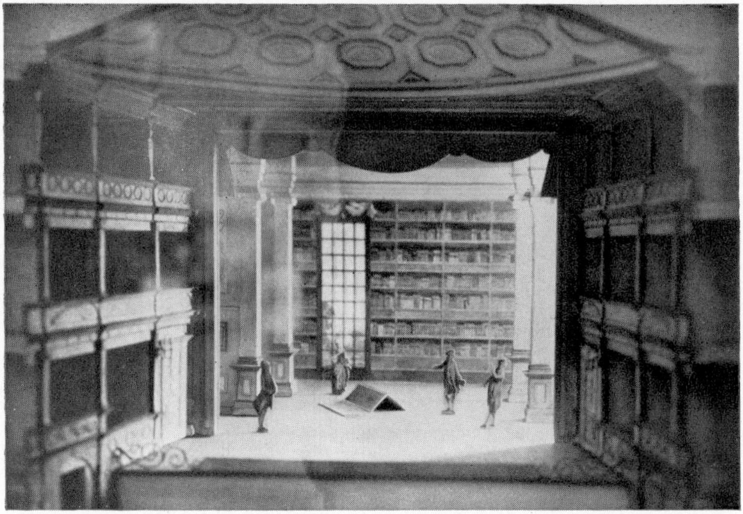

DRURY LANE THEATER IN 1778
Showing the screen scene in Sheridan's *School for Scandal*
(From a model in the Brander Matthews Dramatic Museum of Columbia University)

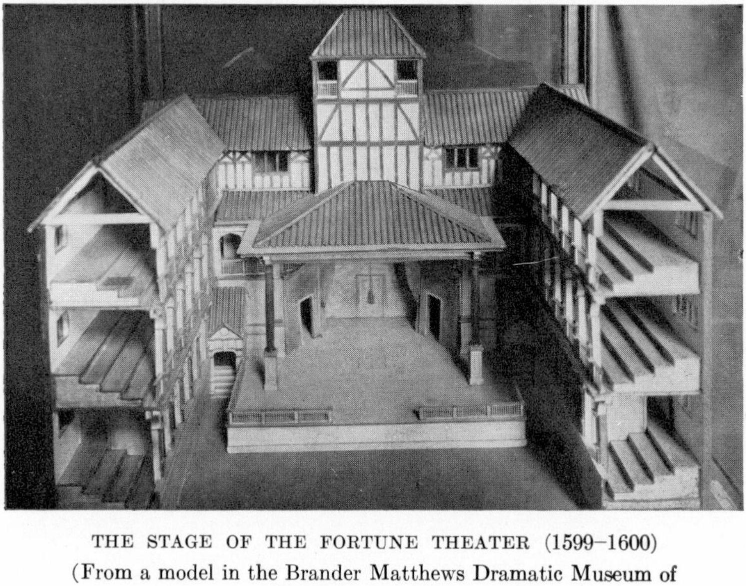

THE STAGE OF THE FORTUNE THEATER (1599–1600)
(From a model in the Brander Matthews Dramatic Museum of Columbia University)

Courtesy of Famous Players-Lasky Corp.

IN THE PALACE OF VERSAILLES

Constantly the motion picture aspires to really artistic standards.

© Underwood & Underwood, N.Y.

THEATER OF DIONYSIUS AT ATHENS

In this theater under sunny skies were played the Greek tragedies, "the crowning glory of Greek literature."

CHAPTER 24

HOW TO STUDY PLOT CONSTRUCTION

PLOT DEVELOPMENT

A plot implies opposing forces. A plot necessarily implies opposition of some kind between forces. In every play leading characters are opposed to something. The struggle may be an external one—for the possession of certain papers, for the love of the heroine, for position in society—or it may be an inward one against some over-powering emotion, temptation, or habit—ambition, jealousy, inaction, pride. The struggle may even be against the forces of Nature, cold, or heat, or mountains, or sea. In the best plays, however, the struggle is both inward and outward. Portia fights for Antonio's liberty; but she also fights for mercy, which is an inward, or moral, struggle. Hamlet struggles against his incapacity for action; Brutus against corruption and selfishness in politics; Viola against the love that "like a worm i' the bud feeds on her damask cheek"; Benedick and Beatrice against false pride. In all these struggles there is something more than a mere chase for some concrete object; there is a struggle of hearts and wills that gives strength and truth to the character drawing of the play. First of all, therefore, we ask about the plot of any play, "Is the struggle an inward or an outward one? If it is inward, how is it outwardly shown to us?"

Protagonist and antagonist. Certain technical terms are used in the discussion of plot construction. The leading figure in the struggle, the character who receives most of the dramatist's attention and who rouses the sympathy of the audience, is called the *protagonist.* In *Julius Caesar*, Brutus is the protagonist; in *The Merchant of Venice*, Portia; in *As You Like It*, Rosalind; in *Hamlet*, Hamlet himself. In some plays, such as Hauptmann's *The Weavers*, a whole social group may be the protagonists. The character who represents the force opposing the protagonist is called the *antagonist*. Thus Antony, Octavius, and Caesar are the antagonists of Brutus in *Julius Caesar;* Shylock is the antagonist of Portia in *The Merchant of Venice*. The hatred of the Capulets and the Montagues, represented by the two families themselves and their followers, is the opposing force in *Romeo and Juliet*. The king and queen are the antagonists of Hamlet. Macduff is the principal antagonist in *Macbeth*. Some plays have little struggle, or plot, and hence have no strong antagonistic force. *As You Like It* is such a play.

Inciting force and preliminary exposition. The point at which the action begins is called the *inciting force*. This does not usually come at the rising of the curtain. Some explanation of the situation and characters is required first. This explanation is called the *preliminary exposition*. In *The Merchant of Venice* the plot does not begin until Bassanio and Antonio negotiate with Shylock for a loan, but the preceding scenes of preliminary exposition familiarize us with these two and their friends and with Portia and Nerissa. In *Hamlet* the plot does not begin until Hamlet first meets the ghost of his father. In *Julius Caesar* there is a good deal of noise and pageantry before Cassius first sows his evil seed in the heart of Brutus.

The climax. The turning point of the struggle, the point where fortune turns definitely for or against the hero is called the *climax*. The climax does not often occur at the end of the play, however. In a Shakespearean play it usually comes somewhere in the third act, about two-thirds of the way through the drama. In *The Merchant of Venice*, for instance, Shylock really began to lose his case the moment that Bassanio chose the right casket, thereby enlisting Portia's aid for Antonio. This is not the highest point of interest in the play—the trial scene is that—but it is the technical turning point.

The climax, or turning point, of *Macbeth* comes when Fleance escapes, for then we know that Macbeth is doomed to failure, that he has murdered Duncan to make the seed of Banquo kings. In *Julius Caesar* the climax and the highest point of interest coincide in Antony's funeral oration. In *Twelfth Night* the climax occurs when Antonio upbraids Viola, thinking her Sebastian; from then on we know that it is only a question of time before Sebastian and Viola meet and everything is straightened out.

Dénouement. The final outcome of the struggle is called the *dénouement* or the *catastrophe.* The word catastrophe does not in this sense necessarily mean an unhappy ending, but simply the end of the struggle. The dénouement or catastrophe is easily found in any play. In *As You Like It* it is the final scene in the forest where the marriages occur and the Duke's kingdom is restored to him. In *Twelfth Night* it is the scene in Olivia's house where the mistaken identities and disguises are explained and everyone, except Malvolio, is made happy. In *The Merchant of Venice* it is the scene in the garden at Belmont where the mystery of the rings and the identity of the young lawyer are cleared up. In *Hamlet* it is the final scene where the king, the queen, Hamlet, and Laertes die.

The rising action and the falling action. That part of the play between the inciting force and the climax is called the *rising action;* that from the climax to the dénouement the *falling action.* A diagram of the construction of a simple play with no sub-plot to complicate matters might resemble this:

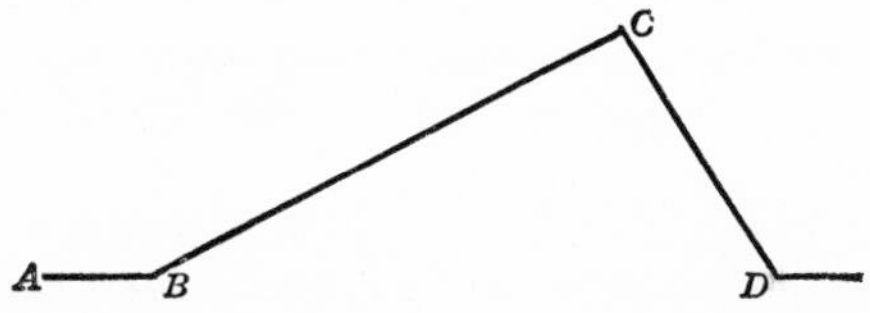

Diagram of the plot construction of a typical Shakespearean play

A to *B* represents the preliminary exposition; *B* the inciting force; *B* to *C* the rising action; *C* the climax; *C* to *D* the falling action; *D* the dénouement. Plays vary, of course, in structure. Some have much preliminary exposition, some none at all. Some end at the climax; some, after a short rising action and a climax, have an *anti-climax.* Some have several climaxes. Some interweave several stories, plots, and sub-plots, each with its inciting force, its climax, and its dénouement. The diagram above disregards sub-plots, giving merely the main structure of an Elizabethan play.

Variations in Elizabethan plot development. Shakespeare did not always construct his plays according to the same pattern. Like every artist he experimented with different forms. For historical plays like *King Henry IV*, Part I, he tried the "framework" scheme of putting the historical parts chiefly in Acts I, III, and V and filling in the framework with the imaginary characters of Falstaff and his companions. In *Romeo and Juliet* and *Othello* the falling action is filled with increasing rather than decreasing suspense. In *Antony and Cleopatra* the structure is loose and episodic; *King Lear* is long and difficult, written beyond the resources of the theater; *Macbeth* is so short as to seem to some critics only a sketch of a play; *Othello* is a masterpiece of perfect plotting. *As You Like It* gets along with little or no plot or action; *Twelfth Night* is full of both.

Plot complications. As the struggle of a play progresses, new elements which complicate matters are usually brought forward. For instance, a play may open with two young men in love with the same girl. Just that situation alone will not make a play. Something has to happen to set the plot in motion. Perhaps the girl expresses a preference for one of the men. The reactions of the rejected suitor thereupon create a new situation. Perhaps he seeks to revenge himself upon his rival. Perhaps he chooses the course of self-sacrifice and then discovers that the other man is unworthy. Whatever he does leads to something further. In any play something happens to develop plot action. This process of developing action from the opening situation is the *plot complication.*

The complicating elements. To judge a play critically one must consider the complicating elements. In *The Merchant of Venice* the opening situation is complicated by Antonio's inability to furnish Bassanio with money and his consequent application to Shylock. The "merry bond" upon which Shylock insists is a further complication. Another complication follows in the elopement of Jessica with one of Antonio's friends which goads Shylock to a passion for revenge. This is followed by the loss of Antonio's ships, the choice of the right casket by Bassanio, the confession of Portia, Portia's sudden resolution to go to Venice, the trial and subsequent ruin of Shylock. But these are not all the elements introduced into the play. To create suspense and to let the audience know the right casket in advance of Bassanio's choosing, Shakespeare brings in the two princes who try their fate. To create humor and additional sentimental interest, he develops a love affair between Gratiano and Nerissa. And finally to eke out his play, after Antonio is saved, he puts in the episode of the rings. Thus we have a fairly complicated story involving many characters and much dramatic suspense, in which many complicating elements are woven together to make one definite, harmonious plot. In criticizing a play, we should ask ourselves whether the complicating elements are few or many; and if many, whether they are knitted firmly together to make a consistent whole.

Difficulty of fitting characters to a ready-made plot. In *The Merchant of Venice,* we feel that the complications are somewhat artificial, invented for the plot-construction rather than resulting from the development of the characters. The story came first, and the characters were made to fit it. This method is artificial but not difficult. It was Shakespeare's way, for he almost never invented his own stories; he borrowed them from various sources. However, he created such lifelike characters that we forget the artificialities of the plot. In *The Merchant of Venice, As You Like It, Twelfth Night,* and *A Midsummer Night's Dream* the complicating elements are all artificial; chance plays too conspicuous a part in them. These plays are nevertheless great because they contain great poetry and great characterization. In *Hamlet* and *Macbeth,* however, the story seems to grow out of the men's characters. Hamlet makes his own tragedy, and so does Macbeth. We must ask ourselves, then, "Are the complicating elements of the play natural outgrowths of human relationships or are they artificial, made in advance without regard to the characters? Is the story human or is it machine-made? Do things happen because people are what they are or just because the dramatist wanted to complicate the plot?"

Originality of the complicating elements. We may also question the originality of the complicating elements. We must not, however, demand that a story be wholly original. The basic situations out of which a story can be made are not very numerous. The story of Cinderella, for instance, is perennially popular. Hundreds of playwrights have taken the situation of the despised Cinderella who finally attains success and, by a little revision of its details, made it sound new. It is perfectly proper that they should, for the Cinderella story has in it elements which are universal. But the outlines of the original story with the wicked stepmother and sisters, the fairy coach, and the glass slipper cannot be used over and over again. These complicating elements must be revised and changed so that the old situation will seem fresh—a new treatment of the ancient theme. For such a treatment of this very story read Barrie's *A Kiss for Cinderella*. *Quality Street* and *What Every Woman Knows* have in them more than one strand of the original Cinderella thread, but they are original plays for all that, because they are fresh in treatment. Stories of mistaken identity, of false accusation, of self-sacrifice, of wandering spirits regenerated by some ennobling influence—all these old themes can be told with originality in the handling of their complicating elements. It is staleness and flatness of treatment to which we rightly object in judging a play, not familiarity of theme.

Complicating elements in a play should be related to life. What matters is not whether complications are old or new or even whether they are probable or improbable, but whether or not they interpret life. A play like *The Comedy of Errors* or *The Taming of the Shrew* may be full of entertaining complications, but it has no relationship to life at all. *The Merchant of Venice* is improbable, but it gives us a picture of real people and it is concerned with actual human values. *The Rivals* is vastly amusing, but not to be taken seriously; *The School for Scandal* goes more deeply under the surface and hence emerges less superficial than its sister piece. In contemporary drama, a melodrama like *The Green Goddess* has no important relation to life, but *The Wild Duck*, *The Cherry Orchard*, *Journey's End*, *The Show-off*, *Loyalties*, *Holiday*, *Anna Christie*, *The Hairy Ape* perhaps even *Once in a Lifetime* and *Of Thee I Sing* seem a part of the very substance of which life is made. Mere complication in a play, then, is significant only as it helps to interpret life.

Sub-plots. Perhaps some of the complicating elements form a little story in themselves. The Elizabethans liked a full story dealing with many characters, so that we rarely find an Elizabethan play like *Othello* with no sub-plots. *The Merchant of Venice*, for instance, contains many stories: the story of the bond, the story of the caskets, the story of the rings. These are so skillfully interwoven, however, that we cannot think of one without the others. For this reason, *The Merchant of Venice* is a striking example of the successful fusion of different plot elements.

Plot structure of *A Midsummer Night's Dream*. *A Midsummer Night's Dream* is another example of different elements which are combined to make a unified play. Here we have the framework of the story in the approaching wedding of Theseus and Hippolyta, into which are inserted the story of the young lovers in the wood, the story of the quarrel and reconciliation of Oberon and Titania, and the story of the rustics and their play of Pyramus and Thisby. Each of these elements is introduced in Act I; in Act II the fairy group is united with the lover group by the complicating effects of the love potion, and with the rustic group by the strange translation of bully Bottom; in Act III these groups are thoroughly fused, and the process of unraveling the complications begins. In the fifth act, by means of the double wedding, the Pyramus and Thisby play, and the final reconciliation and pageant of the fairies, all groups are brought together in a triumphant conclusion. Over the whole is thrown the atmosphere of fairyland which gives the play unity of tone as well as of action.

Plot structure of *The Alchemist*. The most famous example of perfect fusion of complicated plot elements, however, is to be found in Ben Jonson's *The Alchemist*, considered by Coleridge and others to be one of the few perfect plots in existence. Here is a play which observes the classical unities of time and place and yet brings many people with many conflicting motives together so that each is clearly developed, naturally motivated, and skillfully combined with the rest. Not only is all this effected, but the suspense is maintained in increasing degree as the play progresses. At any moment the three tricksters, Subtle, Face, and Doll Common, may be betrayed by: (1) the return of their master, Lovewit, which would ruin them; (2) their own mutual suspicions and jealousies, which would lead to "double crossing"; (3) the increasing suspicions of the gambler, Surly; or (4) the fact that it will be impossible for long to keep so many victims in ignorance of the real state of affairs. The management of the exits and entrances alone in so complicated a play as this is well worth studying. Probably *The Alchemist* is the last word in skillful plotting.

Testing the dramatist's skill in handling complications. In judging the complications of any play then, we must ask: "Does it tell more than one story? If so, are these stories satisfactorily combined so that they are interdependent? Are the complicating elements few or many? artificial or natural, futile inventiveness or old stuff? How is suspense maintained? And last of all is the whole firmly knit together? To answer these questions let us analyze the construction of a few plays.

Opening scenes. The beginning of a play is even more important than the beginning of a novel. With only about two hours at his disposal, the dramatist has not a moment to lose. He must at the outset explain the existing situation with whatever antecedent action is necessary to our understanding of the plot, introduce his characters, get his story under way, and arrest the immediate attention of the audience. In times gone by, a dramatist could drag into his play subordinate characters, the servants or guests of the family, who would discuss the principal characters and explain the situation to the audience. Modern audiences consider such scenes clumsy and devoid of interest even in such a play as Clyde Fitch's *Beau Brummell.* The modern tendency in drama is to reduce the number of characters. Nevertheless, however few or many characters there are, they cannot usually be introduced at once without confusing the audience. As soon as possible after the rising of the curtain, the audience must know who the person speaking is and what his relationship is to other people in the play. Partly for this necessity of introducing and orienting his characters, a dramatist often delays the entrance of the leading character until the audience is somewhat familiar with him through the talk of others.

The dramatist must, however, make his dialogue natural; the audience should not feel that the characters are mouthpieces for the broadcasting of information. Nowadays the audience gains a certain amount of information from the printed program. In Shakespeare's day there were no programs, so that much information had to be given in the opening scenes which, in consequence, were often stilted. In *Romeo and Juliet* Shakespeare brings in a chorus to explain the situation in which "A pair of star-cross'd lovers take their life." In *As You Like It* he makes Orlando, for the benefit of the audience, explain at length to Adam, who obviously was familiar with the situation, his unfortunate position in his brother's house. The whole story is repeated at the entrance of Oliver; shortly afterwards Oliver confides his hatred of Orlando to Charles; and upon the departure of Charles he goes over the whole subject again in soliloquy. Even the untutored people in the pit must by this time have got the matter straight. The

THE DEATH OF TYBALT
From *Romeo and Juliet.*

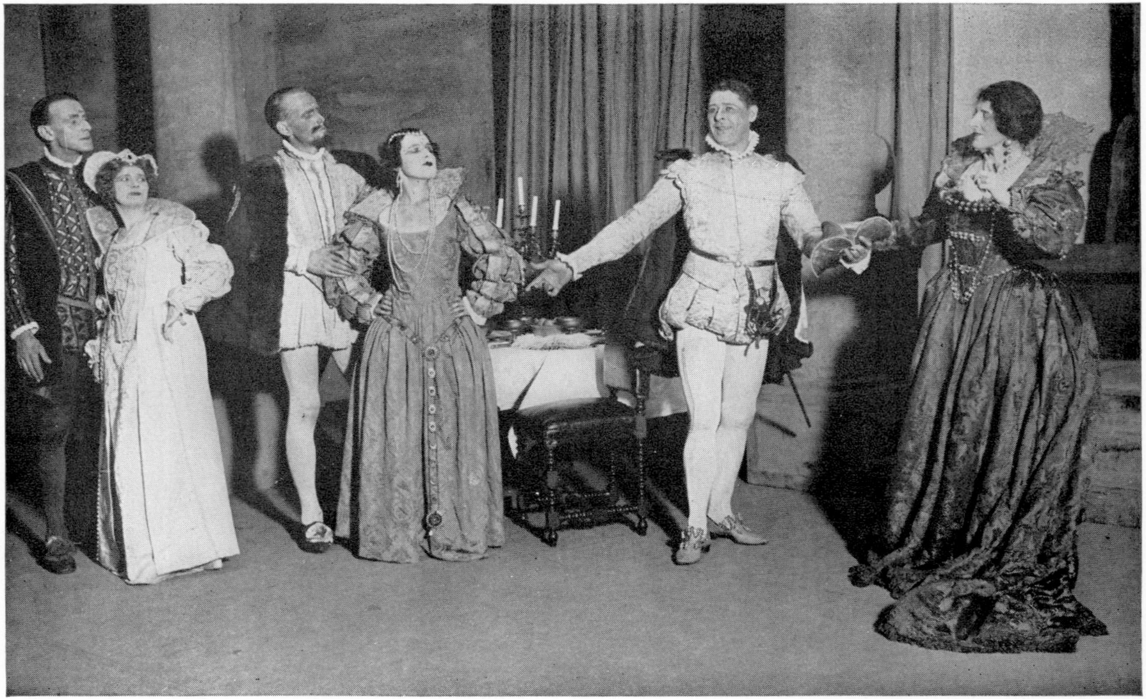

PETRUCHIO TRIUMPHS

From *The Taming of the Shrew* in a modern English production.

situation of Rosalind and Celia at the court is explained in almost as wooden a fashion, although Rosalind manages to give spontaneity to almost all the scenes in which she appears.

Most of Shakespeare's plays are more successful in their opening scenes. *Julius Caesar* begins with a scene of bustling horseplay and confusion and pageantry, all dear to Elizabethan audiences, which at the same time makes clear without delay, time, place, and principal characters. Notice how our attention is first directed to the common people, who are to have a decisive influence on the play, then to Caesar and Antony, and finally to Brutus and Cassius. The proud, sad isolation of Brutus is skillfully suggested at the moment of his first appearance.

Hamlet has a masterly opening scene with the bitter cold night, the shivering sentries ready to start at the slightest sound, the dark shadow of the castle, and the sense of impending, supernatural disaster. The first scene of *Macbeth,* if well acted, holds the imagination of the audience spellbound and at the same time strikes the keynote of the play. *Othello* opens on a dark night in a deserted street with two men plotting in the shadows, thus giving at once an atmosphere of treachery. *Romeo and Juliet* opens with the sudden violence of a street brawl between the Capulets and the Montagues—a significant suggestion of a drama of quick passions.

The rising action and minor crises. Once the preliminary exposition is disposed of, the rising action of a play should lead by rapid degrees of increasing interest to the climax. The rising action of a play is usually the easiest to write since, as new complicating elements are introduced, the interest naturally increases until the turning point of the struggle. The rising action is usually filled with points of interest or *minor crises,* where the suspense is increased because of a new complicating element or a new turn in the struggle. These dramatic moments increase in importance and frequency till the play leads inevitably to a final turning point, the *climax.* In a modern play the most important of these minor crises usually come at the end of each act so that the curtain goes down on a dramatic scene, the climax coming at the end of the next to the last act. In a Shakespearean play such a structure was not practicable because of Elizabethan stage conditions, but the minor crises and the climax are there just the same.

Rising action and climax in *Julius Caesar*. In *Julius Caesar* minor moments of dramatic suspense are provided in increasing number up to the assassination of Caesar. The scene between Caesar and Calpurnia makes us feel that he may not go to the Capitol after all; the short scene between Portia and the soothsayer suggests that the conspiracy may have been discovered; the incident of Artemidorus increases this suspense which is made more intense by the curious behavior of Popilius Lena. All these lead up in a steady crescendo to the tremendous crisis of the murder itself, and then the suspense of the play advances by leaps and bounds to the scene of the funeral oration, the real climax. And even in this funeral scene the final result of the speech is not certain until the very end, when Antony reads Caesar's will. This climax has all the qualities which a climax should have: it comes at the end of a steady series of minor crises, it is inevitable, it has a strong emotional appeal, and it is decisive.

In judging the rising action of any play we should ask these questions: Does the interest rise with the rising action to the climax of the play? Does the author introduce minor crises, moments of dramatic tension, of increasing intensity, as the play progresses? Is the final climax the natural outgrowth of all that has gone before it? Is the climax a decisive turn in the struggle? Has it a strong emotional appeal?

The falling action. So far as suspense is concerned the falling action is the hardest part of the play to write. Once the turning point has been reached, it is difficult to avoid an emotional relaxation that may lead to loss of interest. It is noticeable that the interest in a good many of Shakespeare's plays lags during the fourth act, the one which usually follows the climax. In *Macbeth* the height of the interest is reached at the banquet scene; when Macbeth sees the ghost of Banquo and learns that Banquo's son has escaped, his nerves give way and he betrays himself.

The falling action of *Macbeth* and *Hamlet*. After the climax we feel sure of the end. Consequently the fourth act drags a little. The scene in the witches' cave and the murder of Lady Macduff and her child are fairly successful attempts to keep up the interest, but nothing can make the long scene between Malcolm, Ross, and Macduff in England anything but dull so far as the main interest in the play goes. The fourth act of *Hamlet* is even more halting. After the play and the closet scene, the interest lags undeniably until the fifth act.

Successful falling action in Shakespeare. In some plays Shakespeare is most successful in developing his falling action. The fourth act of *The Merchant of Venice*, for example, is the most interesting act in the play, because of the emotional tension of the court scene. The quarrel of Brutus and Cassius helps the fourth act of *Julius Caesar* which is otherwise weak. In *As You Like It* no climax is reached until the fourth act when the appearance of Oliver in the forest and the swooning of Rosalind at the news of Orlando's heroism make us feel that the dénouement of the comedy is near. After this, the unraveling of the plot is rapid. *Othello* has no well-defined climax; the fourth act contains moments of as great tension as any in the play. In judging any play, we should, therefore, note especially how the falling action is managed. Does the action drag after the climax, to pick up again toward the end of the play, or does the author succeed in making the falling action as interesting as all that has gone before it? If he is thus successful, by what means does he attain his success? Is it by delaying the climax to almost the end of the play, thereby making the falling action short and fast? Is it by the introduction into the falling action of scenes dramatically interesting in themselves, a *retarding point*, so-called? Is the interest in the reactions of the characters to the climax sufficient to carry the falling action? Or are the after effects of the climax uncertain enough to create suspense till the end of the play?

The principles governing dénouement. The same artistic principles that govern the ending of any story apply to the drama as well. The ending should be logical and hence satisfactory, but not necessarily happy. A happy ending to *Hamlet* or *King Lear* or *Macbeth* would be irrelevant. But to have ended *As You Like It* or *A Midsummer Night's Dream* unhappily would have been downright treachery to the audience. The nature of the story, that is, the whole trend of its plot and characters, and the purpose of the author in telling the story should be considered. If *Romeo and Juliet* is to be the short and blissful tragedy of young love, there would certainly be nothing gained by letting the young lovers go on to an unromantic old age. If Lear and Cordelia have lived and suffered through five harrowing acts, no one in the audience should begrudge them the peace of death. Kent says truly to the grieving Edgar:

> Vex not his ghost; O, let him pass! he hates him
> That would upon the rack of this tough world
> Stretch him out longer.

If John Galsworthy's *The Silver Box* is to teach the bitter lesson of social and economic injustice that it sets out to teach, it cannot give in to the public's weakness for a happy ending; Mrs. Jones must suffer unjustly or the lesson of the play will be lost on the audience. Ibsen's *A Doll's House* would lose its whole point if Nora remained with her husband. The idea behind Barrie's *The Admirable Crichton* would have been inexcusably falsified if Crichton had married Lady Mary. Whether or not we like the ending of a play, we must be clear-sighted enough to see whither the plot has been tending, what the characters are making of their lives, what the purpose of the author is, and then we must accept the inevitable ending whatever it be.

SECURING DRAMATIC EMPHASIS AND ECONOMY

The principle of dramatic emphasis. *In a play everything has to be concretely shown to the audience. The author cannot depend on his own comment as he can in a novel; his play must stand or fall by what is said and done on the stage.* Accordingly, if he wishes to produce a certain effect, he has to use a scene or character for that purpose. In *The School for Scandal* if we are to believe in the inherent generosity of the gay Charles Surface, we must see him doing something recklessly fine; accordingly we have the famous picture scene in which he refuses to part with his uncle's portrait. Later in the same play we *see* the hypocritical Joseph caught in the net of his own weaving. In *The Rivals*, it is demonstrated to us by speech and action that Lydia Languish is foolishly sentimental, that Jack Absolute is resourceful and "nervy," that Sir Anthony Absolute has an ungovernable temper, that Faulkland is insanely jealous, that Sir Lucius O'Trigger loves a fight, that Bob Acres is a coward. In *Twelfth Night* we are *witnesses* of the quarrel between Sir Toby and Malvolio and its results, of the cowardice and silliness of Sir Andrew, of the courage and humor and feminine charm of Viola. In *The Taming of the Shrew* we *see* the effects of Katherina's shrewish behavior, and the methods by which Petruchio cures her; and in the end her speech and actions prove to us that she is cured. In a modern play like *Loyalties* the theme of the play, that people would rather be loyal than just, is *demonstrated* to us by the *speech* and *actions* of the characters. In *The Emperor Jones* we *hear* the relentless tom-toms and see the visions with which fear tortures the doomed Jones. This necessity of *showing* an audience emphatically what the dramatist wants stressed is called *the principle of dramatic emphasis.*

Dramatic contrast. A favorite method of securing dramatic emphasis is contrast. Most intensely dramatic plays are full of contrast. Strikingly different characters are placed side by side. A scene of strong emotional tension is relieved by a humorous remark or a humorous episode. A period of calm is followed by one of storm and stress, or vice versa. No dramatist was ever more fond of this device of contrast than Shakespeare. *Macbeth* is filled with startling antithesis. Almost the first words of the play are contradictory:

> Fair is foul, and foul is fair.

Macbeth has "reaped golden opinions of all sorts of people" when the play opens, but at the end his name "blisters the tongue." "A little water clears us of this deed!" exclaims Lady Macbeth after the murder of Duncan, but later she moans in her sleep, "All the perfumes of Arabia will not sweeten this little hand." The gentle, trusting Duncan is contrasted with his black and treacherous host. The hours of Macbeth's triumphs are transformed into the hours of his greatest agony. The scene where Macbeth, emerging from the chamber of Duncan with Duncan's blood upon his hands, stands with his wife shivering and whispering, is followed by the coarse comedy of the drunken porter.

All Shakespeare's plays use contrast in this same way. In *Julius Caesar* there is a telling contrast between the fierce bitterness, jealousy, hurt pride, and hot anger of the quarrel scene and the quiet, peaceful tenderness of the scene between Brutus and his little page. In *The Winter's Tale* passages of almost revolting ugliness and violence are followed by poetry of the most delicate beauty, such as Perdita's:

> daffodils
> That come before the swallow dares, and take
> The winds of March with beauty; violets dim,
> But sweeter than the lids of Juno's eyes
> Or Cytherea's breath.

The imagery shifts from the violence of Paulina's:

> What studied torments, tyrant, hast for me?
> What wheels? racks? fires? what flaying? boiling?
> In lead or oils?

to the boyish enthusiasm of Florizel's:

> What you do
> Still betters what is done. When you speak, sweet,
> I'd have you do it ever; when you sing,
> I'd have you buy and sell so, so give alms,
> Pray so; and, for the ordering your affairs,
> To sing them too. When you dance, I wish you
> A wave o' the sea, that you might ever do
> Nothing but that.

In *The Merchant of Venice* the broken, despairing bitterness of Shylock's final humiliation is followed by careless banter about rings and the romantic glamour of Lorenzo's and Jessica's "lyrical boy-and-girl love" in the garden where "the sweet wind doth gently kiss the trees" and "the moonlight sleeps sweet upon this bank." Contrast is a telling dramatic device.

Other dramatic devices. There are, of course, other dramatic devices. Some scenes serve almost wholly to create suspense by *foreshadowing*. Such are the scenes in *Julius Caesar* between Portia and the soothsayer, the scene of the storm, and the scene in which Artemidorus appears. Some scenes merely convey information about the plot or the characters or the general situation of the play. The opening scene of *Julius Caesar* does this; in fact, this is the purpose of the opening scene of most plays. Other scenes serve to establish character. Thus the scene between Antony, Octavius, and Lepidus in *Julius Caesar* shows the character of the triumvirate; the scenes between Brutus and Portia, between Brutus and Lucius, reveal the tender, domestic side of Brutus; the scene between Brutus and Ligarius shows the influence of Brutus over the truly patriotic men of Rome. Other scenes suggest a lapse of time. Thus in *Julius Caesar* the scene at the camp near Sardis immediately preceding the tent scene suggests the lapse of time as well as gives information; so, too, does the scene between Malcolm, Macduff, and Ross, in the fourth act of *Macbeth*.

Scenes made necessary by stage conditions. Occasionally in Elizabethan drama, scenes were inserted because stage conditions made them necessary. Scenes requiring many properties were set up on the rear of the stage which could be curtained off from that part of the stage which projected into the pit. When two scenes requiring different scenery followed each other, it was necessary to insert between them a short scene requiring no setting. This short scene was acted on the front of the stage while the setting was arranged at the back behind the curtain. Elizabethan audiences tolerated no intervals between scenes. After the trial scene in *The Merchant of Venice*, therefore, we have a short scene in the street while the next scene in Portia's garden is being arranged behind the curtains. Such instances are common in Shakespearean drama.

The obligatory scene. The obligatory scene occurs in drama as well as in fiction. This is the scene which the author is under obligations to show us because he has prepared us for it in advance. In *The Merchant of Venice* the court scene is obligatory; we expect it and we should not be satisfied merely to be told about it afterward. In *Julius Caesar* there have been enough differences of opinion between Brutus and Cassius to make the quarrel scene obligatory. In *Twelfth Night*, once Viola has encountered Antonio, we expect her to find her lost brother; and when we hear the plot against Malvolio, we expect a scene in which it works out. Obligatory scenes exist in every drama.

Managing entrances and exits. A practical difficulty in managing the characters in a play lies in the way they are brought on and off the stage, into the play and out of it. Exits and entrances must occur as naturally as possible, and frequently they must be dramatically effective. A character cannot merely come in when he is needed and go out as soon as the author is through with him, and yet he must come and go at the right times. To manage this is no insuperable difficulty, but carelessness on the part of the dramatist sometimes makes exits and entrances obviously mechanical. *Julius Caesar*, an admirably constructed play, contains excellent examples of natural yet dramatically effective management. The second scene of Act I, for instance, serves skillfully to introduce the characters so that the audience will know each one; to characterize by a few deft touches the leading speakers: Antony, Brutus, Cassius, and Caesar; and to set the plot in motion. Yet all these people are brought forward and dismissed so naturally that the technical skill with which it is all done passes almost unnoticed. The scene in the garden of Brutus, the assassination scene, the funeral scene, and the quarrel scene are all managed with the same skill. In *As You Like It*, however, the workmanship is less careful. At the beginning of the play people come in and perform their business rather mechanically, and the action is decidedly spasmodic, as if the dramatist were himself anxious to escape to the Forest of Arden. Le Beau and Charles the wrestler are at times little more than very obvious means of conveying information and getting the plot started. To drag in a character arbitrarily and then to dismiss him as arbitrarily is not careful technique. And to call two characters, one of whom is not really essential, by the same name as is done in *As You Like It* is mere indifference. In *Julius Caesar*, however, all the characters, except possibly the poet, are an integral part of the action; even Ligarius serves a necessary purpose and is not forgotten after the purpose has been accomplished. Notice, then, the way in which characters are brought on to the stage and how naturally they are disposed of when they are no longer needed. Notice, too, the use the author makes of his subordinate characters, whether they are of assistance to the play or introduced as a convenient but not essential means to an end. Perhaps the best subject for a study of these details is Ben Jonson's *The Alchemist*.

Artistic economy. The final principle in the art of playwriting is the principle of artistic economy. It is imperative that good dramatic literature observe this principle which demands that there be no waste of material, no diffusion of attention, and no lack of interest in a play. It is not too much to say that in a perfectly constructed play not a scene is unnecessary, not a character unessential, not a line without its purpose. After selecting his material, a dramatist must go over it again and again, rigorously cutting out what will not be of some dramatic service to him. Almost any fault of construction is preferable to "talkiness," futile engulfing of incident, character, and even ideas in a sea of talk. If a dramatist is to write a good play about Abraham Lincoln, as Drinkwater has, he cannot expect to show all of Lincoln's life in one evening's performance. He must select only those incidents which he thinks will most dramatically emphasize what manner of man his hero was; and he must make his selection with severe economy, no matter how attractive the unessential material may be.

When Drinkwater wrote a play about Mary Stuart, he did not try to show us every fascinating incident in her career; he confined the action of his play to a single night, the night of the murder of her secretary, David Rizzio; but in that short space he managed to suggest to us his clue to the mystery of the romantic Queen of Scots. Clyde Fitch selected with an eye to dramatic emphasis the incidents which reveal the life and character of Beau Brummell.

Shakespeare and artistic economy. Shakespeare cannot show us the whole of Macbeth's life. He selects what he thinks will be most dramatically effective. There are often things we should like to know about a character in a play, but the principle of artistic economy does not permit a dramatist to gossip about his characters in the manner of Thackeray. In *Othello*, as well as in *Julius Caesar*, there is scarcely a superfluous line. Even Shakespeare, however, is not always entirely obedient to the demands of artistic economy; much of his work is too hurried and careless for that; but the fact that the principle is frequently in evidence even in his most crowded work is sufficient proof of its vital importance.

Watch the next play that you see, then, for its artistic economy. Does the author use his material like a careful workman, avoiding waste and useless duplication and futile digressions, or is he extravagant with it, with no regard for value and no taste for proper emphasis?

Summary. To have action a play must have opposing forces. The conflict of these forces makes the plot. The chief figures in the plot are called *protagonists* and *antagonists*. A plot is built up from *preliminary exposition* to a *moment of inciting force*, *rising action*, *climax*, *falling action*, and *dénouement*. The *beginning* must be *clear*, *brief*, and *interesting*. The *complications* which keep the plot going must have some relation to human life. The *climax* should come at the end of a series of minor crises, be inevitable, decisive, and have strong emotional appeal. The *falling action* should be natural and interesting. The *dénouement* should be logical and satisfactory.

Dramatic emphasis must be maintained by demonstrating every point to the audience. Every scene of the play must have a dramatic purpose, and some scenes are obligatory. Exits and entrances must be managed dramatically and naturally. All plays must observe the principle of *artistic economy*.

COMPREHENSION QUESTIONS

1. *Vocabulary:* struggle, protagonist, antagonist, rising action, preliminary exposition, falling action, moment of inciting force, climax, dénouement, complicating elements, dramatic emphasis, obligatory scene, artistic economy.

2. Why must a play involve struggle if it is to have action?
3. Point out protagonists and antagonists in two plays you have read or seen recently.
4. What qualities should the preliminary exposition have? Why is the preliminary exposition of *Hamlet* superior to that of *As You Like It* or *The Rivals?* Criticize the preliminary exposition of some play or moving picture you have seen recently; for instance, *Camille*.
5. In any play you have read or seen, point out some of the minor crises which occur before the climax.
6. Define *climax*. What specific qualities should a climax have?
7. Why is the falling action hard to write? Compare the falling action of *Macbeth*, *Hamlet*, *Othello*, and *Romeo and Juliet*. What do modern playwrights mean by "third-act trouble"?
8. What is the principle of dramatic emphasis? Illustrate it by reference to some play.
9. Point out by examples how playwrights secure dramatic emphasis by using some tangible object on which to focus the attention of the audience; for instance, the caskets in *The Merchant of Venice*, the skull in *Hamlet*, and the chain of nuggets in *The Great Divide*.
10. Explain and illustrate what is meant by *obligatory scene*.
11. Explain and illustrate what is meant by *artistic economy*.

APPRECIATION PROBLEMS AND REVIEW QUESTIONS

1. Choose one of the following plays, read it, or review it if you have studied it before, and point out the complicating elements as we have done on page 330 for *The Merchant of Venice*. Show each circumstance that serves to set the action of the play in motion, complicate the plot, and finally unravel the complication. Do these complications form a logical chain of events, or are they erratic or disconnected? Which arise from accident and which from human nature? Do they serve to bring out and develop the characters or are they merely tricks to keep the story moving?

Barrie	*Quality Street*
Philip Barry	*Holiday*
Henri Becque	*The Vultures*
Benavente	*The Bonds of Interest*
Rose D. Franken	*Another Language*
Galsworthy	*Escape, Justice, Loyalties*
Goldsmith	*She Stoops to Conquer*
Ibsen	*A Doll's House, An Enemy of the People, Hedda Gabler*

Jonson	*The Alchemist*
George Kelly	*The Show-off*
Philip Massinger	*A New Way to Pay Old Debts*
Molnar	*The Swan*
Shakespeare	*A Midsummer Night's Dream, Much Ado about Nothing, Othello, Romeo and Juliet*
Shaw	*Arms and the Man, The Devil's Disciple*
Sheridan	*The Rivals, The School for Scandal*
Eugene Walter	*The Easiest Way*
Wilde	*Lady Windermere's Fan*

2. Sometimes a whole act or scene will be built up like a play, forming a complete little drama in itself with an inciting force, a rising action, climax, falling action, dénouement, minor crises, suspense, surprise, and so on. Beaumont and Fletcher, the chief successors of Shakespeare, made such scenes the main basis of their plays. Study the following scenes to show how each is really a dramatic unit in itself:

The Admirable Crichton, Act III, Crichton's day of triumph
Androcles and the Lion, outside the arena
Dear Brutus, Act II, midsummer eve
Holiday, the crisis in the nursery
Julius Caesar, Act III, the funeral oration or, Act IV, the quarrel in the tent
The Merchant of Venice, Act IV, the pound of flesh
Othello, Act III, scene 3, Iago shapes human destinies
Romeo and Juliet, Act III, scene 1, the death of Mercutio
The School for Scandal, the picture-gallery scene, the screen scene
Twelfth Night, the duel between Sir Andrew and Viola

3. What is the struggle which constitutes the plot of one of the following plays?

Maxwell Anderson	*Elizabeth the Queen, Mary of Scotland*
Samuel Nathaniel Behrman	*Biography*
Karel M. Capek	*R.U.R.*
Rose D. Franken	*Another Language*
Galsworthy	*Strife*
Sidney Coe Howard	*The Silver Cord*
Ibsen	*An Enemy of the People, Rosmersholm, Hedda Gabler*
William Vaughn Moody	*The Great Divide*

O'Neill	*Mourning Becomes Electra*
Rostand	*Cyrano de Bergerac*
Shakespeare	*As You Like It, Hamlet, Macbeth, Othello, Twelfth Night*
Robert Cedric Sherriff	*Journey's End*
John Van Druten	*Young Woodley*

4. Explain how sub-plots are woven in with main plots in *The Merchant of Venice* and *Twelfth Night*. Which play do you consider more skillful in this respect?

5. In one of the plays in the lists in Problems 1 and 3 find scenes used:
   (*a*) for contrast, (*b*) for comic relief, (*c*) for foreshadowing, (*d*) to convey information, (*e*) to establish character, (*f*) to establish setting, (*g*) to suggest lapse of time.

6. In one of the plays listed in Problems 1 or 3 discuss the use of the *obligatory scene.*

7. Examine carefully the structure of *Macbeth*. It is the shortest of Shakespeare's tragedies—so short that some critics have thought some of it to be lost.
   (*a*) Do you think anything essential to the action is missing? (*b*) Are there any digressions? any places where the action halts? (*c*) Which scene seems to receive undue emphasis in proportion to what it contributes to plot and character? (*d*) The scene of the murder of Lady Macduff has been criticized as an introduction of unnecessary brutality. Do you agree with this criticism? Why, or why not? If this scene is omitted, what is lost to the play? (*e*) The speeches of Hecate and the dialogue connected with them are by some critics attributed to another author than Shakespeare. Is this because of their inferior style? Do you think them structurally necessary to the play? (*f*) Where is the inciting force of the play? the preliminary exposition? (*g*) Which scenes comprise the rising action? (*h*) Where is the climax? (*i*) Which scenes comprise the falling action? (*j*) Where is the catastrophe? (*k*) Point out what each act and scene contributes to plot, character, setting, and theme. (*l*) What is your judgment of the dramatic structure as a whole? (*m*) Draw a diagram illustrating the structure of *Macbeth.*

8. Comment on the beginning of *Othello*, on the use of minor crises, on plot complications and the way in which they are worked out.

9. Write an essay on the three especially effective devices for securing emphasis in *Macbeth.*
   (*a*) use of contrast, (*b*) use of irony, (*c*) the iteration of certain words, phrases, and ideas.

10. Show how the outward and inward (that is, the moral and physical) struggles in *Macbeth* are inseparable at every point.

11. In *Macbeth,* is the banquet scene inevitable, climactic, strongly emotional, decisive? Discuss each point.

12. Find in *Othello* scenes used for dramatic emphasis, for contrast, for relief, for foreshadowing, for conveying information, for establishing character, for suggesting a lapse of time.

13. Discuss the principle of artistic economy as illustrated by these plays:

Drinkwater	*Abraham Lincoln*
St. John Ervine	*Jane Clegg*
Galsworthy	*Loyalties*
Susan Glaspell	*Trifles*
Isabella Augusta Gregory	*The Rising of the Moon*
Ibsen	*Rosmersholm*
Molnar	*Liliom*
Shakespeare	*Othello*
Synge	*Riders to the Sea*
Sutton Vane	*Outward Bound*

CHAPTER 25

WHAT TO LOOK FOR IN STUDYING CHARACTERS

Reality in characterization. Shakespeare, as we have seen, usually took an old story or an old play and rewrote it. Often he built up his plots from several stories which he combined. At first he was not wholly successful in making characters do naturally the things arbitrarily demanded of them by the plot. The characters in his early plays are not always well-rounded, living people. In *A Midsummer Night's Dream* Hermia and Helena are scarcely individualized at all; Oberon and Titania are as unreal as fairies may well be; but Puck and Bottom are strongly individualized. In the later comedies there is a distinct advance in character drawing. Shylock is such a human creation that he nearly distracts our interest from the plot; to many people *The Merchant of Venice* is the tragedy of Shylock rather than the romance of Portia. The character of Viola gives a fragrant charm to *Twelfth Night;* and Sir Andrew, Sir Toby, Maria, and Malvolio are distinct characters who might exist independent of the main action of the story. *As You Like It* is filled with charming people who make us forget the absurdity of the story. *Much Ado about Nothing* contains Benedick and Beatrice and Dogberry, and for them we tolerate the rather unsatisfactory love story of Hero and Claudio. These plays show the ability to create real people; the characters make the play in spite of the plot.

Artificiality in characterization. But notice the improbabilities in character drawing that result from the artificial stories into which Shakespeare has thrust some of his people. No one can condone the conduct of Jessica in *The Merchant of Venice;* yet no one can blame her, for she is a creature of the plot. To account for Shylock's hatred Shakespeare could not but be inconsistent here. In *Twelfth Night* the obliging cheerfulness with which Orsino transfers his affections from Olivia to Viola and the equally astounding match between Olivia and Sebastian are inconceivable; yet if these things did not happen, there would be no story. In *As You Like It*, the sudden conversion of Duke Frederick, the remarkable reform of Oliver, and the rapid attachment of Oliver and Celia who "no sooner met but they looked, no sooner looked but they loved, no sooner loved but they sighed, no sooner sighed but they asked one another the reason, no sooner knew the reason but they sought the remedy," are occurrences certainly not consistent with human nature outside the Forest of Arden. Outside the Forest of Arden, we fear that Orlando would have seen through Rosalind's disguise at once. But if the characters had acted consistently, what would have become of the story? In all these plays, Shakespeare has borrowed stories with ready-made plots, weaving them into plays; but he has created such real people for them that we feel surprised and hurt when they cease momentarily to be real in order to go through with the plot. We expect them to take the plot into their own hands.

Adapting characters to plot. In his greatest plays, however, Shakespeare has so wonderfully adapted character to plot that the whole story seems to proceed from the inner lives of the characters. All the sources of the main plot of *Hamlet* are not known, though the story was certainly not original with Shakespeare; but when we read or see the play we are interested only in the problem that the *character* Hamlet presents; everything that happens seems to proceed from that unfathomable spirit. In *Macbeth* the tragedy emerges inevitably from the dark mists of Macbeth's guilty thoughts. The plot of *Othello* proceeds directly from the principal characters involved. Every character in *Julius Caesar* shapes the course of his own life. Our first interest in the characters of a play, then, should be in relation to the plot. Do they make the plot or does the plot make them?

Plays revolving about one dominant character. Frequently the whole action of a play revolves about one central figure. In comparison with this central figure, the other characters are mere figureheads in the plot; they may be slightly individualized, but they are interesting mainly in their relationship to the overshadowing figure of the play. *Hamlet* is such a play. The Queen, Ophelia, and Horatio come in for a share of our attention, but without the fascinating central figure there could be no serious interest in the play. *Macbeth*, too, exists for the sake of its two protagonists; the others, Macduff, Ross, Lenox, Duncan, Malcolm, are but faintly outlined figures, emphasized chiefly as they throw light on that guilty pair. Many modern plays revolve thus about one dominant character, for instance, *Cyrano de Bergerac*, *The Show-off*, *Peter Pan*, *The Emperor Jones*. *Julius Caesar*, *King Lear*, *Othello*, *As You Like It*, on the other hand, have a variety of interesting characters. It is hard to say whether Brutus or Cassius or Antony in *Julius Caesar* offers the actor most opportunities.

Opportunities for the actor. In reading a play, always keep in mind the actor's point of view. What part or parts should you prefer to play? What "stage business" should you insert at such and such a point? Does this line call for a gesture and that for a certain facial expression? What tone of voice should be used here? A play is written to be acted; the reader who does not as he reads make himself a potential actor misses the pleasure of reading drama. Who could read the long scene between Brutus and Cassius in *Julius Caesar* ignoring the tone of Cassius' voice, the malignant glint in his eyes, or that sarcastic smile of his

> As if he mock'd himself and scorn'd his spirit
> That could be mov'd to smile at anything?

What reader can afford to pass over the glorious opportunities for the actor in Antony's funeral oration? Does not the quarrel between Brutus and Cassius lose half its humanity if one cannot read it with appropriate tone and gesture? In *Macbeth* what should you have Macbeth and his wife do after the banquet is over and the guests have gone? How should you indicate the weariness, the pathetic tenderness, the bleak despair of Lady Macbeth's brief sentences now that the crisis is past and she has failed? Who but a potential actress can get the real pathos out of the sleep-walking scene? In *As You Like It*, Rosalind must have animation, changing expression, boyish grace, spontaneity of voice and gesture if she is to be a real person. "O coz, coz, coz, my pretty little coz," she cries between smiles and tears to the understanding Celia, "that thou didst know how many fathom deep I am in love!" But if we follow her through the play with the imagination of an actress, we *shall* know. Every tone, every fleeting expression, every careless gesture will cry out for us that "young Orlando hath tripped up the wrestler's heels and her heart both in an instant." To portray the character of Hamlet is many an actor's highest ambition. There is hardly a line in all that long part which is not known to players and audience before the performance begins; yet each actor hopes to give a fresh interpretation, to pluck out anew the heart of Hamlet's mystery. And every reader should seek this, too, for the true reader of plays is at heart an actor; and the actor, as well as the author, is a creator of the part.

What is good acting? Probably there is no wiser comment on acting than Hamlet's advice to the players. What, in contemporary English, does he tell them? Chiefly, he says, the art of acting is "to hold the mirror up to nature." Yet at the same time the actor must build up his characterization with loving care for detail, so that he will seem to live the part. He must create for himself and communicate to the audience a mood and a personality but he must never overdo ("tear a passion to tatters") or underdo it, ("come tardy off"). He must respect the play and not use it merely as a means of exploiting his own personality, and he must value the opinion of the few cultivated persons in the audience more than the applause of the unthinking mob. His gestures, his walk, his poise, his voice, his by-play must all be used in the portrayal of character, not clumsily disregarded or exaggerated to get a cheap effect.

Acting on the screen. A few visits to the movies will demonstrate to any thinking person that most stars and directors have not taken Hamlet's advice too seriously. A great many players, of course, do not pretend to be artists. They realize, no doubt, that they are chosen as types, and they are wisely content to be their pleasant and personable selves. Such people never really become ridiculous or reprehensible in their acting, for they know that it is better to underact than to overdo, and they manage to make a little naturalness and a great deal of personal attractiveness or individuality go a long way. A few others shamelessly exploit their own personalities or physical specialties, sometimes even their private lives and emotions; their "art" too often is blatant exhibitionism. Since the arrival of talking pictures, many experienced actors and actresses from the stage, such as the Barrymores, Marie Dressler, Ruth Chatterton, Helen Hayes, Leslie Howard, Paul Muni, May Robson, Katharine Hepburn, and Alice Brady have come to show the screen what competent acting is really like. Notice how much more resourceful such people are. They know something about inflecting the voice, about significant facial expression, telling gestures, bodily poise. Usually, but not always, they are at some pains to portray a character instead of merely repeating a stereotyped impersonation. The theater has taught them how to time their lines and movements so that they "get across" to an audience. Of course, none of these pretends to be a great artist, and some of them are guilty of annoying mannerisms, but they do know the business of acting. To date, with the exception of Charlie Chaplin, the screen has produced no authentic genius; but good actors and actresses are teaching us that:

(1) The player should respect his play, his part, his fellow players, and his audience.
(2) He should have imagination enough to create character for us instead of merely exploiting his own personality.
(3) He should have a technical equipment in his voice, facial expression, bodily poise, gestures, and by-play that enables him to project the character as he conceives it.

Methods of characterization. The methods of characterization in a play are similar to those in fiction with one important exception. The author cannot, of course, insert his own comment, description, or analysis. He must show the character by what he says or does or by the effect he has on others. There is, of course, a wide range of interpretation possible for the actor, as we have pointed out. The playwright's chief means is dialogue. Shakespeare was able to reveal what characters were thinking and feeling by soliloquies; modern playwrights usually get along without them. That means that what is said on the stage must be doubly effective: it must characterize as well as advance the story or situation. To give the dialogue this necessary dramatic emphasis and still keep it natural is an art in itself.

The second means at the dramatist's disposal is action, which has, naturally, to be visualized by the reader. On the stage the actor's by-play of "stage business" may tell volumes. Watch any good actor or actress for these bits of illuminating action. Lastly the dramatist may use indirect methods; that is, he may reveal a character by the reaction of others toward him, for instance Malvolio in *Twelfth Night* or Charles Surface in *The School for Scandal,* or even by making his dress or the place where he lives, as in Barrie's *A Kiss for Cinderella* or *The Old Lady Shows Her Medals,* show what he is like. In the next play you read, try to classify and analyze the dramatist's methods of characterization.

Number and range of characters. The number and range of characters in a dramatist's work are also a good indication of the depth of his power and the breadth of his sympathies. Most dramatists work within a comparatively restricted field. As you read more widely in the drama, you will soon be able to identify the typical Ibsen or Pinero heroine, to expect the same sort of people and the same sort of talk in all plays by Maeterlinck or by Shaw, to look for the whimsical sentiment that characterizes Barrie. These authors do a certain kind of thing well, but outside of their peculiar sphere they are not usually successful. One cannot imagine Shaw indulging in the mysticism of *The Blue Bird* and *Péllèas and Mélisande* or Maeterlinck dazzling us with the brilliant perversities of *Caesar and Cleopatra* and *Pygmalion.* And as for Barrie, you may take him or leave him, but you will not find another like him.

Depth and range of Shakespeare's insight into character. Shakespeare is different. It has been said that we cannot find the man Shakespeare through his style because he has a different style for every character. Cassius says just what we expect Cassius to say from what we know of him; Brutus has a different way of looking at things and a different manner of speech; Octavius is sharply individualized in a few laconic speeches; and Mark Antony is unmistakably Mark Antony. Shakespeare seems to put himself, as if by psychic magic, into the place of each character and to think and feel and speak with him. Notice the differentiation between Macbeth and his wife. See how the hurt pride and passionate but inarticulate tenderness of Cassius' nature are revealed in but a few words. Read the graveyard scene in *Hamlet.* How differently and yet how truly does the dialogue reveal each speaker! In *The Merchant of Venice* we can hear the very tones of Shylock's voice as he speaks; it is no wonder that few actors have failed to make the part interesting. There seems to be no limit to the range of Shakespeare's power to characterize. We have such diverse creations as the bestial Caliban and the innocent Miranda side by side in *The Tempest*. He sees into the souls of Cleopatra, the serpent of old Nile, and Ophelia, the rose of May, with equal intuition. Lady Macbeth and Desdemona, Celia and Audrey, the wolfish Regan and the sparkling Beatrice, all are equally real. He sees clearly the pathos of old age in King Lear:

LEAR. Pray do not mock me.
I am a very foolish fond old man,
Fourscore and upward, not an hour more nor less;
And to deal plainly,
I fear I am not in my perfect mind.
Methinks I should know you, and know this man;
Yet I am doubtful; for I am mainly ignorant
What place this is; and all the skill I have
Remembers not these garments; nor I know not
Where I did lodge last night. Do not laugh at me;
For, as I am a man, I think this lady
To be my child Cordelia.
COR. And so I am, I am.
LEAR. Be your tears wet? yes, 'faith. I pray, weep not:
If you have poison for me, I will drink it.
I know you do not love me; for your sisters
Have, as I do remember, done me wrong:
You have some cause, they have not.
COR. No cause, no cause.
LEAR. Am I in France?
KENT. In your own kingdom, sir.
LEAR. Do not abuse[1] me.
DOCT. Be comforted, good madam: the great rage,
You see, is kill'd in him: and yet it is danger
To make him even o'er the time he has lost.
Desire him to go in; trouble him no more
Till further settling.
COR. Will 't please your highness walk?
LEAR. You must bear with me:
Pray you now, forget and forgive: I am old and foolish.

He sympathizes, too, with the careless exuberance of youth in Mercutio:

[1] Deceive.

O, then, I see Queen Mab hath been with you.
She is the fairies' midwife, and she comes
In shape no bigger than an agate-stone
On the fore-finger of an alderman,
Drawn with a team of little atomies
Athwart men's noses as they lie asleep;
Her waggon-spokes made of long spinners' legs,
The cover of the wings of grasshoppers,
Her traces of the smallest spider web,
Her collars of the moonshine's watery beams,
Her whip of cricket's bone, the lash of film,
Her waggoner a small grey-coated gnat,
Not half so big as a round little worm
Prick'd from the lazy finger of a maid;
Her chariot is an empty hazel-nut
Made by the joiner squirrel or old grub,
Time out o' mind the fairies' coachmakers.
And in this state she gallops night by night
Through lovers' brains, and then they dream of love;
On courtiers' knees, that dream on curtsies straight,
O'er lawyers' fingers, who straight dream on fees;
O'er ladies' lips, who straight on kisses dream,
Which oft the angry Mab with blisters plagues,
Because their breaths with sweetmeats tainted are.
Sometime she gallops o'er a courtier's nose,
And then dreams he of smelling out a suit;
And sometime comes she with a tithe-pig's tail
Tickling a parson's nose as a' lies asleep,
Then dreams he of another benefice:
Sometime she driveth o'er a soldier's neck,
And then dreams he of cutting foreign throats,
Of breaches, ambuscadoes, Spanish blades,
Of healths five-fathom deep; and then anon
Drums in his ear, at which he starts and wakes,
And being thus frighted swears a prayer or two
And sleeps again.

He understands equally well the simple manliness of Horatio, who has been

As one, in suffering all, that suffers nothing,
A man that fortune's buffets and rewards
Hast ta'en with equal thanks,

and the strange combination of sensuality and imagination in Falstaff, who, on being told that he owes God a death on the battlefield of honor, philosophizes:

'Tis not due yet; I would be loath to pay him before his day. What need I be so forward with him that calls not on me? Well, 'tis no matter; honour pricks me on. Yea, but how if honour prick me off when I come on? how then? Can honour set to a leg? no; or an arm? no; or take away the grief of a wound? no. Honour hath no skill in surgery, then? no. What is honour? a word. What is that word honour? air. A trim reckoning! Who hath it? he that died o' Wednesday. Doth he feel it? no. Doth he hear it? no. Is it insensible, then? yea, to the dead. But will it not live with the living? no. Why? detraction will not suffer it. Therefore I'll none of it. Honour is a mere scutcheon; and so ends my catechism.

Quite different from this is the Elizabethan enthusiasm shown by Hotspur in the same play:

By heaven, methinks it were an easy leap,
To pluck bright honour from the pale-faced moon,
Or dive into the bottom of the deep,
Where fathom-line could never touch the ground,
And pluck up drowned honour by the locks!

The depth and range of Shakespeare's knowledge of human nature distinguish him from all other dramatists.

What to consider in studying number and range of characters. In studying the number and range of any dramatist's characters we ask ourselves certain questions. Are the characters few or many? Are they drawn from one class of society or from all classes? Are they individualized or merely typical? Does the author excel in portraying one type or is he master of several? Can you identify him by the sort of people he writes about?

"Stock" characters. You may have noticed that the players in the average stock company are listed according to the type of character which they habitually play. Thus we have a leading man and a leading woman, a pair of "second leads," a "character" man and woman, a "juvenile," an "ingenue." This is really a sad commentary on the characters in a good many plays; they are really nothing but stock figures designed to supply the average company with acting material. These plays have a "comedy part," a "character part," an inevitable sub-plot for the juvenile and the ingenue, a "heavy character part" usually for the villain, and the "big scenes" for the leading actors. The characters are moved by easy machine-made motives, and their reactions are conventional means of advancing the plot. It would be discouraging to discover just what percentage of the plays written for amateur and professional performance in this country is thus constructed.

Distortions of life on the screen. Perhaps the easiest way in which you can observe this sort of mechanical character drawing is to go to the moving pictures. It is true that the industry is making rapid strides and that much sincere and hard work on the part of individual players and directors goes into the pictures. But far too many of them are stupid ready-made stories about stuffed puppets concocted to please the most unthinking part of the audience, a process cynically known to moviemen as "dumbing up" the films. In any good motion picture you can find short scenes which at once strike home with their intimate truth, but few pictures are as a whole sincere. The settings alone are frequently plain indications that the director cares more about giving the public what it wants to see than what it might actually see in real life. No doubt we have all seen homes of the rich in the movies built on the lines of the Grand Central Station of New York City and romantic heroines go from abject poverty to garish riches with appalling nonchalance. Even a high-school freshman knows that the movies are often crass and silly misrepresentations of life. For it is only in them that college students spend all their time and thousands of dollars in perpetual rah-rah gayety, that aviators seem to be continually involved in adolescent feuds over beautiful blondes and high-powered brunettes, that country people are all simple and quaint and good, and city people all extravagant and pleasure-mad and cynical. In real life silken sirens with mysterious, hypnotic eyes and languid manners are rarely, if ever, seen by the eye of man; in the movies there is sure to be at least one siren traveling, heavily veiled, from Omsk to Peiping, drifting somewhere east of Suez with a romantic past behind her. And why must the screen portray all Westerners as breezy, rough-cut diamonds who ride hard and fight hard and play hard; all Mexican señoritas as tempestuous, human hot tamales with quaint accents and a marked preference for English swear words; all aged mothers as worn with sorrow and suffering, loyal to wicked sons who all but knock them down and walk on them; all soldiers, sailors, and marines as overgrown boys whose vocabularies are limited to "Sez you?" and "Oh, yeah?"; all beautiful drawing-room heroines as gallant, silently suffering and slightly embittered? Why *must* detectives and policemen always chew cigars and wear their hats in the house? Why *must* business men be incapable of understanding their wives, and gridiron heroes fall in love with the Sweetheart of Sigma Chi and win the game at the last minute in spite of a bursting appendix and a misunderstanding with the coach? The satire of plays like *Beggar on Horseback* and *Once in a Lifetime* is indeed richly deserved if some moving pictures are an indication of American taste.

Improving moving pictures. Of course there are good motion pictures. Lubitsch has provided us with a type of screen comedy that is masterly in its light, droll cynicism; his pictures skate gracefully and intelligently over thin ice with never so much as a fraction of false emphasis. Extravaganza, wit, irony, gayety, and the lightest touch on deeper chords of feeling combine to make such pictures masterpieces of impudent comedy. *His Double Life, Monte Carlo, Le Million,* and *Trouble in Paradise* need no further justification for their being than the brilliant drolleries they provide. On the serious side, the screen has occasionally given us masterly pictures of human life, sometimes poignant, thoughtful, tender, or even terrifying as in *Maedchen in Uniform, A Farewell to Arms, I Am a Fugitive from a Chain Gang, Eskimo, Poil de Carotte, Little Women, Berkeley Square.* Often one may find scenes of almost startling beauty or reality projected with marvelous photographic skill. But why is it that these triumphs of art over banality are the exceptions rather than the rule? The answer is, of course, that the commonplace films are what the public wants. Directors and players are not to blame. The motion picture will never free itself from the bonds of meretricious cheapness, falsity, and banality until the audience learns to despise these things. It is for the intelligent citizens to demand that characters on the stage and screen be human with natural motives and reactions, that the pictures have some truth and some beauty.

Improbabilities in some Shakespearean characters. Here, again, we go back to Shakespeare for typical illustrations of what is improbable as well as for what is masterly in characterization. As we have seen, in some of his earlier plays the characters were fitted into an artificial plot. No real man would have married Olivia so abruptly as Sebastian does in *Twelfth Night;* the sudden change of heart in Orsino and in Olivia herself is, to put it mildly, surprising. That Oliver's experience under the oak tree in *As You Like It* should have brought about so miraculous a transformation of his character is not convincing; indeed, his original villainy does not seem to have had any natural basis. To tell the truth, the whole plot of *As You Like It* is absurd; so, too, are the plots of *A Midsummer Night's Dream*, *Twelfth Night*, *The Comedy of Errors*, *Much Ado about Nothing*, and many another of Shakespeare's plays.

Shakespearean characters often rise above the plot. With Shakespeare there is this difference: once he has accepted the absurd plot, his characters frequently become alive, too real for their surroundings. Sometimes they even interfere with his plot. In *Measure for Measure* it has been pointed out that Barnardine was created to serve the plot by being executed; but he became so real that Shakespeare apparently had not the heart to make way with him. Shakespeare is commonly accused of killing off Mercutio in *Romeo and Juliet* because he was becoming a dangerous rival to Romeo in the sympathies of the audience. There is little doubt that Shylock was originally intended as a comic figure; but he became so human as his character took shape in Shakespeare's mind that he turned tragic instead, thereby creating for future commentators on *The Merchant of Venice* a perplexing problem. Jaques, who has no business in *As You Like It* anyway, becomes very much alive and walks about holding up the action and commandeering the interest of the audience. The characters concerned with the plot must get along as well as they can while Jaques, well in the center of the stage, delivers his famous speech:

> All the world's a stage,
> And all the men and women merely players:
> They have their exits and their entrances;
> And one man in his time plays many parts,
> His acts being seven ages. At first, the infant,
> Mewling and puking in the nurse's arms:
> Then, the whining school-boy, with his satchel
> And shining morning face, creeping like snail
> Unwillingly to school: and then the lover,
> Sighing like furnace, with a woeful ballad
> Made to his mistress' eyebrow. Then a soldier,
> Full of strange oaths and bearded like the pard,
> Jealous in honor, sudden and quick in quarrel,
> Seeking the bubble reputation
> Even in the cannon's mouth. And then the justice
> In fair round belly with good capon lined,

With eyes severe and beard of formal cut,
Full of wise saws and modern instances;
And so he plays his part. The sixth age shifts
Into the lean and slipper'd pantaloon,
With spectacles on nose and pouch on side,
His youthful hose, well saved, a world too wide
For his shrunk shank; and his big manly voice,
Turning again toward childish treble, pipes
And whistles in his sound. Last scene of all,
That ends this strange, eventful history,
Is second childishness, and mere oblivion,
Sans teeth, sans eyes, sans taste, sans everything.

Characters such as these rise above the plot, but they cannot get out of it.

Masterly character development. There is no trouble with the logical development of the characters in Shakespeare's plays; in his greatest tragedies the reactions of the characters to every turn in the action are always intuitively right and their development as the play proceeds is felt to be inevitable. It is wonderful to contemplate in the few pages of *Macbeth* the transformation of a man's soul revealed with stern justice but infinite compassion. The stages of Macbeth's degradation are mercilessly revealed as the play proceeds, and yet the character keeps our sympathies to the end. But notice how different his reactions are from those of Lady Macbeth. Each develops inevitably according to the forces within; yet each has similar experiences. Study the development of Brutus and Cassius in *Julius Caesar*. How fatally the obstinate blind idealism of Brutus pursues him through the play, how gradual is his disillusionment, how welcome his final peace. We feel that he could not have done otherwise; he was true to the best light he had. Notice, too, how gradually the character of Cassius is revealed. We find him envious, bitter, scheming, shrewd, but possessed of a strain of patriotism, an unerring insight into human nature, a sort of subconscious awe of the innate righteousness in Brutus. These characteristics develop as we follow him through success and failure; and we learn, before the play is over, to respect and admire him with all his weaknesses. Never do we feel that he does or says anything untrue to his nature as Shakespeare conceived it.

The development of characters should seem inevitable. We find this same inevitableness of reaction and development in all of Shakespeare's greatest characters and greatest plays. It is worth your while to see what these people do at each crisis; what flash of insight into their souls is given by each of these significant moments. And when you have finished a play, go back over it watching the course of the character's development; it will seem to you then a well-defined trail leading in an inevitable direction. Such should be the impression of the motives and reactions and consequent development of the characters in any great play. With this in mind, study the next play that you see.

The importance of dialogue. The dialogue of a play is, of course, the chief means of revealing character as well as of advancing plot. It is, therefore, more important than the dialogue of a work of prose fiction.

In the first place, dialogue must serve to tell the story without noticeable digressions, that is, it ought always to contribute something toward plot, character, or setting. The dialogue of some plays is so fascinating in itself that the author is apt to let his characters talk on and on while the development of story and character is temporarily halted. In Shakespeare's plays, there is often useless conversation which is dispensed with in most modern productions. On the other hand, some of his plays are marvels of condensation. There is scarcely a speech in the whole play of *Julius Caesar* that does not serve some legitimate purpose.

Dialogue adapted to individual characters. In the second place, the dialogue should be adapted to the character speaking. In *As You Like It* one cannot imagine Audrey, who replies to Touchstone's rhetoric with commendable caution:

> I do not know what poetical is. Is it honest in deed and word? Is it a true thing?

exchanging clever, irresponsible banter with Rosalind and Celia. In *Romeo and Juliet* every word the Nurse utters is distinctly "in character" with the garrulous, vulgar, shallow, but likable old woman she is:

> NURSE. I am a-weary, give me leave awhile:
> Fie, how my bones ache! what a jaunce have I had!
> JUL. I would thou hadst my bones, and I thy news.
> Nay, come, I pray thee, speak; good, good nurse, speak.
> NURSE. Jesu, what haste! can you not stay awhile?
> Do you not see that I am out of breath?
> JUL. How art thou out of breath, when thou hast breath

To say to me that thou art out of breath?
The excuse that thou dost make in this delay
Is longer than the tale thou dost excuse.
Is thy news good, or bad? Answer to that;
Say either, and I'll stay the circumstance:
Let me be satisfied, is 't good or bad?

NURSE. Well, you have made a simple choice; you know not how to choose a man. Romeo! no, not he; though his face be better than any man's, yet his leg excels all men's; and for a hand, and a foot, and a body, though they be not to be talk'd on, yet they are past compare. He is not the flower of courtesy, but, I'll warrant him, as gentle as a lamb. Go thy ways, wench; serve God. What, have you din'd at home?

JUL. No, no! But all this did I know before.
What says he of our marriage? What of that?

NURSE. Lord, how my head aches! what a head have I!
It beats as it would fall in twenty pieces.
My back o' t'other side, O, my back, my back!
Beshrew your heart for sending me about,
To catch my death with jauncing up and down!

JUL. I' faith, I am sorry that thou art not well.
Sweet, sweet, sweet nurse, tell me, what says my love?

NURSE. Your love says, like an honest gentleman, and a courteous, and a kind, and a handsome, and, I warrant, a virtuous,—Where is your mother?

JUL. Where is my mother! why, she is within:
Where should she be? How oddly thou repliest!
"Your love says, like an honest gentleman,
Where is your mother?"

NURSE. O God's lady dear!
Are you so hot? marry, come up, I trow;
Is this the poultice for my aching bones?
Henceforward do your messages yourself.

JUL. Here's such a coil! come, what says Romeo?

NURSE. Have you got leave to go to shrift to-day?

JUL. I have.

NURSE. Then hie you hence to Friar Laurence' cell;
There stays a husband to make you a wife.

Sir Andrew Aguecheek in *Twelfth Night* distinguishes himself forever by the shallow vanity and the hopeless stupidity of his every sentence. Casca's words in *Julius Caesar* reveal him as superstitious, boorish, and self-important. Only rarely does Shakespeare fail to vary his dialogue to suit the character speaking.

Dialogue usually heightened for dramatic effect. In the third place, the dialogue is almost necessarily heightened for dramatic effect. The dramatist must touch only the high places in conversation; he has not time to set down the thousand irrelevancies and banalities of our everyday speech. It is practically necessary for him to emphasize story and character by making people speak more cleverly, stupidly, eloquently, or pathetically than they would in real life. The stupidity of Dogberry in [1] *Much Ado about Nothing* has to be accentuated. Ophelia has to be made pathetic in a few words; the dramatist cannot stop to record the different ideas and sensations that go through her mind. Consequently he makes her speech much more significant than it would ordinarily be in a brief sentence or two. Indeed, her heartbroken half-murmured responses to Hamlet's brutality in the so-called nunnery scene are among the most intensely touching things in all Shakespeare:

HAMLET. I did love you once.
OPHELIA. Indeed, my lord, you made me believe so.
HAMLET. You should not have believed me . . . I love you not.
OPHELIA. I was the more deceived.

In *As You Like It* the characters never seem at loss for answers; one might think with Jaques that they had all been acquainted with goldsmiths' wives and conn'd them out of rings. The retort courteous, the quip modest, the reproof valiant, all are much in evidence; and every sally of wit or absurdity is given with apparent spontaneity and relish. Surely people in real life would at least occasionally pause for breath. But in the drama there is no time for the barren stretches of daily talk; the dramatist must choose what is essential and dash on with his play. The principle of dramatic emphasis must be observed.

The question of realistic dialogue. The dialogue of a play should be felt to proceed from the springs of character, and in this sense should be true to life. But, as we have just seen, it has to be selective.

[1] See Act III, Scene 3.

There is no reason why it should not be the language of the imagination of the author instead of the direct speech of everyday people. It is interesting to compare an experiment in realistic dialogue, John Masefield's *The Tragedy of Pompey the Great*, with the poetic language of Shakespeare's *Julius Caesar*. Certainly the characters in the latter are not less human because they speak in blank verse. In real life no one would be likely to indulge in Hamlet's extended soliloquies; yet if these offenses against reality were removed from the play, how much of its truth would go with them! Since the day of Ibsen, the great Norwegian dramatist, there has been a widespread prejudice against the use of soliloquies and asides, or any obvious departure from the speech of real life in the dialogue of a play. But whether the dramatists who follow the example of Ibsen in this respect have added enough reality to their work to make up for what they have lost in imaginative expression is an open question. At any rate, Shakespeare's plays would be less great without their soliloquies. Dialogue, then, may be true without being realistic.

Special qualities in dialogue. Finally we may consider the essential value of the dialogue apart from the play itself. It is not necessary that a play contain passages in themselves of permanent intellectual or literary value, but such passages, of course, contribute that much greatness to it. If the dramatist has moments of outstanding eloquence, like Antony's speech in *Julius Caesar*, of depth of insight like Hamlet's speech "To be or not to be," of tremendous imaginative power like the heath scenes in *King Lear*, of tender poetic beauty like the love scenes in *Romeo and Juliet*, of ironical keenness like the seven ages of man speech in *As You Like It*, or of passionate human protest like Shylock's defense of his race in *The Merchant of Venice*, the play will live. Consequently any special qualities the dialogue of a play may have are worth looking for and remembering.

Summary. The characters are the people who carry out the actions of the play. Sometimes they are merely instruments in the plot; at other times they control the plot themselves. The dramatist must manage them naturally so that their motives and reactions, exits and entrances seem real. Some dramatists have a wider range of characterization than others; Shakespeare has the widest of all. The characters are developed by action and dialogue. Dialogue should be related to the plot or theme of the play, adapted to individual characters, and emphasized for dramatic effect. It may or may not be realistic, but it should be character revealing. In some plays it has significance and value in itself apart from the story of the play. Here again Shakespeare's dialogue excels all others.

COMPREHENSION QUESTIONS

1. *Vocabulary:* plot, characters, dialogue, motives, reactions, "stock characters," realistic dialogue, poetic dialogue, number and range of characters, "purple passages."
2. Explain in your own words the difference between characters who are merely instruments for carrying out the plot and characters who through their own natures shape the course of the plot.
3. Why do we lose faith in the reality of Oliver and Duke Frederick in *As You Like It?*
4. Show how the demands of the plot interfere with the real development of the following characters:
   (*a*) the lovers in *A Midsummer Night's Dream*, (*b*) the twins in *The Comedy of Errors*, (*c*) Jessica in *The Merchant of Venice*, (*d*) Claudio in *Much Ado about Nothing.*
5. Point out some plays you have read which revolve around one central character. Explain how every important thing that happens in the play is conditioned by these dominant figures. Suggested titles:

Barrie	*Mary Rose*
Drinkwater	*Abraham Lincoln*
Clyde Fitch	*Beau Brummell*
Galsworthy	*Old English*
Hauptmann	*Drayman Henschel, Rose Bernd*
George Kelly	*The Show-off*
O'Neill	*The Emperor Jones, The Hairy Ape*
Josephine Preston Peabody	*The Piper*
Rostand	*Cyrano de Bergerac*
Shakespeare	*Hamlet*

6. Explain by illustration why the management of exits and entrances is in itself a difficult task. Study entrances and exits in:

Goldsmith	*She Stoops to Conquer*
Jonson	*The Alchemist*
Shakespeare	*As You Like It, Julius Caesar, Othello, Twelfth Night*
Sheridan	*The Rivals, The School for Scandal*

7. What do we mean by saying that Shakespeare excels all other dramatists in the depth and range of his insight into character? Illustrate with examples from five of his plays you have read.
8. What do we mean by *stock characters?* Illustrate from a play or moving picture you have recently seen. What were some Elizabethan *stock characters?*
9. In two Shakespearean plays point out characters that are real in spite of a machine-made plot. At what point in the play does the plot make them act unnaturally?
10. What are the three qualities of good dramatic dialogue?
11. What do we mean by saying that dialogue must be "heightened for dramatic effect"? Illustrate.
12. Look for qualities of special excellence in the dialogue of some play or motion picture you have recently seen. Then compare this dialogue with that in a play by Shakespeare, Sheridan, Shaw, or O'Neill. Which is greater? why?
13. Point out what *Hamlet* or *Macbeth* would lose if all the dialogue were made strictly realistic.
14. What does a play gain by the omission of asides, soliloquies, and other artificial devices? What does it lose without them?

APPRECIATION PROBLEMS AND REVIEW QUESTIONS

1. The following plays present a character study in dramatic form. Analyze the protagonist carefully, paying special attention to his motives, reactions, and development as the play progresses.

   (*a*) By what special means does the author present the character? (*b*) What attractions does the part offer the actor? (*c*) Is the characterization complete and human enough to be of permanent value? (*d*) Would the play and its protagonist appeal to an audience? (*e*) Does the part need to be acted to be fully appreciated? (*f*) Is the character worth studying?

   Be sure to support your answers by specific reference to the play. Quote when you can.

Maxwell Anderson	*Elizabeth the Queen, Mary of Scotland*
Samuel Nathaniel Behrman	*Biography*
Bulwer-Lytton	*Richelieu*
Clemence Dane	*Will Shakespeare*
Drinkwater	*Abraham Lincoln, Cromwell, Mary Stuart, Robert E. Lee*
Clyde Fitch	*Beau Brummel*
Galsworthy	*Old English*

Ibsen	*Hedda Gabler, Peer Gynt, The Wild Duck*
George Kelly	*Daisy Mayme, The Show-off*
Gregorio Martinez Sierra	*The Kingdom of God*
Molière	*L'Avare, Tartuffe*
O'Neill	*The Hairy Ape*
Rostand	*Cyrano de Bergerac*
Shakespeare	*Coriolanus, Hamlet, Macbeth*
Synge	*The Playboy of the Western World*
Tennyson	*Becket, Queen Mary*

2. Study the character development in a moving picture. Comment on the motives and actions of the characters.

   (*a*) Why do they act as they do? (*b*) Do they fail to be lifelike because of the exigencies of the plot? (*c*) Are any of them "stock figures"? (*d*) Are the situations the natural result of their characters and actions, or are they hackneyed, used merely to "put across" the story. (*e*) Are the characters original? (*f*) Are their problems special or universal? (*g*) Which of their reactions are illuminating?

3. Analyze one of the following characters:

Audrey	Falstaff	Lear
Brutus	Hotspur	Mercutio
Caliban	Jaques	Miranda
Cordelia	Juliet	Viola

What motives determine their actions? Are these motives true to their natures? Are the actions that result from these motives consistent with the character as the dramatist built it up? To what extent is the character influenced by other characters in the play? by circumstances over which he has no control? by his own strength or weakness? by moral principles?

4. Discuss the dialogue in one of the following plays for its special qualities of dramatic emphasis, intrinsic interest, power to reveal character, wit, humor, poetic charm, eloquence, realism, imagination, unreality, truth, universal significance, etc. Select passages that have value or interest in themselves apart from their connection with the plot.

Maxwell Anderson	*Elizabeth the Queen, Mary of Scotland*
Gordon Bottomley	*King Lear's Wife, The Lady Gruach*
D'Annunzio	*Francesca da Rimini, La Gioconda*
Dunsany	*King Argimenes and the Unknown Warrior*

James Elroy Flecker	*Hassan*
Maeterlinck	*Pélléas and Mélisande*
O'Neill	*Marco Millions, The Hairy Ape*
S. Phillips	*Paolo and Francesca*
Rostand	*Cyrano de Bergerac*
Shakespeare	*Antony and Cleopatra, Hamlet, Henry IV, Macbeth, The Tempest,*
Shaw	*Caesar and Cleopatra, Saint Joan*
Sheridan	*The School for Scandal*
Synge	*Deirdre of the Sorrows, Riders to the Sea*
Yeats	*Cathleen ni Houlihan, Deirdre, The Land of Heart's Desire*

5. In one of the following plays which characters are created merely to serve the author's purpose?

Drinkwater	*Abraham Lincoln*
Galsworthy	*Strife, Loyalties*
O'Neill	*Marco Millions, Mourning Becomes Electra, Days Without End*
Shakespeare	*As You Like It, A Comedy of Errors, Two Gentlemen of Verona*

6. Write an essay on the number and range of Shakespeare's characters using the following plays as illustrations:

As You Like It	*A Midsummer Night's Dream*
King Henry IV	*Romeo and Juliet*
Macbeth	*The Tempest*
The Merchant of Venice	

7. Pick out the *stock characters* in one of the above plays.

8. In *Macbeth* show how the action proceeds out of the characters—that is, is determined by them, rather than they by it. Is the motivation always natural? (Consider here the flight of Malcolm and Donalbain, and Malcolm's scene with Macduff in England.)

9. Discuss the use of subordinate characters in *Macbeth.* Are they strikingly or faintly delineated? For what special purposes are these characters used? Which seem to you more human, Ross, Lenox, Malcolm, and their group, or the less important group consisting of the Gentlewoman, the Doctor, and Lady Macduff? Characterize each of these as well as you can, using quotations. Comment on the naturalness of Lady Macduff's little son. Look up other children in the plays of Shakespeare.

Can you distinguish between Ross and Lenox by their conspicuous traits? What is Macduff's great scene? why? Are there any *stock characters* in *Macbeth?* Adapt this exercise to *Hamlet.*

10. Relate some dramatic scene in *Macbeth* as you think one of the subordinate characters would tell it. For example, the Gentlewoman describes the sleep-walking scene; Lenox tells about the ghost at the banquet; Banquo describes the meeting with the witches to Ross and Angus. In Walter De la Mare's *Henry Brocken* the Doctor gives his opinions.

11. Discuss the character of Banquo in *Macbeth,* his motives, reactions, and his moral position in the play. Read what Professor Bradley says about him in *Shakespearean Tragedy.*

12. Using the characters of Macbeth and Lady Macbeth as examples, show the depth of Shakespeare's insight into human nature.

(*a*) What was the character of each at the beginning of the play? In what respects were they alike? different? Explain how their characters supplement each other. Could either have sinned so irretrievably alone? How were they regarded by others at the beginning? How far right is Lady Macbeth's analysis of her husband's nature? By what motives were they impelled up to the time of the murder? How did the motives of each work upon the other until the deed was done? (*b*) Contrast the reactions of each immediately after the murder. Is there any indication that here for the first time Lady Macbeth feels that she does not wholly understand her husband? Compare and contrast the development of the two after the second act. Why does Macbeth plunge deeper and deeper into blood? What indications are there of Lady Macbeth's shrinking, of her unwillingness or inability to go to the same lengths? In what respects is the development of each characteristic? What conspicuous traits of each are brought out in the banquet scene? What influences outside his nature impel Macbeth to action? (*c*) Is there any counterpart to the witches' influence on Macbeth in the case of Lady Macbeth? What characteristic in her takes the place of imagination in Macbeth? By what touches is the tender side of both suggested? Trace the course of Lady Macbeth's dream in the sleep-walking scene. Find the source of each of her thoughts. Why is the candle by her bedside pathetic? What do you think happened to her between this scene and her death? (*d*) Find all the indications of Macbeth's mental, moral, and physical degradation in the last act. What is now his attitude toward life? Is it what you would expect him to have? Are there any traces here of the man he once was? Why is the spectacle of his mental, moral, and physical ruin so impressive?

13. Take Macbeth at what you think is the decisive moment of his career. (*a*) Show what manner of man he was. (*b*) Show what his position in life was. (*c*) Show what motives impelled him to action at this crisis. (*d*) Trace the result of this decisive action upon his later life, showing at each step how all might have been different had he acted differently.

14. Try Problem 13 with *Hamlet*, *Julius Caesar*, *King Lear*, or *Othello*.

15. One of the most striking things about Shakespeare is his ability to make a single word or phrase, particularly at a crisis, reveal unsuspected depths of characterization. Almost never do his characters fail at a crisis to say and do the psychologically inevitable thing. Examples are:

(*a*) Lady Macbeth's "Had he not resembled my father as he slept, I had done it," (*b*) Romeo's quiet "Well, Juliet, I will lie with thee tonight," (*c*) Portia's "You see me, Lord Bassanio, where I stand," (*d*) Brutus' "Remember March, the Ides of March remember," (*e*) Ophelia's "I was the more deceived," (*f*) Emilia's "My husband!" (*g*) Sir Toby's "Dost thou think because thou art virtuous there shall be no more cakes and ale?"

See if you can find such illuminating passages in one of the following Shakespearean plays. Try to explain why each scene is a sort of epitome of the characters involved.

Antony and Cleopatra, Cleopatra and the messenger, Act II, scene 5
"I am dying, Egypt, dying," Act IV, scene 15
"The bright day is done," Act V, scene 2
As You Like It, "Now I am in a holiday humor, and like enough to consent," Act IV, scene 1
Hamlet, "O limed soul," Act III, scene 3
"Would it were not so!—you are my mother," Act III, scene 4
"Alas, poor Yorick!" Act V, scene 1
Henry IV, Part II, Falstaff loses a wager, Act V, scene 5
Julius Caesar, The quarrel, Act IV, scene 3
King Lear, Regan shows her colors, Act II, scene 4
The storm symphony, Act III, scenes 2, 4, 6
Much Ado about Nothing, In the church, "Kill Claudio," Act IV, scene 1
Othello, Emilia and Desdemona, Act IV, scene 3
"Put out the light!" Act V, scene 2
Romeo and Juliet, "A plague on both your houses!" Act III, scene 1
"Ancient damnation!" Act III, scene 5
"At the point of death," Act V, scene 3

Troilus and Cressida, "False Cressid," Act V, scene 2
Twelfth Night, Viola and Olivia, Act I, scene 5

16. One of the exercises in which high-school students are most likely to fail is an assignment to characterize any given person in a play or novel. Try your hand at these characters in this way:
(*a*) First make a list of things about the character that distinguish him from others in the play. Who is he? What is he? What is he like? List his chief traits, his chief motives, his most illuminating reactions. (*b*) Then refer to scenes or quote passages that illustrate these traits. (*c*) Then notice if he develops (as Macbeth does, for instance) in the course of the play. If so, try to trace this development giving specific references. (*d*) Then consider in what respects he is individual (like himself) and in what respects he is typical (like others in his class). (*e*) Is the characterization as a whole convincing? Try this exercise with one of the following:

Beatrice	Iago
Caliban	Jack Absolute
Candida	Marco Polo
Cleopatra	Mercutio
Cyrano de Bergerac	Nora Helmer
Dick Falder	Peer Gynt
The Emperor Jones	Regan
Mrs. Erlynne	Dr. Stockmann
Gregers Werle	Viola
Hedda Gabler	

17. *Julius Caesar* is a good example of an old play that still seems modern. It was written about 1601 and it deals with ancient history, taken in some cases almost literally from North's translation of Plutarch's *Lives.* Yet as a study of politics and politicians it is strangely modern. We can find the same problems and types today: the question of personal loyalties in conflict with public duties, the struggle of the political idealist to maintain his ideals in spite of cynical associates, the inability of the dreamer to cope with practical problems. Today there are practical politicians like Cassius who combine a cynical view of men with flashes of patriotism; easily swayed, self-important minor "bosses" like Casca, who think they know more than they do; egotists like Cicero, who will "never follow what other men begin"; personal friends like Ligarius who will follow a man they admire anywhere, regardless of his principles; demagogues like Antony who know how to sway the people by oratory and cheat them afterward. In fact, there is a striking similarity between the whole character and vision of Brutus and those of Woodrow Wilson.

With these things in mind, write an essay on *Julius Caesar* as a play of politics and politicians, being careful to stress its modernity. Quote where you can.

18. Here is a suggestion for studying the following modern dramatists so that you can understand them and discuss their work intelligently. Unlike Shakespeare, each has a somewhat limited range and marked personal idiosyncrasies which affect his work.

(*a*) In Henrik Ibsen, look for:

(1) presentation of a social problem, (2) an individual pitted against social laws or conventions, (3) a tendency to present his women as stronger, more intelligent, more individualistic than men, (4) a tendency to concentrate on inward development and inward struggle in his characters rather than on action, (5) a tendency to show what ruin comes to individuals through their failure to see clearly themselves and others, (6) respect for sanity, self-knowledge, balanced realism, contempt for muddle-headedness, sentimentality, and hypocrisy, (7) the roots of his plays are in what has happened before the play begins, (8) realistic dialogue, setting, and situations, (9) use of symbolism, (10) conflict between the ideal and the actual.

Suggested titles:

A Doll's House	*Ghosts*	*Peer Gynt*
An Enemy of the People	*The Lady from the Sea*	*Rosmersholm*
Hedda Gabler	*Little Eyolf*	*The Wild Duck*

(*b*) In John Galsworthy look for:

(1) presentation of a social or economic problem, (2) preoccupation with injustice to individuals, (3) impartiality in showing fairly the point of view of all his characters, (4) tendency to arrive at no solution of the problem, (5) compassion for the victims of social or economic injustice, (6) artistic economy in the development of stories to bring out his ideas, (7) good psychology but few memorable characters, (8) tendency to build up his plays on a principle of parallel structure, showing first one side of the question and then the other, (9) strongly English point of view—English ideals, English psychology, English self-consciousness, English background, English style.

Suggested titles:

The Eldest Son	*Loyalties*	*The Silver Box*
Escape	*The Mob*	*The Skin Game*
Justice	*The Pigeon*	*Strife*

(*c*) In Sir James Barrie look for:

(1) whimsical humor in characterization, dialogue, and descriptive comment, (2) sentiment verging on sentimentality, (3) a fondness for fantastic situations and characters, (4) true and even bitter ideas underlying his humor or fancy, (5) fondness for the Cinderella type of heroine, (6) quaintness—sometimes too much of it, (7) much charm of style, and occasionally of characters, (8) tendency to use women or elflike people as his protagonists.

Suggested titles:

The Admirable Crichton
Dear Brutus
A Kiss for Cinderella
Mary Rose
Peter Pan
Quality Street
What Every Woman Knows

(*d*) In Eugene O'Neill, look for:

(1) Preoccupation with human beings as *victims*—of their own natures, of society, of circumstances, (2) frequent experimentation with the artistic resources of the theater—great attention to setting, lighting, symbolic devices, and so on, (3) compassionate but pessimistic philosophy of life, (4) tendency to make his characters represent psychological types and conform to psychological formulas, especially Freudian formulas, (5) considerable eloquence, with a power of language sometimes verging on poetry, frequent intensity, but usually far short of genius, (6) a combination of stark realism and poetic symbolism in both style and setting, (7) a tendency to manipulate people and events so as to bring out an idea, to make individual experiences typical, (8) occasional melodrama, (9) variety of forms and styles, (10) interest in impact of life on the individual.

Suggested titles:

Ah, Wilderness!
All God's Chillun Got Wings
Anna Christie
Days Without End
Dynamo
The Emperor Jones
The Hairy Ape
Marco Millions
Mourning Becomes Electra
Strange Interlude

(*e*) In George Bernard Shaw look for:

(1) ideas in preference to plot or characterization, (2) a tendency to repeat stock ideas and stock characters in play after play, (3) perverse delight in making fun of conventional ideas and customs, especially if they are British, (4) brilliant dia-

logue—combining *wit, humor, epigram, paradox,* poetic eloquence, (5) hatred of sentimentality, muddle-headedness, hypocrisy, (6) indifference to conventional demands of the theater, particularly as to length and as to plot structure. (7) ability to rise occasionally above mere wit, humor, and epigram to scenes of genuine human power, (8) keen social satire.

Suggested titles:

Androcles and the Lion
Back to Methuselah
Caesar and Cleopatra
Candida
The Devil's Disciple
Heartbreak House
Major Barbara
Man and Superman
Saint Joan
You Never Can Tell

HAMLET IN MODERN DRESS

English actors in an unconventional presentation.

HAMLET STAGED WITH ALL THE RESOURCES OF THE MODERN STAGE DESIGNER

CHAPTER 26

HOW SETTING CREATES ATMOSPHERE

Contemporary dramatists collaborate with stage managers. The setting of a play is important for at least two reasons. It may be directly influential on the plot and characters as we have seen in the study of prose fiction. It may also create atmosphere. Of recent years, dramatists have collaborated more and more with stage managers, directors, and electricians in order to avail themselves of the resources of the modern theater. One has only to recall plays like O'Neill's *The Emperor Jones*, *Dynamo*, and *Mourning Becomes Electra* to realize the great importance of lighting, scenery, and mechanical effects in the modern theater. Elmer Rice's *Street Scene*, Kaufman and Connelly's *Beggar on Horseback*, and Vicki Baum's *Grand Hotel* deliberately make use of stage effects which would have been unthinkable on the stage of the Globe or the Drury Lane or Wallack's.

Plays with essential setting. In some plays, of course, the setting is part of the play. Thus *A Midsummer Night's Dream* has to take place in a fairy wood, and Prospero's island is the central fact of *The Tempest*. Barrie calls attention to the importance of the setting of *Quality Street* by naming the play for it; in *The Admirable Crichton*, he has to have an uninhabited island, in *Mary Rose* a haunted one, in *Dear Brutus* an enchanted forest. Other plays in which setting is important are easy to recall: *Riders to the Sea*, *The Good Hope*, *Anna Christie*, *Outward Bound*, *Sun-up*, *Mourning Becomes Electra*, *Rain*.

Setting, of course, may be dramatically effective even if it is not essential to the action.

Setting and atmosphere. There is a good deal in having the action occur at an appropriate place, in using the setting to create an appropriate atmosphere for an event. It is not necessary that Casca and Brutus be won over to the conspiracy on the night of a fearful storm, but certainly the terror of the night creates an atmosphere of dramatic suspense which adds tremendously to the play. Macbeth might very well listen to the forces of evil on a bright sunny day, but it is far more effective dramatically to have the play steeped in the atmosphere of night and terror, on the blasted heath, in the rude banquet hall lit by flaring torches, in weird underground caverns, and in the castle halls at midnight where unearthly chills and black shadows and hollow echoes are gathered. The sun appears only once in the whole play and then as if for purposes of contrast. Duncan remarks that the castle has a pleasant seat and that the birds are nesting happily in every available nook and cranny of its sunny walls, but the audience already suspects it to be the breeding place of treachery and murder.

The whole play of *As You Like It* is a notable example of the charm that atmosphere can throw over a play through setting alone. There is little to describe the Forest of Arden. People fleet the time there carelessly as they did in the Golden Age of mankind; they lie under the greenwood tree and tune their songs to the music of the birds; in those inaccessible forests they lose and neglect the creeping hours and become good-humored, happy, pleasantly irresponsible, and strangely susceptible to the influence of love. The whole story seems possible because of the atmosphere of the Forest of Arden, but surely it is an impossible forest with its startling combinations of fauna and flora, its palm trees and oaks, its sheep, its hungry lionesses, and its green and gilded snakes. No one can say that the action of the play needed such a setting, but without the Forest of Arden we feel that the plot and the characters would have been as childishly absurd as they are in the story from which Shakespeare borrowed them.

Problems of the stage manager. It must be remembered that Shakespeare created most of his effects through poetry; he did not depend on elaborate scenic effects as the modern dramatist does. In reading a play from the modern point of view, however, we have to give a thought to the problems of the stage manager. How shall we arrange the scene for Antony's funeral oration? By what lighting effects shall we suggest the garden of Capulet where the inconstant moon "tips with silver all the fruit-tree tops"? And how shall we create an actual picture of that dim monument where lies Juliet, whose "beauty makes this vault a feasting presence full of light"? In *King Lear* how shall we produce the howling storm on the heath where the poor old man seeks shelter from the wind and the rain in a madman's hovel? How shall we portray the mysterious shadows and rounded towers of the castle at Elsinore where the ghost walks at midnight? What stage arrangement is best for the play within the play in *Hamlet?* Again, what sounds and colors shall we use? We must select music for Capulet's ball; we must reproduce the sound of the masques and merrymaking that covers up Jessica's flight from her father and the roar of battle that closes *Julius Caesar* and *Macbeth.* We must furthermore choose costumes and scenery so that the colors harmonize with action and mood, at the same time making an effective stage picture. What Rosalind and Juliet shall wear is no unimportant detail. An actor's make-up for Shylock or Macbeth is often a part of his conception of the character. All these considerations are interesting and significant; one must read a play with them in mind if one is to read imaginatively. But important as they are, details of setting should never attract so much attention to themselves that they distract attention from the play and its people. There is no need to spend thousands of dollars and employ hundreds of people to present a play of any kind. Shakespeare had no conception of the useless extravagance that could be lavished on a production of *Julius Caesar* or *The Merchant of Venice.* Settings should be artistically in keeping with the mood of the story but not flagrantly conspicuous in themselves.

Moving pictures have great scenic resources. Naturally the moving pictures can accomplish wonders in making the setting give atmosphere in comparison with which the best efforts of the stage pale into insignificance. The scenic resources of the screen seem, indeed, almost limitless. It can supply natural backgrounds of beauty or grandeur merely for the cost of a trip "on location." It can increase dramatic significance tenfold by focusing the camera on a detail of the setting which would pass unnoticed in the theater. It can present a scene from many points of view in quick succession, any one of which might be impossible on the stage. It can graphically show the passing of time, the most varied aspects of social life, the past life and the nature of characters, a vast panorama or a complicated kaleidoscope of life which plays can indicate but clumsily or not at all. In its power to produce big scenes, to utilize great masses of people, and at the same time to give startling emphasis to details, it is, as its publicity experts so frequently tell us, truly epic.

Magical effects, dreamlike phantasmagoria, scenes of bizarre beauty or terror, can be designed and animated by an imaginative director with detail, variety, and scope beyond the wildest dreams of the producers of plays. The world of Nature, wind and rain, heat and cold, moonlit clouds, the drama of under-sea life, the exotic charm of far-away lands—all these and much more are the cinema's gift to anyone who can spare a few cents for admission fee. Many pictures which are dramatically mediocre or worse are thrillingly beautiful pictorially. Scenes from *Night Flight*, *Thunder over Mexico* and *Eskimo* come to mind at once. Nor are the resources of the camera confined to the spectacular; it can evoke, as in *Little Women* and *Cavalcade*, the most intimate and gentle moods that leave the beholder with a faint nostalgia for the time not so long ago—when life seems to have been less complicated. Except for its lack of color and depth, the moving picture has more artistic possibilities than the legitimate theater.

Summary. Setting is the background of time and place in a play. In modern plays it often demands close coöperation between the dramatist and stage manager. In some plays it is essential to the action, and in others it contributes atmosphere. A play should be read with the details of setting in mind. The moving pictures command tremendous resources of scenic effect.

COMPREHENSION QUESTIONS

1. *Vocabulary:* setting, atmosphere.
2. Define setting.
3. Point out plays you have read in which the setting is essential, explaining why in each case.
4. In a play or motion picture you have seen recently point out evident efforts on the part of producer or director to secure atmosphere through setting.
5. Explain the difference between the symbolic setting of the Elizabethan stage and the realism of our own stage as mastered by the late David Belasco.
6. What artistic advantages has the cinema over the theater?

PROBLEMS IN APPRECIATION

1. Why is the modern dramatist much more dependent on the coöperation of the stage manager and electrician than the dramatists of other periods have been? Cite examples.
2. Investigate modern attempts to use symbolism in setting; for instance, in the motion picture production of *Dr. Jekyll and Mr. Hyde.*
3. Investigate the history of theatrical lighting.
4. Plan or arrange settings for three scenes from three Shakespearean or eighteenth-century plays.
5. Write descriptions to give the setting and atmosphere of three scenes from Shakespeare.
6. Investigate the stage conditions of the eighteenth century. How did they affect acting and play writing?

CHAPTER 27

WHAT MAKES DRAMATIC LITERATURE LIVE

Does the drama endure? One might think that a form of composition so hampered by artificial restrictions and so dependent on the approval of the public for its support would not produce anything of permanent value. On the whole, perhaps, final oblivion is the fate of the majority of plays; nevertheless there are dramas read, studied, and acted today that were written for audiences in ancient Greece long before the birth of Christ. There is something imperishable, apparently, about the tragedies of Aeschylus, Sophocles, and Euripides, and the comedies of Aristophanes. It is more than three hundred years since the first edition of Shakespeare's plays was published, and yet at the present time these same plays draw crowded houses. The same immortality seems inherent in the comedies of Molière in France; they will probably never cease to be read as long as the French language is read and spoken. Yet surely times have changed. Manners and customs are different. Theatrical construction and theatrical equipment have made tremendous strides since the first London theater was built in 1576.

Audiences in ancient Greece were hardly the same type that today crowd to see Galsworthy's *Loyalties*, Barrie's *What Every Woman Knows*, or Kaufman and Ryskind's *Of Thee I Sing;* but these same audiences also crowd to see *Hamlet*, *Romeo and Juliet*, and *The Merchant of Venice*, and our best actors and actresses like to appear in these. There must be some reason for the longevity of these perennial favorites. What is it?

A play may be of permanent value as entertainment. To begin with, the permanent worth of a play depends in no small measure on the purpose for which it was written. Broadly speaking, of course, all plays are written for entertainment; there is no reason why they should not be produced so long as they continue to entertain the public. In the hands of spirited actors, *She Stoops to Conquer*, *The School for Scandal*, and *The Rivals* still remain good entertainment; as such they will probably continue to be revived. Probably many contemporary light comedies like Barry's *Holiday*, Shaw's *Candida*, and Kelly's *The Show-off* will be revived years from now for the same reason.

A play may be of permanent value as a story. But most plays that live have deeper qualities than that of amusement. Many of them live for the story they tell because it is a story which is as likely to appeal to one age as to another. *Romeo and Juliet* will live because it is the story of young love; until another play manages to develop the same theme with the same lyrical intensity, it will be preëminent. *The Merchant of Venice* has an improbable story, but it is so rich in characterization and so filled with suspense that it will always be a good acting play; audiences seem never to tire of it. Any contemporary play that thus tells a good story well has an equal chance of longevity, unless, of course, another dramatist offers a better version of the same general theme.

A play may be of permanent value as a study of character. Other plays live for the characters they create. *The Merchant of Venice* will live so long as there are actors because Shylock is a powerful character that can be made impressive by an actor of even average ability. *Hamlet* will always fascinate actors and audiences because the more one studies the melancholy Dane, the more interesting he becomes. *Cyrano de Bergerac* has a most compelling central figure in addition to splendor of style. *Julius Caesar* has at least three acting parts of almost equal importance. Any actress with brains and ability is likely to wish to portray Nora Helmer in *A Doll's House*, Rebecca West in *Rosmersholm*, or Hedda Gabler in the play of that name; the very complexities and difficulties of these rôles attract them. In like manner *Beau Brummell*, *The Emperor Jones*, *Cyrano de Bergerac*, and *Old English* offer opportunities for which any actor would be grateful. And parts like Portia, Rosalind, Beatrice, Viola, Juliet, Ophelia, Cordelia, Cleopatra, and Lady Macbeth will make up an almost inexhaustible store of opportunities for actresses for centuries to come.

A play may be of permanent value as an exposition of an idea. Some plays live purely because of their theme. The weaknesses at which Molière aimed his shafts of satire were not wholly weaknesses of his time; they are weaknesses inherent in human nature; and so long as human nature remains fundamentally unchanged, *Tartuffe*, *L'Avare*, and *Le Bourgeois Gentilhomme* will be of permanent value. The theme of the *Œdipus Rex* of Sophocles is an eternal one, for, like Œdipus, no man can wholly escape the common heritage of his kind. Like Hamlet, men will always find something in their natures too weak for the perfect accomplishment of the tasks set before them. Unbridled ambition, lust, jealousy, revenge, patriotism, love, and self-sacrifice will always be themes that humanity can understand; when they are set forth as powerfully as they are in *Macbeth*, *Antony and Cleopatra*, *Othello*, *The Merchant of Venice*, *Julius Caesar*, *Romeo and Juliet*, and *Measure for Measure*, there is little likelihood that the play which embodies them will ever die.

On the other hand, should the problem of labor and capital be satisfactorily solved, Galsworthy's *Strife* would cease to be of permanent interest. Should the evils he attacks in *Justice* and *The Silver Box* disappear, these plays would lose their present significance. Already the aggressive feminism of some of Ibsen's heroines is becoming a bit old-fashioned; the theme of *A Doll's House*, which once caused a furor, does not now attract a passing comment. But *What Every Woman Knows* about men in the play she will probably always know; and the theme of that play will probably be eternally interesting. The attitude toward aristocracy and democracy illustrated by *The Admirable Crichton* is a fundamental attitude, not likely to be changed by time; hence its theme may endure. That little masterpiece *Riders to the Sea* will be as fundamentally true a thousand years from now as it is today; its tragedy of simple men who are victims of the great forces of Nature is likely to be an eternal one.

Vitality, characterization, and significance necessary to dramatic longevity. Of course to prophesy longevity for any particular play is reckless business at best. It takes extraordinary *vitality*, extraordinary *power of characterization*, and *universal significance*, to keep a play alive. If it is to endure, it must have the life and power to make itself seem true to all people at all times. Probably even good plays as true as George Kelly's *The Show-off*, *Craig's Wife*, and *Daisy Mayme* will not live if they are too local in their significance. If characters in a play seem more American, or English, or Russian, or Spanish than human, they will not appeal to everyone. The characters in Chekhov's plays, for instance, are distinctively Russian, yet they have enough of all humanity in them to make them understandable. The people in *The Wild Duck*, in *The Power of Darkness*, in *Cyrano de Bergerac*, in *The Lower Depths*, in *The Kingdom of God*, in *Riders to the Sea*, and perhaps in *Candida*, *Loyalties*, *What Every Woman Knows*, and *Anna Christie*, though distinctly racial, are yet universal. Besides that, these plays rise, as Galsworthy says every good play should, "to a spire of meaning." In them human situations are made so clear and illuminating and so charged with thought and feeling, that the reader feels them truly to "hold the mirror up to Nature." So the final reason for permanent values in drama, as in all literature, is the depth and truth with which it portrays thoughts and feelings that are of universal significance.

Why Shakespeare lives. It is because he can thus reveal the human heart superlatively well that Shakespeare is called the greatest writer of all ages. He is unique in his power to reveal the secret places of our souls in phrase after phrase of almost miraculous insight. That is why we go back to his plays again long after their machine-made plots, their stretches of tedious foolery, and their passages of undeniable bombast have ceased to interest us. It is unlikely that any human being would ever be placed in the somewhat unbelievable situations in which the characters of *Hamlet*, for example, find themselves. But far too many human beings have felt

> the whips and scorns of time,
> The oppressor's wrong, the proud man's contumely,
> The pangs of dispriz'd love, the law's delay,
> The insolence of office, and the spurns
> That patient merit of the unworthy takes,

and all have felt that

> dread of something after death,
> The undiscover'd country from whose bourn
> No traveller returns,

and have regarded with wonder

> this most excellent canopy the air, this brave o'erhanging firmament, this majestical roof fretted with golden fire.

We have all speculated with fascination on the subject of death; we have known "what 'tis to love"; we have felt the insidious grasp on our souls of that monster, habit, "who doth all sense eat"; and we, too, have felt "how weary, stale, flat, and unprofitable seem all the uses of this world." Indeed it has become a commonplace to say that the play of *Hamlet* covers the gamut of all the emotions, save religious devotion, that man has felt. Every man, in truth, is Hamlet; and every man sees himself in Hamlet. The conflicting emotions, the perplexities of the character are universal, hence its universal fascination. The same universal, permanent appeal is found in most of Shakespeare's plays, whether it be the rapture of young love in *Romeo and Juliet*, the irresponsible gayety of *As You Like It*, the boisterous good fellowship of Sir Toby and his companions "rousing the night owl with a catch" in *Twelfth Night*, the unbridled, savage outbursts of human passions and the pitiless pelting of the storm in *King Lear*, or the peaceful acquiescence of Prospero in *The Tempest:*

> we are such stuff
> As dreams are made on; and our little life
> Is rounded with a sleep.

In the last analysis, if a drama has vitality and humanity and meaning, it will live.

Summary. Plays have a higher rate of mortality than any other form of literature. If they survive, it may be because they are permanently entertaining, because they have permanent story value, because they offer permanent attractions to actors and actresses, because they deal with a universal theme. But whatever the source of interest in a play, it must have extraordinary vitality, extraordinary power of characterization, and universal significance, if it is to have permanent artistic value. Shakespeare at his best, obviously meets all these requirements.

COMPREHENSION QUESTIONS

1. State the chief reasons why some plays survive from one generation to another. Give examples.
2. Explain what we mean by dramatic vitality, vital characterization, and universal significance. Illustrate.

PROBLEMS IN APPRECIATION

1. For which of the reasons listed in this chapter do you think the following plays have survived?

Aeschylus	*Agamemnon*
Anonymous	*Everyman*
Euripides	*Medea*
Goethe	*Faust*
Ibsen	*Hedda Gabler, Peer Gynt*
Molière	*L'Avare, Tartuffe*
Rostand	*Cyrano de Bergerac*
Shakespeare	*Hamlet, Macbeth, Romeo and Juliet*
Sheridan	*The School for Scandal*
Sophocles	*Antigone, Oedipus Tyrannus*
Synge	*Riders to the Sea*

2. Do you know any modern plays or moving pictures which you think may survive ten years? twenty-five? fifty? two hundred? Defend your answer.

3. The plays listed in this problem attempt to show dramatically some aspect of the life of an historical person. Notice that in such a play a dramatist must do at least three things:

   (*a*) He must select his material, since a man's life cannot be dramatized in two hours. (*b*) He must choose such episodes as will most dramatically emphasize the character of his protagonist. (*c*) He must choose episodes that will be likely to arouse and hold the interest of an audience in a theater; in other words, his play must be *dramatic.*[1]

   These things are obligatory; apart from them he may, if he chooses, exercise his imagination, especially with minor characters. Consider the extent to which all this is done in one of the following plays:

Maxwell Anderson	*Elizabeth the Queen, Mary of Scotland*
Bulwer-Lytton	*Richelieu*
Drinkwater	*Abraham Lincoln, Mary Stuart*
Agnes MacLeish	*Richard of Bordeaux*
Marlowe	*Edward II*
Masefield	*Philip the King, The Tragedy of Pompey the Great*
Louis Napoleon Parker	*Disraeli*
Rostand	*L'Aiglon*

[1] See page 282.

Schiller	*Maria Stuart, William Tell*
Shakespeare	*Antony and Cleopatra, King Richard II, King Richard III*
Shaw	*Caesar and Cleopatra, The Great Catherine, The Man of Destiny, Saint Joan*
Swinburne	*Chastelard, Bothwell, Mary Stuart*
Tennyson	*Becket, Queen Mary*

4. The following plays are all *problem plays*, that is, they seek through the medium of the theater to focus attention on some social problem. In each of them an individual is, somehow or other, in conflict with existing social or economic conditions. Each play involves not only individual destinies but social theories.

(*a*) What, in each case, is the problem presented? (*b*) Who represents the individual, and who, or what, represents society? (*c*) What characters and circumstances cause the problem? (*d*) What solution, if any, is offered? (*e*) Does the problem seem natural? (*f*) Would it occur often in real life or is it the special problem of particular individuals? (*g*) Is it important enough to be of interest to an audience? (*h*) How is it made into an effective play? (*i*) Is the play ineffective because there is too much talk and too little drama? (*j*) Is the problem still as significant as it was when the play was written? (*h*) Do you think the play will last?

Refer specifically to the play in answering these questions. Quote when you can. See pages 321–322.

Barrie	*The Admirable Crichton*
Philip Barry	*Holiday*
Lewis Beach	*The Goose Hangs High*
Björnson	*Beyond Human Power, A Gauntlet*
Eugène Brieux	*The Red Robe*
Karel M. Capek	*R.U.R.*
Chekhov	*The Cherry Orchard*
Rachel Crothers	*Mary the Third, Nice People*
Galsworthy	*Justice, The Pigeon, Strife*
Giuseppe Giacosa	*Like Falling Leaves*
Hauptmann	*The Weavers*
Paul Hervieu	*The Trail of the Torch*
Sidney Coe Howard	*The Silver Cord*
Ibsen	*Ghosts, The Wild Duck*
Gregorio Martinez Sierra	*The Kingdom of God*
O'Neill	*All God's Chillun Got Wings*

Pinero	*The Second Mrs. Tanqueray*
Channing Pollock	*The Enemy, The Fool, The House Beautiful*
Shakespeare	*Measure for Measure, Troilus and Cressida*
Shaw	*Candida, Major Barbara, Man and Superman, Saint Joan*
Tolstoy	*The Power of Darkness*

5. The following plays seek to present ideas dramatically.
   (*a*) In each case what is the idea presented? (*b*) Do you think it is worth writing a play about? (*c*) Is it the kind of idea that can be made into a play; that is, is it essentially dramatic? (*d*) Is it true? (*e*) Is it significant? (*f*) Is it expressed in effective drama? (*g*) Does the play suffer too much from talk about the ideas, or do the ideas seem to come out naturally in the course of the play?

Do not answer by *yes* or *no;* use specific references to the play. Quote where you can.

Maxwell Anderson and Laurence Stallings	*What Price Glory?*
Andreyev	*The Life of Man*
Solomon Ansky	*The Dybbuk*
John Doyd Balderston	*Berkeley Square*
Barrie	*The Admirable Crichton, Dear Brutus, Mary Rose*
Robert Bracco	*Phantasms*
Karel M. Capek	*The Insect World, R.U.R.*
Alberto Casella and Walter Ferras	*Death Takes a Holiday*
Paul Claudel	*The Tidings Brought to Mary*
D'Annunzio	*La Gioconda*
José Echegaray	*The Great Galeoto*
Galsworthy	*Escape, The Pigeon, Loyalties*
Goethe	*Faust*
Harley Granville-Barker	*The Madras House*
Hauptmann	*The Sunken Bell*
Hervieu	*The Trail of the Torch*
Ibsen	*An Enemy of the People, Ghosts, The Master Builder, Peer Gynt, Rosmersholm, The Wild Duck*
Jerome K. Jerome	*The Passing of the Third Floor Back*
Charles Rann Kennedy	*The Servant in the House*

Gregario Martinez Sierra	*The Kingdom of God*
Somerset Maugham	*Rain*
O'Neill	*The Great God Brown, The Hairy Ape*
Pirandello	*As You Desire Me, Henry IV, Right You Are If You Think So, Six Characters in Search of an Author*
Elmer Rice	*We the People*
Schnitzler	*The Lonely Way*
Shaw	*The Apple Cart, Candida, The Devil's Disciple, Getting Married, Saint Joan*
Robert Cedric Sherriff	*Journey's End*
Augustus Thomas	*As A Man Thinks, The Witching Hour*
Tolstoy	*The Power of Darkness*
Sutton Vane	*Outward Bound*
Zangwill	*The Melting Pot*

6. The following plays have a satirical purpose, that is, they are making fun of something.

(*a*) In each case what is ridiculed? (*b*) Is the ridicule fair? (*c*) What scenes and passages and characters make the ridicule most apparent? (*d*) Is the satire subtle or obvious? (*e*) Is it directed against universal human weakness or of a particular age, type of people or race? (*f*) Would the play, if presented before people who most need its lesson, actually benefit them? (*g*) Is the play wholly comic or is there pathos mingled with satire?

Refer specifically to the play. Quote where you can.

Aristophanes	*The Frogs, Lysistrata*
Barrie	*Alice-Sit-by-the-Fire*
Beaumont and Fletcher	*The Knight of the Burning Pestle*
Dolly Byrne and Gilda Varesi	*Enter Madame*
Congreve	*The Way of the World*
Frank Craven	*The First Year*
Rachel Crothers	*Expressing Willie*
Gilbert	*The Mikado, Pinafore*
George Kaufman and Marc Connelly	*Beggar on Horseback, Merton of the Movies, To The Ladies*
George Kelly	*The Torch Bearers, The Show-off*
Milne	*The Dover Road*
Molière	*The Bourgeois Gentleman, The Imaginary Invalid*

Molnar	*The Swan*
O'Neill	*Marco Millions*
Shaw	*Androcles and the Lion, Arms and the Man, The Doctor's Dilemma*
Sheridan	*The Rivals, The School for Scandal*
Synge	*The Playboy of the Western World*
Tolstoy	*The Fruits of Culture*
Jesse L. Williams	*Why Marry?*

7. The following plays attempt deliberately to teach a lesson.
(*a*) In each play what is the lesson? (*b*) To whom is it addressed? (*c*) Is it a needed lesson? (*d*) How does the play attempt to make it forceful? (*e*) Does the author ever preach so much that the play ceases to be dramatically effective? (*f*) Does the lesson come out naturally and inevitably in the play, or does the play seem to be made to fit the lesson? (*g*) Does the characterization ever suffer from the author's eagerness to point out his moral? (*h*) Which characters give the most direct utterance to the lesson? (*i*) What is the chief danger confronting a dramatist writing a play of this sort?
Use specific references. Quote when you can.

Maxwell Anderson	*Both Your Houses*
Barrie	*The Admirable Crichton*
Björnson	*Beyond Human Power*
Rachel Crothers	*Mary the Third*
St. John Ervine	*Mixed Marriage*
Rose D. Franken	*Another Language*
Sidney Coe Howard	*The Silver Cord*
Ibsen	*The Pillars of Society, The Wild Duck*
Henry Arthur Jones	*Michael and His Lost Angel*
Maeterlinck	*The Blue Bird*
Gregorio Martinez Sierra	*The Kingdom of God*
Somerset Maugham	*Rain*
William Vaughn Moody	*The Faith Healer*
Anne Nichols	*Abie's Irish Rose*
Channing Pollock	*The Enemy, The Fool, The House Beautiful*
Elmer Rice	*We the People*
Shakespeare	*Measure for Measure, The Tempest*
Sheridan	*The School for Scandal*
Robert Cedric Sherriff	*Journey's End*
Tolstoy	*The Power of Darkness*

John Van Druten	*Young Woodley*
Sutton Vane	*Outward Bound*
Yeats	*The Hour Glass*

8. The following plays are primarily concerned with human beings—only secondarily with ideas or problems. Each, despite its having on it the stamp of time and place and nationality, has about it something universal. Thus in a way it shows us people, experiences, and feelings which are common to us all—and sometimes expresses them so eloquently that we feel it is speaking to us, about us, for us. In each the complication is not machine-made but the result of conflicts in human nature and human feelings that are universal.

(*a*) Explain wherein one of them deals with and expresses these common human things. (*b*) Is it local and racial as well as universal? Quote to illustrate your answer. (*c*) What feelings and motives struggle in it? (*d*) Quote passages that seem to have *vitality, universal significance*, or *eloquence*. (*e*) What characterizations strike you as particularly deep and true?

George Abbott and Ann Preston Bridgers	*Coquette*
Maxwell Anderson	*Elizabeth the Queen, Mary of Scotland*
Anonymous	*Everyman*
Barrie	*What Every Woman Knows*
Henri Becque	*The Vultures*
Benavente	*La Malquerida*
Browning	*A Blot in the 'Scutcheon*
Chekhov	*The Cherry Orchard, The Three Sisters, Uncle Vanya*
Corneille	*The Cid*
D'Annunzio	*Francesca da Rimini*
Dryden	*All for Love*
St. John Ervine	*Jane Clegg*
Euripides	*Medea*
Benito Peréz Galdos	*The Duchess of San Quentin, The Grandfather*
Goethe	*Faust*
Gorki	*The Lower Depths*
Hauptmann	*Drayman Henschel, Hannele, Rose Bernd, The Rats, The Weavers*
Hermann Heijermans	*The Good Hope*
Ibsen	*Ghosts, Rosmersholm, The Wild Duck*
George Kelly	*The Show-off*

Vandamm Studio

A SCENE FROM *AS YOU LIKE IT*

Modern actors recapture the joyous humor of Shakespeare's foresters

A SCENE FROM *JOURNEY'S END*

Human vitality and courage conquer the gloom of the trenches.

Gregorio Martinez Sierra	*Cradle Song, The Kingdom of God*
Molnar	*Liliom*
Sean O'Casey	*Juno and the Paycock, The Plough and the Stars*
O'Neill	*Ah, Wilderness!, Desire under the Elms, Mourning Becomes Electra, The Straw*
S. Phillips	*Paolo and Francesca*
Racine	*Bérénice, Esther, Phèdre*
Strindberg	*Comrades, The Father*
Sudermann	*Magda, The Vale of Content*
Synge	*Riders to the Sea*
Tolstoy	*Redemption, The Power of Darkness*

9. The following plays are examples of fantastic drama; that is, they are frankly impossible and yet they express underlying truths about human beings and human life.

(*a*) In each case what is fantastic about each play? (*b*) What is also true? (*c*) Is the truth to be found in human nature, human institutions, or in the underlying idea of the play? (*d*) Are any of these plays purely imaginary without any underlying truth at all? (*e*) What, if any, is the advantage of presenting ideas thus allegorically? (*f*) Do any of these plays contain passages that are true or beautiful in themselves? (*g*) Are any of the characters realistic? (*h*) Which characters are fantastic? (*i*) Does the author make the fantastic characters seem real? (*j*) Quote especially poetic passages.

John Lloyd Balderston	*Berkeley Square*
Barrie	*The Admirable Crichton, Dear Brutus, A Kiss for Cinderella, The Legend of Leonora, Mary Rose, Peter Pan*
Karel M. Capek	*The Insect World, R.U.R.*
Alberto Casella and Walter Ferris	*Death Takes a Holiday*
De la Mare	*Crossings*
Dunsany	*The Gods of the Mountain, If, King Argimenes and the Unknown Warrior*
James Elroy Flecker	*Hassan*
Hauptmann	*Hannele, The Sunken Bell*
Ibsen	*The Lady from the Sea, Peer Gynt*
Percy Mackaye	*The Scarecrow*
Molnar	*Liliom*

Noyes	*Sherwood*
O'Neill	*The Fountain, Lazarus Laughed, Marco Millions*
Josephine Preston Peabody	*The Piper*
Rostand	*Chanticleer*
Shakespeare	*A Midsummer Night's Dream, The Tempest*
Synge	*Deirdre of the Sorrows*
Yeats	*Deirdre, The Land of Heart's Desire*

10. The following plays, though not impossible, are romantic; that is, they show life heightened, idealized, more brightly colored than it is.

    (*a*) What happenings in them are romantic rather than realistic? (*b*) What characters have *romantic appeal?* (*c*) What about the setting is romantic? (*d*) What passages appeal to the imagination? (*e*) Do you prefer romantic or realistic plays? (*f*) Contrast one of these with a realistic play you have read.

Barrie	*Quality Street*
Bulwer-Lytton	*Richelieu*
Hugo	*Hernani, Ruy Blas*
O'Neill	*The Fountain, Marco Millions*
Louis Napoleon Parker	*Pomander Walk*
S. Phillips	*Paolo and Francesca, Ulysses*
Pinero	*The Amazons*
Rostand	*Cyrano de Bergerac, The Far-away Princess*
Shakespeare	*As You Like It, Cymbeline, The Merchant of Venice, Romeo and Juliet, Twelfth Night, The Winter's Tale*
Synge	*Deirdre of the Sorrows*

Part Four

THE ESSAY AND OTHER PROSE NON-FICTION

Nearly everybody in the modern world reads prose: advertisements, newspapers, magazines, textbooks, travel-books, history, and biography. All this reading serves some purpose. Usually it supplies information. Sometimes it provides entertainment. Most of it is thrown aside after a single perusal. Some prose, however, is recognized at once as having value in itself. Even when the facts which it presents become out-dated, it is still read with pleasure and regarded as literature.

In Part Four we shall try to explain why some prose writing aside from the drama and the novel is of enduring value. We shall concentrate our attention upon the chief non-fictional prose form, the essay. Here you will find a discussion of the nature of the essay, of its various forms, and of the way in which it can most profitably be studied.

In these chapters, too, you will find a discussion of biography, a form of prose writing which has recently become very popular. There is also a chapter on such miscellaneous types as history, memoirs, oratory, translations, letters, and diaries.

Before beginning to study these chapters you can well review essays by such standard essayists as Addison, Steele, Irving, Emerson, and Holmes. Of course you will also wish to bring to bear your acquaintance with contemporary writers who are represented in collections of modern essays and who write for the magazines which appeal to thoughtful people. Then, too, you will wish to browse among the various biographies such as Strachey's *Queen Victoria* on the shelves of libraries, and among the miscellaneous works which contain the best thoughts of the best minds.

Part Four represents a fresh opportunity for you to become interested in the work of men who are primarily thinkers, and who love to analyze human emotions, experiences, and ideas. To study their work requires concentration and thoughtful reading. The reward for your effort will be a knowledge of some of the world's most interesting personalities, a sense for prose style, and an acquaintance with stimulating ideas and ideals.

CHAPTER 28

WHAT THE ESSAY IS

The essay as a literary form. What the lyric is to poetry, the essay is to prose. It is the writer's opportunity to give free expression to his ideas about life, as the lyric is his opportunity to express his emotions. The essay is the most informal of literary types, since the one primary characteristic of the essayist is his interest in reflecting about life no matter where his reflections may lead him.

Subject matter of the essay has great variety. The essay may have the dignity of Bacon or the familiarity of Montaigne. Aside from the purely formal essay, which is in no sense personal, the essay is a brief record in prose of the author's personal reactions to some phase of the life about him. Montaigne says,

> It is myselfe I pourtray.

This personal note is found alike in the polished and urbane essays of Addison, the genial and appreciative essays of Irving, the discriminating essays of Agnes Repplier. The subject matter of the essay is as varied as the personalities of its authors. Not many modern essayists wander so far from the implications of the title as Montaigne, but any given volume may treat of most diverse matters. Thus Lamb's *Essays of Elia* contains, among other things, discussions of: "Ears," "All Fool's Day," "My Relations," "Roast Pig," "Dream Children," "Chimney-Sweepers," "Old Actors," "Popular Fallacies." Stevenson's *Virginibus Puerisque* has entertaining, if not profound, things to say about: "Falling in Love," "An Apology for Idlers," "Crabbed Age and Youth," "Walking Tours," "Gas Lamps." Agnes Repplier's *Points of Friction* makes incisive, if not always comforting, comments on: "Dead Authors," "The Cheerful Clan," "The Beloved Sinner," "Money," "Cruelty and Humor." A mere list of titles shows the almost unlimited scope of the essayist's material.

Mood often determines subject. What an essayist has to say depends less on his subject than on his mood and his point of view. Lamb begins his essay on "Ears" with the startling announcement:

> I have no ear,

but he hastens to add that he is not

> by nature destitute of those external twin appendages, hanging ornaments, and (architecturally speaking) handsome volutes to the human capital.

Rather is he

> delicately provided with those conduits,

so that he feels

> no disposition to envy the mule for his plenty or the mole for her exactness in those ingenious labyrinthine inlets—those indispensable sable side-intelligencers.

Neither was he ever, he thanks his stars, in the pillory; nor does he think it within the compass of his destiny that he ever will be. When he says that he has no ear, he means that he has "no ear for music" and on this theme he proceeds to elaborate whimsically; and no one could foresee, himself least of all, where his whim might lead him. In "Popular Fallacies" it leads him to point out that a bully is not always a coward; that a man may laugh at his own jest; that handsome is not as handsome does; that it is often advisable to look a gift horse in the mouth; that pleasures and palaces are sometimes better than home, sweet home; that we ought not always to rise with the lark or lie down with the lamb.

Essayist's views often determine subject. The essay need not, however, deal lightly and carelessly with whims and fancies. It may be a serious, even profound exposition of a subject of importance to the writer or to mankind. Such essays are Emerson's philosophical comments in "Compensation," "Self-Reliance," and "Friendship." Such, too, are Ruskin's reflections in "Roots of Honor," "Time and Tide," and "The Mystery of Life and Its Arts."

The essay may be a satirical or serious comment on the follies and vices of society, suave and not unkindly, as in Addison's comment on the gifted, well-meaning, but useless Will Wimble:

> I was secretly touched with compassion toward the honest gentleman . . . and could not but consider with a great deal of concern how so good a heart and such busy hands were wholly employed in trifles; that so much humanity should be so little beneficial to others, and so much industry so little advantageous to himself. The same temper of mind and application to affairs might have recommended him to the public esteem, and have raised his fortune in another station of life. What good to his country or himself might not a trader or merchant have done with such useful though ordinary qualifications?

or savage with bitter sarcasm as in Swift's "A Modest Proposal."

Frequently essays are written in a spirit of quiet philosophy, such as Sir Thomas Browne's "Urn Burial." Sometimes they are impartial discussions of political questions, such as William Howard Taft's "The Powers of the President." Sometimes they discuss scientific discoveries, social problems, religious thought, education. All these subjects are presented from varying points of view and with varying intensity according to the mood and motive of the author. Whatever its topic the essay is in prose, it is comparatively brief, and it is a record of the personal feelings or views of the author on some subject which interests him.

The essay is usually incomplete. This does not mean that it is unfinished. Any essay is complete in itself, but it does not begin to exhaust the possibilities of its subject matter or even of its author's reactions to that subject matter. It gives us a complete idea of the way the author wishes us to look at his subject within the limits of space and time at his disposal. Addison makes clear his point in his essay on "Party Feeling," but he does not by any means say all that there is to be said on the subject—probably not even all that he has to say about it. Irving makes clear to us what were his chief reactions to Westminster Abbey and Stratford-on-Avon, but he cannot in the space at his disposal include all that he noticed and felt. Emerson cannot in one essay exhaust the possibilities of his ideas on compensation, nor can Macaulay, in the space allowed him for an *Encyclopaedia Britannica* article, tell us all that he knows about Dr. Johnson. An essay is, then, incomplete; it is the expression of the mood, the point of view, the facts of the moment, not a complete study of the subject.

The essay reflects the mood and personality of the author. More direct than other forms of prose literature, it has more of the personal quality in it. The author sets out directly to tell the reader what he personally thinks or feels at that particular moment, and in so doing he is bound to reveal himself. In reading the essay one has the intimate sense of following the facial expressions, the gestures, the tone of voice of the writer. One catches the bitter sneer on Swift's lips, the harsh irony of his voice, as he says of the observance of Sunday:

> What if men of pleasure are forced, one day in the week, to game at home instead of the chocolate-houses? are not the taverns and coffee houses open? . . . Is not that the chief day for traders to sum up accounts of the week, and for lawyers to prepare their briefs? But I would fain know how it can be pretended that churches are misapplied? Where are more appointments and rendezvous of gallantry? Where more care to appear in the foremost box with greater advantage of dress? where more meetings of business? where more bargains driven of all sorts? and where so many conveniences or enticements to sleep?

The flaming scorn, the almost snarling bitterness of Swift's voice are as plainly apparent as the chuckles with which Irving tells about the Christmas music at Squire Bracebridge's church:

> The usual services of the choir were managed tolerably well, the vocal parts generally lagging a little behind the instrumental, and some loitering fiddler now and then making up for lost time by traveling over a passage with prodigious celerity. . . . But the great trial was an anthem that had been prepared and arranged by Master Simon, and on which he had founded great expectation. Unluckily there was a blunder at the very outset; the musicians became flurried; Master Simon was in a fever; everything went on lamely and irregularly until they came to a chorus beginning, "Now let us sing with one accord," which seemed to be a signal for parting company: all became discord and confusion; each shifted for himself, and got to the end as well, or, rather, as soon as he could, excepting one old chorister in a pair of horn spectacles, bestriding and pinching a long sonorous nose; who happened to stand a little apart, and, being wrapped up in his own melody, kept on a quavering course, wriggling his head, ogling his book, and winding all up by a nasal solo of at least three bars' duration.

And equally clear is the gentle sentiment in Thackeray's voice as he tells of the lock of Stella's hair which Swift inclosed in paper marked, "Only a woman's hair":

Do these words indicate indifference or an attempt to hide feeling? Did you ever hear or read four words more pathetic? Only a woman's hair; only love, only fidelity, only purity, innocence, beauty; only the tenderest heart in the world stricken and wounded, and passed away now out of reach of pangs of hope deferred, love insulted, and pitiless desertion:—only that lock of hair left.

In the essay, then, the feelings as well as the ideas of the writer are apparent. Everything is direct, informal, personal. If the writer, like Addison, is an urbane, cultured, witty gentleman of the world, that urbanity, that culture, that sophisticated wit are bound to appear. If, like Irving, he is genial, kindly, sentimental, whole-hearted, these qualities appear in his essays. The principal charm of Lamb's writings lies in the whimsical, imaginative, tender, humorous personality which shines from every page. The enthusiasms, prejudices, and idealism of Emerson can be felt directly. The rough-shod vigor of Carlyle is reflected in the jolt of his sentences and the incoherence of his exclamations.

The essay permits great variety of treatment. Here are no rules, no elaborate technique, no vocabulary of terms to be studied. The essayist writes as he pleases. He may organize his material carefully and present it logically. But he is under no obligation to do so. There is for him no fixed standard. He may improvise as he sees fit. The style is as varied as the subject matter and the moods of the writers. Addison writes in a style that is both smooth and dignified. Browne writes in a rich, poetic style. Washington Irving's style is one of amused tolerance; Carlyle is vigorous and Swift is harshly bitter.

The essay reflects its age. As the essay expresses the mood and personality of its author, so it expresses the mood and personality of the age in which he lived. Like Swift, a writer may be out of sympathy with his age, but he is, in spite of himself, the creature of it. He cannot help revealing it as well as himself. He cannot write his reactions to the life about him without showing what that life was like: what men did, what things in life interested and moved them, what their ideas of literature, science, government, society, and religion were.

A general classification of essays. Free as the essay is in form, there are still certain kinds of essays which have held relatively true to type: the personal essay, the essay of manners, the nature essay, the travel essay, the critical essay in the fields of art and letters, and the philosophical, historical, and scientific essay.

The personal essay. The personal essay has been so much the favorite of essay writers, that many critics refuse the name of essay to any other type. It is a frank revelation of the writer's thoughts on any subject from Bacon's "Of Gardens" to Stevenson's "An Apology for Idlers." The personal essay is a bit of conversation, and is enjoyable in so far as it conveys an interesting idea, is brightly worded, has gayety, humor, or pathos, or stimulates the reader into sympathetic reflection. Above all, the quality of the personal essay depends upon the interest of the personality which it discloses.

It is, of course, impossible to classify personalities. Every human being differs in some respect from every other. Yet men and women are much alike, too, and in the personal essay four types of personality have predominated. These, for convenience, we may call scholarly, emotional, whimsical, and inspirational.

The scholarly personal essay. The scholarly essayist has a keen, bright mind which has been sharpened by much study of men and books. Such writers as Sir Francis Bacon, William Hazlitt, Cardinal Newman, and Agnes Repplier all belong to this type. Their minds are richly stored with learning and their essays are full of allusions to history and literature. They analyze their subjects, taking them apart to view them on every side. They are serious and earnest, eager to find the truth and express it in dignified, expressive language.

The opening sentences of Bacon's "Of Studies" show at once his scholarly mind.

> Studies serve for delight, for ornament, and for ability. Their chief use for delight is in privateness and retiring; for ornament, is in discourse; and for ability, is in the judgment and disposition of business. For expert men can execute, and perhaps judge of particulars, one by one; but the general counsels, and the plots and marshaling of affairs, come best from those that are learned.

The scholarly personal essayist appeals, of course, primarily to readers who like to think hard, to analyze, and to be reminded of the past. The masterly logic, the sharp incisiveness, the cool and assured judgment, the Ciceronian dignity of style which one finds in Cardinal Newman's beautiful prose give the greatest delight to those whose minds are seriously reflective.

When Miss Repplier writes about cats, as in *The Fireside Sphinx*, she makes the cat an historical personage, drawing upon her well-stored mind for endless illustrations from the past. To enjoy such essays of Hazlitt's as "Common Sense" or "On People with One Idea" one needs to recognize scores of allusions to men and books.

The style of the scholarly personal essay aims at clearness, fullness, point, comprehensiveness, dignity, power, and variety.

The emotional personal essay. The emotional personal essayist follows the tradition established by Charles Lamb, the most universally beloved of all personal essayists. The basis of the emotional personal essay is sensitive recollection. Lamb recalled the plays he had seen, the books he had read, the places he had visited, and the people he had known, and let his tender memories play about them gayly, pathetically, humorously, or extravagantly. "Old China," "Dream Children," "The Old Benchers of the Inner Temple," and dozens of other essays show the grace, charm, and tenderness of his sensitive mind.

The subject of the emotional personal essay is not important; what matters is its charm of personality, and the ease, suggestiveness, humor, extravagance, and gayety of its style.

The whimsical personal essay. This essay usually is in the manner of Oliver Wendell Holmes' *Autocrat of the Breakfast Table*, quiet, penetrating, wise, and sensible. The whimsical personal essay usually has a moral concealed in it; its author has thought about life but, like Samuel McChord Crothers, conceals the depth of his thought by a covering of gay banter. The joking is enough in itself to satisfy the reader, but under the joking is usually a lesson worth pondering.

The inspirational personal essay. This type of essay is beautifully exemplified by Robert Louis Stevenson's *Virginibus Puerisque* and "Pulvis et Umbra," which, though light in style and conversational in manner, aim frankly to preach a little sermon which will make its readers better men and women. Stevenson never grew shrill, vituperative, or wrathful as did Thomas Carlyle. As a result his essays have charm, dignity, persuasiveness, and profit. Dealing as they do with the fundamental moral problems of hope, courage, and truth, they outlast changes of fashion and of conduct.

The essay of manners. This type of essay is based upon the lively, satirical observation of the manners, dress, behavior, and customs of contemporary social life. It is the kind of essay which Addison and Steele wrote in *The Tatler* and *The Spectator* and which is written whenever women adopt new and striking fashions of dress, whenever society is in a state of change, or whenever people take an exaggerated interest in games like bridge or golf. Fashions change, but the wit, neatness, and satire of the essay remain. Steele and Addison never grew too serious to be gay and light in style; the essayist of manners in modern magazines is too much interested in preaching a social lesson to retain his light-heartedness. The modern representatives of the true spirit of the essay of manners are the skits and cartoons of humorous magazines and the humorous "columns" of newspapers.

The nature essay. A third type, the nature essay, aims to reflect the world of trees, flowers, birds, mountains, and animals. John Burroughs, Dallas Lore Sharp, Richard Jefferies, and W. H. Hudson, all sensitive observers of Nature, gave their lives to making the city man realize the world of beauty, mystery, and wonder which lies off the beaten track. The nature essay always has a human touch. Though accurate, it is never purely scientific. The facts of natural history which it presents are correct, but they do not exist for themselves. Somewhere in its world is always the presence of man.

The travel essay. The travel essay is not so popular now, when so many people travel, as it was in the nineteenth century when most people had to experience strange lands and peoples in the pages of books. Its interest lies in the reaction of a personality to a new environment. Charles Dickens' *American Notes* is the record of the way in which America impressed him in 1842. In these essays his ardent, eager mind took full control of his judgment. The result is one of the most vivid and most provocative books on nineteenth-century America. On the other hand Washington Irving interprets England of the early nineteenth century with all the charm and kindliness of a man beloved alike in England and America.

The unreflective traveler cannot write travel essays because his travels do nothing for him; he remains after his travels as he was before. As Newman said in his essay "Knowledge Viewed in Relation to Learning":

> Seafaring men, for example, range from one end of the earth to the other; but the multiplicity of external objects, which they have encountered, forms no symmetrical and consistent picture upon their imagination; they see the tapestry of human life, as it were, on the wrong side, and it tells no story. They sleep, and they rise up, and they find themselves, now in Europe, now

in Asia; they see visions of great cities and wild regions; they are in the marts of commerce, or amid the islands of the South; they gaze on Pompey's Pillar, or on the Andes; and nothing which meets them carries them forward or backward, to any idea beyond itself. Nothing has a drift or relation; nothing has a history or a promise. Everything stands by itself, and comes and goes in its turn, like the shifting scenes of a show, which leave the spectator where he was.

The travel essay requires, then, a sensitive, flexible, reflective mind and a sympathetic, persuasive style.

The critical essay. The critical essay contains the record of a thoughtful, analytical mind acting upon literature which it fully understands. Critical essays are of three general types: judicial, appreciative, and biographical.

Judicial criticism is well represented by Matthew Arnold's "The Study of Poetry." Arnold begins with certain judgments which he considers firmly established: that poetry is "a criticism of life"; that it is "the noble and profound application of ideas to life"; that great poetry has "high truth and high seriousness." His method is to subject writers like Chaucer, Gray, and Burns to these judgments and see if they have enduring worth. One may disagree with the judicial critic, but it is impossible not to respect him if he is sincere, thoughtful, thorough, and well read.

Appreciative criticism is well represented by Hazlitt's "My First Acquaintance with Poets." This essay is marked chiefly by its enthusiastic appreciation, what Hazlitt called "gusto." The appreciative critic aims, above all, at interesting readers in his own admiration for a writer. He has no fixed judgments; his infectious enthusiasm is enough.

A variety of appreciative criticism is impressionism. The impressionistic critic is interested not so much in his author as in himself, in what has been called "the adventures of a soul among masterpieces." Many of Lamb's literary essays, "On the Tragedies of Shakespeare," for instance, are pure impressionism. The qualities of the appreciative critic are sensitiveness, wide knowledge of his subject, grace, ease, penetration, and beauty of style.

Biographical criticism aims at the interpretation of a writer through the events of his life. One of the best-known examples of this type of criticism in English literature is Macaulay's "Essay on Boswell's Life of Samuel Johnson." Macaulay tries to explain Johnson through his education, his struggle for recognition in the literary circles of London, and his final success. Like many writers of biographical criticism, Macaulay tended toward picturesque overstatement. The result was that readers remembered Macaulay's highly colored detail and neglected Johnson's really important literary achievements. Biographical criticism is the most misleading of all critical methods, because unimportant but interesting facts often obscure the real literary quality of a writer more than they illuminate it.

The philosophical, historical, and scientific essay. The modern magazine encourages chiefly essays in the fields of social problems, political history, economics, and science. Our modern world changes so rapidly and contains so many people who are well educated, that there is a great demand for discussion of popular topics. Readers naturally want the latest information on all subjects. Hence clearness of exposition and timeliness of subject matter often leave no room for the expression of the writer's personality.

The essays of Thomas Henry Huxley are classic examples of scientific essays. Close reasoning, clarity of expression, and grasp of subject matter raise such an essay as "On a Piece of Chalk" above mere scientific reporting. George Bernard Shaw, Gilbert K. Chesterton, Dean Inge, and L. P. Jacks have shown that powerful personality, brilliant style, and originality of idea can make literature out of the discussion of contemporary topics.

We may be sure that with the further spread of education the essay will broaden in scope and develop other types. Never in history have so many interesting events happened, and never has so large a proportion of the population demanded information about the world and its affairs. Prose rather than poetry has become our natural medium of expression, and the possibilities of prose literature are endless.

Summary. The *essay* is the free expression in prose of a writer's ideas. The subject matter of the essay has great variety. The essay is never a complete presentation of its subject matter. The essay permits great variety of treatment. The essay reflects its age.

The *personal essay* is a frank revelation of a writer's thoughts. There are four varieties of the personal essay: the *scholarly essay*, the *emotional essay*, the *whimsical essay*, and the *inspirational essay*.

The *essay of manners* is based upon the satirical observation of contemporary life. The *nature essay* reflects the outdoor world. The *travel essay* presents the reaction of a personality to a new environment. The *critical essay* contains the record of a thoughtful mind acting upon literature. Critical essays are of three types: *judicial*, *appreciative*, and *biographical*.

Philosophical, *historical*, and *scientific essays* contain a writer's ideas in the fields of social problems, history, and science.

COMPREHENSION QUESTIONS

1. *Vocabulary:* appreciative, essay, Ciceronian, clarity, critical, impressionism, infectious, inspirational, judicial, lyric, multiplicity, philosophy, satirical, scholarly, scope, sophisticated, symmetrical, whimsical, vituperative.
2. *Allusions:*

Montaigne	Thomas Macaulay	Richard Jefferies
Sir Francis Bacon	Thomas Carlyle	W. H. Hudson
Sir Thomas Browne	John Ruskin	Samuel McChord Crothers
Joseph Addison	Ralph Waldo Emerson	Agnes Repplier
Jonathan Swift	Cardinal Newman	George Bernard Shaw
Charles Lamb	Oliver Wendell Holmes	Gilbert K. Chesterton
William Hazlitt	Robert Louis Stevenson	Dean Inge
Washington Irving	John Burroughs	L. P. Jacks

   (*a*) Which of these do you know? (*b*) Which of these have you heard of? (*c*) Find out something about two whom you do not know. (*d*) Tell what you know about two with whom you are familiar.
3. Explain and illustrate what is meant by the statement that the essay has *variety*.
4. How can the essay be *incomplete* without being *unfinished?*
5. Why does the essay easily lend itself to great variety in form and treatment?
6. What is meant by the *personal essay?*
7. Define and exemplify: the *essay of manners*, the *nature essay*, the *travel essay*, the *critical essay*, *philosophical*, *historical*, and *scientific essays*.
8. Explain and illustrate the distinction between *judicial*, *appreciative*, and *impressionistic* criticism. Try to find in a collection of essays an example of one of these.

PROBLEMS IN APPRECIATION

1. In any collection of essays choose:
   (*a*) five which illustrate the variety of subject matter of the essay, (*b*) three which illustrate its incompleteness, (*c*) four which illustrate

different moods and reflect different personalities, (*d*) four which show striking differences in form and treatment.

2. In any collection of essays find examples of the different types of essays mentioned in this chapter.
3. Familiarize yourself with two of the following writers of nature essays:

John Burroughs.	W. H. Hudson	William Beebe
Dallas Lore Sharp	Julian Huxley	

Read and compare two essays by two of these men. Wherein is their treatment of Nature different from that to be found in most nature poets?

4. Read an essay on American life by a foreign visitor to the United States. Wherein does his judgment of this country strike you as true, original, mistaken, or prejudiced?
5. Read and analyze Arnold's "The Study of Poetry." Why is it *judicial* rather than *appreciative* or *impressionistic?* Compare and contrast it with Lamb's "On the Tragedies of Shakespeare."
6. Read a modern biographical essay such as Lytton Strachey's "Florence Nightingale." Compare the method and point of view with Macaulay's "Johnson" or Carlyle's "Burns."

QUESTIONS ON BOOKS YOU HAVE READ

1. Compare Addison's essay on Westminster Abbey with Washington Irving's in *The Sketch Book.* Compare also the way both authors deal with the subject of a stagecoach journey. Which author's writing do you prefer? What differences in personality do you find? in style? in attitude toward the subject matter? in interests? in purpose? Do you think that Irving's essay could have been written in the time of Queen Anne?

2. If the essay expresses the personality of the author, what sort of man is revealed by the Coverley papers which Addison wrote? Do they reveal a personality different from Steele's? from Irving's? from Lamb's? Why is the difference between Addison and Steele not more marked in the essays?

3. Make a list of the places, objects, scenes, incidents, and people in *The Sketch Book* in which Irving seems especially interested. What is the source of his interest in each? Do any of the things in which he is interested reveal definite traits in his character or aspects of his personality? What sort of people interest him most? places? Find evidence of his special interests in literature, of his attitude toward Nature, of his ideas of humor or pathos, of his geniality, of his appreciative but somewhat superficial powers of observation.

4. What qualities make Irving an ideal traveler? What passages in *The Sketch Book* illustrate these qualities? Write an essay on an ideal traveling companion using Irving as your example.

5. How would Jaques in *As You Like It* have described the Christmas festivities at Bracebridge Hall? Try to rewrite the "Christmas Day" essay in the style of Addison, or the "Sunday with Sir Roger" essay in the style of Irving.

CHAPTER 29

HOW TO READ ESSAYS

There are four points of view from which an essay may be studied: its central idea, the method of treating that idea, the author's personality, and the spirit of the age as revealed by these three.

The central idea is the most important. Almost every essay is written to exemplify some one idea. In most of the *Sir Roger de Coverley Papers* the central idea is to be found in some purpose of social reform which the authors wish to impress on their readers. Thus "Moll White" attempts to discourage the persecution of witches; "Will Wimble" to point out the absurdity of limiting the younger sons of great families to two or three professions; "Whigs and Tories" to point out the follies and dangers of the extreme party feeling which existed in the early eighteenth century. The most important thing, then, is to extract the central idea of an essay and, if possible, to sum it up in one sentence. Sometimes this idea is explained definitely and clearly in some paragraph of the essay; sometimes it is only implied; but until you have discovered it and expressed it for yourself, you do not really know what the essay is about. Once having understood this kernel of the essay, you ought next to consider its truth and significance. Is this a true idea or true only from certain points of view or for certain times and certain people? If you do not agree with it, what do you consider the fallacies of the author's position? Can you make application of the idea to the life around you? If you think it is true, what leads you to think so? Can you explain the idea clearly to other people, giving illustrations within the range of your own experience? Does it suggest parallel or related ideas which you think worthy of attention? A study of the thought of any essay carried out in this way will not only assure you of mastery of the particular idea under consideration, but add to your own powers of observation and interpretation.

Getting at the central idea. Let us apply this method of study to Stevenson's "Pulvis et Umbra." The central idea of this inspiring essay is this: Though scientific study shows that man is but dust and a fleeting shadow, yet his possession of noble and unselfish ideals shows that in his nature is something which is above the merely animal.

This idea Stevenson illustrates by many examples drawn from all lands and all classes of people. He attempts to make it universally significant by emphasizing the presence of ideals where we should least expect them: "by camp fires in Assiniboia," "in ships at sea," "in the slums of cities," in India where life is cheap, in dens of vice. If ideals are present in these places, the reader will have no difficulty finding them in his home, his school, and his community.

The reader will be interested in analyzing Stevenson's illustrations from astronomy and natural history. Is the order and coherence of the stellar universe without any relation to the ways of men who inhabit this little planet, the Earth? Does not the social life of animals and insects prove that coöperation and mutual aid are as natural as enmity and competition?

The question then arises: Why does not man develop his higher nature more rapidly? What hinders his achievement of international peace or of the extirpation of crime in all countries? Is Stevenson's hopeful idealism a mere dream?

It is clear that, studied in this way, Stevenson's brief essay is an introduction to what is, perhaps, the fundamental problem of human nature. It should certainly lead to a reading of other related essays such as William James' "A Moral Equivalent for War."

The method of treatment of the essay. With the subject matter of the essay clearly in mind, one may examine the essayist's method of treatment of the essay. His method may be considered under three heads: structure, development, and style.

Structure. The structure of the essay varies from a mere list to the carefully organized plan based upon a logical organization.

In such an essay as Steele's account of the Club, the structure follows the loose method of enumeration. Steele merely names and describes six gentlemen, characterizing each by a few words of description.

Charles Lamb's "Grace before Meat" has a more elaborate structure, though it is merely the loose union of related ideas as in a freely moving conversation. His plan is as follows.

(1) The blessing of food must have originated at a time when a good meal was rare.
(2) Grace might well be said upon other occasions; as, for instance, before reading a new book.
(3) Grace is especially fitting at the poor man's table.
(4) Grace is not fitting at a table richly set.
(5) Milton in *Paradise Regained* has stated my objection (quotation from Milton).
(6) I admire the silent grace of the Quakers.
(7) A short grace is best, especially at such simple meals as were served at my school.

This plan shows Lamb's adherence to his central idea. It is clear that he deliberately avoided any logical plan, however, lest he should lose the charm of informal conversation.

Huxley's essay "On a Piece of Chalk" has the logical structure that its subject warrants. Huxley wanted to prove to an audience, unaware of the immensity of geological changes, that the physical world had undergone and was undergoing slow developments which occupied a tremendous period of years. His method was to proceed from the known to the unknown, what logicians call the method of induction. In its simplest form his plan is as follows.

(1) Everybody knows what chalk is.
(2) A large area of Europe is composed of a deep layer of chalk.
(3) Examined under the microscope, this chalk is discovered to be composed of regular structures.
(4) These structures are the same as the skeletons of minute creatures which compose the mud of the sea bottom.
(5) Hence it is clear that the chalk was once at the bottom of the sea.
(6) Moreover there is evidence that the chalk land was covered by the sea several times.
(7) Hence it follows that tremendous alterations in the surface of the earth have taken place.
(8) Huxley's conclusion is that in the shifting of the land and sea and in the variation of living forms "we have observed nothing but the natural product of the forces originally possessed by the substance of the universe."

The student will find that every essay has a different structure. The important things are, first, to find the structure and, second, to discover that it is not accidental, but is determined by the author's purpose and his methods of thought.

Development. Once the student has found the structure of an essay, he should investigate the essayist's method of developing his ideas.

Some questions he may ask are: How does the author attract the interest and gain the sympathies of the reader? As the essay proceeds, does one notice a definite plan of paragraphing? What transitional devices link paragraphs together? Are there topic sentences? Does the author use concrete details and illustrations? Does the author use anecdotes or allusions? Does the author make use of personal experiences? Is the ending effective for any special reason?

Steele's method of development is the enumeration of significant, concrete details which bring out the character of each member of the Club. Thus, when Sir Roger was young, he "had often supped with my Lord Rochester and Sir George Etherege and kicked Bully Dawson in a public coffee house." The lawyer is

> an excellent critic, and the time of the play is his hour of business; exactly at five he passes through New Inn . . . and takes a turn at Will's till the play begins; he has his shoes rubbed and his periwig powdered at the barber's as you go into the Rose.

Lamb's method is more elaborate. He piles up concrete details with reckless extravagance, drawing upon the Bible, classical mythology, and English poetry for examples. Anecdotes occur freely, and, as in many of his essays, the narrative method is used. His vocabulary is profusely elaborate, and often recondite. Quaintness of diction and ingenuity of phrase are his delight.

Huxley's method is a combination of persuasive logic and scientific accuracy. He is exact and definite in detail, seeking to lead his reader by the hand from the simple piece of chalk to the most profound mysteries of terrestrial history. His essay is an example of the finest kind of teaching. It starts from complete mastery of the most difficult facts and theories. Without condescension it begins instruction on the student's level, and by constant reference to the student's experience leads him gradually to an understanding of as much of the teacher's knowledge as he can comprehend in a single lesson. The way in which each step is established, the transition to the next step, the consolidation of each new position, the play of the teacher's personality, the maintaining of the human touch, the inevitableness of the conclusions reached—all these indicate a masterpiece of persuasive exposition.

Style. Style is the outward expression in words of the inner personality of a writer. It is his way of looking at life made concrete in written language.

Style has two aspects. In the first place, style is the man. It can be felt and described, it can be experienced and sensed but it cannot be analyzed. In the second place, style is the concrete method by which the personality of the man is expressed, the clothes, so to speak, of the personality within.

In studying the first aspect of style, we can use only descriptive words and phrases. Thus we say of Charles Lamb that he had a sweet, kind, sympathetic nature and a quaint, observant mind colored by a gentle melancholy.

We infer these qualities from the words and sentences that he uses, and from his expression of what he saw in his daily life in London. In making this inference, we are really making a technical analysis of the writer's craftsmanship.

In the analysis of style there are always four elements. *There is first a study of the author's words and phrases.* These show not only his ideas, reading, and knowledge, but also the education of the audience for whom he wrote.

In the seventeenth century Sir Francis Bacon chose words which today are clear and simple. In the same century Sir Thomas Browne reveled in words and phrases like "wingy mysteries," "airy subtleties," "supinity," "involved enigmas," and "gross rusticity." Bacon had a clear, scientific, judicial mind; Browne had a quaint, poetic mind stuffed with involved Latin prose.

In the early nineteenth century Charles Lamb often imitated the elaborate words of the time of Shakespeare; William Hazlitt blurted out his mind in words and phrases which definitely belong to his own century. The words and phrases of Oliver Wendell Holmes show the Boston Yankee; the words of Mark Twain show the American from the Middle West, self-educated, plain, humorous, and defiant of convention.

The second element to consider in the analysis of style is the organization of sentences, always a sure indication of a writer's personality. Bacon uses blunt, terse sentences; Addison uses graceful, easy, smoothly constructed sentences; Lamb's sentences are informal, like conversation; Macaulay's are neat, mechanical patterns.

The third element is a consideration of the writer's structure, his method of architecture, the way in which he builds his words and phrases into a complete, coherent, and organized whole. Sometimes a structure is built up by a series of answers to a question. Sometimes it is an antithesis: one idea is contrasted with another. Sometimes it is an explication: the hidden parts of an idea are brought to light one after another and explained. Sometimes, too, a structure is merely a series of illustrations of one or more ideas.

Finally there is the matter of rhythm, one of the most interesting aspects of style. Prose, like poetry, has its rhythms which vary from the full organ music of Browne's "Urn Burial" to the grave eloquence of Newman's *The Idea of a University.* Prose rhythm differs from poetic rhythm primarily in its irregularity. It never properly becomes meter, that is, rhythm with a regular recurrence of accent and cadence. When it does, as sometimes in the prose of Dickens, it seems labored, sentimental, and artificial. There is no better exercise for the formation of a sense for style than the attempt to hear the rhythm of beautiful prose read aloud naturally and easily.

The student of style will be aware of Steele's well-bred simplicity and of the easy grace which for more than two hundred years has made the *Tatler* and the *Spectator* models of "elegant" English style.

In Lamb he will be conscious of gayety, sly humor, and extravagant whimsicality. Lamb's diction and phrasing have the quaintness which comes from the conscious use of old-fashioned language. Lamb's style is interesting, too, for its varied rhythms, sometimes startlingly abrupt, sometimes richly figured with elaborate cadences.

Huxley's style is sometimes severely plain, sometimes unusually poetic, always colloquial, always sincere. It is the style of the persuasive lecturer who watches the faces of his audience, keeps them interested, carries them with him, and makes the most of their understanding of every point.

The author's personality in the essay. From a study of idea, structure, development, and style, the reader can form an idea of the author's personality.

Macaulay in his "Essay on Johnson" shows his wide learning in the fields of history and politics and his special learning in the eighteenth century. Lamb shows his knowledge of London and his acquaintance with Elizabethan literature in all his essays. The student may ask himself such questions as: What references and allusions most reveal the author's education? What does the essay tell me of the author's station in life? What sort of people did he mingle with? Was he a man like Hazlitt (see "On Going on a Journey") who preferred his own company? In what branches of human activity did he have experience?

The essayist's temper or turn of mind. Is the essayist imaginative or practical? Does he observe deeply or merely with close superficial attention? Does he like to draw general conclusions from what he sees? Is he humorous, whimsical, bitter, gentle, ironical, sympathetic, witty, enthusiastic, keen, profound, idealistic, disillusioned, sensible, restrained, emotional? What sort of picture could you draw of his character from what you read between the lines of the essay?

The effect of personality on subject matter. Finally the reader may consider the ways in which the essayist's personality affects his attitude toward the subject matter of his essay. Different essayists have often written of the same subject. Defoe and Steele both wrote essays on the education of women. The reader can make an interesting comparison between the hard common sense of Defoe and the generous, humorous idealism of Steele. Matthew Arnold and Walter Pater both wrote essays on Wordsworth. With the same subject their different personalities give two quite different interpretations of the poet.

The spirit of the age as revealed in the essay. Another profitable source of study in any essay is the life of the times as revealed in it.

In the seventeenth century. In the seventeenth century, when men were moved by moral and philosophical motives forgotten in the crowded excitement and adventure of the Renaissance and the Age of Discovery that had preceded, the essay was usually the expression of the writer's personal attitude toward moral, philosophical, or religious questions. Thus, Sir Francis Bacon writes:

The virtue of prosperity is temperance; the virtue of adversity is fortitude. . . . Prosperity is not without many fears and distastes; and adversity is not without comforts and hopes. . . . Certainly virtue is like precious odors, most fragrant when they are incensed or crushed: for prosperity doth best discover vice; but adversity doth best discover virtue.

In the eighteenth century. In the eighteenth century men were more interested in society and in general questions of politics and literature than in these problems of ethics and philosophy. Hence the essays of the period were social, critical, or didactic. Thus in 1753 Lady Mary Wortley Montague writes:

You should encourage your daughter to talk over with you what she reads . . . take care she does not mistake pert folly for wit and humor, or rhyme for poetry, which are the common errors of young people. . . . The second caution to be given her . . . is to conceal whatever learning she attains, with as much solicitude as she would hide crookedness or lameness. The parade of it can only serve to draw on her the envy, and consequently the most inveterate hatred, of all he and she fools, which will certainly be at least three parts in four of all her acquaintance.

Earlier in the century Addison expressed the perennially popular complaint against the extravagant dress of "the younger generation":

To speak truly, the young people of both sexes are so wonderfully apt to shoot out into long swords or sweeping trains, bushy head-dresses or full-bottomed periwigs, with several other encumbrances of dress, that they stand in need of being pruned very frequently, lest they should be oppressed with ornaments and overrun with the luxuriancy of their habits.

These comments are social, tinged, like Polonius' advice to Laertes, with sensible worldliness. The purpose of the essay in the eighteenth century was not to probe serious questions, but to skim safely over the surface,

to enliven morality with wit and to temper wit with morality.

Addison, observing that

The mind that lies fallow but a single day sprouts up in follies that are only to be killed by a constant and assiduous culture,

sought to introduce to a shallow people sane, but not profound ideas. to bring philosophy out of closets and libraries . . . to dwell in clubs and assemblies, at tea tables and coffeehouses.

In the nineteenth century. In another hundred years, men of the nineteenth century reflected in their essays the awakened love of Nature, the growth of humanitarian interest, the rapid strides of scientific discovery, and the enthusiasm for literature which characterized their age. Coleridge said:

The Englishman who without reverence—a proud and affectionate reverence—can utter the name of William Shakespeare stands disqualified for the office of critic.

And Hazlitt writes a very paean of praise:

Hamlet is a name; his speeches and sayings but the idle coinage of the poet's brain. What then, are they not real? They are as real as our own thoughts. Their reality is in the reader's mind. It is *we* who are Hamlet. This play has a prophetic truth, which is above that of history. Whoever has become thoughtful and melancholy through his own mishaps or those of others . . . whose bitterness of soul makes him careless of consequences, and who goes to a play as his best resource to shove off, to a second remove, the evils of life by a mock representation of them—this is the true Hamlet.

But literature was not the only concern of the essayists. Ruskin was primarily interested in beauty, Carlyle in the dignity of labor, Newman in the problems of faith. History, too, came in for a share of enthusiastic interest. Thus DeQuincey writes of Joan of Arc:

The shepherd girl that had delivered France—she, from her dungeon, she, from her baiting at the stake, she, from her duel with fire, as she entered her last dream—saw Domrémy, the fountain of Domrémy, saw the pomp of forests in which her childhood had wandered.

This mission had now been fulfilled. The storm was weathered; the skirts even of that mighty storm were drawing off. The blood that she was to reckon for had been exacted; the tears that she was to shed in secret had been paid to the last. . . . And in her last fight upon the scaffold she had triumphed gloriously; victoriously she had tasted the stings of death. For all, except this comfort from her farewell dreams, she had died—died, amidst the tears of ten thousand enemies—died, amidst the drums and trumpets of armies—died, amidst peals redoubling upon peals, volleys upon volleys, from the saluting clarions of martyrs.

The essays of Thomas Huxley reflect the scientific interest of the time. Leigh Hunt, William Hazlitt, and Robert Louis Stevenson in their personal essays reflect the varied interests of themselves and their generation. Matthew Arnold developed his ideas on culture, coining such catch phrases as "sweetness and light" and "culture and anarchy."

In the twentieth century. The twentieth-century essay, too, reflects its age. So far the century has been overshadowed by the Great War and its results, which challenge the existing ideas of democracy, of government, of social relationships, of education. The contemporary essay which we find in magazines, in anthologies, and in individual collections, helps us to understand the age in which we live, an age with keen interest in literature, Nature, social, ethical, and religious problems, science, art, and history. G. K. Chesterton, Hilaire Belloc, Stuart P. Sherman, Stephen Leacock, Samuel McChord Crothers, Christopher Morley, Agnes Repplier, and Max Beerbohm all represent from differing points of view the spirit of this perplexing and rapidly changing modern age.

Summary. In studying an essay, first extract its *central idea.* In studying the *method of treatment of the essay*, look for its *structure*, its *development*, and its *style.* In studying *style*, examine the author's *words and phrases*, his *organization of sentences*, the way in which words and phrases are built into an *organized whole*, and the *rhythm* of the sentences. As a result of this study the reader will find out the author's *personality.* Finally, study the *spirit of the age* as revealed in the essay.

COMPREHENSION QUESTIONS

1. *Vocabulary:* colloquial, condescension, extravagance, geological changes, extravagance, induction, ingenuity of phrase, logicians, moral equivalent, quaintness of diction, social life of animals and insects, stellar universe, structure, terrestrial history, whimsicality.
2. *Allusions:*

Addison and Steele	*Sir Roger de Coverley Papers*
Huxley	"On a Piece of Chalk"
James	"A Moral Equivalent for War"
Lamb	"Grace before Meat"
Steele	"The Club"
Stevenson	"Pulvis et Umbra"

3. What are the four points of view from which an essay may be studied?
4. What are the most important questions to ask oneself about the subject matter of any essay which one is studying?
5. What are three convenient heads under which to study the method of treatment of an essay?
6. Compare and contrast the methods of development in the essays by Steele, Lamb, and Huxley analyzed in this chapter.
7. How does an essay give a reader insight into the personality of the author?
8. Why does an essay necessarily reflect the spirit of the age in which it was written?
9. What aspects of contemporary life should you expect to find reflected in a volume of essays by a contemporary writer?
10. What aspects of eighteenth-century life are revealed in the essays of Addison and Steele?
11. What aspects of nineteenth-century life are revealed in essays of the nineteenth century?

PROBLEMS IN APPRECIATION

1. Point out the central idea in one of the *Spectator* papers. What sentence contains the kernel of its central idea? What are the chief steps by which it is developed? What are the principal illustrations used?

2. In any collection of essays, make a study of the method of treatment of four essays under the headings of structure, development, and style.
   Under *structure*, point out:
      (*a*) the progress of the ideas, (*b*) the contribution of each paragraph to the main idea, (*c*) the relationship between paragraphs, (*d*) the use of transitions, (*e*) digressions, if any, (*f*) general plan of the structure.
   Under *development*, point out:
      (*a*) illustrations or examples, (*b*) any qualifications, limitations, or concessions to points of view different from that of the author, (*c*) means by which each paragraph is "filled in," (*d*) use of topic sentences.
   Under *style*, point out:
      (*a*) choice of words, (*b*) phrasing—ability to find combinations of words to express ideas, (*c*) sentence structure, (*d*) use of figurative language and allusions, (*e*) general qualities of style, such as clarity, wit, force, humor, eloquence, imagination, concreteness, (*f*) personal qualities of the author revealed in the style.

3. In any collection of modern essays, pick out three essays which show widely differing temperaments. Illustrate these differences by references

to the subject matter. Then try to find out something about the authors to support your theories.

4. Investigate the life of one of the following essayists and show how his personal background is reflected in his work: Swift, Lamb, Irving, Macaulay, Shaw, Chesterton.
5. In a collection of essays by contemporary authors, or in a book by one contemporary essayist, find all the references to contemporary life.
6. From the results of this study, write an essay on the American spirit in the 1920's or the 1930's.

QUESTIONS ON BOOKS YOU HAVE READ

1. In what respect does the plan of Emerson's "Self-Reliance" or "Compensation" differ from that of most expository essays?
2. Try to find five qualities of Emerson's style with three quotations to illustrate each quality.
3. Make a study of the ideas in Emerson's "Self-Reliance" or "Compensation."

   (*a*) What is the central idea of the essay? What sentences specially bring it out? (*b*) Make a list of quotable passages. Explain each one using your own illustrations. (*c*) Point out ideas in the essay which you think are inspiring even though not wholly true. With what ideas do you disagree? (*d*) What examples and allusions does Emerson use to illustrate his ideas? With which are you unfamiliar? Can you substitute examples of your own?
4. To what extent do you think Emerson was influenced by the age in which he lived?
5. Use the Coverley papers as illustrative material for a theme on the subject matter of the eighteenth-century essay. Find in them examples of both satirical and serious comment on the follies and vices of society, on political problems, on popular beliefs and superstitions, on education, on contemporary ideals, on animals, on popular literature, on travel, on the theater, etc.
6. Find ten Coverley papers which show an evident desire for reform. State in one sentence the purpose of each. What is the method of attack used in each case? In what respect were the weapons used particularly adapted to the nature of the warfare?
7. Compare an individual essay from the Coverley papers with an individual essay of the nineteenth or twentieth century which is similar

to it in subject matter but different in style, atmosphere, point of view, treatment, etc. To what extent do these differences show how times, manners, and ways of thinking have changed? Does the comparison reveal some things which have not changed?

8. Name some of our contemporary periodicals which carry out the *Spectator* idea. Take *The New Yorker* as an example. In any issue of *The New Yorker* point out attacks on contemporary abuses, follies, and manners through satire and ridicule rather than through invective. Compare special aspects of *The New Yorker* with special aspects of the *Spectator* papers, commenting on and accounting for similarities and differences.
9. What aspects of life in the eighteenth century are revealed in the Coverley papers? For instance, what do they tell you about men and women of fashion, about popular literature, about gardens and country life, about sports and amusements, about religion, about politics, about superstitions, about classes of society, etc.? Which papers reveal each of these? Write a long theme on the life of the eighteenth century as revealed in the Coverley papers.
10. Analyze Irving's humor; that is, point out the sort of things that seem humorous to him, the particular ways by which he tries to make the reader see the humor, and the special characteristics of his humor. Does it resemble the humor of any other author you know? Compare the humor of Irving with that of Addison, Lamb, Dickens, Hawthorne, George Eliot, Stevenson, Lewis Carroll, Barrie.
11. Characterize in some detail Macaulay's style. Illustrate with quotations. Find examples of short, forceful sentences, of strong contrasts, of concrete illustrations, of balance (of nouns, adjectives, phrases, sentences), of rapid detail, of logical paragraph development, of climax, of topic sentences, of skillful transitions, of hyperbole.
12. Compare Macaulay's "Life of Samuel Johnson" with his "Addison," "Madame d'Arblay," "Clive," or "Warren Hastings." Find examples of striking similarities. Quote passages in the other essays which seem parallel to passages in his "Johnson."

CHAPTER 30

HOW TO STUDY BIOGRAPHY

Biography, *autobiography*, and *memoirs* are related forms. A biography is the true story of a person's life told by another. An autobiography is the true story of a person's life told by himself. Memoirs are collections of facts, anecdotes, and opinions about people, places, and public events of the author's lifetime; they do not necessarily include an account of the author's life.

These three types of writing stand on the borderline between history and literature of permanent interest. Hundreds of biographical books are printed every year. Most of them serve some useful purpose, but most are soon forgotten. To survive, biographical writing must contain new facts, must present facts with interest, must show that the author has a notable grasp of his subject, and must have artistic form and style.

Why is there such a great interest in biography?

Biography presents interesting facts. The simplest explanation of the interest in biography is that almost everyone is interested in what other people are doing. Most "news" concerns personalities. "I am a man," said a Roman writer, "therefore all things which concern men are of interest to me."

We all wish to see famous men and women, to know what they are like, to share to some extent in their lives. It is this hope of being, in a way, a part of them, which induces some people to collect autographs and photographs of celebrities or possessions such as books, clothing, and furniture which famous people once owned. On a far more intellectual level is the desire to read about what they said and did.

Biography illuminates human nature. Since the usual circle of experience is small, an excellent way to learn about human nature is to read biography. Gamaliel Bradford, one of the most original modern biographers, maintained that "human identity" and "human difference" constituted the basis of biography. He lists as the fundamental elements of identity in human nature in which we all share, the following: love, especially in its tragic aspects; ambition, or the "hunger for success"; money, the way in which it is gained, held, and lost; depression and disgust with life; sickness, physical and moral; and religious doubt and faith. The elements of difference Bradford found chiefly in the kinds and degrees of success which men have achieved.

It is obvious that our knowledge of human nature is increased by the biographies of great men, because men are great by virtue of their intensity of experience, their representative quality, and their extraordinary achievements. What we all have in little, they have in the large. We may fly an airplane on a short journey, but Lindbergh flew from New York to Paris; we may dominate our little group, but Napoleon created an empire; we may love our fellow men, but Lincoln freed a whole race from slavery.

Biography enlivens historical events. How dull history is without the interest of its reflection in human lives! Carlyle, indeed, went so far as to believe that history is nothing but the record of the lives of great men. He said:

> As I take it, Universal History, the history of what man has accomplished in this world, is at bottom the History of the Great Men who have worked here. They were the leaders of men, these great ones; the modelers, patterns, and in a wide sense creators, of whatsoever the general mass of men contrived to do or to attain; all things that we see standing accomplished in the world are properly the outer material result, the practical realization and embodiment, of Thoughts that dwelt in the Great Men sent into the world: the soul of the whole world's history, it may justly be considered, were the history of these.

This is, of course, an extreme statement, and it is not accepted by modern scientific historians. Nevertheless, as an adjunct to the understanding of history, literature, or science, biography is invaluable.

Biography vivifies social history. More and more we are coming to look upon history as the record of how men lived in the past. Carl Sandburg's *Abraham Lincoln: the Prairie Years* is most interesting in bringing out of obscurity the daily life of the Western pioneers. Hamlin Garland's *A Son of the Middle Border* tells vividly how boys and girls lived in the Old West, what they wore, what they did in school, what games they played, what their dreams and ideals were. In the pages of Michael Pupin's *From Immigrant to Inventor* we enter the homes of people of an older generation, we understand their minds, their struggles, and their ideals. In such a book, history becomes a living record of social change and progress. On this point Bradford says:

> After all, the individual human being is the center of the world, and perhaps no better key [than biography] can be chosen to help human beings to understand the world. The human being is all of history. He makes it and in turn is made by it. . . . Get at the man, and you will have double interest in the work. Know the man, or try to know him, and the work will have new significance and far more widely reaching interest.

Biography gives inspiration to the ordinary man. From the pages of biography, readers undoubtedly derive much inspiration for their own lives. Their ideals are strengthened; their hopes are raised by finding that others have surmounted difficulties greater than theirs. The story of Booker T. Washington in *Up from Slavery* or of Pasteur in Vallery-Radot's *The Life of Pasteur* has helped hundreds of readers to a better understanding of life. Great men, as Carlyle said,

> are profitable company. We cannot look, however imperfectly, upon a great man, without gaining something by him. He is the living light-fountain, which it is good and pleasant to be near.

Biography adds to our knowledge of the truth. Anything which really tells the truth about life helps to make the human mind free. Nowhere are we so blinded by prejudices as in our views of other people. We often believe about others what we wish to believe rather than what is true. Biographies, by clearing their subjects from myth, fancy, and the tinsel of hero worship, rescue their readers from falsehood and misconception.

Lytton Strachey's *Queen Victoria* shows the real woman beneath the royal figure; James Truslow Adams' *The Adams Family* shows a much misunderstood group of men as they really were. Of course, in the process of removing varnish the portrait beneath is sometimes damaged, but a little damage is preferable to a complete misconception. We know much more about Washington, Lincoln, and Shakespeare than readers knew fifty years ago. These great figures do not suffer in the light of truth; they become more human.

FIVE TYPES OF BIOGRAPHY

The historical record. The historical record is the most common type, and is usually not literature, except by accident. It aims to give a clear, faithful chronicle of events. Its value lies in its completeness, accuracy, and freedom from prejudice. Thayer's *The Life and Times of Cavour* and Morley's *The Life of William Ewart Gladstone* are models of biographical research. They have become standard books of reference, indispensable to students of history.

The laudatory biography. The laudatory biography, which sets out to praise its subject, often ends in what amounts to falsehood. It is often cheap and trivial like the old life of Washington by Parson Weems which gave currency to stories like that of the cherry tree and the boy who could not tell a lie. On the other hand, it may achieve remarkable results. George Herbert Palmer's *The Life of Alice Freeman Palmer* has become a classic because of its charm of subject and the sincerity and good taste of the author. Similarly, Eliot's *The Life of John Gilley* is a beautiful tribute to a simple Maine fisherman. Laudatory biographies may, then, have value if their subject deserves praise, and if the praise is given with dignity, restraint, and truth.

The critical biography. As a reaction against the biography which is an historical record and the laudatory biography, there has arisen in the last ten years the critical biography. The best of this type is Strachey's *Queen Victoria* (1921). The critical biographer makes up his mind as to the inner truth of a person's life. This idea, about which his interpretation is centralized, is the result of a critical analysis of a mass of facts. The biographer emphasizes only those which bear directly upon his interpretation. Throughout the critical biography, the reader feels an active, discriminating intelligence at work, at its best judicial, calm, reasonable, and analytical.

Sometimes, of course, the temptation is strong to be ironical at the expense of the subject. Sometimes, too, the critical biographer yields to a temptation to drag into the light unpleasant facts which, for one reason or another, have been concealed or neglected. In so far as "debunking" really dissipates lies and tells the truth, it is commendable in biographical writing. Often, however, it degenerates into a love for unsavory details for their own sake. When it becomes sensational, cheap, and vulgar, it is obviously bad.

The psychological biography. This type interprets its subject by an analysis of his mind according to the many theories of present-day psychologists. Psychological biographers are interested not in events for their own sake, but for the light which they throw upon a person's temperament, motives, and all the hidden processes of his mind.

The great biographer of this type is Gamaliel Bradford who invented the term "psychography" for his work. His interest lay in the interpretation of his subject's mind through details the importance of which the ordinary observer would neglect. He maintained that the art of biography consisted in getting at the "soul" of a man or woman. This "soul" he felt, though revealed sometimes in great dramatic crises, was more often revealed in minor acts. The psychological importance of these minor details it is, in his view, the biographer's duty to interpret.

The novelized biography. This type of biography was made popular by André Maurois' *Ariel: The Life of Shelley.* Many lives shape themselves with a little assistance into a form resembling that of a novel. By careful selection of events the biographer gives the story of his subject's life a kind of plot. What can he do for conversations and for dramatic scenes?

In some cases he can quote, as direct discourse, passages from his subject's writings. Often, however, he depends upon *inference.* From what he knows to have occurred, he infers other events which are consistent with the subject's character and which might well have occurred. Whether they did or not no one can tell. As fact, therefore, novelized biography is useless. As an imaginative picture of a man and his times it may, especially when the biographer has a good conscience, be most illuminating.

THE ANALYSIS OF BIOGRAPHY

The writer's plan. In the study of biography the student should first try to discover the writer's plan. This may be of several kinds. In the first place, there is the *simple chronological scheme* whereby the subject's life is divided into periods. Thus Joseph Quincy Adams' interesting life of Shakespeare considers the dramatist's family, his boyhood life, his working life in London, and his life in retirement at Stratford.

Another plan is dominated by a *theme.* Thus Edward Dowden's *Shakespeare: His Mind and Art* interprets the dramatist's adult life as dominated by a series of emotional crises which end in peace. The subjection of a biography to a theme is always interesting and sometimes true. It involves, however, an imaginative interpretation which is often misleading.

Still another plan is the *collection of facts, anecdotes, and documents* about each event in a subject's life. Sir Sidney Lee's authoritative life of Shakespeare follows this plan. It is not nearly so readable as either of the other lives, but it is a most important reference work for students.

A fourth plan may be called *the inductive method.* This consists in making the subject tell his own story as far as possible. The biographer presents all possible direct material such as letters and conversations, provides the necessary introductions and links, and lets the reader infer for himself what kind of person his subject was. The two most famous biographies in English are of this type: Boswell's *The Life of Samuel Johnson* and Lockhart's *Life of Scott.*

The writer's method of securing coherence. All biographical writing requires a certain amount of selection, condensation, and arrangement so that the progress of the subject's life may be made clear to the reader. What the student should watch is the means by which the biographer makes clear to him the subject's growth and development.

Some biographers stress certain dominant qualities. This is a favorite method with the writers of psychological biography. Having decided that Byron, for instance, suffered from a feeling of inferiority because of his deformed foot, the biographer stresses instances of this suffering throughout his life. This may be called the method of "iteration." It involves, of course, subordination of some details and an extra emphasis upon others.

Biographers frequently stress the motives of their subjects. As people seldom know their own motives, and rarely leave any evidence of their motives in documents, this involves a good deal of inference.

Another consideration is the relation in the biographer's mind between character and circumstance. Some writers believe strongly that a man's character decides his fate; others believe no less strongly in the influence of environment. Sandburg's *Abraham Lincoln: the Prairie Years* stresses social backgrounds; Palmer's *The Life of Alice Freeman Palmer* stresses the innate, spiritual force of a woman who would have been successful in any environment.

Finally, the student may look for the biographer's method of explication, that is, the method by which his view of the subject is gradually unfolded. Biographers usually employ a certain amount of expository analysis. Some stress narrative as Maurois does in *Byron* and *Disraeli*. Some prefer description. Others collect large numbers of anecdotes.

In the end, of course, what matters is not the method, but the total view presented. To quote Carlyle again:

> . . . if an individual is really of consequence enough to have his life and character recorded for public remembrance, we have always been of opinion that the public ought to be made acquainted with all the inward springs and relations of his character. How did the world and man's life, from his particular position, represent themselves to his mind? How did coexisting circumstances modify him from without; how did he modify these from within? With what endeavors and what efficacy rule over them; with what resistance and what suffering sink under them? In one word, what and how produced was the effect of society on him; what and how produced was his effect on society? He who should answer these questions, in regard to any individual, would, as we believe, furnish a model of perfection in Biography.

Summary. *Biography* is the true story of a person's life told by another. Biography presents *interesting facts*, *illuminates human nature*, *enlivens historical events*, *vivifies social history*, gives *inspiration* to the ordinary man, and adds to our *knowledge of the truth*. The biography which is an *historical record* gives a *faithful chronicle of events*. The *laudatory* biography *praises* its subject. The *critical* biography presents only those events which *support his interpretation* of the subject. The *psychological* biography is an *analysis* of the subject's *mind*. The *novelized* biography gives an *imaginative picture* of the subject's life.

In studying biography study the writer's *plan*. Then study his *method of securing coherence*.

COMPREHENSION QUESTIONS

1. *Vocabulary:* authoritative, autobiography, biography, dominant qualities, chronological, expository analysis, identity, imaginative interpretation, inductive method, inference, intensity of experience, iteration, laudatory, memoirs, method of explication, novelized, psychological, representative quality, social history, spiritual force, theme.
2. *Allusions:*

Gamaliel Bradford	
Carl Sandburg	*Abraham Lincoln: the Prairie Years*
Hamlin Garland	*A Son of the Middle Border*
Michael Pupin	*From Immigrant to Inventor*
Booker Washington	*Up from Slavery*
Vallery-Radot	*The Life of Pasteur*
Lytton Strachey	*Queen Victoria*
Adams	*The Adams Family*
George Herbert Palmer	*The Life of Alice Freeman Palmer*
Thayer	*The Life and Times of Cavour*
Morley	*Life of William Ewart Gladstone*
Eliot	*The Life of John Gilley*
Maurois	*Ariel*
Joseph Quincy Adams	*Shakespeare*
Dowden	*A Life of William Shakespeare*
Lee	*A Life of William Shakespeare*
Boswell	*The Life of Samuel Johnson*
Lockhart	*Life of Scott*
Maurois	*Byron, Disraeli*
Carlyle	

3. Explain and illustrate five good reasons for reading biography.
4. Show from your reading that biography gives inspiration to the ordinary man.
5. Define, with examples, the five types of biography mentioned in this chapter.
6. Name the three methods of writing biography explained here and give one example of each.
7. How may coherence in biography be secured by:
   (*a*) stressing dominant qualities, (*b*) stressing motives, (*c*) stressing the interaction of character and circumstance.

   Give one example of each method.

PROBLEMS IN APPRECIATION

1. Here is a simple outline for a book report on any biography. Try it in writing a review of a short biography, such as Strachey's *Florence Nightingale*, Ludwig's *Three Titans*, Belloc's *Joan of Arc*, Barrie's *Margaret Ogilvy:*

   (*a*) The chief events of the subject's life. His period. His station in life. (*b*) The interest and significance of the subject's life. (*c*) The chief traits of the subject's character and personality with examples. (*d*) People, surroundings, and events which influenced the subject. (*e*) The author's attitude toward the subject. (*f*) Your own opinion of the book.

2. Here are some questions which can form the basis for a book report on an autobiography:

   (*a*) Who is the subject of the book? When and where did he live? For what is he known? (*b*) What did the subject do? What did he see? Whom did he know? What was he like? (*c*) What were his motives for writing the book? What impression of his character do you get? (*d*) Mention events and personalities which affected the subject's life. Discuss some of his reactions to them. (*e*) What experiences did the subject have that were especially interesting or significant? (*f*) What is your opinion of the value of the book?

3. After having read any biography, study the purpose for which it was written with the aid of the following questions:

   (*a*) Is it written in a spirit of hero worship, to inspire others; in a depreciatory spirit, to remove a sentimental, romantic, or idealistic conception caused by previous works; from a psychological point of view, to seek an explanation for interesting or puzzling behavior; in a scientific spirit, merely to lay facts before the reader? Give examples and illustrations. (*b*) Does the life of the subject suggest problems which are of interest to the author? Explain. (*c*) Is the author interested in the life of the times in which the subject lived? If so, has he considered the effect of contemporary events, persons, and ideas upon his subject? Explain.

4. Having read any biography or autobiography, study the effect of the author's own ideas and personality on his treatment of the subject matter. Answer the following questions:

   (*a*) Is there evidence that he is seeking to be impartial and dispassionate? (*b*) Does he at any time reveal prejudices or predilections which make you question his impartiality? (*c*) Does he seek to excuse or condemn faults? Does he interpret the psychology of his subject in the light of a psychological theory? (*d*) Does he suppress or misrepresent facts? (*e*) Is his comment ironical, over-enthusiastic, smart, moral, sentimental, compassionate, critical?

5. Study with the aid of the following questions the means by which an author secures coherence in biography or autobiography.
   (*a*) Does he use a chronological order or does he follow some other plan? (*b*) Does he regard his subject from some fixed point of view, such as a psychological, historical, economic, social, or moral theory? (*c*) Does he regard his subject as a member of some class, an example of some type, or a factor in the development of his times? (*d*) Does he seek to make the subject tell his own story as far as possible?

6. With the aid of the following questions study the thoroughness with which an author has prepared himself to discuss his subject. To do this, you will need to read more than one book.
   (*a*) Does the author seek to include a wealth of material, or has he sifted and selected his material? If the latter, what principle seems to have guided him in his choices? (*b*) What use does he make of portraits, illustrations, diagrams, and quotations from such original sources as opinions of contemporaries, letters, and diaries? (*c*) Are his judgments or his statements of fact ever at variance with those of other authorities on the subject? (*d*) Has he included a bibliography or footnotes for the guidance of the reader?

7. With the aid of the following questions study the literary skill with which a biographer has organized his material and done his work.
   (*a*) Has the book a clear and effective plan? (*b*) Has it narrative vividness and narrative skill? Does it make events and people live for the reader? (*c*) Can the author both analyze and dramatize his characters? (*d*) Has the author power of visualization? (*e*) Does he use much author's comment? If so, has he humor, wit, irony, insight? (*f*) Has he any eloquent or emotional passages which move the reader? (*g*) Is his style on the whole simple or rhetorical? (*h*) Can he pass over what is trivial and emphasize what is salient?

CHAPTER 31

READING MISCELLANEOUS TYPES OF PROSE NON-FICTION

History. History is the written record of what man has done, attempted, thought, and felt in the past. It does not properly come within the scope of this book, but as much history is actually prose literature it deserves consideration as such.

The difficulties of writing history are tremendous. To begin with, it involves a minute and painstaking investigation of all the facts. Once the exact facts have been obtained, they must be put together with due attention to the importance of each fact so that the course of events, the influence of one generation on another will be clearly brought out. Besides this, events and characters must be made real; yet the historian must not forget that he is writing of a period when ways of thought as well as many other things were different from what they are in his generation. He must use his imagination to project himself into the past and make it vivid to the reader, and in doing this he must not stray from the facts. Even the minutest deviations from the truth seriously mar the historian's standing among his colleagues. In addition, he must pass judgment on characters, criticize policies and events, and interpret the whole as best he can. It is easily seen that such a task involves grave difficulties. What an historian gains in force and vividness, he is likely to lose through inaccuracy or prejudice; what he gains in accuracy is at the expense of imaginative power. Recently the tendency of the historian has been to overlook minor inaccuracies for the sake of making the whole book a vivid picture of the past. Such a book is frankly personal in its judgments, interpretations, and reactions, and hence is not always a trustworthy guide. But it is more interesting reading than the strictly accurate, unimaginative account which chronicles the past without making it live for the reader. H. G. Wells' *The Outline of History* and Hendrik van Loon's *The Story of Mankind* are contemporary examples of literary history which gives vivid pictures.

Memoirs. Memoirs are collections of facts, anecdotes, and opinions about people, places, and public events of the author's lifetime. The interest in memoirs lies in the light which they throw upon human beings and human events. History is necessarily scientific, analytical, and expository; memoirs are the narrative and descriptive record of life as seen by one who can record his likes, dislikes, and prejudices. In the pages of memoirs the past lives again.

The importance of memoirs depends upon the wit, wisdom, and experience of the writer. Then, too, memoirs are interesting in so far as the period which they describe is interesting. The memoirs of important figures of the Great War such as David Lloyd-George necessarily give to historians facts and impressions of the greatest value. There is also, of course, the literary criterion. If the writer of memoirs has imagination, vivid narrative and descriptive power, and, above all, style, his volumes will be read with special interest because of their artistic value.

Oratory. *Oratory* is the name given to highly impassioned speeches made on special occasions for special purposes. This form of literature was highly developed by the Greeks and Romans to whom we owe our conventional form of the oration as well as some immortal examples of oratorical literature in the speeches of Demosthenes and Cicero. The conventional form of an argumentative oration includes an introduction, a statement of the question, a main argument, carefully divided into points, a refutation, and a conclusion or peroration. There is much deviation from this form, however; as speeches for special occasions, involving no formal argument, cannot follow it closely, and as many argumentative orations disregard the classical models.

The oration is of chief interest historically; the occasions on which such speeches were delivered have become historic, and the speeches live as records. The great orations of history, however, have a literary value. The masterly construction of an eloquent unanswerable argument deserves attention as literature. It has the qualities of attention to form, command of language, and worth of ideas that are to be found in all works of literature. Some of the more eloquent passages of oratory have become famous as examples of literary power.

Translations. A form of literature that seldom receives the attention it deserves is the translation. We are not accustomed to think of the translation as original work, but it surely requires more skill than the writing of an informal essay. The good translator must have a thorough knowledge of at least two languages and literatures, as well as an instinctive sense of literary appreciation; he must also have the ability to transcribe from one language to another not only the ideas, the form, and the spirit of a piece of literature, but even the subtle shades of meaning and the beauties of expression that often have no exact parallel. Few able translators get the full share of credit they deserve and still fewer attain literary distinction. Try, for example, to put into satisfactory English a passage from Virgil that appeals to you, or from Daudet, if you read French; or from Goethe, Dante, Cervantes. Your clumsy inaccuracy will perhaps exasperate you. You will then realize the full difficulty of good translation.[1]

Letters. There is a peculiar fascination about the familiar letters of famous men and women. They contain the very words which famous people wrote in moments when the public was least in their minds, when they were their natural selves, informally conversing with chosen friends. From the informal letters of Robert Louis Stevenson, for instance, one realizes his real charm, his good humor, his courage, and his wit in a way which is far more intimate than any impression which one gets from his essays. Familiar letters are the direct revelation of a personality and of the times in which that personality lived. They have often great personal interest even when they have no literary merit. If, however, they are written by a literary artist, they are often gems which shine no less brightly because they are sometimes neglected for his more formal work.

Some letters, of course, are written with an eye to publication like those of Lord Chesterfield and Lady Mary Wortley Montague. Such letters are like essays, though they have an informality lacking in even personal essays.

[1] An excellent example of artistic translation is *Readings from the Literature of Ancient Greece* and *Readings from the Literature of Ancient Rome*, in English Translations, by Dora Pym, New York, 1923.

The value of letters of both the familiar and the informal type depends upon the degree to which they reveal the writer, the skill with which they are adapted to the reader, and their literary style. At their best, letters are among the permanent treasures of our literature.

Diaries. Diaries are the most intimate personal revelations in literature. The best diaries are literature only by accident. They came into being not to interest the public but for the writer's own sake. To the pages of her diary Frances Burney, later Madame d'Arblay, confided all the emotions and ambitions which the etiquette of an English court forced her to conceal beneath a mask. More famous than the diary of the eighteenth-century English novelist and society girl is the diary of Samuel Pepys, a document unique in English literature. It is astoundingly unconscious and frank. As a picture of seventeenth-century London it is historically invaluable. Its real greatness, however, is its vividness as a record of human nature. In actual life we conceal our motives and our emotions even from ourselves. The record of motives and emotions in the novel, though often intensely interesting, is nevertheless imaginary. But in a diary like that of Pepys we have the real record of a human soul, appallingly honest and completely self-revealing. In all literature there is no record quite like that of the seventeenth-century government official who, in his unconscious power, wrote a book of undying interest.

Summary. *History* must be true to the facts of the past; at the same time it should have imaginative power. *Memoirs* are interesting as a writer's collection of facts and opinions about people and events of his lifetime. The literary value of *orations* depends upon their form, command of language, and worth of ideas. A good *translation* shows accurate knowledge of the original and literary ability in the use of English. Good *letters* reveal the writer, are adapted to the reader, and have style. An interesting *diary* is the frank record of a human soul.

COMPREHENSION QUESTIONS

1. What is history?
2. What are the chief difficulties in writing history?
3. Do you know any histories which combine vividness and interest with scholarly accuracy?
4. What are memoirs?

5. For what reasons may memoirs have value?
6. What is oratory?
7. What are the rhetorical divisions of the classic oration?
8. What qualities must an oration have to be of literary value?
9. What qualities are demanded of a good translation?
10. Do you know any famous translations?
11. Why do letters sometimes survive as literature?
12. Why have some diaries gained a permanent place in literature?
13. *Allusions:*

H. G. Wells	Cervantes
Van Loon	Lord Chesterfield
Virgil	Lady Mary Wortley Montague
Daudet	Madame d'Arblay
Goethe	Samuel Pepys
Dante	

Part Five

THE GREAT WRITERS

ONE of the most interesting of all literary studies is the history of English and American literature. Such a study gives the student a knowledge of the intellectual life of two great countries. It shows how men's minds react to their times. It introduces the student to a body of reading which is the common experience of all men and women of intellectual tastes. It recovers from the past some of the most interesting of the world's personalities.

Such a history we cannot provide in the short space of Part Five. We can, however, tell you the main facts in the lives of the greatest English writers and give you some information about the books which they wrote. For your help in choosing among the most important contemporary writers we have provided some information about contemporary Americans as well as Englishmen.

The facts which we present will, we hope, be useful to you in themselves. We have, however, another purpose, to stimulate you to read for yourself in the wide field of literature in the English language and to become acquainted with many interesting poems, plays, novels, and essays which are not ordinarily studied in the classroom.

CHAPTER 32

THE GREAT POETS

GEOFFREY CHAUCER

1343 (?)–1400

Chaucer's life. Geoffrey Chaucer, the first great English poet, was born in London about 1343. His father was a prosperous wine merchant, his mother a woman of good family. In his boyhood he became a page in a noble family where he saw much of the fashionable life of courtly circles. As a young man he served in the English army in France where he was taken prisoner. The king himself contributed a large sum of money toward his ransom, and on his return to England in 1360, he entered the royal service as a special messenger.

Thereafter for forty years he appears again and again in the records as confidential agent to the reigning sovereign, as Controller of the Customs, as Clerk of the King's Works, in short, as a very busy man of affairs, and as an associate of noblemen. By 1366 he had married. By 1387 his wife had died, but Chaucer himself lived on until 1400.

One would not have expected a busy public servant to distinguish himself in the world of letters. Yet while this successful courtier was occupied in London, and while he was traveling to France and Italy on important business, he found time to write poetry which is equaled in bulk, quality, and influence only by that of the greatest poets in English.

At a time when the polite language of England was French and the learned language Latin, Chaucer chose to write in the simple, vigorous, colloquial English of London. That his poems were popular is proved by their preservation in scores of manuscripts. In the fifteenth century when printing was introduced into England by William Caxton, poems by Chaucer were among the earliest printed English books.

First poetic period: before 1372. His first poems, written before 1372, followed popular French models. The most notable is *The Book of the Duchess.* This is an elegy written in commemoration of Blanche, the first wife of John of Gaunt. It uses the artificial medieval form of the dream. In a dream Chaucer hears the bereaved husband lament the death of his wife. He then tells to Chaucer the tale of his courtship and marriage. The poem, written in the simple tetrameter couplet, contains pretty pictures of hunting, of a medieval palace room, and of the forest. It shows the conventional ideas of woman and of love.

Second poetic period: 1372–1380. After 1372 Chaucer wrote more mature poems showing partly the French tradition and partly a new Italian influence. *The House of Fame* and the tragedies which later appear in *The Monk's Tale* come in this period. *The House of Fame,* like *The Book of the Duchess,* is a vision written in tetrameter couplets. It contains a series of little tales drawn chiefly from classical sources, a description of the temple of Fame and an account of various petitions to Fame. It has some attempt at characterization and humor, but is chiefly of interest to students of literature rather than to the general reader.

The Monk's Tale is interesting chiefly because it shows the medieval idea of tragedy. In Chaucer's time there was no theater in the modern sense. To him a tragedy was the story of a person of high degree who fell into misery "and endeth wrecchedly." *The Monk's Tale* is a series of stories telling the tragic fate of characters in the Bible, in Greek mythology, and in ancient and medieval history. It shows the influence of the Italian writers, Dante and Boccaccio.

Third poetic period: 1380–1386. After 1380 the full effect of Chaucer's travels to Italy and his reading of Italian literature is seen.

In *The Legend of Good Women* he tells stories of famous women who died for love and who, therefore, according to the ideas of his time, achieved greatness. He says that the poem was written to atone for his translation of the French poem *The Romaunt of the Rose* which is a satire upon woman's traditional fickleness and falsity. Some of the stories are poignant and pathetic; others have little interest except for the special student. The Prologue to *The Legend of Good Women* contains one of the most beautiful, lyrical descriptions of the English spring time ever written.

Chaucer's great work of this period is *Troilus and Cressida.* In this poem Troilus, a Trojan prince who had long scoffed at lovers falls in love suddenly with Cressida, a beautiful young widow whose father has deserted to the Greeks besieging Troy. According to the medieval love convention Troilus must sigh and sicken for a long time before he even speaks to Cressida. The meetings between the two are cleverly contrived by Troilus' friend Pandarus, a merry man who is Cressida's uncle. For a time the love between the two prospers, but the lovers are parted when Cressida's father sends for her, offering a Trojan prisoner in exchange. Troilus is overcome with woe. Cressida promises to return in ten days. But a Greek soldier, Diomede, wins her heart and Troilus is left to pine until he dies in battle. Cressida is the type of fair, false woman; Troilus the gallant lover who fulfills all the conventional requirements of medieval love. The poem has been called "the first novel in English." It is, indeed, a romance of extraordinary beauty, pathos, and subtle psychology, and has become, in the last few years, a favorite among readers of English literature.

Fourth poetic period: 1387–1392. After 1387 Chaucer wrote the work by which he is best known, "The Prologue" to the *Canterbury Tales*, and some of the tales themselves.

It was on an April evening that Chaucer, as he says, fell in with "nine and twenty" pilgrims at the Tabard Inn at Southwark across the river from London. They were starting on a pilgrimage to the shrine of St. Thomas à Becket at Canterbury. The next morning they set out, a cross section of English society, led by the jolly, free-spoken host Harry Bailly. To beguile the journey they told stories.

Some of the pilgrims were undoubtedly actual people whom Chaucer knew, the host, the "shipman," and the "man of law" among them. The rest are representative of English life: courtly people, the Knight and the Squire; professional men, the Lawyer, the Physician, and the Scholar; people of the Church, the Prioress, the Priest, the Monk, the Parson, and the rascally Pardoner; business men, the Manciple and the Merchant; craftsmen, the Sailor, the Miller, and the Cook; and representative types as the rich Farmer, the Peasant, and the Wife of Bath. All of them are characterized brilliantly, minutely, and sometimes satirically by direct portraiture, by their speech and actions, and by the tales they tell.

The stories themselves are a cross section of medieval literature. Chaucer usually took his stories from well-known sources as was the custom even in Shakespeare's time two hundred years later. When he invented a story, he invented a source for it also.

"The Miller's Tale" is a "fabliau," a coarse, vulgar, funny story of common life. "The Knight's Tale" is a "courtly romance," full of glowing description and adventures of love and combat. "The Tale of Sir Thopas" is a "burlesque romance," a parody of the interminable popular tales of heroes and their impossible deeds. "The Second Nun's Tale" is a "saint's legend," a story based upon the life of a popular saint, his holiness and the miracles he performed, and his martyrdom. Here Chaucer tells of St. Cecilia. "The Nun's Priest's Tale" is a "beast fable," an allegory in which human nature is cleverly satirized by the deeds and characteristics of animals.

The idea of a journey as a framework for a set of tales with the characters carefully dramatized was original with Chaucer, though the simple idea of tales in a framework is as old as the *Arabian Nights* and had been used in Chaucer's lifetime by Boccaccio in Italy.

Fifth poetical period: 1393–1400. After 1393 Chaucer wrote the later tales of the Canterbury series and shorter poems.

Chaucer's achievement. Chaucer's achievements are at least six in number. His verse is always fluid, easy, simple, and, if read with full pronunciation of all syllables and with due attention to his final "e's," most melodious. His descriptions of people and places are like a richly figured tapestry. His sense for characterization and for dramatic fitness is excelled only by Shakespeare. He had extraordinary intellectual power, and his comments on life and character are thoroughly modern. His humor and pathos are almost beyond praise. His influence upon later poets is very marked. Into English literature he introduced two important verse forms, the heroic couplet and the rime royal. The heroic couplet consists of five-foot iambic lines rhymed in pairs. The rime royal is a seven-line stanza.

Five hundred years after his death Chaucer's position as a favorite English poet is unassailable.

Chaucer's imaginative world. The world of Chaucer's imagination is interesting because of his frank curiosity about life whether good or evil. He is never sordid, but he never glosses over evil doing. He was intensely interested in woman and provides brilliant pictures of the full-blooded physically minded woman in the Wife of Bath, of the saintly woman in Constance, of the conventional aristocratic lady in the Prioress, and of the woman who could keep a bargain in Patient Griselda. He loved courtliness, gentleness, good breeding, dignity, and devotion to duty. He exposed rascality humorously and with good nature. Above all he loved the beauty and freshness of the English country in spring time.

Chaucer's prose. Chaucer also wrote some prose. His best-known work is a scientific treatise on the astrolabe, a medieval astronomical instrument. This was written for his son Lewis. He also translated some of the work of Boethius, a post-classical philosopher very popular in Chaucer's time.

SUGGESTIONS FOR FURTHER STUDY

1. A comparison of Chaucer's "The Pardoner's Tale" and Rudyard Kipling's "The King's Ankus" in the *Second Jungle Book.*
2. A comparison of Masefield's *Reynard the Fox* with Chaucer's tales.
3. Standards of politeness in Chaucer's time as shown in the Knight, the Squire, and the Prioress in "The Prologue" to the *Canterbury Tales.*
4. Chaucer's interpretation of knighthood in "The Knight's Tale."
5. An imaginary picture of the pilgrims at dinner in the Tabard Inn.
6. How does Chaucer reveal himself in "The Prologue"?
7. What human qualities and traits of character does Chaucer admire?

USEFUL BOOKS

The best complete edition of Chaucer is the Cambridge edition, edited by F. N. Robinson. The best modernized version is by Tatlock and MacKaye. A standard work on Chaucer's period is *Medieval People* by Eileen Powers. A scholarly compendium of facts about Chaucer and his works is *A Chaucer Handbook* by R. D. French. Good studies of Chaucer are *The Poetry of Chaucer* by R. K. Root, *Chaucer and His Poetry* by G. L. Kittredge, and *Geoffrey Chaucer* by J. L. Lowes.

EDMUND SPENSER

1552 (?)–1599

Edmund Spenser has long been known as "the poet's poet" chiefly because of his unusual command over metrical forms, his brilliant imagination, his use of elaborate ornament, his influence upon later writers, and his lack of popular appeal. Relatively few people now read his poetry, but those who do, admire it greatly. It requires for appreciation rather intimate knowledge of men and affairs of the sixteenth century, and a love of fanciful beauty.

Spenser's life. Spenser was born in London about 1552. His family was apparently not rich, because he had what we should call "scholarships" at an important London school and at Pembroke College, Cambridge University. He apparently made friends easily. At Cambridge he knew intimately Gabriel Harvey, an eminent classical scholar who was friendly with many of the men of letters of the day.

After leaving college in 1576, Spenser studied and wrote. He had come to know Sir Philip Sidney, the famous poet, courtier, and soldier, and other noblemen of the court. In 1580 he was appointed secretary to the lord-deputy of Ireland. Ireland was then a conquered country, constantly in rebellion, and constantly harried by English armies. Spenser later wrote in prose his "View of the State of Ireland" which shows him as a vigorous official who believed in the rigid suppression of the conquered people.

For his services, Spenser received a grant of several thousand acres of Irish territory and Kilcolman Castle. In 1586, he was appointed secretary to the council of Munster in Ireland.

In 1589 he returned to London for a visit, and was received with honor by the court and by Queen Elizabeth, who granted him a small pension. He had the exile's love of the great city, and the idealist's disgust for the complexity and intrigues of political life.

In 1591 he returned to Ireland. In 1594 he married Elizabeth Boyle whom he seems to have loved with poetic ardor. In 1595 he made another visit to London. He returned to Ireland in 1597 and was appointed sheriff of Cork. In that year another rebellion broke out. Spenser's house was burned, but he and his family escaped death.

In 1597 he went to London again, where he seems to have been poor and where he was neglected by those in power. He died in 1599 and was buried near Chaucer's grave in Westminster Abbey.

The Shepherd's Calendar. In 1579 Spenser published his first volume of poetry, *The Shepherd's Calendar*. It contains twelve poems, one for each month, and is full of allusions to men and events now known chiefly to scholars. Its interest for the modern reader lies in the fact that it is an example of "pastoral poetry," a form as old as the Greek poet Theocritus (B.C. 270) who wrote charming little descriptions of the life and loves of shepherds. Pastoral poetry became highly conventionalized in Latin literature, and even more artificial in Renaissance Italy and France.

Since the language of shepherds conventionally was rough and unpolished, Spenser used words and forms some of which he had found in Chaucer and other early writers, and some of which he invented. The poems in Spenser's series are bound together by a love story. Some are allegorical, some philosophize about life, some discuss the religious problems of the day.

Spenser's love poetry. Like all the poets of his time, Spenser wrote a series of sonnets, the "Amoretti" (1595). These sonnets commemorate with great dignity and beauty the episodes of a courtship, presumably his own courtship of Elizabeth Boyle. To commemorate his marriage, he wrote what is certainly the finest marriage hymn in English, the "Epithalamion." In its imaginative phrasing, its rich and adorned imagery, and its fervent, impassioned emotion, it recalls the Biblical Song of Songs. This he published with his sonnets.

Other poems. "Mother Hubberd's Tale" (1591) is a political satire, written on the model of the medieval "beast-legend." "Colin Clout's Come Home Again" (1595) is an autobiographical poem which tells of his journey to London. In 1596 he published an elegy on the death of Sir Philip Sidney, "Astrophel"; "Prothalamion," a poem written for the marriage of a friend; and "Four Hymns," poems inspired by the most exalted and imaginative parts of Plato's philosophy.

The Faerie Queene. Spenser's great work is his romantic epic, *The Faerie Queene* (1590), in power and size one of the world's great poems. Spenser worked under the influence of medieval romances as they had been changed by Renaissance poets, particularly by the Italian poet Ariosto (1474–1533) in his *Orlando Furioso.* Spenser conceived of an allegorical poem in "twelve books, fashioning XII morall vertues" but only six were completed: "The Legend of the Knight of the Red Crosse or of Holinesse"; "The Legend of Sir Guyon or of Temperaunce"; "The Legend of Britomartis or of

Chastity"; "The Legend of Cambel and Triamond or of Friendship"; "The Legend of Artegall or of Justice"; and "The Legend of Calidore or of Courtesie." As each book has twelve cantos, even the uncompleted work to the modern reader seems formidable. As narrative the poem is slow and unwieldy. Knights are sent forth on adventures by Gloriana, queen of fairyland. But their adventures are lost in the maze of allegory in which the poem wanders. Everything is allegory, sometimes three allegories at once. Spenser's personal affairs; England's political affairs; the religious controversies of the sixteenth century; the allegory of the conflict of vice and virtue; all these are interwoven in prodigal profusion, rich and lovely with poetic imagery, glowing romance, and luxuriant descriptions. Nowhere is the Renaissance ideal of poetic beauty more copiously illustrated. The cantos flow like majestic rivers.

The poem was immediately recognized as great. After fifty years it suffered a period of neglect. Then, in the eighteenth century, interest in Spenser revived. *The Faerie Queene* became the happy playground of poetic minds. Its stanza was used again and again. Now the poem is sure of its place as one of the few really great long poems of European culture.

Undoubtedly Spenser thought of himself as a moral teacher. To him the good and the beautiful were one. He hated vice because it was ugly, and loved virtue as bright and glorious. He had no clearly reasoned philosophy; he felt the truth of courage, loyalty, temperance, and justice as he felt the richness of summer foliage, the coolness of a silvery waterfall, or the brilliance of a cloudless day. To read Spenser with enjoyment one must surrender to his luxuriant imagination and the flowing rhythms of his varied, musical verse.

SUGGESTIONS FOR FURTHER STUDY

1. Spenser's sonnets.
2. The allegory in Book I of *The Faerie Queene.*
3. Spenser in Ireland.
4. Spenser's friends.
5. Pastorals.
6. The Spenserian stanza.
7. Beautiful passages in *The Faerie Queene.*
8. Spenser's poetic language.

USEFUL BOOKS

The best one-volume edition of Spenser is the Cambridge edition, edited by R. E. Neil Dodge. For Spenser's allegory see *Studies in Spenser's Historical Allegory* by E. A. Greenlaw. For some of Spenser's ideas, see *Chivalry in English Literature* by W. H. Schofield. For a general survey, see the chapter on Spenser in *The Cambridge History of English Literature.*

JOHN MILTON
1608–1674

The poetry of John Milton has always had a special interest for Americans. Milton's political and intellectual sympathies were with the Puritans who settled New England. As the author of *Paradise Lost*, particularly, he gave supreme expression to their religious ideals. His great poem was standard reading in America for nearly three centuries, and his minor poems have long been studied in schools as representative of the best in English literature.

Milton's life. Like Chaucer and Spenser, Milton was born in London. His father's business was that branch of the law which is concerned with drawing up such documents as wills, deeds, and contracts. His father was a man of taste and learning with a special love for music.

To an excellent home training, Milton added an education at a London school and at Christ's College, Cambridge University. He was gifted in languages, music, and mathematics, and wrote poetry both in English and in Latin. He intended to become a clergyman in the English church. Early in college, however, finding that his sympathies were with the Puritans, he gave up his intended career to become a writer and scholar.

From 1632 to 1638 he lived in retirement at Horton, seventeen miles from London, studying at leisure classical, Italian, and English literature.

In 1638 he left England for a foreign tour, spending much time in Italy where he met many Italian celebrities. Late in 1638 he learned that the English Puritans were about to break out in revolt. He decided to return, but it was not until late in 1639 that he reached England.

In 1640 he undertook to teach a few pupils, but he was soon drawn into the service of the new Puritan government as a writer of pamphlets and as "Latin secretary," that is, as officially in charge of foreign correspondence. In 1643, he married a girl of Royalist family who left him after a few weeks. She returned to him in 1645 and died in 1654. The marriage was never really happy.

For twenty years Milton devoted himself to public service and to expressing his radical ideas on church government, divorce, and the freedom of the press. Incessant study and writing had affected his eyes, and in 1652 he became totally blind. In 1656 he married again, this time happily, but his wife died in 1658.

The restoration of King Charles II in 1660 overturned Milton's world. How, as one of the leading Puritans, he escaped execution is not known, but he continued to live in London in obscurity, blind, and relatively poor. His mind, however, was unimpaired, and he devoted himself to the production of his greatest literary works. He married for the third time in 1663. Toward the end of his life he was recognized as a great poet. In 1674 he died.

Milton's early work: 1625–1640. The poems of Milton's youth show him as a happy, serious-minded, thoughtful student with a great interest in travel and a great capacity for friendship. His religious feeling was strong, but not fanatical. His Puritanism was in no sense narrow or bigoted.

The youthful Milton is clearly seen in his four poems: "L'Allegro," "Il Penseroso," "Lycidas," and "Comus." The first two are companion poems showing two moods, cheerfulness and serious reflection. Both poems are calm, thoughtful, and high-minded. They reveal a young man who loved reading, walking, talking to country folk, and listening to music. They show that he knew English fairy lore and the plays of Jonson and Shakespeare, and that he had studied astronomy and philosophy. The two poems are written in a meter which is sometimes gay and sometimes pensive and reflective. They reveal a scholarly mind which never loses touch with humanity; which is kindly, sympathetic, and understanding. Everywhere in the poems is evidence of a sense of beauty in many forms: in Nature, in the world of art, in music, and in architecture.

"Lycidas," one of the greatest elegies of the world's literature, was written on the death of a college acquaintance, Edward King. It was contributed to a memorial volume. King was not a close friend, and the poem is rather a general lament for youth cut short than an outpouring of personal grief. Its ideas and imagery are not so important as is the glorious music of its haunting rhythms. Only those whose sense of music in poetry has been fully developed can understand the enthusiasm which lovers of poetry feel for this matchless elegy.

"Comus" is a masque written for a marriage celebration at a great nobleman's castle. It is not specially dramatic, but it contains beautiful passages of noble philosophy. No finer expression of Puritan moral idealism was ever written than some of the speeches in "Comus." Unfortunately the modern reader has to do without the music to the masque, the costumes, the pageantry, the rich setting at Ludlow Castle, and the pomp and festivity of the occasion.

Milton's middle period: 1640–1660. The twenty years which went into the service of Cromwell and the Puritan Commonwealth gave little opportunity for poetry. Most of Milton's sonnets, however, were written in this period. For them he used the Italian form of octave and sestet rather than the popular Elizabethan form of three quatrains and a concluding couplet. At their best, as in "On the Late Massacre in Piemont" and "On His Blindness" they show to what heights grandeur of thought and nobility of imagination could be raised in verse of sonorous, musical power.

In general Milton's energy in these years went into his prose essays and pamphlets. Today, in spite of their ornate, rhythmic style and their intellectual power, they have interest chiefly for special students. They require for complete appreciation an intimate knowledge of the politics and the social conditions of the time. Moreover they are all the products of violent controversy, and in controversy Milton knew nothing of the qualities which we value today: subtlety, persuasiveness, good humor, generosity, and openness of mind. Milton's argumentative weapon was the sledge hammer. It is perhaps enough if we recognize his modernity of ideas, his social and religious liberalism, and his tremendous scholarship. Bitter and violent as he usually was in his prose, he fought for the ideas of the future against equally bitter proponents of the ideas of the past.

Milton's great poems. Had Milton's life not been spared in 1660, the world would never have known three poems in the truly grand style: *Paradise Lost, Paradise Regained,* and *Samson Agonistes.*

At the age of fifty-eight, blind, worn in health, in a social world which had no respect for his ideals and his traditions, having escaped death only by a lucky chance, he might well have considered his life's work done. With heroic resolution he turned to the composition of an epic which he had long had in mind.

He had thought of many subjects, among them King Arthur, but in the end he chose the grandest which religion could suggest, the fall of man through the agency of Satan, and man's redemption through the agency of Jesus Christ.

Paradise Lost was published in 1667 in ten books and in 1674 in twelve books. It is a grand poem on a grand theme. It opens with the revolt of the angels led by Satan, with their expulsion from Heaven, and their building the palace of Pandemonium in Hell. Under Satan's powerful and courageous leadership, the fallen angels determine upon revenge. Their opportunity comes with the creation of the earth and with the innocence of Adam and Eve in Paradise. Satan travels to the garden of Eden, accomplishes the fall of man through the temptation of Eve, and is triumphant. But Adam and Eve receive assurance that in the end God will save fallen humanity through his Son.

The power of the poem lies first of all in its theme. Then one must recognize the simplicity, sweep, and grandeur of the poet's imaginative treatment of the theme. Third, the blank verse of the poem has a swelling music like that of an organ, rich, deep-toned, varied, and impressive. Further, the characterization of Satan is tremendous. His dauntless courage, his intellectual power, his resolution, and his leadership are all fitting to one who was chief of God's angels. Then, too, the poem is full of dramatic incidents and moving descriptions. Furthermore one cannot forget the quiet, pastoral charm of portions of the poem. As Tennyson said in his "Milton":

> Me rather all that bowery loneliness,
> The brooks of Eden mazily murmuring,
> And bloom profuse and cedar arches
> Charm . . .

Of course, the poem demands that the reader have a well-stored mind, a sympathy for the Biblical narrative, an understanding of Puritan idealism, and an appreciation of Milton's blank verse harmonies. One must bring much to the poem if he would capture some portion of its riches.

In 1671 Milton published *Paradise Regained* as a sequel to *Paradise Lost.* Like most sequels, it lacks the power of the earlier work.

With it he published a drama in the Greek form, *Samson Agonistes.* With concentrated unity and severe restraint in style, Samson is presented just before his death. He is taunted by the false Dalila and the Philistine giant, Harapha. He, himself, feels deep chagrin at his weakness. Realizing, however, that his physical power has returned, he permits himself to be led out for a sport to the Philistines. At the end of the dramatic poem, a messenger recites how Samson has secured revenge by pulling down the temple upon himself and his mocking enemies.

Samson Agonistes was long overshadowed by Milton's great epic, but it is now valued at its true worth. Readers now understand that it is more than the story of Samson; it is the voice of the poet, himself, in his blindness crying out against the evil days on which he has fallen. As he cries at the end of the drama:

> Nothing is here for tears, nothing to wail
> Or knock the breast; no weakness, no contempt,
> Dispraise, or blame; nothing but well and fair,
> And what may quiet us in a death so noble.

With the change in religious ideas Milton no longer interests readers as a great Puritan prophet. But there is no real loss, for with the change we see the greatness of his artistry and understand better his personality.

SUGGESTIONS FOR FURTHER STUDY

1. Passages in "Comus" and "Lycidas" that seem "universal," that is, in touch with ideas, feelings, and experiences common to all people at all times.
2. "L'Allegro" and "Il Penseroso" as a composite portrait of a young man of the Renaissance.
3. Milton's references to his blindness.
4. Milton as a public servant.
5. The picture of Satan in *Paradise Lost,* Book I.
6. Compare Milton's account of the Creation with the account in Genesis.
7. Milton's views on education.
8. *Samson Agonistes* as a Greek drama.
9. Milton's Puritanism.

USEFUL BOOKS

The best one-volume edition is the Cambridge, edited by William Vaughn Moody. Milton's prose works are published in the Everyman series. A compendium of facts about Milton is *The Milton Handbook* by J. H. Hanford. Milton's influence upon English poetry is fully presented in *The Influence of Milton on English Poetry* by R. D. Havens. A short study of Milton is *Milton* by Walter Raleigh. Matthew Arnold has an essay, "Milton," in *Essays in Criticism*, second series. For a general survey see the chapter on Milton in *The Cambridge History of English Literature.*

ALEXANDER POPE

1688–1744

The poetry of Pope is an introduction to the age of Queen Anne when polite society ruled in London, and when elegance, ease, and brilliance were prized above all other qualities. By the eighteenth century, the glory of the Renaissance and the religious earnestness of the seventeenth century had passed away. "The age of prose and reason," as Matthew Arnold called it, had its virtues. But in the work of Pope we see its least attractive aspects: its artificial correctness, its social conventionalities, its imitation of classical literature, and its malicious satire.

Pope's life. Throughout his life Pope labored under two disabilities: he was a Roman Catholic and he was physically weak and deformed. His Catholicism prevented his receiving a regular education or his taking part in public life, since Catholics were severely restricted in their activities. His bodily weakness kept him much at home and made him spiteful and malicious.

The record of his life is brief and uneventful. He cultivated the society of noblemen and writers. He was friendly with Addison, Steele, Swift, and many writers less famous. He made large sums of money by his writings and built a house at Twickenham, near London. He had a strong affection for his father and mother, and he never married. He was constantly involved in quarrels with publishers and with other writers, but his own reputation remained high in public esteem. He was long regarded as an important moralist and social critic. He died in 1744.

First period: 1709–1717. His work falls into three periods. The first contains his most brilliant and sparkling poetry.

In 1709 he published some pastorals which follow the conventional model, and which, considering the artificiality of the pastoral form, are not without their charm.

In 1711 he wrote his *Essay on Criticism*, a poem in heroic couplets. In beautifully finished, witty, and pointed epigrams, he assembled the chief commonplaces of eighteenth-century criticism. The poem is so brightly and tellingly phrased that many of its couplets have passed into the common stock of quotations which everyone knows.

The chief critical ideas of the poem are these: always keep in mind an author's purpose; be sound in your scholarship; follow "nature," that is, the normal standard of human conduct as it is recognized in the best cultivated society; make the classical writers your model; insist upon "correctness," that is, a careful adherence to standard critical rules; admire good taste and restraint; in poetry observe how sound echoes sense. Intellectually these critical standards do not go very deep; but they are clear and they make for elegance, polish, smoothness, and ease.

In 1712 he published his sparkling satire of polite society *The Rape of the Lock*. He expanded it in 1714. The poem is a mock epic and makes delightful fun of social customs and of the shallow life of a fashionable young lady. Its style burlesques the so-called "epic machinery": the familiar epic expressions, the extended similes, the intervention of deities, the invocations to the muses, and the epic battles. Lords and ladies replace classic heroes, attendant sylphs replace pagan divinities, a card game becomes an epic conflict, and a quarrel over a lock of hair causes a mighty struggle in society.

"Windsor Forest" (1713) is a descriptive poem, continuing the pastoral tradition. "An Elegy on an Unfortunate Lady" and "Eloisa to Abelard," both published in 1717, show as much genuine emotion as Pope's critical rationalism could compass.

Second period: 1719–1728. In the eighteenth century there was a great vogue for English translations of the classics. Since the *Iliad* and the *Odyssey* were regarded, next to Virgil's *Aeneid*, as the greatest works of classical antiquity, Pope undertook to translate them. John Dryden (1631–1700) whom Pope revered as his master, had translated the *Aeneid* twenty years before. As Pope's classical knowledge was limited, he secured the assistance of certain scholars, and with their help his *Iliad* and *Odyssey* were published at intervals from 1715 to 1725. By this time Pope's work had become fashionable. Society "took up" his translation and his success made him rich. "A very pretty poem, Mr. Pope," said Bentley, the famous classicist, "but you must not call it Homer." For nearly one hundred and fifty years, however, readers in England and America preferred to read their Homer in Pope's "modernized" version.

In 1725 Pope edited Shakespeare's works. Lacking, as he did, any real knowledge of Elizabethan England, and with little genuine feeling for Shakespeare, his edition is not one of the more important contributions to Shakespearean scholarship.

In 1728 he published *The Dunciad* in which he mercilessly satirized all the writers whom he despised and hated. These were his "dunces." Pope honestly believed that true culture and even civilization itself were in danger of extinction by "dullness," as he called pedantry. He could not foresee that the downfall of the age of prose and reason would come from a revival of emotion and an interest in the life of outdoor Nature and simple people rather than from excessive and tasteless learning.

Third period: 1733–1744. The most important work of this period is the *Essay on Man*, once regarded as a great moral poem, but now valued for its epigrammatic terseness and the light which it throws upon the philosophy of its time.

Pope was not a great thinker. He had none of Milton's depth, sincerity, or passionate moral force. Hence his poem seems now superficial, and lacking in coherence and depth of thought. Modern readers prefer his less pretentious but more entertaining *The Rape of the Lock*.

He also published satires directed at prominent social figures and centering on such vices as hypocrisy, gluttony, pride, and avarice. Toward the end of his life he published his letters with elaborate falsifications which remained undiscovered for a hundred years.

Pope's place in English literature. It is hard for the twentieth century to do Pope justice. His personality is to us unattractive, we have little knowledge of the social group which he knew so well, and his classical criticism and moral philosophizing now seem remote and dull.

Yet we must recognize that he was truly representative of his time and that he had a great influence upon later writers. Hence he cannot be neglected. Moreover for finish, polish, and epigrammatic force in poetry he remains unsurpassed.

SUGGESTIONS FOR FURTHER STUDY

1. A comparison of a passage from Pope's *Iliad* with one from Dryden's *Aeneid.*
2. A comparison of a passage from Pope's *Iliad* with the same passage from the modern translation by Lang, Leaf, and Myers.
3. A comparison of a passage from Pope's *Odyssey* with passages from the following translations: Chapman's (sixteenth century), Morris (nineteenth century), and T. E. Lawrence (twentieth century).
4. Irony, satire, and burlesque in *The Rape of the Lock.*
5. A study of the *Essay on Man* to find examples of epigrammatic terseness, elevation of ideas, reasonable philosophy, conventional attitude toward life.
6. Familiar quotations from Pope.
7. The heroic couplet.
8. Pope's relations with Horace Walpole and Lady Mary Wortley Montague.
9. A comparison of Pope and Gay.

USEFUL BOOKS

The best one-volume edition is in the Globe series, edited by A. W. Ward. This does not contain the translations, which must be looked for in older editions. In connection with the translation of Homer, see Matthew Arnold's essay "On Translating Homer." The best general articles are in *The Cambridge History of English Literature* and the *Encyclopaedia Britannica.* The latest life of Pope is by Edith Sitwell. An older and more conservative life is in the English Men of Letters series, by Leslie Stephen.

WILLIAM WORDSWORTH

1770–1850

The romantic movement. In 1798 began a new movement in English literature which historians have agreed to call the "romantic movement." The new romantic writers substituted for the classic ideals of the age of Pope and Johnson complete freedom of the individual to write about life as he saw it without regard for social conventions. All about them the old life was breaking up. The American Revolution, the French Revolution, the change in social and industrial life—these made life seem new, vigorous, exciting, and free. Wordsworth said:

Bliss was it in that dawn to be alive,
But to be young was very heaven!—Oh! times,
In which the meager, stale, forbidding ways
Of custom, law, and statute, took at once
The attraction of a country in romance!

The new freedom to which, of course, such men as Thomson, Gray, Collins, Blake, and Burns in the eighteenth century had pointed the way, showed itself in the form and subject matter of literature. The new poetry wrote about life out of doors, flowers and trees, storms and mountains; about humble, simple people; about the hopes and aspirations of lovers of liberty; about the emotions and experiences of ardent, sensitive souls; about the joys of discovery felt by the lover of art and literature; about old stories drawn from legend, history, and simple religious faith; about the Greek and Roman classics seen in the light of a new interpretation. These things and hundreds of others were felt intensely and given a meaning that was new and deeply emotional.

Wordsworth's life. Wordsworth was born in a village in northern England in 1770. His father was a prosperous lawyer, his mother a descendant of gentlefolk. Both parents had died before Wordsworth was fourteen and he was left much to himself, boarding in the village and attending a small school. He followed the usual boyish pursuits of fishing, swimming, skating and was fond of long solitary walks. Outdoor life in one of the most picturesque portions of England made a deep impression upon him.

At St. John's College, Cambridge University, he did not distinguish himself as a scholar. He represents himself as something of an idler, but he read steadily and spent much time out of doors. The influence of Nature was increasing.

In 1791 he visited France, then in a state of revolution. He sympathized strongly with the revolutionaries and would have thrown in his lot with a small group of young enthusiasts had he not been forced to return to England in 1792.

He followed no regular occupation, being interested primarily in poetry. His first published works were two descriptive poems in the formal manner of the eighteenth century, "An Evening Walk" and "Descriptive Sketches," both published in 1793.

His determination to be a poet and nothing else was strengthened by the devotion of his sister Dorothy. When in 1795 a friend bequeathed to him enough money for a frugal independence, Dorothy joined him at Grasmere. From his father's estate he later received a sum of money, and his income was further increased in 1802 through his marriage with Mary Hutchinson. In 1813 he received a public appointment with a fair income and no duties, and in 1842 a government pension. He lived in simple style in the beautiful Lake country and always had leisure to devote himself to his life interest, poetry. He died in 1850.

Influences on his life. The effect of the French Revolution upon Wordsworth was lasting. His enthusiasm, however, passed away when he found that the Revolution brought the Reign of Terror, a European war, and the Napoleonic empire instead of the promised brotherhood of man. Revolting now from radicalism, Wordsworth became the stanchest of conservatives.

More important was the influence of his sister Dorothy. She strengthened his Nature worship and in every way devoted herself to the development of his poetic power, suggesting, criticizing, inspiring. The influence of his friend, Samuel Taylor Coleridge, was also very strong. To Coleridge's philosophical and critical mind and romantic imagination, he owed much.

Most important was the influence of Nature. From the contemplation of lakes, trees, and mountains he absorbed a passionate faith in the inspiring and healing power of Nature. He speedily acquired the belief that humble folk who lived in the country are the wisest and best of men. He felt that their language, simple and unadorned, was superior for poetical purposes to the more elaborate language of the educated people in cities. He believed, too, that men learned best by "a wise passiveness" and by contemplation and reflection rather than by reason and study.

Lyrical Ballads. The publication of *Lyrical Ballads* in 1798 was an important literary event. It showed that the old poetic régime was over and that England had a new poetry. Wordsworth and Coleridge, in planning the volume, definitely regarded it as an innovation. Wordsworth's part was to write on simple themes from common life; Coleridge's to use romantic themes which depended on the reader's "willing suspension of disbelief." The second edition in 1800 carried a preface in which Wordsworth stated clearly the poetical doctrines of the two friends.

The volume contained Coleridge's "The Ancient Mariner" and poems of Wordsworth varying from the commonplace, prosaic style of "The Idiot Boy" to the beautiful music of "Lines Composed a Few Miles above Tintern Abbey." Though coldly received at first, the volume gained influence steadily.

What *Lyrical Ballads* did was to establish the main doctrines of the new poetry: that beauty in poetry could come from humble themes; that poetry needed, not elaborate and conventional language, but warmth of emotion and intensity of experience; that imagination was the all-powerful motive force of poetry and that wonder and "emotion recollected in tranquillity" were the poet's necessary inspiration.

Edition of 1807. In 1807 Wordsworth collected his poems in two volumes. In this collection his work reached its high watermark. Such poems as "Ode: Intimations of Immortality," "The Solitary Reaper," and many of his sonnets belong to the greatest English lyrical poetry.

Later work. In 1814 Wordsworth published "The Excursion," a long poem filled with his philosophy and his observations of country life in the Lake district where he lived. It was received by howls of disapproval from the conservative critics, who in this case were right. It is, indeed, a very dull poem.

"The Prelude." For years Wordsworth worked on a poetical autobiography of his youth, "The Prelude." He did not, however, publish it during his life. It was published in 1850, after his death. Had it been published at the same time as "The Excursion" the verdict of critics might have been different. Though very long, "The Prelude" is not dull. It is full of interesting material and contains many very beautiful lines.

Wordsworth's poetical achievement. Historically Wordsworth is of great importance because he, more than any other writer of his time, freed poetry from artificialities of language and from the domination of the heroic couplet.

Then, too, he widened the field of poetic material. Conventional beauty, man-made, was put aside for simple aspects of Nature, for the beauty of humble life, and for simple truths. Who, in the eighteenth century, could have written

> The rainbow comes and goes,
> And lovely is the rose;
> The moon doth with delight
> Look round her when the heavens are bare,
> Waters on a starry night
> Are beautiful and fair.

Third, he expressed beautifully and with complete imaginative power, simple emotions. "The Solitary Reaper," "Michael," and "I Wandered Lonely as a Cloud" bring out a new and striking beauty in a highland lass cutting and binding grain, in a humble sheep herder whose life is desolate, and in a bank of daffodils. Wordsworth showed the world new sources of beauty.

Moreover, he had the gift of phrasing ideas in memorable form. With Shakespeare and Pope he is among the most quoted poets in English literature.

Fifth, he popularized the belief in Nature as a beneficent, life-giving Power. Nature was to him the deepest source of human inspiration.

Finally, he was the most influential poet of the nineteenth century. Tennyson, Arnold, Longfellow, Bryant, and Whitman all show his influence. Even today our poetry in its deliberate search for simplicity and its interest in humble life shows that his poetic teaching still has vitality.

SUGGESTIONS FOR FURTHER STUDY

1. Wordsworth's interest in simple people and ordinary experiences.
2. The suggestive power of Wordsworth's simple diction.
3. Wordsworth's interest in Nature.
4. Examples of Wordsworth's theory that poetry should express and re-create "emotion recollected in tranquillity."
5. A comparison of Milton's and Wordsworth's sonnets.
6. Wordsworth's relationship with Coleridge.
7. Wordsworth's influence on William Cullen Bryant.
8. Wordsworth's sister Dorothy.
9. Wordsworth and the French Revolution.
10. Wordsworth's sonnets.

USEFUL BOOKS

There are excellent one-volume editions of Wordsworth in the Cambridge, Globe, and Oxford series. "The Prelude," which is Wordsworth's poetical autobiography of his youth, has been edited by E. de Selincourt. The complete and authoritative life is in two volumes by George M. Harper. "The Prelude" has been studied at length by Emile Legouis in *The Early Life of William Wordsworth.* A popular book is *Wordsworth: How to Know Him* by C. T. Winchester. *The Journals of Dorothy Wordsworth,* edited by W. Knight, throws light on his relations to his sister. There are important essays by Matthew Arnold and Walter Pater. See also the chapter in *The Cambridge History of English Literature.*

GEORGE NOEL GORDON, LORD BYRON
1788–1824

The effect of the French Revolution on the older poets, Wordsworth and Coleridge, was to drive them to conservatism. In younger men it stimulated an intense desire for freedom, idealism, and beauty. One of the most prominent of the younger group was Lord Byron who became in his day the embodiment of the spirit of youthful revolt and of complete devotion to liberty.

Byron's life. Byron was born in London, but spent his early life in Scotland. His father, a dashing, handsome spendthrift known as "Mad Jack Byron" died when the boy was three. His mother, a Scotch woman unbalanced in temper and behavior, gave her son neither a normal home nor a calm upbringing. At ten he inherited the title, but little money. His inability to live in the style of a lord bothered him. His lameness was an even greater handicap.

At Harrow, one of the famous English preparatory schools, he engaged in sports in spite of his lameness, wrote poetry, and read everything which came in his way. He attended Trinity College, Cambridge University, where he was distinguished more for his unrestrained conduct than for scholarship. He did, however, publish a volume of poems while he was in college, a volume which he called somewhat superciliously *Hours of Idleness.*

In 1809 he took his seat in the House of Lords where he showed considerable political ability. He was, however, too restless to settle down to regular life. He dashed off to the continent, visiting countries unknown to the usual traveler, including Albania.

He returned to a riotous social life, one of the most popular men in London. In 1815 he married an heiress, with whom he lived only a year. Their separation at the birth of their daughter shocked society. Byron left England, never to return. For a time he was in Switzerland where he was joined by the Shelleys. He then went to Italy living for a time at Venice and later at Pisa. The Shelleys followed him to Italy, and Byron was one of the few friends at Shelley's funeral pyre. In 1823 Byron, wearied by a life of triviality, and moved by his passionate devotion to liberty, threw in his lot with the Greek revolutionists who were trying to free their country from Turkish tyranny. Byron gave to the cause of Greek freedom his mind, his fortune, and his life. He died of fever at Missolonghi in 1824.

English Bards and Scotch Reviewers. Byron's early volume, *Hours of Idleness*, had received the scorching criticism meted out to every new poet by the arbiter of British opinion, *The Edinburgh Review*. Byron surveyed his contemporaries, passed his own judgment upon them, and upon the reviewers, and in 1809 published the first of his keen satires, *English Bards and Scotch Reviewers*, an extraordinary performance for a young man of twenty-one.

Childe Harold's Pilgrimage. During his travels Byron wrote such fascinating letters to his men friends that he was urged to publish them. He recast the material in verse using the Spenserian stanza. The result, *Childe Harold's Pilgrimage*, of which the first two cantos were published in 1812, brought him fame overnight. In these cantos Byron takes Harold through Spain, Portugal, and Greece. The third and fourth cantos which came later cover Belgium, Switzerland, and Italy. The poem as a whole has great vitality. It is filled with extraordinarily vivid and quotable descriptions, with occasional touches of satire, with emotional appreciation of Nature, and above all with the romantic personality of Byron: his enthusiasms, his disillusionment, his romantic melancholy. Here, as always, he sounded the personal note.

Satires. The vein of satire opened in *English Bards and Scotch Reviewers* proved rich ore. Byron found much in English life and manners to satirize. He preferred to cloak his biting comments in narrative form, placing his characters in Spain, Italy, and the Orient, but there is no mistaking his uncomplimentary estimate of the English society that had ostracized him. "Beppo," a fairly short humorous tale of Venice, and *Don Juan*, a really long poem, the longest written by Byron, are both in the Italian eight-line stanza called *ottava rima*. They are in the easy style of the Italian medley poem and are full of pointed wit. *Don Juan* illustrates the Byronic temperament fully. It is grave and gay, poetical and nonsensical, comic and tragic, serene and bitter in swift changes. The episode of Haidee and Juan is an idyll of young love, beautifully and sympathetically told. Other incidents border on the absurd. As in *Childe Harold's Pilgrimage* there are exquisite descriptions. But again and again Byron, always afraid of becoming sentimental, pricks the iridescent bubbles he has blown and escapes by laughing at himself and the world in verses which are sometimes mere doggerel, and sometimes true wit.

"The Vision of Judgment," another satire, though most popular in its own time, has less to offer the modern reader. As a reply to the poet Southey's eulogy of King George III, it is full of topical allusions. It is, however, clever and amusing.

Tales. Besides the loosely constructed narratives such as *Childe Harold's Pilgrimage* and *Don Juan* Byron wrote a number of tales, usually with Oriental setting. Their popularity was enormous. The first of these, "The Giaour," appeared in 1813. "Lara," "The Corsair," "Mazeppa," and "The Bride of Abydos" delighted a large public with similar details of unfamiliar scenery, strange customs, high passions, beautiful maidens, and daring men of action.

Dramas. Of Byron's dramas, *Cain* and *Manfred* are the most important. Both of these are impressive. Byron takes the Bible story and interprets Cain with sympathy and understanding. *Manfred* is a tense drama on the old theme of a man's selling his soul to the devil.

Shorter poems. Byron wrote many lyrics and songs, sometimes interspersing his long poems with these. Many of his lyrics were actually written for music and became popular songs, such as "Maid of Athens." Many express Byron's characteristic mood of sad disillusionment. Some, like "The Destruction of Sennacherib" are powerful and splendid.

Byron's poetical achievement. Byron refused to give to poetry the close attention which would make his verses finished. He was a careless workman. But his command over words and rhythms was large, and the vitality of his own personality so great that nearly

MR. WILLIAM

SHAKESPEARES

COMEDIES,
HISTORIES, &
TRAGEDIES.

Publiſhed according to the True Originall Copies.

Martin Droeshout sculpsit London.

LONDON

Printed by Iſaac Iaggard, and Ed. Blount. 1623.

Courtesy of the Library of Harvard University

TITLE-PAGE OF SHAKESPEARE'S "FIRST FOLIO"

The most valuable book in English literature.

TOMB OF CHAUCER, LONDON

everything he wrote throbs with life. He was a great influence, so that proud melancholy, scornful disillusionment, and romantic disparagement of the human race have come to be known as "Byronic." His beauty, his personal charm seem to cling to these aspects of his thinking and young people wear his ideas as they used to wear his flowing ties.

In the second place he stands entrenched in a firm position as a descriptive poet of skill and sensitive appreciation. It was he who set the fashion for love of the violent aspects of Nature—stern mountains and violent storms.

In the third place he was a skillful teller of tales. He could create melodramas with wild adventures and highly colored characters, and he could in smooth informal verse present gay sinners and sweet young maidens.

Finally, his rank as a satirist is very high. As a critic of contemporary society and of human nature as it always will be, he shows himself keenly observant and unerringly just in his estimates.

His influence extends to the present. The term "Byronic" is still applied, poets still follow his lead, and people still delight in reading him.

SUGGESTIONS FOR FURTHER STUDY

1. What is meant by "Byronism"?
2. A comparison of Byron's "The Bride of Abydos" with Masefield's "Enslaved."
3. Byron's "Romanticism."
4. Vigorous and varied rhythms in Byron's poetry.
5. Exultation in wild and passionate emotions in *Childe Harold's Pilgrimage.*
6. Byron's independence, freedom, and courage as seen in "The Prisoner of Chillon."
7. Byron and Greece.
8. Byronic ideas in *Cain* or *Manfred.*
9. The satirical method in *Don Juan.*

USEFUL BOOKS

The best one-volume edition is the Cambridge, edited by P. E. More. Maurois' *Byron* is a very modern life of the poet. Other biographical material will be found in *Byron in Greece* by H. Spender and *The Pilgrim of Eternity* by John Drinkwater. Matthew Arnold's essay, "Byron," gives the Victorian view. The chapter in *The Cambridge History of English Literature* provides an excellent survey.

PERCY BYSSHE SHELLEY
1792–1822

Shelley represents the extreme idealistic side of the romantic revolt. He seemed not to be a creature of earth, but one who dwelt in clouds. He was among the first to rebel against the injustices of the existing social system and to express poetically the desire for a better social order, guided by universal love. He poured forth his aspirations in a torrent of lyric poetry.

Shelley's life. Percy Bysshe Shelley was born in Sussex, the grandson of a baronet. Though the heir to the title, Shelley never inherited it, dying many years before his father. At Eton he was unhappy, loathing the sports emphasized heavily by all English schools, and finding few friends. He read widely, experimented with chemistry, took long walks in the country, and wrote novels. His refusal to endure beatings with fortitude marked him out as peculiar.

At Oxford, where he went in 1810, his unpopularity continued. He made friends with Thomas Jefferson Hogg, a fellow student destined for the law. As a gentleman's son, the heir to a large fortune, Shelley prepared for no profession. He read omnivorously, and continued pranks with chemistry. His career was cut short after a few months by his expulsion, for arrant defiance of authority. The immediate cause was his publication of a boyish pamphlet "On the Necessity of Atheism." Hogg was also expelled. The two boys dashed off to London. Shelley's father tried to make his son apologize, but the only result was a permanent breach between Shelley and his father. Shelley was given an income of two hundred pounds a year and left to his own devices, while Hogg, more amenable, went off to study law. Shelley never lost his belief that his father was a "tyrant."

Other fathers were tyrants, too. A schoolmate of his sisters, Harriet Westbrook, had a father who compelled her to go back to school although she was sixteen. Shelley "rescued" her by running off with her to Gretna Green. He did not believe in marriage, but yielded to her conservative ideas. Now began a period of borrowing money from friends, and from professional money lenders to whom he paid ruinous interest. At his majority, two years later, his father settled upon him an income of a thousand pounds which was still not enough for one of Shelley's princely generosity. He gave away large sums especially to William Godwin, an impecunious writer of great influence at this time.

In 1814 he eloped with Godwin's daughter Mary, carrying out his theory that marriage was dissolved when true communion of spirit ceased. Divorce was then not granted to women, and to men only rarely. Harriet drowned herself later, and Shelley then yielded to Mary's conservatism and married her. He was much grieved because the court refused him the custody of the son and daughter of his first marriage, and, believing more than ever that he was "persecuted," he left England and never returned. He now took up permanent residence in Italy.

Association with Byron stimulated him greatly. Mary's influence declined as she changed from eager girl to grieving mother. In the eight years of her life with Shelley she lost four children. Only the youngest child, a boy, lived to maturity. Neither of Shelley's wives could run a household, and Shelley never lost his careless habits of eating. A handful of raisins and a few bread crumbs were often his only meal. He was much of a valetudinarian and at all times in his life was sure that death was around the corner. Suicide was one of his recurring ideas. In 1822 he was drowned while sailing. In his pockets were a volume of Sophocles, and Keats' poems. His body was burned on the shore, according to Italian law, and the ashes were then buried in the Protestant cemetery at Rome.

Early writings. Shelley's two novels are merely boyish rubbish, based on the popular Gothic romances of the time. "On the Necessity of Atheism" is an attempt to show that there is no basis for belief in the traditional God. "Queen Mab" is a plea for virtue, "Alastor," a longer and more sustained poem, a plea for love. The narratives upon which these are strung are very slight. "The Revolt of Islam" is a long narrative of two people's effort to reform the social order through love. There are interesting passages in this poem about woman's intellectual equality with man.

"Prometheus Unbound." Shelley, intensely interested in abstract truth, in liberty, and in love, takes Prometheus as a symbol of all these. In this dramatic poem Shelley writes with power and beauty his aspirations for the freedom of mankind.

The Cenci. Shelley's one drama written for the stage was not considered suitable, and has rarely been presented. It is forceful, tense, and moving. It shows much understanding of human motive. But the theme, taken from an old murder, is forbidding.

Lyrics. It is in his lyrics that Shelley's poetic gift shows itself at its best. He poured forth lyrics much as a bird sings, to relieve his heart of its weight of emotion. There is always a note of sadness in Shelley. He yielded to the charm of the skylark's song, to the swift onslaught of the west wind, to the sweep of the clouds, to the deep peace of night, but even in joyousness there was an undercurrent of pain. He wrote words for music, "The Indian Serenade," "Music, when soft voices die," and various poems meant to be sung to the guitar or the piano.

"Adonais." Shelley had written to Keats his appreciation many times, and the two had met, but were not close friends, largely because of their different backgrounds and way of life. Keats felt keenly his social and economic inferiority and probably did not understand Shelley's broad sympathies and generosities. When Keats died Shelley was moved to write an elegy which, although ruthlessly ridiculed by contemporary critics, remains one of the most exquisite elegies in English literature. With magnificent music Shelley gives voice to a belief in eternity where man is one with Nature and gives final form to his various images of light, and his expression of the transient quality of human life.

Shelley's poetical achievement. It was not until after his death that Shelley's poetry received recognition. He has gained steadily in esteem but has never been a wide influence. His philosophy, though all important to him, is obscured by the wealth of words with which he cloaked it. He is listened to, not as a teacher, but as a singer of most musical and tenderly affecting lyrics. In a sonnet such as "Ozymandias" his comment on the brevity of life and the emptiness of fame is so aptly phrased that it startles even the most casual reader into reflective thinking. In general Shelley stirs our emotions rather than our minds. His great talent is re-creating his emotional reactions in vivid images and musical phrasing so that we, too, are swept along with the west wind, stirred to wistful longing by the skylark, and pleasantly saddened by the desired coming of night

SUGGESTIONS FOR FURTHER STUDY

1. The word music of Shelley's poems.
2. Moods of joy, exultation, regret, and love in Shelley's poems.
3. The mythology of "Prometheus Unbound."
4. Shelley's poetic imagery.
5. A comparison of "Adonais" with Milton's "Lycidas."
6. Shelley's "romanticism."
7. Shelley's protest against human enslavement to cruelty, meanness, and injustice.
8. Dramatic power in *The Cenci*.

USEFUL BOOKS

The best one-volume edition is in the Cambridge series, edited by G. E. Woodberry. The authoritative life is in two volumes by W. E. Peck. Maurois' *Ariel* is a popular modern life. There is excellent biographical material in *Shelley, Godwin, and Their Circle* by H. N. Brailsford. For Shelley's relations with his first wife, see *Shelley's Lost Letters to Harriet* by Leslie Hotson. For general criticism see the chapter in *The Cambridge History of English Literature.*

JOHN KEATS
1795–1821

Keats, the youngest and shortest-lived of the prominent romantic poets, represented a different aspect of romanticism. He was not influenced by the French Revolution and, unlike Byron and Shelley, felt no passionate yearnings for liberty. His revolt was from the commonplace and ordinary into the world of beauty and of antiquity. He would walk about the streets of London chanting the verses of Chaucer and Spenser, taking special pleasure in forgotten words and phrases. With no direct knowledge of Greek he became, through a translation, an ardent admirer of Homer.

He was also led to a love of Greek culture and Greek art by his visits to museums. In his youth Lord Elgin brought to England a marvelous collection of Greek sculpture. In imagination Keats was carried away from the busy London streets rattling with wagons, to the quiet peace of ancient Athens, the golden age when beauty was in its heyday.

He differed from Byron and Shelley in his close attention to form. Byron was frequently careless in both form and language; Shelley frequently showed impatience with revision; Keats sometimes rewrote his lines five or six times until he found exactly the right words with the right sound and rhythms. A study of his revisions is extremely informative.

Keats' life. Keats was born in London in 1795. His father held a position of responsibility in an inn owned by Mrs. Keats' father. At fifteen Keats was an orphan. His parents had sent him to a good school and had been proud of his literary prizes. His guardians, however, had no sympathy with such occupations. They very soon apprenticed the young boy to a surgeon. Although Keats' interests were decidedly literary he became fairly proficient in surgery, spending some time in the London hospitals. At twenty-one, free from his worldly-minded guardians, he turned to poetry as his sole occupation.

Keats was not strong and when tuberculosis was fast closing his days, he left England for the more kindly climate of Italy. Four months later he died in Rome and was buried there in 1821.

His illness had prevented his marriage with Fanny Brawne, a young English girl with whom he had been in love for some time.

Early poems. Keats' life was brief, but his talents ripened fast. At twenty he had mastered the sonnet form and had written one of his most famous sonnets, "On First Looking into Chapman's Homer," in which he expressed that sense of wonder and awe which comes upon the voyager in the seas of literature. The sonnet, because of its set form, was always a pleasure to Keats, and he wrote it with much skill. It was in 1817 that the sonnet on Homer appeared in his first published volume, *Poems by John Keats,* and in the next year "Endymion" was published. His third volume, with his fine odes and "The Eve of St. Agnes," appeared in 1820.

Keats' earliest poems have many faults in over-elaborateness and occasional ineptitude of phrase. He was overfond of listing what he observed. But even such a poem as "Sleep and Poetry" shows promise. Keats had keen senses; he brings them all to play in his poetry. No poet has had eyes more quick to take in details of beauty, ears to hear more delicate sounds; and no poet has shown more keen appreciation of the senses of touch and taste. "I Stood Tip-toe" reproduces the sights and sounds Keats caught on his little hill.

"Endymion." Keats took for background the old Greek legend of Endymion in love with the moon. Endymion's longing for the goddess represents Keats' longing for ideal beauty. The poem is highly colored, but contains many fine passages.

"Hyperion." "Hyperion" also turns to Greek legend. Far more mature than the earlier poem, "Endymion," it offers a magnificent picture of the overthrown gods and their desire to regain power. Keats makes the god Hyperion truly majestic. When he attempted to rewrite the poem to make it more philosophical he weakened it.

Tales. Probably influenced by Byron's success with tales, Keats wrote "Isabella, or the Pot of Basil," "Lamia," and "The Eve of St. Agnes." In "Isabella" Keats tries a touch of Byronic satire in one place, but without much success. His was not the satiric temper. The success of "Isabella" lies in its effective simplicity. The pathos is almost never overstrained and although morbid in theme, the tale is quite free from morbidity of effect. The pictures of young love in the beginning and of deep grief at the end are very effective.

"Lamia" takes up the legend of marriage with a snake woman who disappears when she is unmasked.

"The Eve of St. Agnes" is a much slighter tale. It is concerned with the superstition that a girl if she follows certain observances will, on the eve of St. Agnes, see the face of her future husband. In this tale the lover hides in the girl's home, and at the end the two elope. It is a delicate tale, full of rich description. Rarely has cold been made so penetrating with mere words as it is in this poem. Keats' careful workmanship and untiring attention to detail gave this poem rich artistry.

"La Belle Dame sans Merci" is the slightest of the tales. Indeed it is scarcely a tale at all. It is merely the lament of a knight who has been enchanted. It shows Keats' skill in securing effects. Here he pictures the barren shore of a lake "where no birds sing," and in the barrenness of the scene intensifies the desolateness of the knight.

Odes. Keats' "Ode to a Nightingale" and his "Ode on a Grecian Urn" are his most famous odes. Both are beautiful expressions of his emotional experience in hearing the nightingale and in reflecting upon the beauty of an antique Greek vase upon which was pictured a group of villagers at a spring festival. In these odes Keats' poetic power is at its height. For felicity of phrase and melodious verse they have rarely been surpassed. In both, Keats expresses with pensive melancholy the transient quality of human life. Only on the vase will the musician forever play sweet melodies, will the lover find his love always undimmed, his loved one forever fair. Nightingales will sing in time to come, but this individual nightingale will be gone. In these two odes occur some of our most quoted phrases such as "magic casements" from the "Ode to a Nightingale" and from the same poem the picture of Ruth

> when, sick for home,
> She stood in tears amid the alien corn.

The much-disputed statement,

> Beauty is truth, truth beauty,

comes from the "Ode on a Grecian Urn."

Keats' poetical achievement. Keats' influence has been very strong from Tennyson to the present time. His emphasis upon craftsmanship has had excellent following. Many a poet has been led through the example of Keats to perfect verse that might otherwise have been carelessly written. Keats also turned attention to richness of verse, unlike the simplicity of Wordsworth. Again, he taught a new use of the classics. Instead of finding in the classics models for restraint he found a highly colored romanticism. Restraint of form he did emphasize, but for his material he chose the legends of Endymion and Lamia rather than the tales of Greeks and Romans of inspiring deeds.

Keats' greatest achievement, however, is in his presentation of pure beauty. Beauty itself was his interest, not beauty to point a moral or to carry a message. Keats had no lesson to teach. He did not want to call his readers' attentions to social wrongs as Shelley did; to the corrupt state of society as Byron did; to Nature as a great moral teacher as Wordsworth did. Because of this lack of bias his poems have an objective beauty which is especially attractive to young people. But to readers of all ages Keats sings enduring music.

SUGGESTIONS FOR FURTHER STUDY

1. Keats' love of beauty.
2. Keats' poetic imagery.
3. Spenserian influence on Keats.

4. Keats' moods of love, regret, wonder, and worship of beauty.
5. Keats' "romanticism."
6. Keats' sonnets.
7. Keats as a writer of odes.
8. Keats and Leigh Hunt.

USEFUL BOOKS

The best one-volume edition is in the Oxford series, edited by H. B. Forman. The authoritative life is in two large volumes by Amy Lowell. A good short life is in the English Men of Letters series by Sidney Colvin. For general studies see the chapter in *The Cambridge History of English Literature* and the article in the *Encyclopaedia Britannica*. Gamaliel Bradford has an essay in *Bare Souls*. Matthew Arnold wrote an essay on Keats. Keats' letters have been edited by Sidney Colvin. For Leigh Hunt and Keats see *Leigh Hunt* by E. Blunden and the *Autobiography of Leigh Hunt*, edited by E. Blunden.

ALFRED, LORD TENNYSON
1809–1892

Alfred Tennyson was the most popular and most honored poet of the nineteenth century. In his long life he attempted to carry on the noblest ideals of poetry. He kept abreast of the new interest in science and democracy, and retained a calmly assured faith

> that somehow, good
> Will be the final goal of ill.

Life. Alfred Tennyson was born on August 6, 1809, in the beautiful pastoral county of Lincolnshire. His father was a clergyman. Alfred was the fourth of twelve children. He began early to read widely and to write poetry. His literary tastes were encouraged by his father who prepared him for college.

He attended Trinity College, Cambridge, where he joined a small group of intellectuals. Among his friends was Arthur Hallam who had a strong influence upon him.

After his college days he returned to his father's house where he lived for some years writing steadily. In 1833 Hallam died and Tennyson was overcome with grief. He remained in poor health of mind and body for many years.

In 1845 he received a small pension which ended certain financial difficulties. He went abroad, and after a time his health steadily improved. His poems began to bring in money, and in 1850 he married Emily Sellwood to whom he had been engaged for many years.

In 1850 he was appointed Poet Laureate, and henceforth his literary success was assured. From then on, his life was quiet and retired. He was honored by Oxford University, he traveled, and he studied and wrote continuously. As he grew older, he became a great international figure, and was particularly admired in America. In 1884 he received the greatest public honor which England could bestow upon him, a peerage. He was made Baron Tennyson and he took his place in the House of Lords.

In 1892 he died and was buried in Westminster Abbey.

Early poems. Tennyson's early volumes were *Poems, Chiefly Lyrical* (1830) and *Poems* (1833). This poetry was influenced by Byron and Keats and seemed to readers over-ornamented, merely pretty, and sentimental. As a result of the harsh criticism which he received he kept silent for ten years.

In 1842 he published *Poems* in two volumes. He revised his earlier work rigidly and presented for the first time such poems as "Locksley Hall" and "Ulysses." These volumes were well received.

The Princess. In 1847 he published *The Princess*, a long fancifully romantic poem on the education of women, containing such beautiful songs as "Tears, Idle Tears" and "The Bugle Song." His idea of women was typical of the Victorian era. Tennysonian girls were sweet, pretty, playful darlings with golden ringlets. They were carefully protected from a rough, masculine world. Their proper destiny was marriage, after which they settled down into "sainted motherhood."

In Memoriam. In 1850 he published *In Memoriam*, a long elegy composed of single poems in quatrains in memory of Arthur Hallam. In this great poem he expresses the religious doubts and beliefs of his time. The poem shows the progress of a grief-stricken mind from the depths of despair to triumphant faith. It speaks to every earnest reader who has known doubt or grief. It is manly, dignified, elevated, and full of imaginative beauty and noble rhythms.

Maud. In 1855 *Maud* was published. This poem he called a "monodrama." Parts of it are the melodramatic and hysterical ravings of an unbalanced man; other parts are the beautiful expression of passionate love. We object to its sentimental passage; the Victorian public objected to its passion and its lack of restraint.

Idylls of the King. Tennyson had long been interested in the Arthurian legends. In 1859 he published four idylls: "Enid," "Vivien," "Elaine," and "Guinevere." These poems were immediately successful. Their beauty and their narrative charm together with their moral allegory exactly fitted Victorian taste. In later years he continued the series which has remained the most popular of his works.

Enoch Arden. This poem, published in 1864, is a romantic story of a shipwrecked sailor who returned to England to find his wife happily married. The returned husband sacrificed himself to his wife's happiness. The poem was immensely popular.

Dramas. In 1875 Tennyson published the first of a series of poetic dramas, *Queen Mary.* It was played by Sir Henry Irving. He also wrote other plays: *Harold* (1876), *The Cup and the Falcon* (1884), and *Becket* (1884), only the last of which was successful on the stage. He was so much of a reflective poet that he could hardly have become a theatrical writer. All his plays are, however, good reading, particularly for those who know the history on which the dramatic action is based.

Later poems. Other volumes appeared continuously until his death: *Tiresias* (1885), *Locksley Hall Sixty Years After* (1886), *Demeter* (1889), *The Death of Oenone* (1892). In these volumes he showed great beauty of imagery and an extraordinary metrical gift. His treatment of classical themes is particularly successful.

His achievement. Tennyson is one of the great poets who is thoroughly and completely representative of his age. He expressed its noblest ideals in language of great imaginative power.

Furthermore, he was a master of beautiful song rhythms and of pictorial description. As a story teller, too, he showed great power. When occasion demanded, he could be simple and dramatic as in "The Revenge" and "The Charge of the Light Brigade."

His greatest achievement is his mastery of poetic form. No other English poet commanded more various verse forms. So entirely did he dominate the technique of poetry that, for a generation, minor poets in England and America followed the Tennysonian form.

SUGGESTIONS FOR FURTHER STUDY

1. The influence of Keats on Tennyson.
2. The use of Arthurian legend in *Idylls of the King*, Morris' *Defense of Guinevere*, Swinburne's *Tristram of Lyonesse*, and Robinson's *Tristram.*
3. Tennyson's reflections of Victorian science.
4. Religious ideas in *In Memoriam.*
5. Patriotism in Tennyson's poems.
6. Poems of English country life.
7. *Maud* as an expression of Tennyson's "romanticism."
8. A comparison of *Enoch Arden* with Masefield's *The Daffodil Fields.*
9. Tennyson's poetic imagery.
10. Tennyson's use of classical mythology.
11. Dramatic power in *Becket.*

USEFUL BOOKS

The best one-volume edition is in the Cambridge series, edited by W. J. Rolfe. There are excellent general sketches in *The Cambridge History of English Literature* and the *Encyclopaedia Britannica.* A good short life is in the English Men of Letters series, by A. Lyall. Good studies from the Victorian point of view are by Henry van Dyke and Stopford Brooke.

ROBERT BROWNING

1812–1889

Robert Browning was never so popular in his own time as was Tennyson. Instead of representing his age, he foreshadowed the ideals of the post-Victorian generation: strenuousness, virility, self-reliance, disregard for convention, and an interest in passionate emotion and intense drama. His chief interest was in complex, often wicked people in moments of psychological stress.

Life. Browning was born in London on May 7, 1812. His father was a banker and amateur in art. Browning had little regular schooling. He read widely in English literature and had a special interest in Shelley. With his father's approval he decided to devote his life to study and writing.

In 1833 he visited Russia, and in 1834, Italy, to which he became passionately attached. In 1846 he made a romantic marriage with Elizabeth Barrett who, at the time, was far better known as a poet than was he. They settled in Italy where a son was born. In Italy the Brownings passed fifteen happy years.

In 1861 Browning's wife died and he returned to England. His poetry was growing in popularity. He moved constantly in society.

In 1881 the Browning Society was established to study his works which had a reputation for depth and obscurity. He received many honors from universities. He wrote constantly until his death in 1889. He was buried in Westminster Abbey.

Early work. Browning's first poem "Pauline" (1833) is an obvious imitation of Shelley. Browning, himself, later regarded it as immature and destroyed all the copies he could find. "Paracelsus" (1835) and "Sordello" (1840) are narrative poems so obscure in thought, incoherent in expression, and crabbed in language, that they can be neglected by all except close students of his work.

Browning then wrote a series of dramas, only two of which, *A Blot in the 'Scutcheon* and *In a Balcony* have much dramatic power. In all his plays he tended toward minute psychological analysis rather than toward the simple, broad presentation of character which the theater demands.

Dramatic monologues. Browning's best work was published after 1844 in a series of volumes called *Bells and Pomegranates*. Many of these are in a form specially developed by Browning, the dramatic monologue, in which a man or woman in a moment of crisis speaks in such a way as completely to reveal his mind.

One of the best of these poems is "Pippa Passes." Pippa is an Italian mill girl who has her one day's holiday in the year. She wishes she might share in the life of four of the happiest groups of people in her town. As she goes singing on her way we see the four groups as they actually are. With deepest irony Browning shows men and women who are far from happy about to make critical decisions. In each case they make the right decision as they hear Pippa's song.

Other intensely dramatic studies are "The Bishop Orders His Tomb," "My Last Duchess," "In a Laboratory," "Fra Lippo Lippi," "Andrea del Sarto," and "Soliloquy in a Spanish Cloister." Browning's interest was not so much in complex people as in people who were picturesque and emotionally intense. For his subjects he explored forgotten incidents in the history of the Renaissance, especially in Italy and Spain, and romantic legends of the past.

In these dramatic monologues appear some of his most characteristic ideas: that action is better than inactivity, even though action leads to sin; that good eventually triumphs over evil; that "love is best"; and that a man's motives are more important than his achievements.

Other poems. In 1850 he published "Christmas Eve and Easter Day" which should be read with Tennyson's *In Memoriam* as a revelation of religious thought of the Victorian period.

In 1855 he showed his continued interest in picturesque personalities who reveal their characters in monologue in "Men and Women." In 1864 other poems of personal revelation in dramatic speech appeared in "Dramatis Personae."

The Ring and the Book. This long poem, published in four volumes in 1868 and 1869, is Browning's masterpiece. It is a retelling from ten points of view of a murder by one Guido Franceschini in Italy in the sixteenth century. Browning had found a complete report of the case in an "old yellow book." His imagination brought to life the characters and the story lived again.

Guido is the villain of the piece and is given two monologues. Pompilia, Guido's wife and victim, is highly idealized. She represents true womanhood and spiritualized love. Similarly, Caponsacchi, the priest who championed her, is endowed with noble, knightly qualities and is made an eloquent hero. Three popular points of view are presented, that of the defenders of Guido, that of the defenders of Pompilia, and that of the half-interested spectators. The speeches of the lawyers are given with the fullest detail.

The finest monologue in the poem is that of the Pope as the final arbiter of judgment. Here we have the verdict upon the case given by a man of the highest spiritual and ethical ideals, a man who stands above human contention and becomes as near divine as man can hope to be.

The greatness of *The Ring and the Book* does not lie, of course, in its subject, but in Browning's imaginative rendering of the obscure human motives in the story, in the splendid eloquence of much of the verse, and in the intense drama of such monologues as Guido's.

Later poems. After 1870 Browning produced a series of long poems. Some of them are "Prince Hohenstiel-Schwangau," "Fifine at the Fair," and "The Inn Album." They are all difficult and sometimes obscure. They are usually neglected by the reader of today in favor of the shorter poems which are easier to understand.

Browning's chief characteristics. The chief impressions which Browning's poems leave with the reader are: his virility, his idealism, his high ethical standards, his understanding of and sympathy with all human beings, his knowledge of human nature, and his defiant optimism.

His verse is often difficult and confused, his allusions sometimes cryptic and recondite. As in "Caliban upon Setebos" he often shows an overfondness for the grotesque.

Read in a wise selection, however, he is always interesting and always intensely human. No other English poet has more strength, vividness, courage, and variety. Aside from Shakespeare, no other poet ever showed so much dramatic power.

SUGGESTIONS FOR FURTHER STUDY

1. Browning's background of reading.
2. Browning's optimistic philosophy.
3. A study of a dramatic monologue with the following questions in mind: (*a*) Who is talking? to whom? in what circumstances? (*b*) What motives and traits of character are suggested in the poem? How are they suggested? (*c*) How is the background of time and place conveyed to the reader? (*d*) What hints of Browning's philosophy does the poem give you?
4. Guido, Pompilia, Caponsacchi, and the Pope in *The Ring and the Book.*
5. Difficulties in Browning's style.
6. Browning's metrical forms.
7. Elizabeth Barrett Browning.
8. Browning in Italy.
9. The effect of Pippa on four groups of people in *Pippa Passes.*
10. Browning as a dramatist.

USEFUL BOOKS

The best one-volume edition is in the Cambridge series, edited by H. E. Scudder. For difficult passages in Browning see *The Browning Cyclopaedia* by E. Berdoe and *Handbook to the Works of Robert Browning* by Mrs. Sutherland Orr. *Robert Browning* by G. K. Chesterton is an excellent short study. A good popular book is *Robert Browning, How to Know Him* by W. L. Phelps. The best life of Browning's wife is *Elizabeth Barrett Browning* by Louise Schutz Boas. See also the play, *The Barretts of Wimpole Street*, and *Flush; a Biography* by Virginia Woolf. The letters of the Brownings are available in two volumes. *The Old Yellow Book*, the source of *The Ring and the Book*, is in the Everyman series.

CONTEMPORARY POETRY

About 1914 began a new creative period in poetry. Like the romanticists of the early nineteenth century, the "new poets" aimed at spontaneity, individuality, and sincerity.

The admirers of the "new poetry" claim for it the following characteristics, some of which merely repeat Wordsworth's doctrines stated in his preface to *Lyrical Ballads* in 1800.

(1) The new poetry has discarded conventional poetic language for the natural speech of ordinary men. There is often a conscious attempt to use rough, uncouth, or vulgar speech.
(2) The new poetry is national and local in its interests. It takes its subjects from the commonplace and the familiar.
(3) The new poetry is highly experimental in its form. It often uses regular meters, but it tries to use them in a new way.
(4) The new poetry is hard, clear, and definite. It dislikes prettiness, moralizing, and sentimentality.

Since 1914 there have been hundreds of eager writers of poetry in England and America, many of them showing great originality and power. Only a few of those whose work has been most distinctive can be named here.

Edwin Arlington Robinson. Robinson was born in 1869 in Head Tide, Maine, a little village. His boyhood was passed in the town of Gardiner, near by. He studied at Harvard, leaving without graduating in 1893. He went to New York, earned a meager living in various ways, and published a book of verse, *Captain Craig*, in 1902. This book interested President Theodore Roosevelt so much that he sought out the poet and gave him a position in the New York Custom House. After 1910 Robinson was able to give his entire time to literature.

His chief works are: *Collected Poems* (1921), *Roman Bartholow* (1923), *The Man Who Died Twice* (1924), *Dionysus in Doubt* (1925), and *Tristram* (1927).

Many of his poems are searching, vivid, psychological analyses of New England men and women. Some of them are satirical; some cynical. Others are modern, disillusioned treatments of the Arthurian legends. All his poems are primarily intellectual. The lover of beautiful pictures, singing rhythms, and simple emotions will find little pleasure in Robinson's work. He is a thinker and analyst, a poet of the mind.

Amy Lowell. Miss Lowell was born in Brookline, Massachusetts, in 1874. James Russell Lowell was a distant relative. Abbott Lawrence Lowell, her brother, retired from the presidency of Harvard in 1933. She was privately educated and traveled widely. In 1902 she decided to write poetry. In 1910 she published for the first time. Her first volume, *A Dome of Many-colored Glass* (1912) showed the influence of Keats and Tennyson.

In *Sword Blades and Poppy Seed* (1914) and *Men, Women and Ghosts* (1916) she broke new ground and became the foremost American exponent of "imagism." Her vibrant personality soon made her widely known, and soon everyone was discussing her theories and her poems.

Other books are: *Can Grande's Castle* (1918), *Pictures of the Floating World* (1919), *Legends* (1921), and *What's O'Clock* (1925).

In 1925 she died.

Her poems are sharp, clear, and vivid. She delighted in startling images full of light and color. She was highly experimental and even fantastic in technique, as is shown particularly in her "polyphonic prose." Her intelligence was always sharp and active, and her imagination amazingly brilliant.

Robert Frost. Frost was born in San Francisco in 1875. Ten years later he went to New England where his family had lived for more than two hundred years. In 1892 he entered Dartmouth College where he remained for only a few months. He later worked as a mill hand. In 1895 he married. In 1897 he entered Harvard and studied there for two years. From 1900 to 1912 he farmed, taught school, made shoes, and worked on a newspaper.

In 1912 he went to England with his family. There he published in 1913 his first volume, *A Boy's Will*, the merits of which were immediately recognized. In 1914 he published *North of Boston*, a much better book, which gained him recognition in America.

In 1915 he returned to the United States. Since then he has farmed, lectured, and resided without teaching at the University of Michigan and at Amherst College.

His other volumes of poetry are *Mountain Interval* (1916) and *New Hampshire* (1923).

Frost is the poet of New England farm and country. He is always simple and always faithful to the realities of common life. Many of his poems are, however, rich with symbolic meanings.

His verse is always colloquial in rhythms and his vocabulary simple, but there is no question of his imaginative power. He has, too, a kind of whimsical humor, and his poems show that he looks at life with quiet happiness.

Carl Sandburg. Sandburg was born at Galesburg, Illinois, in 1878. He is of Swedish descent. At thirteen he began earning his living and came to understand and to sympathize with the point of view of workingmen, farmers, and laborers. At twenty he served in the Spanish-American War. After the war he entered Lombard College. In 1914 he was awarded a prize for a group of poems in the magazine *Poetry*. From then on he wrote steadily and became one of the most widely read and discussed writers of the "new poetry."

Sandburg has used chiefly "free verse." He has chosen subjects not generally favored by poets: laborers, people of the slums, and the many activities of the city. Shops, factories, steel mills, and the crude life of Western farms have been his special interest. He has used slang and rough speech, and has glorified energy, strength, and endurance. He has a strong sympathy for those whom industry has exploited: working women, children, and immigrant laborers.

Many of his poems show tenderness and an appreciation of lyric beauty like "Cool Tombs" and "Fog." His greatest achievement has been his finding beauty and human warmth where other men see ugliness and even degradation.

He has given much time to the study of American social history, to the revival of American folk songs, and to writing highly imaginative stories for children.

His best-known volumes are: *Chicago Poems* (1916), *Cornhuskers* (1918), and *Smoke and Steel* (1920).

Edna St. Vincent Millay. Miss Millay, the most popular of the younger contemporary American poets, was born in 1892 at Rockland, Maine. She graduated from Vassar in 1917, and has since spent her life in travel and writing.

She follows traditional forms in most of her poetry, using particularly the sonnet. She has been much influenced by Keats. She writes chiefly of passionate love, intense beauty, and youthful disillusion. She has written poetic dramas. *Aria Da Capo* is a bitter satire on war; *The King's Henchman*, a poetic libretto for an opera.

Her admirers speak chiefly of her lyric gift, her emotional intensity, and her pursuit of sensuous beauty.

Some of her volumes, all small in compass, are: *Renascence* (1917), *Second April* (1921), *A Few Figs from Thistles* (1921), *The Harp Weaver* (1923), and *The Buck in the Snow* (1928).

Walter De la Mare. De la Mare was born in Kent, England, in 1873. His family is descended from French Huguenots who emigrated to England in the eighteenth century.

He was educated in a London school. At seventeen he entered business and for eighteen years worked in a London office.

In 1908, having received a grant from the English government, he gave up business to devote himself to literature. He has written and published steadily since 1902 small volumes of poetry, several novels, and many short stories. His *Collected Poems* were issued in 1920.

His poems fall into two groups: romantic fantasies like "The Listeners," and poems of childhood like "A Child's Day."

His work is marked by extreme delicacy, by a haunting sense of something mysterious beyond our knowledge of ordinary life, and by a remarkable command of poetic music. In the realm of delicate fantasy he is unequaled. His favorite poetic themes are the strangeness of the adult world as children see it, the beauty of silence, shadows, and flowers, and the magic of daydreams. His range of subject is not wide, but in his own field he is always the complete artist.

John Masefield. Masefield was born in 1878 in Herefordshire, England. He attended a village school for a few years. At fourteen he went to sea as an apprentice on a sailing ship which rounded Cape Horn. He learned the realities of life aboard ship, but he learned also to love the beauty of ships and the wonder and romance of the sea.

In 1895 he gave up sea life and found himself in New York with five dollars in his pocket. He did all sorts of odd jobs to keep himself alive. Finally he secured steady work in a carpet factory in Yonkers, New York. He had always hoped to write, and now, having regular wages, he began to buy and read poetry in the hope that he could himself become a poet. Chaucer seems to have given him a great impetus; he then carefully read Keats, Shelley, Milton, and Shakespeare.

In 1897 he returned to England.

His first book, *Salt-Water Ballads*, appeared in 1902. Then followed other poems, some tales in prose, and several plays. In 1911 a verse tale of English village life, *The Everlasting Mercy*, made a notable success. Other long narrative poems followed: *The Widow in the Bye Street* (1912), *Dauber* (1913), and *The Daffodil Fields* (1913).

During the Great War Masefield served with the Red Cross in France and at Gallipoli. He wrote several war books, among them *Gallipoli* (1916), one of the best prose works which the War inspired.

After the War he continued to write narrative poems, among them *Reynard the Fox* (1919), *Right Royal* (1920), and *Enslaved* (1920). He also wrote several novels.

He has received many honors and prizes for his poetry, and in 1930 he succeeded Robert Bridges as Poet Laureate of England.

Masefield's poetry first received attention because of its brutal realism of subject and vocabulary, and because it was a frank and honest treatment of simple and elemental human passions. With the appearance of *Dauber* he was recognized as the greatest of English writers of the sea, and readers recognized his sense of beauty and his delicacy of perception.

All his poems show an understanding of simple human nature and a love of the out-of-doors. He writes with vigor, freshness, and vitality. His verse moves rapidly and often has great delicacy of rhythm.

Even his admirers agree that he has written too much and so fast that some of his poetry is rough and thin. There is no doubt, however, that in imaginative intensity, in perception of beauty, and in range of interest he stands high among contemporary poets.

Alfred Noyes. Noyes was born in Staffordshire, England, in 1880. He received his education at Exeter College, Oxford.

By 1913 he had written eight volumes of poetry. He was so well known that he was invited to lecture on "The Sea in English Poetry" at the Lowell Institute in Boston. Yale gave him an honorary degree, and Princeton made him Professor of Modern English Literature, a position which he held until 1923.

Noyes has been very popular in academic circles because of his scholarship, his conservatism, and his opposition to the "new poetry." In his writings and lectures he has stressed the value of adherence to tradition and to conventional ideals of beauty.

During the Great War Noyes served the British government in the Foreign Office.

Besides writing more than twenty-five volumes of verse, he has edited anthologies and written literary criticism.

Some of the best known of his poems are: *Drake*, "Forty Singing Seamen," "The Barrel Organ," and "The Highwayman."

His chief poetic qualities are his command over lilting rhythms and his ability to dash off a tale with spontaneity and gayety. He makes no demands upon the minds of his readers, and he writes with such evident joy that he captivates those who like their poetry bright, musical, and easy.

Rupert Brooke. Brooke was born in 1884 at Rugby, in England. His father taught in the famous Rugby School. Brooke received the regular education of an English boy of his class and went to Cambridge University.

In search of adventure he traveled to Tahiti in the Pacific. When the War broke out in 1914 he obtained a commission in the British Army. He died in Greece during the British attack upon the Dardanelles in 1915.

He is the most romantic and Byronic of the younger poets. Like Byron he was handsome, magnetic, brilliant, and disillusioned. He traveled about in search of something, he knew not what, and ended with homesickness for what he had left.

The War was to him a real expression of the romance for which he had been vainly seeking. It was perhaps as well for him that he died while the adventure lasted. In the post-War period he would have been utterly miserable.

His collected poems were published in 1915.

Brooke had a great zest for life and the kind of imagination that fills everything with poetry. These qualities are combined with rhythmic freedom and beauty of expression in such poems as "The Old Vicarage, Grantchester" and "The Great Lover."

His occasional moods of romantic exaltation are best seen in his sonnets such as "If I should die, think only this of me" and "Oh! Death will find me, long before I tire."

SUGGESTIONS FOR FURTHER STUDY

1. Choose poems from an anthology of contemporary poetry which illustrate the qualities of "the new poetry" outlined in this section.
2. Choose one poem by each author mentioned in this section. Show how each poem illustrates what is said here about its author.
3. Make a study of a contemporary poet. Point out about each one: (*a*) facts about his life, education, literary theories, (*b*) his chief works, (*c*) his ideas, emotional tone, verse forms, word music, imagery, (*d*) the chief qualities in his work which stamp him as "modern."
4. Make a study of one of the following long poems:

Benét	*John Brown's Body*
De la Mare	*A Child's Day*
MacLeish	*Conquistador*
Masefield	*Dauber*
Master	*Spoon River Anthology*
Noyes	*Drake*
Robinson	*Tristram*

5. Echoes in contemporary poetry of Tennyson, Keats, Byron, and Wordsworth.
6. The village in contemporary poetry.
7. The city in contemporary poetry.

USEFUL BOOKS

The best sources for information about contemporary poetry are:

Monroe and Henderson	*The New Poetry*
Sanders and Nelson	*Chief Modern Poets*
Untermeyer, Louis	*Modern Poetry: American and British* (Combined edition of *Modern American Poetry* and *Modern British Poetry*)

CHAPTER 33

THE GREAT DRAMATISTS

CHRISTOPHER MARLOWE
1564–1593

The first English dramatist of real distinction was Christopher Marlowe.

Life. He was born in Canterbury on February 6, 1564. He attended a school in the town and in 1578 entered what is now Corpus Christi College in Cambridge. He took his bachelor's degree in 1584. By 1587 he had gone to London and had joined a company of players as a writer of plays. Apparently he was not popular with other writers like Nashe, Greene, and Gabriel Harvey; but he had many friends among the noblemen who patronized the theater, notably Sir Walter Raleigh.

His career as a dramatic writer was brief. He was killed in a quarrel in 1593. In his short life, however, he wrote two beautiful poems and four important plays. In addition he made blank verse the literary medium of Elizabethan drama, and received full appreciation from Shakespeare, who was strongly influenced by him.

Poems. The brief pastoral poem, "The Passionate Shepherd," has been justly called a work "of pure fancy and radiant melody without break or pause." "Hero and Leander" (unfinished) is a richly imaginative narrative poem in heroic couplets on the classical story of two famous lovers.

Plays. Marlowe had almost nothing in the way of models. The plays before his time, however interesting historically, were weak in creative power. Marlowe worked out an original method for tragedy, and left an indelible mark on Elizabethan drama.

Tamburlaine the Great, a play in two parts, each of five acts, displays the almost legendary conqueror as the "superman" in whom Elizabethan drama delighted. The conqueror is figured as a man freed from all restraint of kindness, conscience, or altruism, bent upon one goal, the exaltation of his own power.

The play presents a pageant of Tamburlaine's march to power and his love for "divine Zenocrate." Nothing stands before him; kings draw his chariot and he slaughters his enemies by thousands. But he in turn cannot stand before death and human weakness. His beloved queen dies; he grows old and dies in turn. Marlowe seems to say that the tragedy of human greatness lies in the fact that it is human. However great man's lust for power may be, and however he may triumph, in the end his fate is death.

As *Tamburlaine* represents the thirst for power, *Dr. Faustus* represents the thirst for knowledge. Faustus sells his soul for complete experience of all earthly sensations. The play contains many passages of supreme poetic beauty.

In *The Jew of Malta,* the forerunner of Shakespeare's *Merchant of Venice,* Marlowe attempted to depict the tragedy of a man who craved "infinite riches" and who was possessed by a fiendish mania for revenge. The Jew, Barabas, is a monster of craft, greed, and cruelty, a "superman" in deviltry. Inevitably as the play progresses it is forced into what, compared with Shakespeare's play, is mere caricature.

Elizabethan audiences were fond of dramatized history. *Edward the Second* pictures a weak king surrounded by favorites and careless of his people's welfare. It has little of the blustering and even madness of the earlier plays, and none of their splendid poetry. But it has far greater reality, and, were it not overshadowed by Shakespeare's history plays, would be regarded more highly than it often is.

Marlowe's achievement. As a dramatist Marlowe lacked any real knowledge of human nature and of the workings of men's minds. He is really great as a poet. His plays are full of imaginative fire. Such passages as

> Infinite riches in a little room

and

> Was this the face that launch'd a thousand ships
> And burnt the topless towers of Ilium?

and

> O, thou art fairer than the evening air
> Clad in the beauty of a thousand stars

have the special quality of splendid imagination which is the glory of Elizabethan poetry.

Moreover, though Marlowe did not invent blank verse, he developed it into the flexible and musical form which made it the best vehicle for poetic drama. It was from Marlowe that Shakespeare learned the use of blank verse in his great plays.

SUGGESTIONS FOR FURTHER STUDY

1. Elizabethan splendor and extravagance in *Tamburlaine*.
2. A comparison of *The Jew of Malta* with *The Merchant of Venice*.
3. Compare *Edward II* with Shakespeare's *King Richard II* from the following points of view:
   (*a*) use of sources, (*b*) subject matter, (*c*) characterization, (*d*) dramatic effectiveness, (*e*) style.
4. *Dr. Faustus* as an expression of the Renaissance spirit.

USEFUL BOOKS

An excellent one-volume edition of Marlowe is edited by C. F. Tucker Brooke. The *Encyclopaedia Britannica* has a long article on Marlowe. This should be supplemented by *The Death of Christopher Marlowe* by J. Leslie Hotson. A scholarly survey of biographical material is *Marlowe and His Circle* by F. S. Boas. See also *The Cambridge History of English Literature.*

WILLIAM SHAKESPEARE
1564–1616

Life. Shakespeare was the son of John Shakespeare, a merchant of Stratford, and Mary Arden Shakespeare, daughter of a prosperous farmer. In 1568 his father rose to be mayor of the town, but in later years he became poor and lost public office.

Of Shakespeare's early life we actually know very little. We know that he was christened at Stratford on April 26, 1564. From this date we infer that he was born on April 23, since children were commonly christened three days after birth. Since there was a free "grammar school" in Stratford, so-called because Latin grammar was the chief subject taught, we may infer that he was educated there. Of course, as far as facts go, he may never have gone to school at all.

We know that he married Anne Hathaway in 1582. We know that he had three children, two daughters and one son. Aside from such traditions as his having been a schoolmaster and his having left Stratford because he killed game unlawfully on a gentleman's land, we have no other actual knowledge until 1592.

In 1592 Robert Greene, a contemporary playwright, referred in a pamphlet to a man whom he called a "Shake-scene" who used other men's ideas and remodeled old plays and had a "Tygers heart wrapt in a Players hide." From this reference we infer that he meant Shakespeare, since we know that in the third *King Henry VI* play, which is attributed to Shakespeare, there occurs the line "O Tiger's heart wrapt in a woman's hide." Hence we say that by 1592, Shakespeare was a rising playwright in London who must have been in the service of a dramatic company rewriting old plays and working in collaboration, as was the custom, with other playwrights.

We know that he had influential friends because the publisher of the pamphlet apologized for Greene's attack. Moreover "Venus and Adonis" and "The Rape of Lucrece," two long poems published in 1593 and 1594 and bearing Shakespeare's name, were dedicated to the Earl of Southampton in language which implies more than common friendship. Hence we infer that Shakespeare was known at court and probably played before Queen Elizabeth. There is an actual record of a performance before the Queen in 1594 in which his name is mentioned.

In 1598 he was mentioned by name by a critic as the best dramatist in comedy and tragedy. In 1597 he bought a house in Stratford; in 1599 he received in his father's name a coat of arms which made him, technically, a "gentleman." There are actual records of purchases of property and of law suits in which he appeared.

During his lifetime fourteen plays were published apparently based upon texts which were reliable. In 1609 his sonnets were published. Five other plays were apparently "pirated," that is, printed without his consent or that of the company which owned the manuscripts. All these publications are known as "the quartos," from their size.

In 1611 he had stopped writing and had returned to live at Stratford as a well-to-do country gentleman. He died in 1616.

The Folio. In 1623 two friends who had acted in his company published the first collected edition of his plays, the First Folio, a large volume with his portrait. Upon the Folio and the quartos all modern texts are based. The Folio presented twenty plays which had never before been printed, the plays which had been printed in "good" quartos, and two which had appeared only in pirated editions.

Shakespeare, the man. Shakespeare appears in his plays, in the records, and in tradition, as a highly successful dramatist and business man, as an honest man with an excellent reputation, and as a kindly, pleasant person who was well liked and had many friends. It is clear that he noticed everything about him in contemporary life and that he had an extraordinary memory for what he saw, heard, and read. It is evident that he knew Latin well and that he had an excellent command of French. His knowledge of Roman and English history was, for his time, extensive. He knew medieval love stories, Italian tales, and much English literature. He had a special interest in law, medicine, seamanship, hunting, and English folk-lore. He knew much about music and flowers. Above all he had the most extraordinary knowledge of human nature and what we call "psychology" that any writer in any language ever possessed.

Poems. Had Shakespeare never written one play he would still have been famous as a poet. "Venus and Adonis" and "The Rape of Lucrece" are the finest examples of Elizabethan romantic tales founded on classic legend. His Sonnets are the most beautiful in English. Whether or not the story which they unfold has any basis in actual fact is unknown, but there is no doubt about their imagery, their haunting music, and their glorious imaginative power. The songs in his plays place him among the great lyric writers. They deserve special attention not only for their beauty, but for their dramatic effectiveness in the places where they occur.

First dramatic period. The plays written before 1594 show Shakespeare as an experimenter with popular forms and as the adapter of themes used by other writers of his time.

Titus Andronicus is a melodramatic tragedy full of the wildest and most horrible crimes committed by villains of the blackest nature. Aside from one or two passages of descriptive beauty, the play is so strained and violent that many people refuse to believe that Shakespeare wrote it.

The three *King Henry VI* plays and *King Richard II* are history plays probably written in collaboration with Marlowe and others.

Love's Labor's Lost is a witty court comedy obviously modeled upon the work of Lyly.

Two Gentlemen of Verona is a romantic comedy of love, influenced by the plays of Robert Greene. It stresses a popular theme of the time, the conflict between love and friendship, and introduces one of Shakespeare's standard devices, a woman disguised as a boy. The device was useful because all women's parts were played by men or boys.

The Comedy of Errors is an adaptation of a Roman comedy by Plautus. By "errors" is meant mistakes arising from the confusion of people who look alike. Two gentlemen who are twins have twins as slaves, and the resulting "errors" make a merry farce.

Second dramatic period: 1594–1600. This is the period of the great history plays and of romantic comedy.

A Midsummer Night's Dream has three elements of comedy: the mistakes of four lovers who wander about one night in a forest outside Athens; a parallel series of adventures among the fairy folk led by Oberon and Titania; and the production of a play by a group of mechanics, who, though nominally Athenians, are really English.

Romeo and Juliet is the tragic story of two "star-cross'd" lovers who would have been happy had they not belonged to two opposing families. The scene is laid in Italy.

The Merchant of Venice, the scene of which is also laid in Italy, is a romantic comedy. Modern audiences are likely to see the play from Shylock's point of view as more tragic than comic.

The Taming of the Shrew is a farce showing how a masterful young man broke the will of a girl with a temper and made her a good wife.

Much Ado about Nothing is a witty romantic comedy. *As You Like It* tells a romantic story of lovers in the Forest of Arden. *Twelfth Night* is Shakespeare's gayest and most lyrical comedy. One of its characters, Malvolio, is a satire upon the Puritans. We now are inclined to pity him as we do Shylock, though Shakespeare's audience certainly thought that he got what he deserved.

The two parts of *King Henry IV*, and *King Henry V* are a kind of dramatic epic of patriotism. They are famous for the fat Falstaff, the greatest of Shakespeare's comic creations. Falstaff appears again in *The Merry Wives of Windsor*, which tradition says was written by command of Queen Elizabeth who wished to see the fat knight in love.

Third dramatic period: 1600–1608. Shakespeare now turned his attention to tragic themes. Three of the tragedies are based upon Roman history: *Julius Caesar*, *Antony and Cleopatra*, and *Coriolanus.* The last shows a favorite idea with Shakespeare, that an able aristocratic leader is never popular with the fickle, mindless mob.

Four plays are bitter satires upon human nature. They are not tragedies in form, but they are tragic in their deep pessimism. They are *All's Well That Ends Well*, *Measure for Measure*, *Troilus and Cressida*, and *Timon of Athens.*

Three plays show the tragic effect upon men of uncontrolled and misdirected emotion. In *Macbeth* an essentially good man is led by ambition to commit murder. He is punished by his conscience to such an extent that death comes as a welcome release. In *King Lear* a foolish old king, unable to distinguish between true and false affection, is pursued to madness and death by two unfilial daughters. In *Othello* a brave warrior is tormented by jealousy at the instigation of a subtle, soulless villain, Iago. He kills his innocent wife, Desdemona, and himself.

The greatest play of the group is *Hamlet*, the most famous tragedy ever written. Hamlet, a victim of melancholia, seeks revenge for his father's murder. In the end, his delayed revenge brings about the death of all the chief characters. The play is the most intellectual of all the tragedies.

Fourth dramatic period: 1609–1611. Shakespeare ended his dramatic career with a series of dramatized romances which carry their characters through sadness and misfortune to a happy ending. *Pericles* is a dramatization of an old Greek romance. *Cymbeline* tells a mingled story of adventure in ancient Britain and Renaissance Italy. *The Winter's Tale* mingles the blackest jealousy of a king with the serene high-mindedness of a noble queen and a beautiful, pastoral love tale of a prince and princess. In *The Tempest*, which combines beautiful poetry, adventure on a distant island, grotesque characterization, and an idyl of young love, Shakespeare, as the leading character, Prospero, the wise magician, seems to take leave of the stage forever.

Works as a whole. Shakespeare's genius was so great, his field so broad and various, and his poetry at once so powerfully intellectual and so lyrically moving, that readers sometimes forget that he was a man of his time. He was a popular playwright working for a popular stage. Really to understand him, one must know his contemporaries, his theater, and the England of his time.

The themes of which he wrote were those in which his time was interested; the stories which he borrowed for his plots were already familiar to his audiences.

But though working always in harmony with popular taste he constantly rose above it. When he borrowed a plot he always transformed it into something finer. When he made use of characters already invented he made them more human.

To create men and women of permanent human interest, to present them in moments of dramatic intensity which never lose their vividness, and to make them speak in words which ring with a music more than earthly—this was Shakespeare's achievement and the glory of Elizabethan drama.

SUGGESTIONS FOR FURTHER STUDY

1. The following plays not usually studied in schools may be used for reports by individual students:

   Farce: *The Taming of the Shrew, The Comedy of Errors*
   Romantic comedy: *Twelfth Night, Much Ado about Nothing*
   Chronicle play: *King Henry IV*, Parts I and II
   Tragedy: *Othello, King Lear, Antony and Cleopatra, Coriolanus*
   Dramatic romance: *A Winter's Tale, Cymbeline, The Tempest*

2. How many of the following Shakespearean characters do you know? In which play does each appear? What does each do in the play? What are the chief characteristics of each? What are the most famous scenes and speeches of each?

Mercutio	Prince Hal	Imogen
Benedick and Beatrice	Hotspur	Caliban
Dogberry	Polonius	Malvolio
Rosalind	Iago	Ariel
Jaques	Cleopatra	Prospero
Falstaff	Perdita	

3. Shakespeare and Roman history.
4. Shakespeare and Italy.
5. Songs in Shakespeare's plays.

6. Shakespeare and the law.
7. Shakespeare's idea of tragedy.

USEFUL BOOKS

The best one-volume edition is in the Cambridge series, edited by W. A. Neilson. *Hamlet* and *Macbeth* have been edited in a new form with a commentary by Joseph Quincy Adams. The New Cambridge edition of single plays is the most modern edition. For plays not yet published in this edition, the student will find the New Hudson edition most useful. The best lives are by Sidney Lee and Joseph Quincy Adams. The volumes in the Furness Variorum edition are encyclopædic in scope. *Shakespeare's England* edited in two volumes by various authors is a complete survey of Shakespeare's time. For a briefer sketch see *Social Backgrounds of English Literature* by Boas and Hahn.

The following books contain excellent critical material:

Bailey, John	*Shakespeare*
Baker, G. P.	*The Development of Shakespeare as a Dramatist*
Bradley, A. C.	*Shakespearean Tragedy, Oxford Lectures on Poetry*
Knight, G. W.	*The Wheel of Fire*
Naylor, E. W.	*Shakespeare and Music*
Neilson, W. A. and Thorndike, A. H.	*The Facts about Shakespeare*
Smith, D. N.	*Shakespeare Criticism*
Stoll, E. E.	*Shakespeare Studies*
Symonds, J. A.	*Shakespeare's Predecessors*
Wilson, J. D.	*The Essential Shakespeare*

BEN JONSON

1573–1637

In his own day Ben Jonson was looked up to with respect and even reverence by young writers. In the eighteenth century he was often admired above Shakespeare. In the nineteenth century he began to lose prestige. Today no one except serious students of literature reads his works.

The reason for Jonson's decline in popularity is simple. He had a serious dramatic theory on which he patterned all his plays. As long as that theory was popular, he was admired. When, however, readers admired spontaneity, beauty, liveliness and good humor above theories of dramatic art, naturally they neglected a man whose works lack those qualities.

Jonson's life. Jonson was born in Westminster, now a part of London, in 1573. His father, a clergyman, died before his birth. His stepfather was a bricklayer. Tradition says that Ben was, in his youth, a bricklayer, too. About 1593 he served in the army.

His first play, acted in 1598, indicates that he was a practiced writer for the stage. We infer, then, that after 1593 he worked for a theatrical company.

He fought a duel and barely escaped a death sentence for killing his adversary. He quarreled violently with contemporary writers, but by 1605 he appears as a literary leader at the Mermaid Tavern. Here, tradition says, he and Shakespeare spent many an evening of good-fellowship.

He was a favorite with King James I and with the court. Until 1625 his plays were all successful. After King James' death in that year, his plays failed and he turned to writing masques. As he grew older his health failed and he became involved in more quarrels. In 1637 he died. He was buried in Westminster Abbey.

Comedies. Jonson adhered to the old theory of "humors." According to this theory a man's character was dependent upon the adjustment of "humors" within his body. In many men one "humor" or another appears to excess, and hence some men are cowardly, quarrelsome, greedy, boastful, tricky, etc. Jonson believed that comedy ought to satirize these "humors" and thus correct the follies, affectations, and vices of humanity. Jonson's comedies are, therefore, didactic; that is, they aim to teach useful lessons and make men better.

He believed, moreover, that plays ought to adhere to the "rules" of classic criticism. They ought to be unified, and above all, be true to the facts of life as interpreted by serious observers.

His best-known comedies are realistic pictures of London life: *Every Man in His Humor* (1598); *Every Man out of His Humor* (1598); *The Alchemist* (1610); and *Bartholomew Fair* (1614). These plays lack charm, gayety, and good-nature, but they are an admirable gallery of types of the time and show us clearly that human foolishness remains pretty much the same as the years go on.

Volpone (1605) is a story of human wickedness and greed almost passing belief. The scene is laid in Italy. It lacks the historical in-

LIVING ROOM IN SHAKESPEARE'S HOUSE, STRATFORD-ON-AVON

Courtesy of the Metropolitan Museum of Art

"THE PIERCE-NICHOLS HOUSE, SALEM,"
BY FELICIA WALDO HOWELL

The grace, dignity, and charm of the eighteenth century, so well represented in this old house, find adequate expression in the essays of the period.

terest of the London plays, but is an extraordinary study of human meanness at its worst.

Tragedies. Jonson's two tragedies, *Sejanus* (1603) and *Catiline* (1611) are serious, scholarly, intellectual, and well constructed, but, to us, utterly lacking in humanity.

Other work. As a writer of masques Jonson became famous. Unfortunately so much of the masque depended upon costumes, scenery, and music, that his work in this field cannot have as much interest for the reader as have his comedies.

He wrote also some beautifully phrased lyrics, and some literary criticism which, after 1660, had an important influence. His critical ideas are not original, but were borrowed from the Italian criticism of the Renaissance.

His achievement. Jonson's achievement, historically, was important. His theory of humors was adopted by other dramatists and is really not yet obsolete. The serious student who is willing to give Jonson time and attention will find his comedies and his personality of much historical interest.

SUGGESTIONS FOR FURTHER STUDY

1. Jonson's theory of "humors."
2. London life in Jonson's plays.
3. Jonson and Shakespeare.
4. A comparison of Shakespeare's *Julius Caesar* and Jonson's *Catiline.*
5. Objects of Jonson's satire in *The Alchemist.*
6. Jonson's dramatic power in *The Silent Woman.*

USEFUL BOOKS

The most accessible edition of Jonson is in the Everyman series. Selections from his plays will be found in *Chief Elizabethan Dramatists* by W. A. Neilson. For his life see *Ben Jonson* by G. G. Smith in the English Men of Letters series. There is a good essay by C. H. Herford in *Representative English Comedies* edited by C. M. Gayley, volume II. For a general survey see *The Cambridge History of English Literature* and the *Encyclopaedia Britannica.*

LATER DRAMA

Seventeenth century. The London theaters were closed by the Puritans in 1642. With the restoration of King Charles II in 1660 they opened again with heroic plays and "comedies of manners."

The heroic play was a tragedy in rhyme, improbable in plot, presenting characters of preposterous emotions, picturing love as a devastating passion and furnished with a lavish stage setting. A well-known heroic play is Dryden's *The Conquest of Granada.*

The comedy of manners reflected the witty, superficial court of King Charles. Its interest lay in its reflection of a shallow and hypocritical social life. The conversation of the characters sparkled with epigram and wit. William Congreve's (1670–1729) *Love for Love* and *The Way of the World* show with a light touch and flashing wit complete penetration into the characters of people who attempt to live a shallow life without regard for truth or morality.

Eighteenth century and after. In the eighteenth century English drama steadily declined in power and interest. It was rapidly overshadowed by the novel. In the late eighteenth century David Garrick began a revival of Shakespeare's plays. With Oliver Goldsmith's (1728–1774) *She Stoops to Conquer* and Richard Brinsley Sheridan's (1751–1816) *The Rivals* and *The School for Scandal,* comedy had a brief revival of brilliance. But the interest in drama as a literary form speedily declined again, and farces, melodrama, pantomimes, imitations of Shakespeare, and adaptations from the French satisfied theater goers until the modern revival of drama after 1880.

The new drama. After 1880 came a rebirth of interest in the drama. Under the influence of Continental playwrights, particularly of the Norwegian Henrik Ibsen (1828–1906), English dramatic literature came once more to a new and vigorous life. But the old forms were gone. Tragedy and comedy no longer had their old meanings. The conventional division into five acts was disregarded. The new realism insisted upon a drama which should give an accurate picture of life in natural dialogue with a setting accurately reproducing the background of modern life. Among the many dramatists in England and America since 1880, four may be chosen as representative: George Bernard Shaw, J. M. Barrie, John Galsworthy, and Eugene O'Neill.

George Bernard Shaw. Shaw was born in Dublin, Ireland, in 1856. His parents were of English origin, but Shaw always joyously proclaims himself an Irishman.

Shaw's career began in business. Then he wrote novels and reviewed books for a magazine. Later he became an art critic, music critic, and finally dramatic critic. He was always revolutionary in his ideas and tried to interest the British public in such personalities as Ibsen, Nietzsche, Karl Marx, and Wagner. In 1884 he joined a socialist society and worked steadily to spread socialistic doctrine.

Plays Pleasant and Unpleasant appeared in 1898. Immediately it was realized that here was a dramatist who had something new to say. This impression was intensified by *Man and Superman* (1903), his most typical play.

Thereafter Shaw became an international figure. His vivid and pungent satire, his startling paradoxes, the fluent, brilliant speech of his characters, and his own striking personality all made him interesting.

Other interesting plays are: *Androcles and the Lion* (1912), *Pygmalion* (1912), and *Saint Joan* (1923).

All of Shaw's plays try to upset some current social or historical prejudice. His mission has been to jar the world into a recognition of the realities behind superficial appearances.

James Matthew Barrie. Barrie was born in Scotland in 1860. He was educated at Edinburgh University. From 1883 to 1885 he practiced journalism in Scotland. In 1885 he moved to London and soon received recognition for his Scottish novels and sketches.

Barrie began writing for the stage in 1892 with a farce-comedy. Thereafter came a series of gently romantic comedies. In 1903 his success was assured by the presentation of *Quality Street*, *The Admirable Crichton*, and *Little Mary*.

His beautiful fantasy *Peter Pan* (1904) brought him international fame. Later plays were: *Alice-Sit-by-the-Fire* (1905), *What Every Woman Knows* (1908), *Dear Brutus* (1917), and *Mary Rose* (1920).

Barrie is the most beloved of contemporary dramatists. Unlike Shaw he is no preacher; unlike Shaw, too, he is tender, wistful, and somewhat sentimental. When his plays have a lesson as has *Dear Brutus*, the lesson is gently insinuated with whimsical irony and sympathetic characterization. He is, moreover, a thorough theatrical craftsman, as Shaw is not, and his plays are popular favorites for acting.

John Galsworthy. Galsworthy is so important as a novelist that his dramatic activities are sometimes undervalued.

In his plays one sees particularly his humanitarian sympathies and his logical power. All his plays are careful in construction and reasoning.

In Galsworthy's plays theme overshadows characterization. Thus one remembers *The Silver Box* (1909) because with mathematical precision it shows that there is one law for the rich and another for the poor. In *Justice* (1910), so striking is his presentation of the iniquities of the prison system that the play actually brought about changes in the English prisons. In other plays, as in *Loyalties* (1922), he discusses typical moral and social situations which exist in our complex modern life. He shows that life bristles with social difficulties which cause unnecessary personal suffering. He does not, however, attempt to solve the questions which he raises.

Americans can appreciate the moral intensity and the beautiful structure of his plays, but they cannot, as can the English, always enter into their situations with full understanding.

Eugene O'Neill. O'Neill was born in New York City in 1888. His father was a prominent actor. He attended Princeton from 1906 to 1907. Then for seven years he lived a roving, adventurous life. He spent two years at sea. He also lived in the Argentine. In 1914 he studied the writing of drama at Harvard.

After 1914 he became well known for his one-act plays like *Thirst* (1914) and *Ile* (1919).

His first theatrical successes were *Anna Christie* (1920) and *The Emperor Jones* (1920).

In the last ten years O'Neill has become the most interesting dramatist writing in English. He has been highly experimental in many directions. In *The Great God Brown* he uses masks; in *Strange Interlude* two sets of dialogue, one the actual spoken words of the characters, and one the characters' unspoken thoughts. *Marco Millions* is an experiment in making a play out of a series of pictorial episodes.

Lately he has been experimenting with the findings of the "new psychology." *Mourning Becomes Electra* is a trilogy entirely new in form and spirit. It is the most modern form of tragedy, and excited, when it appeared, the widest interest.

His latest plays, *Ah, Wilderness!* and *Days Without End*, show his continued interest in experiment and innovation. The first is a delightfully fresh comedy of adolescent love. The second presents with deep seriousness the idea that a stricken soul can find help and comfort only by faith in God.

Students of the drama are agreed that O'Neill is the most promising dramatist now living.

SUGGESTIONS FOR FURTHER STUDY

1. Dryden's *Conquest of Granada* as an heroic play.
2. A comparison of Shakespeare's *Antony and Cleopatra* with Dryden's *All for Love.*
3. Otway's *Venice Preserved.*
4. Congreve's *The Way of the World* and Sheridan's *The School for Scandal.*
5. Farcical elements in Goldsmith's *She Stoops to Conquer* and Sheridan's *The Rivals.*
6. The following modern plays may be used for reports by individual students:

Ibsen:	*A Doll's House*—the "new woman" asserts herself
	An Enemy of the People—the idealistic individual defies society
	The Wild Duck—the idealistic reformer wrecks a happy home
	Rosmersholm—a study of the influence of ideas, traditions, and emotions on two people
Shaw:	*Arms and the Man*—a satire on romantic ideas of war
	The Devil's Disciple—a satire on Puritanism and romanticism
	Caesar and Cleopatra—Shaw's "debunking" of the romantic notions of Cleopatra
	Candida—the ideal woman makes a womanly choice
	Androcles and the Lion—a satire on various conceptions of Christianity and service
	Saint Joan—Shaw's idea of the rise of Protestantism and nationalism
Galsworthy:	*The Silver Box*—an attack on injustice in the courts
	Strife—the conflict of labor and capital
	Loyalties—loyalty versus justice
	Escape—the individual cannot act alone
Barrie:	*The Admirable Crichton*—aristocracy versus democracy
	Quality Street—the schoolmistress captures the soldier
	What Every Woman Knows—A Scotch lassie with a secret
	Peter Pan—the boy who wouldn't grow up
	Dear Brutus—"if we had our lives to live over"
	Mary Rose—showing that love is "Time's fool"

O'Neill: *The Emperor Jones*—atavistic fear pursues a man
The Hairy Ape—society crushes an outcast
Anna Christie—a woman seeks to free herself from the past
Marco Millions—a satire on commercial progress
All God's Chillun Got Wings—the tragedy of a marriage between a Negro and a white girl
Mourning Becomes Electra—a psychological tragedy of fate, family traditions, and human hatreds

USEFUL BOOKS

The following collections of drama will prove most useful to the student:

Dickinson, T. H.	*Chief Contemporary Dramatists*, series 1, 2, and 3
Matthews, B.	*Chief European Dramatists*
Matthews, B. and Lieder, P.	*Chief British Dramatists*
Moses, M.	*Representative Continental Dramas*
Tucker, S. M.	*Modern Continental Plays*

CHAPTER 34

MASTERS OF THE NOVEL

HENRY FIELDING

1707–1754

The novel owes a great debt to four men of the eighteenth century, Richardson, Fielding, Smollett, and Sterne. The later novelists all borrowed from them in some degree. It was because of their imaginative power and the influence of the many novels which they produced between 1740 and 1771 that the novel became the most popular modern form of literature. The greatest of these four men was Henry Fielding.

Fielding's life. Fielding was born in Somersetshire in 1707 of a younger branch of a noble family. He was educated at Eton. He had a firm grounding in the classics for which he retained a love all his life.

After his school days he lived the life of a fashionable young man in London. He was attracted to the stage, and from 1730 to 1736 produced a series of farces and adaptations. Some of his plays satirized the government which promptly passed a Licensing Act ending Fielding's dramatic career.

In 1737 he began the study of law. In 1740 the success of Richardson's *Pamela,* a novel in the form of letters, induced Fielding to write a satire upon it, *Shamela.* This satire he followed with a novel of his own, *Joseph Andrews,* which was fairly successful.

In 1749 appeared Fielding's most important novel, *Tom Jones: or, the History of a Foundling.* It was widely read, but Fielding continued to work hard at the law.

In 1752 he published *Amelia* which is an attempt to "show up" the wickedness and the follies of London society. He always hated meanness and affectation, and could be bitterly satirical as in *Jonathan Wild* (1743), the story of a noted criminal.

In 1754 Fielding's health broke down. He undertook a sea voyage to Lisbon in the hope of recovery, but he died soon after his arrival.

Characteristics as a novelist. Fielding thought of himself as a moralist. He aimed to rebuke hypocrisy and to show that those who are often thought ridiculous or immoral often have more real goodness of heart than the supposedly good.

Parson Adams in *Joseph Andrews* is a truly good man. Yet he often cuts a ridiculous figure and is very badly treated by the world. Tom Jones is heedless, prodigal, and licentious, but Fielding constantly stresses his chivalry, warmth of heart, and generosity. Amelia is a perfect woman, yet she is not supremely beautiful as is Sophia in *Tom Jones*, and life treats her very shabbily indeed.

His novels are a panorama of English life of his time. He loved to send his hero on a journey so that he could have a series of adventures and meet scores of men and women. Clergymen, innkeepers, doctors, lawyers, men and women of fashion, soldiers, farmers—all these and scores of others live for us in Fielding's pages.

In general his method was to give a cross section of society and a complete picture of a large group of people in their relations to each other. Indeed, he called the novel "a comic epic in prose" and his books have much of the epic quality.

Achievement. Historically, Fielding is of the greatest importance. The later novel learned everything from him. Moreover, as an interpreter of his time he is unrivaled. He tells more of the eighteenth century than most historians, because he makes his world live through his vivid imagination.

Artistically his novels are valuable because of his vitality, his wise appraisal of human nature, and his excellent mind. He had an unusual sense of balance, an inexhaustible sense of humor, and a warm and generous heart.

SUGGESTIONS FOR FURTHER STUDY

1. A study of *Tom Jones* from the following points of view:
   (*a*) construction, (*b*) characterization, (*c*) humor, (*d*) zest for life,

(*e*) reality in action, (*f*) panorama of eighteenth-century life, (*g*) stock situations: coincidence, surprise, mistaken identity, false imprisonment, comic relief, quarrels, reconciliations.

2. *Joseph Andrews* as a "novel of the road."
3. Fielding's ideals of womanhood as seen in *Amelia.*
4. Goldsmith's *Vicar of Wakefield.*
5. Smollett's *Roderick Random.*

USEFUL BOOKS

For general information on the history of the novel see:

Cross, W.	*The Development of the English Novel*
Lovett, R. M., and Hughes, H. S.	*History of the Novel in England*

The authoritative work on Fielding is *The History of Henry Fielding* by W. L. Cross.

JANE AUSTEN

1775–1817

Life. Jane Austen was born in Hampshire in 1775. Her father was a clergyman. She lived the usual life of a girl in a large family in the eighteenth century, being taught at home and being confined to the society of the people in her neighborhood.

In 1801 her family moved to Bath, a fashionable center for rich English people of the time. Her brothers entered the navy. She wrote from girlhood, quietly and unobtrusively, neither her family nor her friends realizing that she would become one of the best-known English novelists. She died in 1817.

Novels. Her best novel, *Pride and Prejudice,* was written in 1797, but not published until 1813. In 1798 she wrote her delightful satire, *Northanger Abbey,* which was not published until 1818. *Sense and Sensibility* appeared in 1811, *Mansfield Park* in 1814, and *Emma* in 1816. *Persuasion* was published with *Northanger Abbey.*

Her novels are partly satirical. In her time came a great vogue for melodramatic novels of mystery and crime, led by Mrs. Radcliffe's *Mysteries of Udolpho.* Accompanying this vogue was a craze for the sentimental and the picturesque. "Sensibility" meant emotionalism and gushing sentiment. *Northanger Abbey* and *Sense and Sensibility* both are a plea for well-reasoned common sense and good-natured realization of what life actually is as opposed to the current fashionable affectations.

Jane Austen is at her best in the study of character. In brief space and with a few touches she makes her characters really live as no one else in her time could. As a result, we have a clear picture of normal, healthy, commonplace life in the early nineteenth century.

Her books have little striking incident. For her girls, marriage was the ultimate and desired fate. They fall sensibly in love with eligible young men. For a while, the foolishness of their families, misunderstandings, or social differences keep the course of love from running too smoothly. In the end they marry happily. The main plot is filled in with clearly drawn characters, mostly fathers, mothers, other young men and women, and clergymen.

Characteristics. Within her field Miss Austen has never been equaled. Her quiet and optimistic realism, her irony, her humor, the beautiful construction of her books, and her perfect prose style place her among the great novelists.

The best comment upon her is Scott's:

> That young lady had a talent for describing the involvements, feelings, and characters of ordinary life which is to me the most wonderful I have ever met with. The big bow-wow I can do myself like any one going; but the exquisite touch which renders commonplace things and characters interesting from the truth of the description and the sentiment is denied to me.

SUGGESTIONS FOR FURTHER STUDY

1. A study of one of the novels of Jane Austen from the following points of view:

   (*a*) absolute reality within a limited scope, (*b*) memorable comic characters, (*c*) satirical wit and humor, (*d*) an intimate knowledge of women and a good knowledge of men so far as a woman has the opportunity to observe them, (*e*) keen insight into human foibles, vanities, and follies, and a keen appreciation of courage, common sense, and good principles, (*f*) hard-headed, unsentimental but just criticism of human weaknesses, such as vanity, selfishness, sentimentality, stupidity, laziness, insincerity, (*g*) a tendency to avoid big emotions and troubles, such as violent passion, misery, guilt, remorse, death, (*h*) careful working out of the plot, using every scene and character purposefully, (*i*) uniformly good characterization.

USEFUL BOOKS

The letters of Jane Austen have been edited by R. B. Johnson. For further information see *The Cambridge History of English Literature* and the *Encyclopaedia Britannica.*

SIR WALTER SCOTT

1771–1832

Life. Scott was born in Edinburgh in 1771. His father was a lawyer. In childhood Scott was in poor health, and all his life he was lame. He was quick, imaginative, and sensitive with a romantic interest in Scottish stories and legends.

He received a formal training at the high school and university at Edinburgh. His real education, however, he gained by a passionate study of literature and by exhaustive research into Scottish history. In youth his health improved, and he became robust and high-spirited.

In 1792 he became a lawyer and later was appointed to various salaried offices.

Scott first attracted attention as a writer of verse tales. *The Lay of the Last Minstrel* (1805) became immediately popular and was followed by *Marmion* (1808), *The Lady of the Lake* (1810), and other poems.

After the publication of *Marmion,* Scott entered into partnership with the Ballantyne brothers in a publishing firm. He paid little attention to the business which was continually in difficulties. The need for money was increased by his purchase of land at Abbotsford and his beginning the building of a pretentious house.

To make money he began writing novels. The first of a long line was *Waverley* (1814). It was published anonymously, and Scott's authorship was not formally revealed until 1827. Meanwhile novel after novel appeared "by the author of *Waverley.*"

After 1814 Scott became rich and famous. He wrote many books besides his novels, entertained lavishly, and carried on official duties. Unfortunately, he did not pay sufficient attention to the publishing house in which he was a partner. It failed in 1825 and Scott found himself owing, as a partner, 130,000 pounds or, in American money, more than half a million dollars.

He refused to go into bankruptcy and determined to earn enough money to free himself from debt. For the last seven years of his life he toiled at this work. When he had earned about a third of the debt, his mind failed, and his friends allowed him to believe that he had paid it all. He died in 1832. The remainder of the debt was paid by the profits of Lockhart's *Life of Scott.* Lockhart was his son-in-law.

Novels. Scott's aim as a novelist was to tell vivid stories of chivalry, daring, and military prowess with a background of history. In general, his novels fall into three groups: the novels of Scottish history, such as *Old Mortality* and *Guy Mannering;* the novels of English history, such as *Ivanhoe* and *Kenilworth;* and the novels of Continental history, such as *The Talisman* and *Quentin Durward.* His historical background generally follows the facts and enlivens our historical knowledge with richly detailed pictures of famous men and famous places. Against this background are placed the fictitious lives of Scottish or English men and women of "gentle" or noble birth.

Scott's method. Scott's usual method was to choose as his hero a young man of good family who had his fortune to make. By setting his hero on a series of adventures, he was able to change his scenes and to bring into his story battles, plots, and various complications. Sooner or later the hero falls in love with a beautiful girl. As her mission in the book is to be married, she has little share in the action. Often a villain crosses the hero's path, but good always triumphs over evil. An older man, often a general, a chieftain, or a king usually plays a part in the plot.

Scott was fond of bringing into his story comic ladies of middle age, old hags or witches, strange people like gipsies, and a variety of Scottish types who usually speak in Scottish dialect. Once in a while a beautiful dark lady befriends the hero and shows herself a truly noble, self-sacrificing character. She never marries the hero.

The backgrounds of his novels are full of castles, dark, paneled rooms, caves, and forests. Always, too, there are historical essays attached which often occupy whole chapters.

Intellectually, the novels are simple. Scott's view of life was that of the strong, healthy, chivalrous, good-natured gentleman. Hence his books contribute little to the reader's knowledge of life. Scott aimed primarily at providing wholesome, enjoyable entertainment.

Achievement. So popular did Scott's novels become, and so widely imitated were they in other countries, that he may fairly be said to have established the historical novel as an important form of literature.

It must be admitted, however, that as the years have passed, Scott's popularity has waned. His novels now seem over-simple, conventional, and too full of historical discussion. Yet it is doubtful whether his gayety, his power of creating climax and suspense, and his picturesqueness can ever quite lose their charm.

SUGGESTIONS FOR FURTHER STUDY

1. The following novels are of special interest:

   The Talisman—a tale of the Crusades somewhat shorter than *Ivanhoe*
   Redgauntlet—dealing with Jacobite uprisings in Scotland and England—about the same period as Stevenson's *Kidnapped*
   Kenilworth—dealing with Queen Elizabeth, the Earl of Leicester, and the ill-fated Amy Robsart
   The Abbot—a tale of the romantic Mary Stuart, interesting to compare with Hewlett's *The Queen's Quair*
   The Heart of Midlothian—a Scottish romance dealing with the love of two sisters
   Quentin Durward—a romance of the time of Louis XI of France and Charles of Burgundy
   Rob Roy—Scott's highwaymen and one of the best heroines in fiction
   The Bride of Lammermoor—a tragic romance, the basis of the opera *Lucia*

2. In studying Scott, the student should look for the following characteristics:

   (*a*) a tendency to start with an interesting situation and then to delay the reader by detailed description, (*b*) insufficient variety in style—long and involved sentence and occasionally inflated dialogue, (*c*) great variety in use of background, characters, and episodes, (*d*) many exciting and dramatic scenes with much suspense, (*e*) great reality in presentation of romantic characters, (*f*) rather conventional love stories, (*g*) much use of conventional material, (*h*) high, if somewhat romantic ideals of chivalry and honor, (*i*) complete absence of social criticism.

USEFUL BOOKS

The authoritative life is Lockhart's in many volumes. Scott's story is interestingly told in a brief biography *A Great Rich Man* by Louise Schutz

Boas. A more formal biography is by John Buchan. For criticism see the histories of the novel.

CHARLES DICKENS
1812–1870

Life. Dickens was born in 1812 in a little town in southern England. His father was a clerk in a navy office. His early childhood was happy and later served him for material in *David Copperfield* and *Great Expectations.* When he was a growing boy the family moved to London. Here his father fell into debt and was imprisoned in the Marshalsea prison. Dickens was sent to work in a blacking factory and there for two years suffered privation and humiliation which he never forgot.

In 1824 he was rescued from poverty and sent to school. Later he became a reporter on various newspapers. He traveled about England, storing up for future use his impressions of inns and travelers.

In 1831 appeared *Sketches by Boz*, a collection of "stories" of contemporary London life. In 1836 began the publication which was to make him famous, *The Posthumous Papers of the Pickwick Club.* When it appeared in book form in 1837, all England was talking about Pickwickians and the new young novelist.

Thereafter Dickens led a crowded literary life. He published novels constantly, traveled, lectured, and gave readings. He soon became as well known in America as in England. In 1842 he visited the United States and wrote his impressions in *American Notes.* The book aroused a tempest of resentment. He made a second visit in 1867 with much better feeling.

In 1870 he died. He was buried in Westminster Abbey.

Novels. Dickens made his great reputation by a series of character studies beginning with *Pickwick Papers* and including such books as *Oliver Twist, Nicholas Nickleby, The Old Curiosity Shop,* and *Martin Chuzzlewit.* These books are full of enthusiastic humor, abundant sentiment, and the exaggerated caricature in which he delighted. They contain, too, examples of Dickens' violent humanitarianism. For instance, *Oliver Twist* is an attack upon poorhouses and *Nickleby* an exposé of the "poor schools" of Yorkshire.

The great interest in these books, however, lies in their characters.

Everyone who read books in the nineteenth century came to know Fagin, Bill Sikes, Squeers, Little Nell, Pecksniff, and Mrs. Gamp.

Dickens' next period established his reputation which had been made from 1837 to 1843. The optimism of "A Christmas Carol" (1843) was entirely suited to Victorian ideals. *Dombey and Son* (1848) seems now one of the most sentimental and theatrical of his books; it was, in its day, immensely popular. *David Copperfield* (1850), which is mainly autobiographical, is one of the great classics. It was Dickens' own favorite.

Dickens' third period is one of experiment and uneven performance. *Bleak House* (1853) is a rambling satire upon the injustice and inefficiency of British legal procedure, and *Hard Times* (1854) is an argument against new economic theories.

In *A Tale of Two Cities* (1859) Dickens produced a classic in the field of the historical novel. It was influenced by Carlyle's *French Revolution*. *Great Expectations* (1861) is much better organized and more concentrated than most of Dickens' novels. Next to *Copperfield* it is often regarded as his best novel. It is a masterpiece in the creation of character and background.

In *Our Mutual Friend* (1865) he entered the field of the mystery novel which he cultivated further in *The Mystery of Edwin Drood*. This novel was interrupted by his death in 1870. The solution of its plot has long been a question about which lovers of mystery stories have argued.

Achievement. "I rest my claim," said Dickens, "to the remembrance of my country on my published works." That readers will long remember him there is no doubt. His claim rests not upon his interpretation of life or his artistry, but upon his imagination. He created, with enthusiasm, humor, and faith in human nature, a gallery of characters and of episodes which constitutes a world of his own. It may not be close to the actual world of nineteenth-century England, but in its own way it is unforgettable.

SUGGESTIONS FOR FURTHER STUDY

In reading Dickens, notice the following characteristics:

(*a*) a constant temptation on the part of the author to overdo his humor, his pathos, and his whole story, (*b*) a fondness for scenes which would be theatrically effective, so that one could readily imagine his scenes on the stage or screen, (*c*) somewhat conventional love stories, (*d*) conventional devices for carrying out his complication—coincidences, disappearances, lost documents, missing heirs, figures from the past, disguises, manly heroes, and sneaking villains, (*e*) great gusto and zest, especially in scenes of conviviality, eating, drinking, and traveling, (*f*) genius for making odd or humorous characters live, (*g*) compassion for the suffering of the poor and the helpless, leading to a passion for social reform.

USEFUL BOOKS

The standard life of Dickens is in three volumes by John Forster. Two excellent one-volume studies are by G. K. Chesterton and George Gissing. The histories of the novel give extended notice to Dickens. There is a full discussion of Dickens in the *Encyclopaedia Britannica.* Many special studies of Dickens have been made. An interesting one is *Charles Dickens as a Legal Historian* by W. S. Holdsworth. Light is thrown upon Dickens' theatricality in *Charles Dickens and the Stage* by E. T. Pemberton. The Dickens enthusiast will take pleasure in *The Dickens Dictionary* by W. A. Wheeler, an exhaustive reference book.

WILLIAM MAKEPEACE THACKERAY
1811–1863

Life. Thackeray was born in 1811 in India. Like most children of Indian birth he was sent to England to be educated. He entered Charterhouse School in London in 1822. References to his school life appear in *Vanity Fair* and *The Newcomes.* In 1829 he entered Trinity College, Cambridge. He was no scholar, and was more interested in friendships and literary work than in his studies. He left college in 1830. His brief college life he wrote of later in *Pendennis.*

In 1830 he traveled in France and Germany. Later he made use of this experience also in his novels. In 1831 he returned to England to study law. He inherited some money which he lost partly in bad investments and partly in gambling. He then went to France to study art.

In 1837, having returned to England, he began a busy life writing sketches, stories, essays, and poems for the magazines. Not until 1848 did he have any real success. Then, with the publication of *Vanity Fair* he was recognized as a great novelist.

From 1848 on, Thackeray published a series of novels which gained for him an increasing circle of readers. He lectured in England and America and edited a popular English magazine. He died in 1863.

Novels. Thackeray's major novels form a series which should be read in succession.

Henry Esmond (1852) is a story of life in the early eighteenth century. The chief figure is the grave, austere Esmond who writes his memoirs. Then there is the beautiful Beatrix, willful, intelligent, and ruthless, who captivates everyone. Lady Castlewood, the sweet, quiet Englishwoman so much beloved by Victorian novelists, becomes Esmond's wife. Esmond emigrates to America and becomes a successful "planter." The historical background is very rich, with all the literary and military notables of Queen Anne's time moving in and out of the story.

The Virginians (1859) carries on the Esmond family into the late eighteenth century. The story is not so vivid as in *Esmond*, but the historical background is even more fully developed. The portrait of Beatrix Esmond grown old is the most brilliant part of the book.

Vanity Fair (1848) introduces two new groups representative of London merchants, the Osbornes and the Sedleys. Into respectable London life enters the adventuress, Rebecca Sharpe, one of the most vivid women in literature. With extraordinary skill Thackeray moves the characters through the stirring years of the early nineteenth century in and out of a beautifully woven web of episode. One of the most interesting characters is the Marquis of Steyne who represents the dissolute, aristocratic life of the time.

Early Victorian life forms the background of *Pendennis* (1850) and *The Newcomes* (1855). These novels are practically coincident in time. *Pendennis* is partly autobiographical. It contains the portrait of Major Pendennis, the bachelor clubman, who represents the worldly, cynical point of view of fashionable society.

The Newcomes is the story of a family told by Pendennis. It is Thackeray's most ambitious book and has the largest canvas. Though it has not the brilliant vividness of *Vanity Fair*, it is full of interesting episodes and varied characters. Colonel Newcome is the great figure of the book, a kind of modern Don Quixote, one of the gentlest and most lovable of men.

Thackeray also wrote some shorter novels, notably *Barry Lyndon*

(1844), an ironical picture of an eighteenth-century rascal, and many essays, sketches, and poems.

His aim. Thackeray was, consciously, a realistic satirist. His aim was to present formal society in such a way as to tell the truth about its shallowness, affectation, snobbery, and meanness. He also wished to give credit, where it was due, for nobility, kindness of heart, and natural goodness. None of his characters is all bad or all good. He tries to be entirely fair, and particularly to strip from life the veil of false romance.

He felt that as novelist he had a right to talk about his characters, and did so. He said that it was his privilege

> occasionally to step down from the platform, and talk about them; if they are good and kindly, to love and shake them by the hand; if they are silly, to laugh at them confidentially in the reader's sleeve; if they are wicked and heartless, to abuse them in the strongest terms politeness admits of.

Achievement. Thackeray's great achievement is his picture of English society. There was nothing like it in English fiction before him.

Then, too, he had great ability in presenting vivid and dramatic incident. The meeting of Prince Charles, Henry Esmond, and Viscount Castlewood, and Rawdon Crawley's encounter with Lord Steyne in *Vanity Fair* are among the immortal scenes in fiction.

Furthermore, his power of characterization was unexcelled. He never descended to caricature, and he never relied for interest upon the grotesque or farcical.

Finally, he was a master of pure, simple style. He loved the eighteenth century, and he learned the secret of its grace, charm, and urbanity. His skill in writing, added to his good humor, his refusal to become shrill or excited, and his genuine sentiment make him the favorite novelist of a multitude of readers.

SUGGESTIONS FOR FURTHER STUDY

In any of Thackeray's novels, find examples of:

(*a*) realism—that is, an attempt to show truly how his characters' minds work and how their moral qualities affect their lives, (*b*) humor, chiefly satirical, (*c*) compassion for human trouble, sometimes verging on sentimentality, (*d*) appreciation of ironical and dramatic effects, (*e*) tendency to over-indulgence in author's comment, (*f*) fine characterization, (*g*) elaborate development of background through introduction of many minor characters, (*h*) variety in style, shown in dramatic narration, humor, pathos, irony, and dialogue, (*i*) fine moral idealism, marred occasionally by Victorian priggishness.

USEFUL BOOKS

The novelist, Anthony Trollope, wrote the short life of Thackeray in the English Men of Letters series. *Thackeray and His Daughter* edited by Hester T. Ritchie presents much material for an understanding of Thackeray. There is an essay on Thackeray in *Victorian Prose Masters* by W. C. Brownell. For those who read Thackeray extensively, *A Thackeray Dictionary* by I. G. Mudge will be useful.

THE BRONTËS

No more interesting or gifted group exists among novelists than the three Brontë sisters, Anne, Emily, and Charlotte. They lived apart from the world in a remote section of England; they had little except imaginative experience of life; and they all died young. As time goes on, however, their place among the great figures of literature grows more and more secure.

Anne Brontë. Anne was the youngest of the Brontë family of three daughters and one son. She was born in 1820 and died in 1849. Her novels, *Agnes Gray* (1847) and *The Tenant of Wildfell Hall* (1848) are interesting chiefly as pictures of middle-class life seen by a shy, gentle girl deeply sensitive to pain and suffering.

Emily Brontë. Emily was born in 1818 and died in 1848. She had the most vivid imagination of the three and a mind which flashed like lightning. Her novel *Wuthering Heights* is a masterpiece of poetic intensity, passionate emotion, and grim power. It tells an almost unbelievable story of love, hate, and revenge in a lonely district of Yorkshire. To read the book is an unforgettable experience.

Charlotte Brontë. Charlotte was born in 1816. She attended a school which she hated. It is portrayed in *Jane Eyre*. In 1835 she became a governess. In order to advance in the teaching profession she entered, in 1842, a school in Brussels. Her Belgian experiences were later used in *Villette*.

In 1844 she returned to her family at Haworth in Yorkshire. The girls began publishing in 1846 as "Currer, Ellis and Acton Bell," pseudonyms which they retained. In 1847 Charlotte's *Jane Eyre* was published with immediate success.

The death of her sisters was a great blow, but she bravely completed *Shirley* which contains a portrait of Emily. It was published in 1849. In that year she visited London, and for the first time in her life had some experience of society.

In 1853 she published *Villette.* In 1854 she married. In 1855 she died.

Novels. The Brontë sisters wrote their inner lives in their books. Their novels contain a revealing record of emotional strain, idealized feeling, and dramatized aspirations. In all of them a young girl, subdued and shy, wins happiness in marriage. Contrasting with the girl is usually a florid, vivid personality who overshadows her. The men are all Byronic and masterful with generous hearts and powerful minds beneath a rough exterior.

The backgrounds of the novels are all the product of imaginative, sensitive minds acting upon autobiographical material such as Yorkshire, the governess' impressions of society, and Brussels.

The importance of the Brontës lies not in any message or in their intellectual interpretation of life. It lies rather in their individuality and their emotional intensity.

SUGGESTIONS FOR FURTHER STUDY

In reading the novels by the Brontës, notice particularly the following characteristics:

(*a*) The girls live an intense emotional and imaginative life under a mask of self-control. (*b*) The men are often projections of a girl's romantic imagination rather than men such as we meet in everyday life. (*c*) There is great reality in the depiction of stormy emotions. (*d*) There is considerable theatricality in plot. (*e*) There is much use of background for atmosphere. (*f*) There is a complete absence of both humor and sentimentality. (*g*) The view of life is personal not social.

USEFUL BOOKS

The standard work on the Brontës, *The Life of Charlotte Brontë* by Mrs. Gaskell, is still the best book for the beginner. Briefer lives are by A. Birrell and E. F. Benson. The modern authoritative work is *The Brontës; Life and*

Letters in two volumes by Clement Shorter. The new biography has been busy with the Brontës. Two examples of modern biography are: *The Brontë Sisters* by Ernest Dimnet and *Charlotte Brontë, a Psychological Study* by Rosamund Langbridge.

GEORGE ELIOT
(MARY ANN EVANS)
1819–1880

Life. The girl who later became known to the world as George Eliot was born in Warwickshire in 1819. Her father was a business man. The important part of her education was gained by keeping house for her father and by reading widely in English and foreign literatures.

In 1851 she began editorial work in London and associated with a noted group of liberal writers and thinkers. She entered into a marriage with George Henry Lewes, philosopher and writer. Their married life was ideal, and Lewes was a conscientious and able literary adviser.

The publication of *Adam Bede* in 1859 gave her recognition as a novelist. Novels followed in succession: *Silas Marner* (1861), *Romola* (1863), *Middlemarch* (1872), and *Daniel Deronda* (1876).

Lewes died in 1878 and George Eliot later married J. W. Cross. She died in 1880.

Characteristics. George Eliot was primarily concerned with moral problems, particularly with the problem of moral weakness. All her stories contain a contrast of the weak with the strong. Thus Romola is contrasted with Tito and Adam Bede with Arthur Donnithorne.

Another of her interests is the way in which quiet endurance of a hard fate is often relieved by self-sacrificing love. This is shown in *Silas Marner*.

She had a great interest in people's motives. In *Middlemarch* and *Daniel Deronda* there are long passages of psychological analysis.

Her most attractive quality is her sympathy for and understanding of English country people in their natural environment. This is seen most clearly in *The Mill on the Floss* which is partly autobiographical.

She was primarily an intellectual writer and made much use of analytic exposition. Her seriousness, scholarship, and profundity made a great impression on her time.

SUGGESTIONS FOR FURTHER STUDY

1. The following novels are of particular interest:

   Adam Bede—notable for the fidelity and humor of its picture of country life, for scenes of great emotional power, and for logical psychological analysis

   The Mill on the Floss—a story of brother and sister in which an idealistic girl becomes involved in two tragic love affairs

   Romola—an impressive study of moral degeneration, and an elaborate picture of Florence in the time of Savonarola

   Middlemarch—a picture of an English village and all its people. Rich in characterization, but somewhat over-weighted with moral earnestness. Should be compared with Bennett's *The Old Wives' Tale*

2. Note the following characteristics of the novels of George Eliot: (*a*) her ability to construct a plot involving one or more social groups so that all their interactions seem to grow naturally out of human nature, (*b*) her insight into human nature, (*c*) her intense interest in moral problems, (*d*) her ability to present simple country folk with truth and humor, (*e*) her tendency to introduce philosophical and moral comment, (*f*) her insight into masculine psychology.

USEFUL BOOKS

The standard life of George Eliot is by J. W. Cross in three volumes containing her letters and journals. A shorter life is by Oscar Browning. A very modern life is *George Eliot and Her Times; a Victorian Study* by E. S. Haldane. There is an essay on her work in *Victorian Prose Masters* by W. C. Brownell. For intensive study, students will find useful *A George Eliot Dictionary* by I. G. Mudge.

THOMAS HARDY

1840–1928

Life. Hardy was born in Dorsetshire in 1840. His family had long been in the West of England. After an education in local schools, he entered an architect's office. He was successful in his profession and did not publish novels until 1871. He then began a long series of novels which ended in 1895, when he returned to poetry which had been the literary interest of his youth. At his death in 1928 he was honored as much for his poetry as for his novels, especially for his great work, *The Dynasts,* a dramatic poem dealing with the Napoleonic Wars.

Novels. Hardy's first successful novel was a pretty country tale *Under the Greenwood Tree* (1872) which shows his understanding of the country people of Dorsetshire and Wiltshire, the district which he called "Wessex." *Far from the Madding Crowd* (1874) is a much more serious and even somber book. In this novel appear many types of character which he afterward used: the beautiful, willful girl who brings tragedy to some men and happiness to others; the strong, quiet countryman who is successful because he is completely attuned to his environment; and the man from the city, the alien who never adjusts to Wessex.

The Return of the Native (1878) is Hardy's greatest book. With somber Egdon Heath as a setting, and with a variety of peasant types as a background, two groups of people move in tragic paths through complications brought about partly by Fate and partly by their own natures.

The Mayor of Casterbridge (1886) is like a Greek tragedy. It tells of the rise to power of a man neither all good nor all bad, and his slow, relentless decline to utter insignificance and a miserable death.

The Woodlanders (1887) is a tragedy in monotone. In the Wessex woods modern sophistication encounters native conservatism and strength. This time, however, the nobility and dignity of the woodland people go down to a drab and fruitless end, while the less worthy characters achieve a certain amount of happiness.

Tess of the D'Urbervilles (1891) roused a storm of discussion. It is a tragedy of a woman naturally good who comes to a bad end through the narrowness and prejudice of society and through the malignancy of Fate.

Jude the Obscure (1895) is a novel of despair. For the unlucky Jude nothing can come right. He is born to misery and dies in frustration. The book contains some of the most bitterly tragic scenes in the English novel.

Characteristics. Hardy was in complete revolt against Victorian conventions of morality and religion. He was a believer in Fate as the ruling power in the life of man. All humanity, from his point of view, struggles with environment, and success is a matter of pure chance. It has little to do with inner worth. He stands aloof from his characters except in *Tess* and *Jude*. He sympathizes deeply with them, crying out in bitter irony against false ideals, unfair prejudices, and the unjust Fate which make them what they become.

He is interested in Nature as an active force in life and in country people who live close to Nature. His novels are full of incident and are dramatic, even, at times, melodramatic.

Achievement. Hardy represents the feeling of revolt with which men after 1870 began to throw off Victorian conservatism. He is thus of great importance, historically.

He is also important for his treatment of tragic themes with relentless sincerity.

His view of womanhood, often, except in *Tess*, critical and disparaging, foreshadowed the new position which women have taken in modern life.

His greatest achievement is his complete interpretation of Wessex and its folk. He made the district peculiarly his own.

Finally, he brought the novel to a point where for thoroughness, sincerity, and fearless treatment of tragic themes it could compete with poetry and the drama.

SUGGESTIONS FOR FURTHER STUDY

In reading Hardy's novels notice the following characteristics:

(*a*) control of his art—everything in the story contributes to an inevitable end, carefully planned and worked up to a climax, (*b*) weakness for melodramatic scenes, (*c*) over-use of coincidence and chance which work his characters' ruin, (*d*) appreciation of country life and rustic humor, (*e*) vivid pictorial background, often symbolic, (*f*) preoccupation with the theory that men are the victims of an unkind fate which they struggle in vain to escape, (*g*) tendency to overdo irrational impulsiveness in his characters, especially his women, (*h*) much use of dramatic irony, (*i*) fondness for describing local customs and superstitions.

USEFUL BOOKS

The best study of Hardy is the beautifully written *The Art of Thomas Hardy* by Lionel Johnson. A scholarly study is *Thomas Hardy, Poet and Novelist* by S. C. Chew. For authoritative biographical material see *The Early Life of Thomas Hardy* and *The Later Years of Thomas Hardy* both by

Florence Emily Hardy. A short modern life is *The Life of Thomas Hardy* by Ernest Brennecke.

CONTEMPORARY NOVELISTS

The novel has become the chief literary form of today. Never before have so many novels been written with so much skill, beauty, variety, and sincerity.

The novel has become startlingly experimental. Novels are now much shorter than they used to be. Under the stimulus of the short story and the moving picture, novels center upon single characters, situations, and incidents.

In structure, novels have ceased to follow traditional patterns. Willa Cather's *Death Comes for the Archbishop* is a condensed biography without a plot. Virginia Woolf's *To the Lighthouse* adopts the freedom of a reverie, as do all "stream-of-consciousness" novels. In general, fiction tries to hold the reader by securing a sense of living reality rather than by working up suspense and climax.

From the multitude of contemporary novelists two may be chosen because their work has received general recognition and because their place in literature is secure, Joseph Conrad and John Galsworthy.

Joseph Conrad. Conrad was born in Ukraine in 1857. His parents were exiled Polish patriots. His father interested him in English literature. He became a seaman in the British merchant marine and rose through the various ranks to end as master of a vessel.

He had the nature of an artist and a sure understanding of the people whom he observed in his travels. With a deep desire to render in artistic form the life which he experienced, he began writing novels.

He published *Almayer's Folly* in 1895, *The Nigger of the Narcissus* in 1897, and *Lord Jim* in 1900. *Lord Jim* is a masterpiece of realistic detail, romantic adventure, idealistic aspiration, and psychological analysis. Many other novels followed, all of which brought him a wider public and increasing fame. He died in 1924.

His beautiful style, his descriptive power, and his interpretation of life at sea and in the Far East would have been enough to make him an important writer. What makes him truly great is his interpretation of human character and his passionate interest in and understanding of human motives.

Some of his other works are: *Nostromo* (1904), *Chance* (1913), and *Victory* (1915).

John Galsworthy. Galsworthy, unlike Conrad, was thoroughly English. He was born in 1867 of an aristocratic old English family. He was educated at Harrow and Oxford. By training he was a lawyer, but his chief interests were always literary.

Galsworthy began by writing a series of novels illustrating various aspects of English society. *The Man of Property* (1906) is a study of the rich property-holding class in London. The Forsyte family is studied through various members and in various situations to show that it has made money its god, and thus destroyed beauty and freedom.

The Country House (1907) is a sympathetic study of the land-holding class in the country. In this novel is no thesis, but rather an attempt to render the kind of life which a country squire and his family lead and the complications which ensue when alien ideas cross their path.

Fraternity (1909) is a satire upon men and women who profess social idealism but have no real strength of character.

The Patrician (1911) is a picture of the high nobility. It presents the thesis that when young people are imbued with ideals of caste, they will live up to them and sacrifice their personal ideals and emotions.

Other novels followed until in 1920 Galsworthy picked up the main character of *The Man of Property*, Soames Forsyte, and continued his life in *In Chancery*. This was followed by *To Let* (1921).

In 1922 the three Forsyte novels were published as *The Forsyte Saga*. A large public began to read with delight the greatest novel of a family in English. Readers saw that it was more than a study of social conditions, more than a novel of ideas, more even than an extraordinary study of a single character. It was the biography of a generation in transition from nineteenth-century conservatism to the bewildered confusion of our own time.

This great study of Soames Forsyte, his family, and his friends Galsworthy continued in *The White Monkey* (1924), *The Silver Spoon* (1926), and *Swan Song* (1928). The six novels of the Forsyte series are a great achievement.

When Galsworthy died in 1933, he was at work upon another family chronicle, two sections of which had been published, *Maid in Waiting*

© Underwood & Underwood, N.Y.

JOHN GALSWORTHY

The Forsyte Saga has made him one of the great English novelists.

Courtesy of Edward Steichen

CARL SANDBURG

With rugged sincerity and warm humanity Sandburg has vivified American life in modern verse.

and *Flowering Wilderness*. Both novels are far below the Forsyte series in power and interest. After his death the third novel of the series appeared, *One More River*.

SUGGESTIONS FOR FURTHER STUDY

1. The following novels of Conrad are of special interest:

   "Youth"—a long short story of the indomitable spirit of youth
   The Nigger of the Narcissus—a picture of the sea and of seamen
   Typhoon—sailors and a sailing ship in a terrible storm
   Lord Jim—a man retrieves his lost honor. A background of tropical sea, sky, and jungle
   Victory—a man seeks to escape from life, but in the end is entangled with human greed, love, and gratitude
   Almayer's Folly, *An Outcast of the Islands*, and *The Rescue*—Europeans exiled in the tropics seek vainly to escape
   Chance—strangely woven human relationships. Deals more elaborately with feminine psychology than any other novel by Conrad
   Nostromo—centers about a valuable silver mine in South America

2. In studying Conrad note especially the following characteristics: (*a*) a complicated narrative method involving frequent shifts in point of view, (*b*) interest in psychology, (*c*) variety in subject matter and characters, (*d*) realism in psychology and ironical comment; romance in descriptive background, exciting scenes, and treatment of women, (*e*) pictorial power, (*f*) style. Vaguely suggestive, steeped in melancholy and romance, (*g*) literary philosophy—"to intensify the expression of things so that the heart and inner meaning may become vividly real," (*h*) recurrent themes and types:

   (1) the elusive, romantic woman, (2) the sagacious, taciturn older man, (3) the fearless, honor-haunted youth, (4) the generous romanticist, (5) the cowardly scoundrel, (6) the inscrutable oriental, (7) characters confined in fear and darkness, (8) the "besieged-island" motif.

3. In the study of the novels of Galsworthy notice the following characteristics:

   (*a*) balance—that is, ability to keep his sense of justice in equilibrium with his human sympathies, so that he shows both sides of questions fairly and sympathetically, (*b*) a consequent tendency to arrive at no decisive conclusion because he sees so clearly the good and bad in the old and new, and the discrepancy between human idealism and human nature; and perhaps, too, a consequent lack of vividness and emotional vitality in characterization, (*c*) a fondness for presenting the conflict between the new and the old, (*d*) an interest in social and economic problems as they affect human beings, (*e*) a tendency to underscore characters to bring out a point, (*f*) love of English countryside expressed in artistic description, (*g*) ability to round out a character (Soames) or to suggest one by economical means (Annette), (*h*) English sentiment and idealism (Old and Young Jolyon, Jon, and Michael Mont) combined with pessimism as to final solutions, (*i*) artistic plot development, but frequent sacrifice of construction to characterization, (*j*) compassion for human unhappiness.

CHAPTER 35

THE GREAT ESSAYISTS

JOSEPH ADDISON and RICHARD STEELE

1672–1719 1672–1729

Addison's life. Addison was born in 1672 in Wiltshire. His father was a prominent clergyman. He attended Charterhouse School, and later had a distinguished career at Oxford.

He was popular in court circles, received a good pension, and went abroad in 1699. A change in government left him to his own resources, and in 1703 he returned to England.

For several years he held political appointments. In 1711 he began writing for the *Spectator* and in 1713 he wrote for the *Guardian.* In the same year his drama *Cato* had a great success, not because of any artistic merit, but because both political parties, the Whigs and the Tories, used it for political purposes.

After the death of Queen Anne in 1714 Addison wrote nothing of any interest. He continued his political activities and associated with the leading writers of the time. Pope satirized him bitterly, and he quarreled with Steele. But on the whole his closing years were happy except for his ill-health. He died in 1719 and was buried in Westminster Abbey.

Character. Addison was apparently a rather stiff, kindly, precise, scholarly man with high ideals of dignified conduct. He had many friends. He was loyal and energetic with a firm sense of responsibility. In general, he held, in his time, the respect, admiration, and quiet affection of most of his contemporaries.

Steele's life. Steele was born in Dublin in 1672. His father was an attorney. He attended Charterhouse School where he first met

Addison. He also went to Oxford where the friendship between the two men continued.

Steele left the university to enter the army and rose to a captaincy. In 1700 he fought a duel and was so overcome with remorse that he always opposed dueling. In 1701 he published a treatise on morals, *The Christian Hero*, which argued for a change from the low moral standards of the late seventeenth century. In 1701 he began writing for the stage and produced a series of sentimental comedies.

In 1709 Steele began the first of his periodicals, the *Tatler*, published three times a week. It ended in 1711. Immediately, with Addison who had written some papers for the *Tatler*, he began the *Spectator* which ran daily until the end of 1712. In 1713 he began the *Guardian*, again with Addison's assistance. It ran less than a year. Then, without Addison, he published a series of short-lived periodicals.

He was a busy politician and held many offices. In 1715 he was knighted. Toward the end of his life he was harassed by debts and ill-health. He died in Wales in 1729.

Character. Steele was impulsive, warm hearted, high minded, and extravagant. He had a vein of originality which Addison lacked. He had also more energy and imagination than his friend. The two complemented each other, and made admirable associates.

The *Spectator*. The fame of the *Spectator* rests first upon its historical importance. With the *Tatler* it was the first really successful effort to use the essay for periodical purposes. It immediately became a classic and influenced the form and style of the essay for nearly two hundred years.

Second, it is an excellent mirror of its time. Addison and Steele were earnest social critics. There is no doubt that the ideals upheld by the *Spectator* strengthened the moral reforms of the eighteenth century. For a hundred years at least the essays of Addison and Steele were "required reading" for men and women who sought elegance and refinement.

In the third place, the essays presented in Sir Roger and his friends a series of portraits and character sketches which anticipated the novel. Even now, the characters in the Club remain as fresh as those in many novels.

Finally, the *Spectator* has always been a model of English style. As Samuel Johnson said in his life of Addison:

Whoever wishes to attain an English style, familiar but not coarse, and elegant but not ostentatious, must give his days and nights to the volumes of Addison.

SUGGESTIONS FOR FURTHER STUDY

1. Addison and Steele as critics of the eighteenth century.
2. The eighteenth-century coffeehouses.
3. A comparison of Addison and Steele.
4. Other eighteenth-century periodicals: *The Rambler, The Idler, The World.*
5. Addison as literary critic.
6. Politics in Queen Anne's time.
7. Addison's *Cato.*
8. Johnson's *Life of Addison.*
9. Steele's *Letters.*
10. Addison as a poet.

USEFUL BOOKS

For the background of Addison and Steele, see *Social Life in the Reign of Queen Anne* by J. Ashton and *Social Backgrounds of English Literature* by Boas and Hahn. The best short life of Addison is by W. J. Courthope in the English Men of Letters series; the best short life of Steele is by Austin Dobson. The letters of Steele have been edited by R. B. Johnson.

JONATHAN SWIFT
1667–1745

Life. Swift was born in Dublin in 1667 of English parentage. He was brought up by relatives. He attended Trinity College, Dublin, without making any mark as a scholar. Nevertheless he became, in 1689, secretary to Sir William Temple, an eminent diplomat and man of letters.

He later became a clergyman in the Church of England. He resided in Ireland and made frequent trips to England. In 1710 he entered the service of the ruling Tory party and remained high in favor with them until their fall in 1714.

Thereafter he lived in Ireland as dean of St. Patrick's Cathedral in Dublin. In 1742 he became insane. In 1745 he died.

Swift's personal life is of the greatest interest. His relations with his friends, especially with the ladies whom he called "Stella" and "Vanessa" have long been the subject of research. The letters collected in the *Journal to Stella* give a fascinating picture of his daily life in London and of the prominent people whom he knew.

Work. Though Swift was not strictly an essayist, he is included in this survey because of his many miscellaneous writings in prose, his association with essayists, and his contribution to the development of English prose style. Swift's striking intellectual power, his savage and relentless irony, and his bitter hatred of sham, affectation, and oppression made him a merciless satirist. The modern reader, however, cannot understand his works without a thorough knowledge of the early eighteenth century.

Only one work remains, aside from the letters to Stella, which everyone can enjoy. That is the immortal *Gulliver's Travels.* Originally it was a sweeping satire on international politics, war, science, and the writers of travels, real or fanciful.

He builds up the imaginary kingdoms of Lilliput and Brobdingnag with rigid mathematical accuracy and extraordinary imaginative power. What he thought of humanity can be seen in the voyage to the kingdom of horses. It must always be remembered that Swift bitterly hated evil and hypocrisy. All his life he suffered intensely from the world. In a way, the key to his satire is found in the epitaph over his tomb in his cathedral,

> Here lies the body of Jonathan Swift, dean of this cathedral; where bitter anger can no longer tear at his heart. . . .

SUGGESTIONS FOR FURTHER STUDY

1. *Gulliver's Travels* as a satire.
2. London life as seen in the *Journal to Stella.*
3. The work of Sir William Temple.
4. Swift's satirical power as seen in *A Modest Proposal* and *Essay on a Broomstick.*
5. Swift in Ireland.

USEFUL BOOKS

The best short life is by Leslie Stephen in the English Men of Letters series. The best modern life is by Carl Van Doren. There are excellent studies in the *Encyclopaedia Britannica* and in *The Cambridge History of English Literature*. There is a most interesting essay by the novelist Thackeray in *English Humorists*.

CHARLES LAMB

1775–1834

Life. Lamb was born in London in 1775. His father was a lawyer's clerk. He went to Christ's Hospital School where he met the poet Coleridge. He was deeply interested in the older English literature, at that time not much read.

In 1792 he entered the East India House as a clerk. He remained in the employ of the East India Company for more than thirty years.

In 1796 his sister Mary, to whom he was devoted, went insane and killed their mother. She recovered from the insane attack, and Charles took charge of her. She suffered recurrences of insanity from time to time which saddened his whole life.

Lamb spent his life in London, working in his office, going to the theater, writing essays, and associating with the many friends who were attracted to him. In 1825 he retired from business with a good pension. He died in 1834.

Writings. With his sister Mary, Charles Lamb wrote that famous children's classic, *Tales Founded on the Plays of Shakespeare*. He wrote other books for children, some poetry, and several plays. He also edited selections from the dramatists of Shakespeare's time with excellent critical notes.

His fame will always rest on his *Essays of Elia*. These cover a variety of subjects: memories of his youth, interesting places and people in London, humorous reflections upon life, fantasies, and criticisms of literature and the theater.

The essays are characterized by humor, tenderness, whimsical imagination, and critical insight. His style is founded upon the quaint prose of the seventeenth century. So rich is his imaginative power, and so beautiful the rhythm and structure of his prose that his work, small as it is in quantity, ranks with the world's great essays.

SUGGESTIONS FOR FURTHER STUDY

1. Lamb as a poet.
2. Lamb as a playwright.

3. Lamb's criticisms of Shakespeare.
4. London as seen in the *Essays of Elia.*
5. Humor in Lamb's essays.

USEFUL BOOKS

The one indispensable work on Lamb is the *Life* in two volumes by E. V. Lucas. There is a short life by A. Ainger in the English Men of Letters series. A useful collection of the less well-known work of Lamb is *Charles Lamb in Essays and Letters* by M. G. Fulton. Gamaliel Bradford has an essay on Lamb in *Bare Souls.* Walter Pater has written on Lamb in *Appreciations.*

THOMAS BABINGTON MACAULAY

1800–1859

Life. Macaulay was born in Leicestershire in 1800. His father was prominent in the movement for the abolition of Negro slavery in the British Empire. Thomas attended Trinity College, Cambridge, where he had a distinguished scholarly career.

In 1825 he began his literary work with an essay on Milton in the *Edinburgh Review.* In 1830 he entered the House of Commons where he made a brilliant record.

In 1834 he sailed for India to assume a high position in the Indian government. He remained there until 1838.

On his return to England he reëntered politics. He published essays constantly. His great success, however, was his *History of England,* the first volumes of which were published in 1848. The work earned for him the equivalent of more than one hundred thousand dollars, was translated into a dozen foreign languages, and brought him academic honors. In 1857 he was raised to the peerage as a baron.

His health at this time was failing, and he died in 1859.

Achievement. Macaulay's fame rests upon the brilliance and vividness of his style. His encyclopædic mind encompassed a tremendous range of facts in history and literature. These, well digested and logically organized, he presented in prose which delighted his readers.

Macaulay had no original ideas. He believed that Victorian England had reached an enviably happy position, and he believed that the past was full of fascinating facts, incidents, and personalities. His essays swept his readers off their feet with their fluency and their concreteness.

His essays and his history can still be read with pleasure. It should always be remembered, however, that modern historical and biographical research render most of his statements only partially true.

SUGGESTIONS FOR FURTHER STUDY

1. Reports on Macaulay's essays on "Milton," "Madame d'Arblay," "Lord Clive," and "Warren Hastings" from the following points of view:
   (*a*) encyclopædic mind, (*b*) clear organization, (*c*) concrete vividness, (*d*) exaggeration, (*e*) force and fluency, (*f*) British prejudices, (*g*) conventional ideas.
2. Macaulay as historian.
3. Macaulay as poet.
4. Macaulay's political career.

USEFUL BOOKS

The best work on Macaulay is *The Life and Letters of Lord Macaulay* by G. Otto Trevelyan in two volumes. There is a good short life by J. C. Morison in the English Men of Letters series.

THOMAS CARLYLE
1795–1881

Unlike the brilliant, optimistic Macaulay who glorified material success, Thomas Carlyle, like a prophet of old, preached to Victorian England a spiritual message.

Life. Carlyle was born in Scotland. He was educated in the stern, religious Scottish way and brought up in poverty. He was intended for the ministry and educated at Edinburgh University. He later taught school.

In 1828, after his marriage with Jane Welsh, he went to live at Craigenputtock, a dreary, remote Scottish farm. He had decided to earn his living by writing. He had little success, and he therefore moved to London in 1831.

In 1833 *Sartor Resartus* appeared but attracted favorable attention only in America. With the publication of *The French Revolution* in 1837 recognition began. Thereafter, Carlyle became known as one of the great leaders of Victorian thought. He lectured and wrote steadily producing essays, historical sketches, and biographies.

As years went on he felt that the world was going from bad to worse and said so on every possible occasion. He was treated, however, with great respect by his contemporaries who recognized his sincerity and earnestness.

He died in 1881.

Characteristics. Carlyle was a bitter individualist at war with the world and with himself. His harshness expressed itself in his explosive and incoherent style. When he chose, however, he could be vividly picturesque and eloquent.

His deepest belief was in the value of strenuous action, the "everlasting yea" as he called it, or the saving power of work. He glorified strength, the hero, and the "captain of industry." He maintained that men should search out the great leaders and follow them to the death. Theodore Roosevelt's doctrine of "the strenuous life" came directly from Carlyle.

Achievement. Carlyle's fame must rest upon the reader's reaction to his teaching. As a historian he is picturesque and vivid; as a critic he is highly prejudiced. As a teacher he saw the dangers of democracy and prophesied the interest in dictatorship which swept Europe after 1920. He was out of harmony with his own time, but it may well be that he will be recognized as the only teacher of his day who realized what the future would bring forth.

SUGGESTIONS FOR FURTHER STUDY

1. Reports on *Heroes and Hero Worship* and *Sartor Resartus* from the following points of view:
   (*a*) rough, incoherent, but forceful style, (*b*) eloquence, (*c*) strenuous affirmation of the value of work and struggle, (*d*) glorification of the individual over the mob, (*e*) strong prejudices, (*f*) intense individualism.
2. Carlyle's *The French Revolution.*
3. Carlyle's "Essay on Burns."
4. Carlyle's style.

USEFUL BOOKS

The best popular introduction to Carlyle is *Thomas Carlyle: How to Know Him* by Bliss Perry. There are short lives by R. Garnett and J. Nichol.

Long authoritative lives are by J. A. Froude and D. A. Wilson. W. C. Brownell has an essay on Carlyle in *Victorian Prose Masters*.

JOHN HENRY, CARDINAL NEWMAN

1801–1890

Life. Newman was born in London in 1801. His father was a banker. He was educated at Trinity College, Oxford, where he had no great scholarly success. In 1822, however, after a year of hard study, he was elected to a fellowship in Oriel College, Oxford.

In 1824 he entered the ministry of the Church of England. He worked and preached in Oxford. He also traveled abroad. In 1833 he joined the Oxford Movement, a group of Church of England clergymen who worked for certain reforms in church practice and government. In 1845 he joined the Roman Catholic Church.

In 1854 he went to Dublin to head a new Catholic university, but he was not successful as an administrator. He lectured on "The Idea of a University." These lectures, when published, formed one of his most famous books.

Ten years later an attack upon him by the novelist Kingsley brought out his *Apologia pro Vita Sua*, one of the great autobiographies of literature.

In 1879 he was made a cardinal. In 1890 he died.

Achievement. Newman's influence as a religious teacher was immense upon Protestants and Catholics alike. He had a brilliant, logical mind, a wide range of reading, a deep knowledge of theology, and a passionately spiritual view of religion.

His style is bright, fresh, spontaneous, clear, and dignified. He had a strong feeling for beautiful prose rhythm. It is the style of a man whose learning is never obtrusive, whose mind is always clear, and whose feelings are sensitive and sincere.

SUGGESTIONS FOR FURTHER STUDY

1. Reports on *The Idea of a University*, *The Grammar of Assent*, and *Apologia pro Vita Sua*, Parts I and VII from the following points of view:
   (*a*) beauty and clarity of style, (*b*) eloquence, (*c*) exactness, (*d*) defense of individual faith.
2. Newman as a poet.

USEFUL BOOKS

The following books will be found useful for a full study of Newman:

Barry, W.	*Cardinal Newman*
Hutton, R. H.	*Cardinal Newman*
Reilly, J. J.	*Newman as a Man of Letters*
Ward, W. P.	*The Life of John Henry Cardinal Newman*

MATTHEW ARNOLD

1822–1888

The Victorian period was an era of great teachers who were also great writers of prose. One of the most distinguished of the group which included Carlyle, Newman, John Ruskin, and Thomas Henry Huxley, was Matthew Arnold. He took as his mission the criticism of literature and the teaching of ideals of "culture."

Life. Arnold was born in a small town near London in 1822. His father was the famous headmaster of Rugby and he, himself, had a distinguished career at Oxford.

He was fellow of Oriel from 1845–1847, and for four years thereafter a private secretary. In 1851 he became an inspector of government schools. He retained this position for thirty-five years, traveling constantly, and working hard visiting schools and writing reports.

He first published volumes of poems: *The Strayed Reveller* (1849), *Empedocles on Etna* (1852), and *Poems* (1853). His poetry is thoughtful, dignified, and musical.

His prose works, which established his fame as critic and thinker, began with the publication of lectures which he delivered at Oxford from 1857–1867. Thereafter followed other volumes until the close of his life.

He visited America in 1883 and 1886 on lecture tours. In 1888 he died.

Arnold's ideas. Certain ideas appear constantly in Arnold's writings. He maintained that there is a standard of the highest and best in literature and that this standard ought to govern the study of poetry. He believed that the best way to reach a high standard of taste was to familiarize oneself with beautiful lines and passages—"touchstones," as he called them. Further, he insisted that great literature came from minds which had sound and important ideas about life—that poetry was a "criticism of life."

He hated all ideas which were commonplace, dull, conventional, and illogical. To the stupid people or "philistines," as he called them, he opposed the upholders of "culture" or "sweetness and light." He disliked loud-voiced reformers, but he was consistently liberal in his views.

In all his work he maintained a high ethical standard. He wrote in a beautifully simple style, persuasive and eloquent, with an abundance of quotable phrases.

The best introduction to his works is through the essays on "The Study of Poetry" and "Wordsworth" and the volume *Culture and Anarchy*.

SUGGESTIONS FOR FURTHER STUDY

1. Arnold as a poet. Read "Dover Beach," "Rugby Chapel," "The Forsaken Merman," "Requiescat," "The Strayed Reveller," "Self-Dependence."
2. A comparison of Arnold's essay on Wordsworth with Pater's essay.
3. Arnold's ideas about poetry.
4. Arnold's ideas of culture.
5. Arnold's style.

USEFUL BOOKS

The best popular introduction to the work of Matthew Arnold is *Matthew Arnold: How to Know Him* by S. P. Sherman. A good short life is by H. W. Paul in the English Men of Letters series. An excellent selection from his work is *Selections from the Prose Works of Matthew Arnold* in the Riverside College Classics. An excellent essay on Arnold is in *Three Studies in Literature* by L. E. Gates.

ROBERT LOUIS STEVENSON
1850–1894

Life. Stevenson was born in Edinburgh in 1850. His father was a civil engineer. As a child Stevenson's health was poor and he received an irregular education at schools and at home. He made some progress in engineering and he studied law, but his chief interest lay in writing.

Much of his adult life was spent in travel, partly in Europe, and partly in the United States. In 1888 he went to the South Seas for his health. In 1894 he died in Samoa, famous throughout the English-speaking world as a writer of children's verse, of novels, and of essays.

Works. In 1885 he published *A Child's Garden of Verses* which speedily became a children's classic. The poems are simple and charming, with a true understanding of the psychology of childhood.

His novels are all romances. *Treasure Island* (1882) is the finest romance of pirates, sea adventure, and treasure hunting in English literature. *Prince Otto* (1885) is a love story with a setting in an imaginary German principality. It began the vogue which such stories as *Graustark* and *The Prisoner of Zenda* imitated on a lower level. *Kidnapped* and *The Master of Ballantrae* exploit Scottish history somewhat in the manner of Scott though more simply and vividly. *Weir of Hermiston* (1896), left unfinished at his death, is a tale of the conflict of youth and age. It promised to be his most mature novel.

His short stories, "The Sire of Malétroit's Door," "The Strange Case of Dr. Jekyll and Mr. Hyde," and "A Lodging for the Night" are vivid, romantic, and perfect in form.

As an essayist and critic Stevenson showed himself a thinker and teacher of high ethical, social, and artistic ideals. He was eternally young, optimistic, gay, courageous, and charitable. These qualities are clearly seen in *Travels with a Donkey* (1897), *Virginibus Puerisque* (1881), and *Familiar Studies of Men and Books* (1882).

Stevenson's style, like Lamb's, was consciously modeled upon that of older writers. It is always easy and graceful. Sometimes it is sharply dramatic; sometimes carefully elaborated; sometimes colloquial and humorous; sometimes, as in his essay "Pulvis et Umbra," nobly eloquent.

Personally, as is seen in his *Letters*, Stevenson was one of the most charming of men. He was beloved by his friends and by his readers, and remains one of the most romantically alluring figures in literature.

SUGGESTIONS FOR FURTHER STUDY

1. Stevenson as a novelist. Read *Treasure Island, Kidnapped, The Master of Ballantrae,* and *Prince Otto.*
2. Stevenson's conception of romance. See essays in *Memories and Portraits.*
3. Stevenson as critic. See *Familiar Studies of Men and Books.*
4. Stevenson as poet.

5. Stevenson's short stories.
6. Stevenson in America.
7. Stevenson in the South Seas.
8. Stevenson's style.

USEFUL BOOKS

A good popular introduction is *Stevenson* by R. Rice. Stevenson's *Letters* are an indispensable source for a knowledge of his life. Other works are:

Balfour, G.	*The Life of Robert Louis Stevenson*
Raleigh, W.	*R. L. Stevenson*
Stewart, J. A.	*R. L. Stevenson, Man and Writer*

A very modern life is *The True Stevenson: a Study in Clarification* by G. S. Hellman.

CONTEMPORARY PROSE

Among contemporary English prose writers the following may be mentioned.

Hilaire Belloc is a prolific writer in prose and verse. He has written several biographies of leaders of the French Revolution. His light, humorous essays have been particularly popular. Interesting volumes of essays are: *On Nothing and Kindred Subjects, On Everything,* and *On Anything.*

E. V. Lucas has specialized in essays of travel. He has something of the quality of Charles Lamb on whose work he has made himself an authority. Some volumes of his essays are: *The Open Road, A Wanderer in London, Old Lamps for New, Luck of the Year.*

Gilbert K. Chesterton has been even more prolific in his writing than Belloc. He has written in every literary form. His essays have consistently preached against fads and superstitions with a brilliantly paradoxical style. Representative volumes are: *Heretics, Orthodoxy, The Uses of Diversity.*

L. P. Jacks is a philosopher who has the knack of presenting difficult ideas in lucid and attractive form. *The Magic Formula* is a volume of selections from his work, made by himself.

Lytton Strachey wrote the most influential modern biography, *Queen Victoria.*

Among critics may be mentioned J. C. Squire, Rebecca West, and Lascelles Abercrombie.

American prose writers have reached such a high level of competence, clarity, and interest that it is difficult to choose even a few names. Among the best-known are the following.

William Beebe is a scientist who knows how to write about his observations of Nature with charm and even eloquence. Some of his volumes are: *Jungle Peace, The Log of the Sun, The Edge of the Jungle.*

Gamaliel Bradford was for many years the greatest American writer of biography. Among his volumes are: *Lee, the American, American Portraits*, and *Damaged Souls.*

Samuel McChord Crothers long carried on the tradition of Oliver Wendell Holmes in the familiar personal essay. Among his volumes are: *The Pardoner's Wallet, The Pleasures of an Absentee Landlord*, and *The Dame School of Experience.*

Walter Prichard Eaton is a dramatic critic. His more important literary work comprises essays on life in the country. Some volumes are: *In Berkshire Fields* and *On the Edge of the Wilderness.*

In recent years Walter Lippman has become America's foremost journalistic writer. His forceful style, logical mind, and freedom from prejudice make him, for thousands of readers, a guide to national and international affairs.

Agnes Repplier has consistently maintained in her essays the best traditions of English literature. Among her books are: *The Fireside Sphinx, Counter Currents*, and *Points of Friction.*

INDEX